DEATH NOTE
How to use it
XXXVI

- There are male and female gods of death, but it is neither permitted, nor possible for them to have sexual relations with humans. The gods of death also cannot have sex with each other.

死神にはオス・メスがあるが、
人間との生殖行為は許されないし不可能であり、
死神同士も交尾はしない。

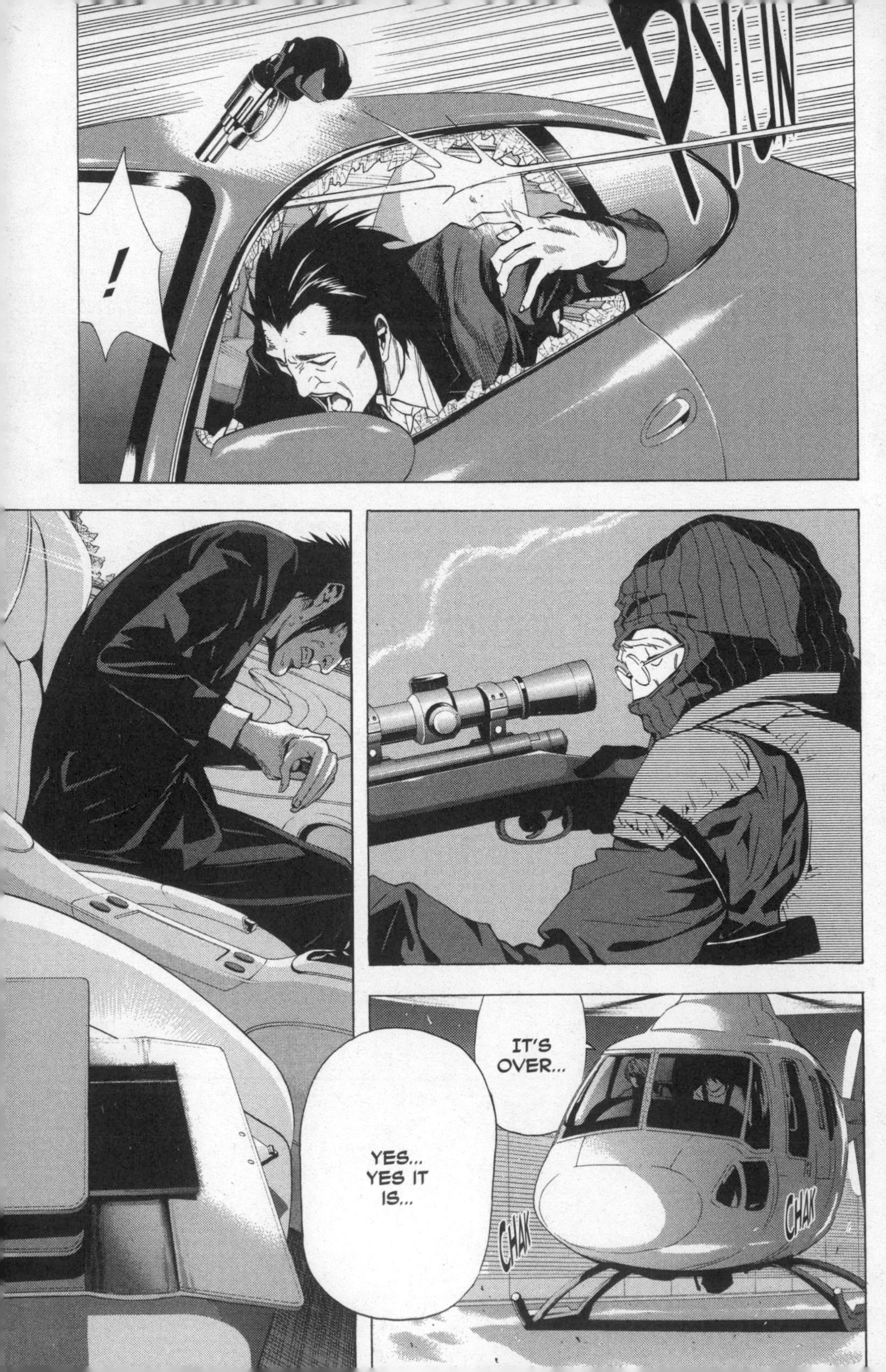
PYUN
!
IT'S OVER...
YES... YES IT IS...
CHAK
CHAK

DEATH NOTE

Black Edition
III

Story by Tsugumi Ohba   Art by Takeshi Obata

Original Graphic Novel Edition Volume 5

Original Graphic Novel Edition Volume 6

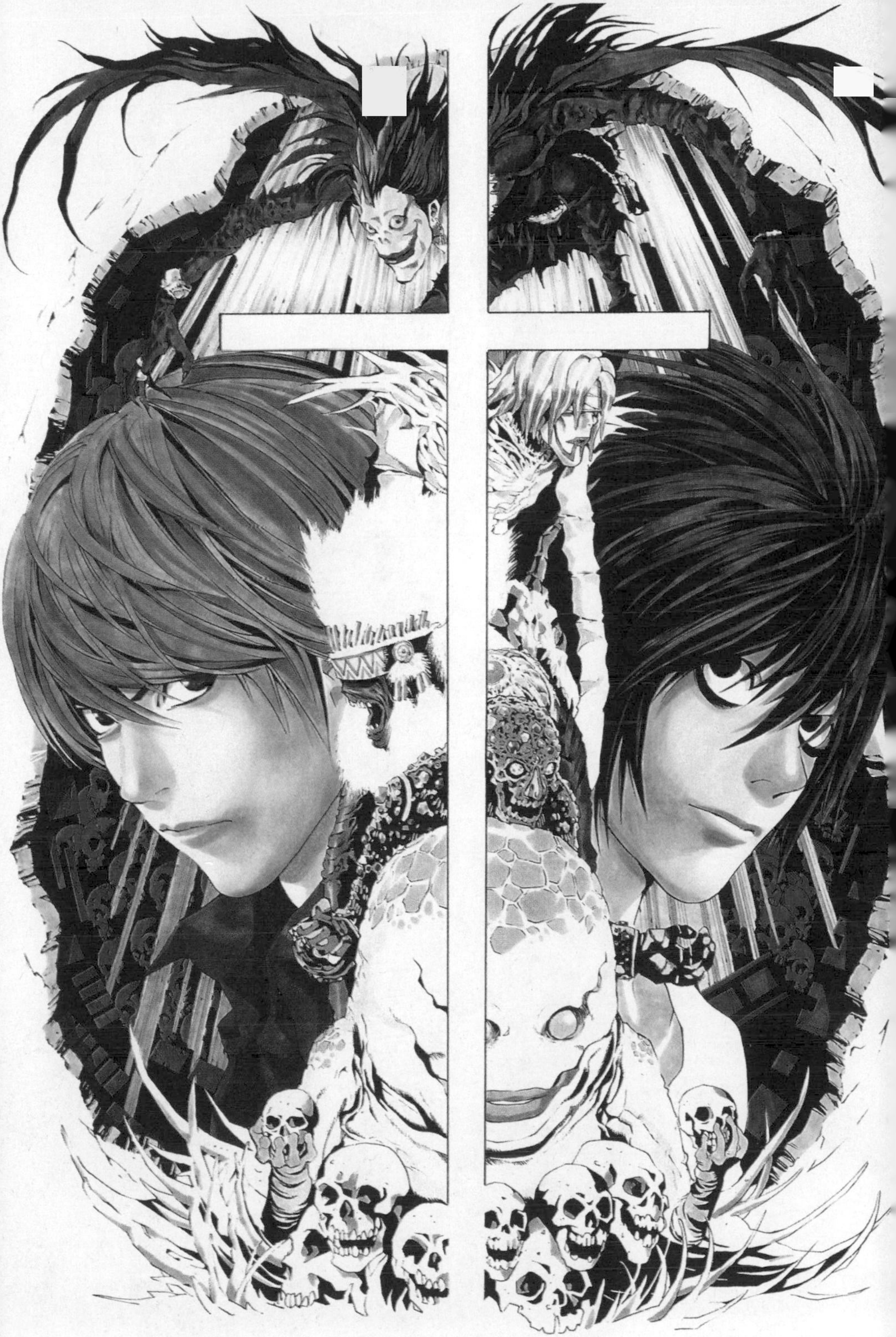

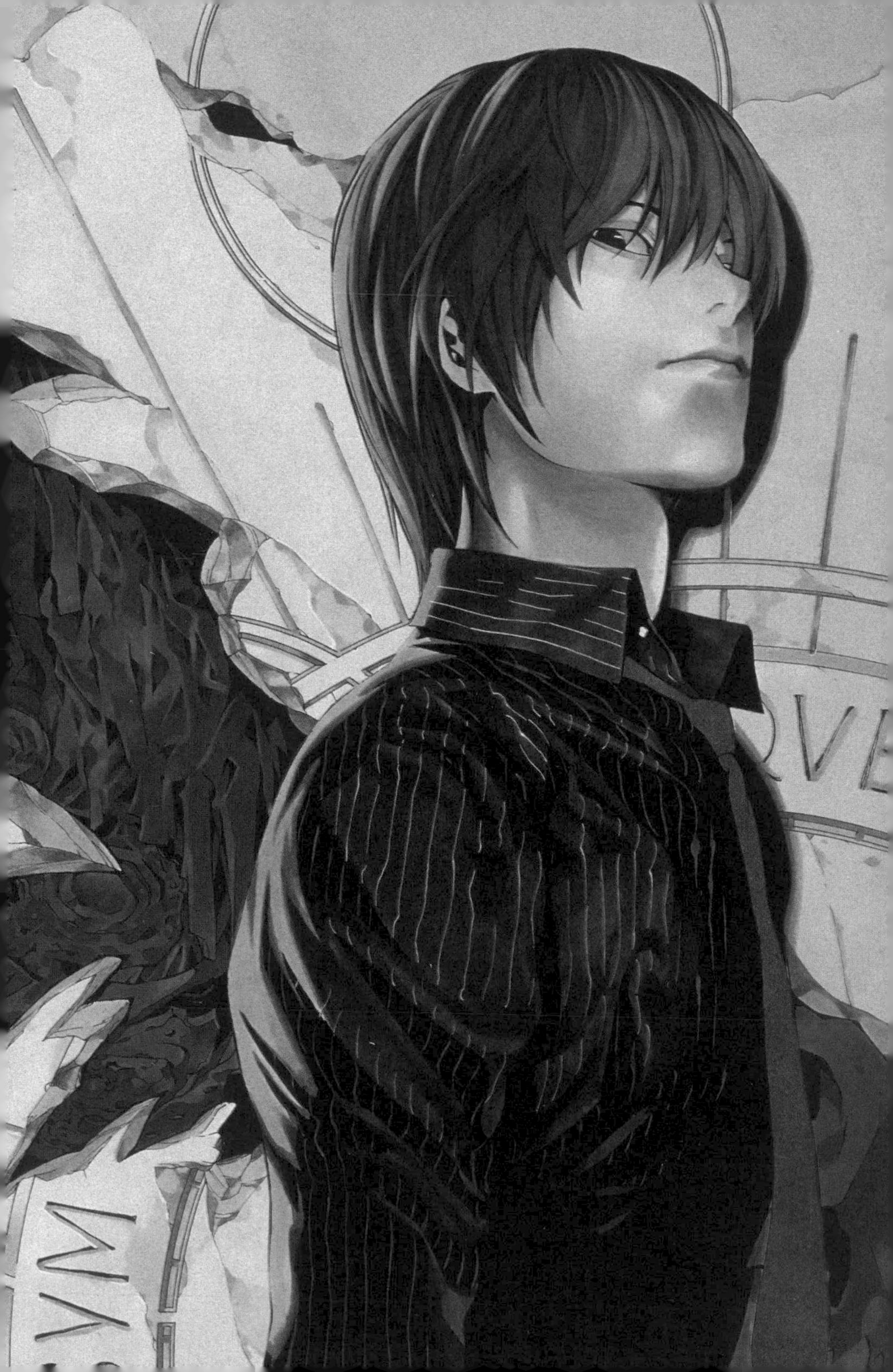

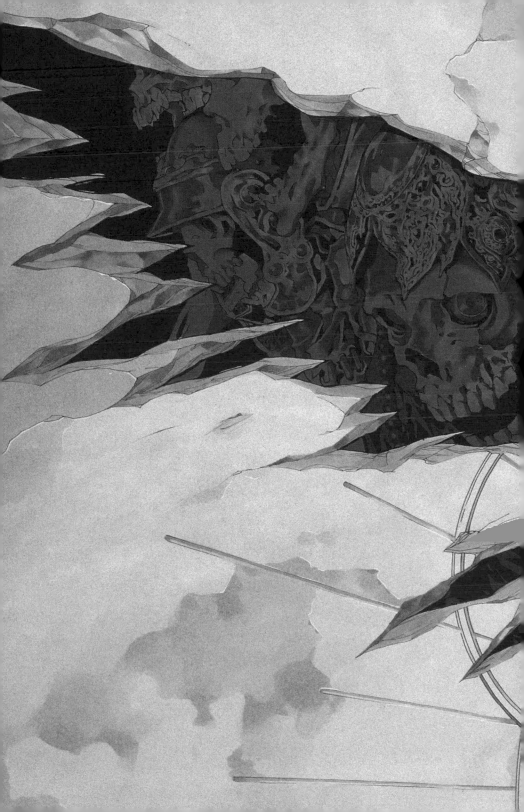

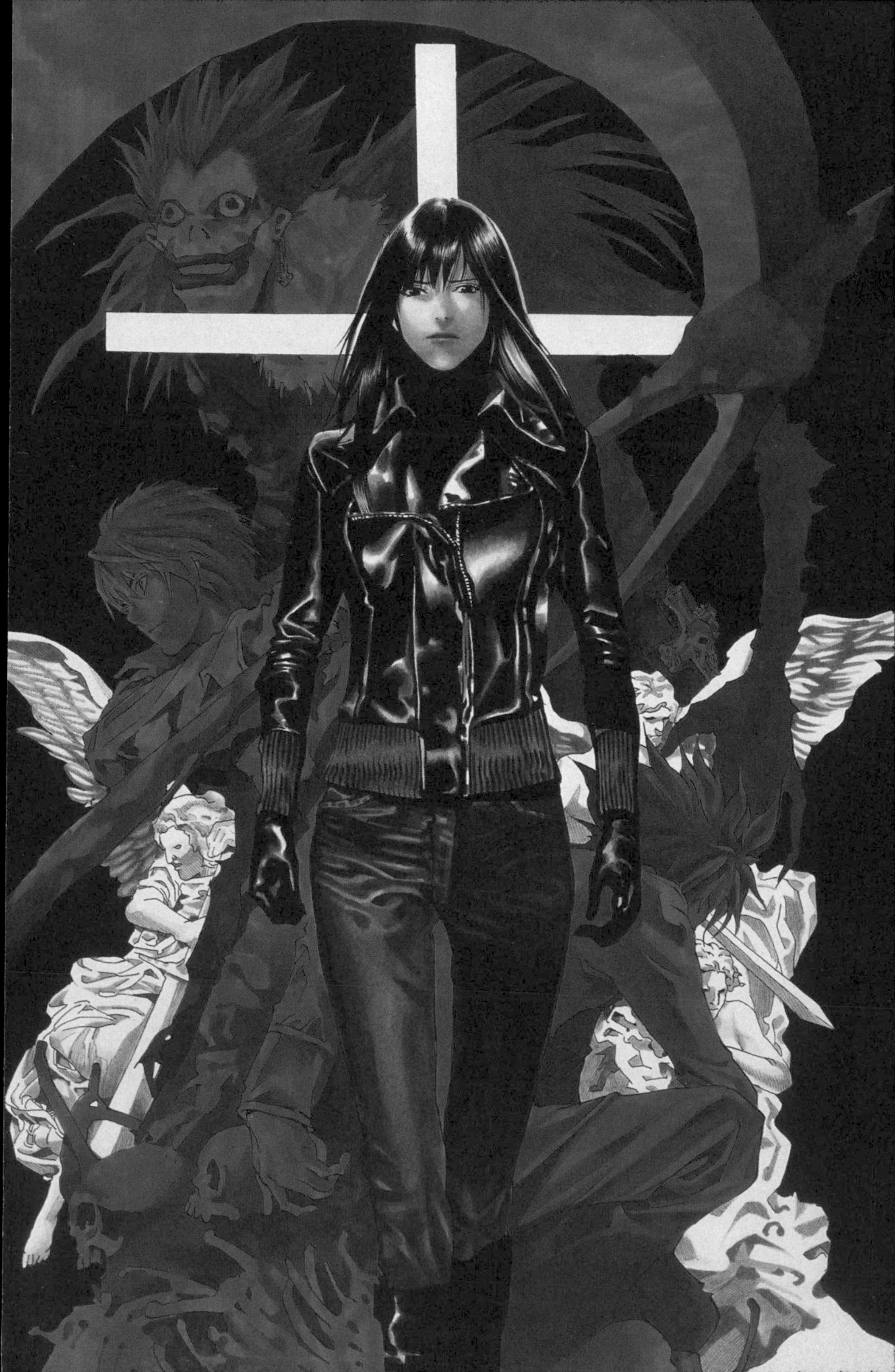

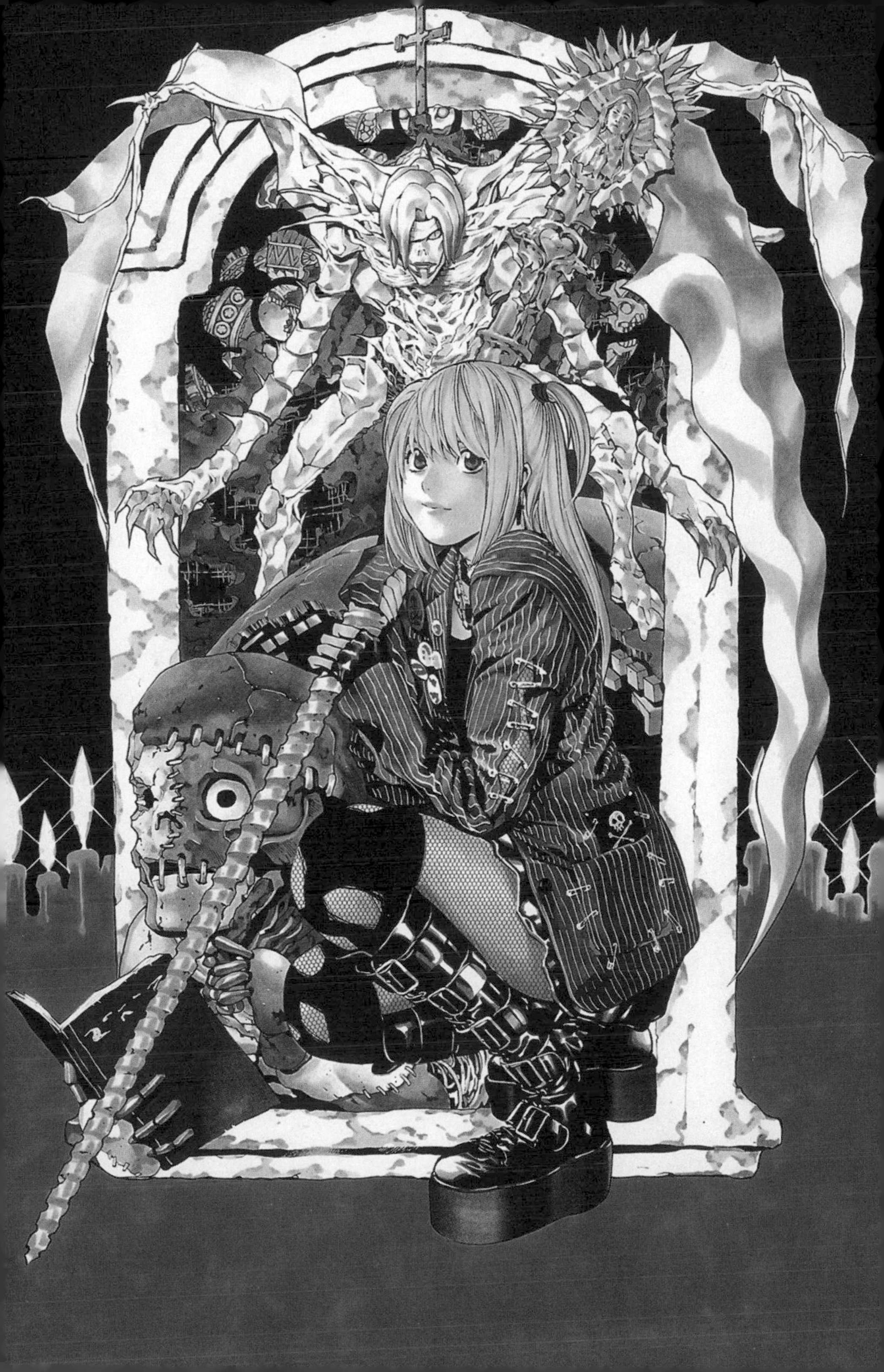

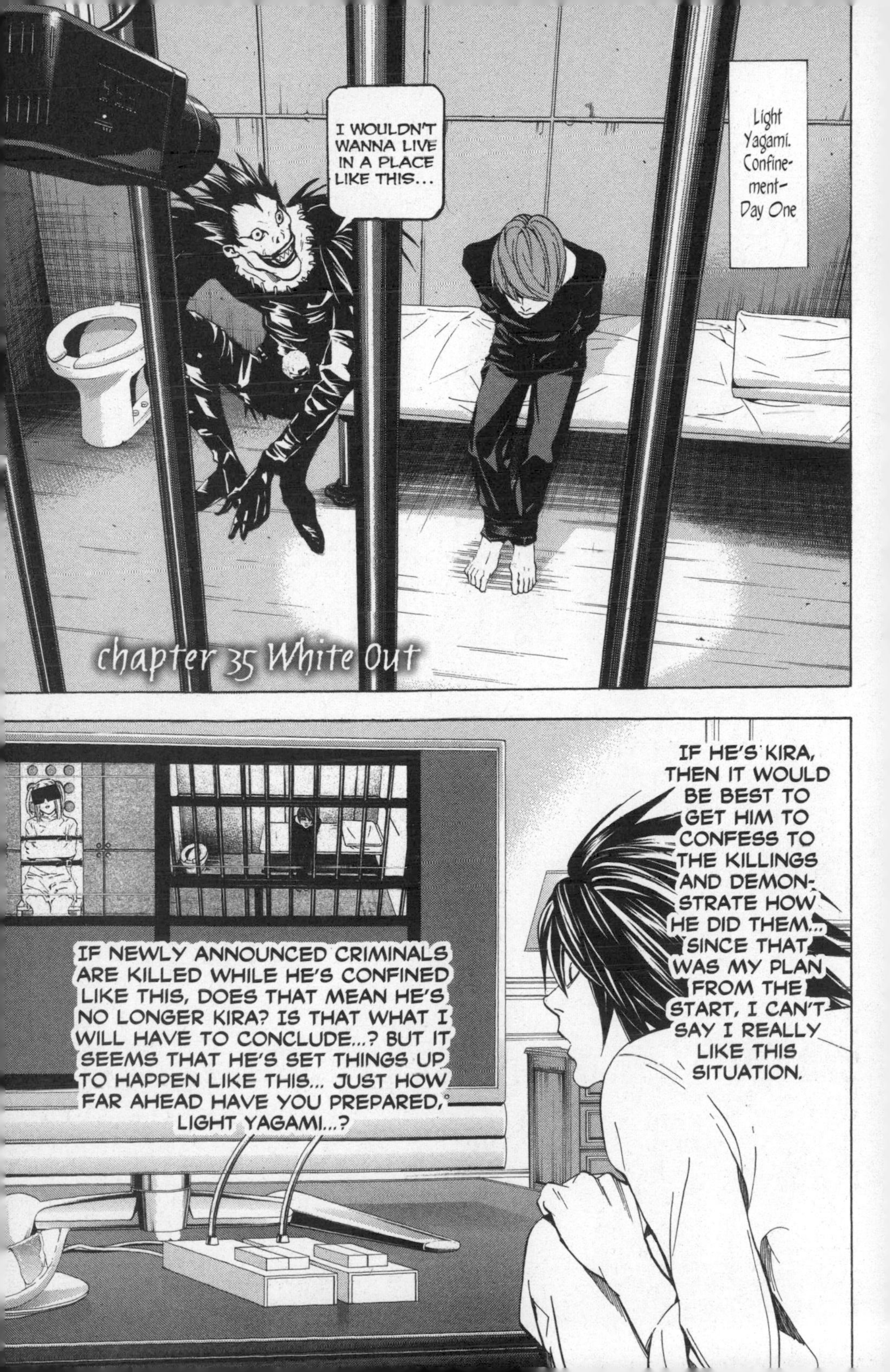
Light Yagami. Confinement- Day One
I WOULDN'T WANNA LIVE IN A PLACE LIKE THIS...
chapter 35 White Out
IF HE'S KIRA, THEN IT WOULD BE BEST TO GET HIM TO CONFESS TO THE KILLINGS AND DEMONSTRATE HOW HE DID THEM... SINCE THAT WAS MY PLAN FROM THE START, I CAN'T SAY I REALLY LIKE THIS SITUATION.
IF NEWLY ANNOUNCED CRIMINALS ARE KILLED WHILE HE'S CONFINED LIKE THIS, DOES THAT MEAN HE'S NO LONGER KIRA? IS THAT WHAT I WILL HAVE TO CONCLUDE...? BUT IT SEEMS THAT HE'S SET THINGS UP TO HAPPEN LIKE THIS... JUST HOW FAR AHEAD HAVE YOU PREPARED, LIGHT YAGAMI...?

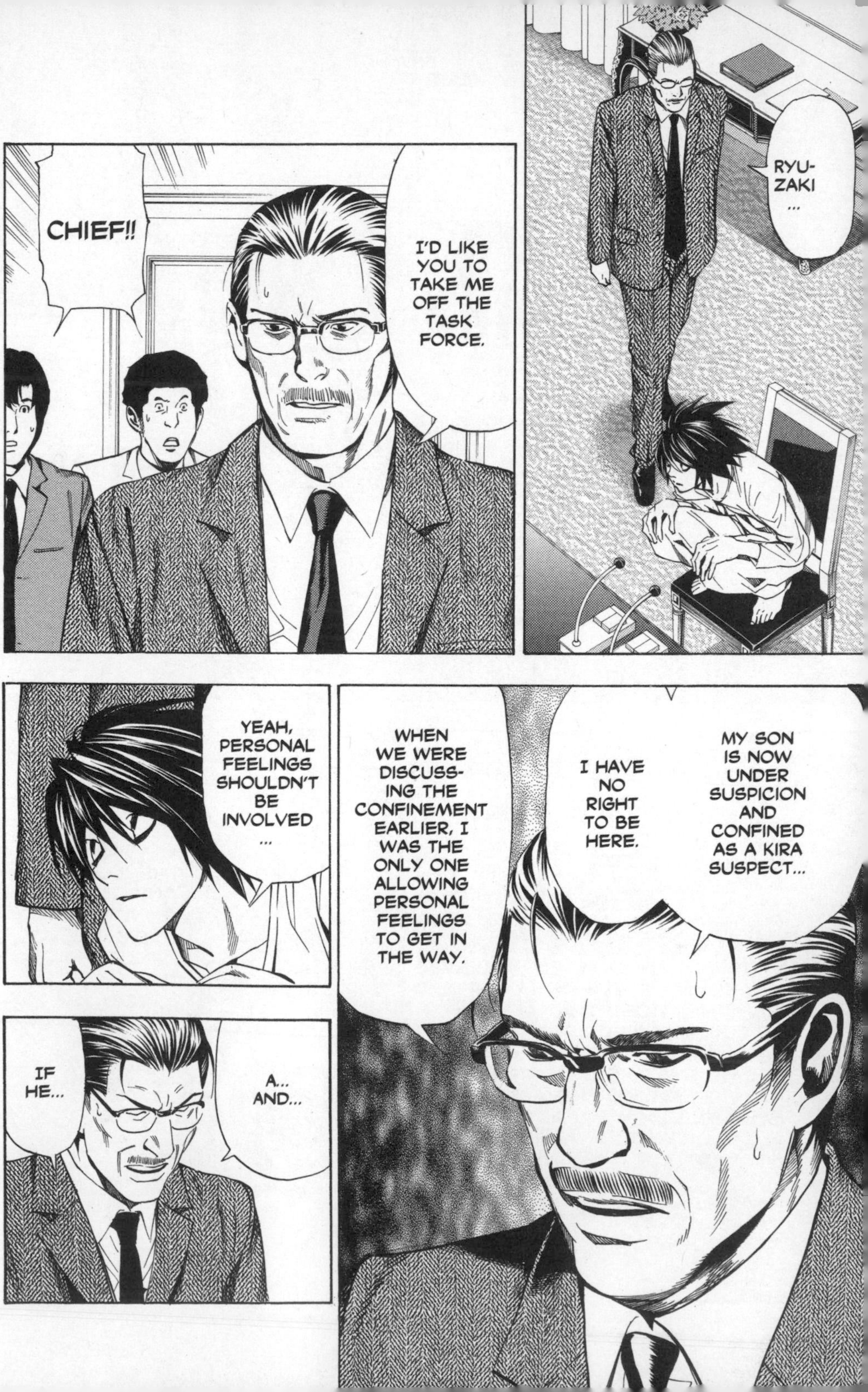
RYU-ZAKI ...
I'D LIKE YOU TO TAKE ME OFF THE TASK FORCE.
CHIEF!!
MY SON IS NOW UNDER SUSPICION AND CONFINED AS A KIRA SUSPECT...
I HAVE NO RIGHT TO BE HERE.
WHEN WE WERE DISCUSSING THE CONFINEMENT EARLIER, I WAS THE ONLY ONE ALLOWING PERSONAL FEELINGS TO GET IN THE WAY.
YEAH, PERSONAL FEELINGS SHOULDN'T BE INVOLVED ...
A... AND...
IF HE...

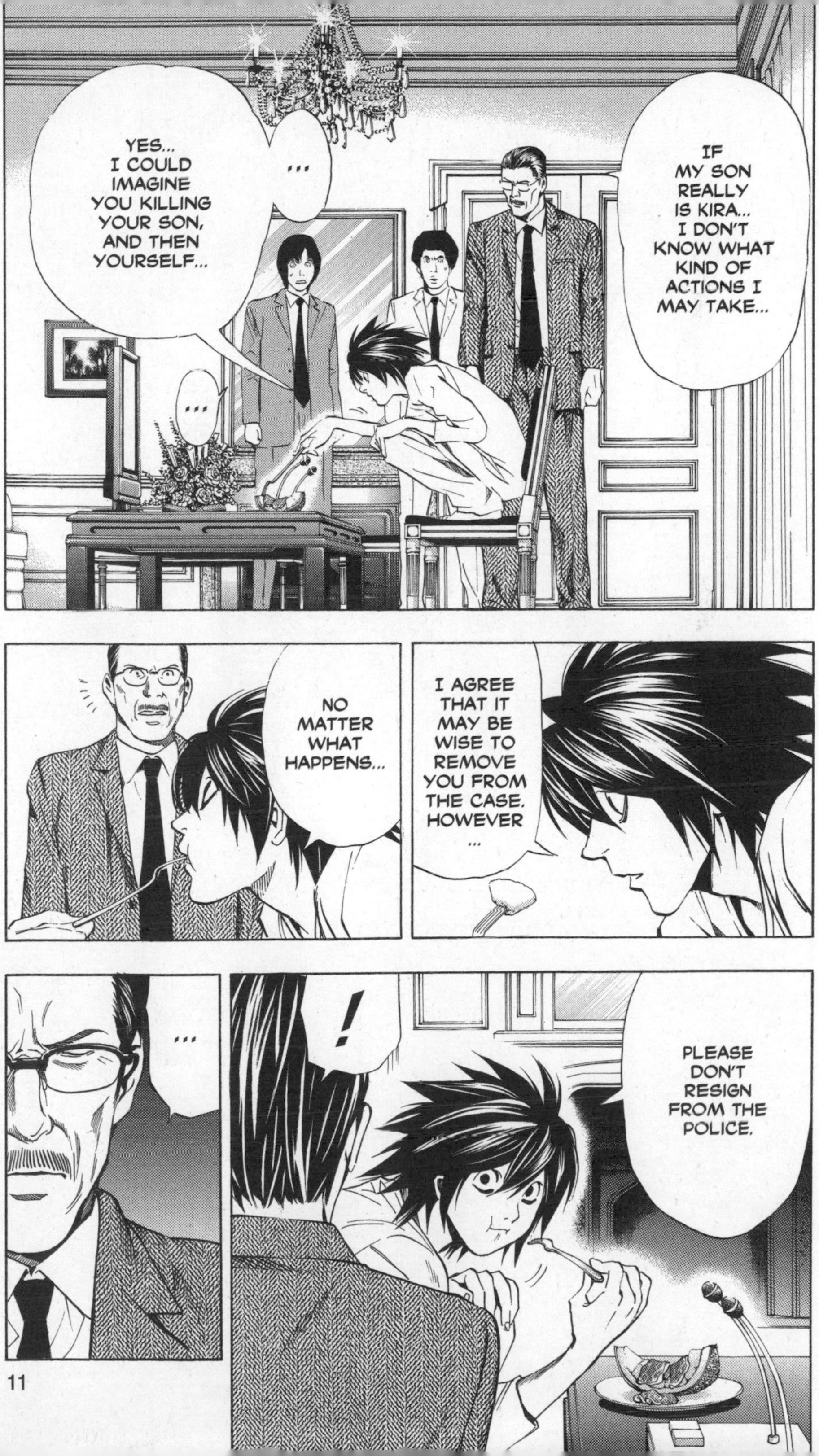
IF MY SON REALLY IS KIRA... I DON'T KNOW WHAT KIND OF ACTIONS I MAY TAKE...
...
YES... I COULD IMAGINE YOU KILLING YOUR SON, AND THEN YOURSELF...
...
I AGREE THAT IT MAY BE WISE TO REMOVE YOU FROM THE CASE. HOWEVER ...
NO MATTER WHAT HAPPENS...
PLEASE DON'T RESIGN FROM THE POLICE.
!
...

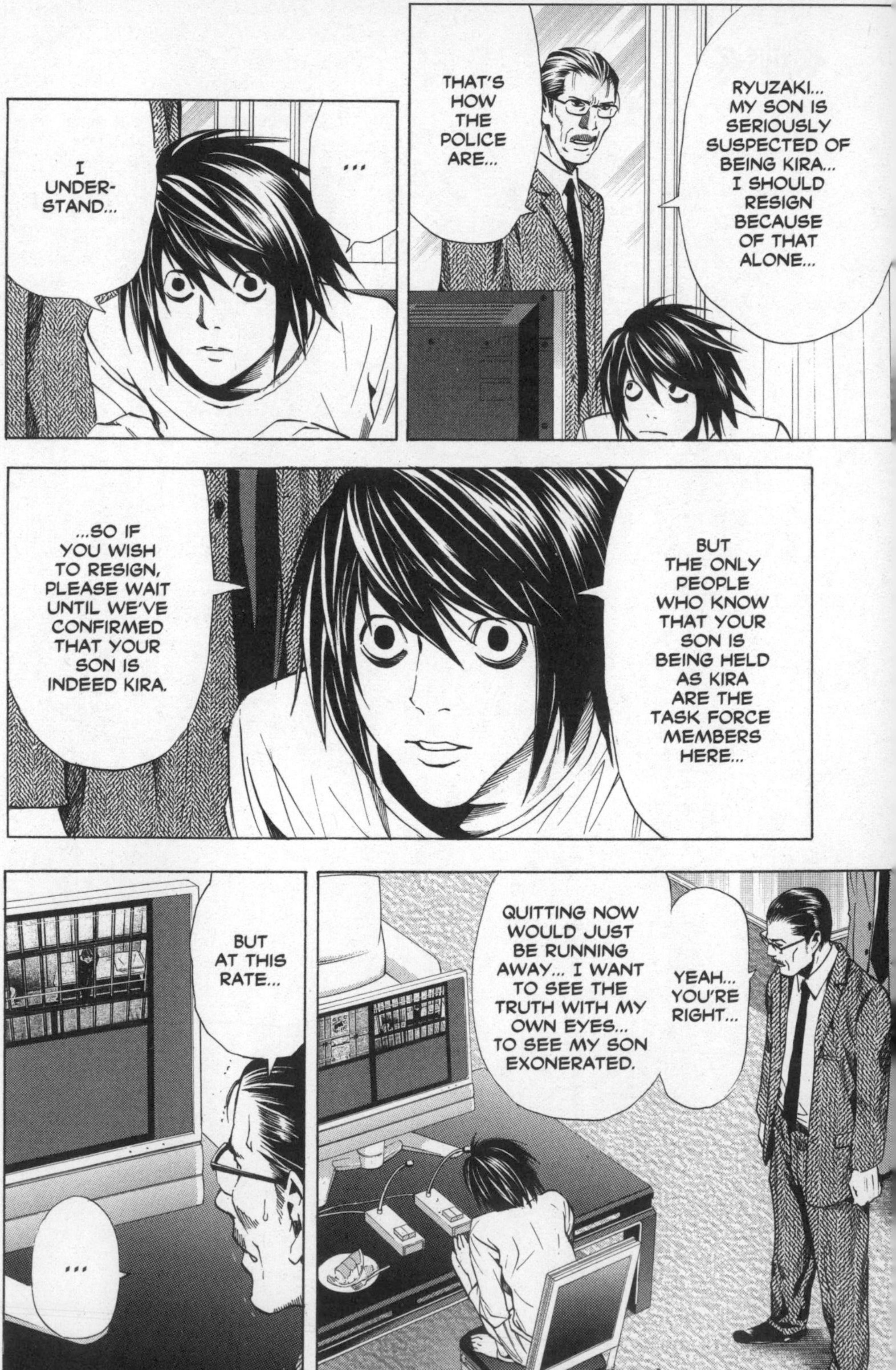
RYUZAKI... MY SON IS SERIOUSLY SUSPECTED OF BEING KIRA... I SHOULD RESIGN BECAUSE OF THAT ALONE...
THAT'S HOW THE POLICE ARE...
...
I UNDER-STAND...
BUT THE ONLY PEOPLE WHO KNOW THAT YOUR SON IS BEING HELD AS KIRA ARE THE TASK FORCE MEMBERS HERE...
...SO IF YOU WISH TO RESIGN, PLEASE WAIT UNTIL WE'VE CONFIRMED THAT YOUR SON IS INDEED KIRA.
YEAH... YOU'RE RIGHT...
QUITTING NOW WOULD JUST BE RUNNING AWAY... I WANT TO SEE THE TRUTH WITH MY OWN EYES... TO SEE MY SON EXONERATED.
BUT AT THIS RATE...
...

READ THIS WAY

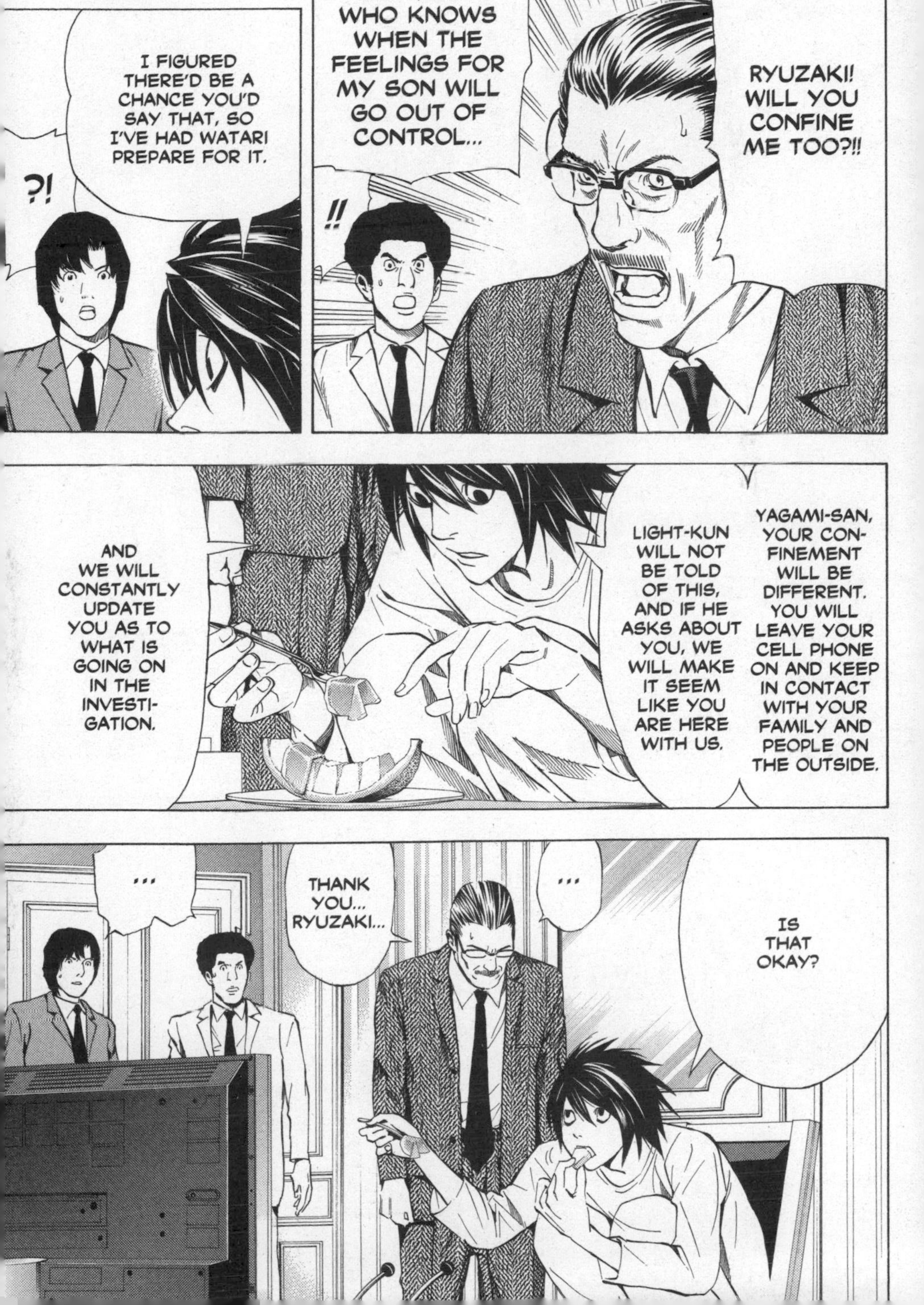
RYUZAKI! WILL YOU CONFINE ME TOO?!!
I'M CALM NOW, BUT WHO KNOWS WHEN THE FEELINGS FOR MY SON WILL GO OUT OF CONTROL...
!!
I FIGURED THERE'D BE A CHANCE YOU'D SAY THAT, SO I'VE HAD WATARI PREPARE FOR IT.
?!
YAGAMI-SAN, YOUR CON-FINEMENT WILL BE DIFFERENT. YOU WILL LEAVE YOUR CELL PHONE ON AND KEEP IN CONTACT WITH YOUR FAMILY AND PEOPLE ON THE OUTSIDE.
LIGHT-KUN WILL NOT BE TOLD OF THIS, AND IF HE ASKS ABOUT YOU, WE WILL MAKE IT SEEM LIKE YOU ARE HERE WITH US.
AND WE WILL CONSTANTLY UPDATE YOU AS TO WHAT IS GOING ON IN THE INVESTI-GATION.
IS THAT OKAY?
...
THANK YOU... RYUZAKI...
...

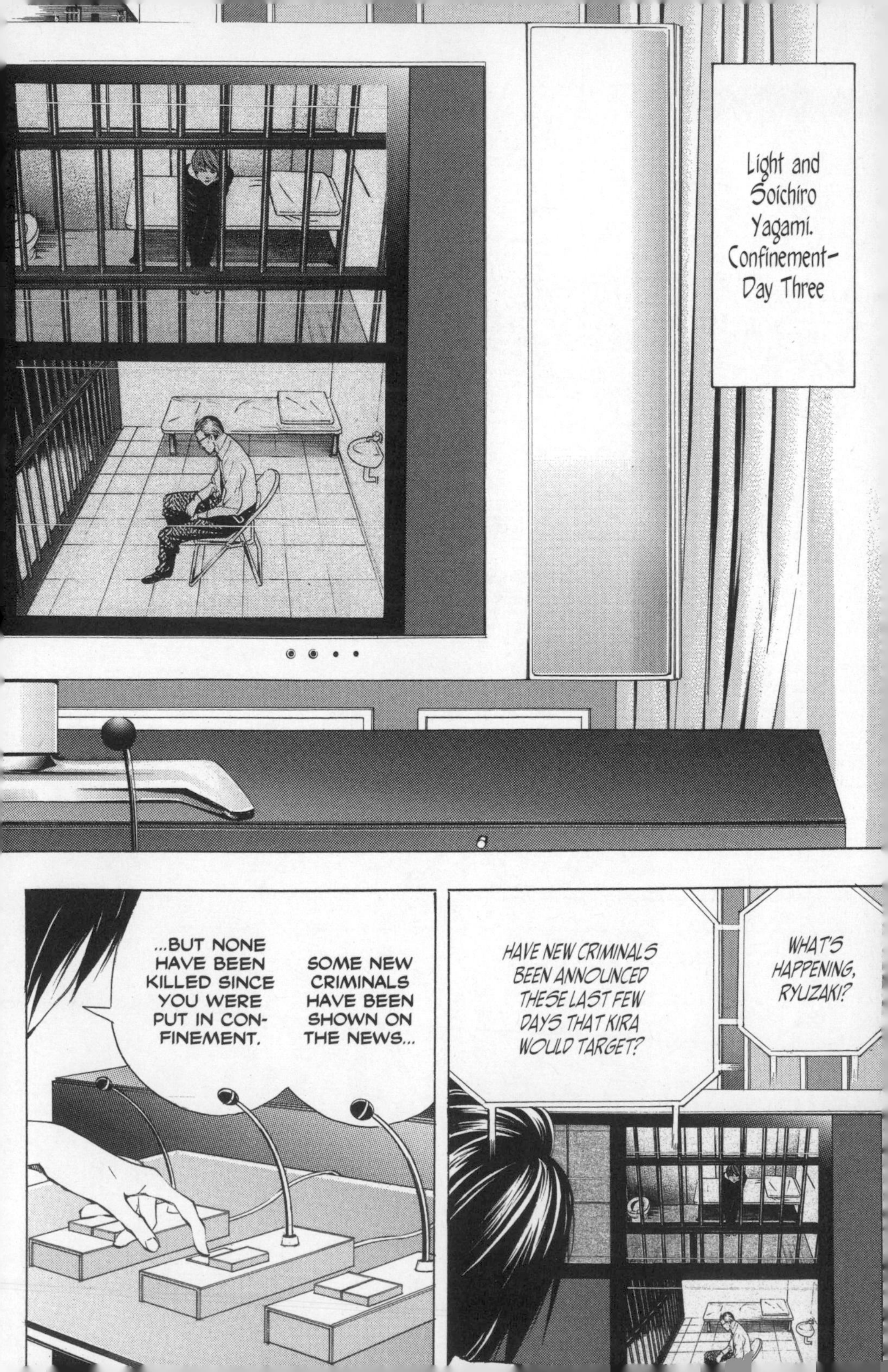
Light and Soichiro Yagami. Confinement– Day Three
WHAT'S HAPPENING, RYUZAKI?
HAVE NEW CRIMINALS BEEN ANNOUNCED THESE LAST FEW DAYS THAT KIRA WOULD TARGET?
SOME NEW CRIMINALS HAVE BEEN SHOWN ON THE NEWS...
...BUT NONE HAVE BEEN KILLED SINCE YOU WERE PUT IN CONFINEMENT.

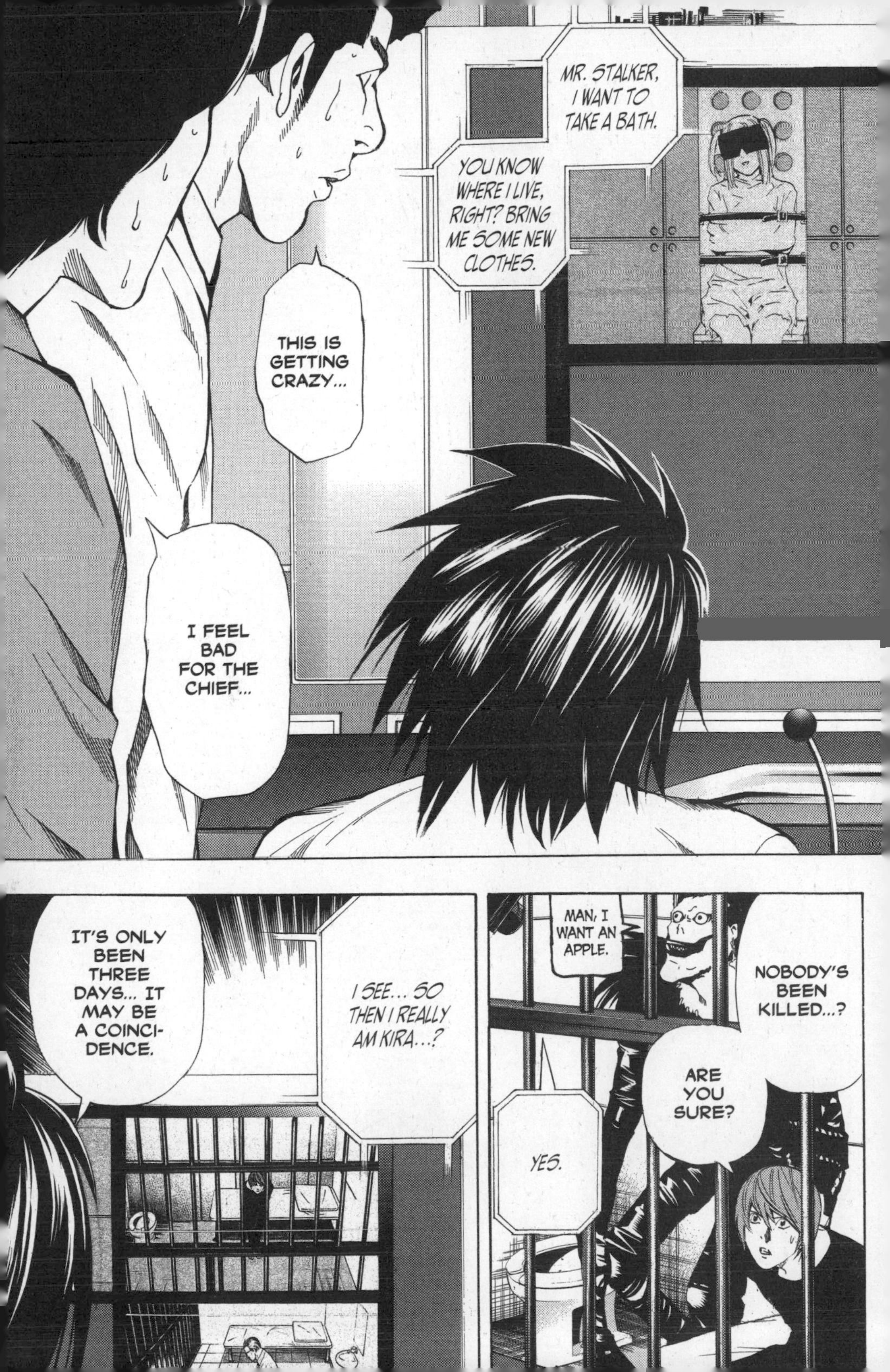
MR. STALKER, I WANT TO TAKE A BATH.
YOU KNOW WHERE I LIVE, RIGHT? BRING ME SOME NEW CLOTHES.
THIS IS GETTING CRAZY...
I FEEL BAD FOR THE CHIEF...
NOBODY'S BEEN KILLED...?
MAN, I WANT AN APPLE.
ARE YOU SURE?
YES.
I SEE... SO THEN I REALLY AM KIRA...?
IT'S ONLY BEEN THREE DAYS... IT MAY BE A COINCIDENCE.

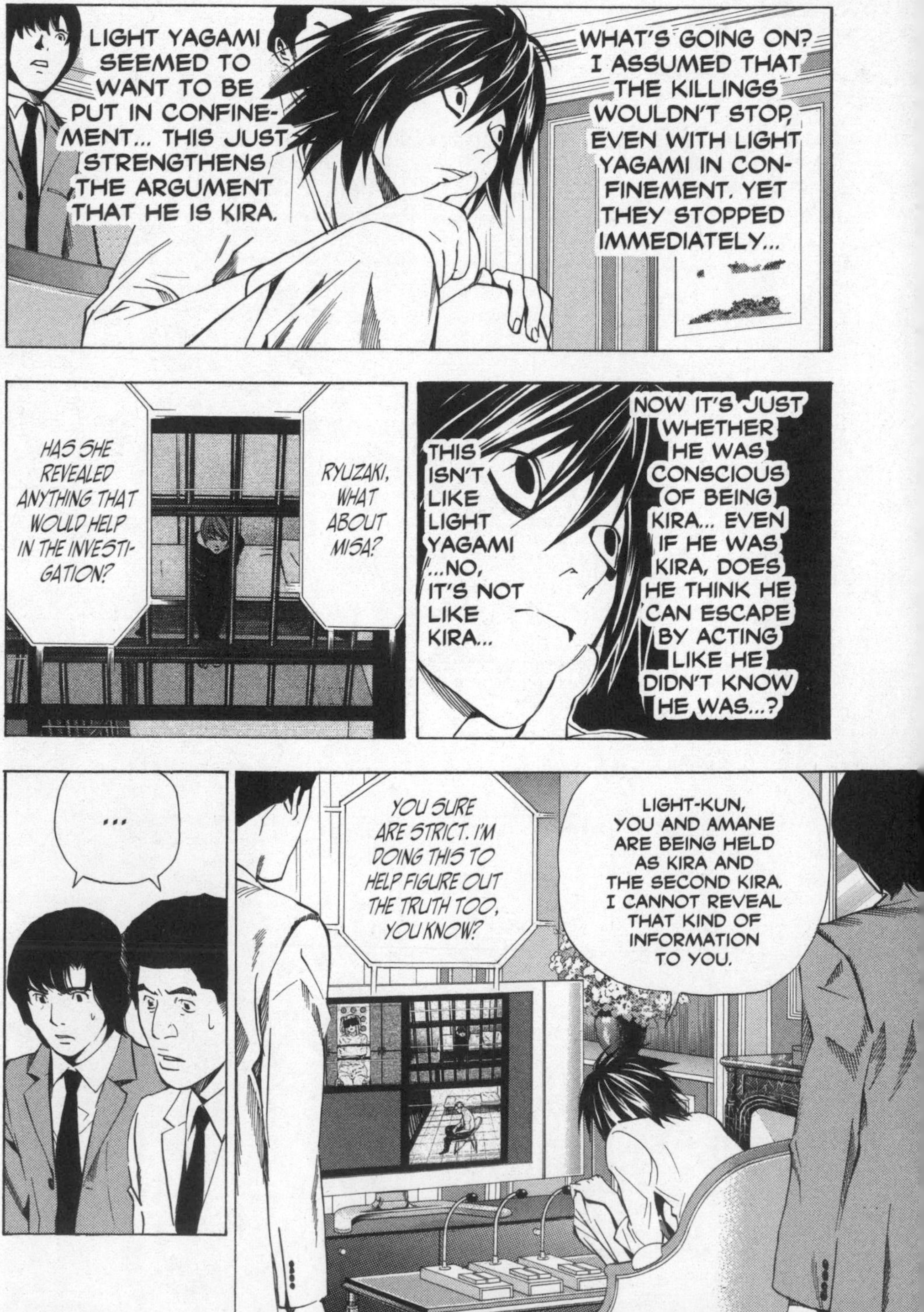
WHAT'S GOING ON? I ASSUMED THAT THE KILLINGS WOULDN'T STOP, EVEN WITH LIGHT YAGAMI IN CONFINEMENT. YET THEY STOPPED IMMEDIATELY...
LIGHT YAGAMI SEEMED TO WANT TO BE PUT IN CONFINEMENT... THIS JUST STRENGTHENS THE ARGUMENT THAT HE IS KIRA.
NOW IT'S JUST WHETHER HE WAS CONSCIOUS OF BEING KIRA... EVEN IF HE WAS KIRA, DOES HE THINK HE CAN ESCAPE BY ACTING LIKE HE DIDN'T KNOW HE WAS...?
THIS ISN'T LIKE LIGHT YAGAMI ...NO, IT'S NOT LIKE KIRA...
RYUZAKI, WHAT ABOUT MISA?
HAS SHE REVEALED ANYTHING THAT WOULD HELP IN THE INVESTIGATION?
LIGHT-KUN, YOU AND AMANE ARE BEING HELD AS KIRA AND THE SECOND KIRA. I CANNOT REVEAL THAT KIND OF INFORMATION TO YOU.
YOU SURE ARE STRICT. I'M DOING THIS TO HELP FIGURE OUT THE TRUTH TOO, YOU KNOW?
...

READ THIS WAY

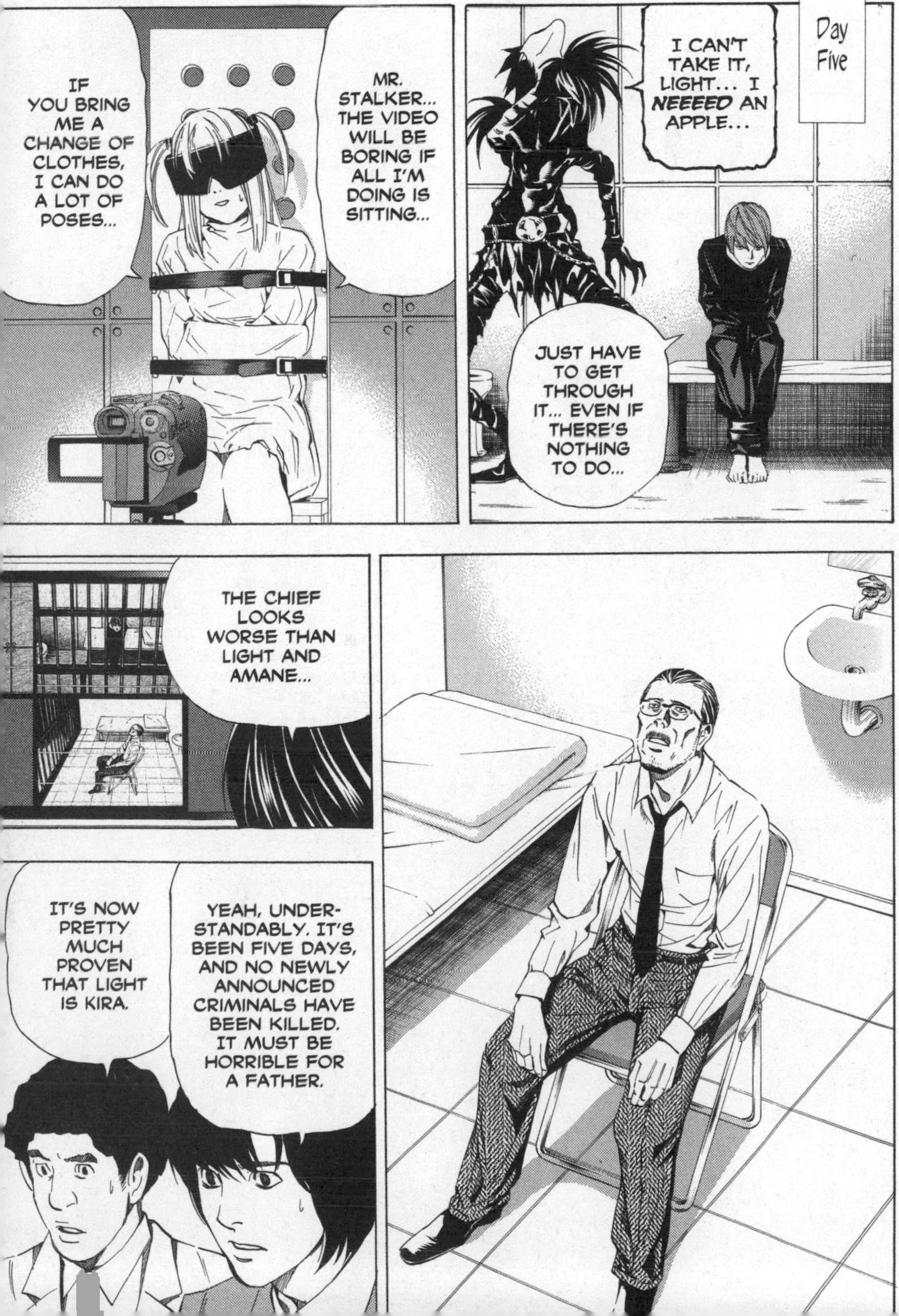
Day Five
I CAN'T TAKE IT, LIGHT... I *NEEEED* AN APPLE...
JUST HAVE TO GET THROUGH IT... EVEN IF THERE'S NOTHING TO DO...
MR. STALKER... THE VIDEO WILL BE BORING IF ALL I'M DOING IS SITTING...
IF YOU BRING ME A CHANGE OF CLOTHES, I CAN DO A LOT OF POSES...
THE CHIEF LOOKS WORSE THAN LIGHT AND AMANE...
YEAH, UNDER-STANDABLY. IT'S BEEN FIVE DAYS, AND NO NEWLY ANNOUNCED CRIMINALS HAVE BEEN KILLED. IT MUST BE HORRIBLE FOR A FATHER.
IT'S NOW PRETTY MUCH PROVEN THAT LIGHT IS KIRA.

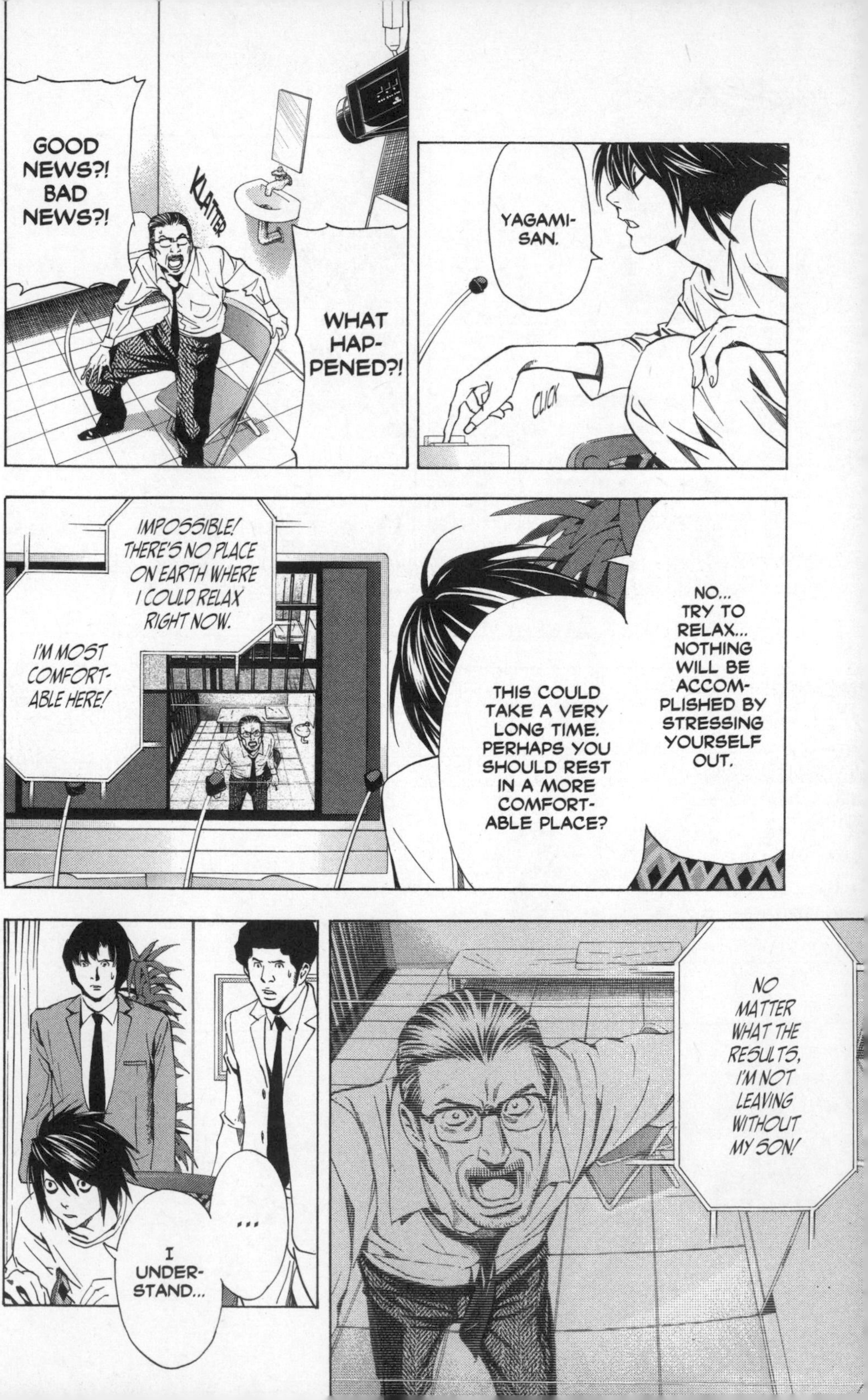
YAGAMI-SAN.
CLICK
GOOD NEWS?! BAD NEWS?!
KLATTER
WHAT HAPPENED?!
NO... TRY TO RELAX... NOTHING WILL BE ACCOMPLISHED BY STRESSING YOURSELF OUT.
THIS COULD TAKE A VERY LONG TIME. PERHAPS YOU SHOULD REST IN A MORE COMFORTABLE PLACE?
IMPOSSIBLE! THERE'S NO PLACE ON EARTH WHERE I COULD RELAX RIGHT NOW.
I'M MOST COMFORTABLE HERE!
NO MATTER WHAT THE RESULTS, I'M NOT LEAVING WITHOUT MY SON!
...
I UNDERSTAND...

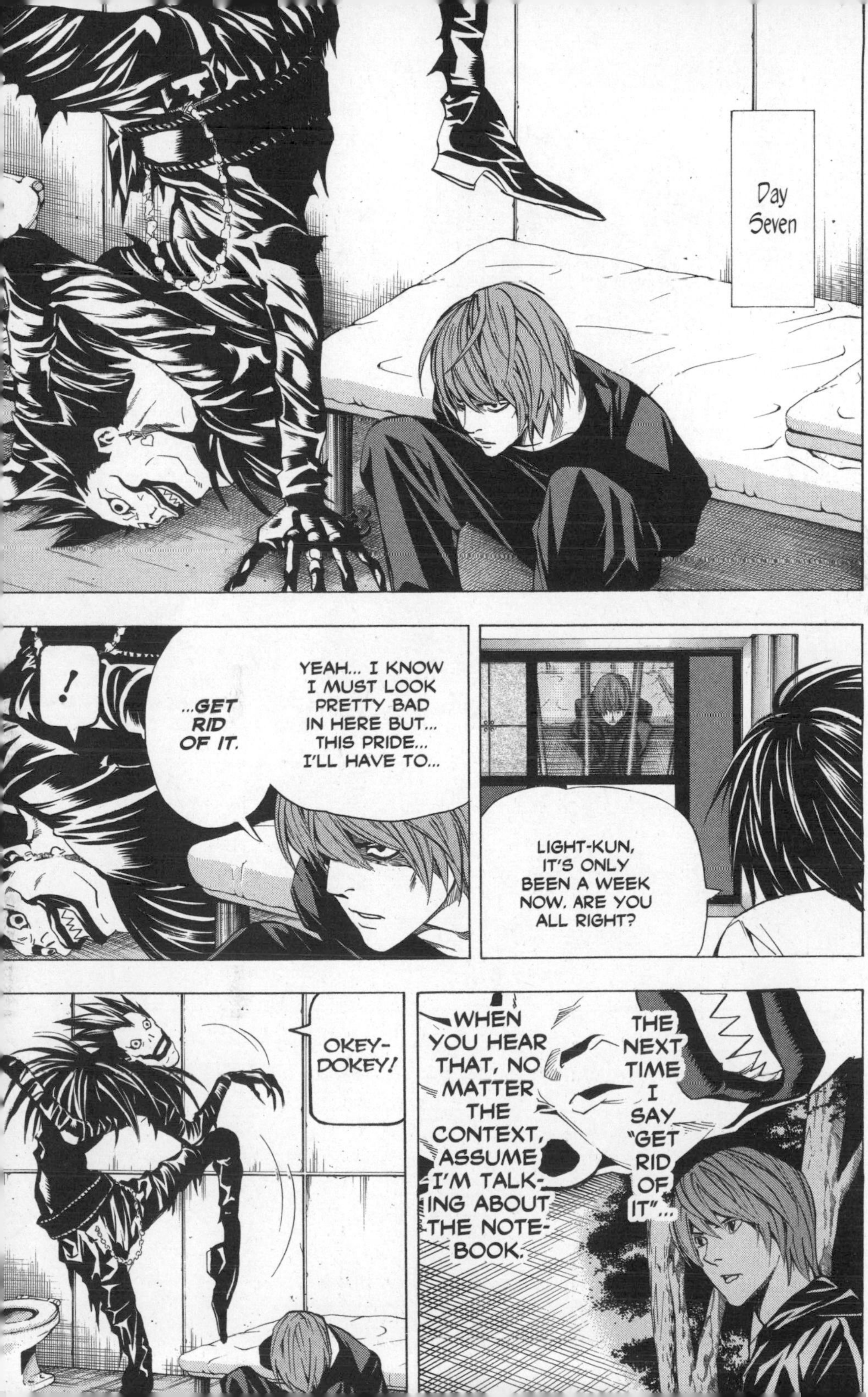
Day Seven
LIGHT-KUN, IT'S ONLY BEEN A WEEK NOW. ARE YOU ALL RIGHT?
YEAH... I KNOW I MUST LOOK PRETTY BAD IN HERE BUT... THIS PRIDE... I'LL HAVE TO...
...GET RID OF IT.
!
THE NEXT TIME I SAY "GET RID OF IT"...
WHEN YOU HEAR THAT, NO MATTER THE CONTEXT, ASSUME I'M TALKING ABOUT THE NOTEBOOK.
OKEY-DOKEY!

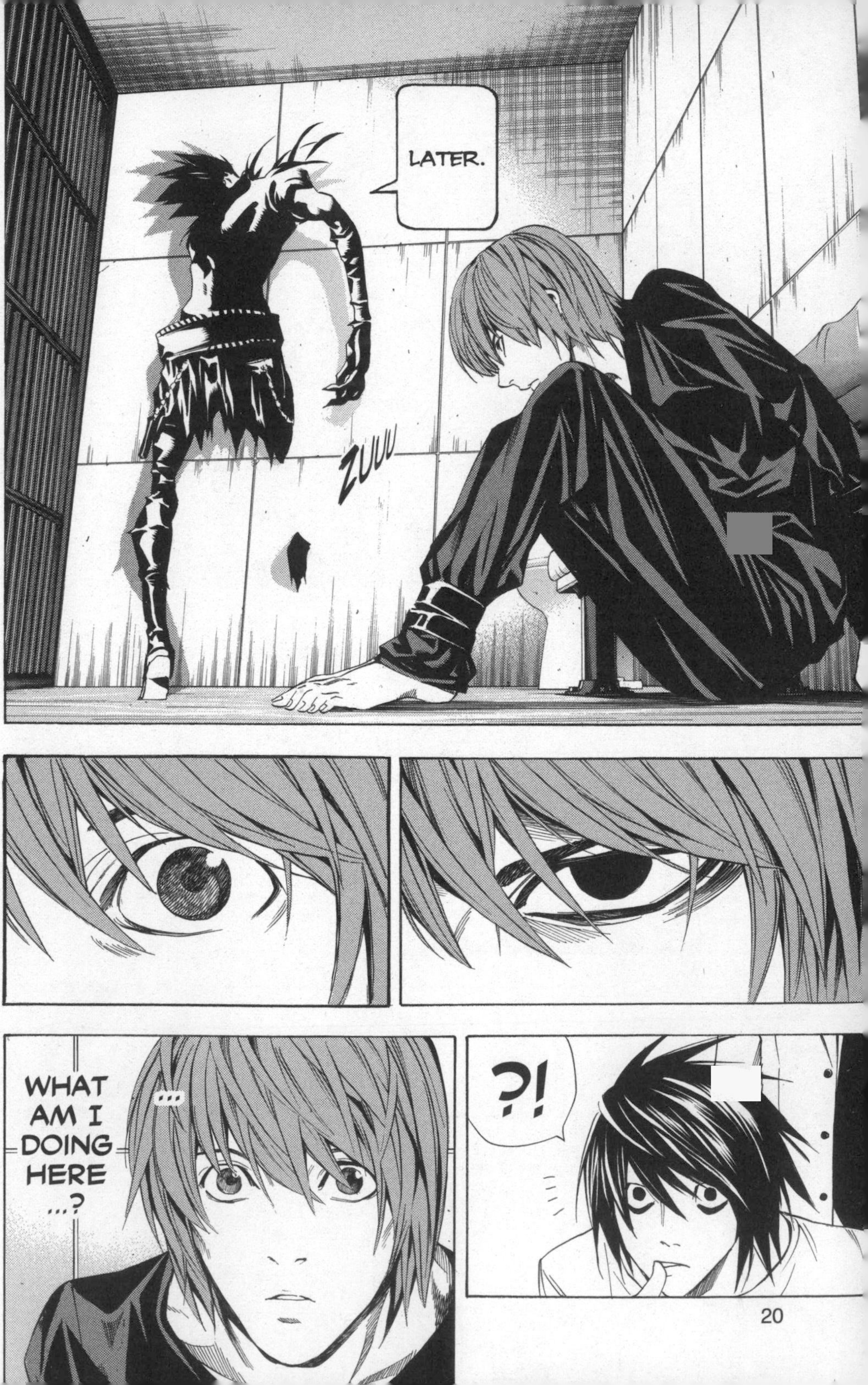
LATER.
ZUUU
?!
...
WHAT AM I DOING HERE ...?

READ THIS WAY

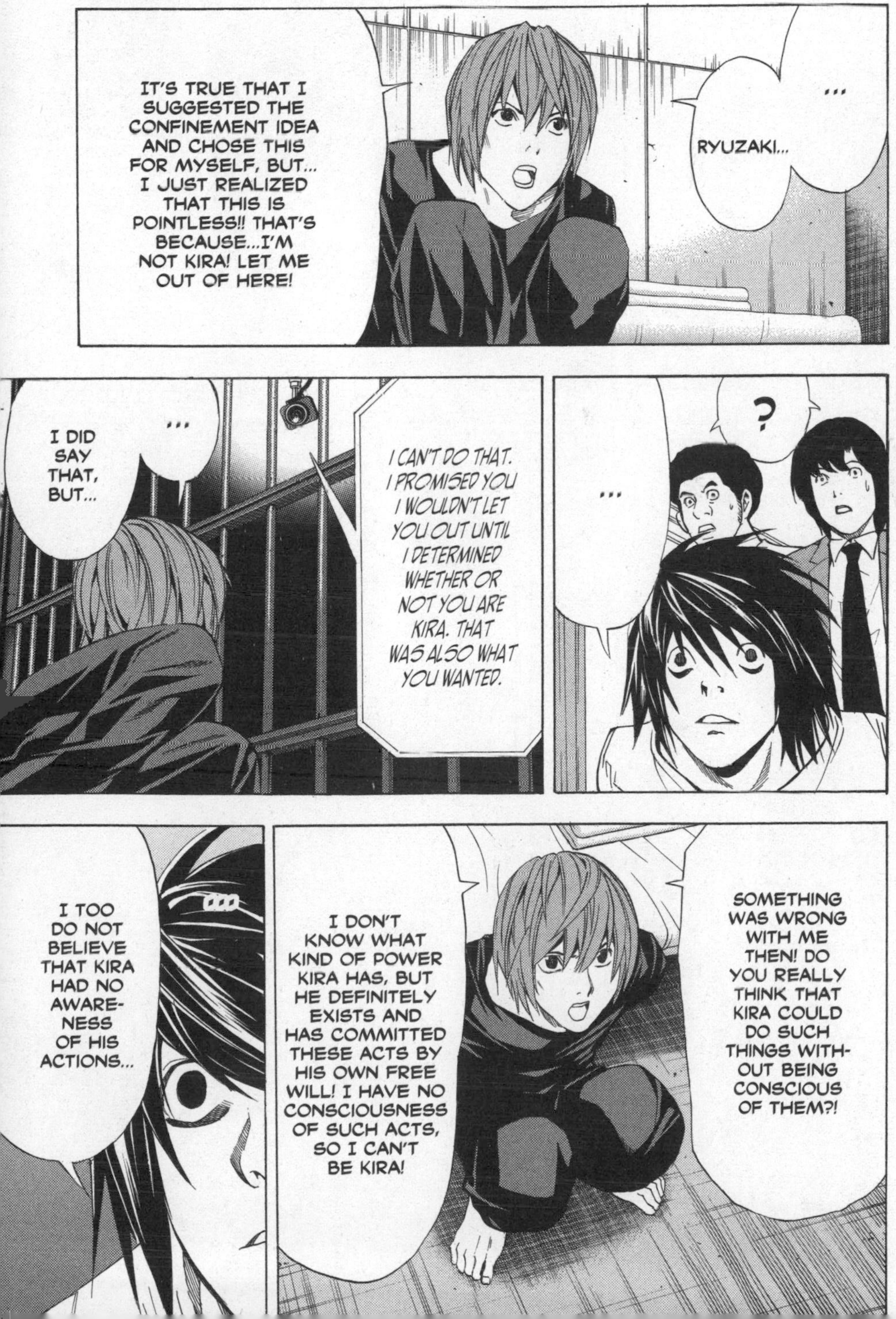
...
RYUZAKI...
IT'S TRUE THAT I SUGGESTED THE CONFINEMENT IDEA AND CHOSE THIS FOR MYSELF, BUT... I JUST REALIZED THAT THIS IS POINTLESS!! THAT'S BECAUSE...I'M NOT KIRA! LET ME OUT OF HERE!
?
...
I CAN'T DO THAT. I PROMISED YOU I WOULDN'T LET YOU OUT UNTIL I DETERMINED WHETHER OR NOT YOU ARE KIRA. THAT WAS ALSO WHAT YOU WANTED.
...
I DID SAY THAT, BUT...
SOMETHING WAS WRONG WITH ME THEN! DO YOU REALLY THINK THAT KIRA COULD DO SUCH THINGS WITH-OUT BEING CONSCIOUS OF THEM?!
I DON'T KNOW WHAT KIND OF POWER KIRA HAS, BUT HE DEFINITELY EXISTS AND HAS COMMITTED THESE ACTS BY HIS OWN FREE WILL! I HAVE NO CONSCIOUSNESS OF SUCH ACTS, SO I CAN'T BE KIRA!
I TOO DO NOT BELIEVE THAT KIRA HAD NO AWARE-NESS OF HIS ACTIONS...

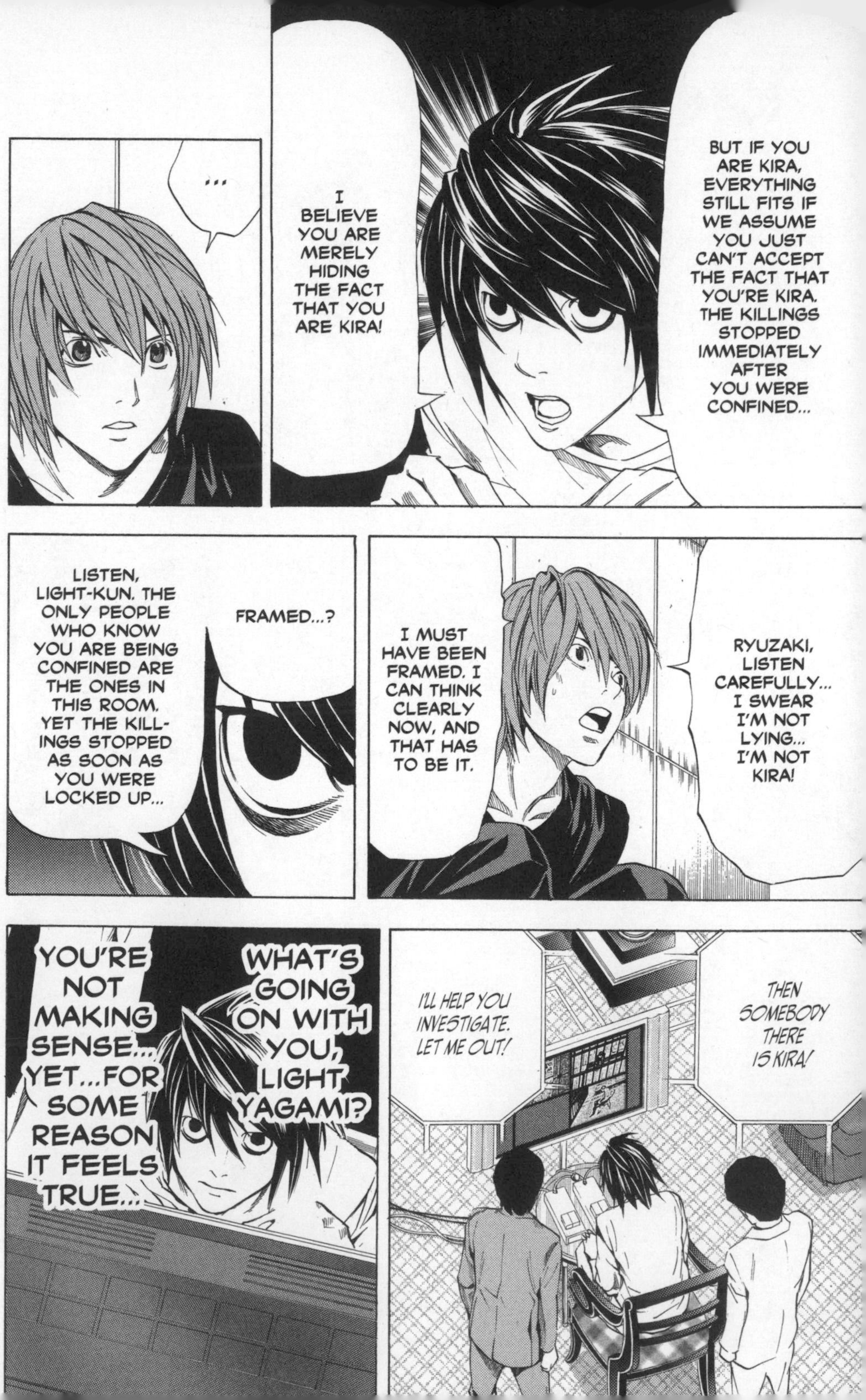
BUT IF YOU ARE KIRA, EVERYTHING STILL FITS IF WE ASSUME YOU JUST CAN'T ACCEPT THE FACT THAT YOU'RE KIRA. THE KILLINGS STOPPED IMMEDIATELY AFTER YOU WERE CONFINED...
I BELIEVE YOU ARE MERELY HIDING THE FACT THAT YOU ARE KIRA!
...
RYUZAKI, LISTEN CAREFULLY... I SWEAR I'M NOT LYING... I'M NOT KIRA!
I MUST HAVE BEEN FRAMED. I CAN THINK CLEARLY NOW, AND THAT HAS TO BE IT.
FRAMED...?
LISTEN, LIGHT-KUN. THE ONLY PEOPLE WHO KNOW YOU ARE BEING CONFINED ARE THE ONES IN THIS ROOM. YET THE KILL-INGS STOPPED AS SOON AS YOU WERE LOCKED UP...
THEN SOMEBODY THERE IS KIRA!
I'LL HELP YOU INVESTIGATE. LET ME OUT!
WHAT'S GOING ON WITH YOU, LIGHT YAGAMI?
YOU'RE NOT MAKING SENSE... YET...FOR SOME REASON IT FEELS TRUE...

READ THIS WAY

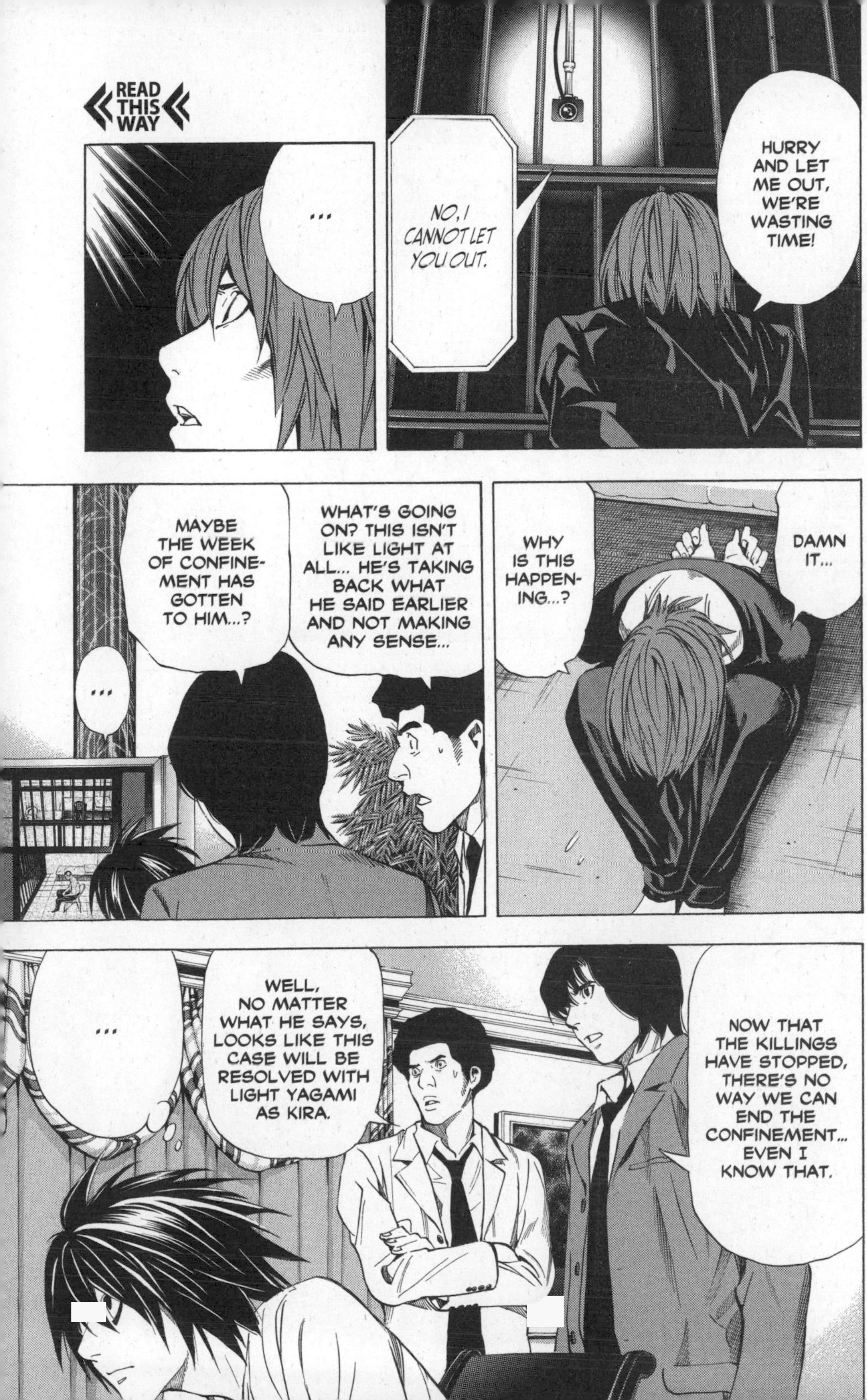
HURRY AND LET ME OUT, WE'RE WASTING TIME!
NO, I CANNOT LET YOU OUT.
...
DAMN IT...
WHY IS THIS HAPPENING...?
WHAT'S GOING ON? THIS ISN'T LIKE LIGHT AT ALL... HE'S TAKING BACK WHAT HE SAID EARLIER AND NOT MAKING ANY SENSE...
MAYBE THE WEEK OF CONFINEMENT HAS GOTTEN TO HIM...?
...
NOW THAT THE KILLINGS HAVE STOPPED, THERE'S NO WAY WE CAN END THE CONFINEMENT... EVEN I KNOW THAT.
WELL, NO MATTER WHAT HE SAYS, LOOKS LIKE THIS CASE WILL BE RESOLVED WITH LIGHT YAGAMI AS KIRA.
...

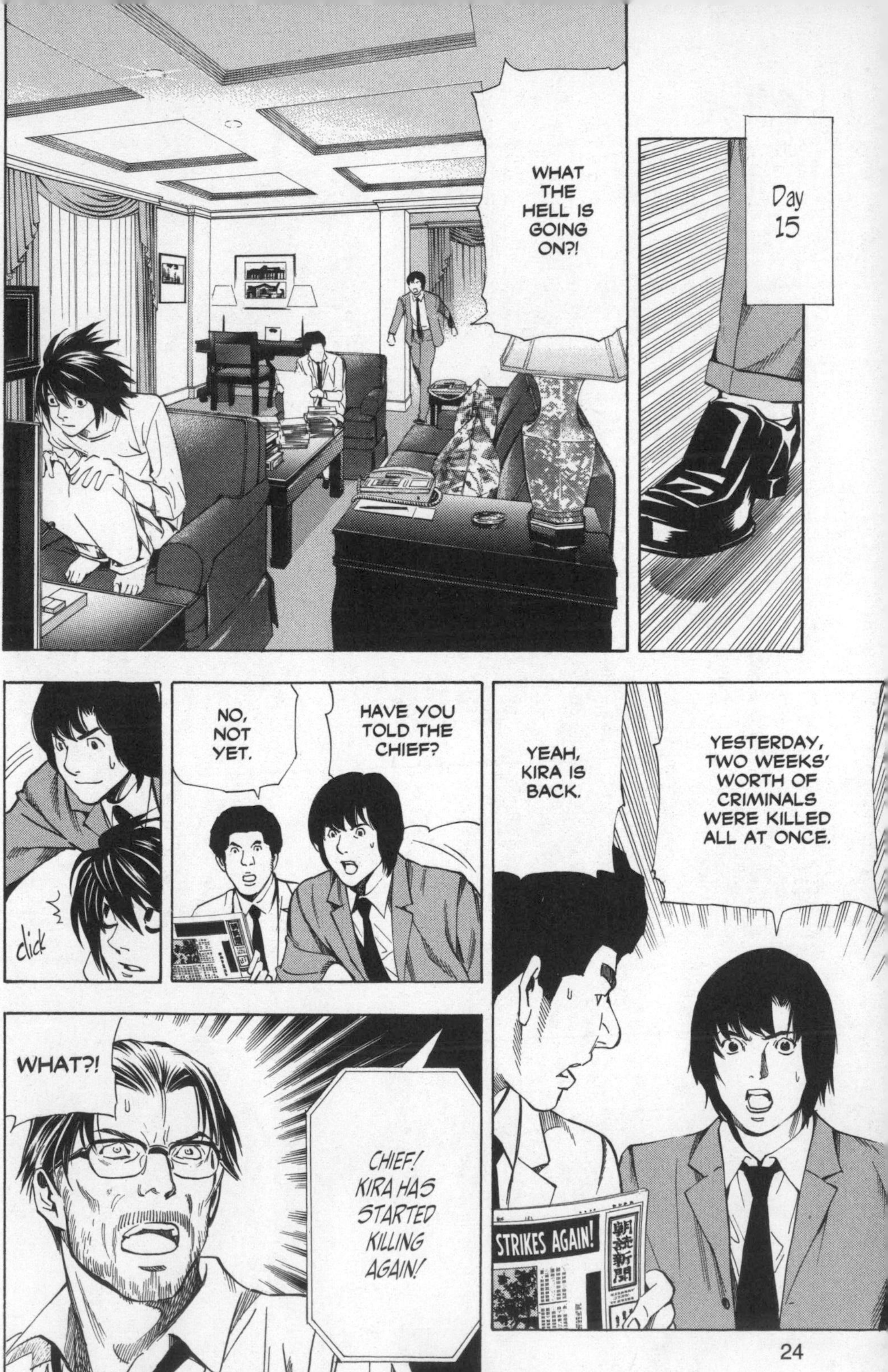

Day 15
WHAT THE HELL IS GOING ON?!
YESTERDAY, TWO WEEKS' WORTH OF CRIMINALS WERE KILLED ALL AT ONCE.
YEAH, KIRA IS BACK.
STRIKES AGAIN!
HAVE YOU TOLD THE CHIEF?
NO, NOT YET.
click
CHIEF! KIRA HAS STARTED KILLING AGAIN!
WHAT?!

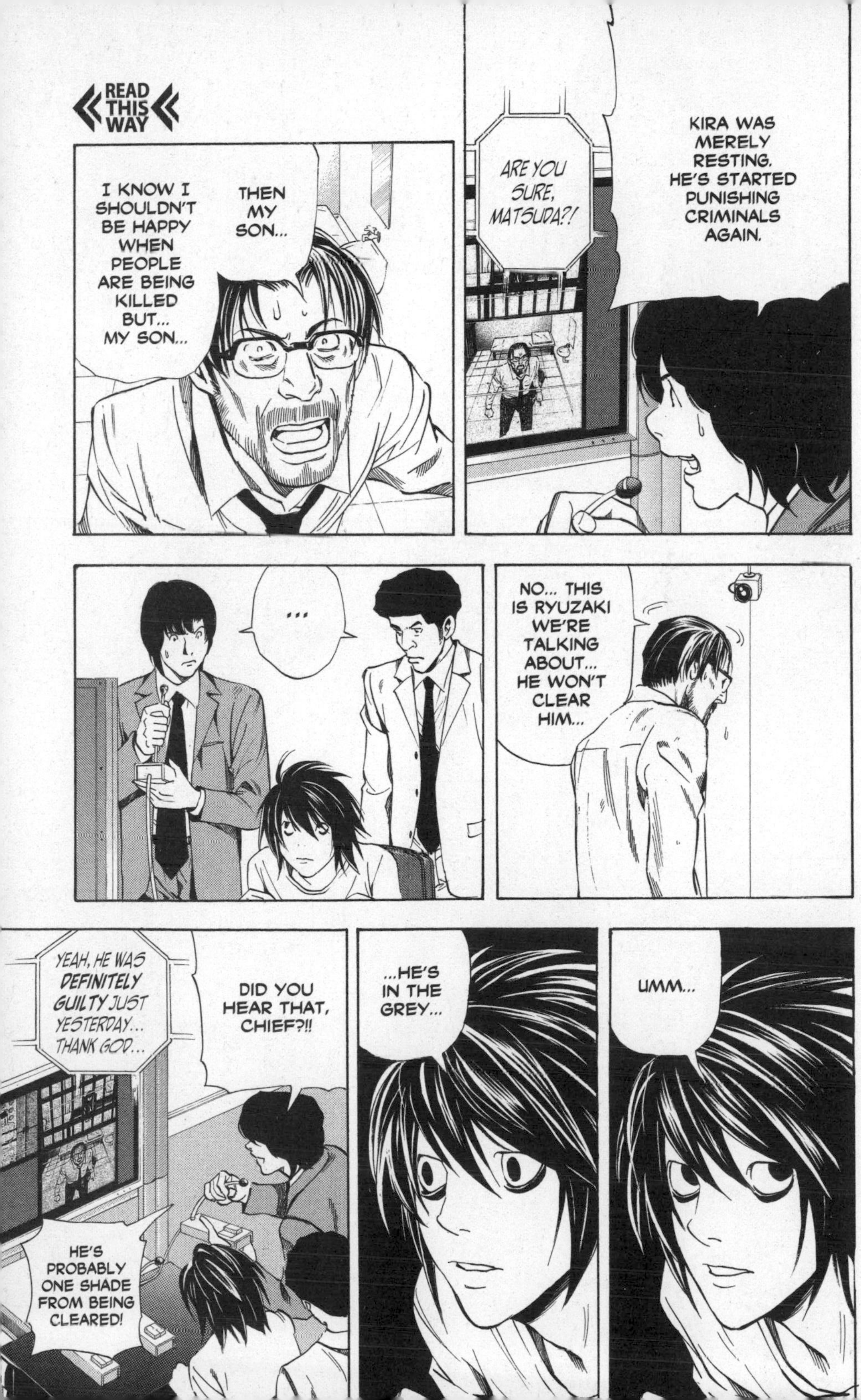
READ THIS WAY
KIRA WAS MERELY RESTING. HE'S STARTED PUNISHING CRIMINALS AGAIN.
ARE YOU SURE, MATSUDA?!
THEN MY SON...
I KNOW I SHOULDN'T BE HAPPY WHEN PEOPLE ARE BEING KILLED BUT... MY SON...
NO... THIS IS RYUZAKI WE'RE TALKING ABOUT... HE WON'T CLEAR HIM...
...
UMM...
...HE'S IN THE GREY...
DID YOU HEAR THAT, CHIEF?!!
YEAH, HE WAS DEFINITELY GUILTY JUST YESTERDAY... THANK GOD...
HE'S PROBABLY ONE SHADE FROM BEING CLEARED!

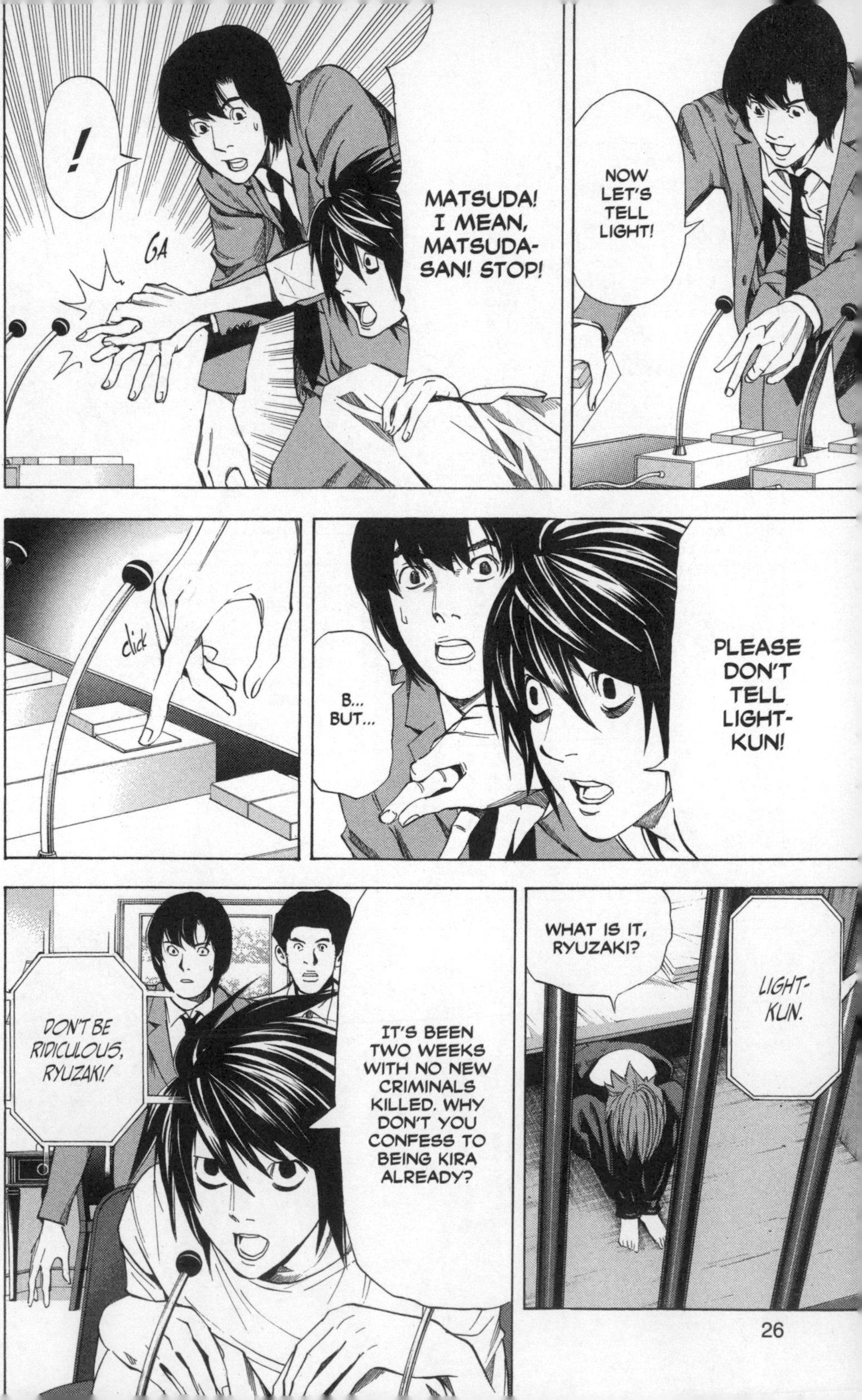
NOW LET'S TELL LIGHT!
MATSUDA! I MEAN, MATSUDA-SAN! STOP!
!
GA
PLEASE DON'T TELL LIGHT-KUN!
B... BUT...
click
LIGHT-KUN.
WHAT IS IT, RYUZAKI?
IT'S BEEN TWO WEEKS WITH NO NEW CRIMINALS KILLED. WHY DON'T YOU CONFESS TO BEING KIRA ALREADY?
DON'T BE RIDICULOUS, RYUZAKI!

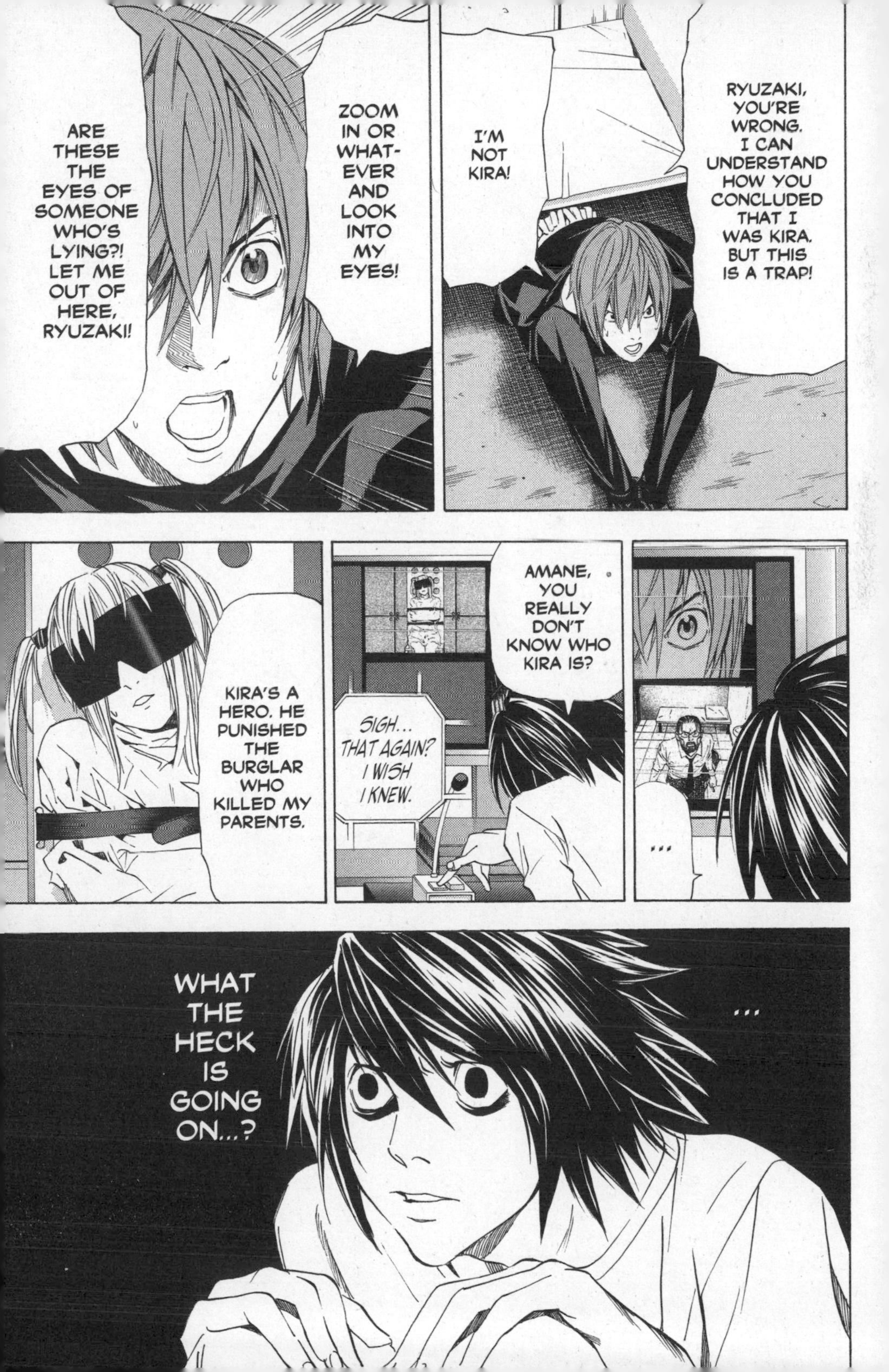
RYUZAKI, YOU'RE WRONG. I CAN UNDERSTAND HOW YOU CONCLUDED THAT I WAS KIRA. BUT THIS IS A TRAP!
I'M NOT KIRA!
ZOOM IN OR WHATEVER AND LOOK INTO MY EYES!
ARE THESE THE EYES OF SOMEONE WHO'S LYING?! LET ME OUT OF HERE, RYUZAKI!
...
AMANE, YOU REALLY DON'T KNOW WHO KIRA IS?
SIGH... THAT AGAIN? I WISH I KNEW.
KIRA'S A HERO. HE PUNISHED THE BURGLAR WHO KILLED MY PARENTS.
...
WHAT THE HECK IS GOING ON...?

DEATH NOTE
How to use it
XXIV

○ The god of death must not stay in the human world without a particular reason. Conditions to stay in the human world are as follows:

死神は無闇に人間界に居てはならない。
人間界に居てよい条件は、

I.　　When the god of death's DEATH NOTE is handed to a human.

Ⅰ．自分が所持していたノートを人間に持たせている時。

II.　　Essentially, finding a human to pass on the DEATH NOTE should be done from the world of the gods of death, but if it is within 82 hours this may also be done in the human world.

Ⅱ．ノートを渡す人間を物色するのは、本来、死神界からするべきではあるが、82時間以内であれば、人間界に居て物色しても構わない。

III.　　When a god of death stalks an individual with an intention to kill them, as long as it is within 82 hours of haunting them, the god of death may stay in the human world.

Ⅲ．人間を殺す目的でより深くその個人を観察する場合も、82時間以内でその人間に憑いていれば人間界に居てもよい。

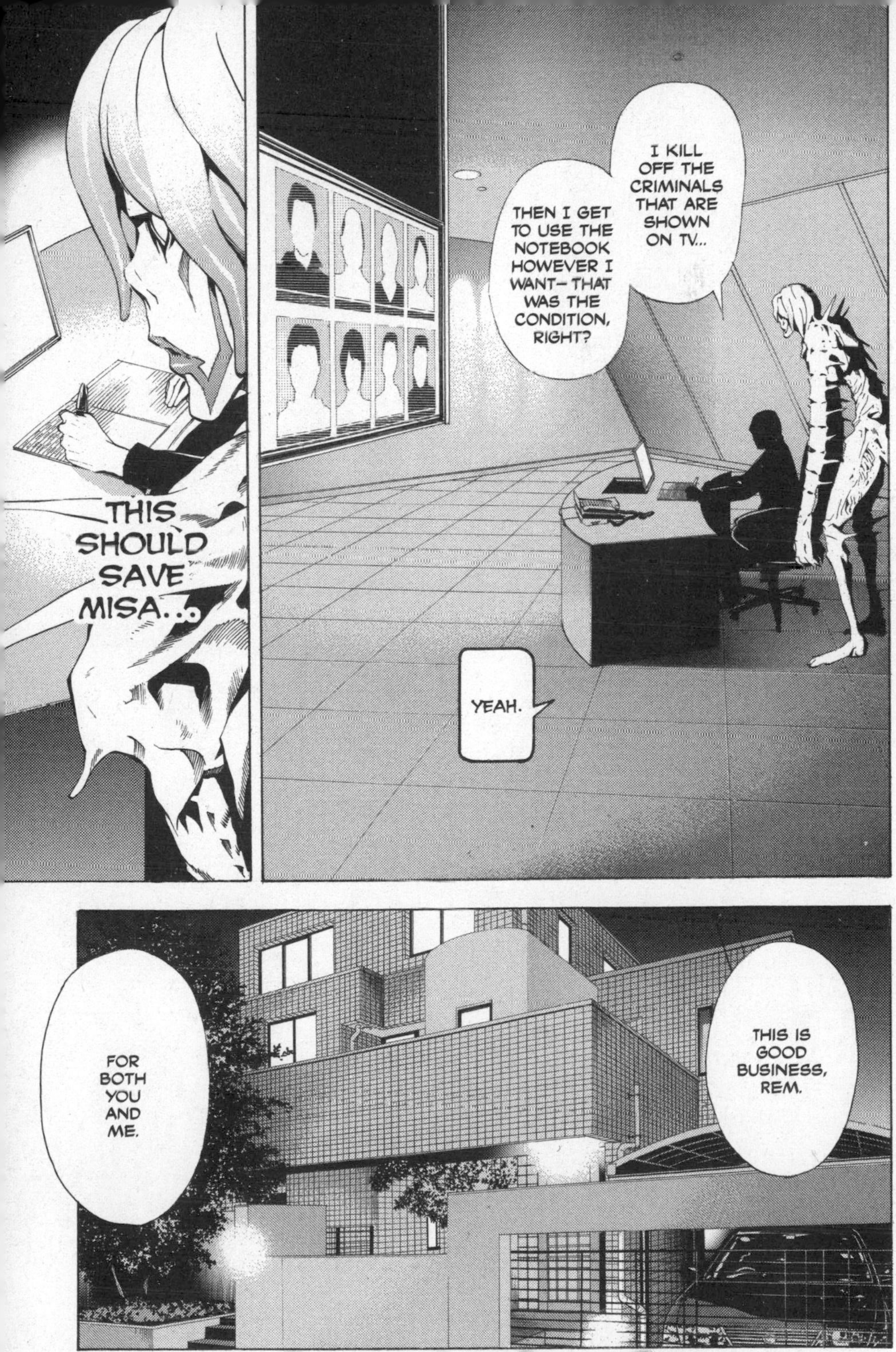
I KILL OFF THE CRIMINALS THAT ARE SHOWN ON TV...
THEN I GET TO USE THE NOTEBOOK HOWEVER I WANT—THAT WAS THE CONDITION, RIGHT?
YEAH.
THIS SHOULD SAVE MISA...
THIS IS GOOD BUSINESS, REM.
FOR BOTH YOU AND ME.

chapter 36 Father and Son

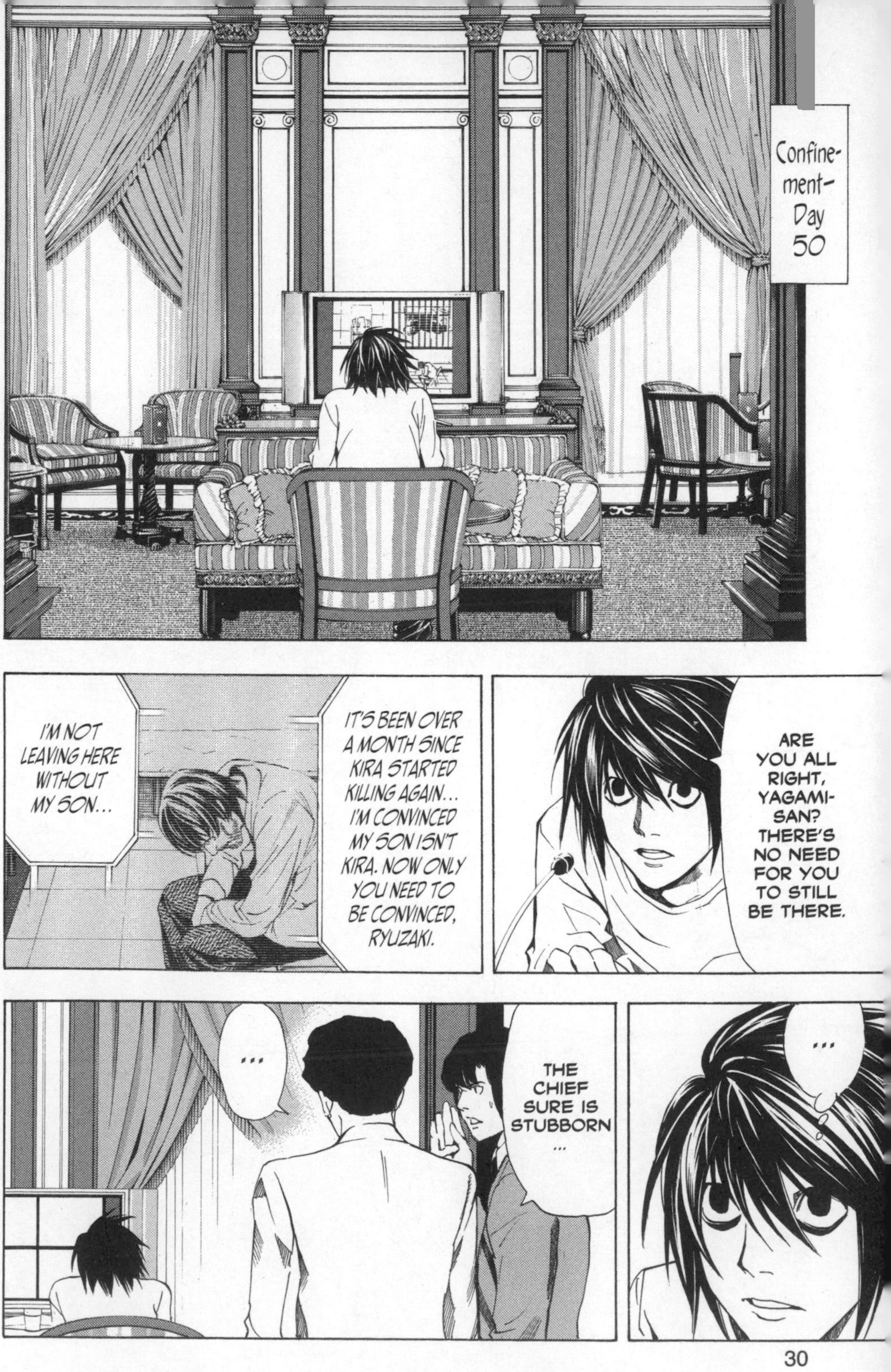
Confinement—Day 50
ARE YOU ALL RIGHT, YAGAMI-SAN? THERE'S NO NEED FOR YOU TO STILL BE THERE.
IT'S BEEN OVER A MONTH SINCE KIRA STARTED KILLING AGAIN... I'M CONVINCED MY SON ISN'T KIRA. NOW ONLY YOU NEED TO BE CONVINCED, RYUZAKI.
I'M NOT LEAVING HERE WITHOUT MY SON...
...
THE CHIEF SURE IS STUBBORN...
...

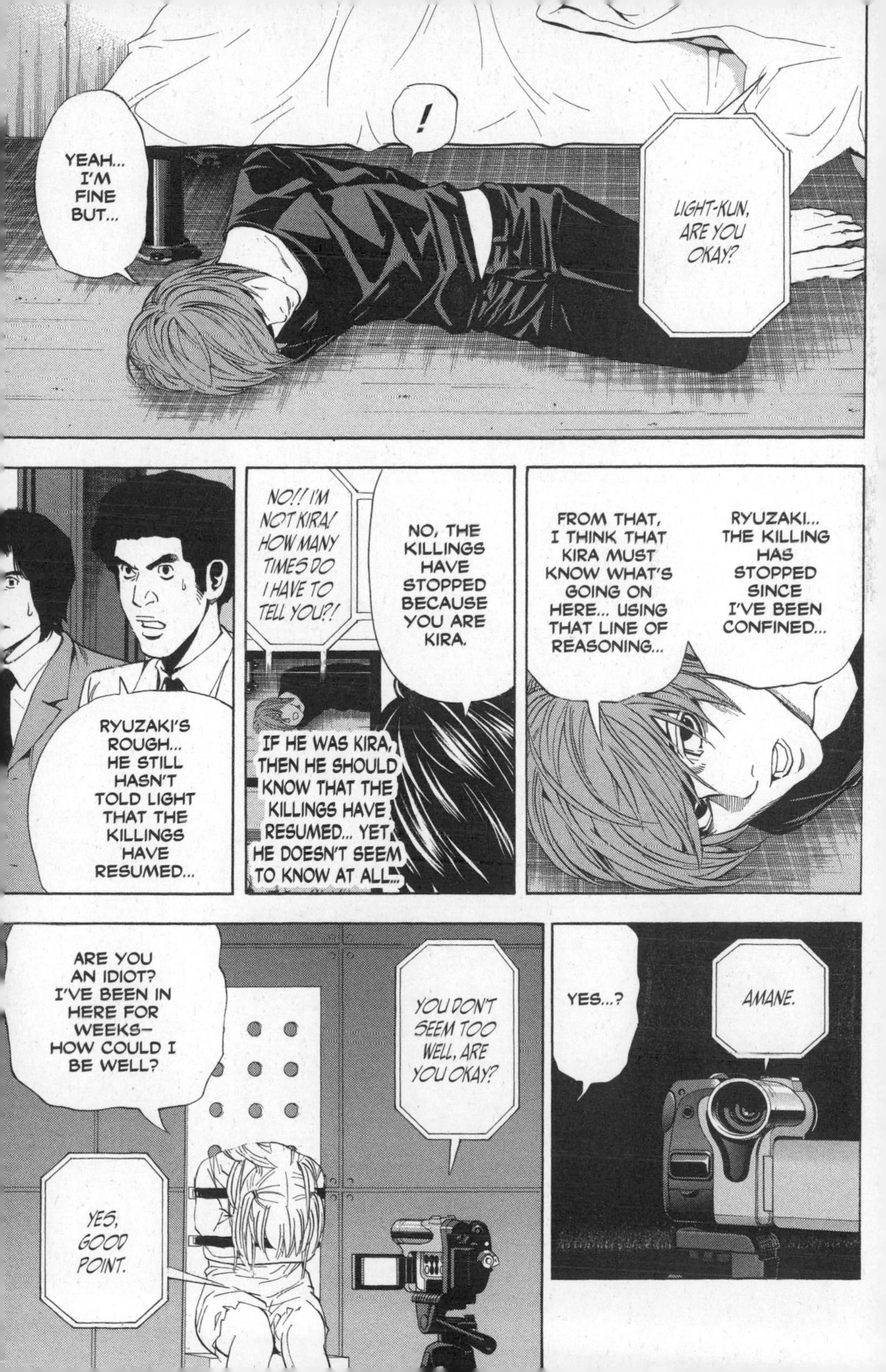
LIGHT-KUN, ARE YOU OKAY?
!
YEAH... I'M FINE BUT...
RYUZAKI... THE KILLING HAS STOPPED SINCE I'VE BEEN CONFINED...
FROM THAT, I THINK THAT KIRA MUST KNOW WHAT'S GOING ON HERE... USING THAT LINE OF REASONING...
NO, THE KILLINGS HAVE STOPPED BECAUSE YOU ARE KIRA.
NO!! I'M NOT KIRA! HOW MANY TIMES DO I HAVE TO TELL YOU?!
IF HE WAS KIRA, THEN HE SHOULD KNOW THAT THE KILLINGS HAVE RESUMED... YET HE DOESN'T SEEM TO KNOW AT ALL...
RYUZAKI'S ROUGH... HE STILL HASN'T TOLD LIGHT THAT THE KILLINGS HAVE RESUMED...
AMANE.
YES...?
YOU DON'T SEEM TOO WELL, ARE YOU OKAY?
ARE YOU AN IDIOT? I'VE BEEN IN HERE FOR WEEKS–HOW COULD I BE WELL?
YES, GOOD POINT.

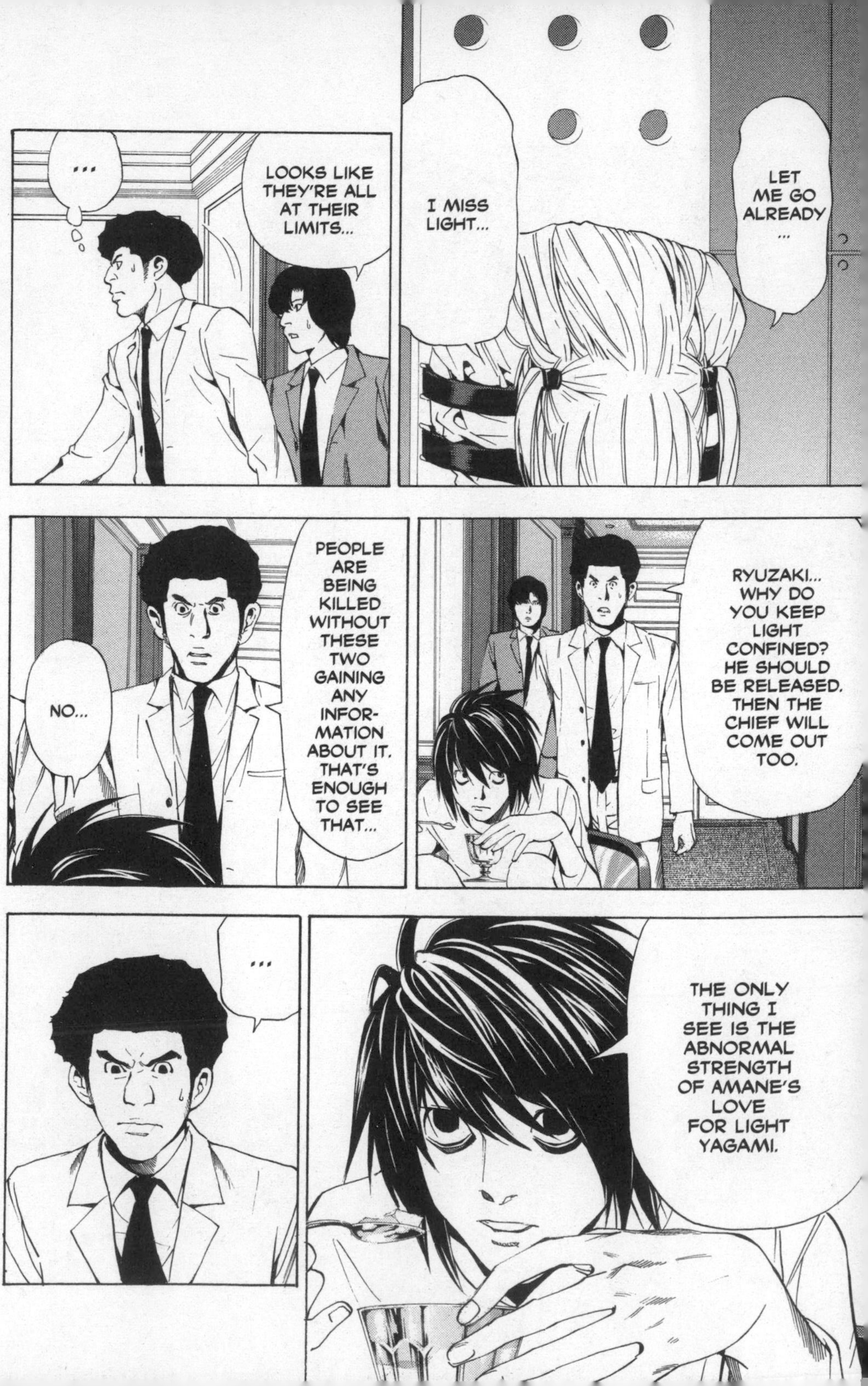
LET ME GO ALREADY ...
I MISS LIGHT...
LOOKS LIKE THEY'RE ALL AT THEIR LIMITS...
...
RYUZAKI... WHY DO YOU KEEP LIGHT CONFINED? HE SHOULD BE RELEASED. THEN THE CHIEF WILL COME OUT TOO.
PEOPLE ARE BEING KILLED WITHOUT THESE TWO GAINING ANY INFOR-MATION ABOUT IT. THAT'S ENOUGH TO SEE THAT...
NO...
THE ONLY THING I SEE IS THE ABNORMAL STRENGTH OF AMANE'S LOVE FOR LIGHT YAGAMI.
...

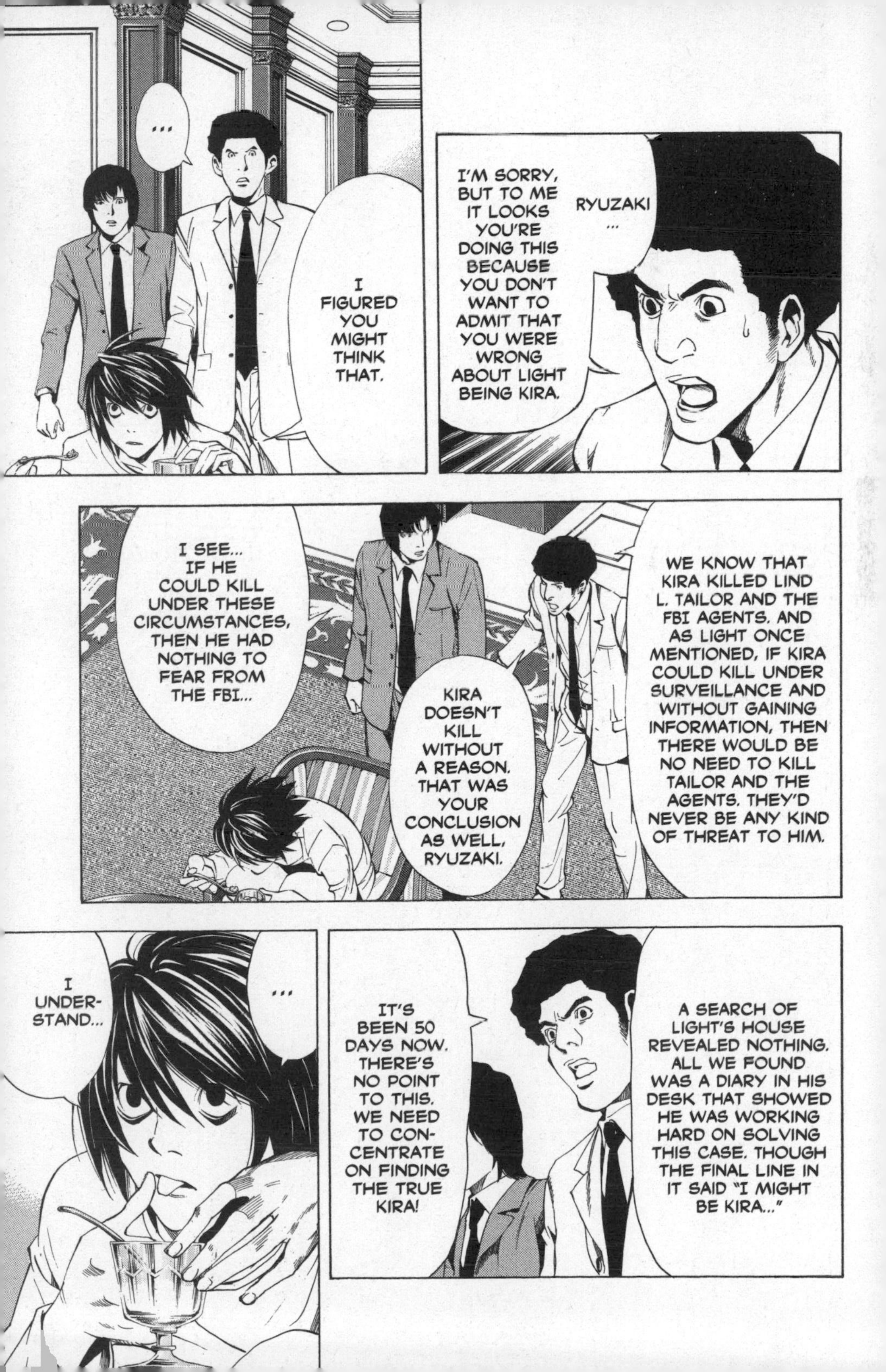
RYUZAKI ...
I'M SORRY, BUT TO ME IT LOOKS YOU'RE DOING THIS BECAUSE YOU DON'T WANT TO ADMIT THAT YOU WERE WRONG ABOUT LIGHT BEING KIRA.
I FIGURED YOU MIGHT THINK THAT.
...
WE KNOW THAT KIRA KILLED LIND L. TAILOR AND THE FBI AGENTS. AND AS LIGHT ONCE MENTIONED, IF KIRA COULD KILL UNDER SURVEILLANCE AND WITHOUT GAINING INFORMATION, THEN THERE WOULD BE NO NEED TO KILL TAILOR AND THE AGENTS. THEY'D NEVER BE ANY KIND OF THREAT TO HIM.
KIRA DOESN'T KILL WITHOUT A REASON. THAT WAS YOUR CONCLUSION AS WELL, RYUZAKI.
I SEE... IF HE COULD KILL UNDER THESE CIRCUMSTANCES, THEN HE HAD NOTHING TO FEAR FROM THE FBI...
A SEARCH OF LIGHT'S HOUSE REVEALED NOTHING. ALL WE FOUND WAS A DIARY IN HIS DESK THAT SHOWED HE WAS WORKING HARD ON SOLVING THIS CASE. THOUGH THE FINAL LINE IN IT SAID "I MIGHT BE KIRA..."
IT'S BEEN 50 DAYS NOW. THERE'S NO POINT TO THIS. WE NEED TO CON-CENTRATE ON FINDING THE TRUE KIRA!
...
I UNDER-STAND...

I WANT TO SPEAK TO YOU DIRECTLY. WILL YOU RETURN TO THE TASK-FORCE HEAD-QUARTERS?

WHAT?

YAGAMI-SAN.

...

FINE...

I WILL SHARE MY CONCLUSION ON THIS CASE. AS LIGHT-KUN'S FATHER, I WANT YOU TO BE THE FIRST TO HEAR IT...

...?!

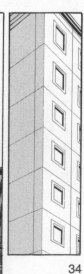

34

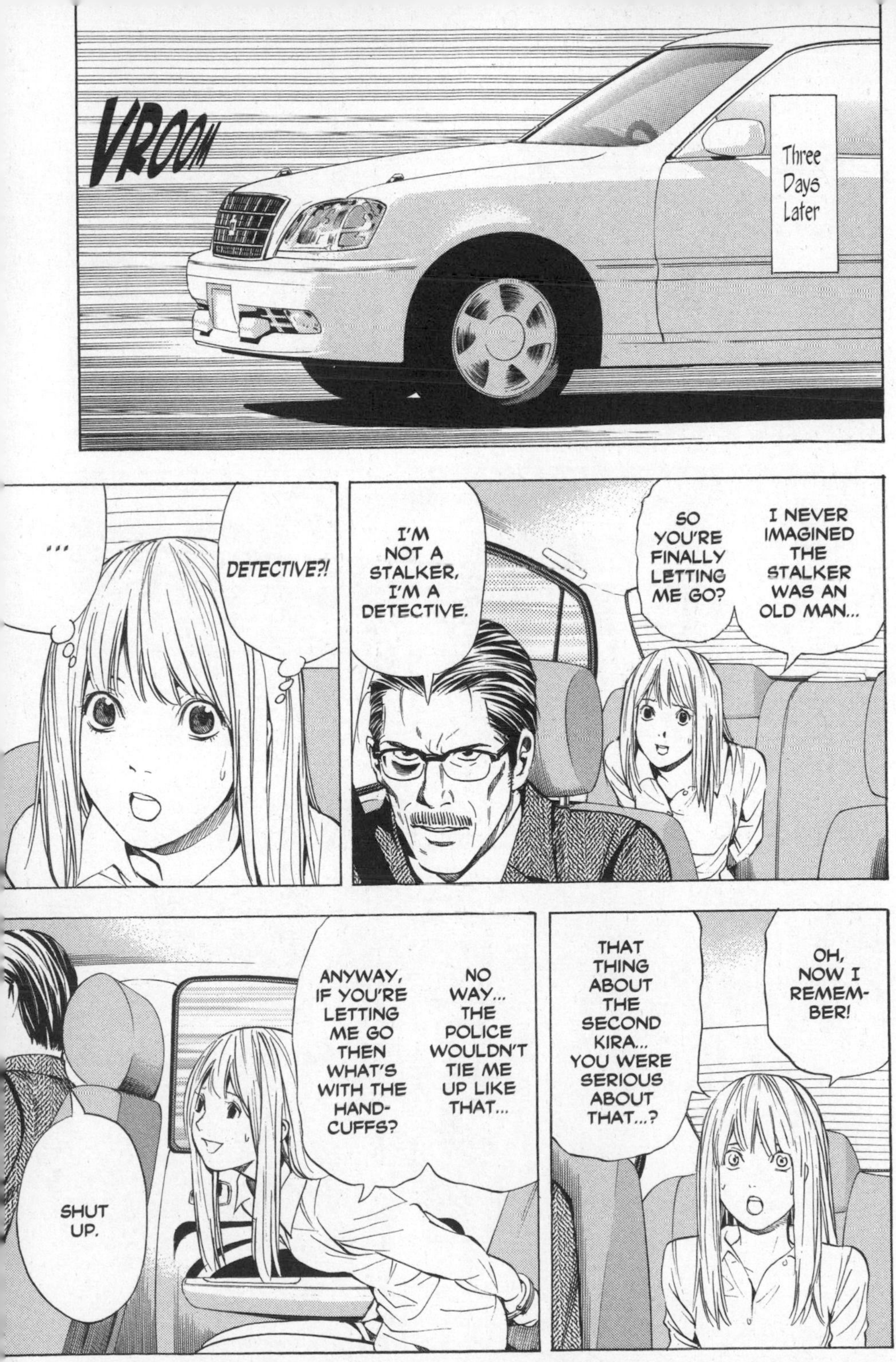
Three Days Later
VROOM
I NEVER IMAGINED THE STALKER WAS AN OLD MAN...
SO YOU'RE FINALLY LETTING ME GO?
I'M NOT A STALKER, I'M A DETECTIVE.
DETECTIVE?!
...
OH, NOW I REMEMBER!
THAT THING ABOUT THE SECOND KIRA... YOU WERE SERIOUS ABOUT THAT...?
NO WAY... THE POLICE WOULDN'T TIE ME UP LIKE THAT...
ANYWAY, IF YOU'RE LETTING ME GO THEN WHAT'S WITH THE HAND-CUFFS?
SHUT UP.

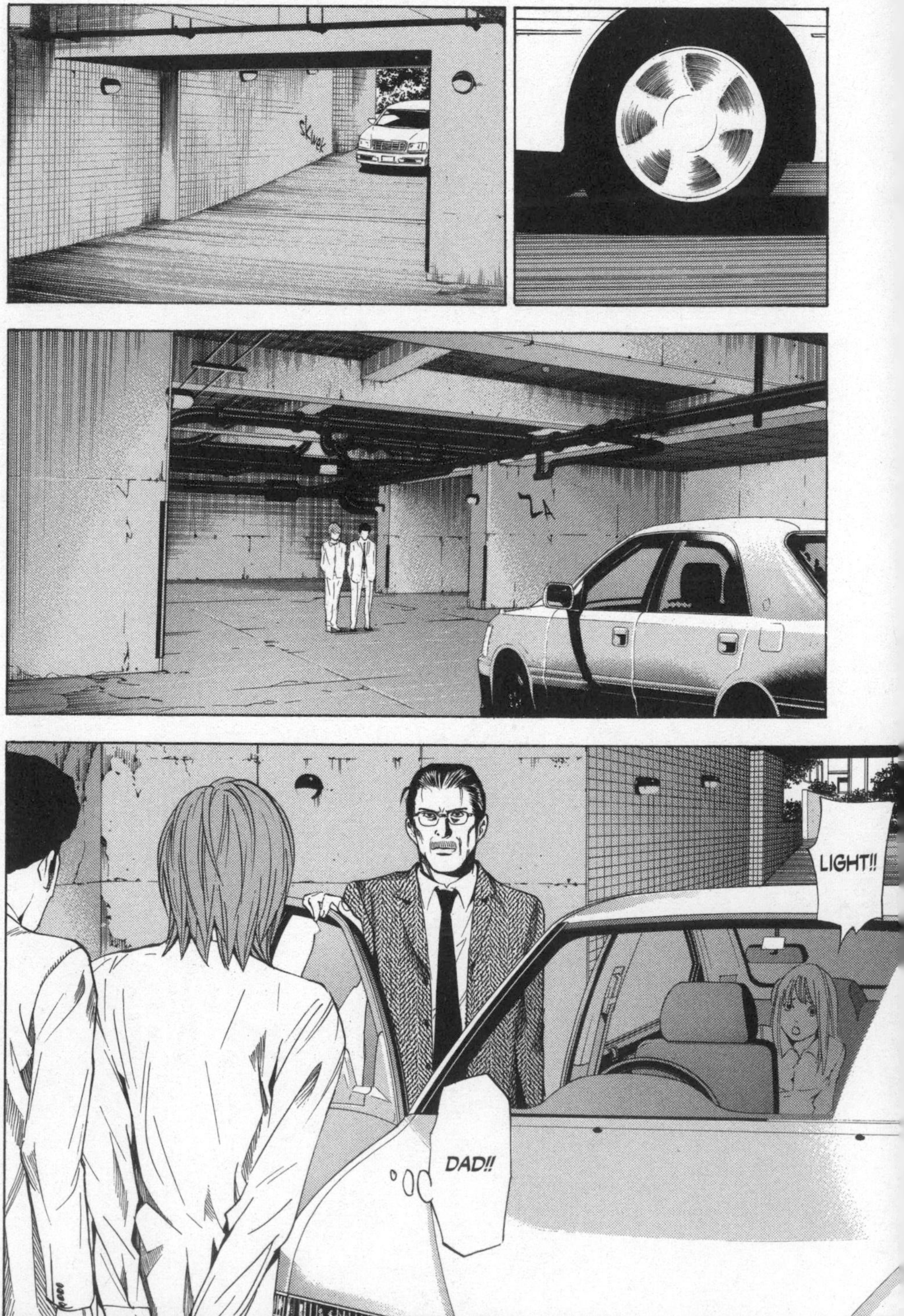
LIGHT!!
DAD!!

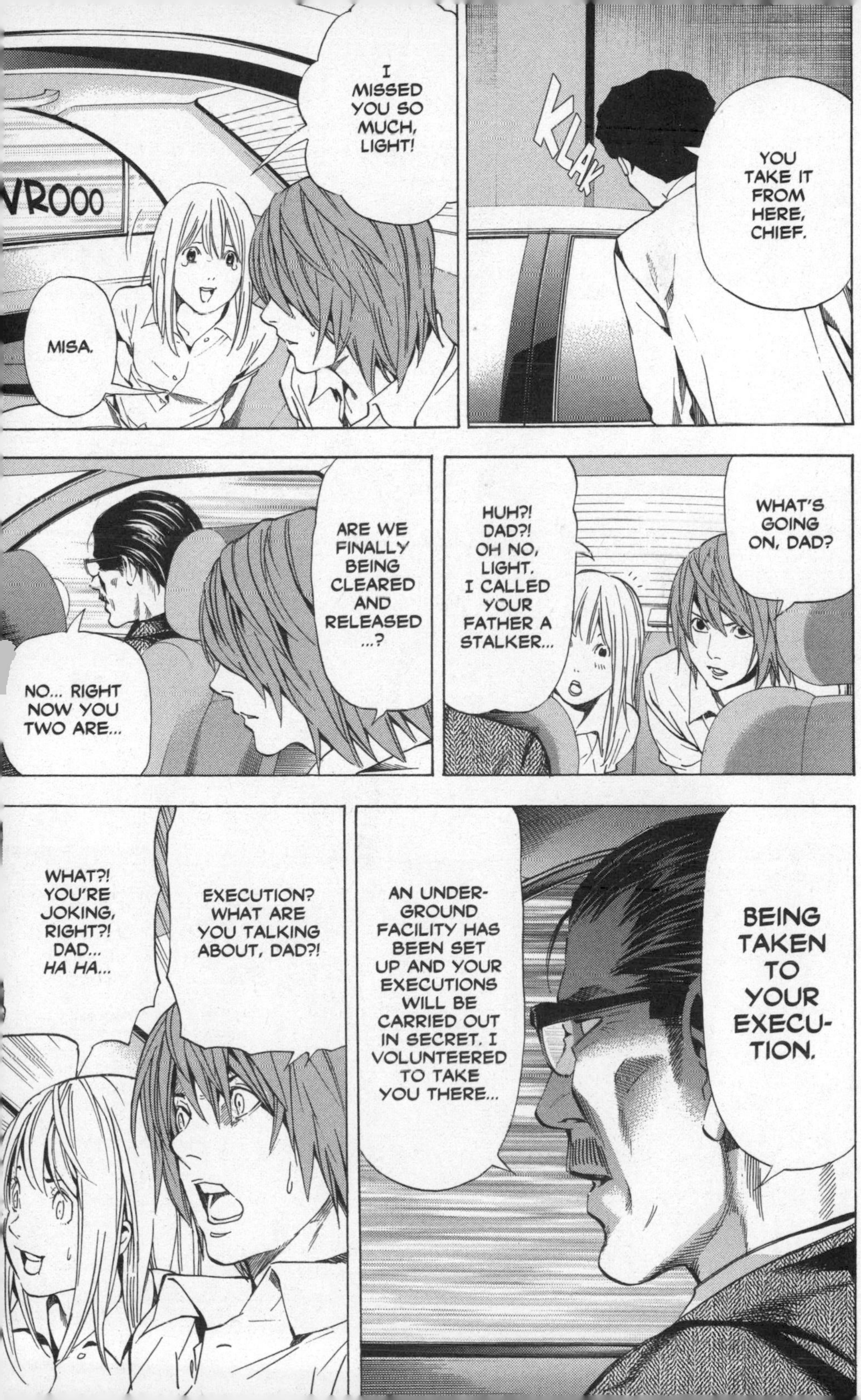
KLAK
YOU TAKE IT FROM HERE, CHIEF.
I MISSED YOU SO MUCH, LIGHT!
VROOO
MISA.
WHAT'S GOING ON, DAD?
HUH?! DAD?! OH NO, LIGHT. I CALLED YOUR FATHER A STALKER...
ARE WE FINALLY BEING CLEARED AND RELEASED...?
NO... RIGHT NOW YOU TWO ARE...
BEING TAKEN TO YOUR EXECUTION.
AN UNDERGROUND FACILITY HAS BEEN SET UP AND YOUR EXECUTIONS WILL BE CARRIED OUT IN SECRET. I VOLUNTEERED TO TAKE YOU THERE...
EXECUTION? WHAT ARE YOU TALKING ABOUT, DAD?!
WHAT?! YOU'RE JOKING, RIGHT?! DAD... *HA HA*...

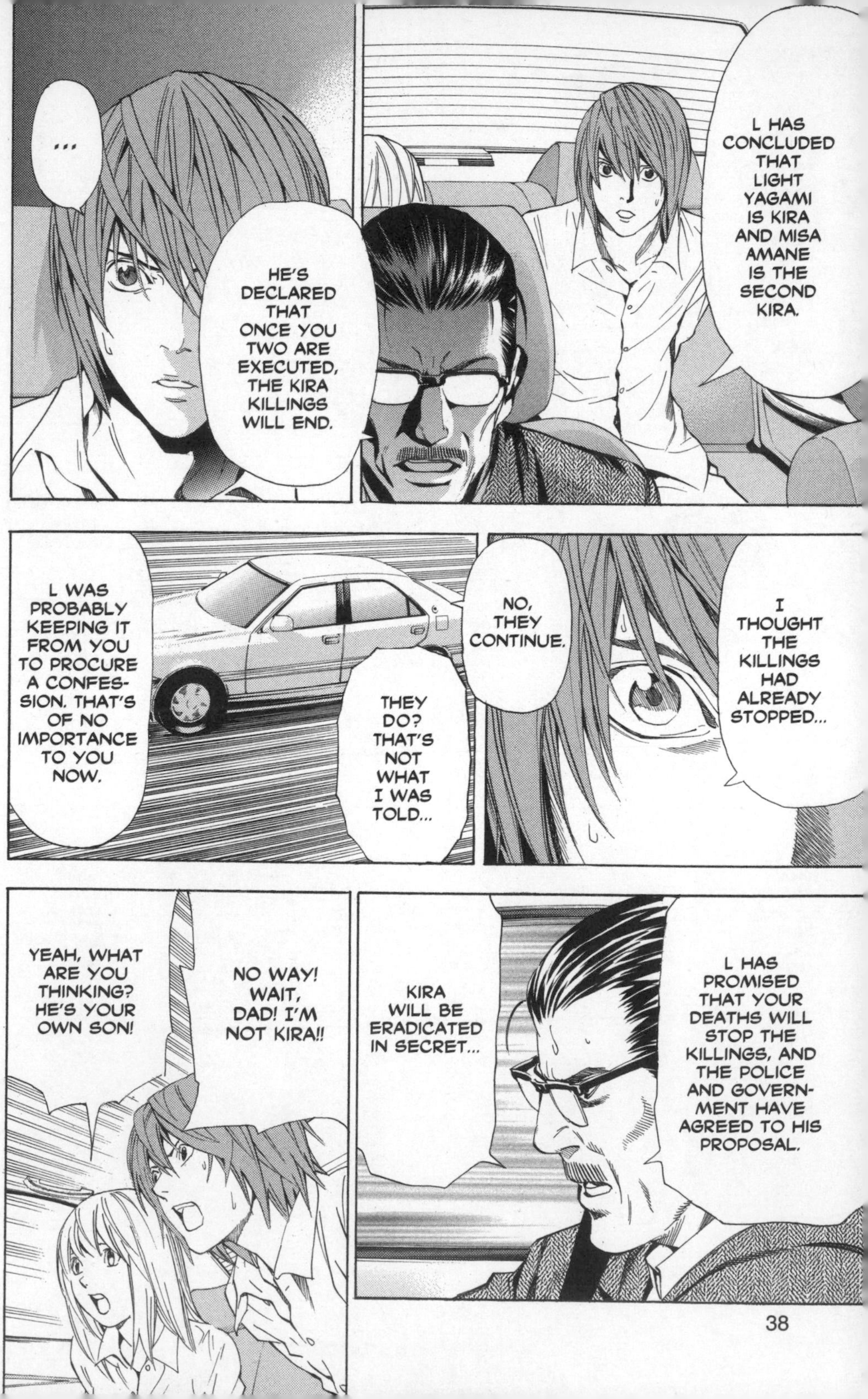
L HAS CONCLUDED THAT LIGHT YAGAMI IS KIRA AND MISA AMANE IS THE SECOND KIRA.
HE'S DECLARED THAT ONCE YOU TWO ARE EXECUTED, THE KIRA KILLINGS WILL END.
...
I THOUGHT THE KILLINGS HAD ALREADY STOPPED...
NO, THEY CONTINUE.
THEY DO? THAT'S NOT WHAT I WAS TOLD...
L WAS PROBABLY KEEPING IT FROM YOU TO PROCURE A CONFES-SION. THAT'S OF NO IMPORTANCE TO YOU NOW.
L HAS PROMISED THAT YOUR DEATHS WILL STOP THE KILLINGS, AND THE POLICE AND GOVERN-MENT HAVE AGREED TO HIS PROPOSAL.
KIRA WILL BE ERADICATED IN SECRET...
NO WAY! WAIT, DAD! I'M NOT KIRA!!
YEAH, WHAT ARE YOU THINKING? HE'S YOUR OWN SON!

READ THIS WAY

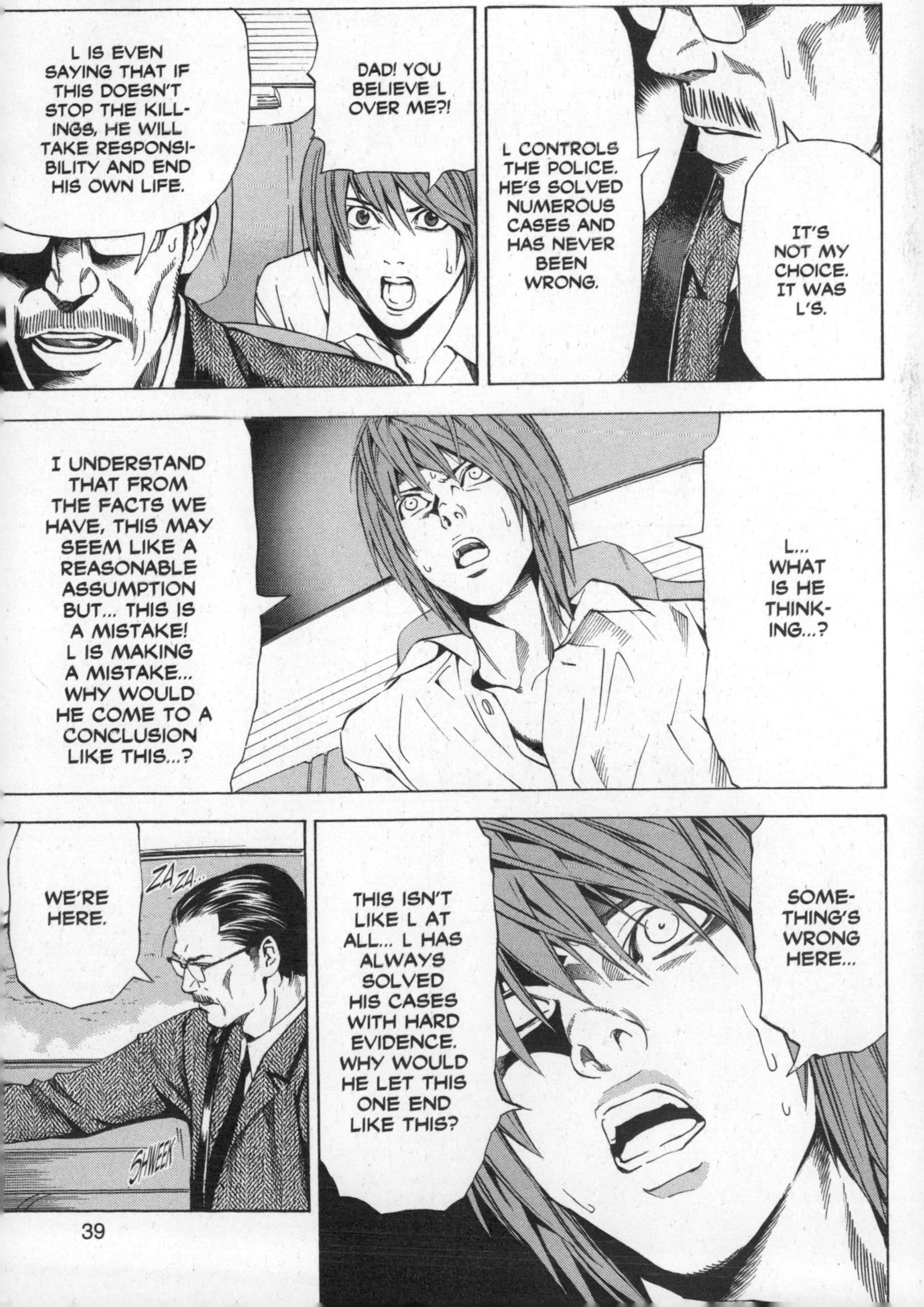

IT'S NOT MY CHOICE. IT WAS L'S.
L CONTROLS THE POLICE. HE'S SOLVED NUMEROUS CASES AND HAS NEVER BEEN WRONG.
DAD! YOU BELIEVE L OVER ME?!
L IS EVEN SAYING THAT IF THIS DOESN'T STOP THE KILL-INGS, HE WILL TAKE RESPONSI-BILITY AND END HIS OWN LIFE.
L... WHAT IS HE THINK-ING...?
I UNDERSTAND THAT FROM THE FACTS WE HAVE, THIS MAY SEEM LIKE A REASONABLE ASSUMPTION BUT... THIS IS A MISTAKE! L IS MAKING A MISTAKE... WHY WOULD HE COME TO A CONCLUSION LIKE THIS...?
SOME-THING'S WRONG HERE...
THIS ISN'T LIKE L AT ALL... L HAS ALWAYS SOLVED HIS CASES WITH HARD EVIDENCE. WHY WOULD HE LET THIS ONE END LIKE THIS?
ZA ZA...
WE'RE HERE.
SHWEEK

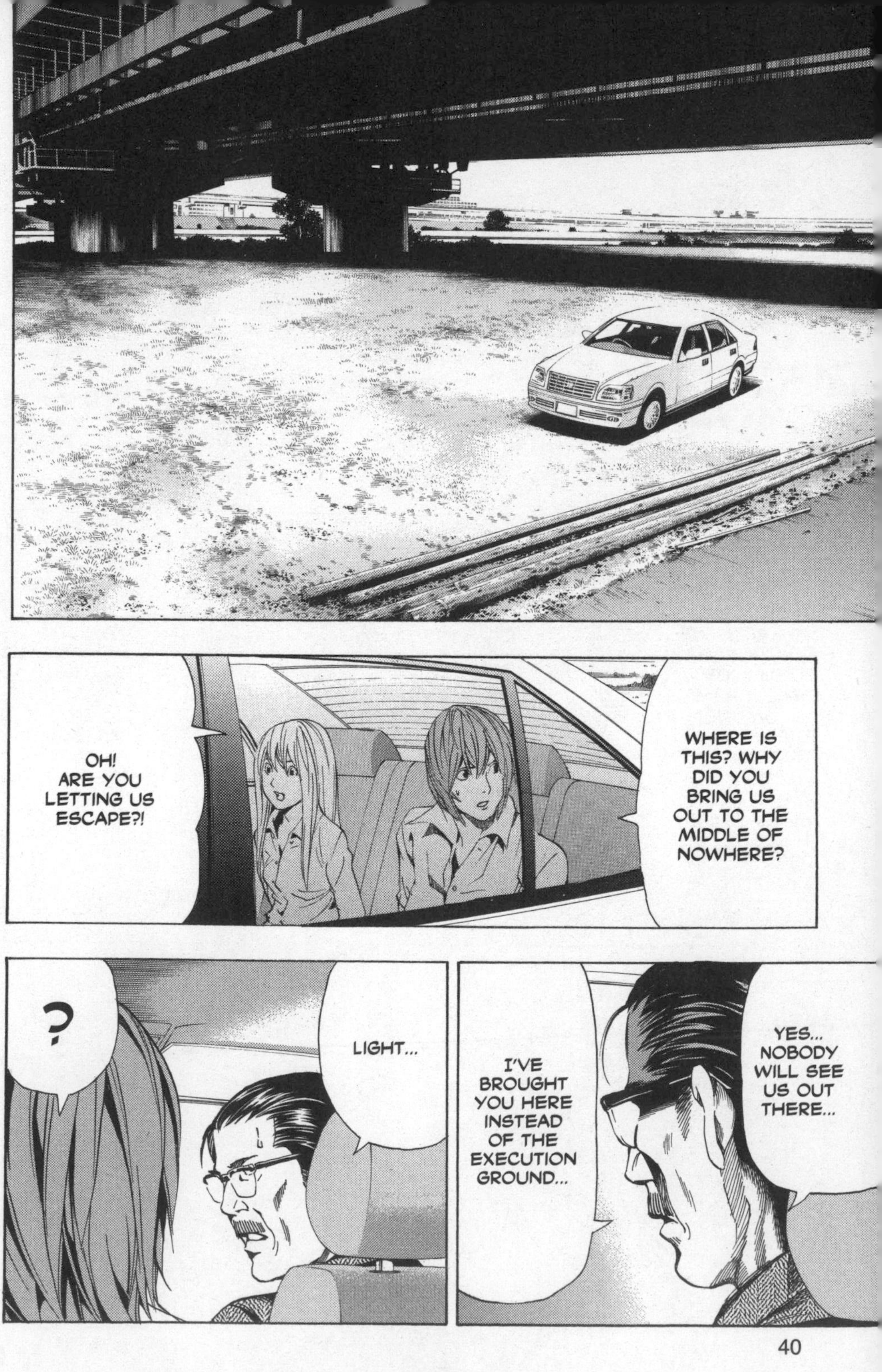
WHERE IS THIS? WHY DID YOU BRING US OUT TO THE MIDDLE OF NOWHERE?
OH! ARE YOU LETTING US ESCAPE?!
YES... NOBODY WILL SEE US OUT THERE...
I'VE BROUGHT YOU HERE INSTEAD OF THE EXECUTION GROUND...
LIGHT...
?

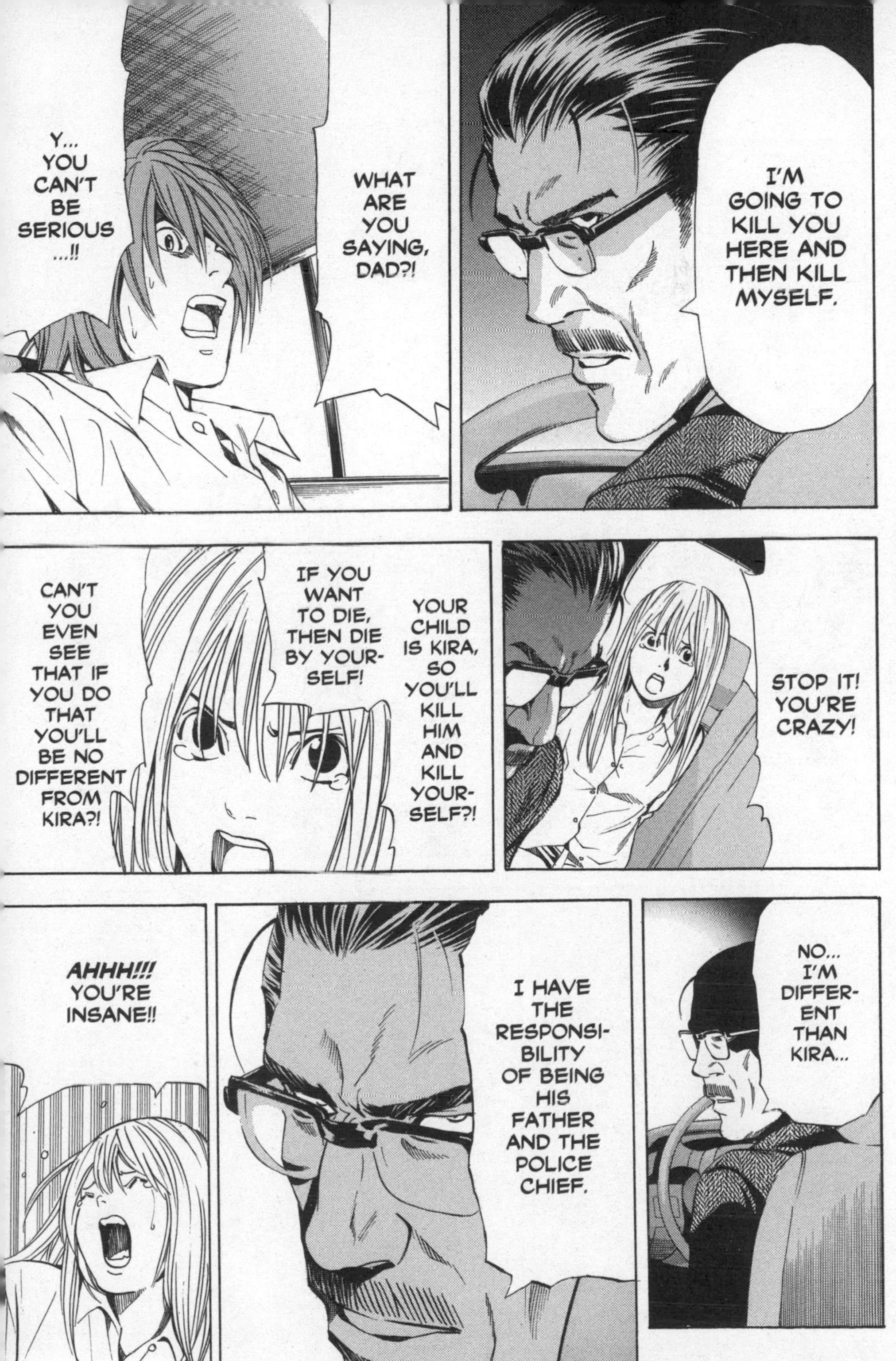
I'M GOING TO KILL YOU HERE AND THEN KILL MYSELF.
WHAT ARE YOU SAYING, DAD?!
Y... YOU CAN'T BE SERIOUS ...!!
STOP IT! YOU'RE CRAZY!
YOUR CHILD IS KIRA, SO YOU'LL KILL HIM AND KILL YOURSELF?!
IF YOU WANT TO DIE, THEN DIE BY YOURSELF!
CAN'T YOU EVEN SEE THAT IF YOU DO THAT YOU'LL BE NO DIFFERENT FROM KIRA?!
NO... I'M DIFFERENT THAN KIRA...
I HAVE THE RESPONSIBILITY OF BEING HIS FATHER AND THE POLICE CHIEF.
AHHH!!! YOU'RE INSANE!!

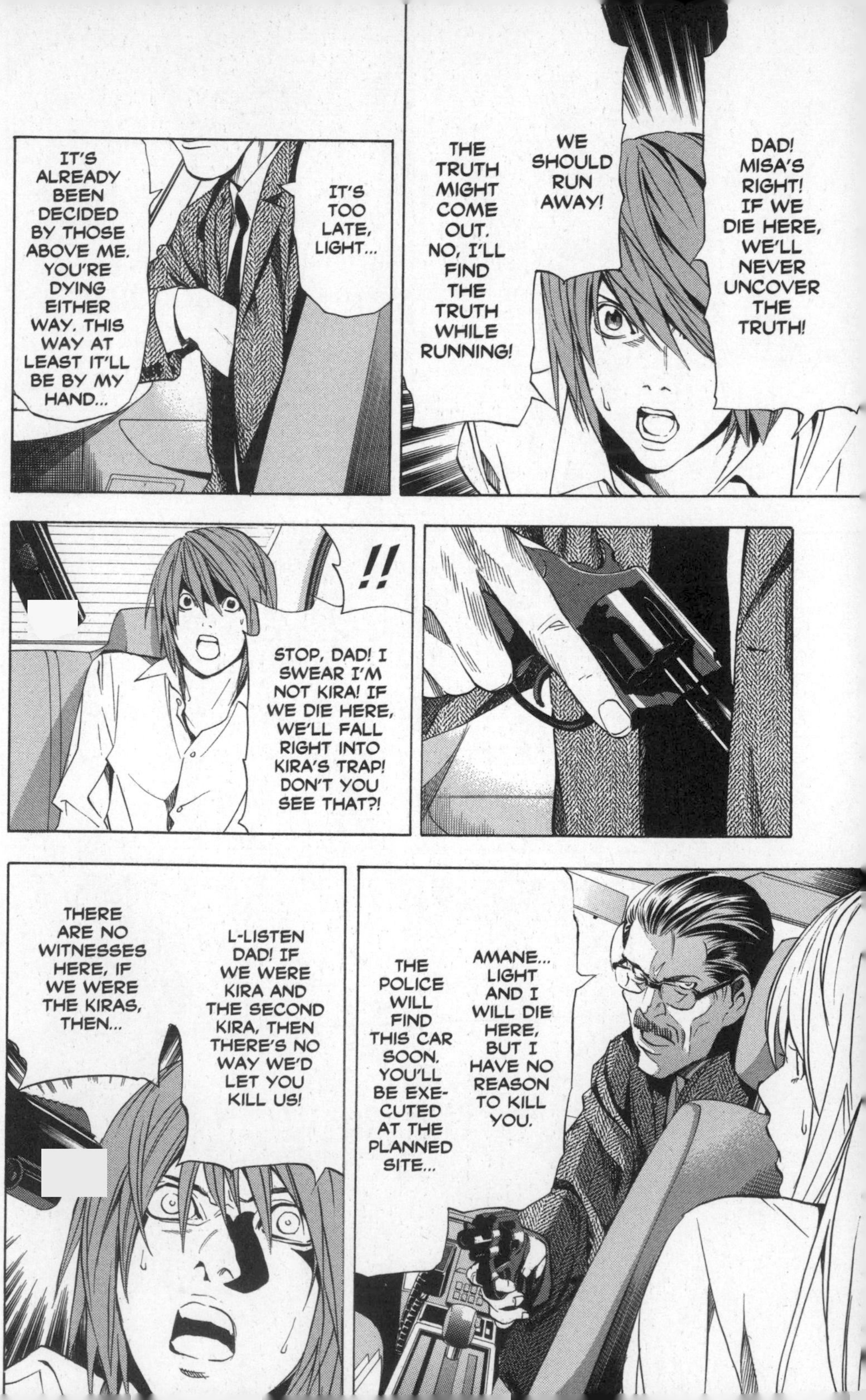
DAD! MISA'S RIGHT! IF WE DIE HERE, WE'LL NEVER UNCOVER THE TRUTH!
WE SHOULD RUN AWAY!
THE TRUTH MIGHT COME OUT. NO, I'LL FIND THE TRUTH WHILE RUNNING!
IT'S TOO LATE, LIGHT...
IT'S ALREADY BEEN DECIDED BY THOSE ABOVE ME. YOU'RE DYING EITHER WAY. THIS WAY AT LEAST IT'LL BE BY MY HAND...
!!
STOP, DAD! I SWEAR I'M NOT KIRA! IF WE DIE HERE, WE'LL FALL RIGHT INTO KIRA'S TRAP! DON'T YOU SEE THAT?!
AMANE... LIGHT AND I WILL DIE HERE, BUT I HAVE NO REASON TO KILL YOU.
THE POLICE WILL FIND THIS CAR SOON. YOU'LL BE EXE-CUTED AT THE PLANNED SITE...
L-LISTEN DAD! IF WE WERE KIRA AND THE SECOND KIRA, THEN THERE'S NO WAY WE'D LET YOU KILL US!
THERE ARE NO WITNESSES HERE, IF WE WERE THE KIRAS, THEN...

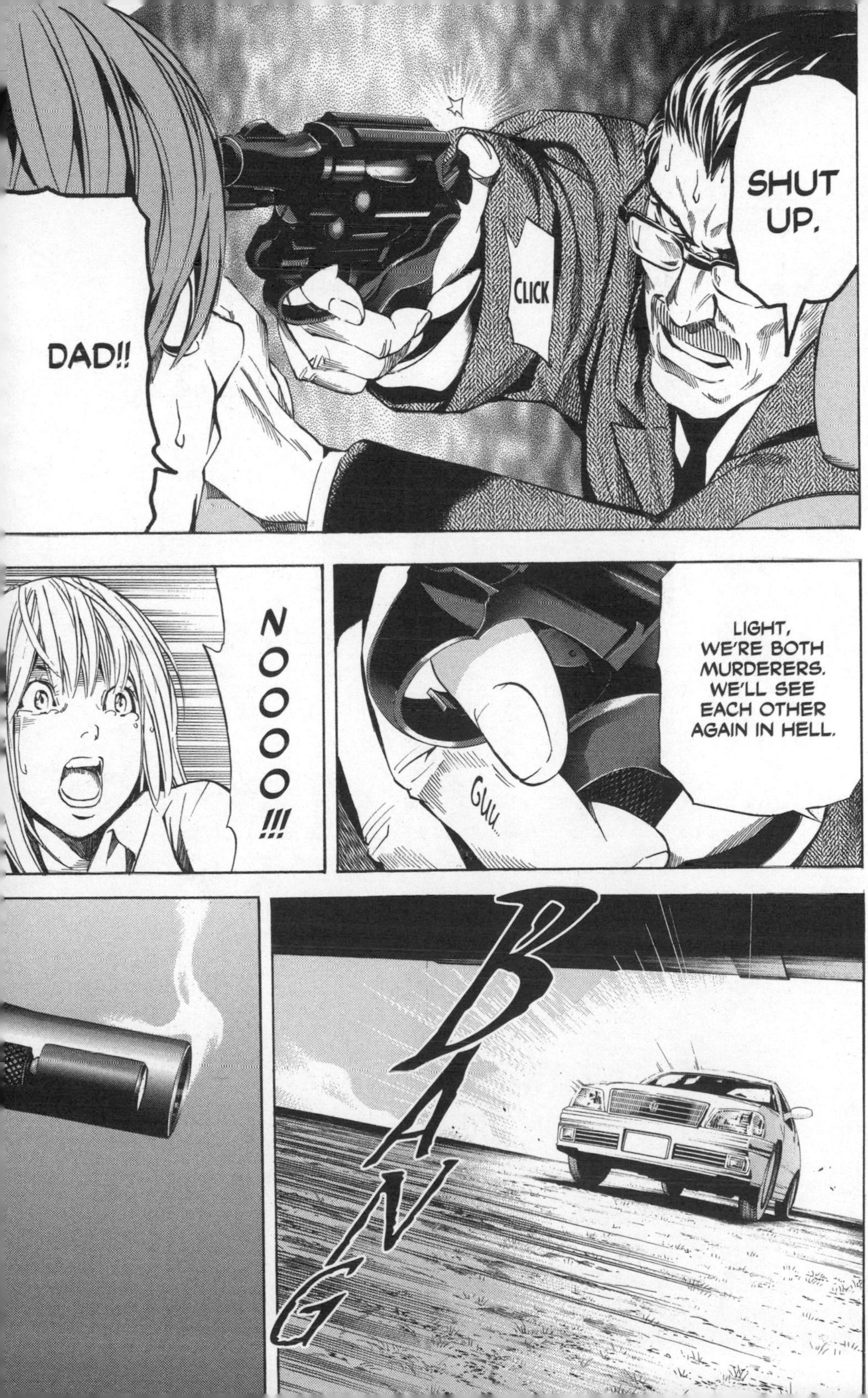
SHUT UP.
CLICK
DAD!!
LIGHT, WE'RE BOTH MURDERERS. WE'LL SEE EACH OTHER AGAIN IN HELL.
GUU...
NOOOOO!!!
BANG

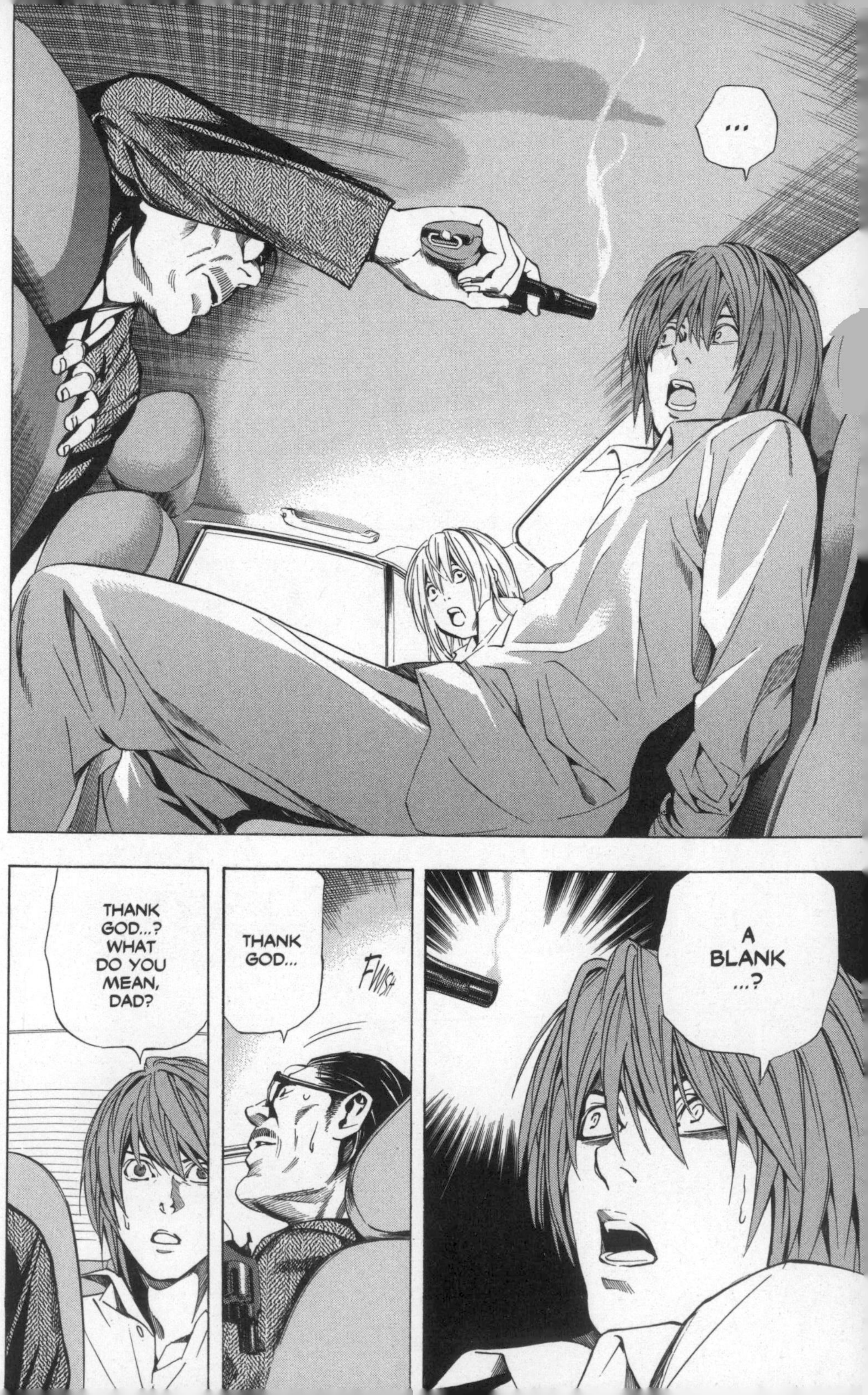
...
A BLANK ...?
FWISH
THANK GOD...
THANK GOD...? WHAT DO YOU MEAN, DAD?

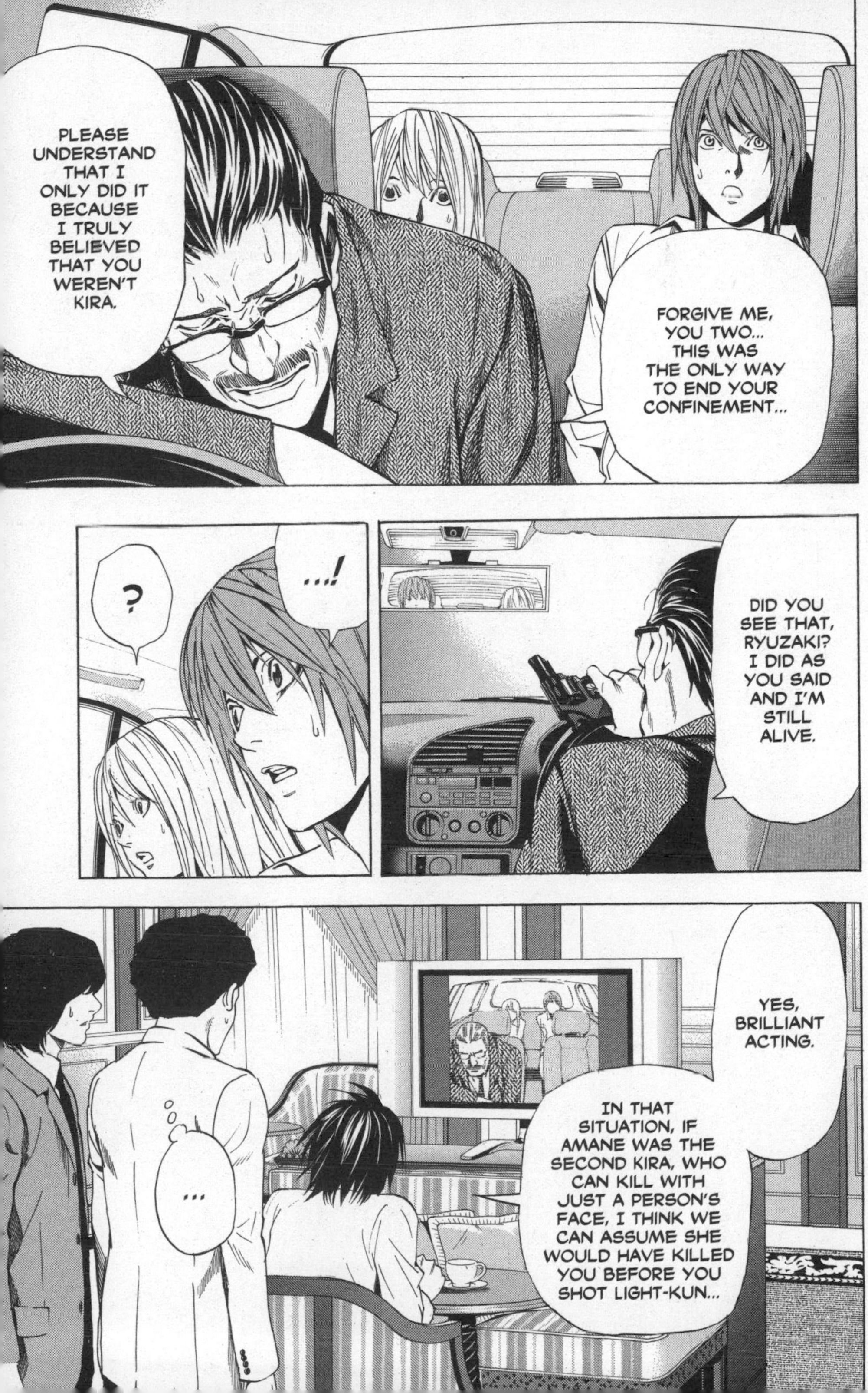
FORGIVE ME, YOU TWO... THIS WAS THE ONLY WAY TO END YOUR CONFINEMENT...
PLEASE UNDERSTAND THAT I ONLY DID IT BECAUSE I TRULY BELIEVED THAT YOU WEREN'T KIRA.
DID YOU SEE THAT, RYUZAKI? I DID AS YOU SAID AND I'M STILL ALIVE.
...!
?
YES, BRILLIANT ACTING.
IN THAT SITUATION, IF AMANE WAS THE SECOND KIRA, WHO CAN KILL WITH JUST A PERSON'S FACE, I THINK WE CAN ASSUME SHE WOULD HAVE KILLED YOU BEFORE YOU SHOT LIGHT-KUN...
...

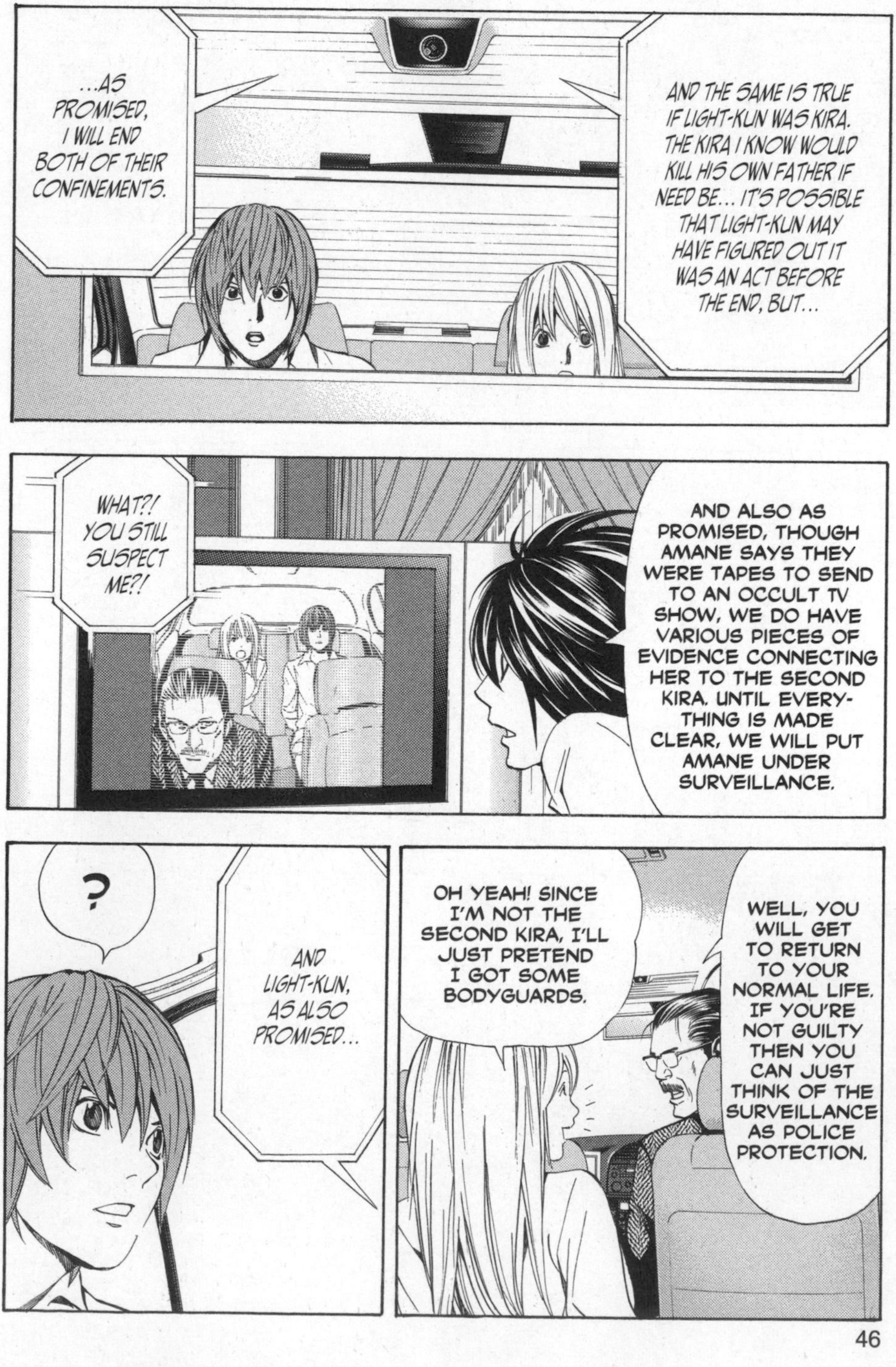
AND THE SAME IS TRUE IF LIGHT-KUN WAS KIRA. THE KIRA I KNOW WOULD KILL HIS OWN FATHER IF NEED BE... IT'S POSSIBLE THAT LIGHT-KUN MAY HAVE FIGURED OUT IT WAS AN ACT BEFORE THE END, BUT...
...AS PROMISED, I WILL END BOTH OF THEIR CONFINEMENTS.
AND ALSO AS PROMISED, THOUGH AMANE SAYS THEY WERE TAPES TO SEND TO AN OCCULT TV SHOW, WE DO HAVE VARIOUS PIECES OF EVIDENCE CONNECTING HER TO THE SECOND KIRA. UNTIL EVERY-THING IS MADE CLEAR, WE WILL PUT AMANE UNDER SURVEILLANCE.
WHAT?! YOU STILL SUSPECT ME?!
WELL, YOU WILL GET TO RETURN TO YOUR NORMAL LIFE. IF YOU'RE NOT GUILTY THEN YOU CAN JUST THINK OF THE SURVEILLANCE AS POLICE PROTECTION.
OH YEAH! SINCE I'M NOT THE SECOND KIRA, I'LL JUST PRETEND I GOT SOME BODYGUARDS.
AND LIGHT-KUN, AS ALSO PROMISED...
?

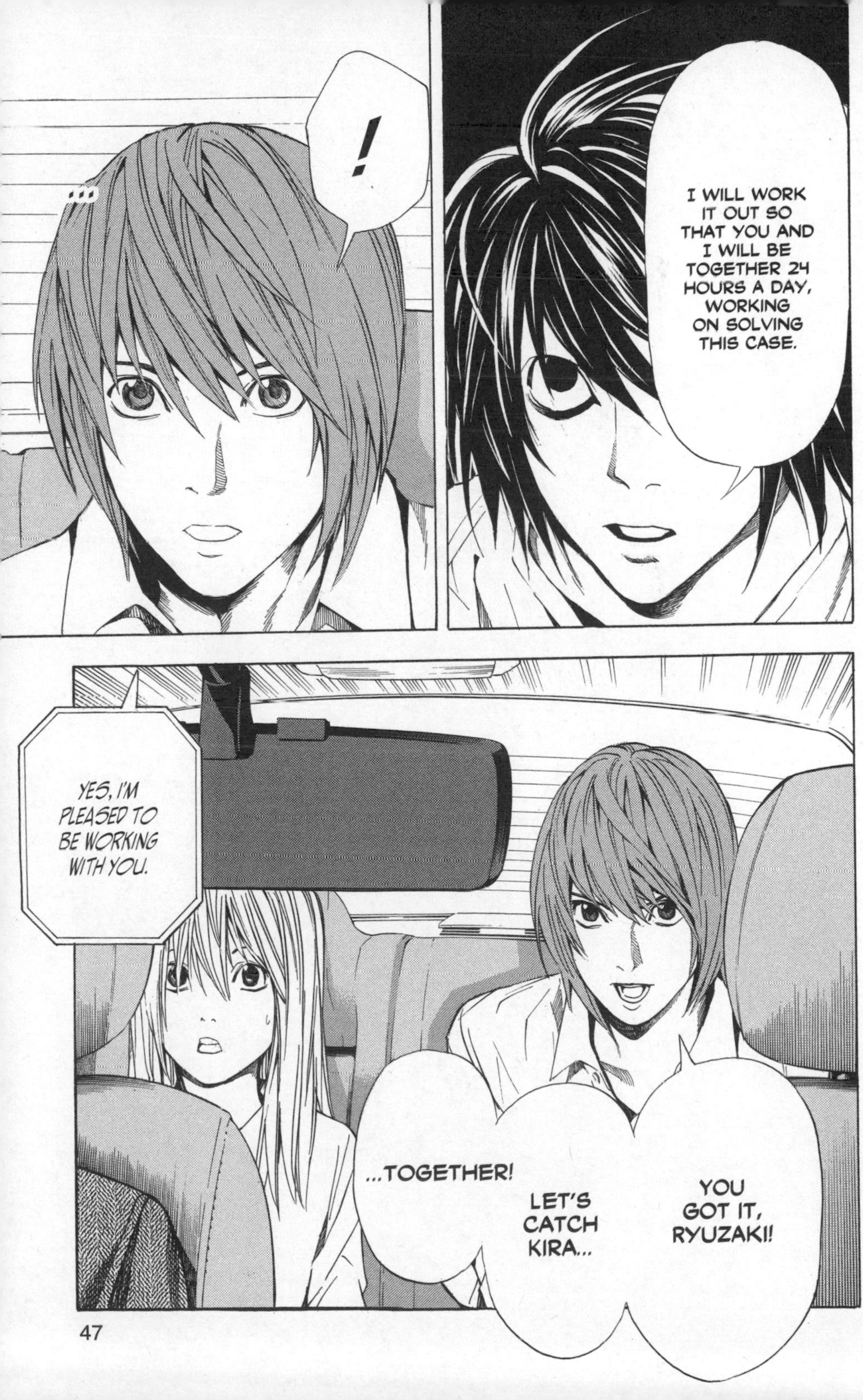
I WILL WORK IT OUT SO THAT YOU AND I WILL BE TOGETHER 24 HOURS A DAY, WORKING ON SOLVING THIS CASE.
!
...
YES, I'M PLEASED TO BE WORKING WITH YOU.
YOU GOT IT, RYUZAKI!
LET'S CATCH KIRA...
...TOGETHER!

DEATH NOTE
How to use it
XXV

○ The god of death must not hand the DEATH NOTE directly to a child under 6 years of age (based on the human calendar).

死神は人間にデスノートを直接渡す場合、
人間界単位で満6歳に満たない人間にノートを渡してはならない。

○ The DEATH NOTE must not be handed to a child under 6 years of age, but DEATH NOTES that have been dropped into the human world, and are part of the human world, can be used upon humans of any age with the same effect.

満6歳未満の人間に渡してはならないが、
人間界に落とし人間界の物になったノートは、
何歳の人間に使われようとその効力は同じである。

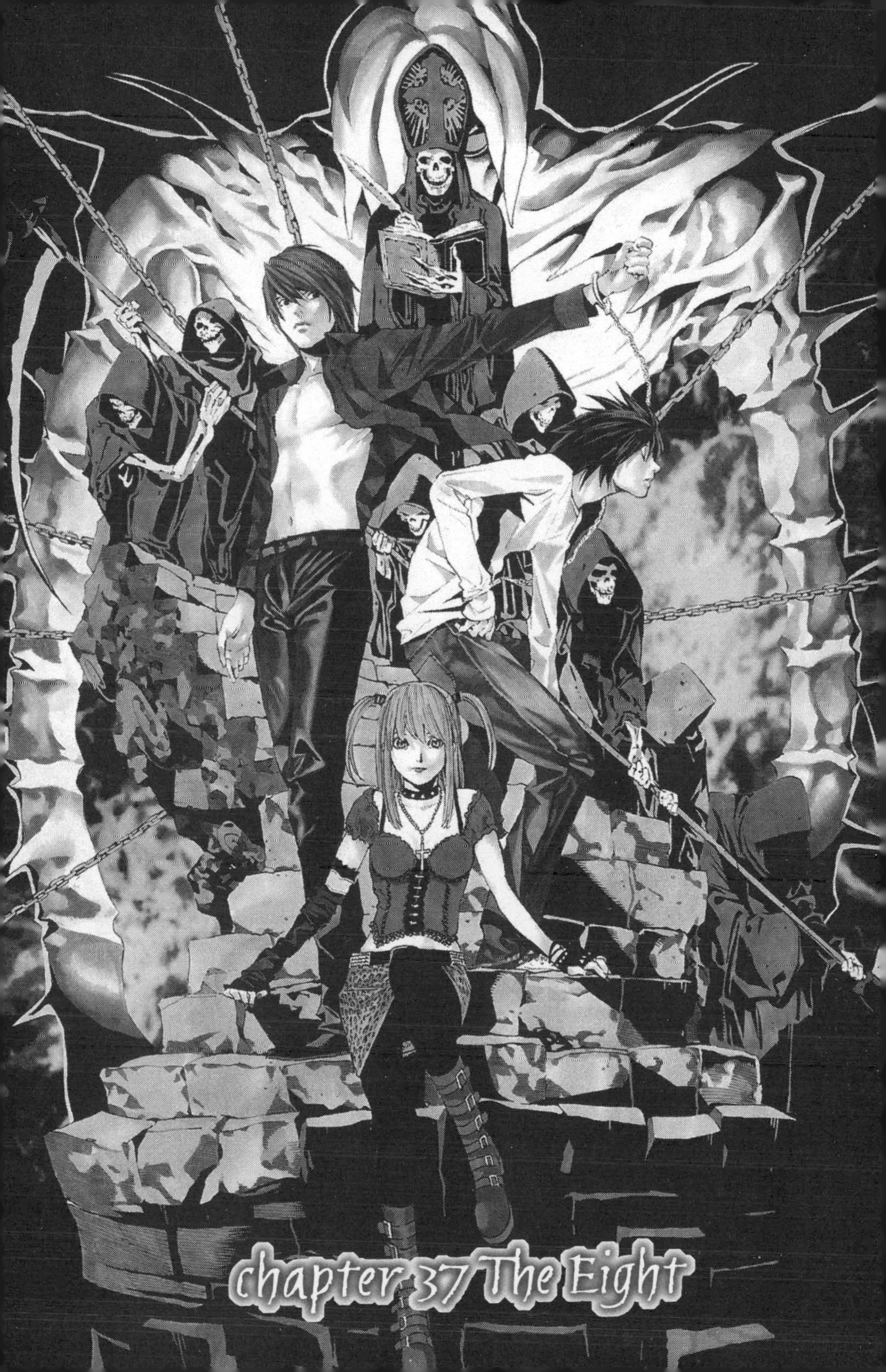
chapter 37 The Eight

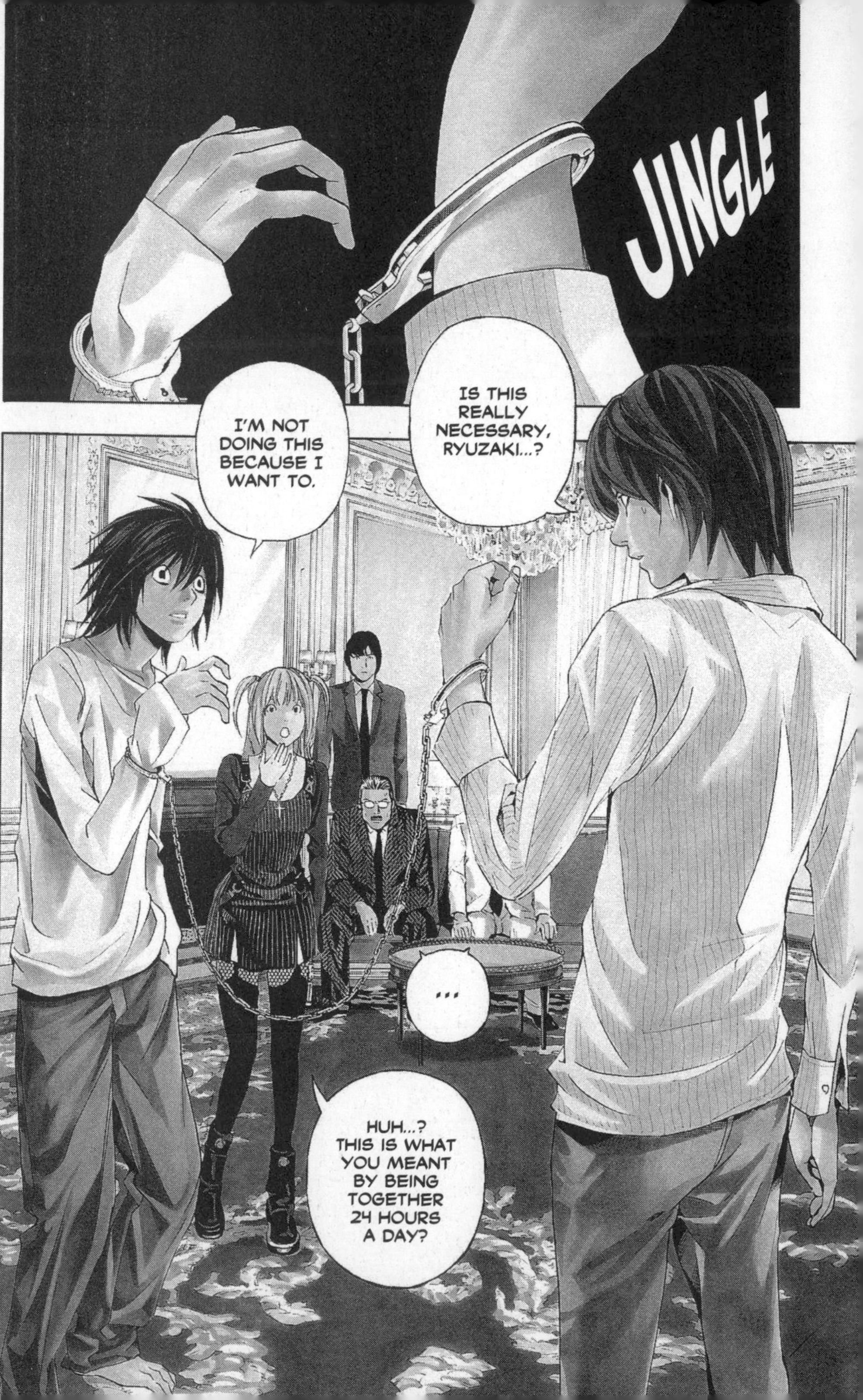
JINGLE
IS THIS REALLY NECESSARY, RYUZAKI...?
I'M NOT DOING THIS BECAUSE I WANT TO.
...
HUH...? THIS IS WHAT YOU MEANT BY BEING TOGETHER 24 HOURS A DAY?

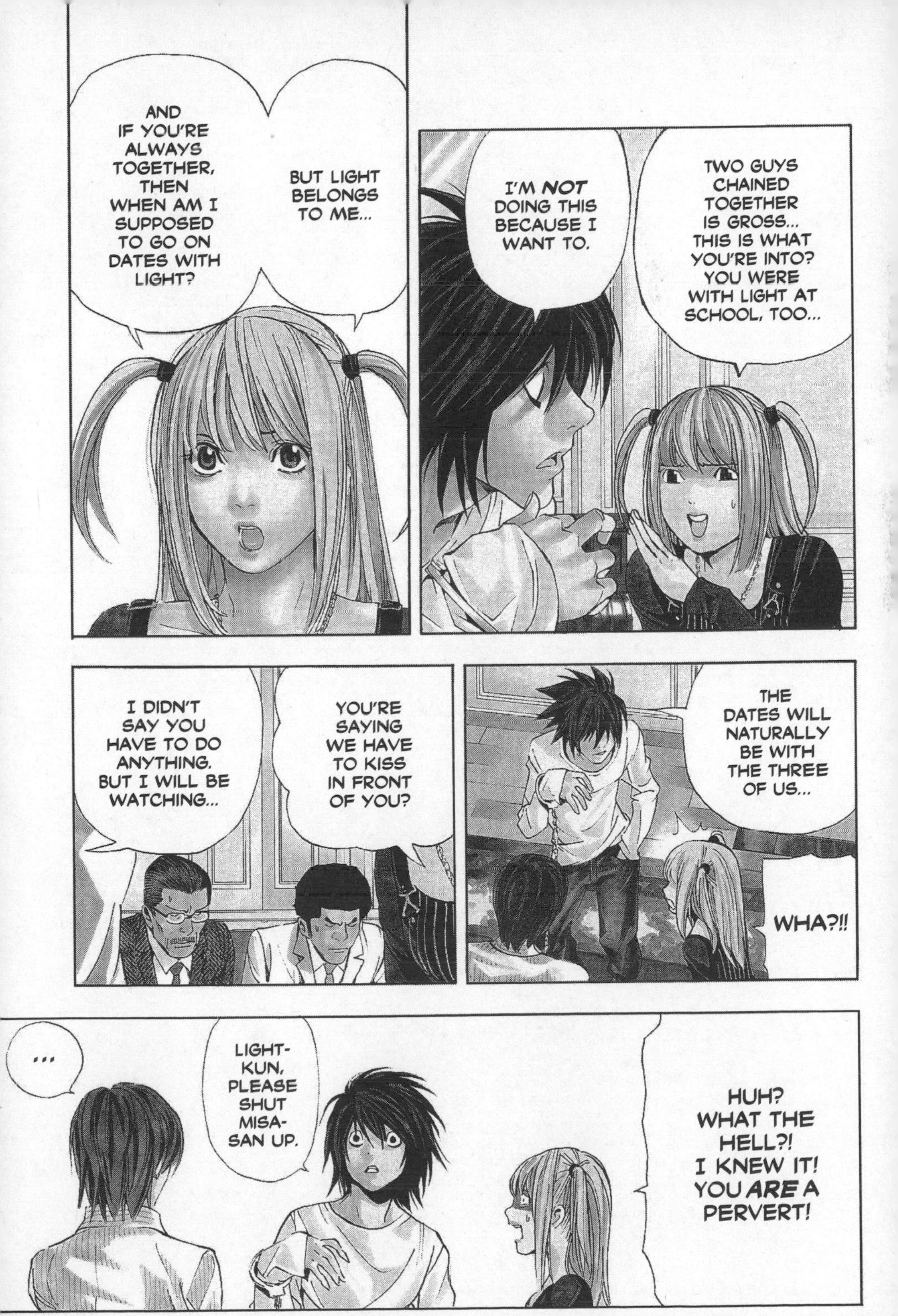
TWO GUYS CHAINED TOGETHER IS GROSS... THIS IS WHAT YOU'RE INTO? YOU WERE WITH LIGHT AT SCHOOL, TOO...
I'M **NOT** DOING THIS BECAUSE I WANT TO.
BUT LIGHT BELONGS TO ME...
AND IF YOU'RE ALWAYS TOGETHER, THEN WHEN AM I SUPPOSED TO GO ON DATES WITH LIGHT?
THE DATES WILL NATURALLY BE WITH THE THREE OF US...
WHA?!!
YOU'RE SAYING WE HAVE TO KISS IN FRONT OF YOU?
I DIDN'T SAY YOU HAVE TO DO ANYTHING. BUT I WILL BE WATCHING...
HUH? WHAT THE HELL?! I KNEW IT! YOU **ARE** A PERVERT!
LIGHT-KUN, PLEASE SHUT MISA-SAN UP.
...

READ THIS WAY

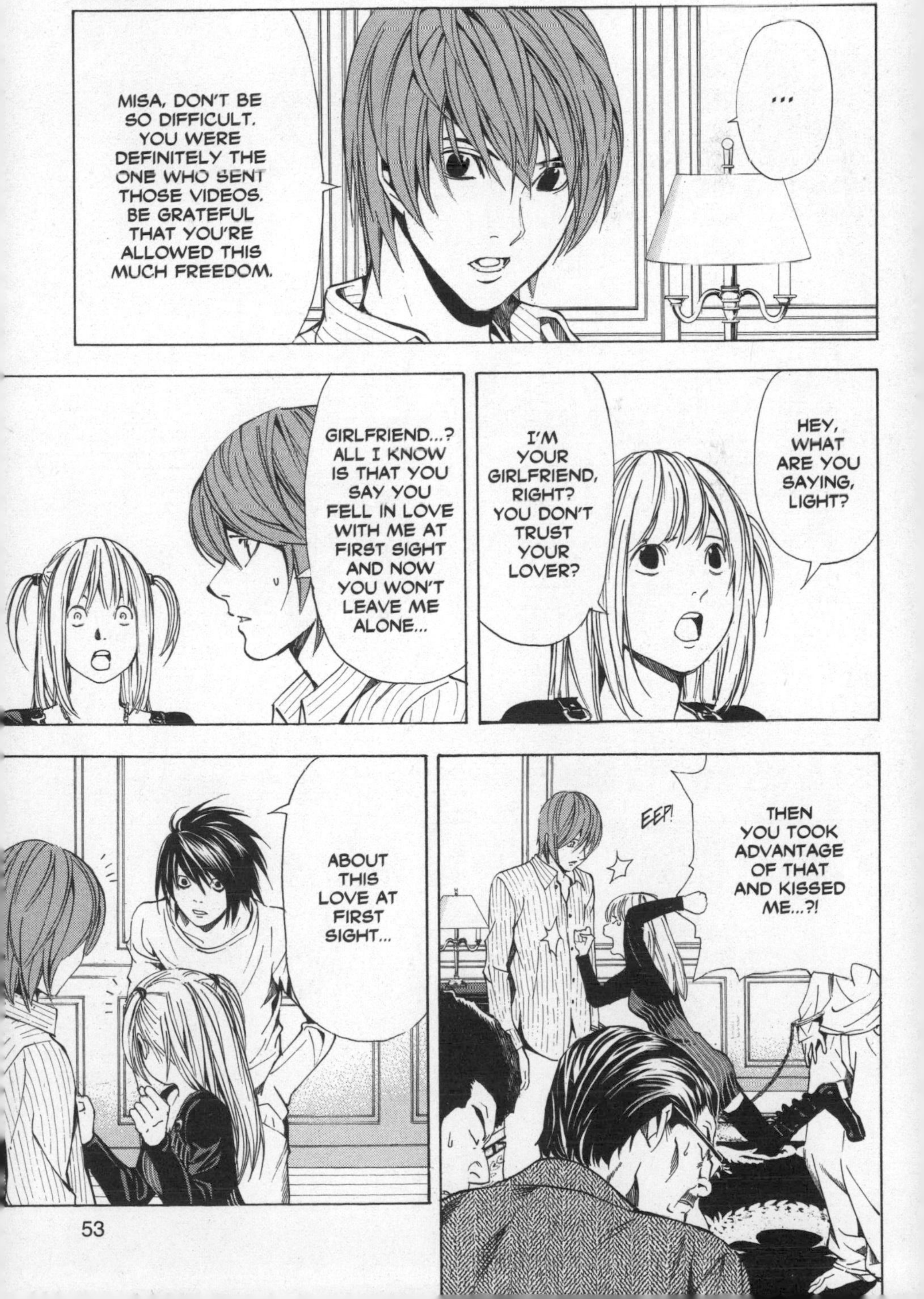
...
MISA, DON'T BE SO DIFFICULT. YOU WERE DEFINITELY THE ONE WHO SENT THOSE VIDEOS. BE GRATEFUL THAT YOU'RE ALLOWED THIS MUCH FREEDOM.
HEY, WHAT ARE YOU SAYING, LIGHT?
I'M YOUR GIRLFRIEND, RIGHT? YOU DON'T TRUST YOUR LOVER?
GIRLFRIEND...? ALL I KNOW IS THAT YOU SAY YOU FELL IN LOVE WITH ME AT FIRST SIGHT AND NOW YOU WON'T LEAVE ME ALONE...
THEN YOU TOOK ADVANTAGE OF THAT AND KISSED ME...?!
EEP!
ABOUT THIS LOVE AT FIRST SIGHT...

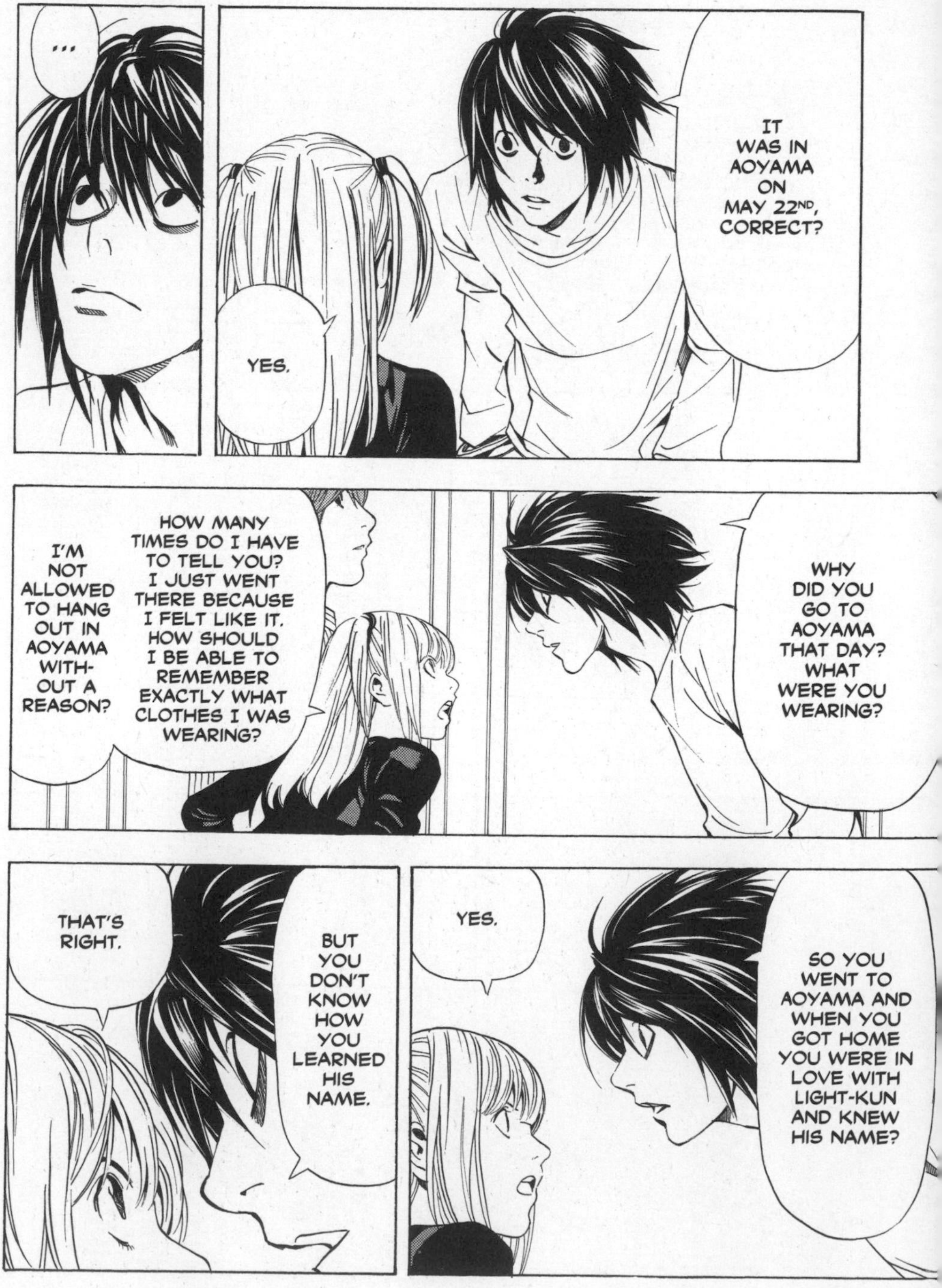

IT WAS IN AOYAMA ON MAY 22ND, CORRECT?
YES.
...
WHY DID YOU GO TO AOYAMA THAT DAY? WHAT WERE YOU WEARING?
HOW MANY TIMES DO I HAVE TO TELL YOU? I JUST WENT THERE BECAUSE I FELT LIKE IT. HOW SHOULD I BE ABLE TO REMEMBER EXACTLY WHAT CLOTHES I WAS WEARING?
I'M NOT ALLOWED TO HANG OUT IN AOYAMA WITH-OUT A REASON?
SO YOU WENT TO AOYAMA AND WHEN YOU GOT HOME YOU WERE IN LOVE WITH LIGHT-KUN AND KNEW HIS NAME?
YES.
BUT YOU DON'T KNOW HOW YOU LEARNED HIS NAME.
THAT'S RIGHT.

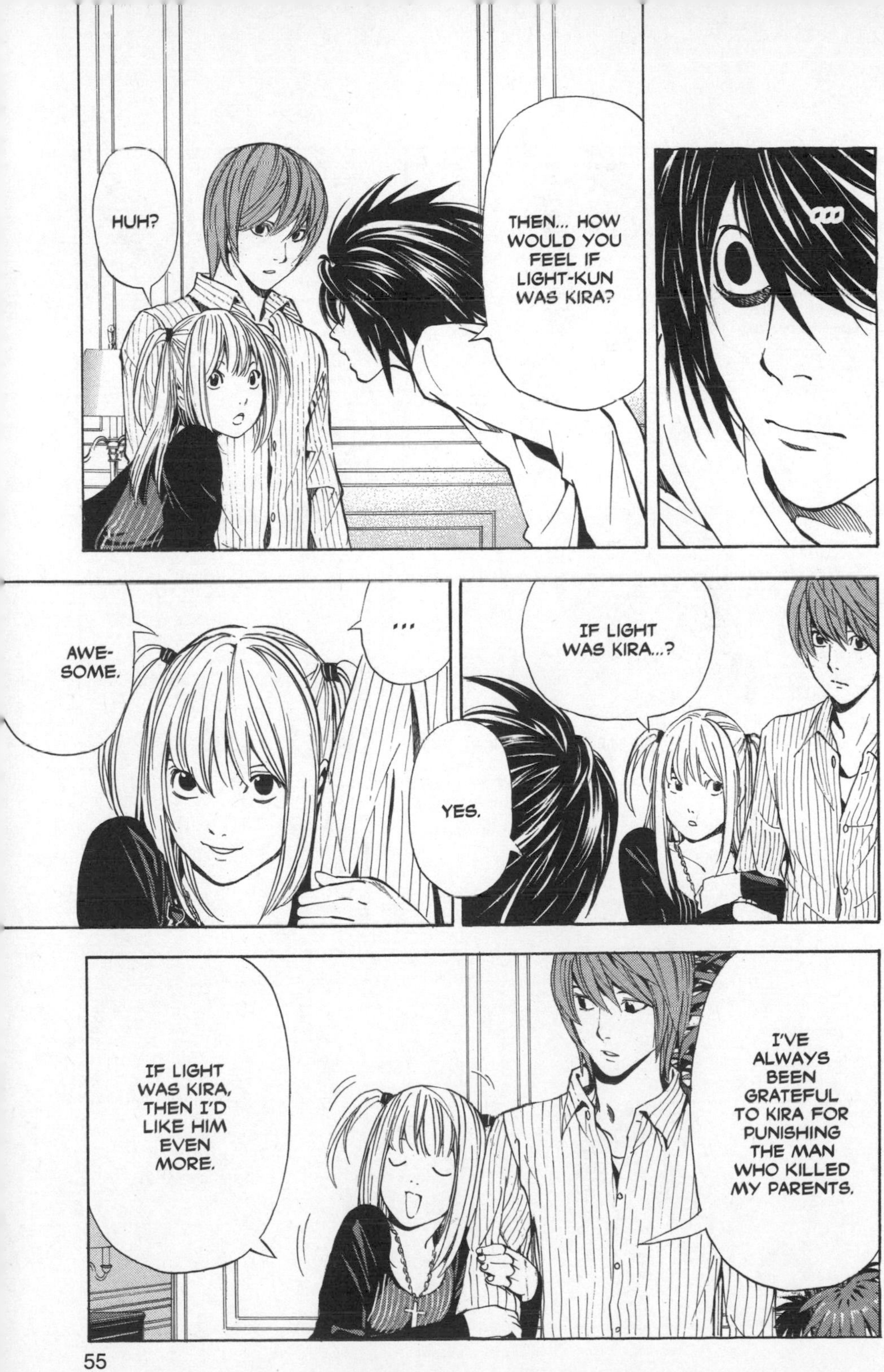
THEN... HOW WOULD YOU FEEL IF LIGHT-KUN WAS KIRA?
HUH?
IF LIGHT WAS KIRA...?
YES.
...
AWE-SOME.
I'VE ALWAYS BEEN GRATEFUL TO KIRA FOR PUNISHING THE MAN WHO KILLED MY PARENTS.
IF LIGHT WAS KIRA, THEN I'D LIKE HIM EVEN MORE.

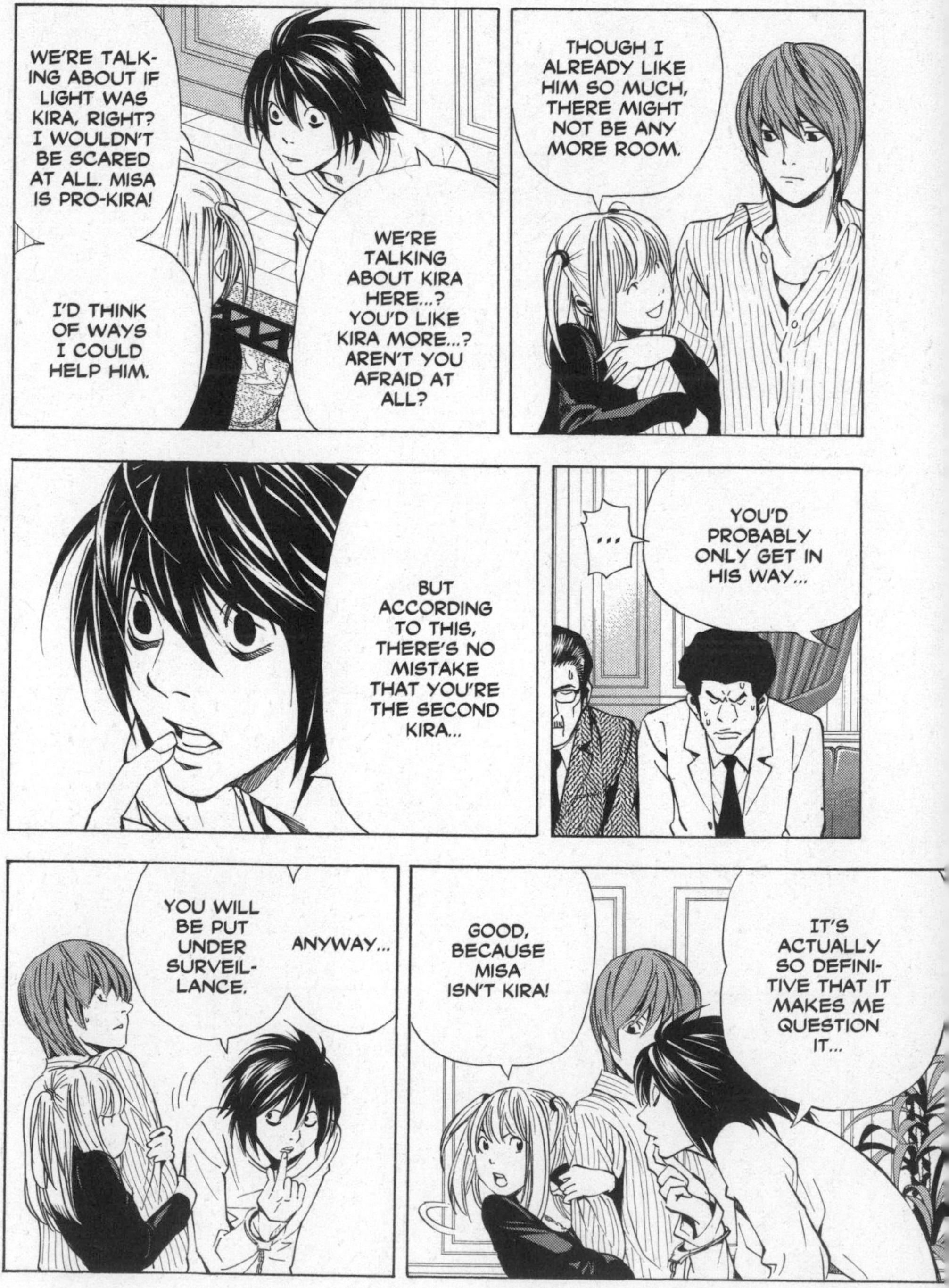
THOUGH I ALREADY LIKE HIM SO MUCH, THERE MIGHT NOT BE ANY MORE ROOM.
WE'RE TALKING ABOUT KIRA HERE...? YOU'D LIKE KIRA MORE...? AREN'T YOU AFRAID AT ALL?
WE'RE TALKING ABOUT IF LIGHT WAS KIRA, RIGHT? I WOULDN'T BE SCARED AT ALL. MISA IS PRO-KIRA!
I'D THINK OF WAYS I COULD HELP HIM.
YOU'D PROBABLY ONLY GET IN HIS WAY...
...
BUT ACCORDING TO THIS, THERE'S NO MISTAKE THAT YOU'RE THE SECOND KIRA...
IT'S ACTUALLY SO DEFINITIVE THAT IT MAKES ME QUESTION IT...
GOOD, BECAUSE MISA ISN'T KIRA!
ANYWAY...
YOU WILL BE PUT UNDER SURVEILLANCE.

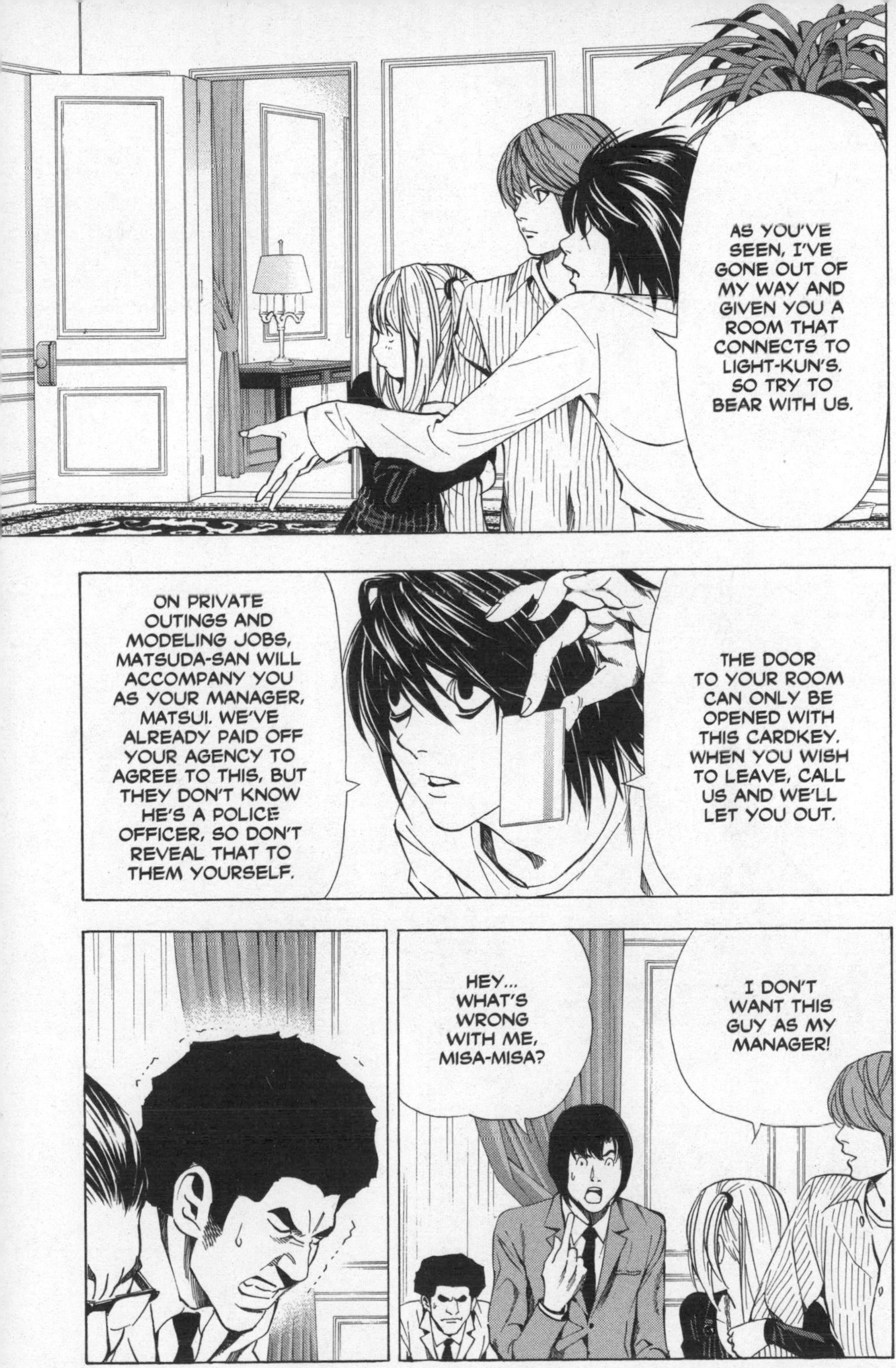
AS YOU'VE SEEN, I'VE GONE OUT OF MY WAY AND GIVEN YOU A ROOM THAT CONNECTS TO LIGHT-KUN'S. SO TRY TO BEAR WITH US.
THE DOOR TO YOUR ROOM CAN ONLY BE OPENED WITH THIS CARDKEY. WHEN YOU WISH TO LEAVE, CALL US AND WE'LL LET YOU OUT.
ON PRIVATE OUTINGS AND MODELING JOBS, MATSUDA-SAN WILL ACCOMPANY YOU AS YOUR MANAGER, MATSUI. WE'VE ALREADY PAID OFF YOUR AGENCY TO AGREE TO THIS, BUT THEY DON'T KNOW HE'S A POLICE OFFICER, SO DON'T REVEAL THAT TO THEM YOURSELF.
I DON'T WANT THIS GUY AS MY MANAGER!
HEY... WHAT'S WRONG WITH ME, MISA-MISA?

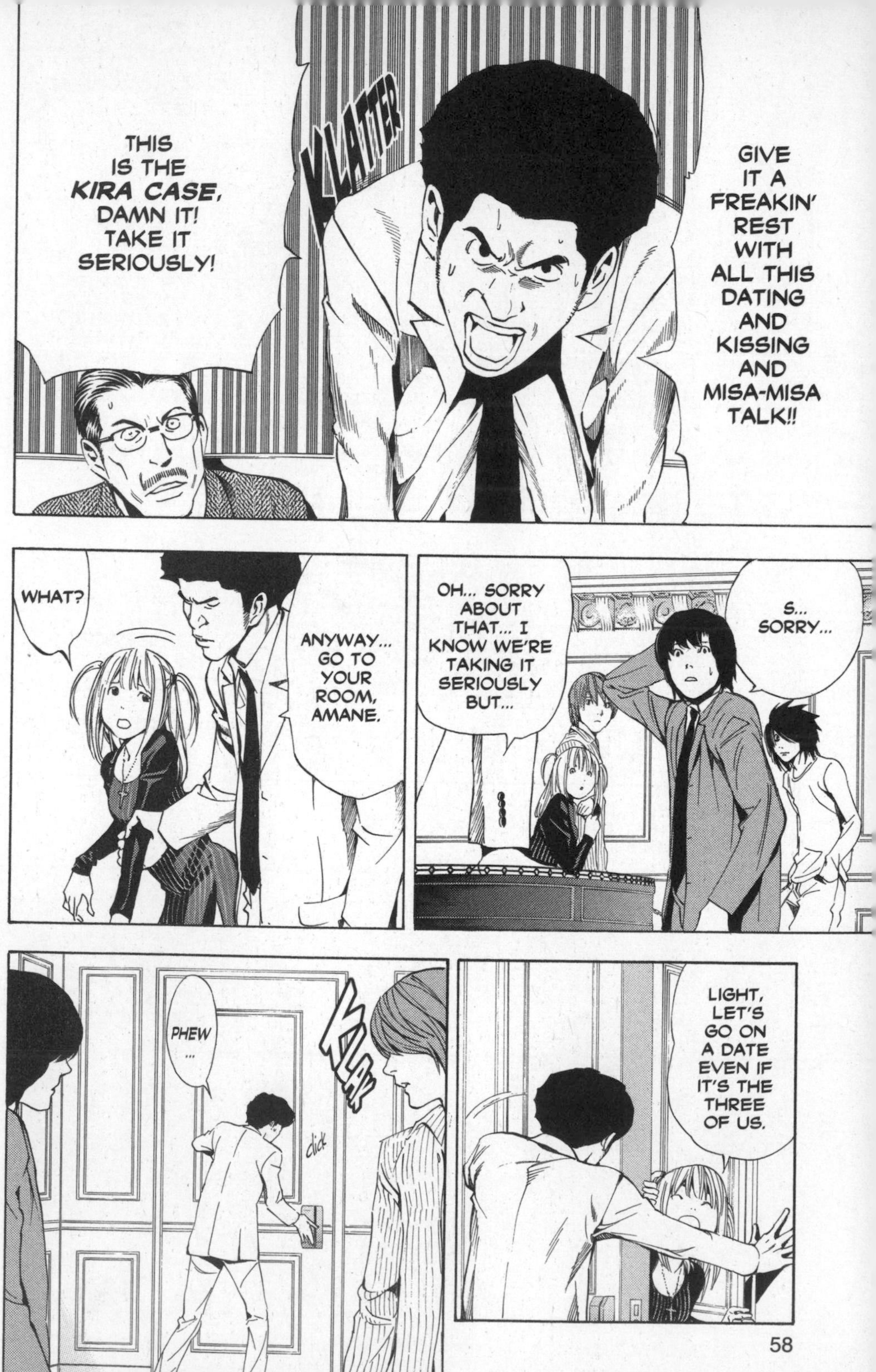
GIVE IT A FREAKIN' REST WITH ALL THIS DATING AND KISSING AND MISA-MISA TALK!!
KLATTER
THIS IS THE *KIRA CASE*, DAMN IT! TAKE IT SERIOUSLY!
S... SORRY...
OH... SORRY ABOUT THAT... I KNOW WE'RE TAKING IT SERIOUSLY BUT...
ANYWAY... GO TO YOUR ROOM, AMANE.
WHAT?
LIGHT, LET'S GO ON A DATE EVEN IF IT'S THE THREE OF US.
KLAK
click
PHEW ...

READ THIS WAY

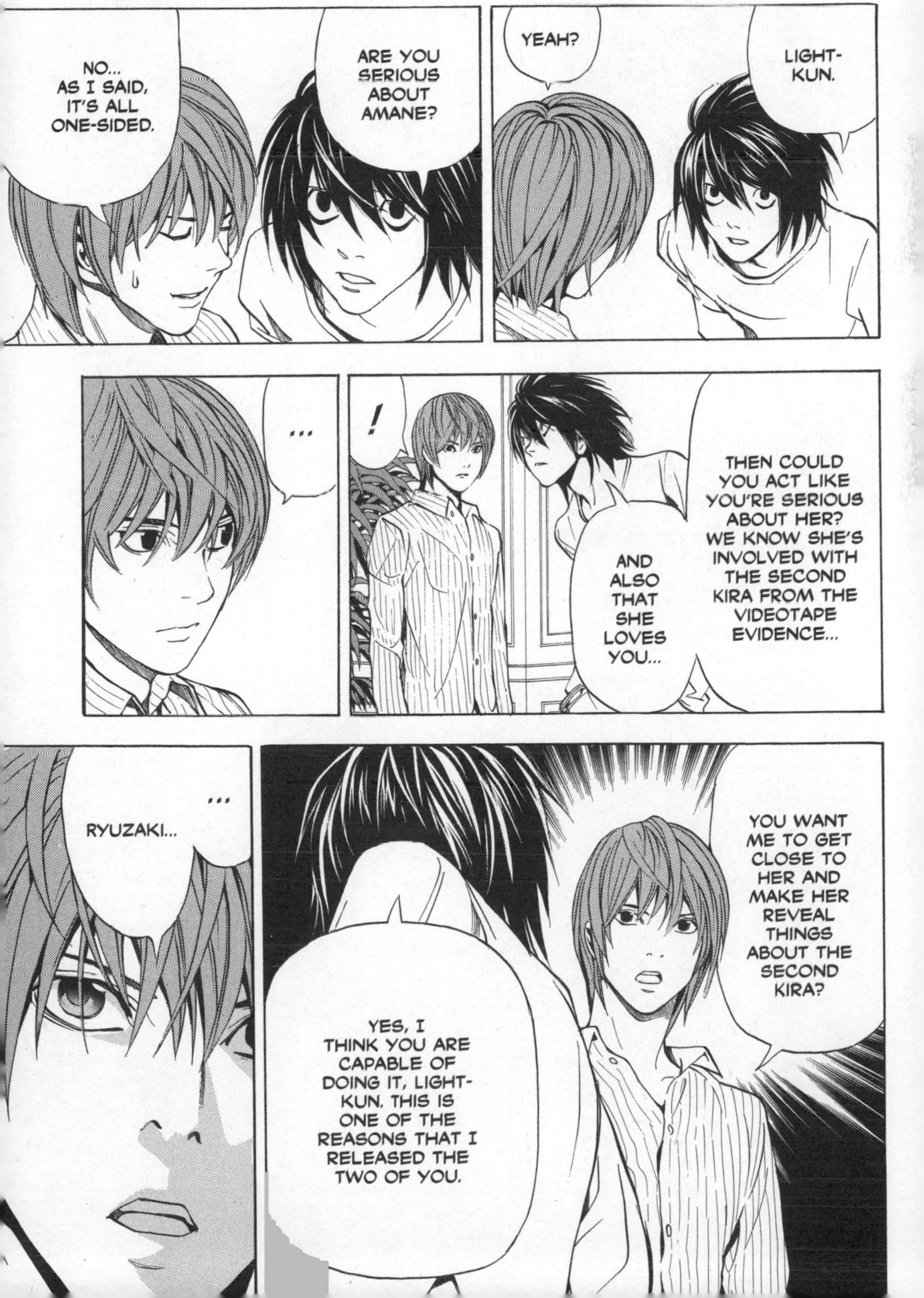
LIGHT-KUN.
YEAH?
ARE YOU SERIOUS ABOUT AMANE?
NO... AS I SAID, IT'S ALL ONE-SIDED.
THEN COULD YOU ACT LIKE YOU'RE SERIOUS ABOUT HER? WE KNOW SHE'S INVOLVED WITH THE SECOND KIRA FROM THE VIDEOTAPE EVIDENCE...
AND ALSO THAT SHE LOVES YOU...
!
...
YOU WANT ME TO GET CLOSE TO HER AND MAKE HER REVEAL THINGS ABOUT THE SECOND KIRA?
YES, I THINK YOU ARE CAPABLE OF DOING IT, LIGHT-KUN. THIS IS ONE OF THE REASONS THAT I RELEASED THE TWO OF YOU.
...
RYUZAKI...

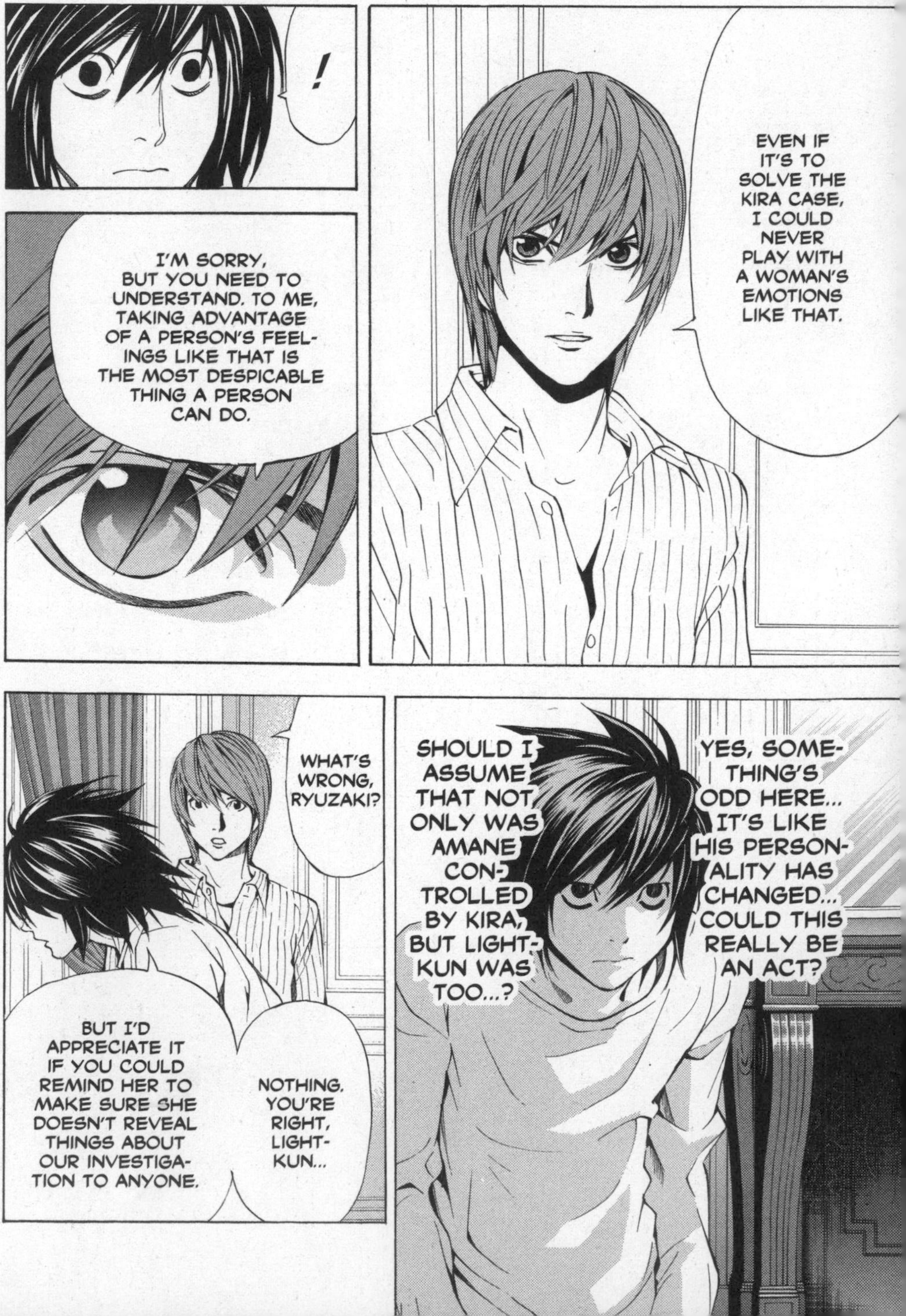
EVEN IF IT'S TO SOLVE THE KIRA CASE, I COULD NEVER PLAY WITH A WOMAN'S EMOTIONS LIKE THAT.
!
I'M SORRY, BUT YOU NEED TO UNDERSTAND. TO ME, TAKING ADVANTAGE OF A PERSON'S FEEL-INGS LIKE THAT IS THE MOST DESPICABLE THING A PERSON CAN DO.
YES, SOME-THING'S ODD HERE... IT'S LIKE HIS PERSON-ALITY HAS CHANGED... COULD THIS REALLY BE AN ACT?
SHOULD I ASSUME THAT NOT ONLY WAS AMANE CON-TROLLED BY KIRA, BUT LIGHT-KUN WAS TOO...?
WHAT'S WRONG, RYUZAKI?
NOTHING. YOU'RE RIGHT, LIGHT-KUN...
BUT I'D APPRECIATE IT IF YOU COULD REMIND HER TO MAKE SURE SHE DOESN'T REVEAL THINGS ABOUT OUR INVESTIGA-TION TO ANYONE.

READ THIS WAY

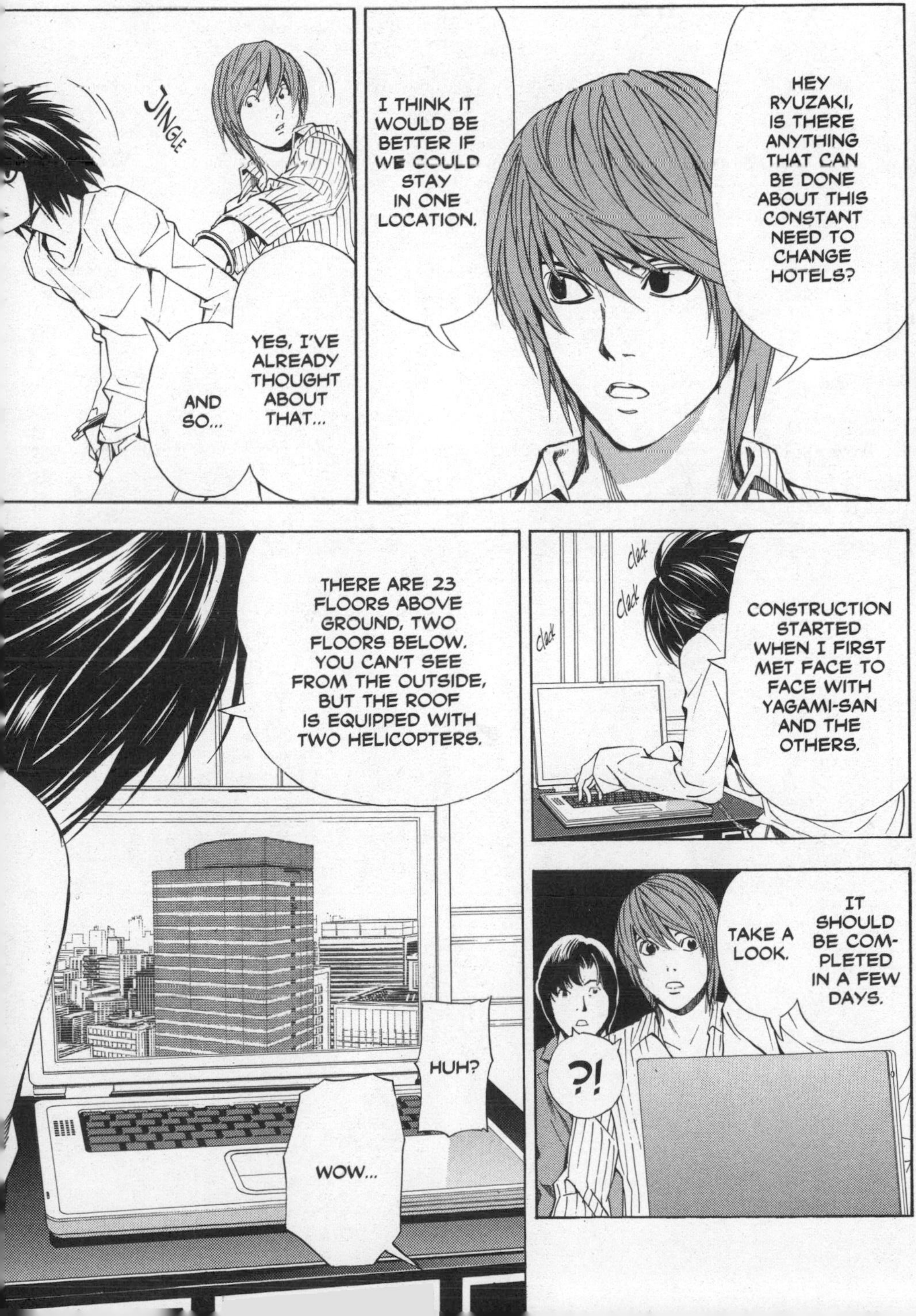
HEY RYUZAKI, IS THERE ANYTHING THAT CAN BE DONE ABOUT THIS CONSTANT NEED TO CHANGE HOTELS?
I THINK IT WOULD BE BETTER IF WE COULD STAY IN ONE LOCATION.
JINGLE
YES, I'VE ALREADY THOUGHT ABOUT THAT...
AND SO...
clack
clack
clack
CONSTRUCTION STARTED WHEN I FIRST MET FACE TO FACE WITH YAGAMI-SAN AND THE OTHERS.
IT SHOULD BE COM-PLETED IN A FEW DAYS.
TAKE A LOOK.
?!
THERE ARE 23 FLOORS ABOVE GROUND, TWO FLOORS BELOW. YOU CAN'T SEE FROM THE OUTSIDE, BUT THE ROOF IS EQUIPPED WITH TWO HELICOPTERS.
HUH?
WOW...

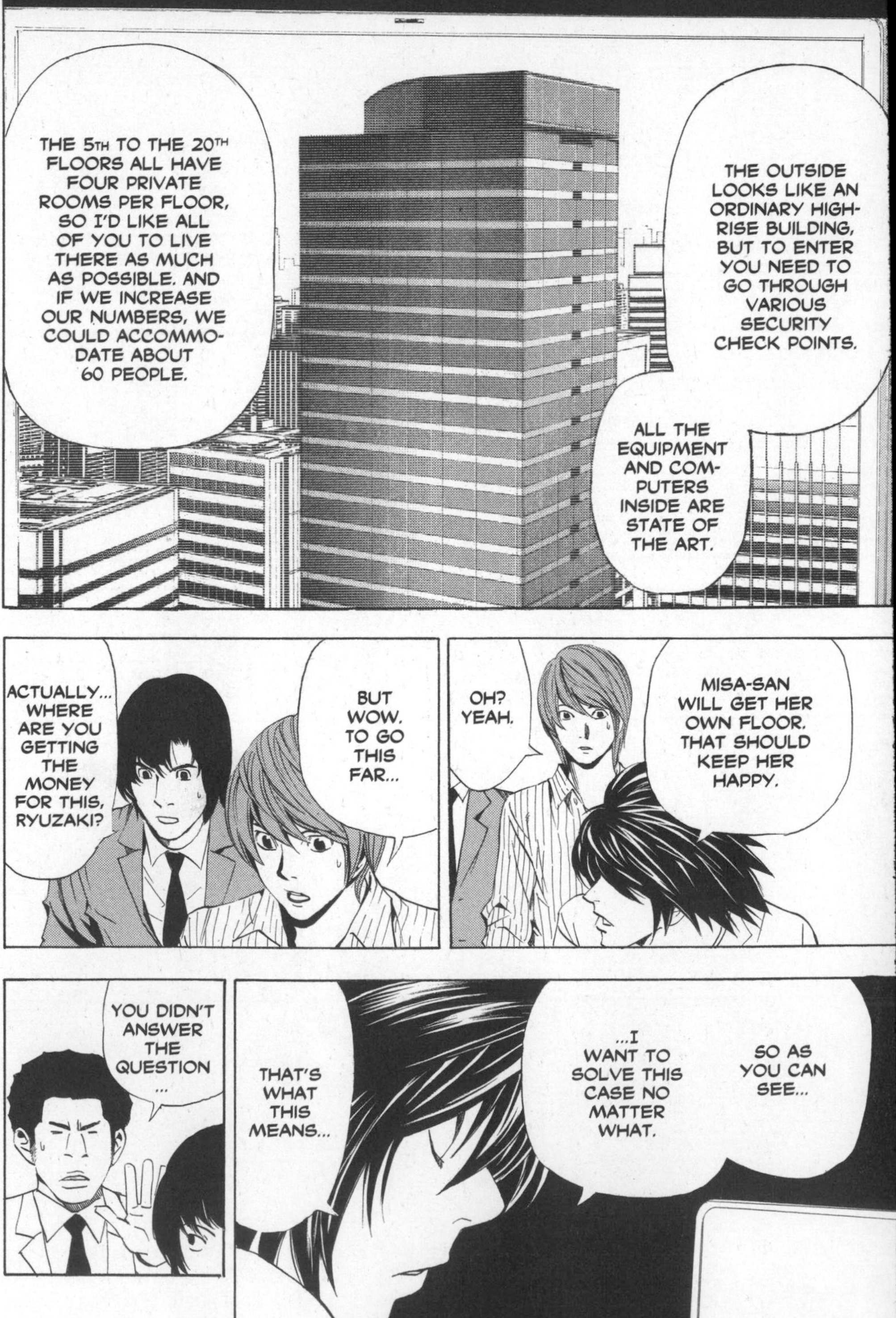
THE OUTSIDE LOOKS LIKE AN ORDINARY HIGH-RISE BUILDING, BUT TO ENTER YOU NEED TO GO THROUGH VARIOUS SECURITY CHECK POINTS.
ALL THE EQUIPMENT AND COMPUTERS INSIDE ARE STATE OF THE ART.
THE 5TH TO THE 20TH FLOORS ALL HAVE FOUR PRIVATE ROOMS PER FLOOR, SO I'D LIKE ALL OF YOU TO LIVE THERE AS MUCH AS POSSIBLE. AND IF WE INCREASE OUR NUMBERS, WE COULD ACCOMMODATE ABOUT 60 PEOPLE.
MISA-SAN WILL GET HER OWN FLOOR. THAT SHOULD KEEP HER HAPPY.
OH? YEAH.
BUT WOW. TO GO THIS FAR...
ACTUALLY... WHERE ARE YOU GETTING THE MONEY FOR THIS, RYUZAKI?
SO AS YOU CAN SEE...
...I WANT TO SOLVE THIS CASE NO MATTER WHAT.
THAT'S WHAT THIS MEANS...
YOU DIDN'T ANSWER THE QUESTION ...

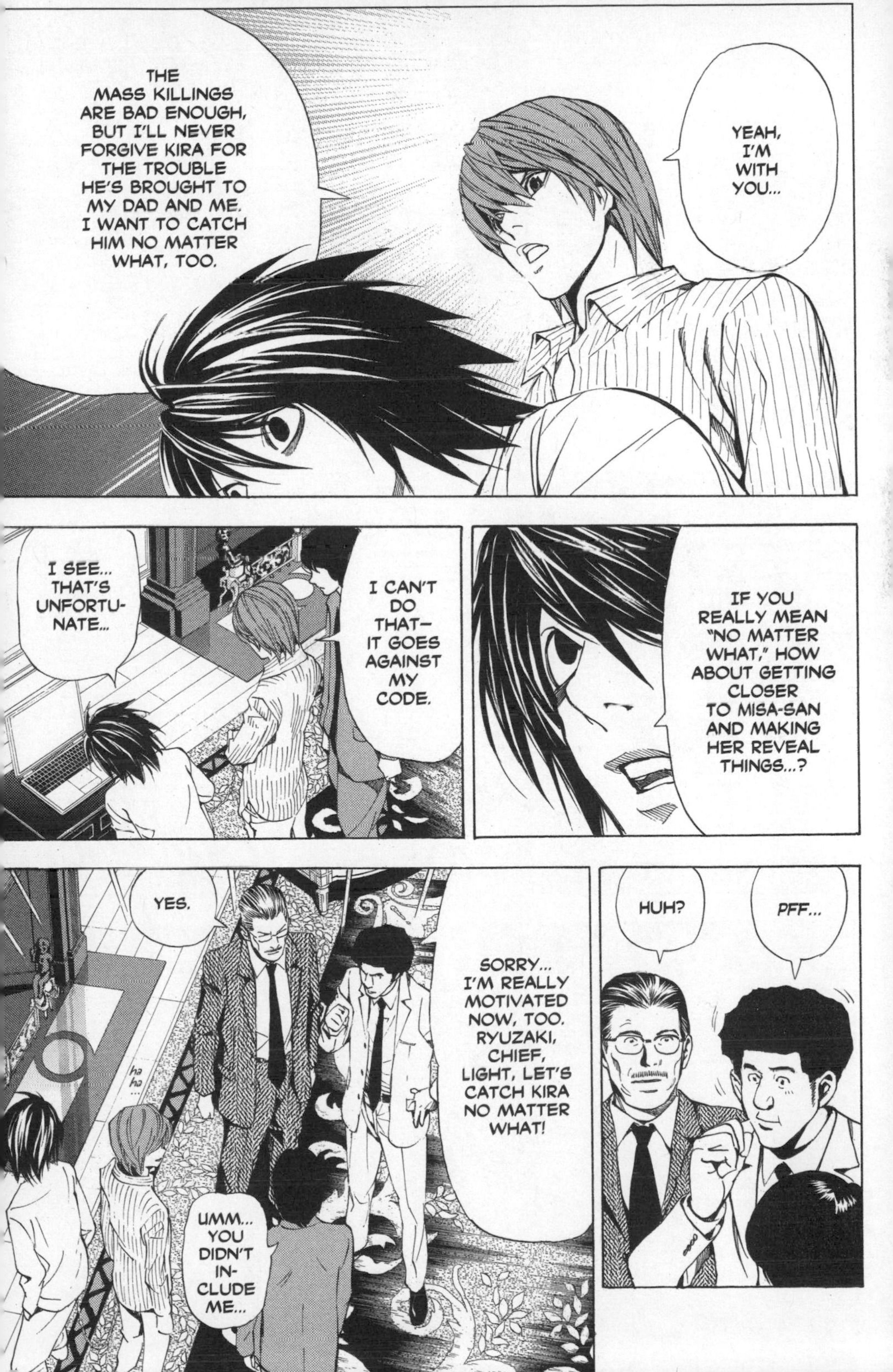
YEAH, I'M WITH YOU...
THE MASS KILLINGS ARE BAD ENOUGH, BUT I'LL NEVER FORGIVE KIRA FOR THE TROUBLE HE'S BROUGHT TO MY DAD AND ME. I WANT TO CATCH HIM NO MATTER WHAT, TOO.
IF YOU REALLY MEAN "NO MATTER WHAT," HOW ABOUT GETTING CLOSER TO MISA-SAN AND MAKING HER REVEAL THINGS...?
I CAN'T DO THAT— IT GOES AGAINST MY CODE.
I SEE... THAT'S UNFORTU-NATE...
PFF...
HUH?
SORRY... I'M REALLY MOTIVATED NOW, TOO. RYUZAKI, CHIEF, LIGHT, LET'S CATCH KIRA NO MATTER WHAT!
YES.
ha ha ...
UMM... YOU DIDN'T IN-CLUDE ME...

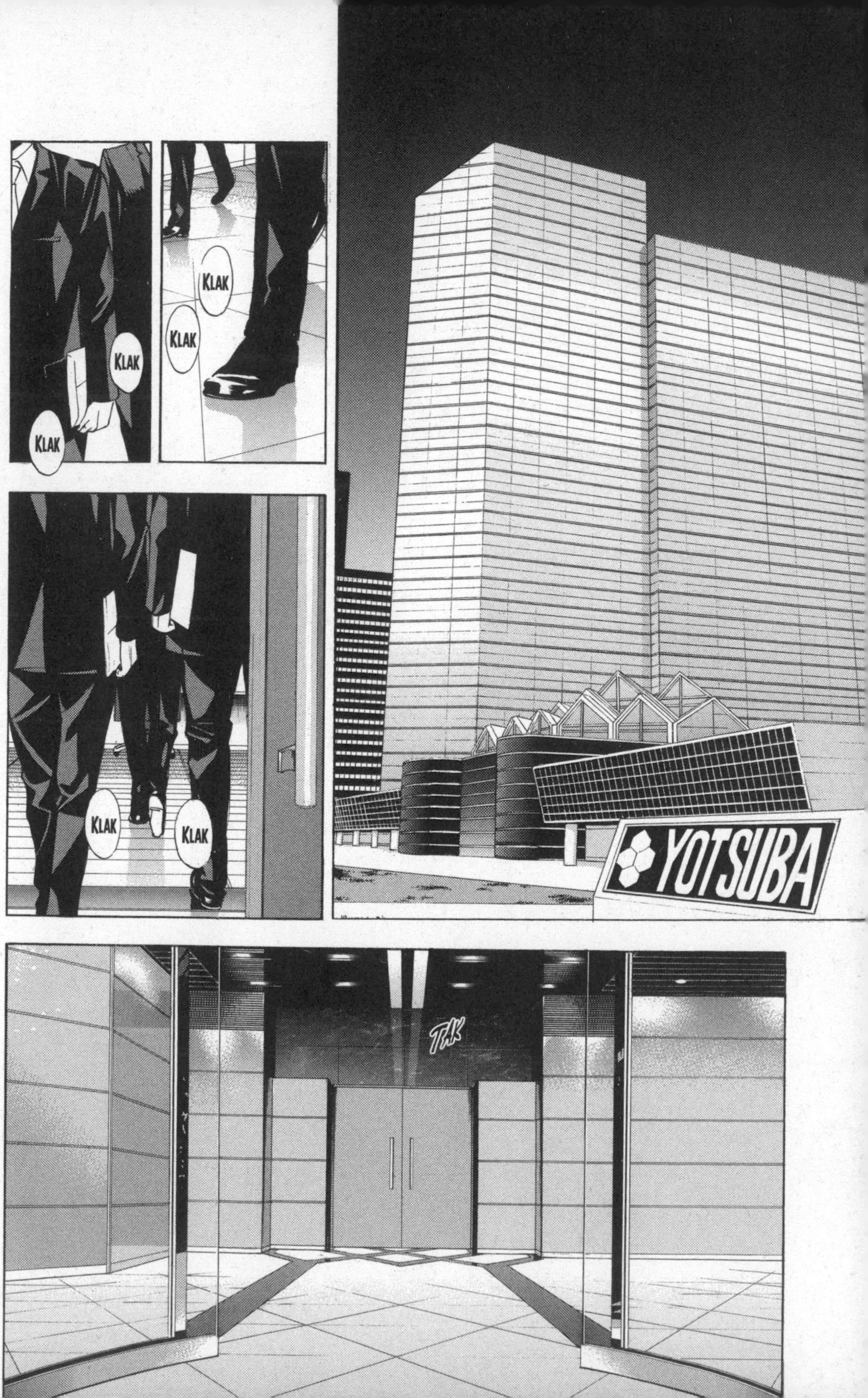
YOTSUBA
KLAK
KLAK
KLAK
KLAK
KLAK
KLAK
TAK

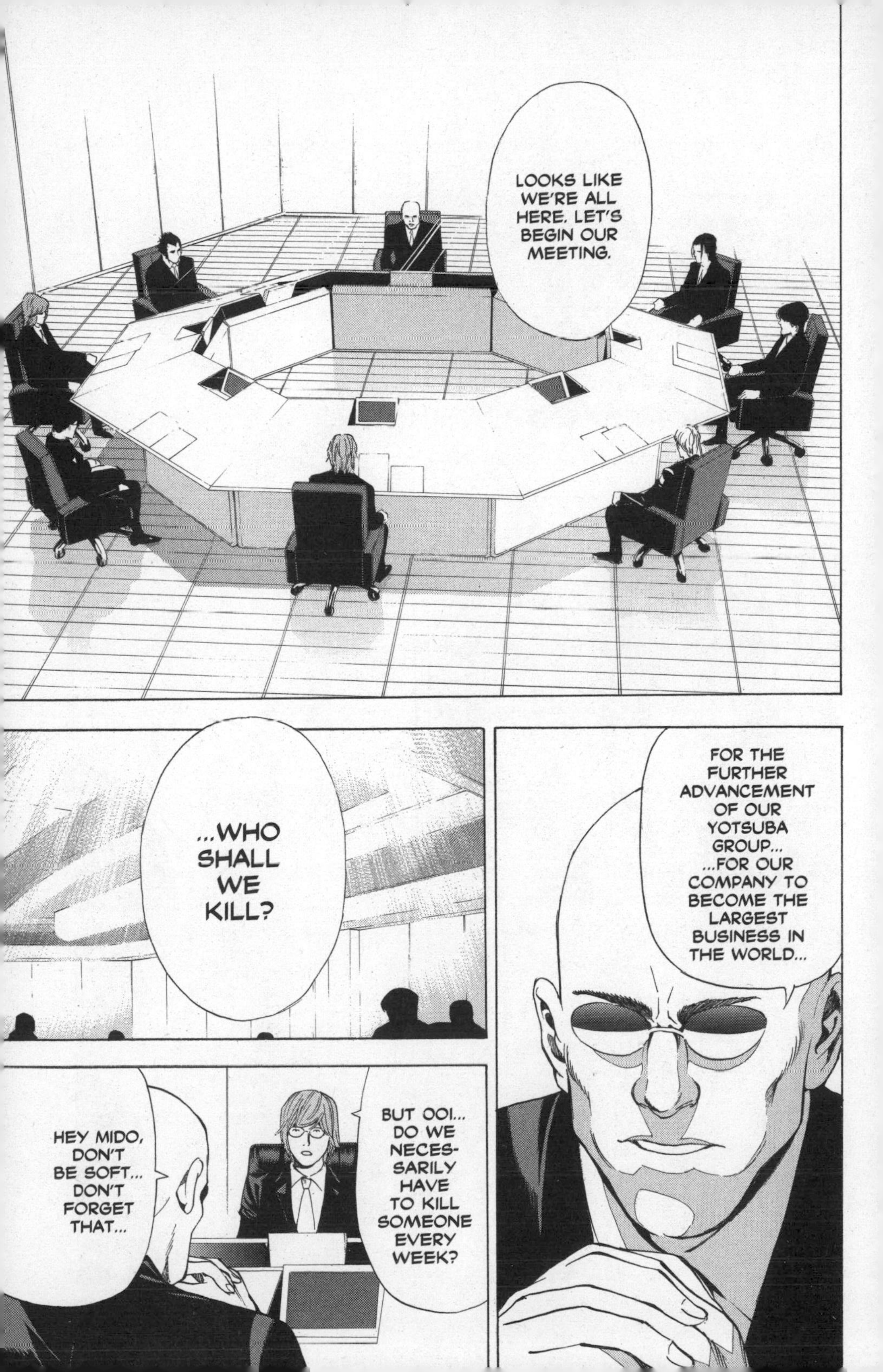
LOOKS LIKE WE'RE ALL HERE. LET'S BEGIN OUR MEETING.
FOR THE FURTHER ADVANCEMENT OF OUR YOTSUBA GROUP... ...FOR OUR COMPANY TO BECOME THE LARGEST BUSINESS IN THE WORLD...
...WHO SHALL WE KILL?
BUT OOI... DO WE NECES-SARILY HAVE TO KILL SOMEONE EVERY WEEK?
HEY MIDO, DON'T BE SOFT... DON'T FORGET THAT...

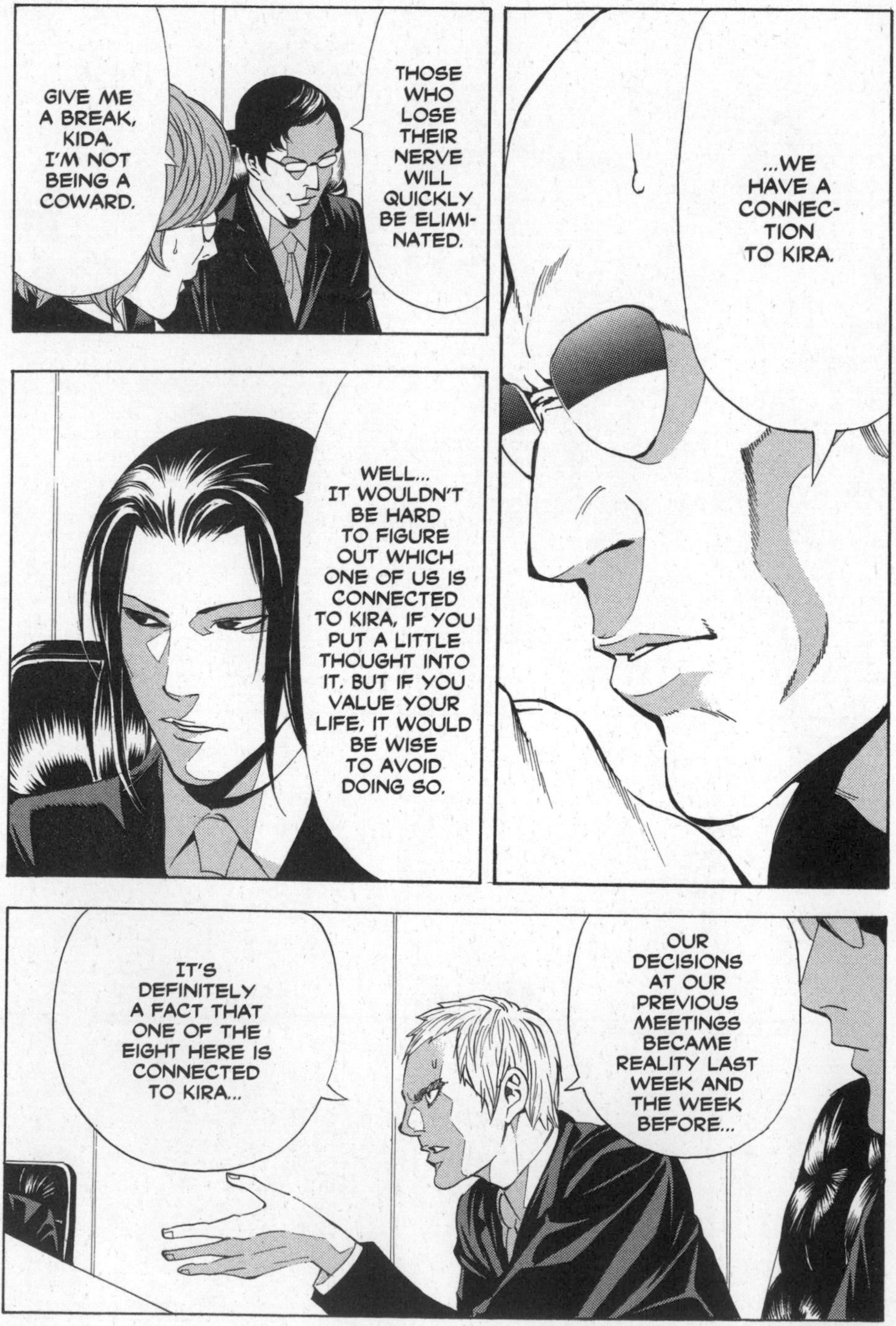
...WE HAVE A CONNECTION TO KIRA.
THOSE WHO LOSE THEIR NERVE WILL QUICKLY BE ELIMINATED.
GIVE ME A BREAK, KIDA. I'M NOT BEING A COWARD.
WELL... IT WOULDN'T BE HARD TO FIGURE OUT WHICH ONE OF US IS CONNECTED TO KIRA, IF YOU PUT A LITTLE THOUGHT INTO IT. BUT IF YOU VALUE YOUR LIFE, IT WOULD BE WISE TO AVOID DOING SO.
OUR DECISIONS AT OUR PREVIOUS MEETINGS BECAME REALITY LAST WEEK AND THE WEEK BEFORE...
IT'S DEFINITELY A FACT THAT ONE OF THE EIGHT HERE IS CONNECTED TO KIRA...

READ THIS WAY

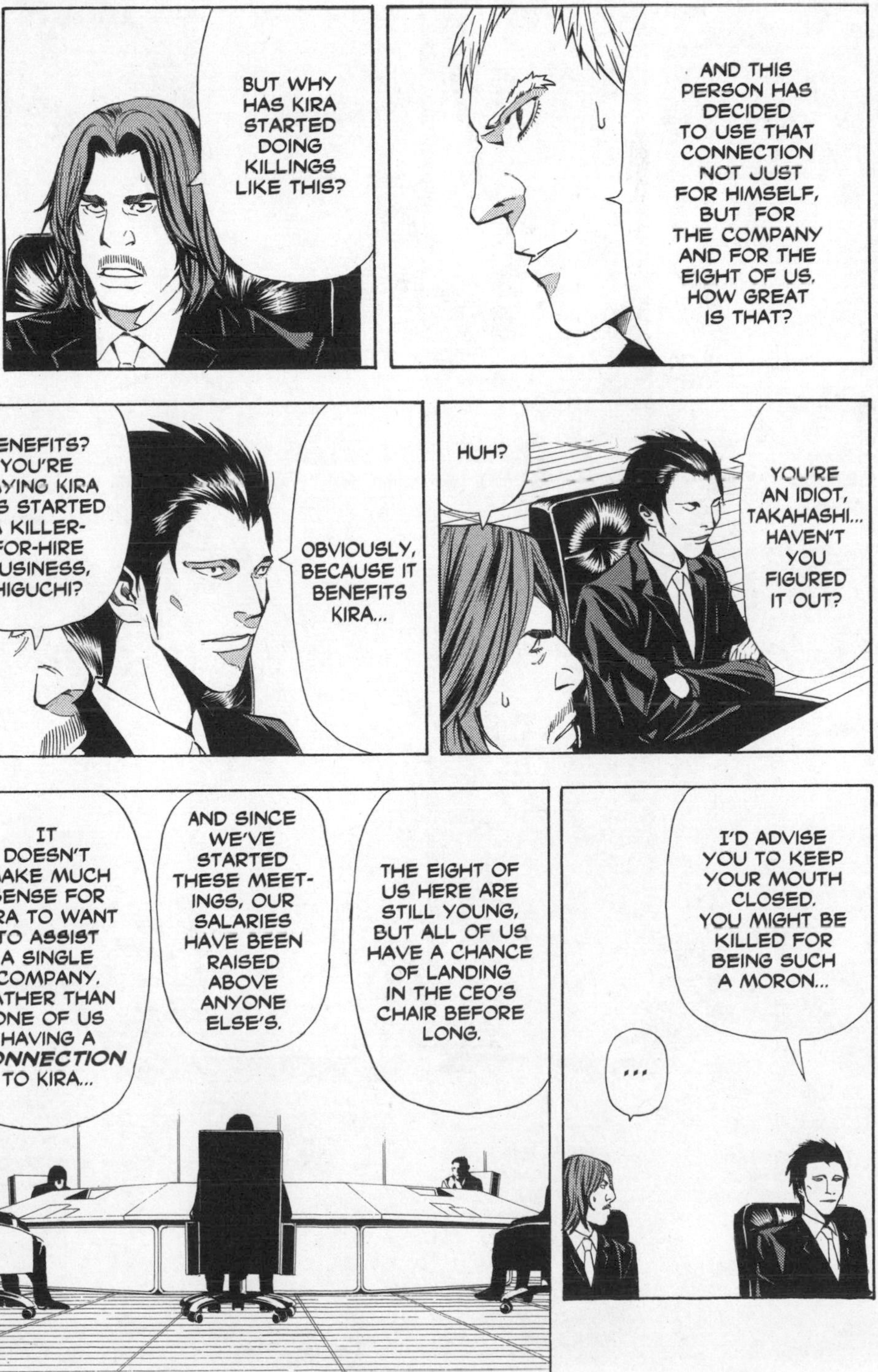
AND THIS PERSON HAS DECIDED TO USE THAT CONNECTION NOT JUST FOR HIMSELF, BUT FOR THE COMPANY AND FOR THE EIGHT OF US. HOW GREAT IS THAT?
BUT WHY HAS KIRA STARTED DOING KILLINGS LIKE THIS?
YOU'RE AN IDIOT, TAKAHASHI... HAVEN'T YOU FIGURED IT OUT?
HUH?
OBVIOUSLY, BECAUSE IT BENEFITS KIRA...
BENEFITS? YOU'RE SAYING KIRA HAS STARTED A KILLER-FOR-HIRE BUSINESS, HIGUCHI?
I'D ADVISE YOU TO KEEP YOUR MOUTH CLOSED. YOU MIGHT BE KILLED FOR BEING SUCH A MORON...
...
THE EIGHT OF US HERE ARE STILL YOUNG, BUT ALL OF US HAVE A CHANCE OF LANDING IN THE CEO'S CHAIR BEFORE LONG.
AND SINCE WE'VE STARTED THESE MEET-INGS, OUR SALARIES HAVE BEEN RAISED ABOVE ANYONE ELSE'S.
IT DOESN'T MAKE MUCH SENSE FOR KIRA TO WANT TO ASSIST A SINGLE COMPANY. RATHER THAN ONE OF US HAVING A CONNECTION TO KIRA...

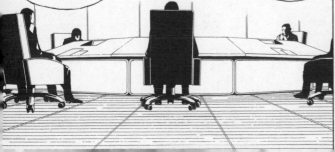

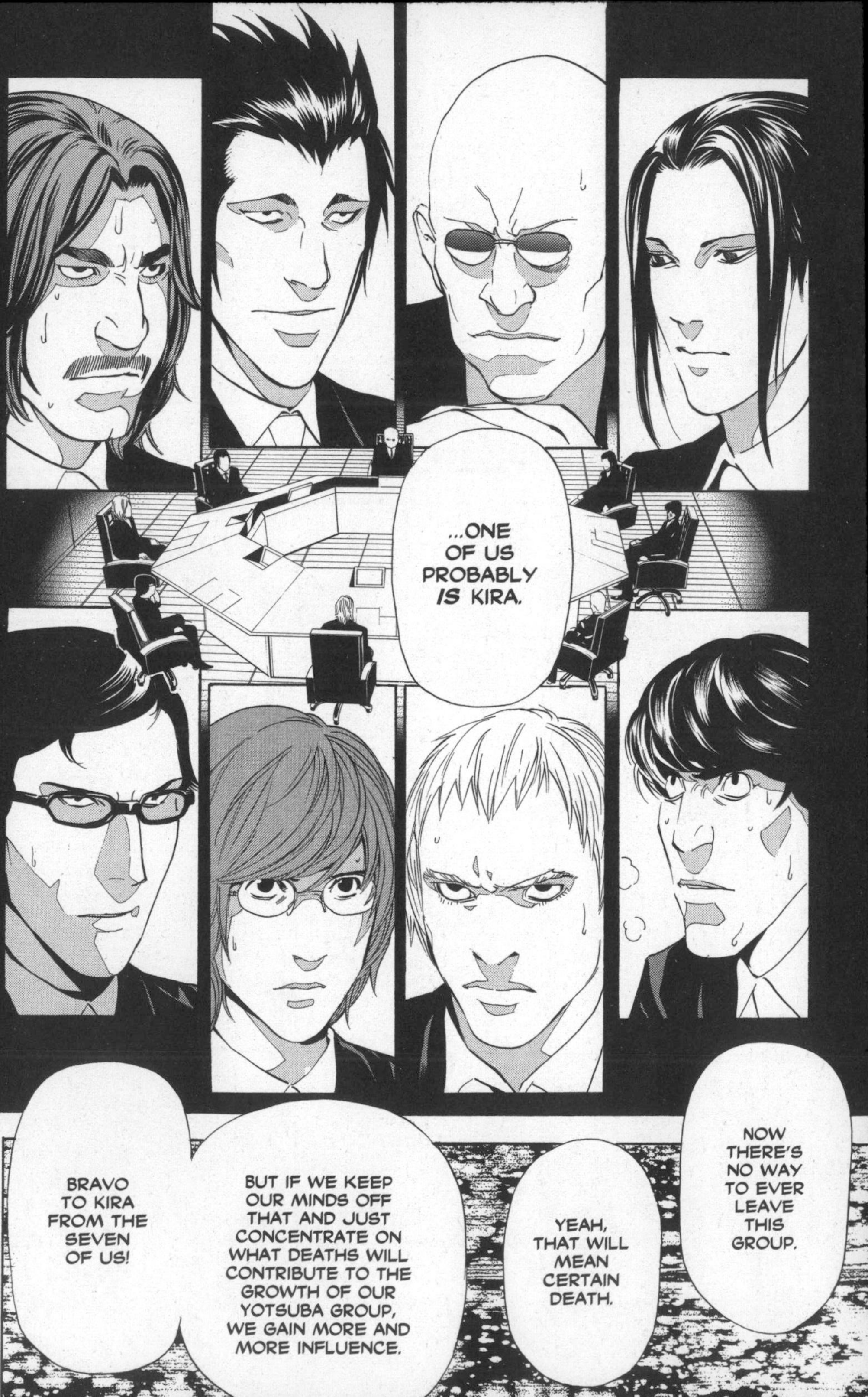
...ONE OF US PROBABLY *IS* KIRA.
NOW THERE'S NO WAY TO EVER LEAVE THIS GROUP.
YEAH, THAT WILL MEAN CERTAIN DEATH.
BUT IF WE KEEP OUR MINDS OFF THAT AND JUST CONCENTRATE ON WHAT DEATHS WILL CONTRIBUTE TO THE GROWTH OF OUR YOTSUBA GROUP, WE GAIN MORE AND MORE INFLUENCE.
BRAVO TO KIRA FROM THE SEVEN OF US!

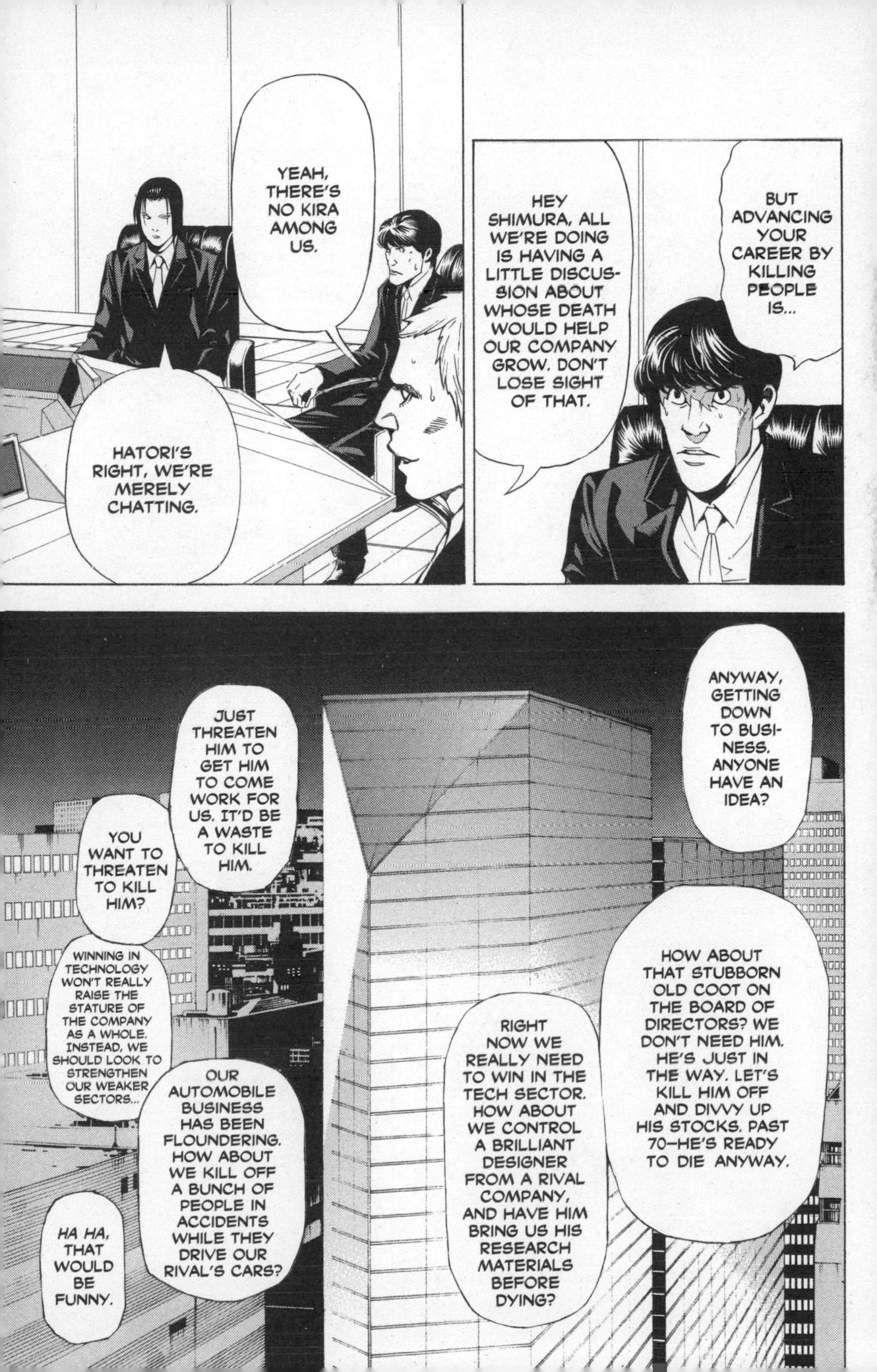
BUT ADVANCING YOUR CAREER BY KILLING PEOPLE IS...
HEY SHIMURA, ALL WE'RE DOING IS HAVING A LITTLE DISCUSSION ABOUT WHOSE DEATH WOULD HELP OUR COMPANY GROW. DON'T LOSE SIGHT OF THAT.
YEAH, THERE'S NO KIRA AMONG US.
HATORI'S RIGHT, WE'RE MERELY CHATTING.
ANYWAY, GETTING DOWN TO BUSINESS. ANYONE HAVE AN IDEA?
HOW ABOUT THAT STUBBORN OLD COOT ON THE BOARD OF DIRECTORS? WE DON'T NEED HIM. HE'S JUST IN THE WAY. LET'S KILL HIM OFF AND DIVVY UP HIS STOCKS. PAST 70—HE'S READY TO DIE ANYWAY.
RIGHT NOW WE REALLY NEED TO WIN IN THE TECH SECTOR. HOW ABOUT WE CONTROL A BRILLIANT DESIGNER FROM A RIVAL COMPANY, AND HAVE HIM BRING US HIS RESEARCH MATERIALS BEFORE DYING?
YOU WANT TO THREATEN TO KILL HIM?
JUST THREATEN HIM TO GET HIM TO COME WORK FOR US. IT'D BE A WASTE TO KILL HIM.
WINNING IN TECHNOLOGY WON'T REALLY RAISE THE STATURE OF THE COMPANY AS A WHOLE. INSTEAD, WE SHOULD LOOK TO STRENGTHEN OUR WEAKER SECTORS...
OUR AUTOMOBILE BUSINESS HAS BEEN FLOUNDERING. HOW ABOUT WE KILL OFF A BUNCH OF PEOPLE IN ACCIDENTS WHILE THEY DRIVE OUR RIVAL'S CARS?
HA HA, THAT WOULD BE FUNNY.

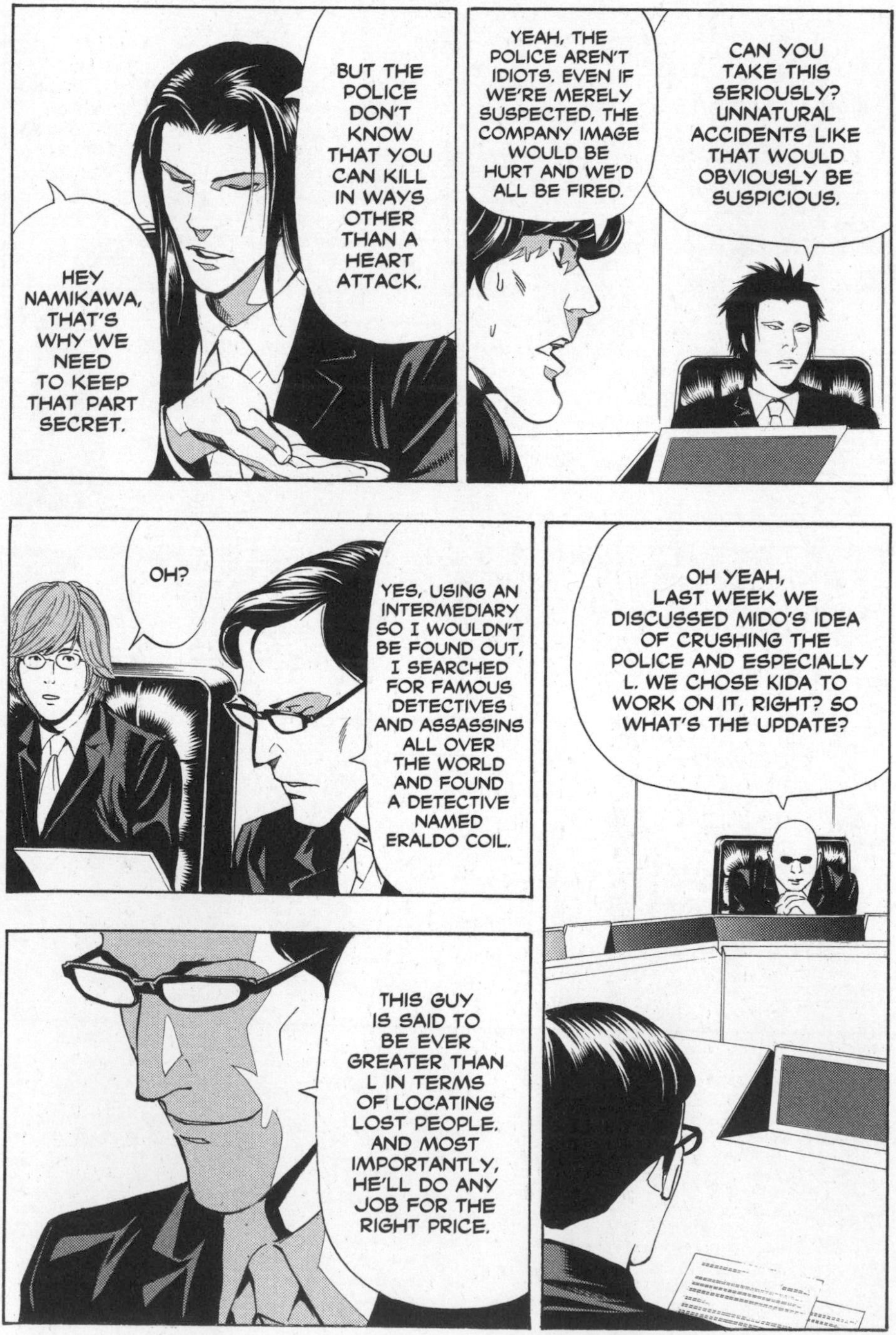
CAN YOU TAKE THIS SERIOUSLY? UNNATURAL ACCIDENTS LIKE THAT WOULD OBVIOUSLY BE SUSPICIOUS.
YEAH, THE POLICE AREN'T IDIOTS. EVEN IF WE'RE MERELY SUSPECTED, THE COMPANY IMAGE WOULD BE HURT AND WE'D ALL BE FIRED.
BUT THE POLICE DON'T KNOW THAT YOU CAN KILL IN WAYS OTHER THAN A HEART ATTACK.
HEY NAMIKAWA, THAT'S WHY WE NEED TO KEEP THAT PART SECRET.
OH YEAH, LAST WEEK WE DISCUSSED MIDO'S IDEA OF CRUSHING THE POLICE AND ESPECIALLY L. WE CHOSE KIDA TO WORK ON IT, RIGHT? SO WHAT'S THE UPDATE?
YES, USING AN INTERMEDIARY SO I WOULDN'T BE FOUND OUT, I SEARCHED FOR FAMOUS DETECTIVES AND ASSASSINS ALL OVER THE WORLD AND FOUND A DETECTIVE NAMED ERALDO COIL.
OH?
THIS GUY IS SAID TO BE EVER GREATER THAN L IN TERMS OF LOCATING LOST PEOPLE. AND MOST IMPORTANTLY, HE'LL DO ANY JOB FOR THE RIGHT PRICE.

READ THIS WAY

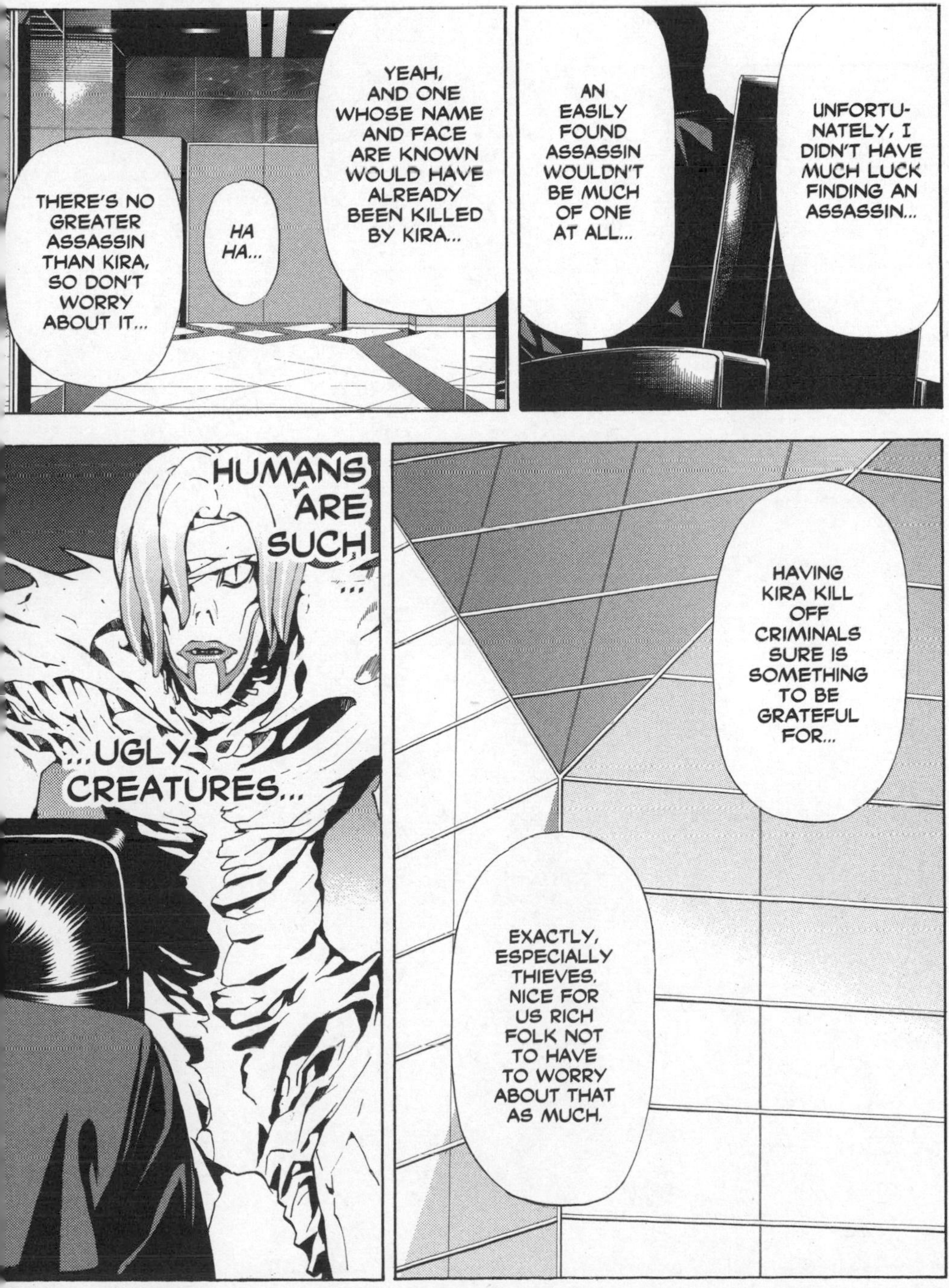
UNFORTU-NATELY, I DIDN'T HAVE MUCH LUCK FINDING AN ASSASSIN...
AN EASILY FOUND ASSASSIN WOULDN'T BE MUCH OF ONE AT ALL...
YEAH, AND ONE WHOSE NAME AND FACE ARE KNOWN WOULD HAVE ALREADY BEEN KILLED BY KIRA...
HA HA...
THERE'S NO GREATER ASSASSIN THAN KIRA, SO DON'T WORRY ABOUT IT...
HAVING KIRA KILL OFF CRIMINALS SURE IS SOMETHING TO BE GRATEFUL FOR...
EXACTLY, ESPECIALLY THIEVES. NICE FOR US RICH FOLK NOT TO HAVE TO WORRY ABOUT THAT AS MUCH.
HUMANS ARE SUCH...
...UGLY CREATURES...

chapter 38 Strike

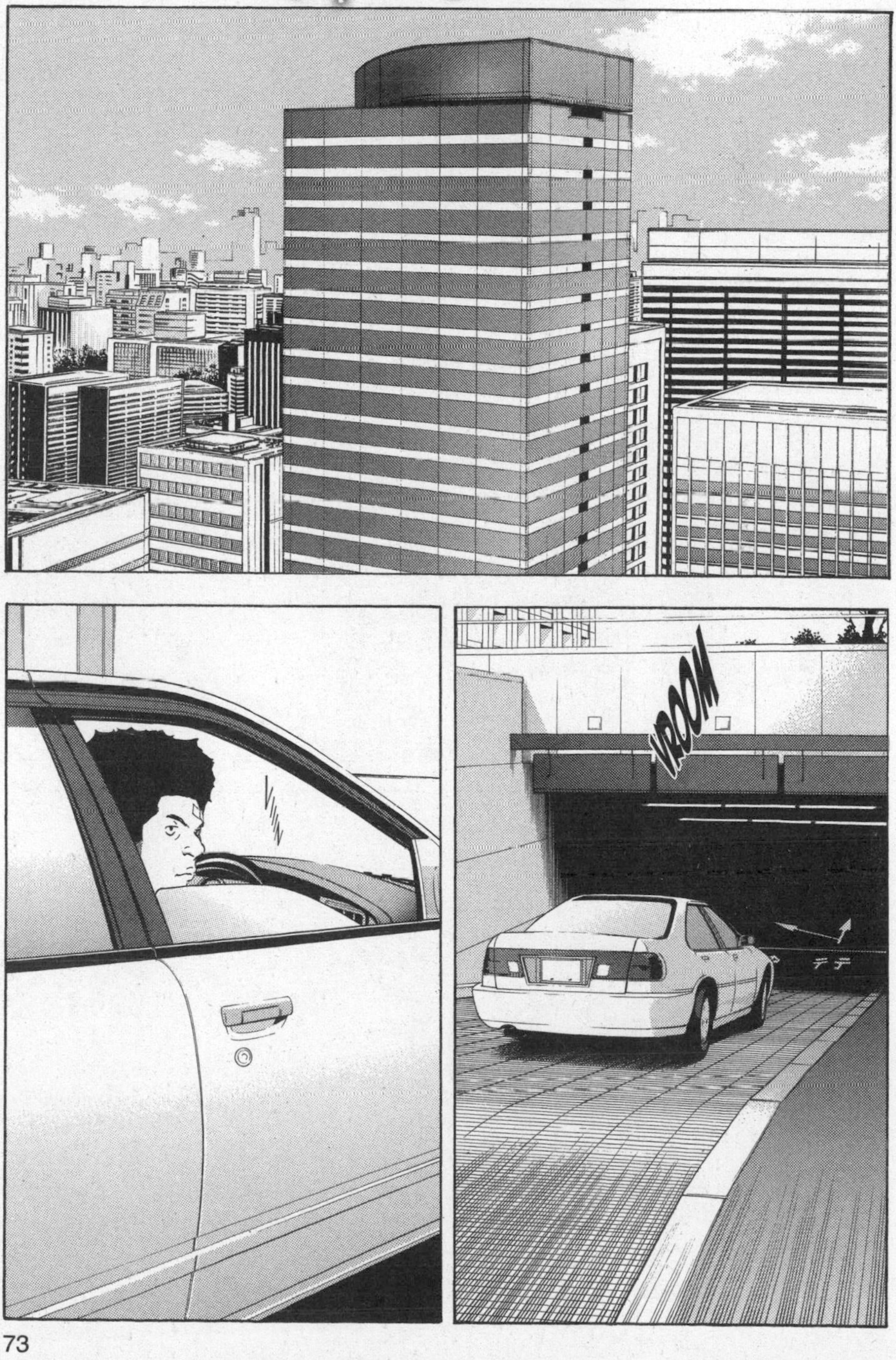
VROOM
VIIN

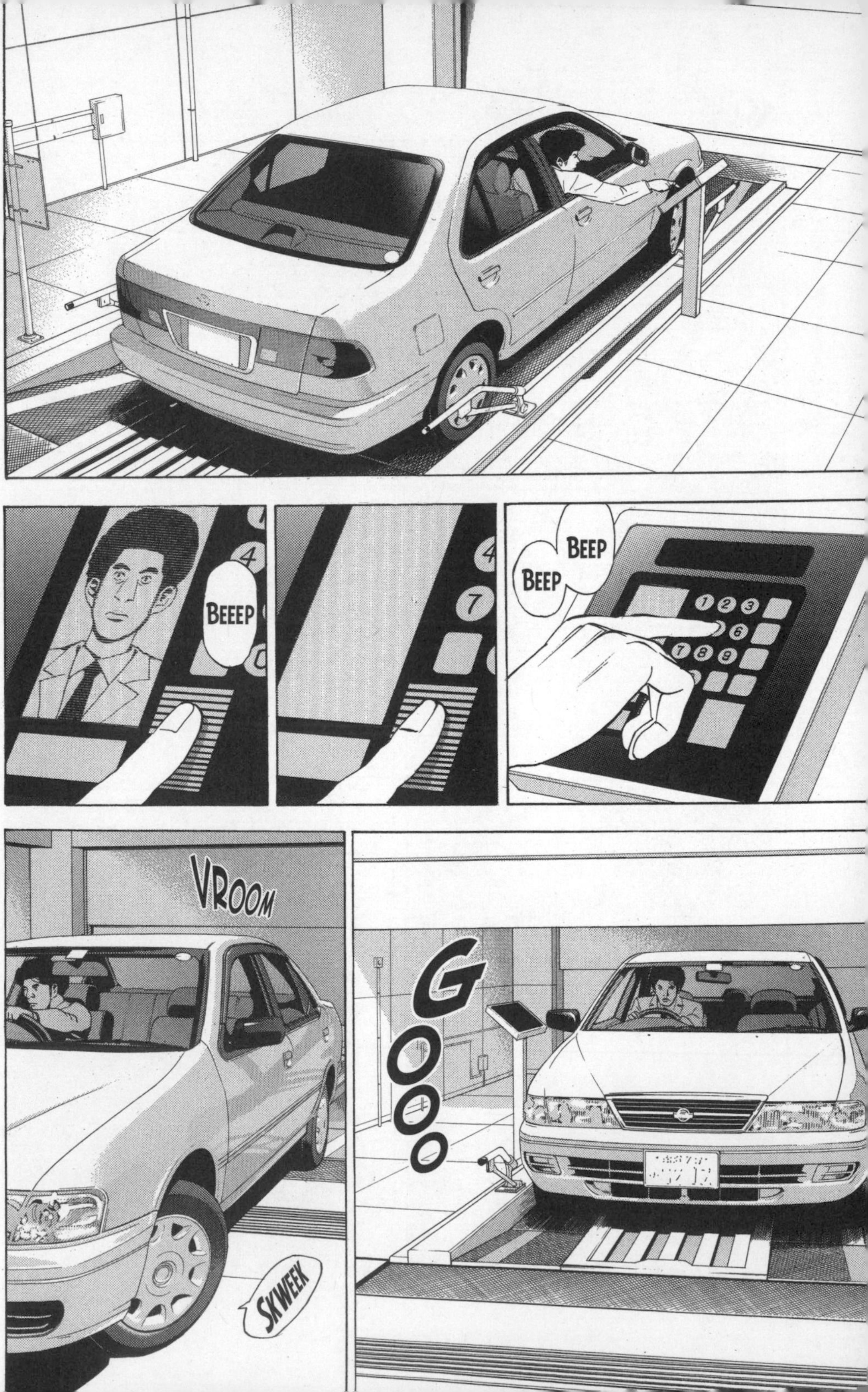
BEEP
BEEP
BEEEP
GOOOO
VROOM
SKWEEK

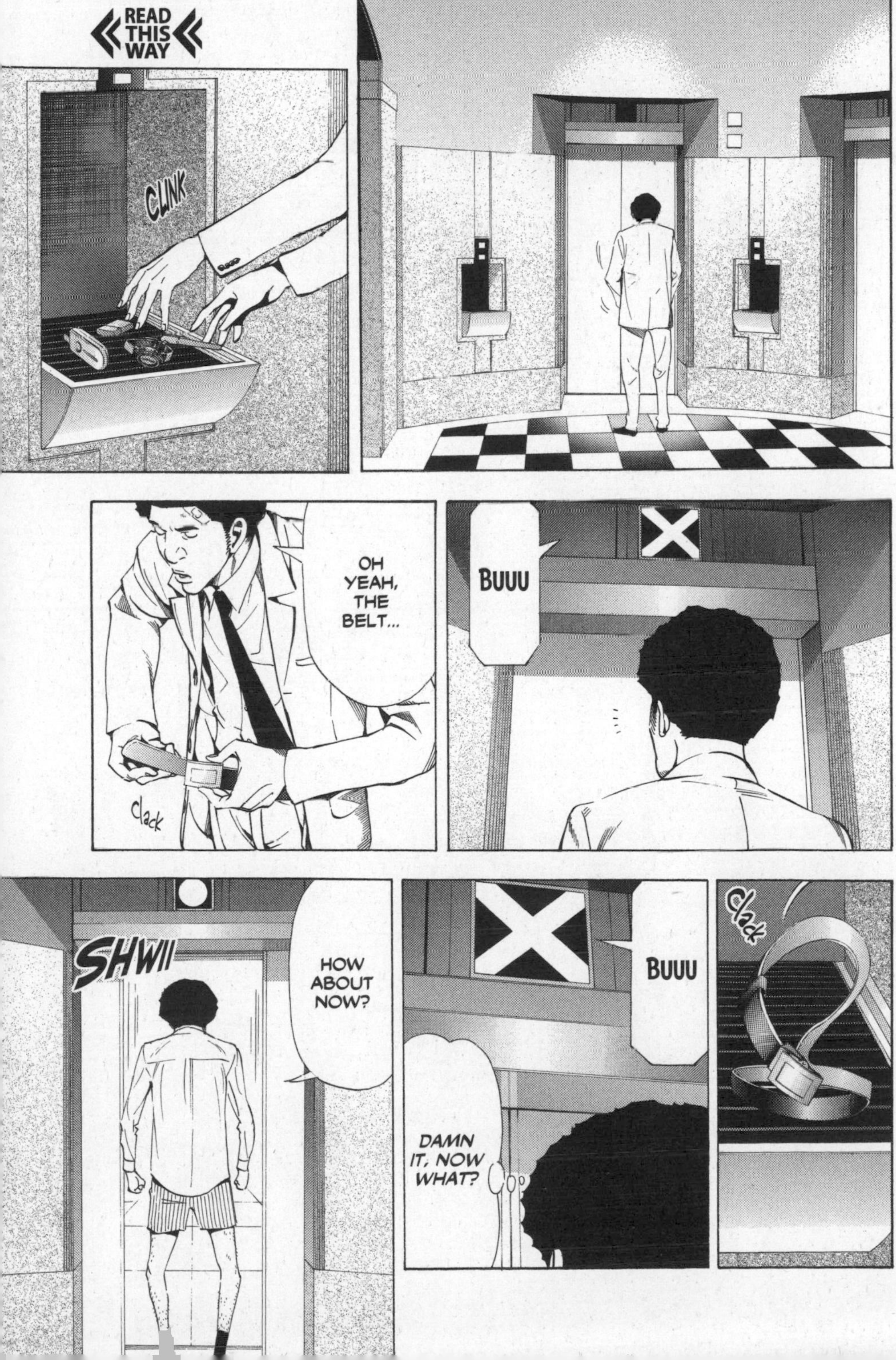
READ THIS WAY
CLINK
BUUU
OH YEAH, THE BELT...
clack
clack
BUUU
DAMN IT, NOW WHAT?
SHWIII
HOW ABOUT NOW?

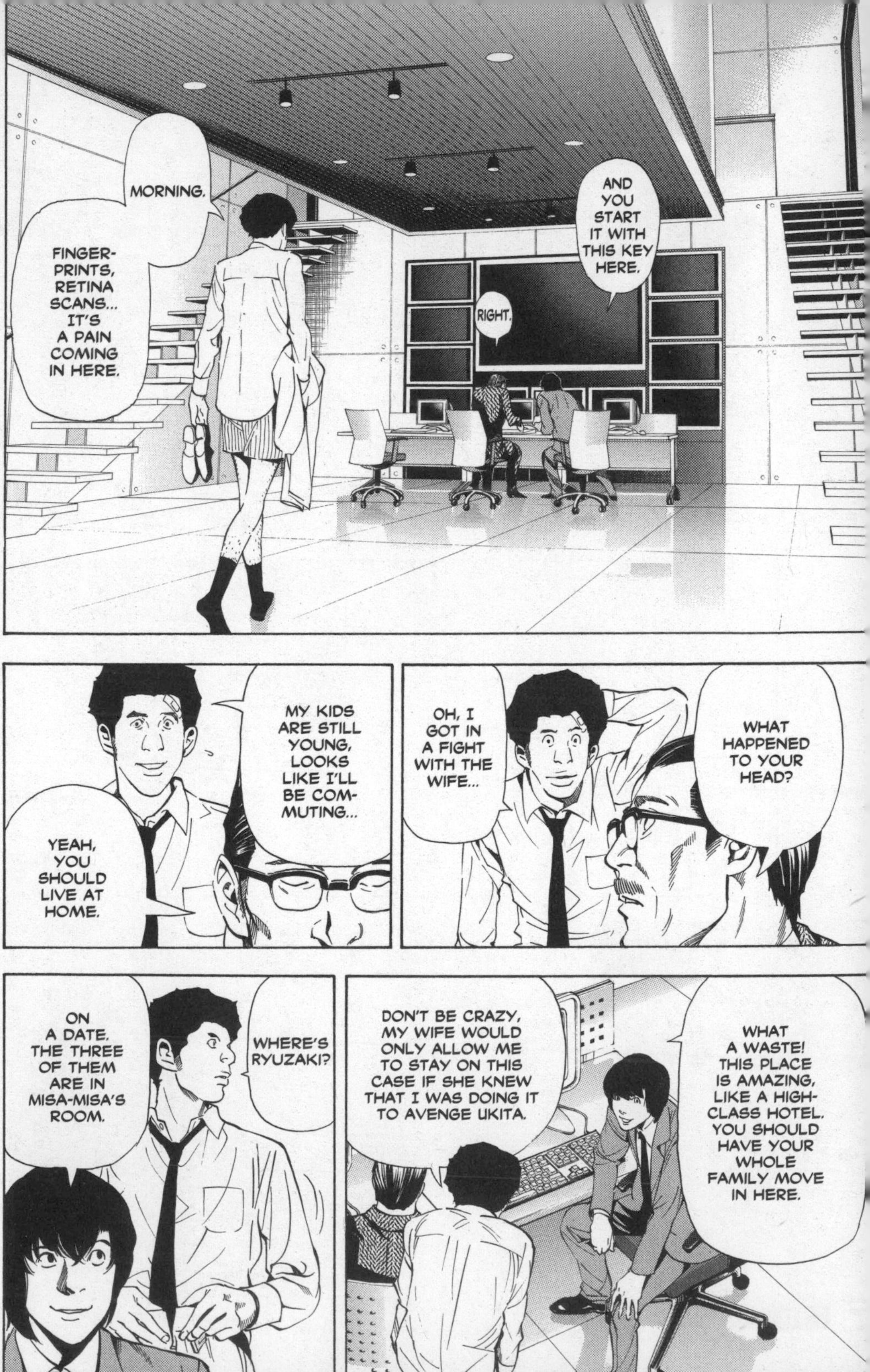
AND YOU START IT WITH THIS KEY HERE.
RIGHT.
MORNING.
FINGER-PRINTS, RETINA SCANS... IT'S A PAIN COMING IN HERE.
WHAT HAPPENED TO YOUR HEAD?
OH, I GOT IN A FIGHT WITH THE WIFE...
MY KIDS ARE STILL YOUNG, LOOKS LIKE I'LL BE COM-MUTING...
YEAH, YOU SHOULD LIVE AT HOME.
WHAT A WASTE! THIS PLACE IS AMAZING, LIKE A HIGH-CLASS HOTEL. YOU SHOULD HAVE YOUR WHOLE FAMILY MOVE IN HERE.
DON'T BE CRAZY, MY WIFE WOULD ONLY ALLOW ME TO STAY ON THIS CASE IF SHE KNEW THAT I WAS DOING IT TO AVENGE UKITA.
WHERE'S RYUZAKI?
ON A DATE. THE THREE OF THEM ARE IN MISA-MISA'S ROOM.

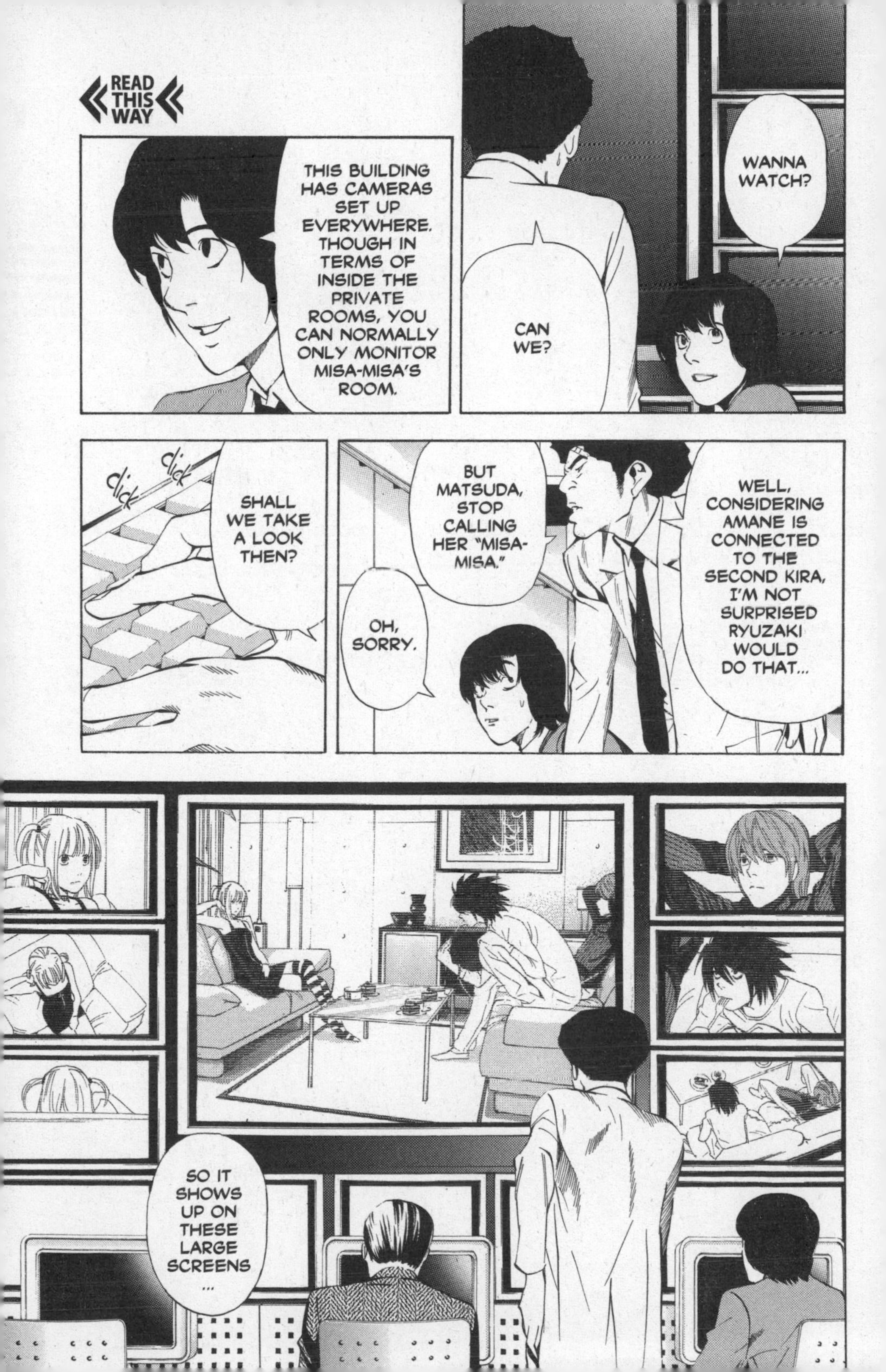
READ THIS WAY
WANNA WATCH?
CAN WE?
THIS BUILDING HAS CAMERAS SET UP EVERYWHERE. THOUGH IN TERMS OF INSIDE THE PRIVATE ROOMS, YOU CAN NORMALLY ONLY MONITOR MISA-MISA'S ROOM.
WELL, CONSIDERING AMANE IS CONNECTED TO THE SECOND KIRA, I'M NOT SURPRISED RYUZAKI WOULD DO THAT...
BUT MATSUDA, STOP CALLING HER "MISA-MISA."
OH, SORRY.
click
click
SHALL WE TAKE A LOOK THEN?
SO IT SHOWS UP ON THESE LARGE SCREENS ...

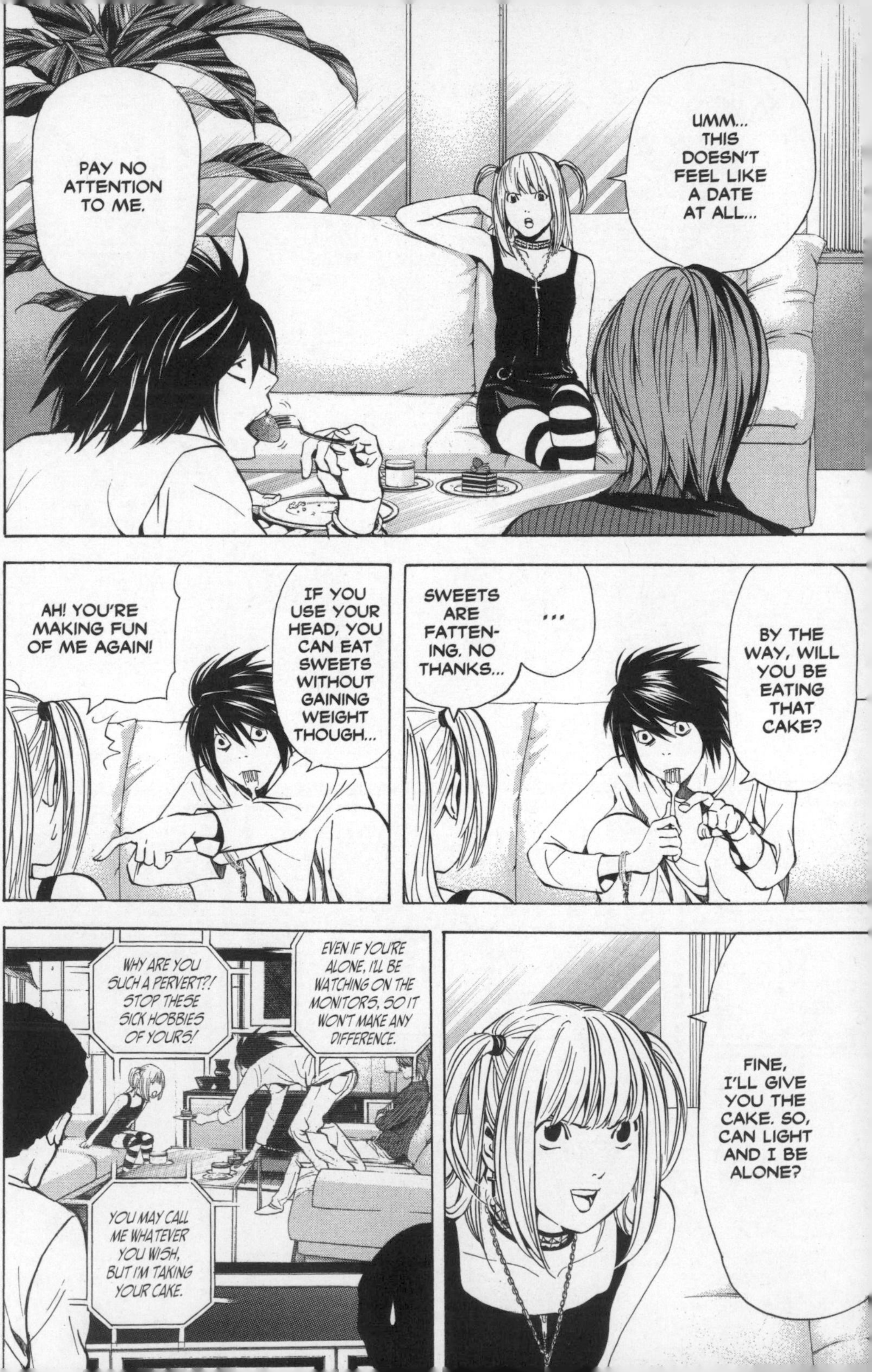

UMM... THIS DOESN'T FEEL LIKE A DATE AT ALL...
PAY NO ATTENTION TO ME.
BY THE WAY, WILL YOU BE EATING THAT CAKE?
...
SWEETS ARE FATTEN-ING. NO THANKS...
IF YOU USE YOUR HEAD, YOU CAN EAT SWEETS WITHOUT GAINING WEIGHT THOUGH...
AH! YOU'RE MAKING FUN OF ME AGAIN!
FINE, I'LL GIVE YOU THE CAKE. SO, CAN LIGHT AND I BE ALONE?
EVEN IF YOU'RE ALONE, I'LL BE WATCHING ON THE MONITORS, SO IT WON'T MAKE ANY DIFFERENCE.
WHY ARE YOU SUCH A PERVERT?! STOP THESE SICK HOBBIES OF YOURS!
YOU MAY CALL ME WHATEVER YOU WISH, BUT I'M TAKING YOUR CAKE.

READ THIS WAY

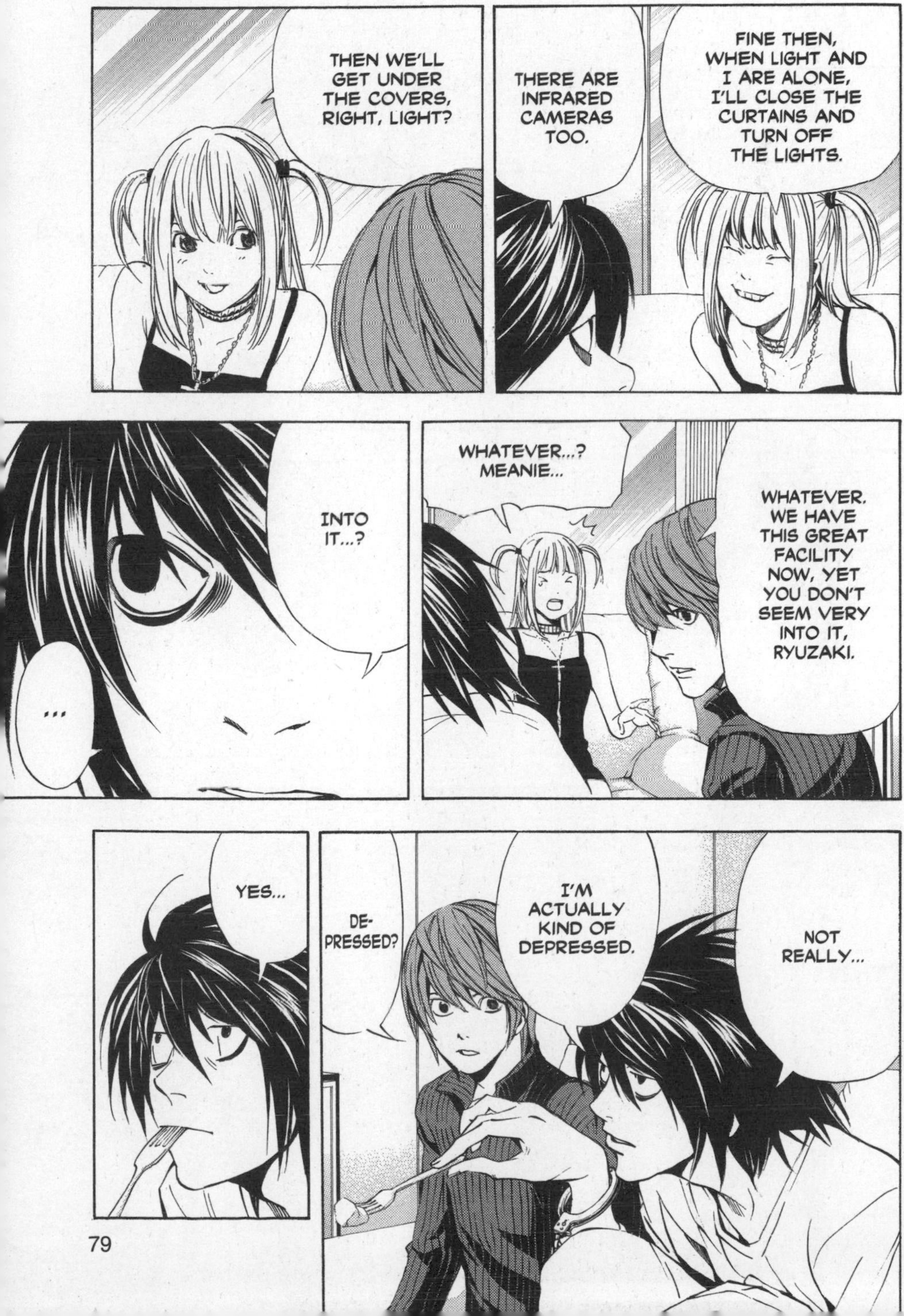
FINE THEN, WHEN LIGHT AND I ARE ALONE, I'LL CLOSE THE CURTAINS AND TURN OFF THE LIGHTS.
THERE ARE INFRARED CAMERAS TOO.
THEN WE'LL GET UNDER THE COVERS, RIGHT, LIGHT?
WHATEVER. WE HAVE THIS GREAT FACILITY NOW, YET YOU DON'T SEEM VERY INTO IT, RYUZAKI.
WHATEVER...? MEANIE...
INTO IT...?
...
NOT REALLY...
I'M ACTUALLY KIND OF DEPRESSED.
DE-PRESSED?
YES...

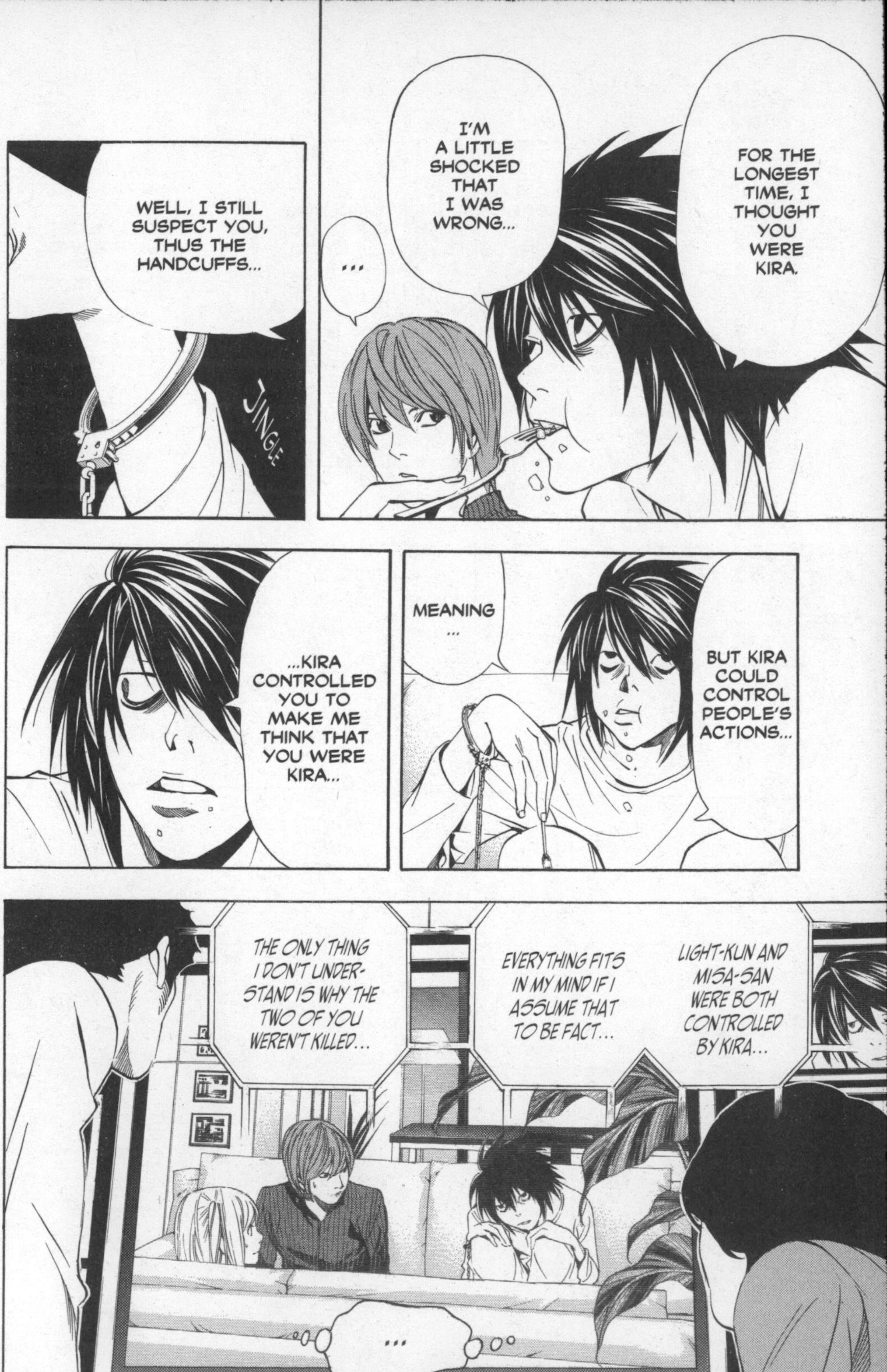
FOR THE LONGEST TIME, I THOUGHT YOU WERE KIRA.
I'M A LITTLE SHOCKED THAT I WAS WRONG...
...
WELL, I STILL SUSPECT YOU, THUS THE HANDCUFFS...
JINGLE
BUT KIRA COULD CONTROL PEOPLE'S ACTIONS...
MEANING ...
...KIRA CONTROLLED YOU TO MAKE ME THINK THAT YOU WERE KIRA...
LIGHT-KUN AND MISA-SAN WERE BOTH CONTROLLED BY KIRA...
EVERYTHING FITS IN MY MIND IF I ASSUME THAT TO BE FACT...
THE ONLY THING I DON'T UNDER-STAND IS WHY THE TWO OF YOU WEREN'T KILLED...
...

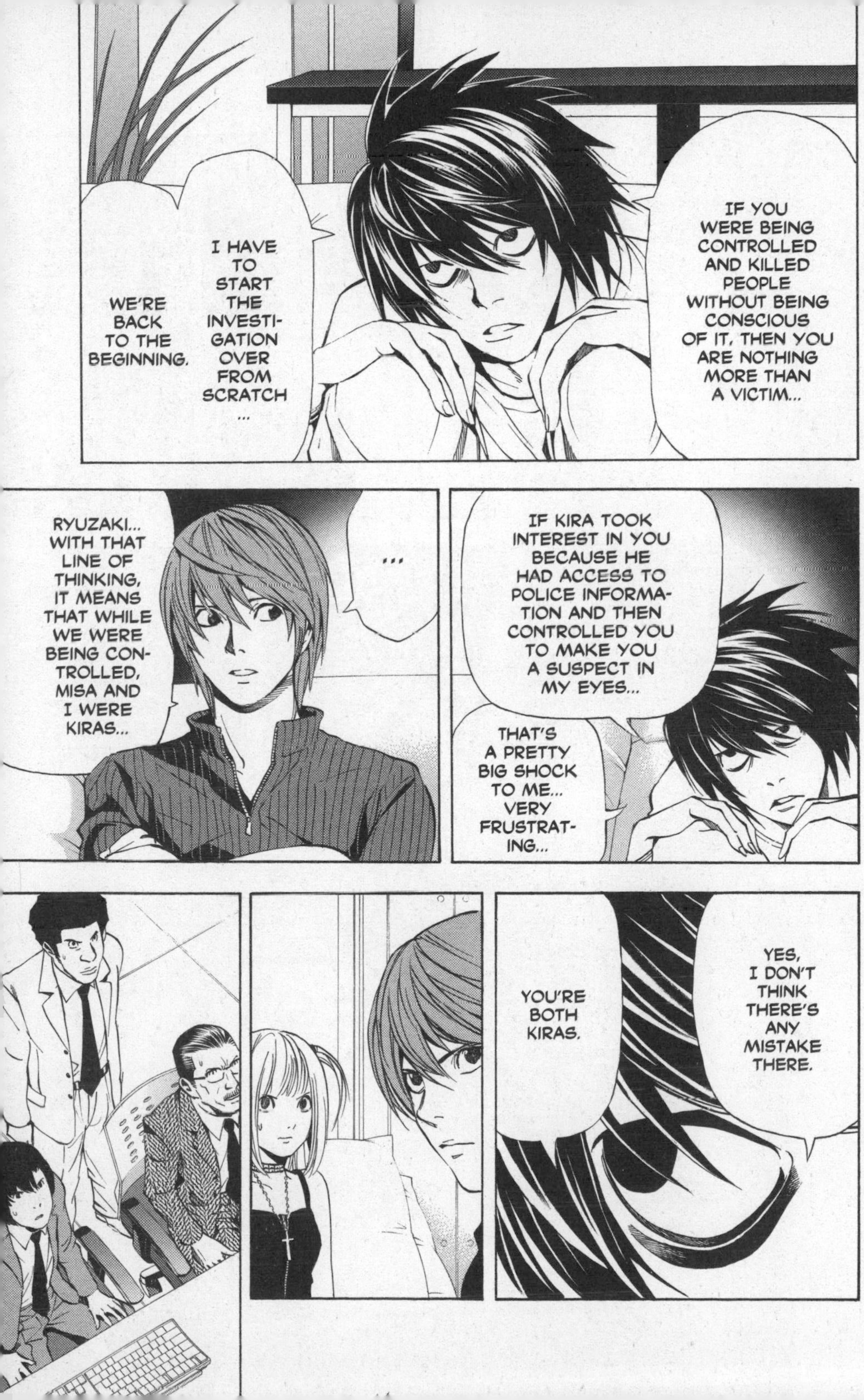
IF YOU WERE BEING CONTROLLED AND KILLED PEOPLE WITHOUT BEING CONSCIOUS OF IT, THEN YOU ARE NOTHING MORE THAN A VICTIM...
I HAVE TO START THE INVESTIGATION OVER FROM SCRATCH ...
WE'RE BACK TO THE BEGINNING.
IF KIRA TOOK INTEREST IN YOU BECAUSE HE HAD ACCESS TO POLICE INFORMATION AND THEN CONTROLLED YOU TO MAKE YOU A SUSPECT IN MY EYES...
THAT'S A PRETTY BIG SHOCK TO ME... VERY FRUSTRATING...
...
RYUZAKI... WITH THAT LINE OF THINKING, IT MEANS THAT WHILE WE WERE BEING CONTROLLED, MISA AND I WERE KIRAS...
YES, I DON'T THINK THERE'S ANY MISTAKE THERE.
YOU'RE BOTH KIRAS.

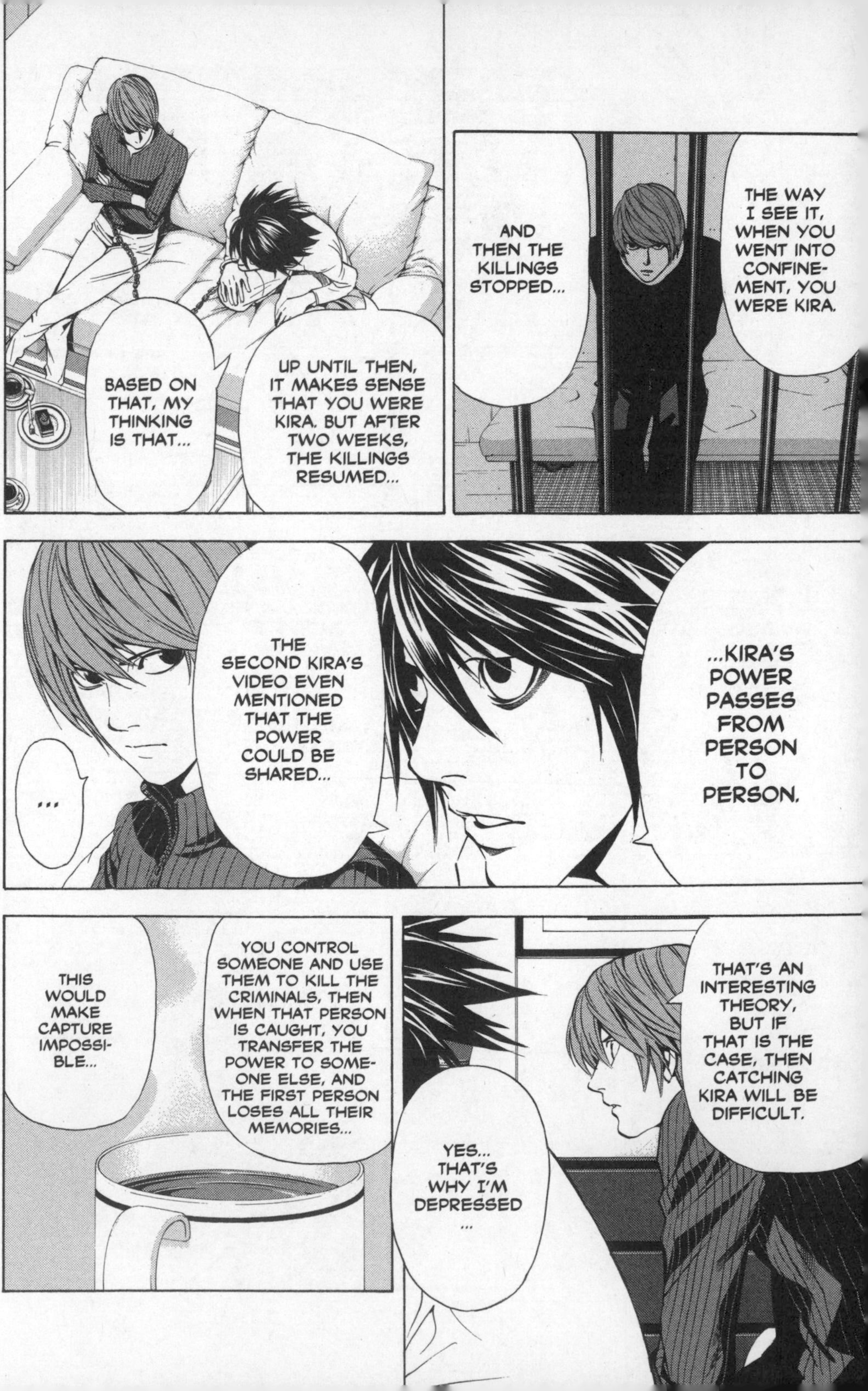
THE WAY I SEE IT, WHEN YOU WENT INTO CONFINEMENT, YOU WERE KIRA.
AND THEN THE KILLINGS STOPPED...
UP UNTIL THEN, IT MAKES SENSE THAT YOU WERE KIRA. BUT AFTER TWO WEEKS, THE KILLINGS RESUMED...
BASED ON THAT, MY THINKING IS THAT...
...KIRA'S POWER PASSES FROM PERSON TO PERSON.
THE SECOND KIRA'S VIDEO EVEN MENTIONED THAT THE POWER COULD BE SHARED...
...
THAT'S AN INTERESTING THEORY, BUT IF THAT IS THE CASE, THEN CATCHING KIRA WILL BE DIFFICULT.
YES... THAT'S WHY I'M DEPRESSED...
YOU CONTROL SOMEONE AND USE THEM TO KILL THE CRIMINALS, THEN WHEN THAT PERSON IS CAUGHT, YOU TRANSFER THE POWER TO SOMEONE ELSE, AND THE FIRST PERSON LOSES ALL THEIR MEMORIES...
THIS WOULD MAKE CAPTURE IMPOSSIBLE...

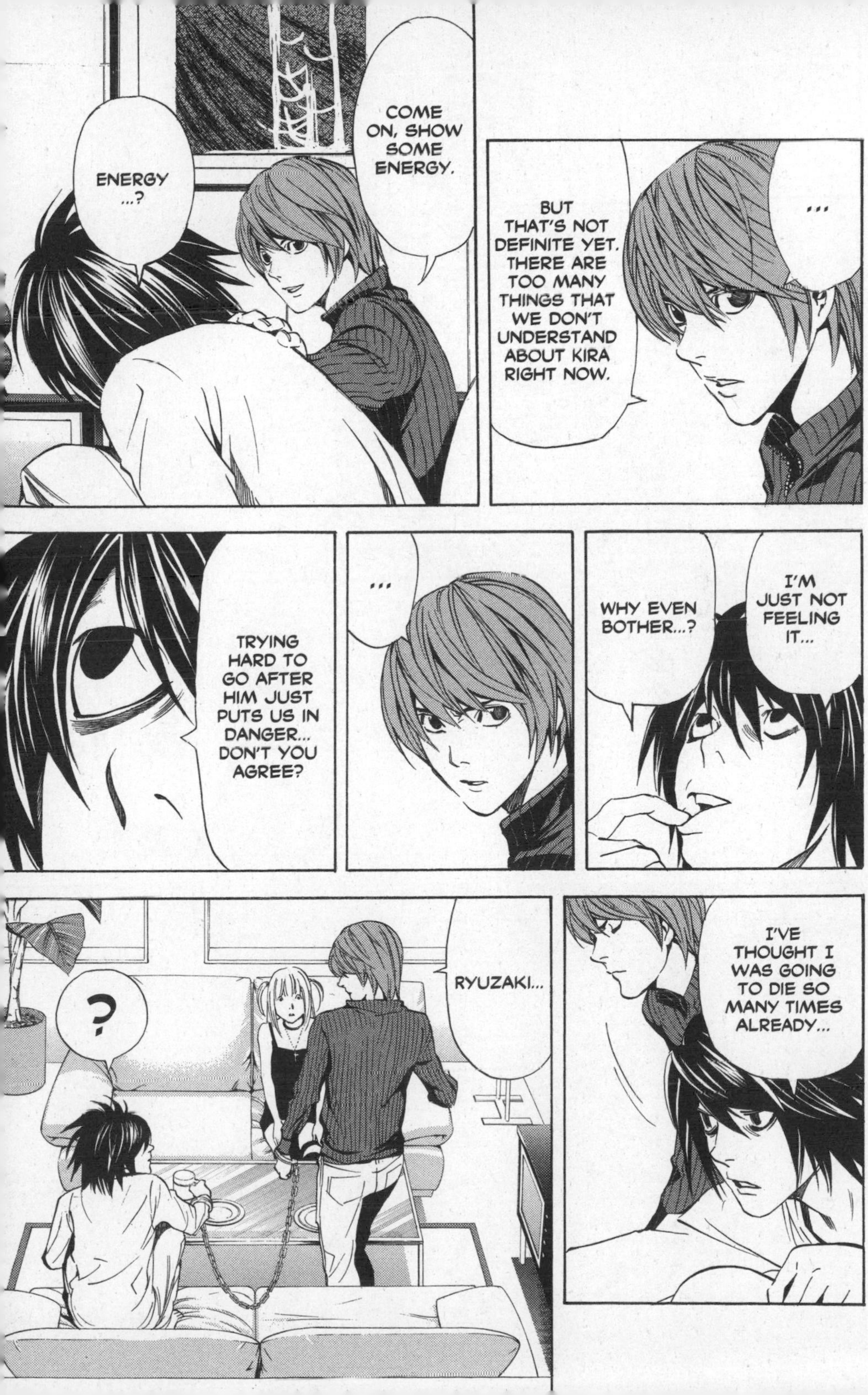
...
BUT THAT'S NOT DEFINITE YET. THERE ARE TOO MANY THINGS THAT WE DON'T UNDERSTAND ABOUT KIRA RIGHT NOW.
COME ON, SHOW SOME ENERGY.
ENERGY ...?
I'M JUST NOT FEELING IT...
WHY EVEN BOTHER...?
...
TRYING HARD TO GO AFTER HIM JUST PUTS US IN DANGER... DON'T YOU AGREE?
I'VE THOUGHT I WAS GOING TO DIE SO MANY TIMES ALREADY...
RYUZAKI...
?

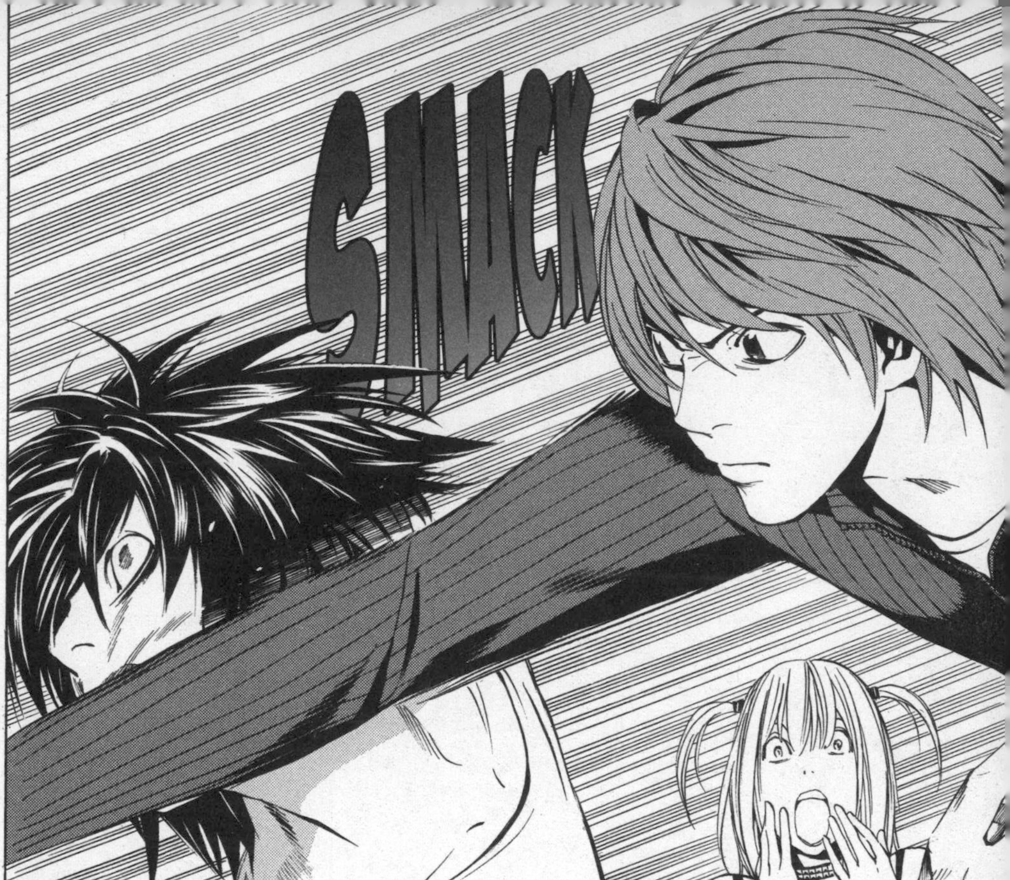
SMACK
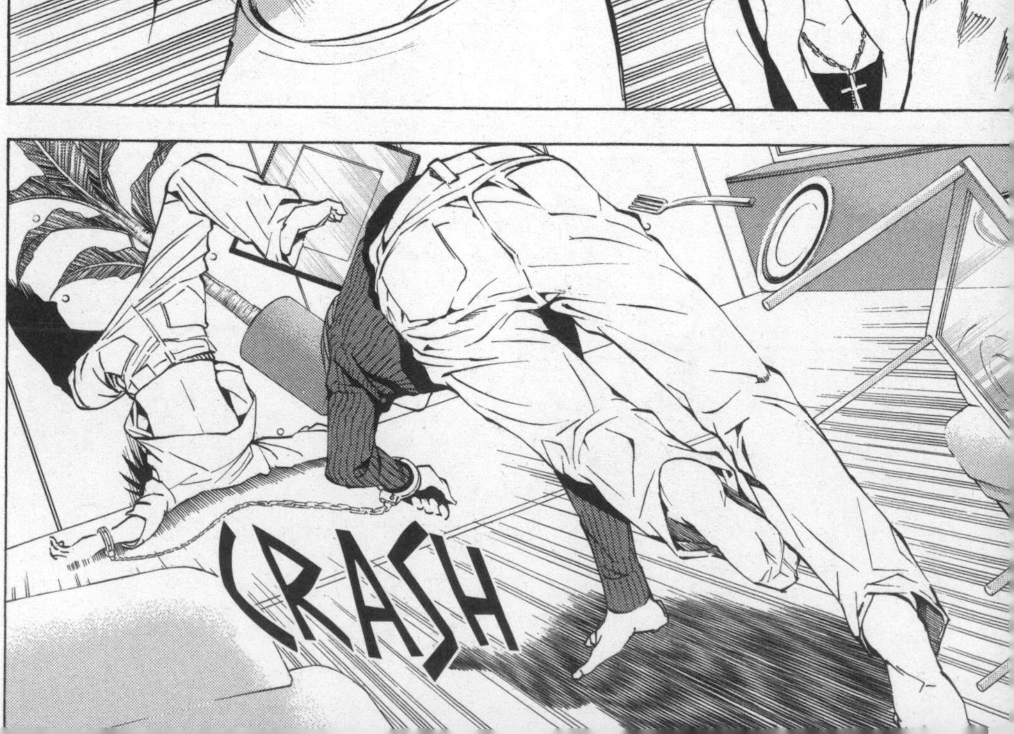
CRASH

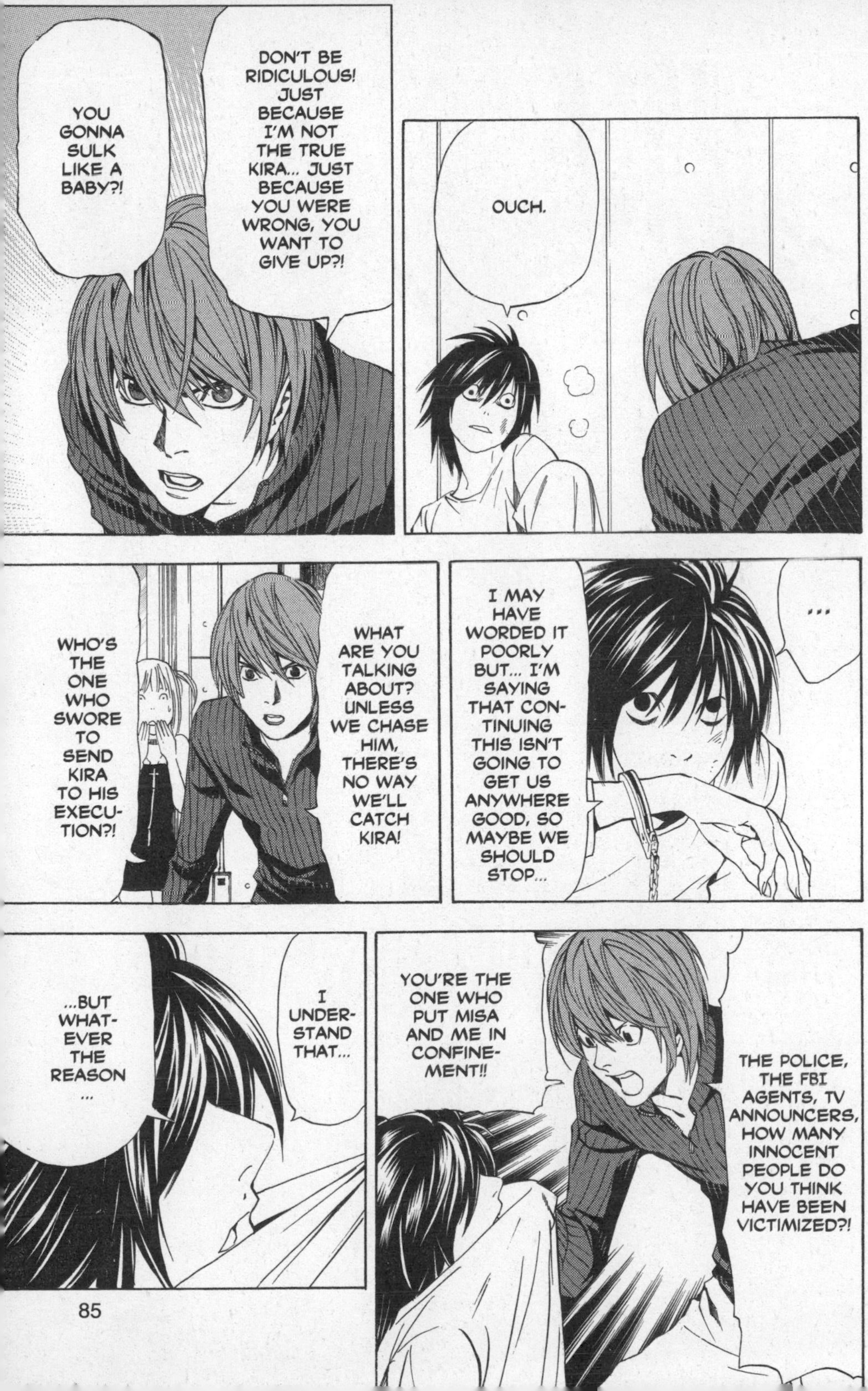
OUCH.
DON'T BE RIDICULOUS! JUST BECAUSE I'M NOT THE TRUE KIRA... JUST BECAUSE YOU WERE WRONG, YOU WANT TO GIVE UP?!
YOU GONNA SULK LIKE A BABY?!
...
I MAY HAVE WORDED IT POORLY BUT... I'M SAYING THAT CON-TINUING THIS ISN'T GOING TO GET US ANYWHERE GOOD, SO MAYBE WE SHOULD STOP...
WHAT ARE YOU TALKING ABOUT? UNLESS WE CHASE HIM, THERE'S NO WAY WE'LL CATCH KIRA!
WHO'S THE ONE WHO SWORE TO SEND KIRA TO HIS EXECU-TION?!
THE POLICE, THE FBI AGENTS, TV ANNOUNCERS, HOW MANY INNOCENT PEOPLE DO YOU THINK HAVE BEEN VICTIMIZED?!
YOU'RE THE ONE WHO PUT MISA AND ME IN CONFINE-MENT!!
I UNDER-STAND THAT...
...BUT WHAT-EVER THE REASON ...

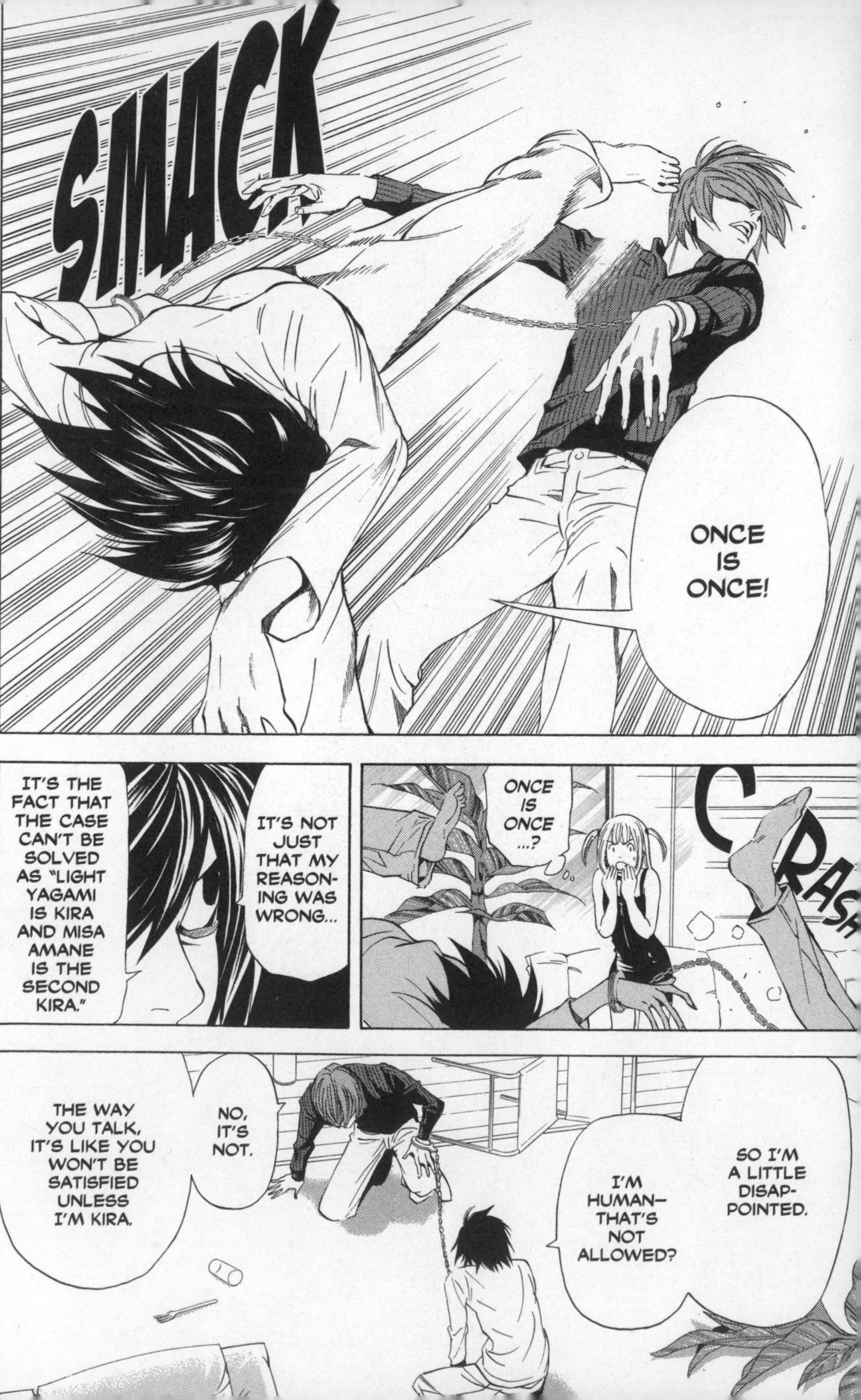
ONCE IS ONCE!
SMACK
CRASH
ONCE IS ONCE ...?
IT'S NOT JUST THAT MY REASONING WAS WRONG...
IT'S THE FACT THAT THE CASE CAN'T BE SOLVED AS "LIGHT YAGAMI IS KIRA AND MISA AMANE IS THE SECOND KIRA."
SO I'M A LITTLE DISAPPOINTED.
I'M HUMAN—THAT'S NOT ALLOWED?
NO, IT'S NOT.
THE WAY YOU TALK, IT'S LIKE YOU WON'T BE SATISFIED UNLESS I'M KIRA.

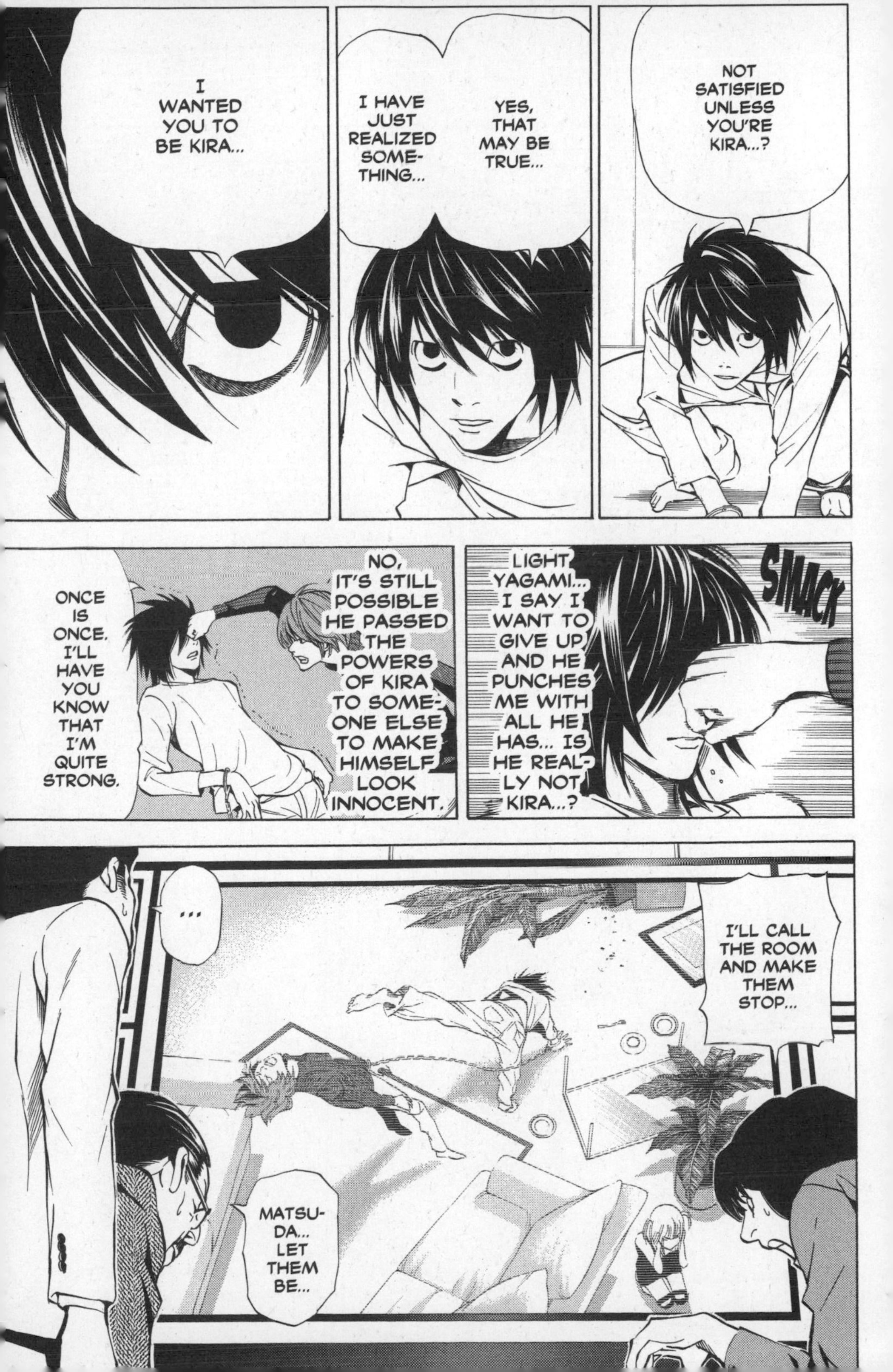
NOT SATISFIED UNLESS YOU'RE KIRA...?
YES, THAT MAY BE TRUE...
I HAVE JUST REALIZED SOMETHING...
I WANTED YOU TO BE KIRA...
SMACK
LIGHT YAGAMI... I SAY I WANT TO GIVE UP AND HE PUNCHES ME WITH ALL HE HAS... IS HE REALLY NOT KIRA...?
NO, IT'S STILL POSSIBLE HE PASSED THE POWERS OF KIRA TO SOMEONE ELSE TO MAKE HIMSELF LOOK INNOCENT.
ONCE IS ONCE. I'LL HAVE YOU KNOW THAT I'M QUITE STRONG.
I'LL CALL THE ROOM AND MAKE THEM STOP...
...
MATSUDA... LET THEM BE...

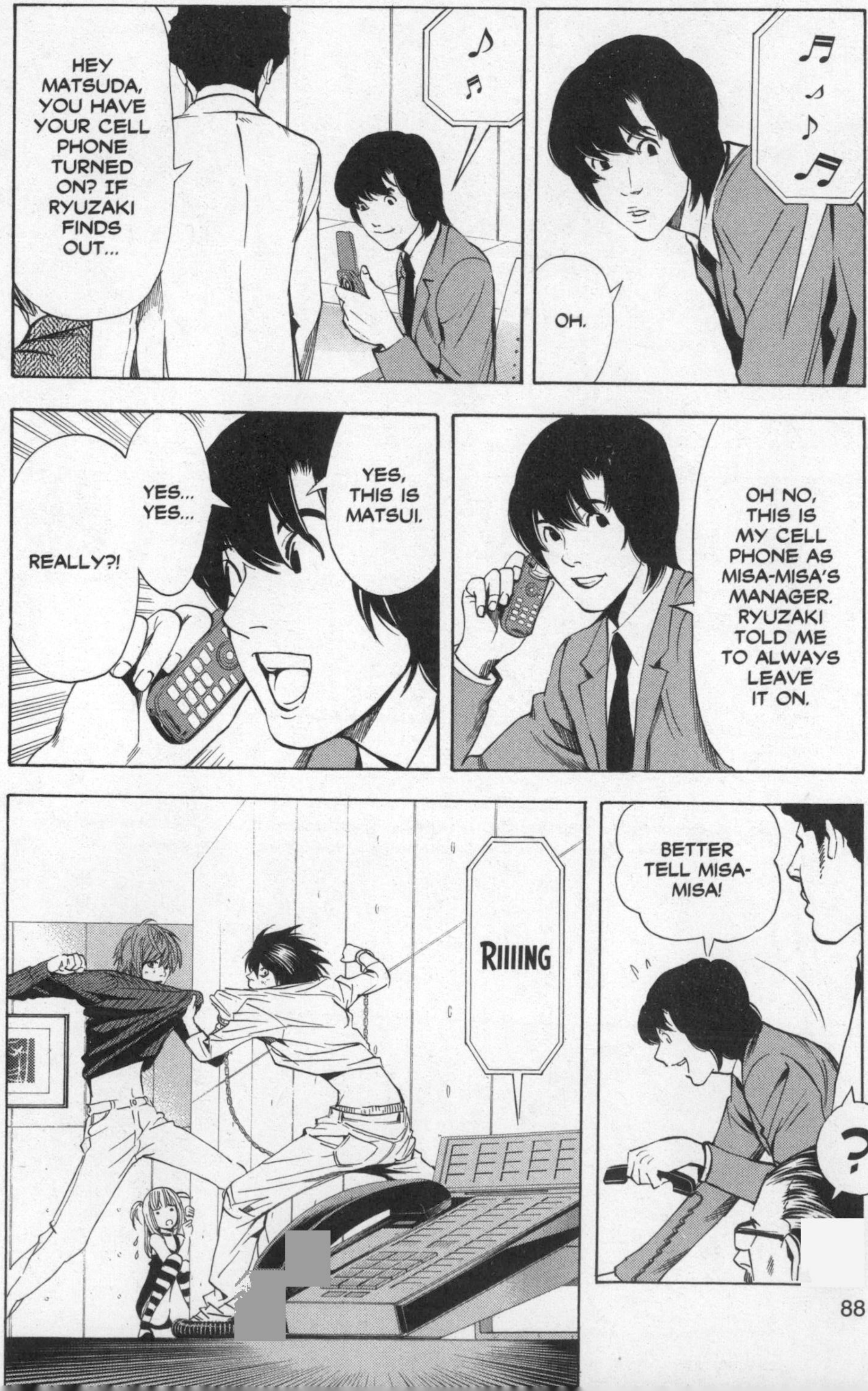
OH.
HEY MATSUDA, YOU HAVE YOUR CELL PHONE TURNED ON? IF RYUZAKI FINDS OUT...
OH NO, THIS IS MY CELL PHONE AS MISA-MISA'S MANAGER. RYUZAKI TOLD ME TO ALWAYS LEAVE IT ON.
YES, THIS IS MATSUI.
YES... YES...
REALLY?!
BETTER TELL MISA-MISA!
?
RIIIING

READ THIS WAY

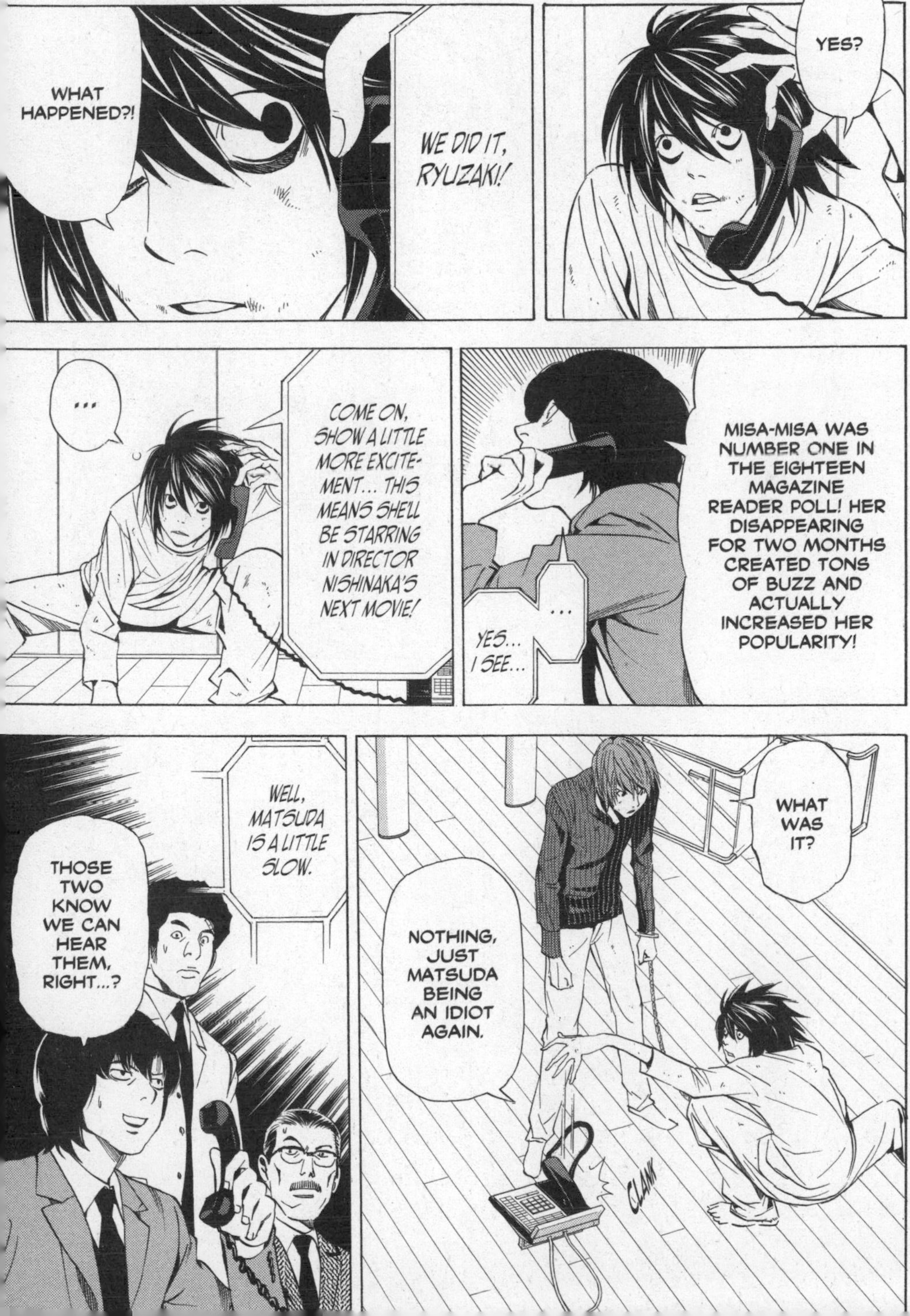
YES?
WE DID IT, RYUZAKI!
WHAT HAPPENED?!
MISA-MISA WAS NUMBER ONE IN THE EIGHTEEN MAGAZINE READER POLL! HER DISAPPEARING FOR TWO MONTHS CREATED TONS OF BUZZ AND ACTUALLY INCREASED HER POPULARITY!
...
YES... I SEE...
COME ON, SHOW A LITTLE MORE EXCITEMENT... THIS MEANS SHE'LL BE STARRING IN DIRECTOR NISHINAKA'S NEXT MOVIE!
...
WHAT WAS IT?
NOTHING, JUST MATSUDA BEING AN IDIOT AGAIN.
CLANK
WELL, MATSUDA IS A LITTLE SLOW.
THOSE TWO KNOW WE CAN HEAR THEM, RIGHT...?

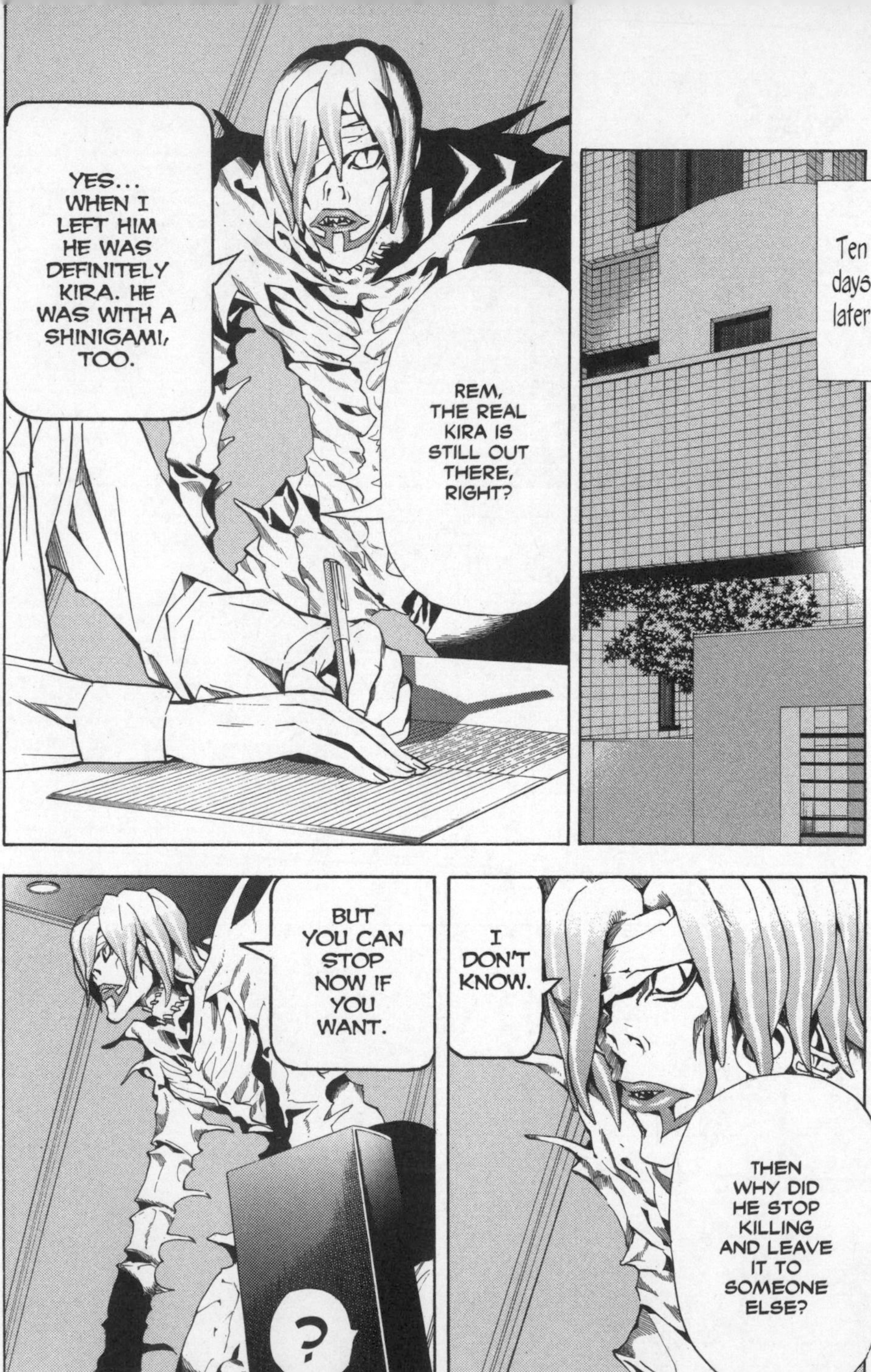
Ten days later
REM, THE REAL KIRA IS STILL OUT THERE, RIGHT?
YES... WHEN I LEFT HIM HE WAS DEFINITELY KIRA. HE WAS WITH A SHINIGAMI, TOO.
I DON'T KNOW.
THEN WHY DID HE STOP KILLING AND LEAVE IT TO SOMEONE ELSE?
BUT YOU CAN STOP NOW IF YOU WANT.
?

READ THIS WAY

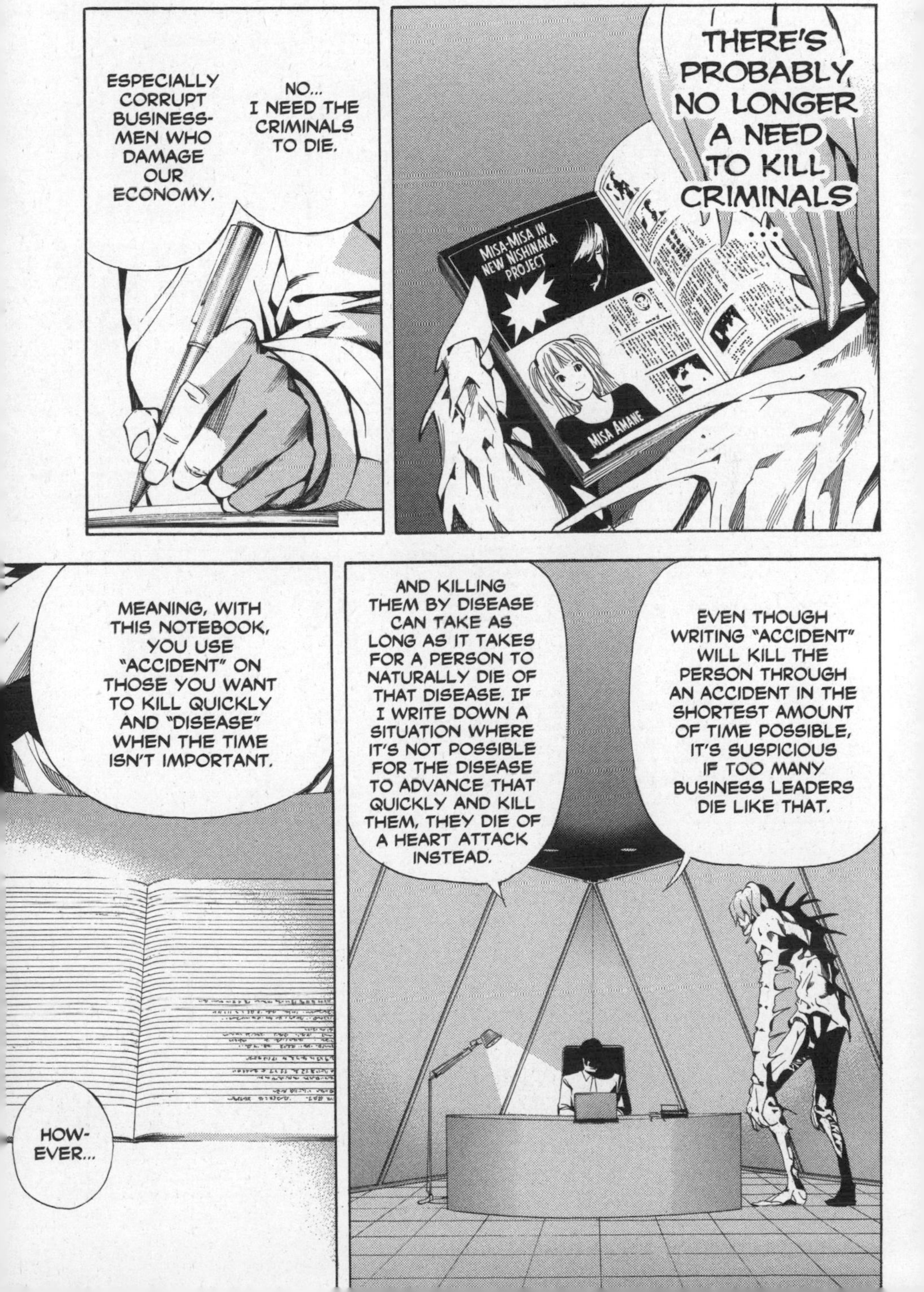
THERE'S PROBABLY NO LONGER A NEED TO KILL CRIMINALS...
MISA-MISA IN NEW NISHINAKA PROJECT
MISA AMANE
NO... I NEED THE CRIMINALS TO DIE.
ESPECIALLY CORRUPT BUSINESS-MEN WHO DAMAGE OUR ECONOMY.
EVEN THOUGH WRITING "ACCIDENT" WILL KILL THE PERSON THROUGH AN ACCIDENT IN THE SHORTEST AMOUNT OF TIME POSSIBLE, IT'S SUSPICIOUS IF TOO MANY BUSINESS LEADERS DIE LIKE THAT.
AND KILLING THEM BY DISEASE CAN TAKE AS LONG AS IT TAKES FOR A PERSON TO NATURALLY DIE OF THAT DISEASE. IF I WRITE DOWN A SITUATION WHERE IT'S NOT POSSIBLE FOR THE DISEASE TO ADVANCE THAT QUICKLY AND KILL THEM, THEY DIE OF A HEART ATTACK INSTEAD.
MEANING, WITH THIS NOTEBOOK, YOU USE "ACCIDENT" ON THOSE YOU WANT TO KILL QUICKLY AND "DISEASE" WHEN THE TIME ISN'T IMPORTANT.
HOW-EVER...

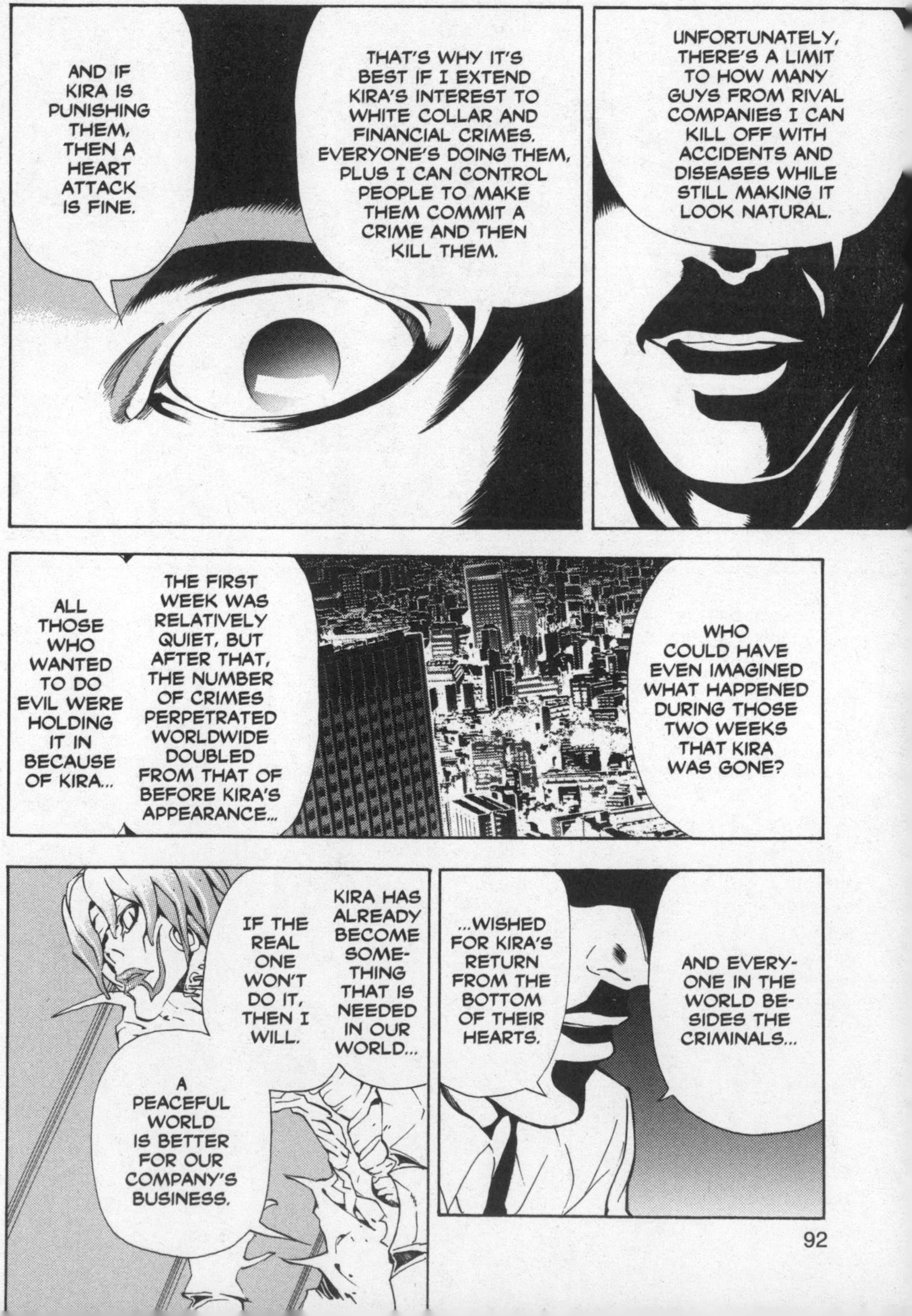
UNFORTUNATELY, THERE'S A LIMIT TO HOW MANY GUYS FROM RIVAL COMPANIES I CAN KILL OFF WITH ACCIDENTS AND DISEASES WHILE STILL MAKING IT LOOK NATURAL.
THAT'S WHY IT'S BEST IF I EXTEND KIRA'S INTEREST TO WHITE COLLAR AND FINANCIAL CRIMES. EVERYONE'S DOING THEM, PLUS I CAN CONTROL PEOPLE TO MAKE THEM COMMIT A CRIME AND THEN KILL THEM.
AND IF KIRA IS PUNISHING THEM, THEN A HEART ATTACK IS FINE.
WHO COULD HAVE EVEN IMAGINED WHAT HAPPENED DURING THOSE TWO WEEKS THAT KIRA WAS GONE?
THE FIRST WEEK WAS RELATIVELY QUIET, BUT AFTER THAT, THE NUMBER OF CRIMES PERPETRATED WORLDWIDE DOUBLED FROM THAT OF BEFORE KIRA'S APPEARANCE...
ALL THOSE WHO WANTED TO DO EVIL WERE HOLDING IT IN BECAUSE OF KIRA...
AND EVERY-ONE IN THE WORLD BE-SIDES THE CRIMINALS...
...WISHED FOR KIRA'S RETURN FROM THE BOTTOM OF THEIR HEARTS.
KIRA HAS ALREADY BECOME SOME-THING THAT IS NEEDED IN OUR WORLD...
IF THE REAL ONE WON'T DO IT, THEN I WILL.
A PEACEFUL WORLD IS BETTER FOR OUR COMPANY'S BUSINESS.

READ THIS WAY

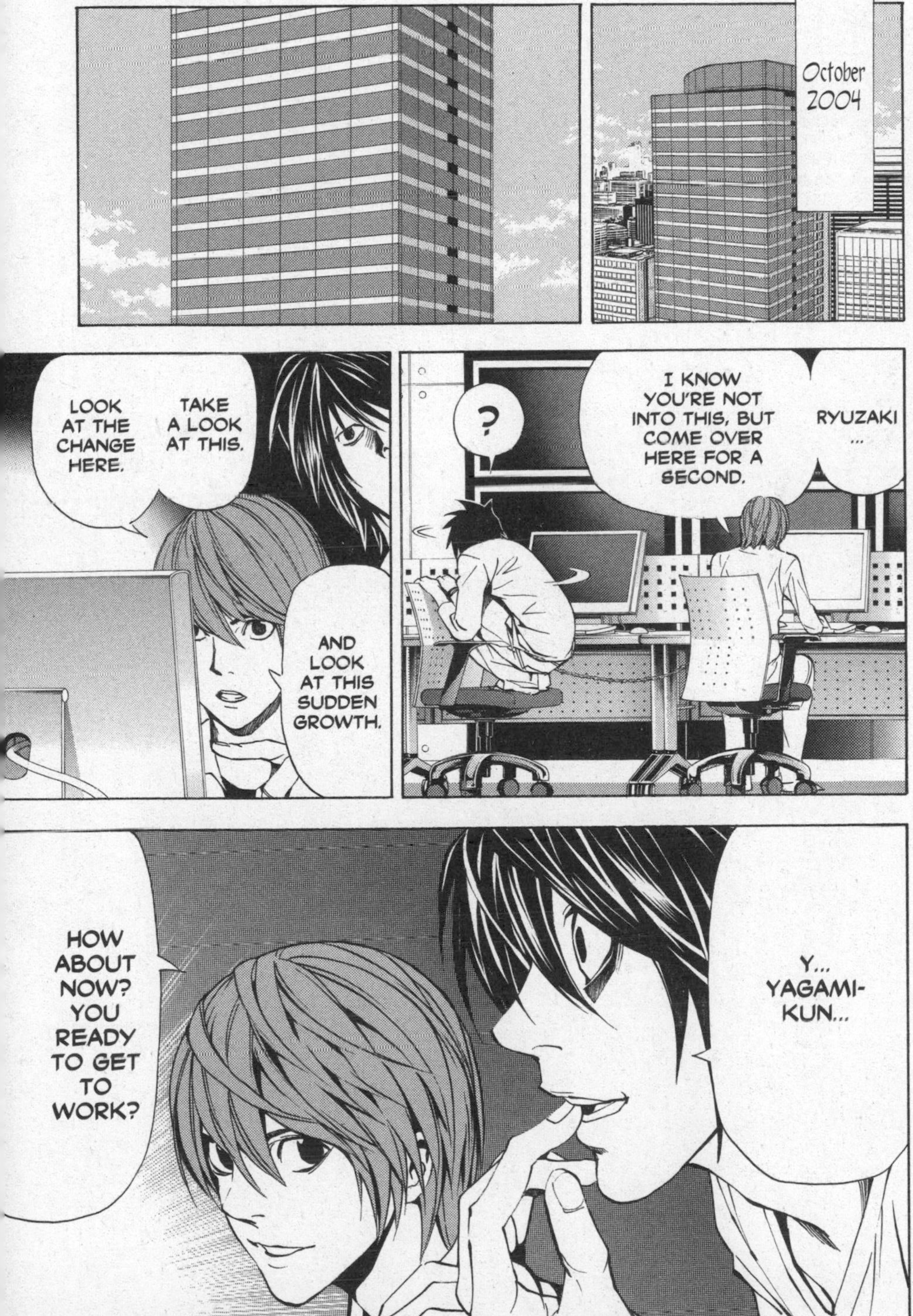
October 2004
RYUZAKI ...
I KNOW YOU'RE NOT INTO THIS, BUT COME OVER HERE FOR A SECOND.
?
TAKE A LOOK AT THIS.
LOOK AT THE CHANGE HERE.
AND LOOK AT THIS SUDDEN GROWTH.
Y... YAGAMI-KUN...
HOW ABOUT NOW? YOU READY TO GET TO WORK?

DEATH NOTE
How to use it
XXVI

● If you just write, "die of accident" for the cause of death, the victim will die from a natural accident after 6 minutes and 40 seconds from the time of writing it.

事故死とだけ書き死の状況を書かない場合は、
そこから6分40秒以後、最短で不自然でない事故に遭い、死亡する。

● Even though only one name is written in the DEATH NOTE, if it influences and causes other humans that are not written in it to die, the victim's cause of death will be a heart attack.

事故死の死の状況は、たとえその時死亡する人間が名前を書かれた者
だけであっても、人間界の環境に多大な影響を与え
その事で後に死者が出るような物は「人を巻き込む」事になる為、
心臓麻痺となる。

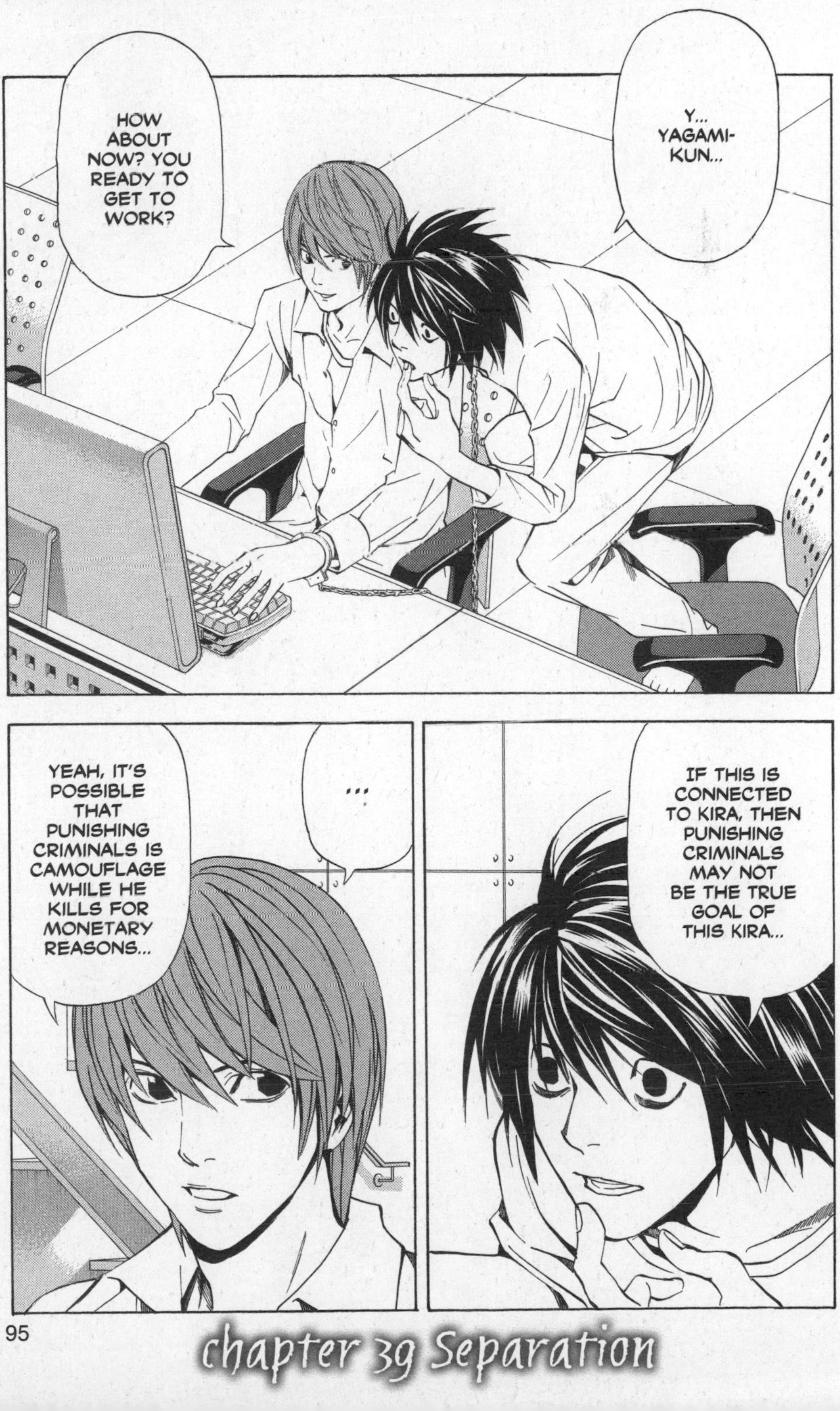
Y... YAGAMI-KUN...
HOW ABOUT NOW? YOU READY TO GET TO WORK?
IF THIS IS CONNECTED TO KIRA, THEN PUNISHING CRIMINALS MAY NOT BE THE TRUE GOAL OF THIS KIRA...
...
YEAH, IT'S POSSIBLE THAT PUNISHING CRIMINALS IS CAMOUFLAGE WHILE HE KILLS FOR MONETARY REASONS...

chapter 39 Separation

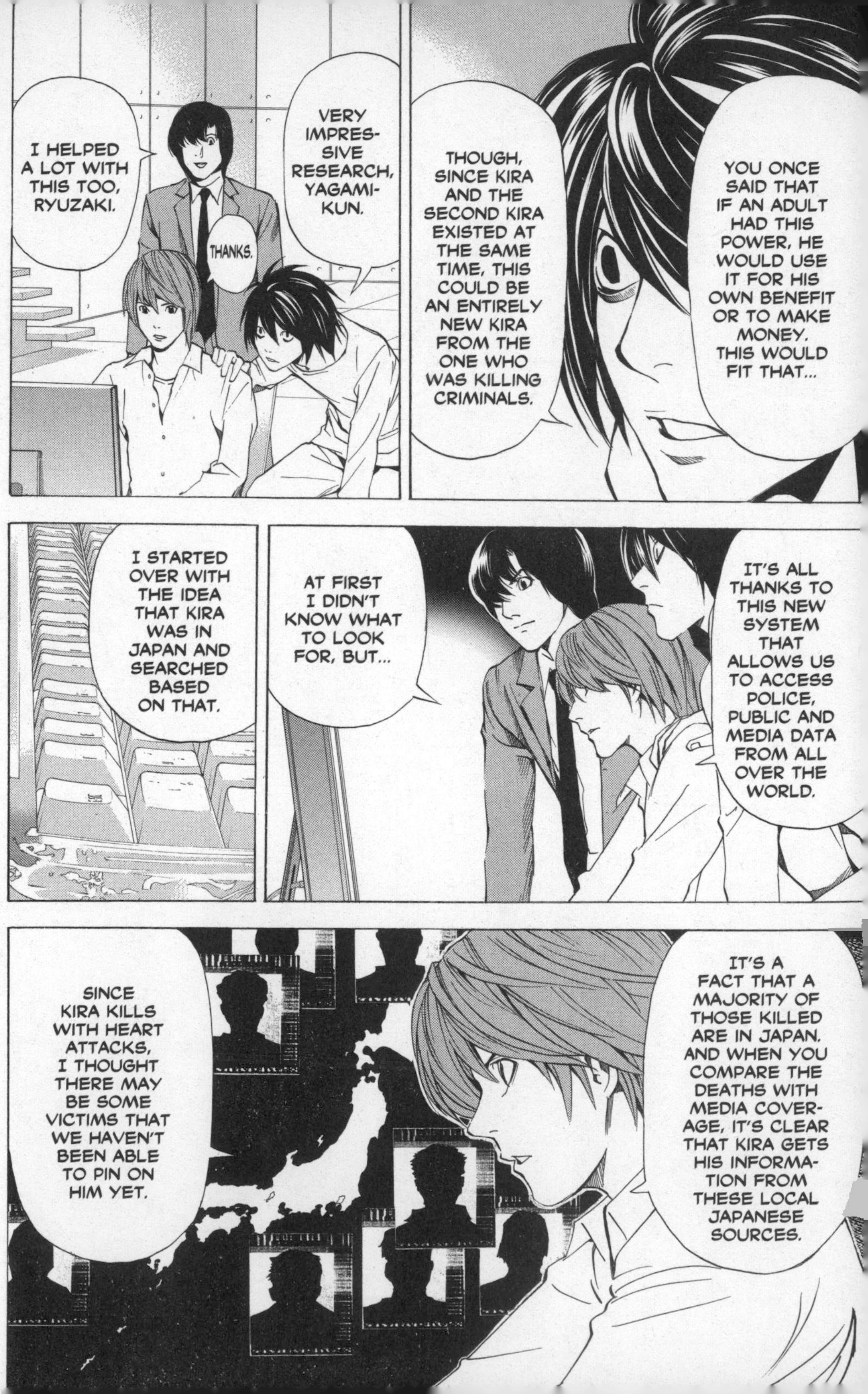
YOU ONCE SAID THAT IF AN ADULT HAD THIS POWER, HE WOULD USE IT FOR HIS OWN BENEFIT OR TO MAKE MONEY. THIS WOULD FIT THAT...
THOUGH, SINCE KIRA AND THE SECOND KIRA EXISTED AT THE SAME TIME, THIS COULD BE AN ENTIRELY NEW KIRA FROM THE ONE WHO WAS KILLING CRIMINALS.
VERY IMPRES-SIVE RESEARCH, YAGAMI-KUN.
THANKS.
I HELPED A LOT WITH THIS TOO, RYUZAKI.
IT'S ALL THANKS TO THIS NEW SYSTEM THAT ALLOWS US TO ACCESS POLICE, PUBLIC AND MEDIA DATA FROM ALL OVER THE WORLD.
AT FIRST I DIDN'T KNOW WHAT TO LOOK FOR, BUT...
I STARTED OVER WITH THE IDEA THAT KIRA WAS IN JAPAN AND SEARCHED BASED ON THAT.
IT'S A FACT THAT A MAJORITY OF THOSE KILLED ARE IN JAPAN. AND WHEN YOU COMPARE THE DEATHS WITH MEDIA COVER-AGE, IT'S CLEAR THAT KIRA GETS HIS INFORMA-TION FROM THESE LOCAL JAPANESE SOURCES.
SINCE KIRA KILLS WITH HEART ATTACKS, I THOUGHT THERE MAY BE SOME VICTIMS THAT WE HAVEN'T BEEN ABLE TO PIN ON HIM YET.

...I QUICKLY NOTICED THREE SUSPICIOUS CASES. TWO COULD BE COINCIDENCE, BUT NOT THREE.

I PLANNED TO CAREFULLY EXAMINE EVERY HEART ATTACK VICTIM OVER THE LAST FIVE MONTHS BUT...

I HELPED A LOT ON THIS, RYUZAKI.

THAT WOULD USUALLY BE AN INCREDIBLE AMOUNT OF WORK, BUT THIS SYSTEM MADE IT RELATIVELY FAST.

SO I SEARCHED FOR ALL THE PEOPLE WHO DIED OF HEART ATTACKS UP TO NOW, INCLUDING NON-CRIMINALS.

ALL THREE WERE IN IMPORTANT POSITIONS IN THE JAPANESE BUSINESS WORLD AND ALL DIED OF HEART ATTACKS.

Roppei Tamiya	Heart Attack	2004.6.27
Kouji Aoi	Heart Attack	2004.7.2
Takeyoshi Moriya	Heart Attack	2004.7.30
Koutaro Ashimoto	Car Accident	2004.6.19
Kenji Tanimi	Car Accident	2004.6.26
Tatsuya Kawajima	Car Accident	2004.7.4

SEKIMARU CORP'S VP OF DEVELOPMENT, ROPPEI TAMIYA. AOI INDUSTRIES' DIRECTOR OF INTEGRATED SYSTEMS, KOUJI AOI. FORMER YOTSUBA VICE-PRESIDENT, TAKEYOSHI MORIYA.

YEAH, AND LOOK...

SO THEN YOU DID FURTHER RESEARCH INTO OTHER DEATHS INVOLVING PEOPLE IN THE BUSINESS WORLD...?

YOTSUBA'S STOCK HAS BEEN RISING STEADILY WHILE SEKIMARU AND AOI'S HAVE PLUMMETED.

SO THEN I RESEARCHED SEKIMARU, AOI, AND YOTSUBA.

click

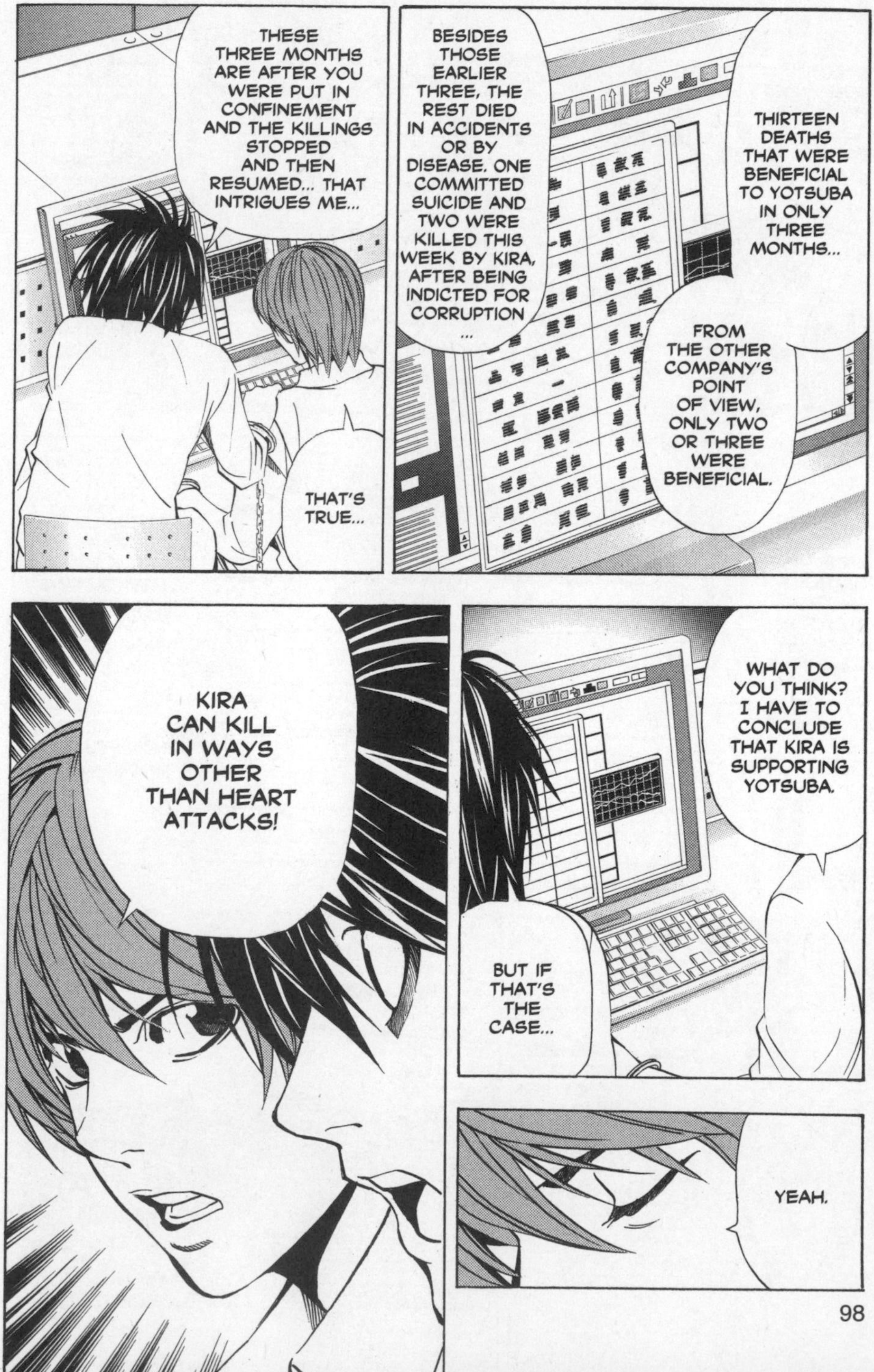
THIRTEEN DEATHS THAT WERE BENEFICIAL TO YOTSUBA IN ONLY THREE MONTHS...
FROM THE OTHER COMPANY'S POINT OF VIEW, ONLY TWO OR THREE WERE BENEFICIAL.
BESIDES THOSE EARLIER THREE, THE REST DIED IN ACCIDENTS OR BY DISEASE. ONE COMMITTED SUICIDE AND TWO WERE KILLED THIS WEEK BY KIRA, AFTER BEING INDICTED FOR CORRUPTION...
THESE THREE MONTHS ARE AFTER YOU WERE PUT IN CONFINEMENT AND THE KILLINGS STOPPED AND THEN RESUMED... THAT INTRIGUES ME...
THAT'S TRUE...
WHAT DO YOU THINK? I HAVE TO CONCLUDE THAT KIRA IS SUPPORTING YOTSUBA.
BUT IF THAT'S THE CASE...
YEAH.
KIRA CAN KILL IN WAYS OTHER THAN HEART ATTACKS!

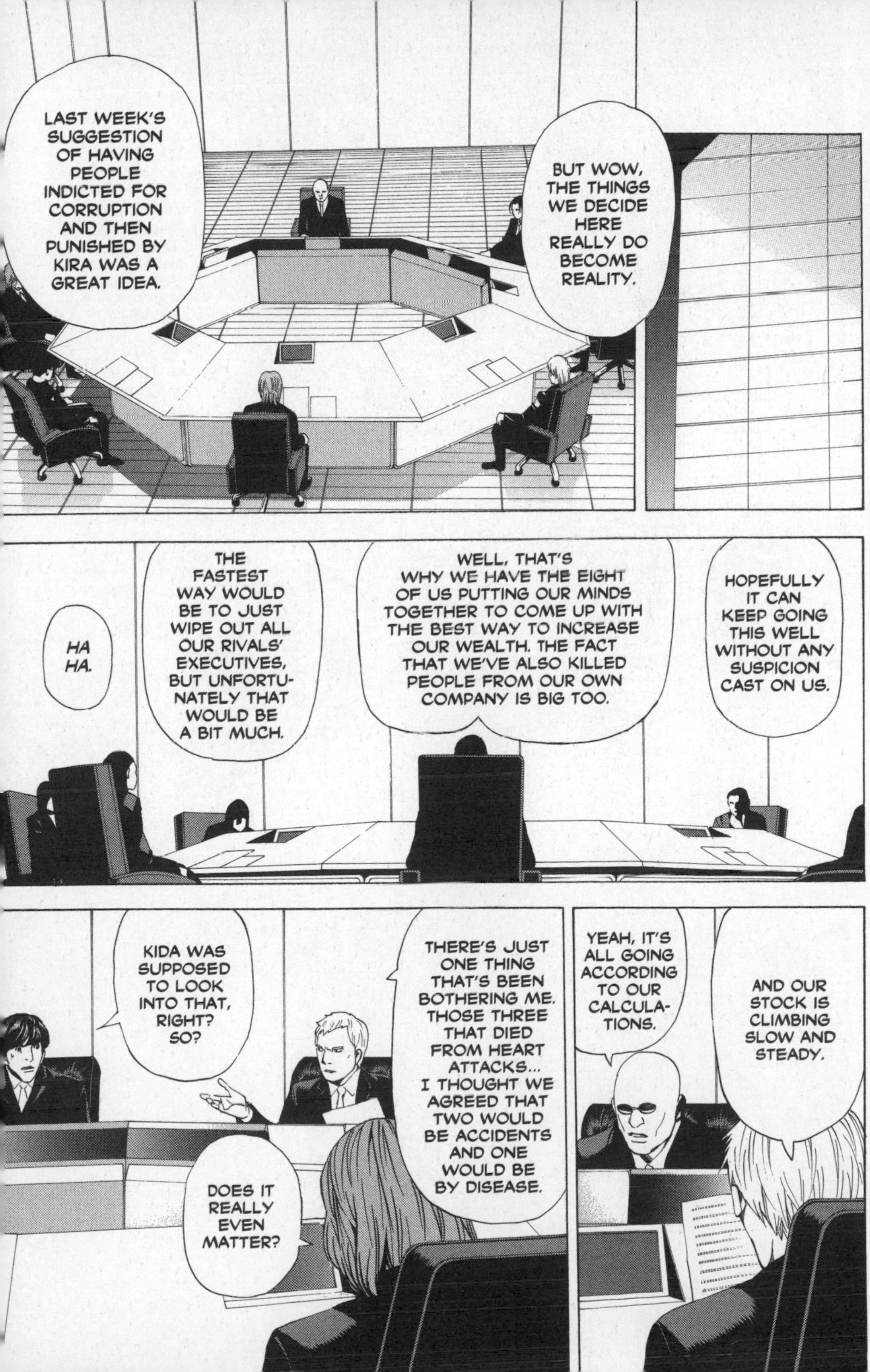
BUT WOW, THE THINGS WE DECIDE HERE REALLY DO BECOME REALITY.
LAST WEEK'S SUGGESTION OF HAVING PEOPLE INDICTED FOR CORRUPTION AND THEN PUNISHED BY KIRA WAS A GREAT IDEA.
HOPEFULLY IT CAN KEEP GOING THIS WELL WITHOUT ANY SUSPICION CAST ON US.
WELL, THAT'S WHY WE HAVE THE EIGHT OF US PUTTING OUR MINDS TOGETHER TO COME UP WITH THE BEST WAY TO INCREASE OUR WEALTH. THE FACT THAT WE'VE ALSO KILLED PEOPLE FROM OUR OWN COMPANY IS BIG TOO.
THE FASTEST WAY WOULD BE TO JUST WIPE OUT ALL OUR RIVALS' EXECUTIVES, BUT UNFORTUNATELY THAT WOULD BE A BIT MUCH.
HA HA.
AND OUR STOCK IS CLIMBING SLOW AND STEADY.
YEAH, IT'S ALL GOING ACCORDING TO OUR CALCULATIONS.
THERE'S JUST ONE THING THAT'S BEEN BOTHERING ME. THOSE THREE THAT DIED FROM HEART ATTACKS... I THOUGHT WE AGREED THAT TWO WOULD BE ACCIDENTS AND ONE WOULD BE BY DISEASE.
KIDA WAS SUPPOSED TO LOOK INTO THAT, RIGHT? SO?
DOES IT REALLY EVEN MATTER?

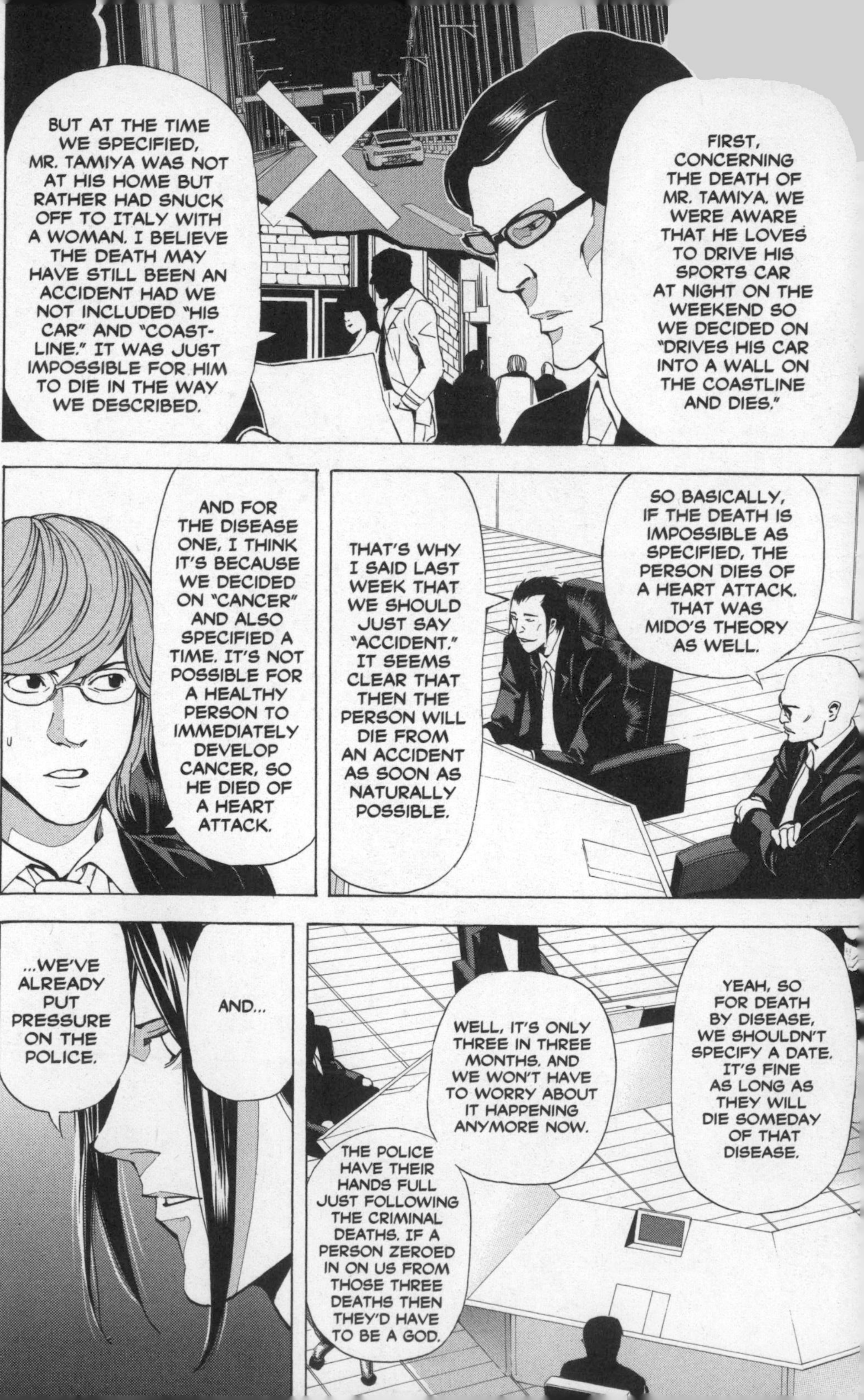
FIRST, CONCERNING THE DEATH OF MR. TAMIYA. WE WERE AWARE THAT HE LOVES TO DRIVE HIS SPORTS CAR AT NIGHT ON THE WEEKEND SO WE DECIDED ON "DRIVES HIS CAR INTO A WALL ON THE COASTLINE AND DIES."
BUT AT THE TIME WE SPECIFIED, MR. TAMIYA WAS NOT AT HIS HOME BUT RATHER HAD SNUCK OFF TO ITALY WITH A WOMAN. I BELIEVE THE DEATH MAY HAVE STILL BEEN AN ACCIDENT HAD WE NOT INCLUDED "HIS CAR" AND "COAST-LINE." IT WAS JUST IMPOSSIBLE FOR HIM TO DIE IN THE WAY WE DESCRIBED.
SO BASICALLY, IF THE DEATH IS IMPOSSIBLE AS SPECIFIED, THE PERSON DIES OF A HEART ATTACK. THAT WAS MIDO'S THEORY AS WELL.
THAT'S WHY I SAID LAST WEEK THAT WE SHOULD JUST SAY "ACCIDENT." IT SEEMS CLEAR THAT THEN THE PERSON WILL DIE FROM AN ACCIDENT AS SOON AS NATURALLY POSSIBLE.
AND FOR THE DISEASE ONE, I THINK IT'S BECAUSE WE DECIDED ON "CANCER" AND ALSO SPECIFIED A TIME. IT'S NOT POSSIBLE FOR A HEALTHY PERSON TO IMMEDIATELY DEVELOP CANCER, SO HE DIED OF A HEART ATTACK.
YEAH, SO FOR DEATH BY DISEASE, WE SHOULDN'T SPECIFY A DATE. IT'S FINE AS LONG AS THEY WILL DIE SOMEDAY OF THAT DISEASE.
WELL, IT'S ONLY THREE IN THREE MONTHS. AND WE WON'T HAVE TO WORRY ABOUT IT HAPPENING ANYMORE NOW.
THE POLICE HAVE THEIR HANDS FULL JUST FOLLOWING THE CRIMINAL DEATHS. IF A PERSON ZEROED IN ON US FROM THOSE THREE DEATHS THEN THEY'D HAVE TO BE A GOD.
AND...
...WE'VE ALREADY PUT PRESSURE ON THE POLICE.

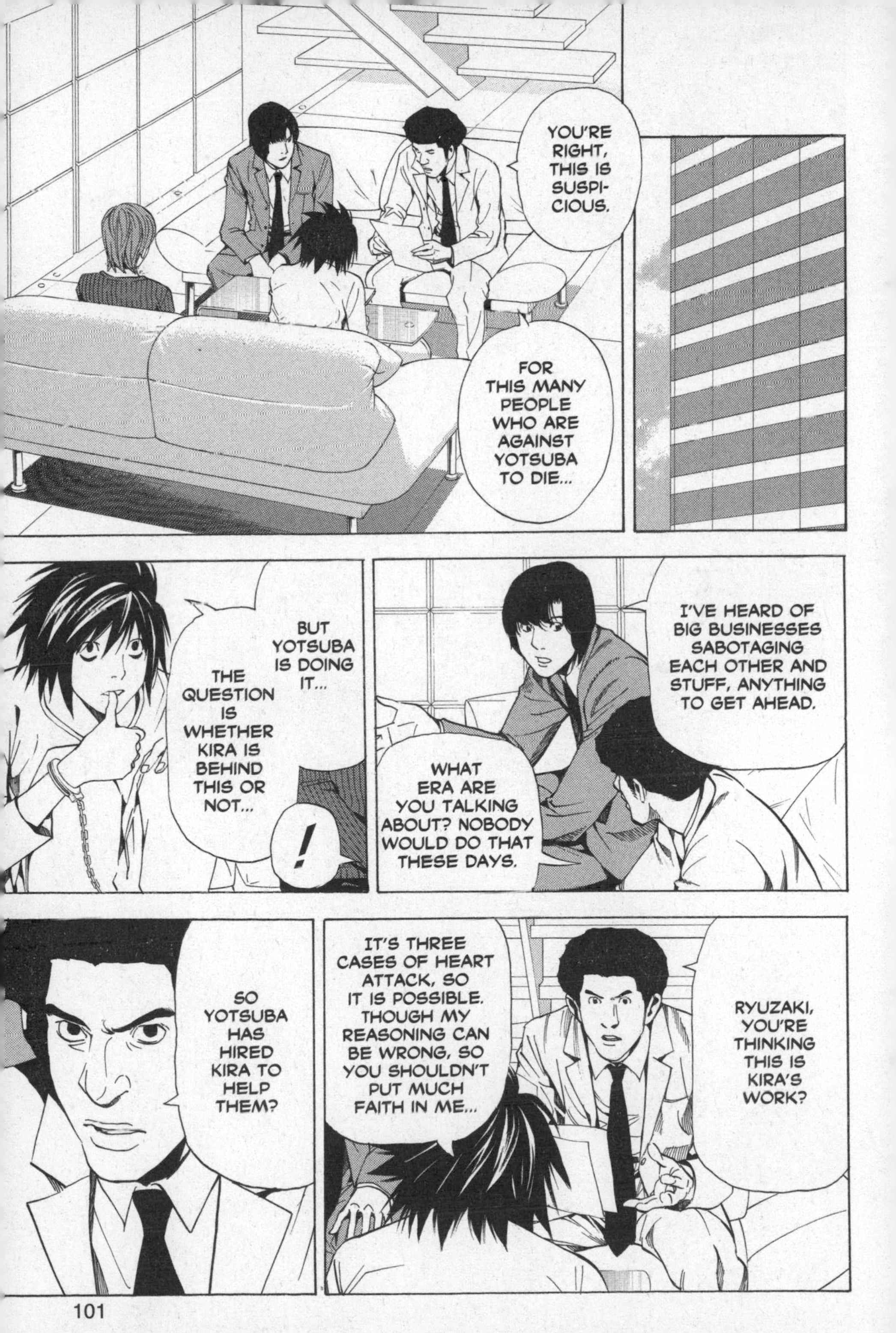
YOU'RE RIGHT, THIS IS SUSPICIOUS.
FOR THIS MANY PEOPLE WHO ARE AGAINST YOTSUBA TO DIE...
I'VE HEARD OF BIG BUSINESSES SABOTAGING EACH OTHER AND STUFF, ANYTHING TO GET AHEAD.
WHAT ERA ARE YOU TALKING ABOUT? NOBODY WOULD DO THAT THESE DAYS.
BUT YOTSUBA IS DOING IT...
THE QUESTION IS WHETHER KIRA IS BEHIND THIS OR NOT...
!
RYUZAKI, YOU'RE THINKING THIS IS KIRA'S WORK?
IT'S THREE CASES OF HEART ATTACK, SO IT IS POSSIBLE. THOUGH MY REASONING CAN BE WRONG, SO YOU SHOULDN'T PUT MUCH FAITH IN ME...
SO YOTSUBA HAS HIRED KIRA TO HELP THEM?

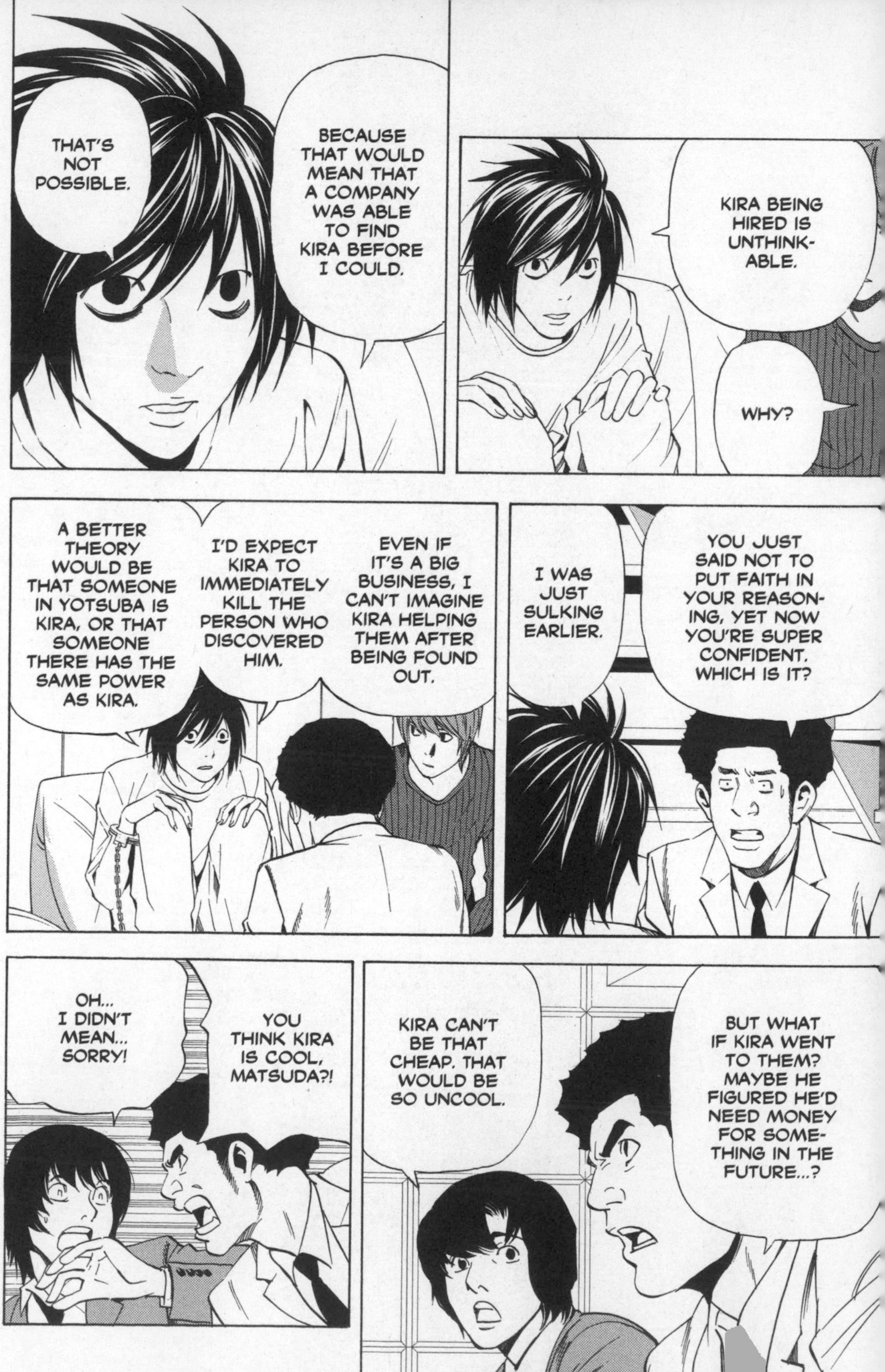
KIRA BEING HIRED IS UNTHINKABLE.
WHY?
THAT'S NOT POSSIBLE.
BECAUSE THAT WOULD MEAN THAT A COMPANY WAS ABLE TO FIND KIRA BEFORE I COULD.
YOU JUST SAID NOT TO PUT FAITH IN YOUR REASONING, YET NOW YOU'RE SUPER CONFIDENT. WHICH IS IT?
I WAS JUST SULKING EARLIER.
EVEN IF IT'S A BIG BUSINESS, I CAN'T IMAGINE KIRA HELPING THEM AFTER BEING FOUND OUT.
I'D EXPECT KIRA TO IMMEDIATELY KILL THE PERSON WHO DISCOVERED HIM.
A BETTER THEORY WOULD BE THAT SOMEONE IN YOTSUBA IS KIRA, OR THAT SOMEONE THERE HAS THE SAME POWER AS KIRA.
BUT WHAT IF KIRA WENT TO THEM? MAYBE HE FIGURED HE'D NEED MONEY FOR SOMETHING IN THE FUTURE...?
KIRA CAN'T BE THAT CHEAP. THAT WOULD BE SO UNCOOL.
YOU THINK KIRA IS COOL, MATSUDA?!
OH... I DIDN'T MEAN... SORRY!

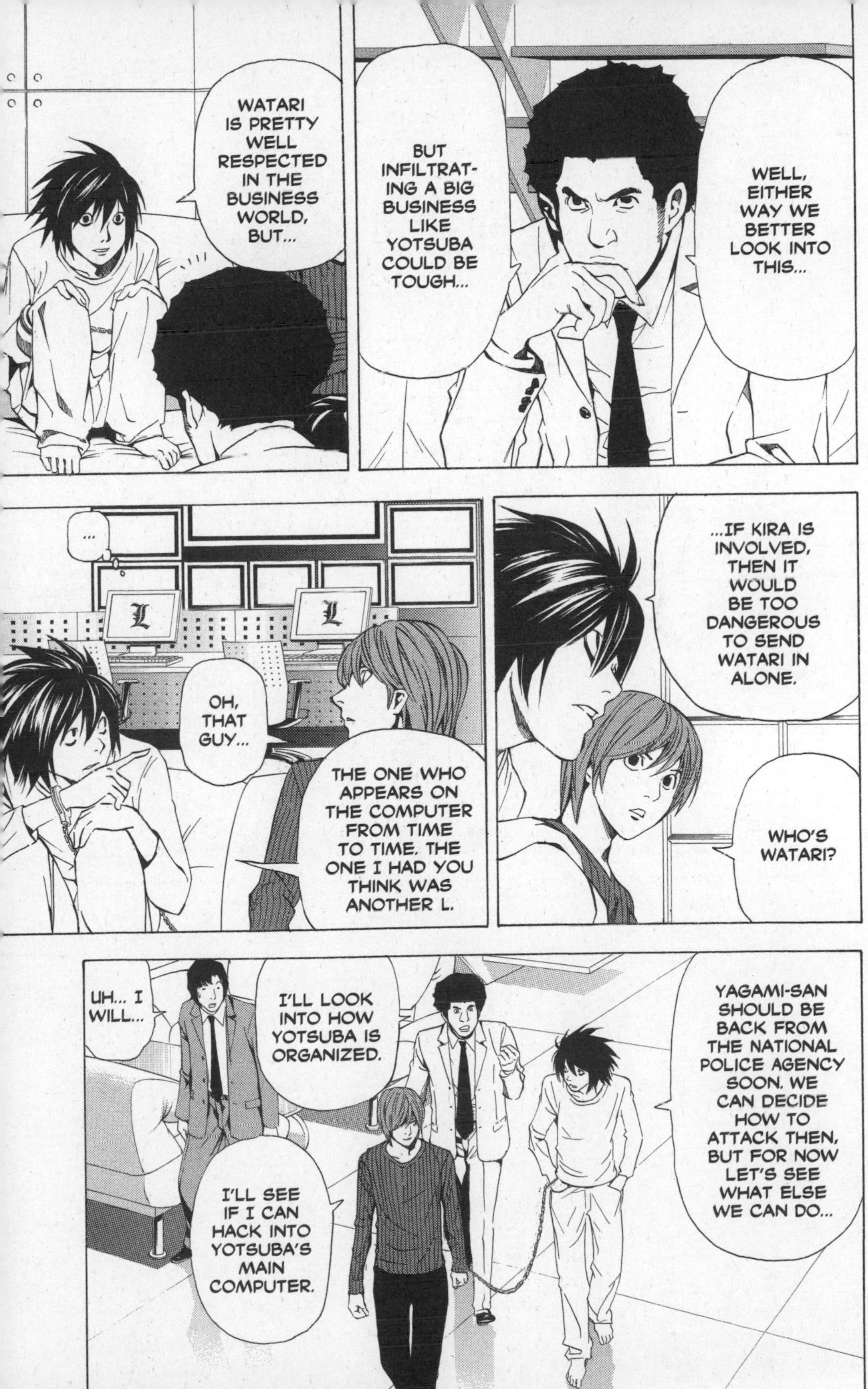
WELL, EITHER WAY WE BETTER LOOK INTO THIS...
BUT INFILTRAT-ING A BIG BUSINESS LIKE YOTSUBA COULD BE TOUGH...
WATARI IS PRETTY WELL RESPECTED IN THE BUSINESS WORLD, BUT...
...IF KIRA IS INVOLVED, THEN IT WOULD BE TOO DANGEROUS TO SEND WATARI IN ALONE.
WHO'S WATARI?
...
OH, THAT GUY...
THE ONE WHO APPEARS ON THE COMPUTER FROM TIME TO TIME. THE ONE I HAD YOU THINK WAS ANOTHER L.
YAGAMI-SAN SHOULD BE BACK FROM THE NATIONAL POLICE AGENCY SOON. WE CAN DECIDE HOW TO ATTACK THEN, BUT FOR NOW LET'S SEE WHAT ELSE WE CAN DO...
I'LL LOOK INTO HOW YOTSUBA IS ORGANIZED.
I'LL SEE IF I CAN HACK INTO YOTSUBA'S MAIN COMPUTER.
UH... I WILL...

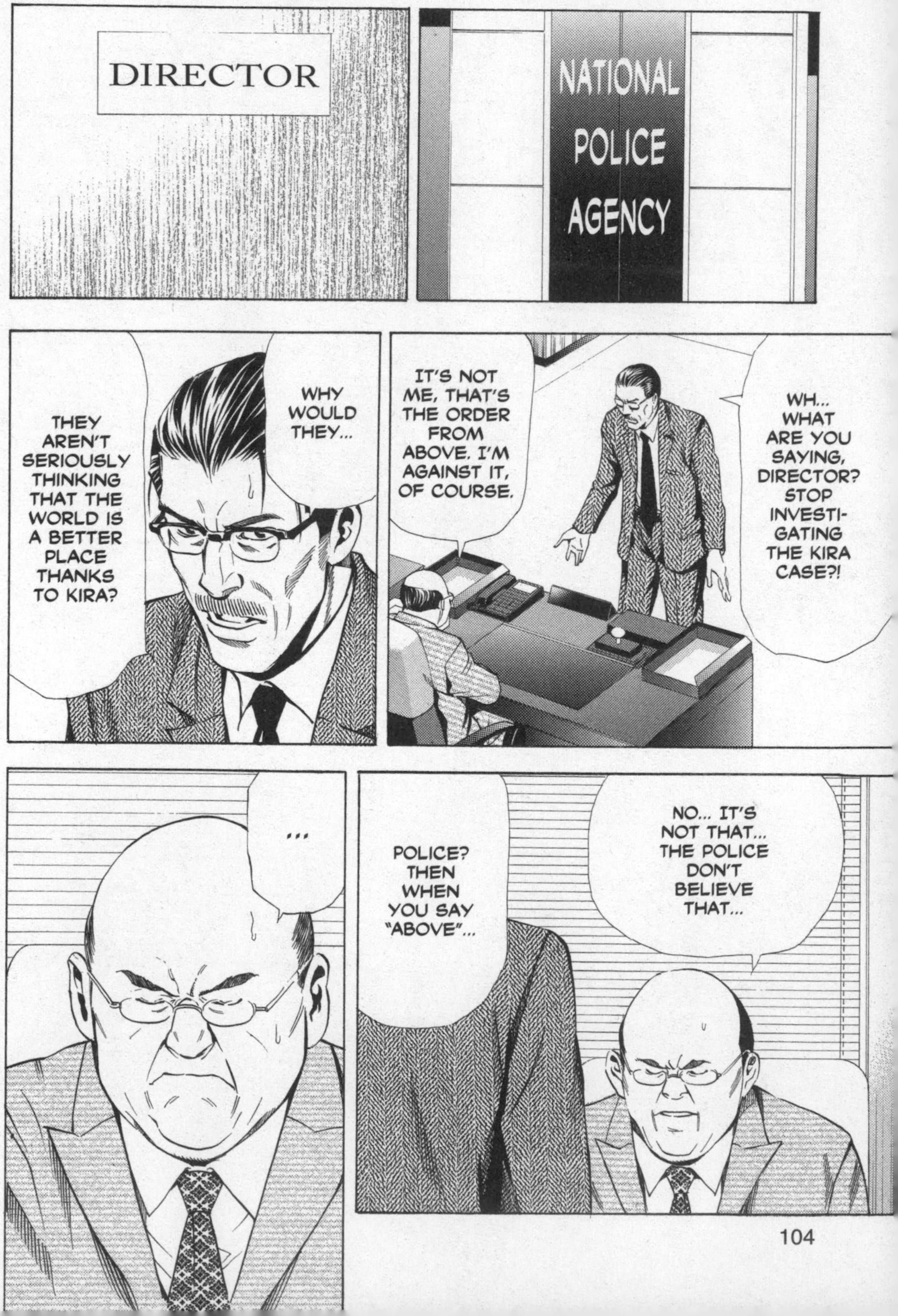
NATIONAL POLICE AGENCY
DIRECTOR
WH... WHAT ARE YOU SAYING, DIRECTOR? STOP INVESTIGATING THE KIRA CASE?!
IT'S NOT ME, THAT'S THE ORDER FROM ABOVE. I'M AGAINST IT, OF COURSE.
WHY WOULD THEY...
THEY AREN'T SERIOUSLY THINKING THAT THE WORLD IS A BETTER PLACE THANKS TO KIRA?
NO... IT'S NOT THAT... THE POLICE DON'T BELIEVE THAT...
POLICE? THEN WHEN YOU SAY "ABOVE"...
...

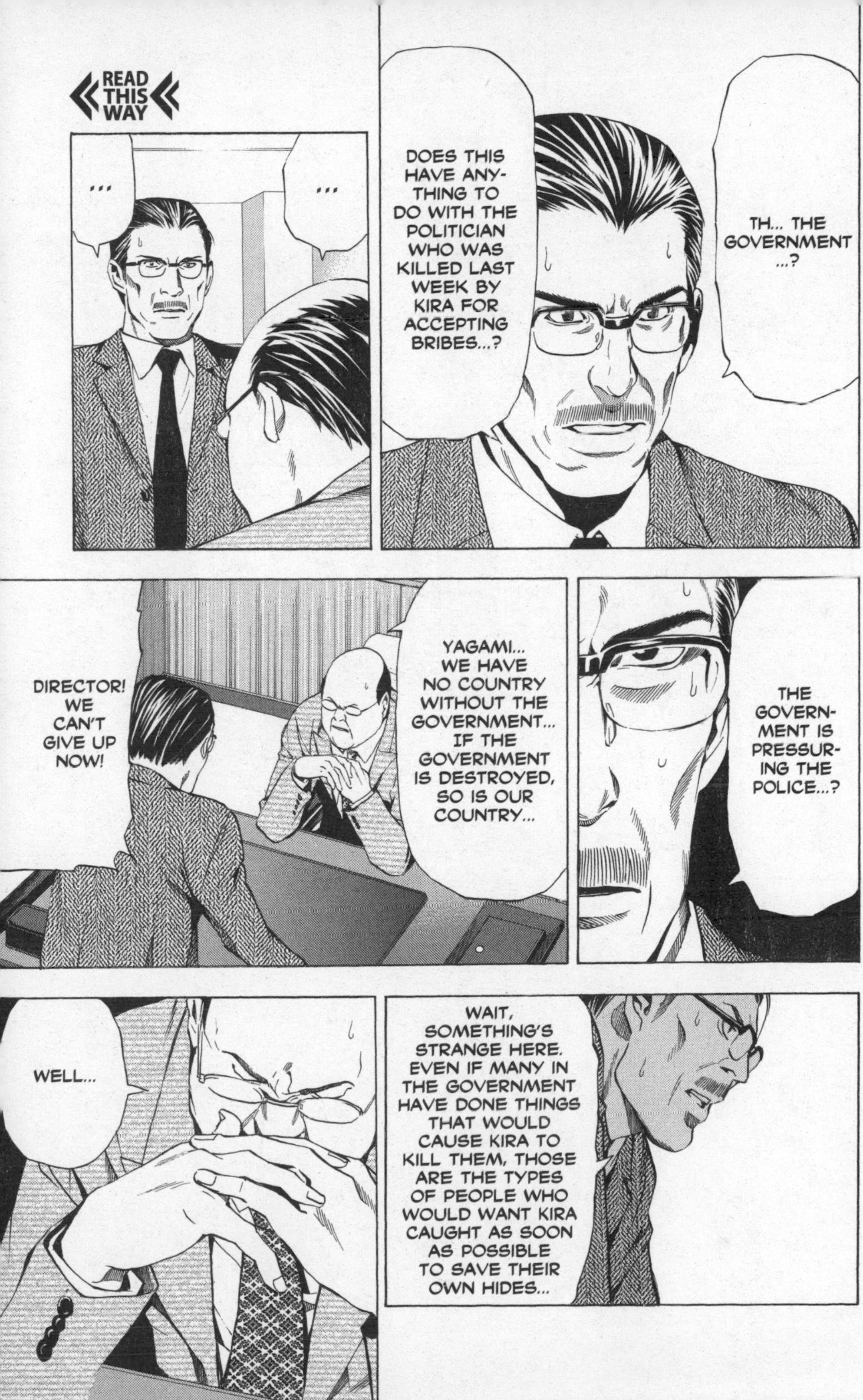
READ THIS WAY
TH... THE GOVERNMENT ...?
DOES THIS HAVE ANYTHING TO DO WITH THE POLITICIAN WHO WAS KILLED LAST WEEK BY KIRA FOR ACCEPTING BRIBES...?
...
...
THE GOVERNMENT IS PRESSURING THE POLICE...?
YAGAMI... WE HAVE NO COUNTRY WITHOUT THE GOVERNMENT... IF THE GOVERNMENT IS DESTROYED, SO IS OUR COUNTRY...
DIRECTOR! WE CAN'T GIVE UP NOW!
WAIT, SOMETHING'S STRANGE HERE. EVEN IF MANY IN THE GOVERNMENT HAVE DONE THINGS THAT WOULD CAUSE KIRA TO KILL THEM, THOSE ARE THE TYPES OF PEOPLE WHO WOULD WANT KIRA CAUGHT AS SOON AS POSSIBLE TO SAVE THEIR OWN HIDES...
WELL...

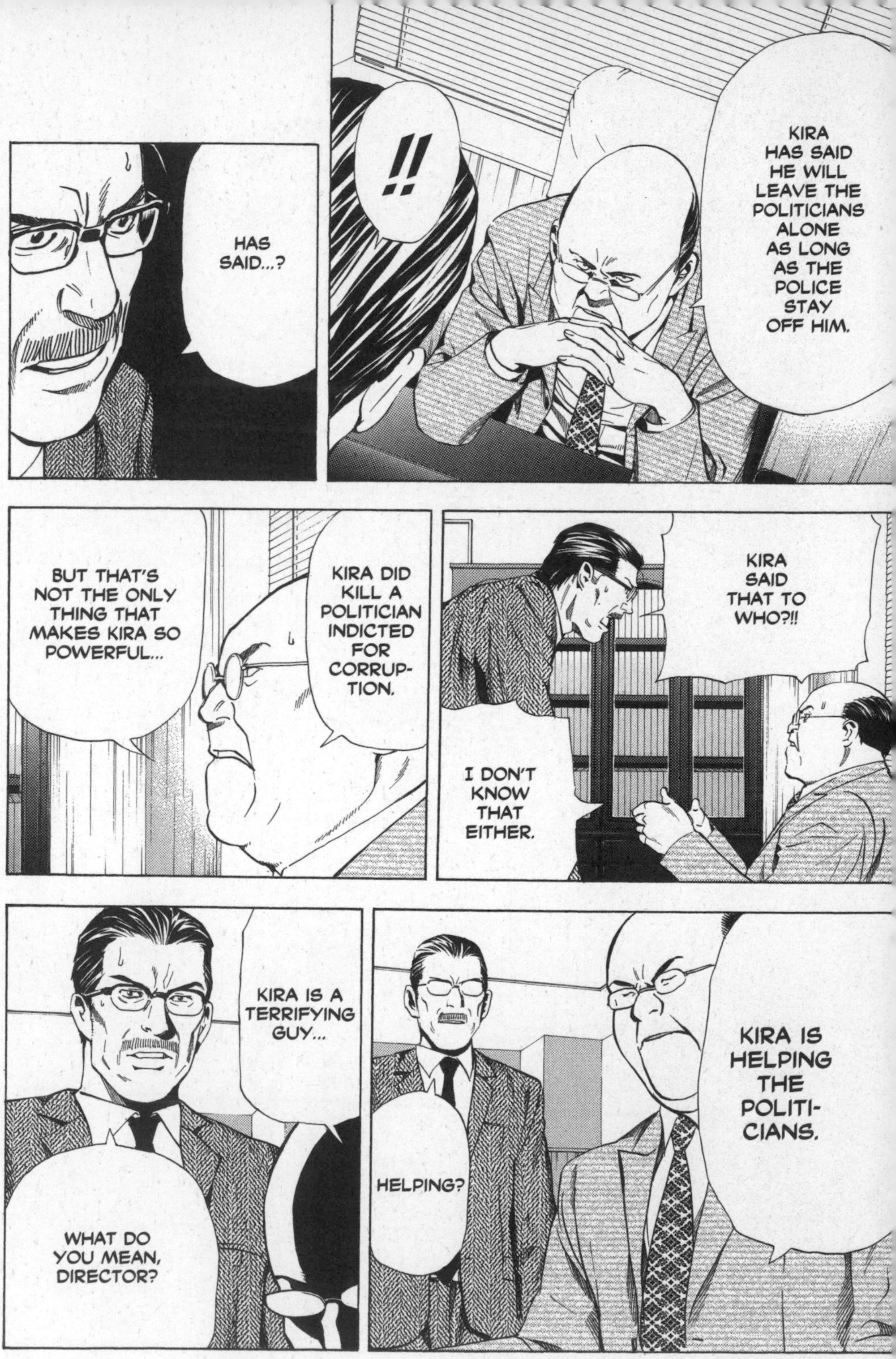
KIRA HAS SAID HE WILL LEAVE THE POLITICIANS ALONE AS LONG AS THE POLICE STAY OFF HIM.
!!
HAS SAID...?
KIRA SAID THAT TO WHO?!!
I DON'T KNOW THAT EITHER.
KIRA DID KILL A POLITICIAN INDICTED FOR CORRUPTION.
BUT THAT'S NOT THE ONLY THING THAT MAKES KIRA SO POWERFUL...
KIRA IS HELPING THE POLITICIANS.
HELPING?
KIRA IS A TERRIFYING GUY...
WHAT DO YOU MEAN, DIRECTOR?

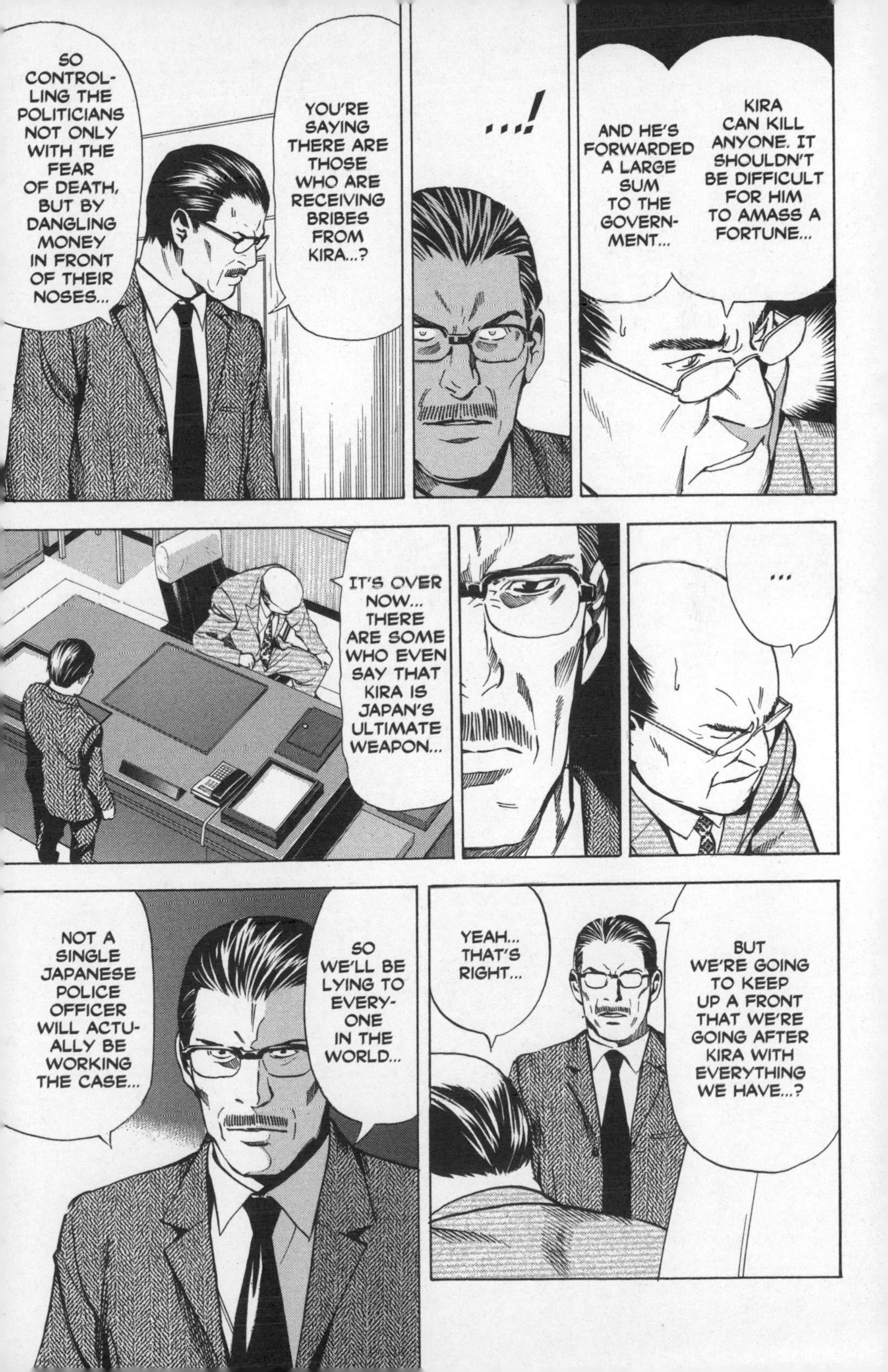
KIRA CAN KILL ANYONE. IT SHOULDN'T BE DIFFICULT FOR HIM TO AMASS A FORTUNE...
AND HE'S FORWARDED A LARGE SUM TO THE GOVERNMENT...
...!
YOU'RE SAYING THERE ARE THOSE WHO ARE RECEIVING BRIBES FROM KIRA...?
SO CONTROLLING THE POLITICIANS NOT ONLY WITH THE FEAR OF DEATH, BUT BY DANGLING MONEY IN FRONT OF THEIR NOSES...
...
IT'S OVER NOW... THERE ARE SOME WHO EVEN SAY THAT KIRA IS JAPAN'S ULTIMATE WEAPON...
BUT WE'RE GOING TO KEEP UP A FRONT THAT WE'RE GOING AFTER KIRA WITH EVERYTHING WE HAVE...?
YEAH... THAT'S RIGHT...
SO WE'LL BE LYING TO EVERYONE IN THE WORLD...
NOT A SINGLE JAPANESE POLICE OFFICER WILL ACTUALLY BE WORKING THE CASE...

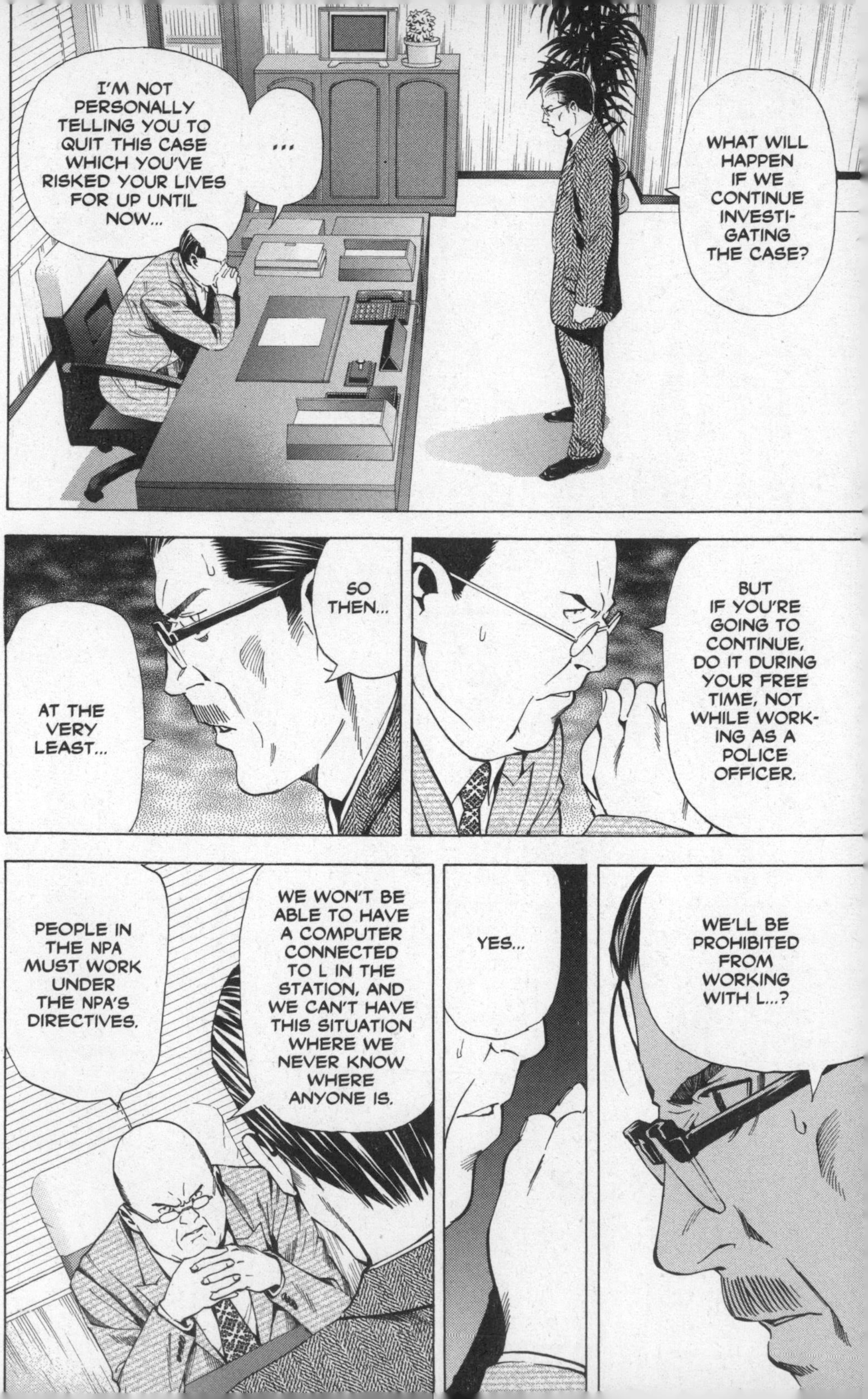
WHAT WILL HAPPEN IF WE CONTINUE INVESTI- GATING THE CASE?
...
I'M NOT PERSONALLY TELLING YOU TO QUIT THIS CASE WHICH YOU'VE RISKED YOUR LIVES FOR UP UNTIL NOW...
BUT IF YOU'RE GOING TO CONTINUE, DO IT DURING YOUR FREE TIME, NOT WHILE WORK- ING AS A POLICE OFFICER.
SO THEN...
AT THE VERY LEAST...
WE'LL BE PROHIBITED FROM WORKING WITH L...?
YES...
WE WON'T BE ABLE TO HAVE A COMPUTER CONNECTED TO L IN THE STATION, AND WE CAN'T HAVE THIS SITUATION WHERE WE NEVER KNOW WHERE ANYONE IS.
PEOPLE IN THE NPA MUST WORK UNDER THE NPA'S DIRECTIVES.

READ THIS WAY

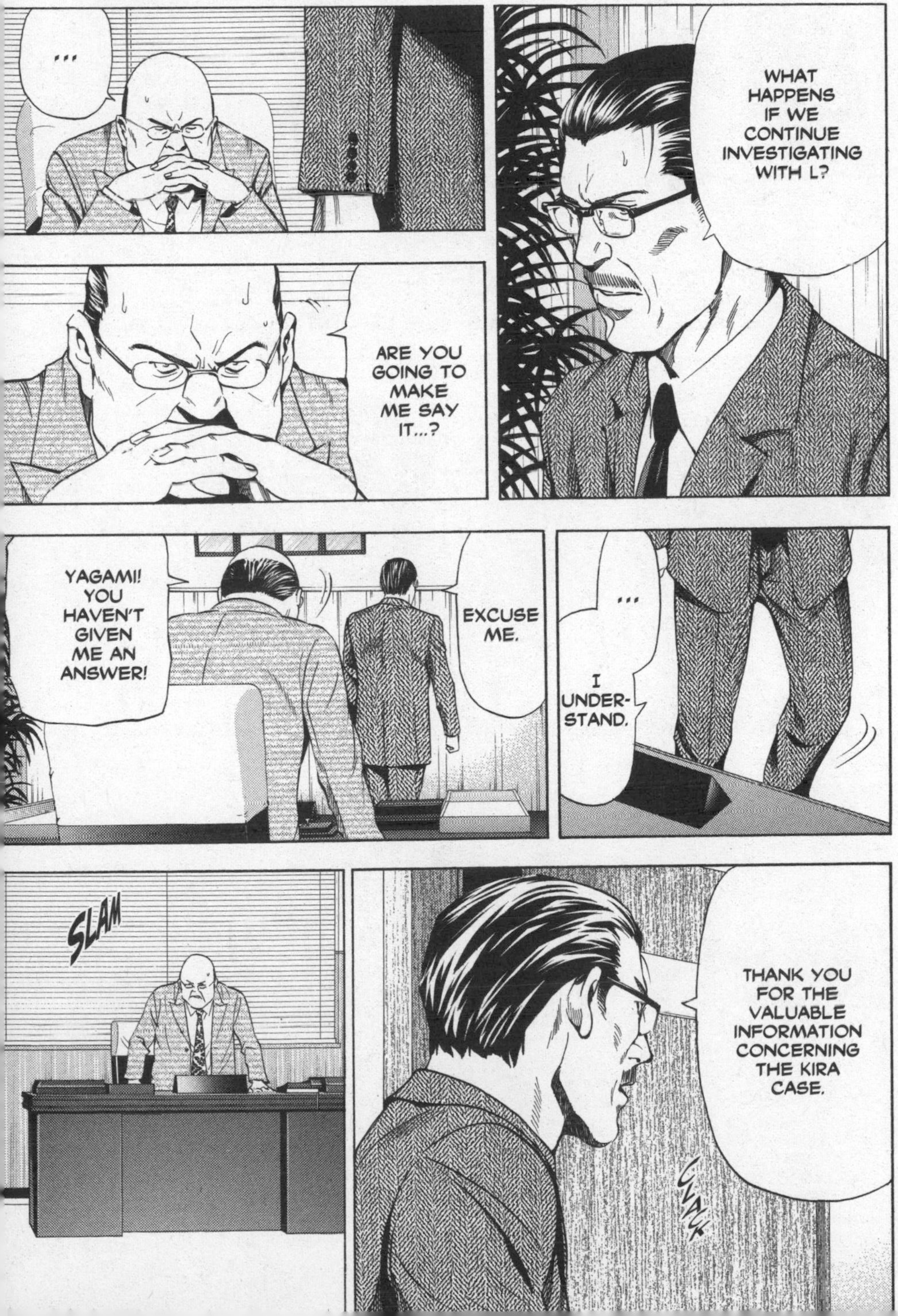
WHAT HAPPENS IF WE CONTINUE INVESTIGATING WITH L?
...
ARE YOU GOING TO MAKE ME SAY IT...?
...
I UNDERSTAND.
EXCUSE ME.
YAGAMI! YOU HAVEN'T GIVEN ME AN ANSWER!
THANK YOU FOR THE VALUABLE INFORMATION CONCERNING THE KIRA CASE.
CLACK
SLAM

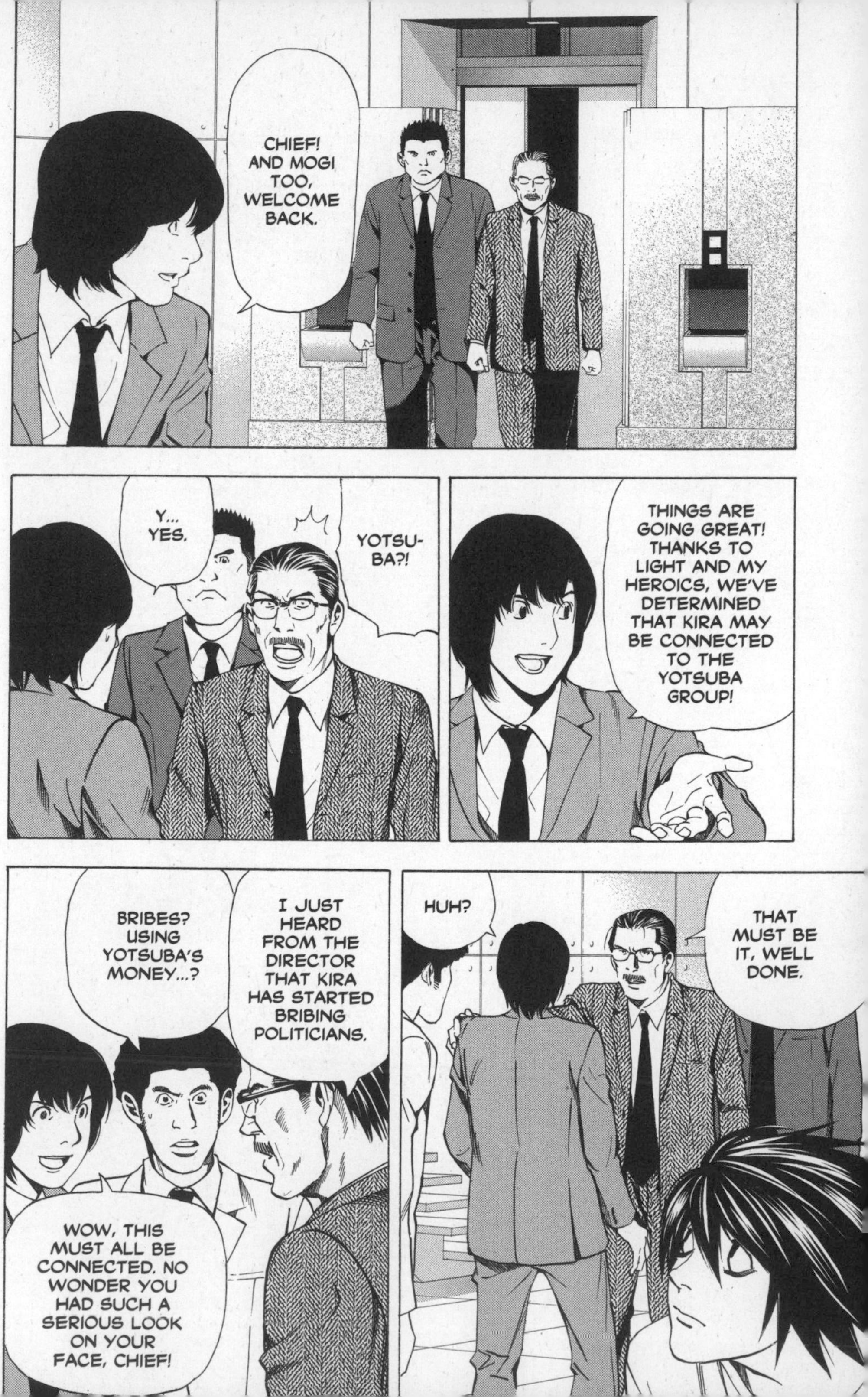
CHIEF! AND MOGI TOO, WELCOME BACK.
THINGS ARE GOING GREAT! THANKS TO LIGHT AND MY HEROICS, WE'VE DETERMINED THAT KIRA MAY BE CONNECTED TO THE YOTSUBA GROUP!
YOTSU-BA?!
Y... YES.
THAT MUST BE IT, WELL DONE.
HUH?
I JUST HEARD FROM THE DIRECTOR THAT KIRA HAS STARTED BRIBING POLITICIANS.
BRIBES? USING YOTSUBA'S MONEY...?
WOW, THIS MUST ALL BE CONNECTED. NO WONDER YOU HAD SUCH A SERIOUS LOOK ON YOUR FACE, CHIEF!

READ THIS WAY

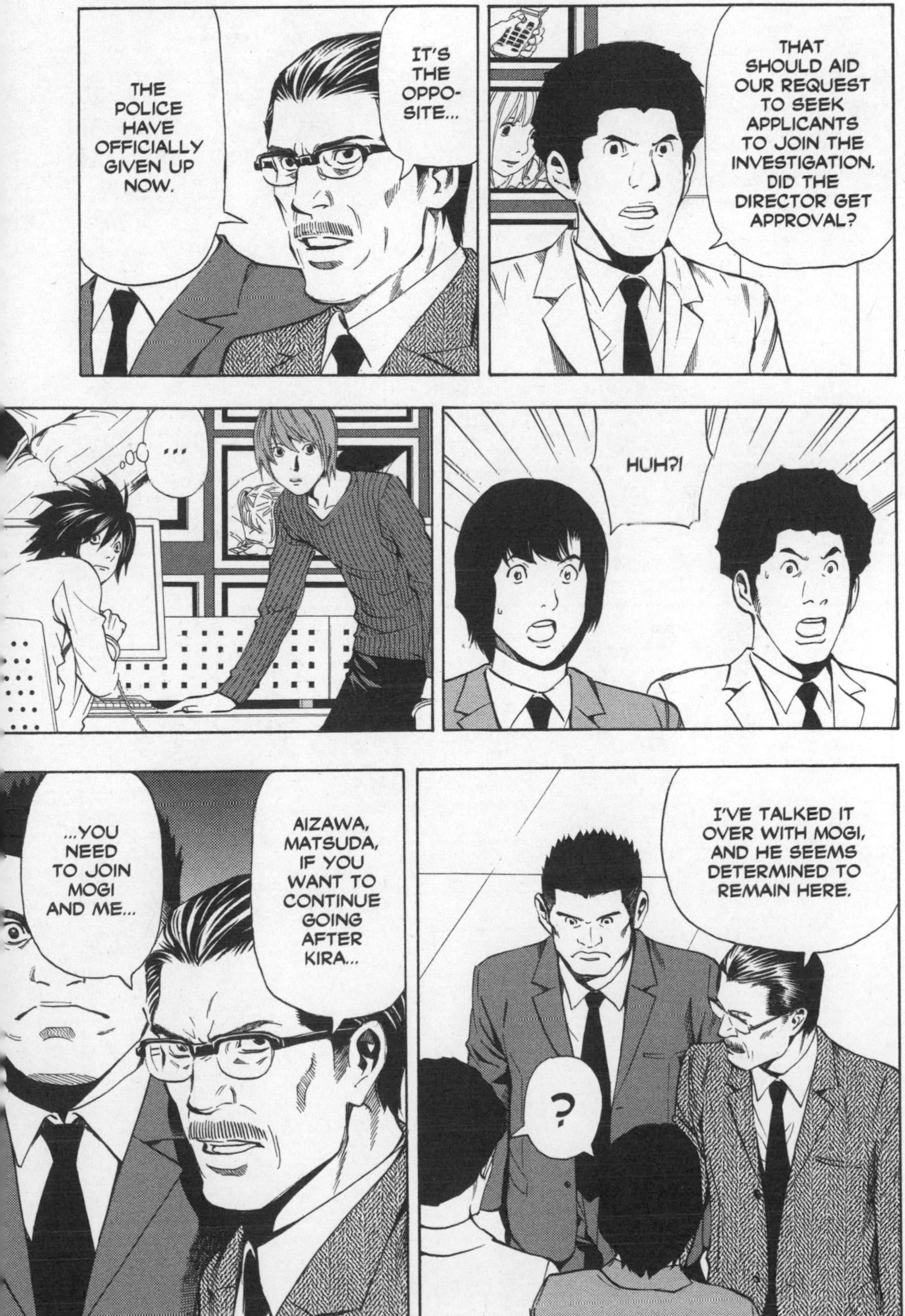
THAT SHOULD AID OUR REQUEST TO SEEK APPLICANTS TO JOIN THE INVESTIGATION. DID THE DIRECTOR GET APPROVAL?
IT'S THE OPPO-SITE...
THE POLICE HAVE OFFICIALLY GIVEN UP NOW.
HUH?!
...
I'VE TALKED IT OVER WITH MOGI, AND HE SEEMS DETERMINED TO REMAIN HERE.
?
AIZAWA, MATSUDA, IF YOU WANT TO CONTINUE GOING AFTER KIRA...
...YOU NEED TO JOIN MOGI AND ME...

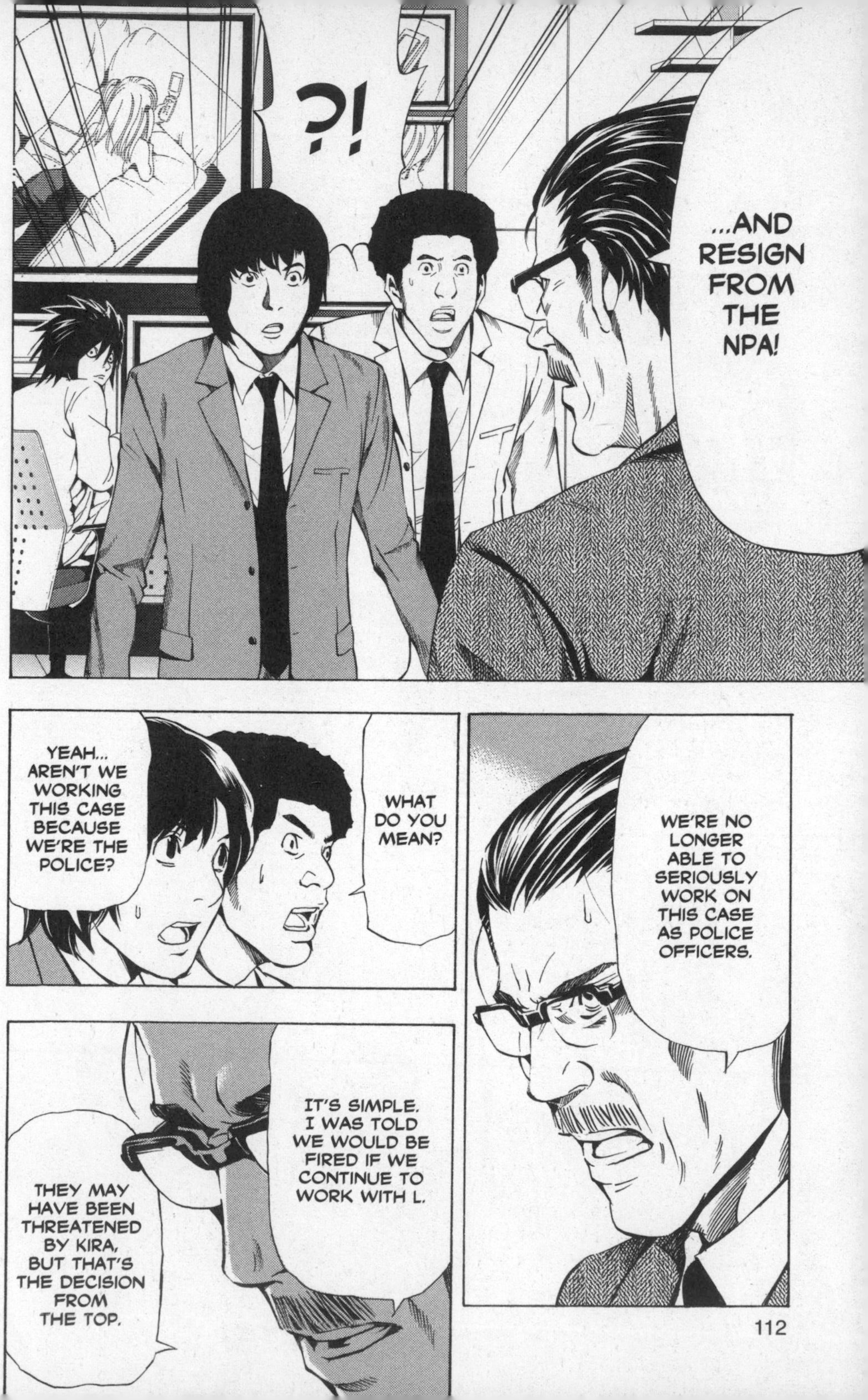
...AND RESIGN FROM THE NPA!
?!
WE'RE NO LONGER ABLE TO SERIOUSLY WORK ON THIS CASE AS POLICE OFFICERS.
WHAT DO YOU MEAN?
YEAH... AREN'T WE WORKING THIS CASE BECAUSE WE'RE THE POLICE?
IT'S SIMPLE. I WAS TOLD WE WOULD BE FIRED IF WE CONTINUE TO WORK WITH L.
THEY MAY HAVE BEEN THREATENED BY KIRA, BUT THAT'S THE DECISION FROM THE TOP.

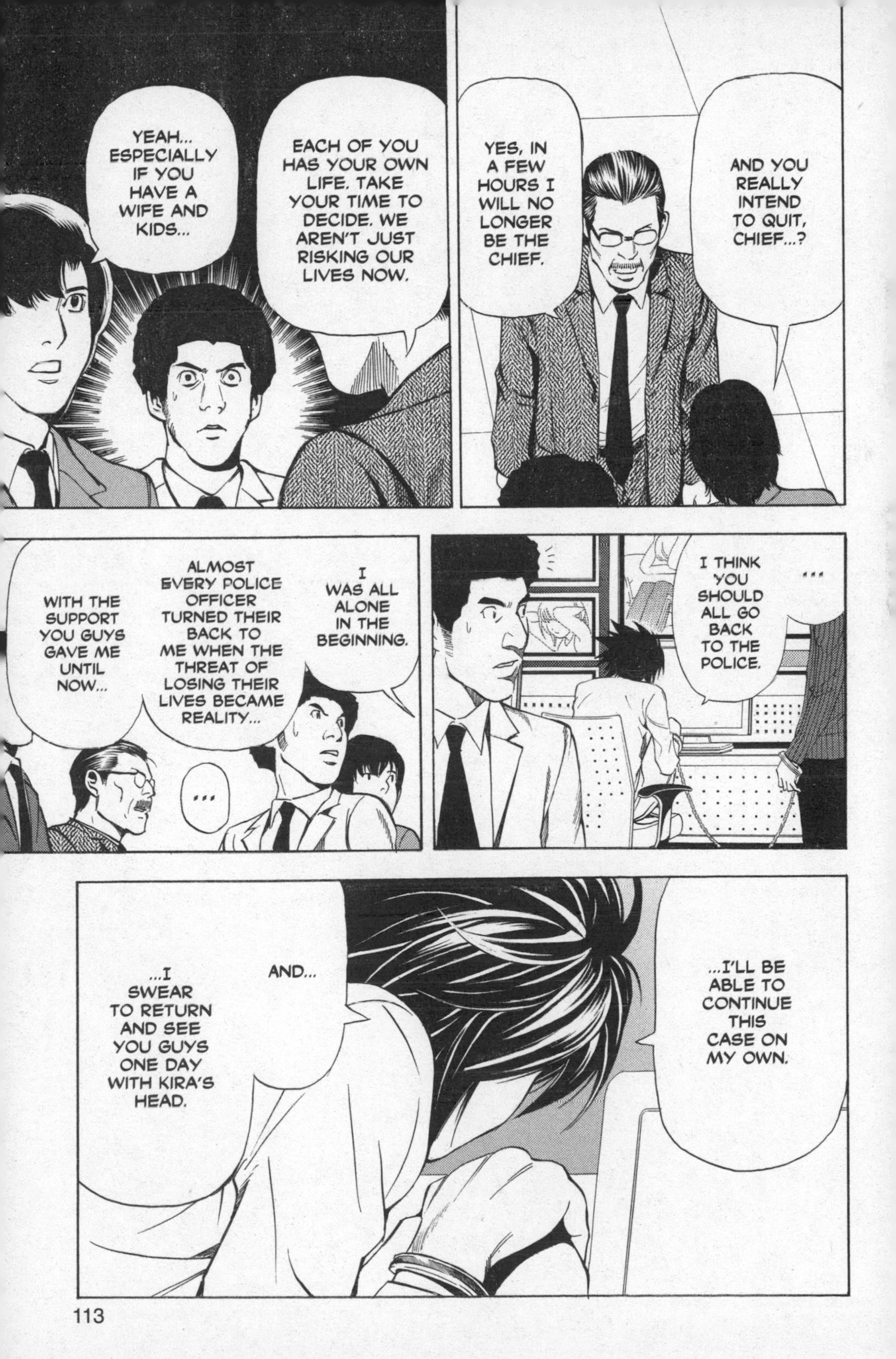
AND YOU REALLY INTEND TO QUIT, CHIEF...?
YES, IN A FEW HOURS I WILL NO LONGER BE THE CHIEF.
EACH OF YOU HAS YOUR OWN LIFE. TAKE YOUR TIME TO DECIDE. WE AREN'T JUST RISKING OUR LIVES NOW.
YEAH... ESPECIALLY IF YOU HAVE A WIFE AND KIDS...
...
I THINK YOU SHOULD ALL GO BACK TO THE POLICE.
I WAS ALL ALONE IN THE BEGINNING.
ALMOST EVERY POLICE OFFICER TURNED THEIR BACK TO ME WHEN THE THREAT OF LOSING THEIR LIVES BECAME REALITY...
WITH THE SUPPORT YOU GUYS GAVE ME UNTIL NOW...
...
...I'LL BE ABLE TO CONTINUE THIS CASE ON MY OWN.
AND...
...I SWEAR TO RETURN AND SEE YOU GUYS ONE DAY WITH KIRA'S HEAD.

DEATH NOTE
How to use it
XXVII

○ If you write, "die of disease" with a specific disease's name and the person's time of death, there must be a sufficient amount of time for the disease to progress. If the set time is too tight, the victim will die of a heart attack 40 seconds after completing the DEATH NOTE.

デスノートに病死と書き、病名と時間を指定をした場合、
その病気の進行に必要なだけの時間指定がされておらず
無理が生じると、書き終えてから40秒後に心臓麻痺となる。

○ If you write, "die of disease" for the cause of death, but only write a specific time of death without the actual name of disease, the human will die from an adequate disease. But the DEATH NOTE can only operate within 23 days (in the human calendar).
This is called the 23-day rule.

病死と書いた場合、病名を書かず時間指定をすれば、
その時間通りに適した病気で死ぬ。
ただし、デスノートで操れる死の時間は人間界単位で23日間以内である。

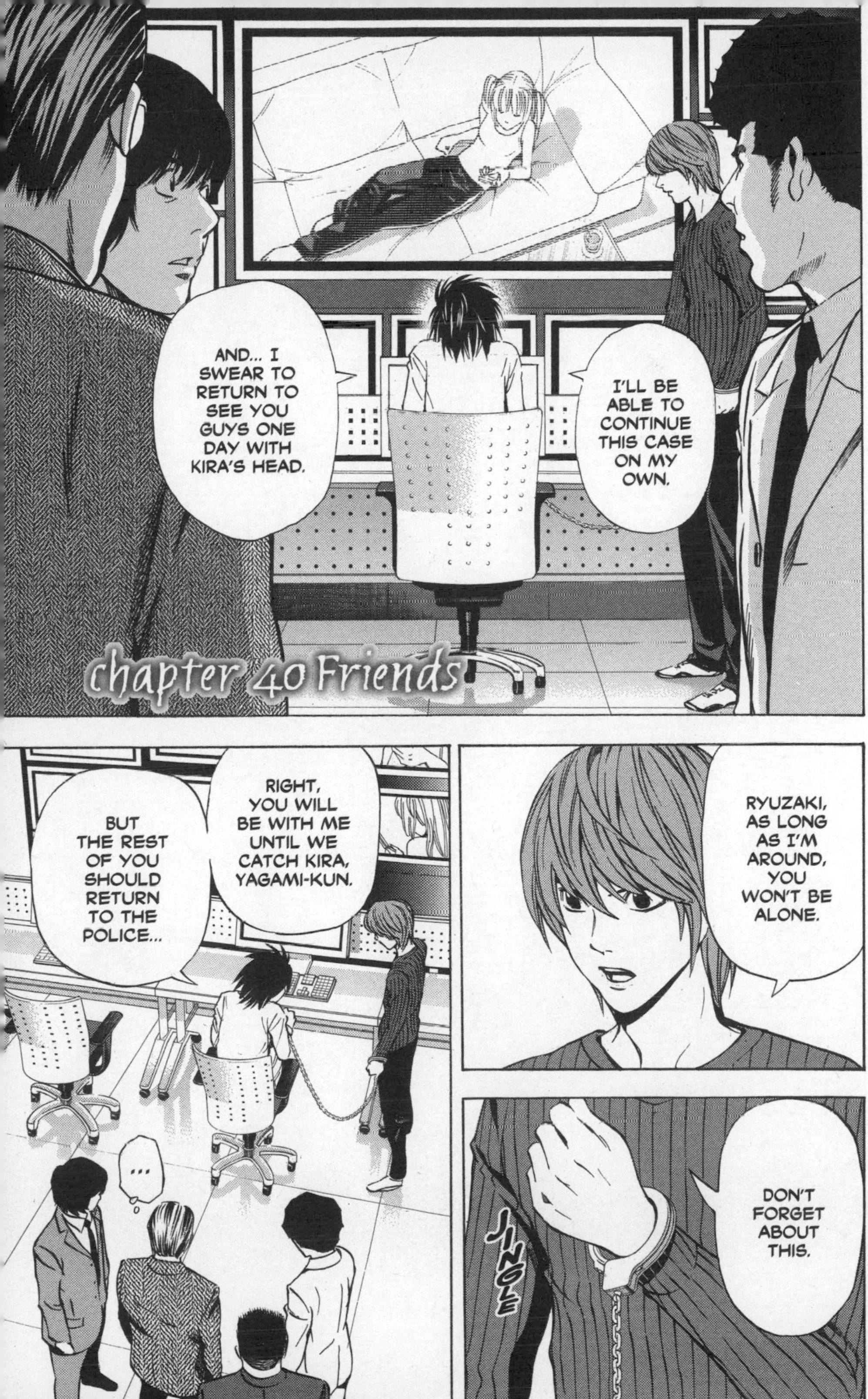
I'LL BE ABLE TO CONTINUE THIS CASE ON MY OWN.
AND... I SWEAR TO RETURN TO SEE YOU GUYS ONE DAY WITH KIRA'S HEAD.
chapter 40 Friends
RYUZAKI, AS LONG AS I'M AROUND, YOU WON'T BE ALONE.
JINGLE
DON'T FORGET ABOUT THIS.
RIGHT, YOU WILL BE WITH ME UNTIL WE CATCH KIRA, YAGAMI-KUN.
BUT THE REST OF YOU SHOULD RETURN TO THE POLICE...
...

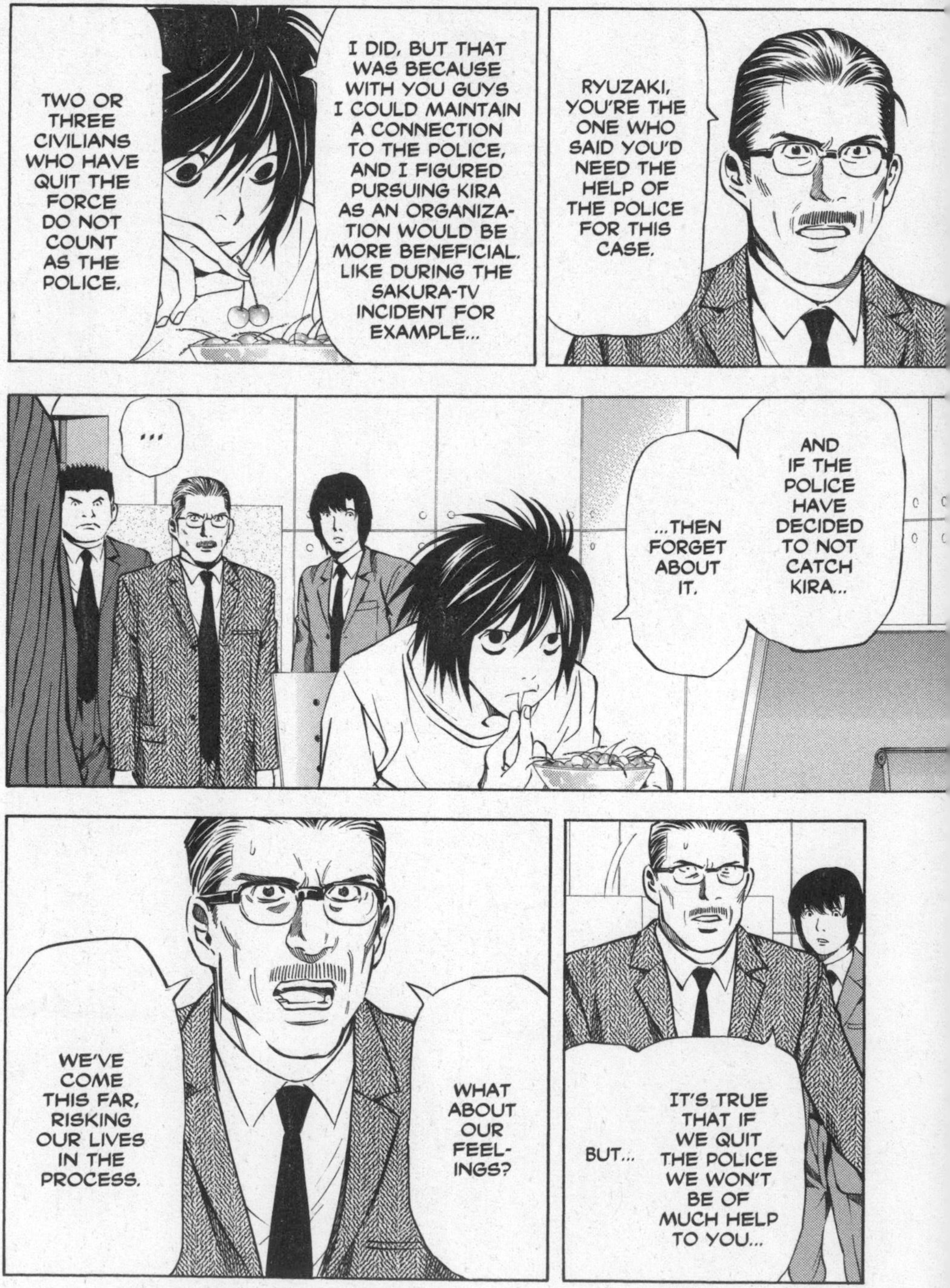
RYUZAKI, YOU'RE THE ONE WHO SAID YOU'D NEED THE HELP OF THE POLICE FOR THIS CASE.
I DID, BUT THAT WAS BECAUSE WITH YOU GUYS I COULD MAINTAIN A CONNECTION TO THE POLICE, AND I FIGURED PURSUING KIRA AS AN ORGANIZATION WOULD BE MORE BENEFICIAL. LIKE DURING THE SAKURA-TV INCIDENT FOR EXAMPLE...
TWO OR THREE CIVILIANS WHO HAVE QUIT THE FORCE DO NOT COUNT AS THE POLICE.
AND IF THE POLICE HAVE DECIDED TO NOT CATCH KIRA...
...THEN FORGET ABOUT IT.
...
IT'S TRUE THAT IF WE QUIT THE POLICE WE WON'T BE OF MUCH HELP TO YOU...
BUT...
WHAT ABOUT OUR FEELINGS?
WE'VE COME THIS FAR, RISKING OUR LIVES IN THE PROCESS.

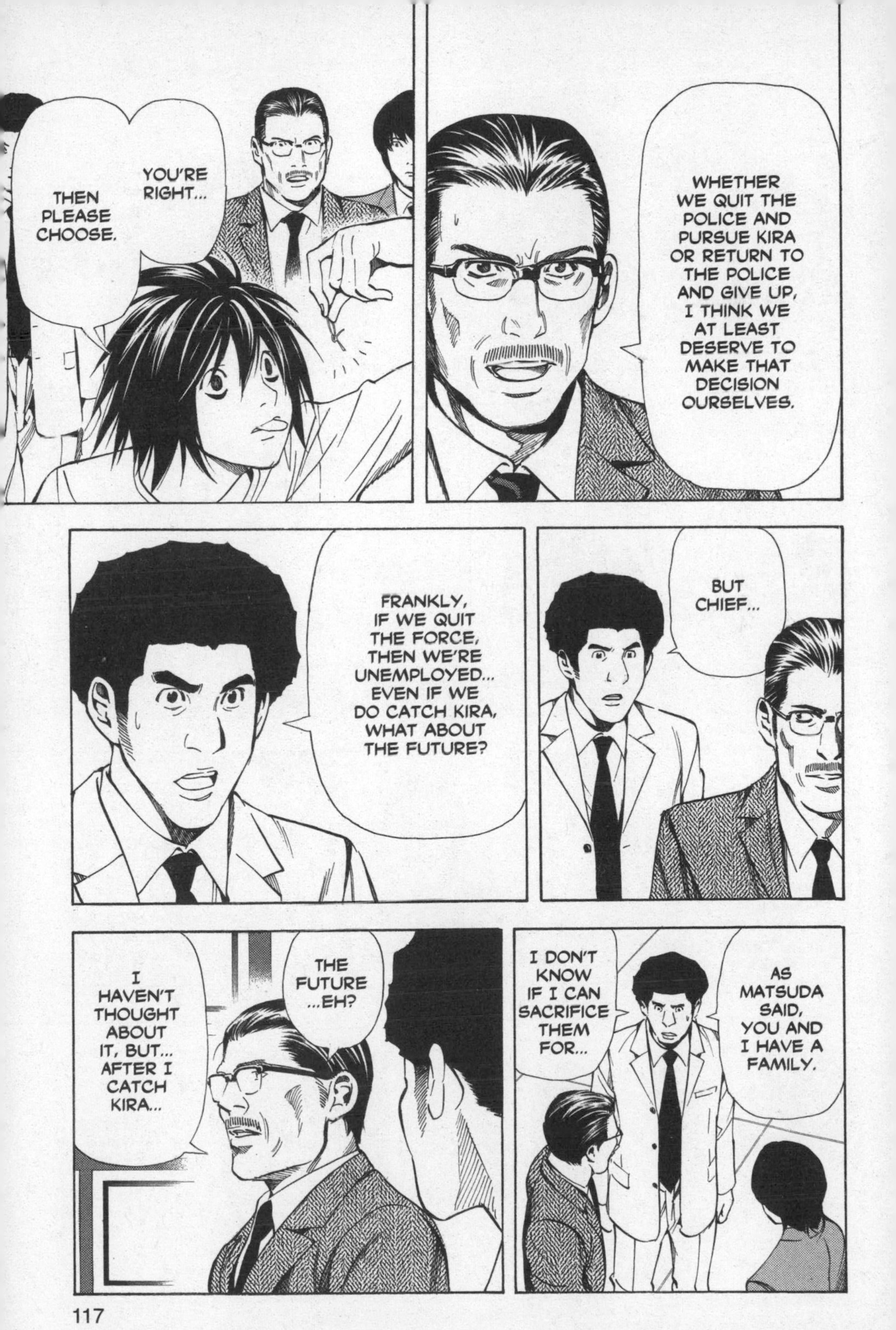
WHETHER WE QUIT THE POLICE AND PURSUE KIRA OR RETURN TO THE POLICE AND GIVE UP, I THINK WE AT LEAST DESERVE TO MAKE THAT DECISION OURSELVES.
YOU'RE RIGHT...
THEN PLEASE CHOOSE.
BUT CHIEF...
FRANKLY, IF WE QUIT THE FORCE, THEN WE'RE UNEMPLOYED... EVEN IF WE DO CATCH KIRA, WHAT ABOUT THE FUTURE?
AS MATSUDA SAID, YOU AND I HAVE A FAMILY.
I DON'T KNOW IF I CAN SACRIFICE THEM FOR...
THE FUTURE ...EH?
I HAVEN'T THOUGHT ABOUT IT, BUT... AFTER I CATCH KIRA...

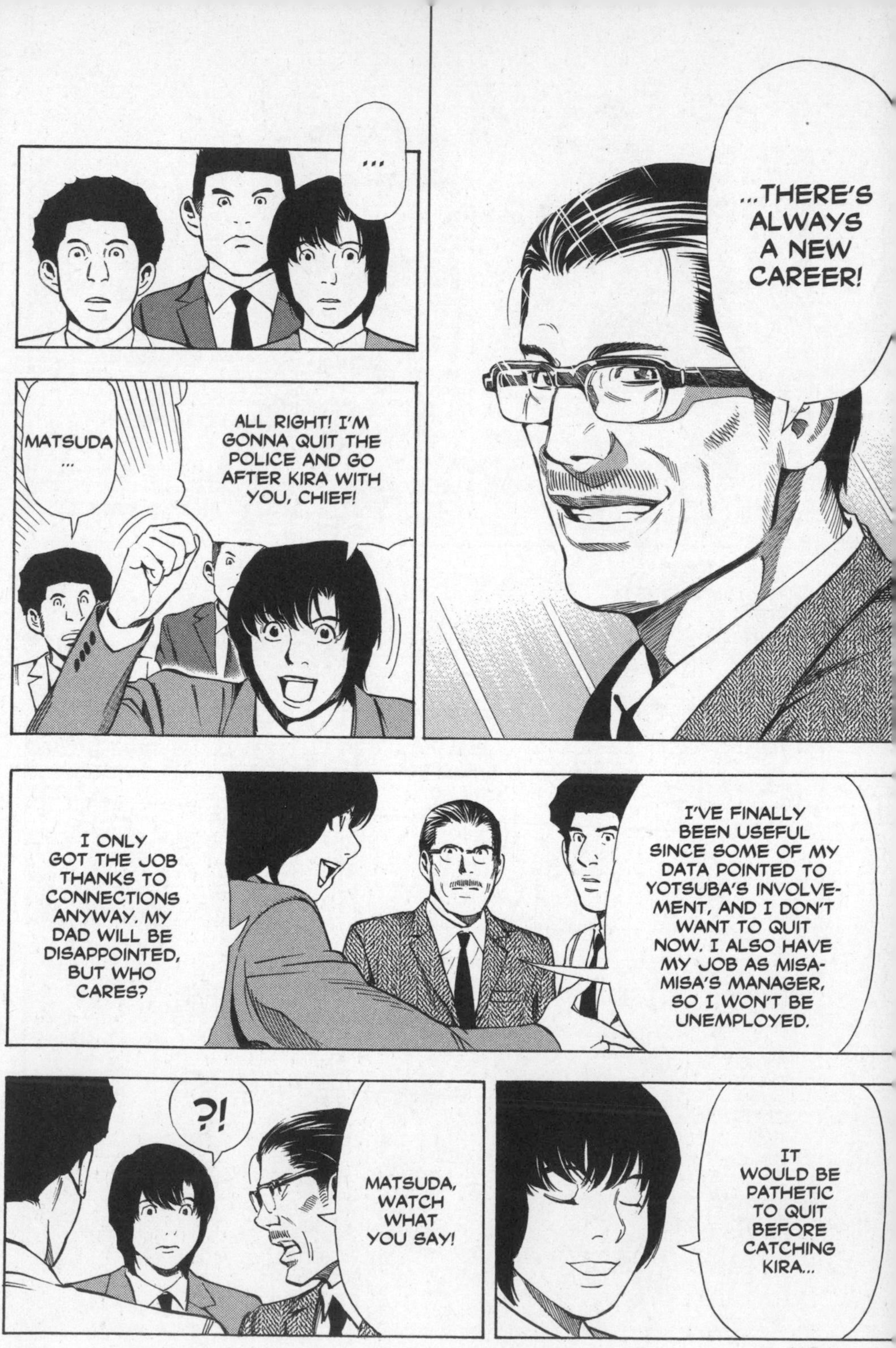
...THERE'S ALWAYS A NEW CAREER!
...
ALL RIGHT! I'M GONNA QUIT THE POLICE AND GO AFTER KIRA WITH YOU, CHIEF!
MATSUDA ...
I'VE FINALLY BEEN USEFUL SINCE SOME OF MY DATA POINTED TO YOTSUBA'S INVOLVE-MENT, AND I DON'T WANT TO QUIT NOW. I ALSO HAVE MY JOB AS MISA-MISA'S MANAGER, SO I WON'T BE UNEMPLOYED.
I ONLY GOT THE JOB THANKS TO CONNECTIONS ANYWAY. MY DAD WILL BE DISAPPOINTED, BUT WHO CARES?
IT WOULD BE PATHETIC TO QUIT BEFORE CATCHING KIRA...
MATSUDA, WATCH WHAT YOU SAY!
?!

READ THIS WAY

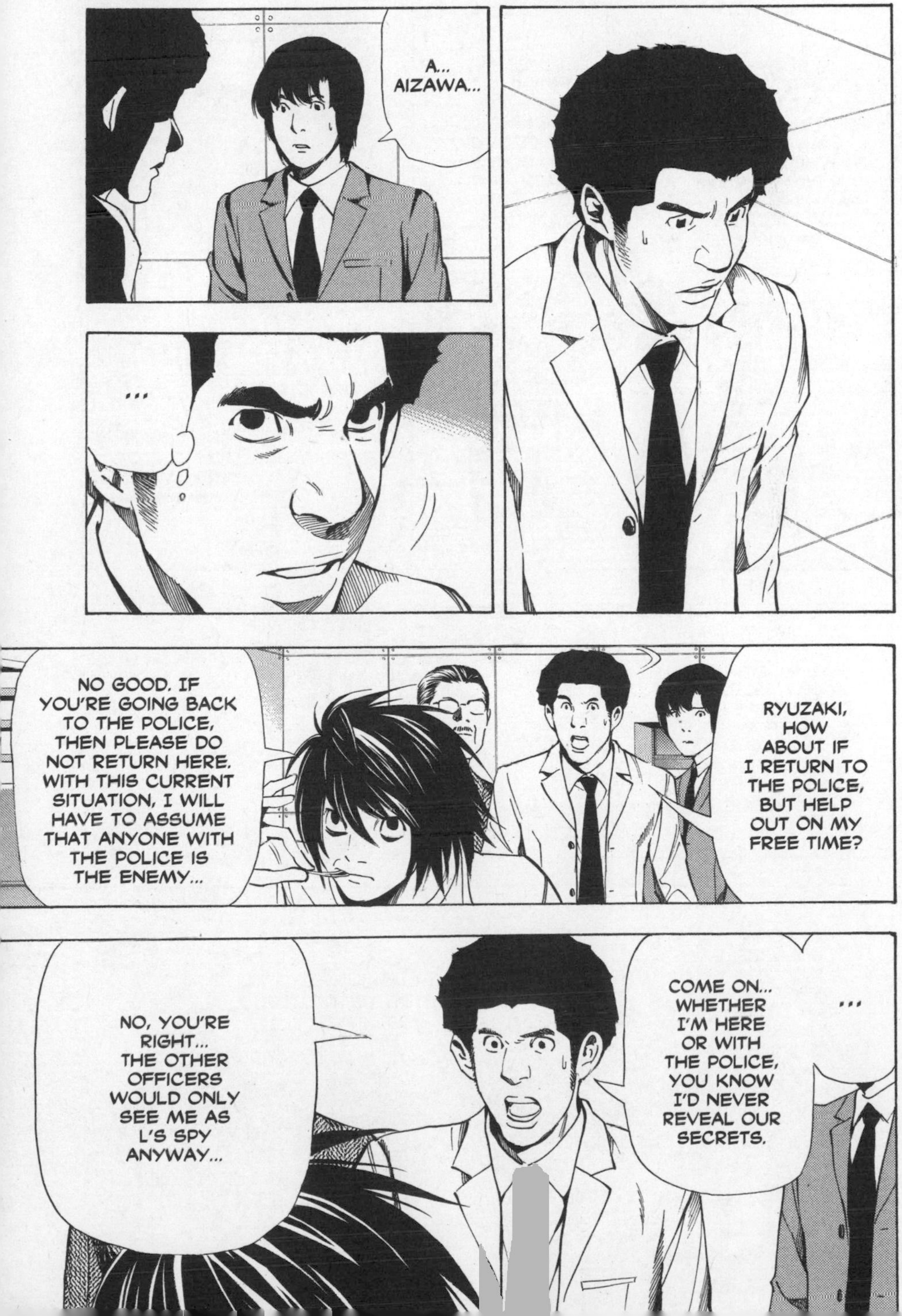
A... AIZAWA...
...
RYUZAKI, HOW ABOUT IF I RETURN TO THE POLICE, BUT HELP OUT ON MY FREE TIME?
NO GOOD. IF YOU'RE GOING BACK TO THE POLICE, THEN PLEASE DO NOT RETURN HERE. WITH THIS CURRENT SITUATION, I WILL HAVE TO ASSUME THAT ANYONE WITH THE POLICE IS THE ENEMY...
...
COME ON... WHETHER I'M HERE OR WITH THE POLICE, YOU KNOW I'D NEVER REVEAL OUR SECRETS.
NO, YOU'RE RIGHT... THE OTHER OFFICERS WOULD ONLY SEE ME AS L'S SPY ANYWAY...

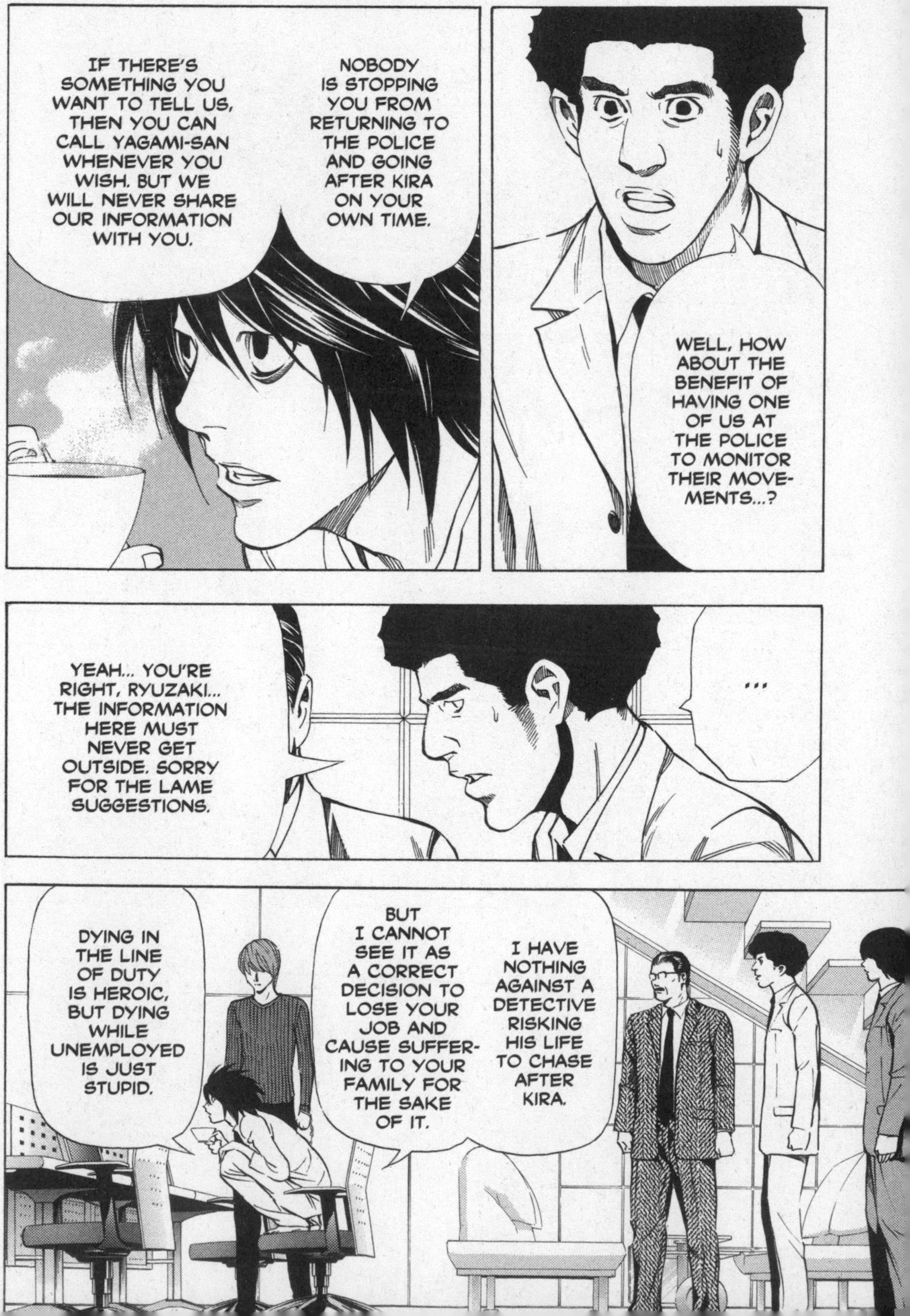
WELL, HOW ABOUT THE BENEFIT OF HAVING ONE OF US AT THE POLICE TO MONITOR THEIR MOVEMENTS...?
NOBODY IS STOPPING YOU FROM RETURNING TO THE POLICE AND GOING AFTER KIRA ON YOUR OWN TIME.
IF THERE'S SOMETHING YOU WANT TO TELL US, THEN YOU CAN CALL YAGAMI-SAN WHENEVER YOU WISH. BUT WE WILL NEVER SHARE OUR INFORMATION WITH YOU.
...
YEAH... YOU'RE RIGHT, RYUZAKI... THE INFORMATION HERE MUST NEVER GET OUTSIDE. SORRY FOR THE LAME SUGGESTIONS.
I HAVE NOTHING AGAINST A DETECTIVE RISKING HIS LIFE TO CHASE AFTER KIRA.
BUT I CANNOT SEE IT AS A CORRECT DECISION TO LOSE YOUR JOB AND CAUSE SUFFERING TO YOUR FAMILY FOR THE SAKE OF IT.
DYING IN THE LINE OF DUTY IS HEROIC, BUT DYING WHILE UNEMPLOYED IS JUST STUPID.

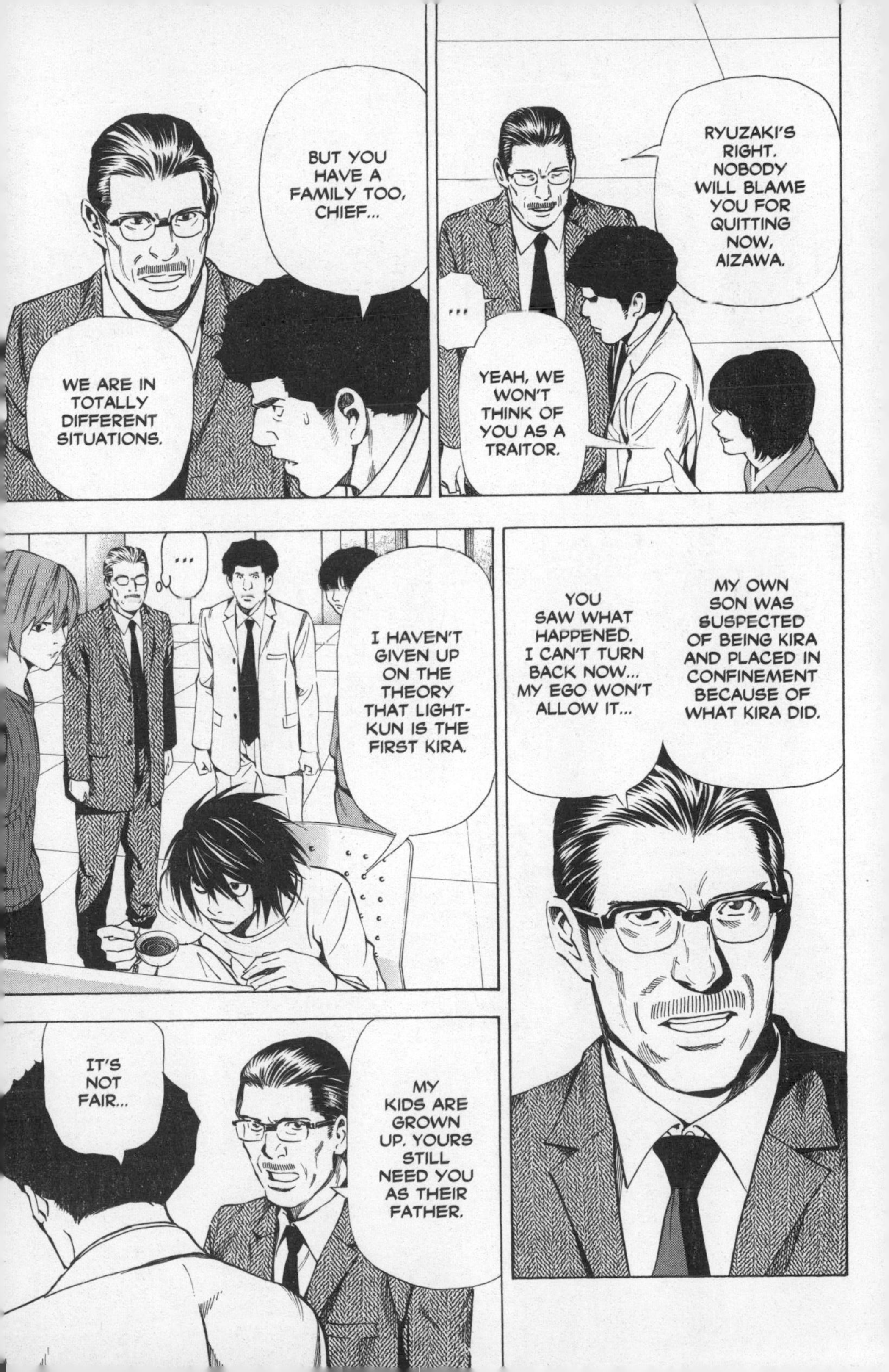
RYUZAKI'S RIGHT. NOBODY WILL BLAME YOU FOR QUITTING NOW, AIZAWA.
...
YEAH, WE WON'T THINK OF YOU AS A TRAITOR.
BUT YOU HAVE A FAMILY TOO, CHIEF...
WE ARE IN TOTALLY DIFFERENT SITUATIONS.
MY OWN SON WAS SUSPECTED OF BEING KIRA AND PLACED IN CONFINEMENT BECAUSE OF WHAT KIRA DID.
YOU SAW WHAT HAPPENED. I CAN'T TURN BACK NOW... MY EGO WON'T ALLOW IT...
...
I HAVEN'T GIVEN UP ON THE THEORY THAT LIGHT-KUN IS THE FIRST KIRA.
MY KIDS ARE GROWN UP. YOURS STILL NEED YOU AS THEIR FATHER.
IT'S NOT FAIR...

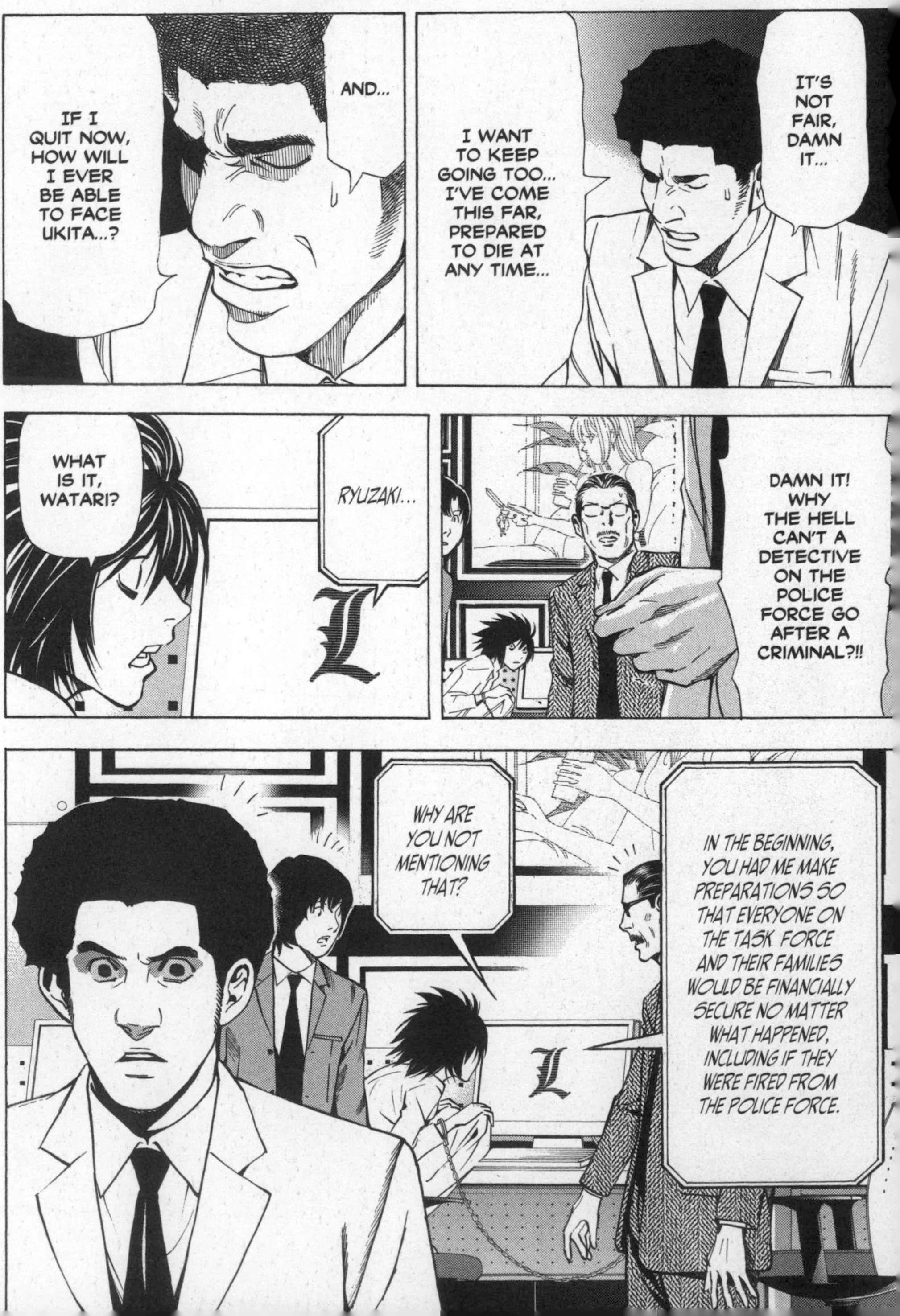
IT'S NOT FAIR, DAMN IT...
I WANT TO KEEP GOING TOO... I'VE COME THIS FAR, PREPARED TO DIE AT ANY TIME...
AND...
IF I QUIT NOW, HOW WILL I EVER BE ABLE TO FACE UKITA...?
DAMN IT! WHY THE HELL CAN'T A DETECTIVE ON THE POLICE FORCE GO AFTER A CRIMINAL?!!
RYUZAKI...
WHAT IS IT, WATARI?
IN THE BEGINNING, YOU HAD ME MAKE PREPARATIONS SO THAT EVERYONE ON THE TASK FORCE AND THEIR FAMILIES WOULD BE FINANCIALLY SECURE NO MATTER WHAT HAPPENED, INCLUDING IF THEY WERE FIRED FROM THE POLICE FORCE.
WHY ARE YOU NOT MENTIONING THAT?

READ THIS WAY

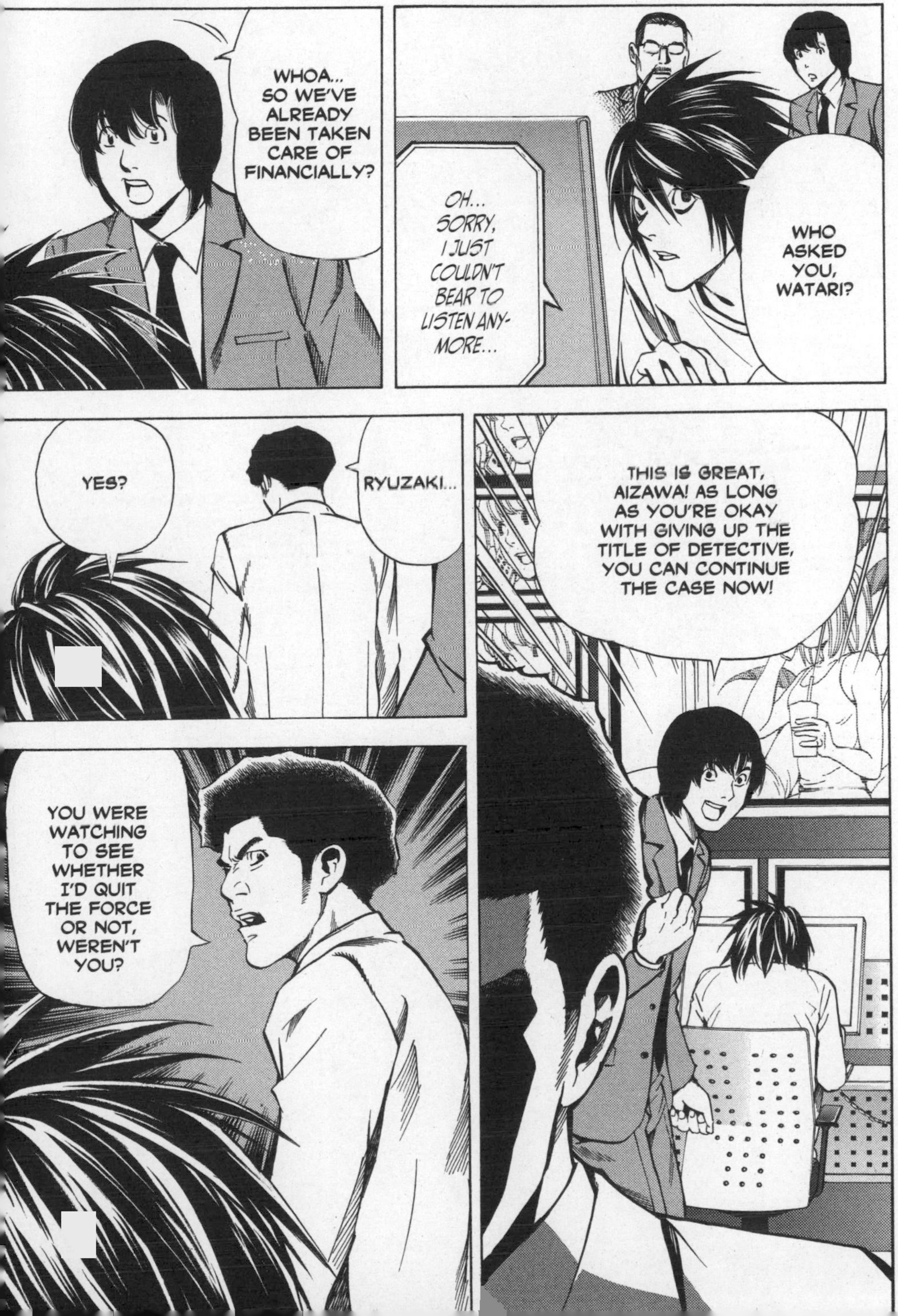
WHO ASKED YOU, WATARI?
OH... SORRY, I JUST COULDN'T BEAR TO LISTEN ANYMORE...
WHOA... SO WE'VE ALREADY BEEN TAKEN CARE OF FINANCIALLY?
THIS IS GREAT, AIZAWA! AS LONG AS YOU'RE OKAY WITH GIVING UP THE TITLE OF DETECTIVE, YOU CAN CONTINUE THE CASE NOW!
RYUZAKI...
YES?
YOU WERE WATCHING TO SEE WHETHER I'D QUIT THE FORCE OR NOT, WEREN'T YOU?

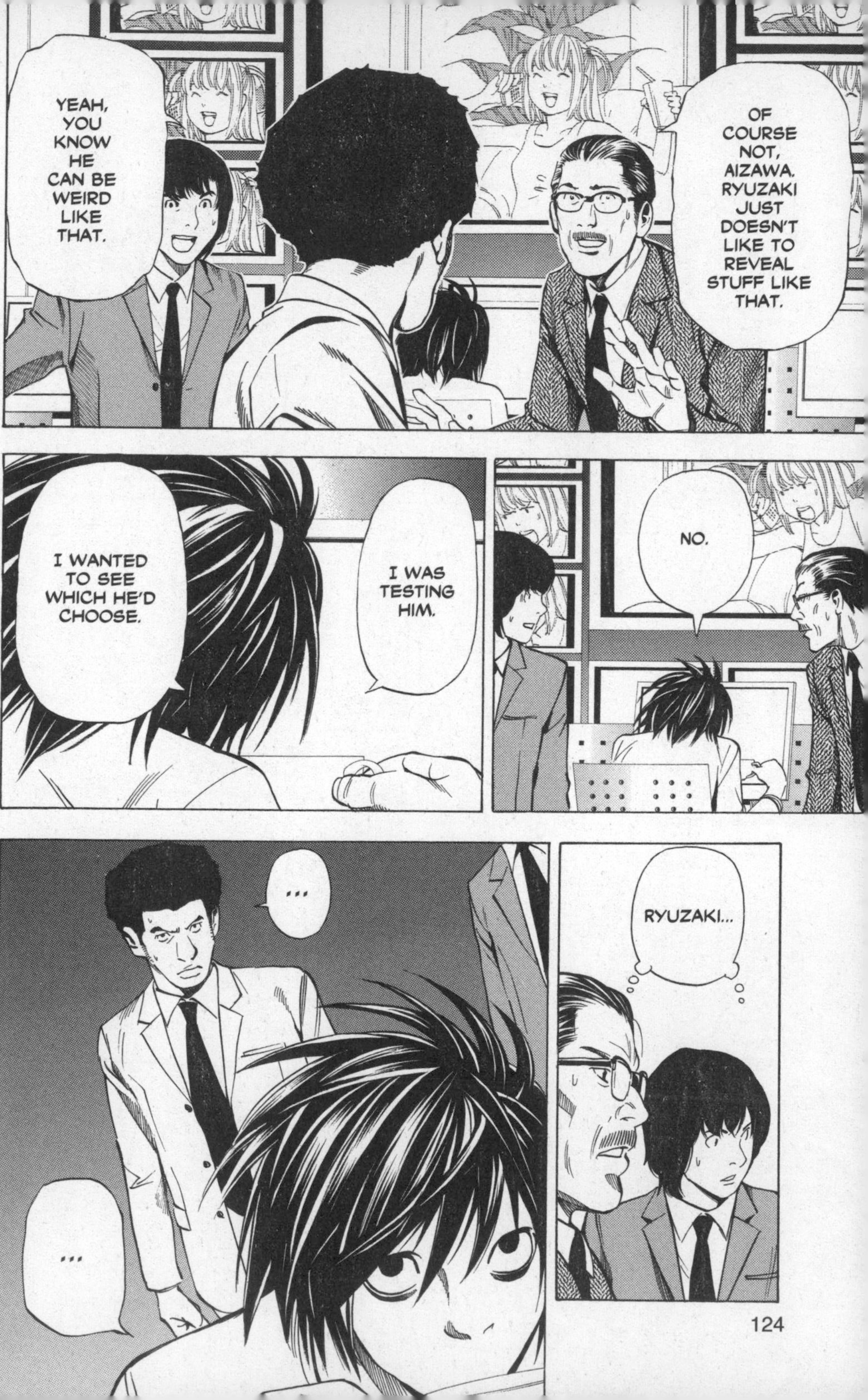
OF COURSE NOT, AIZAWA. RYUZAKI JUST DOESN'T LIKE TO REVEAL STUFF LIKE THAT.
YEAH, YOU KNOW HE CAN BE WEIRD LIKE THAT.
NO.
I WAS TESTING HIM.
I WANTED TO SEE WHICH HE'D CHOOSE.
RYUZAKI...
...
...

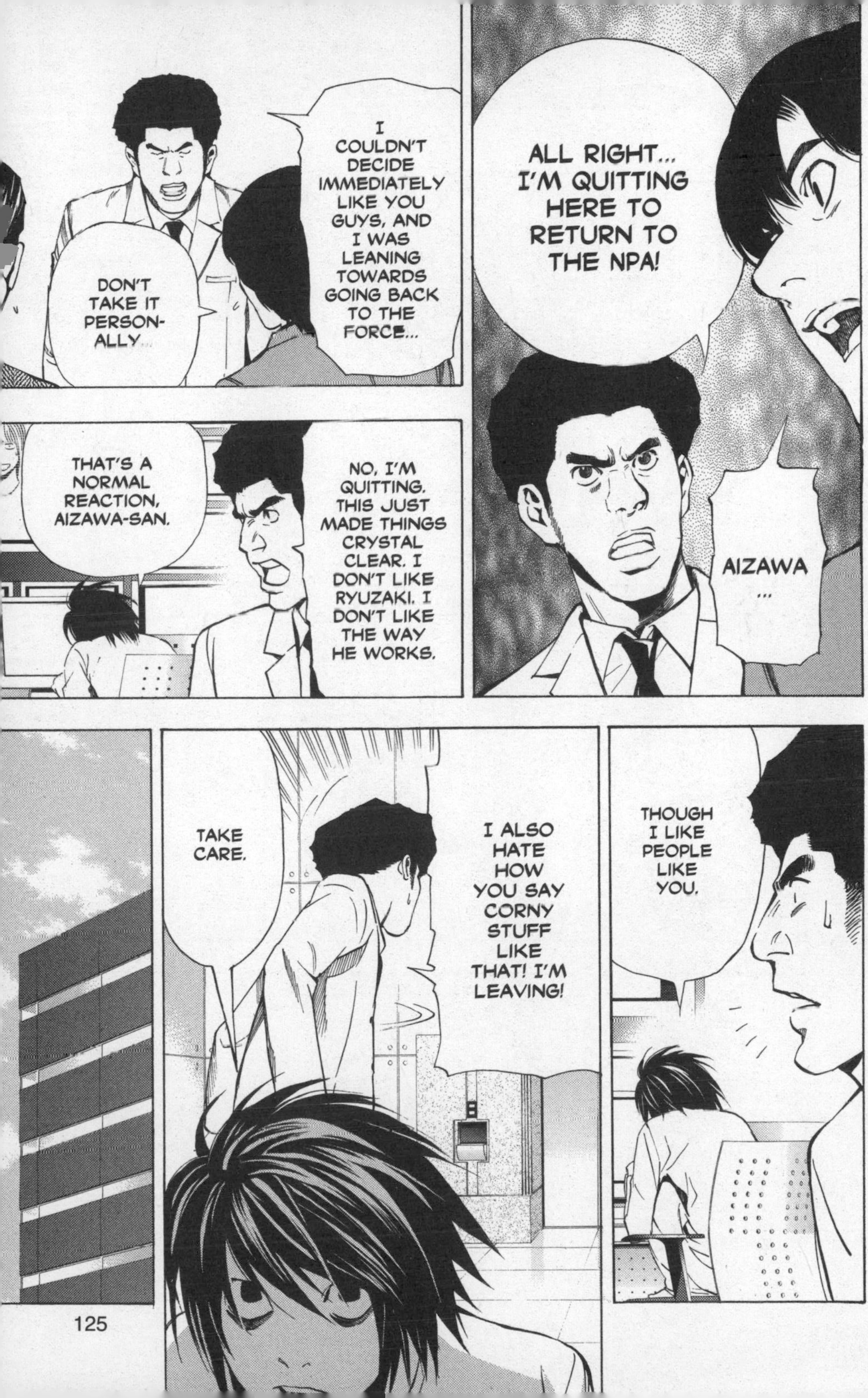
ALL RIGHT... I'M QUITTING HERE TO RETURN TO THE NPA!
AIZAWA ...
I COULDN'T DECIDE IMMEDIATELY LIKE YOU GUYS, AND I WAS LEANING TOWARDS GOING BACK TO THE FORCE...
DON'T TAKE IT PERSON-ALLY...
NO, I'M QUITTING. THIS JUST MADE THINGS CRYSTAL CLEAR. I DON'T LIKE RYUZAKI. I DON'T LIKE THE WAY HE WORKS.
THAT'S A NORMAL REACTION, AIZAWA-SAN.
THOUGH I LIKE PEOPLE LIKE YOU.
I ALSO HATE HOW YOU SAY CORNY STUFF LIKE THAT! I'M LEAVING!
TAKE CARE.

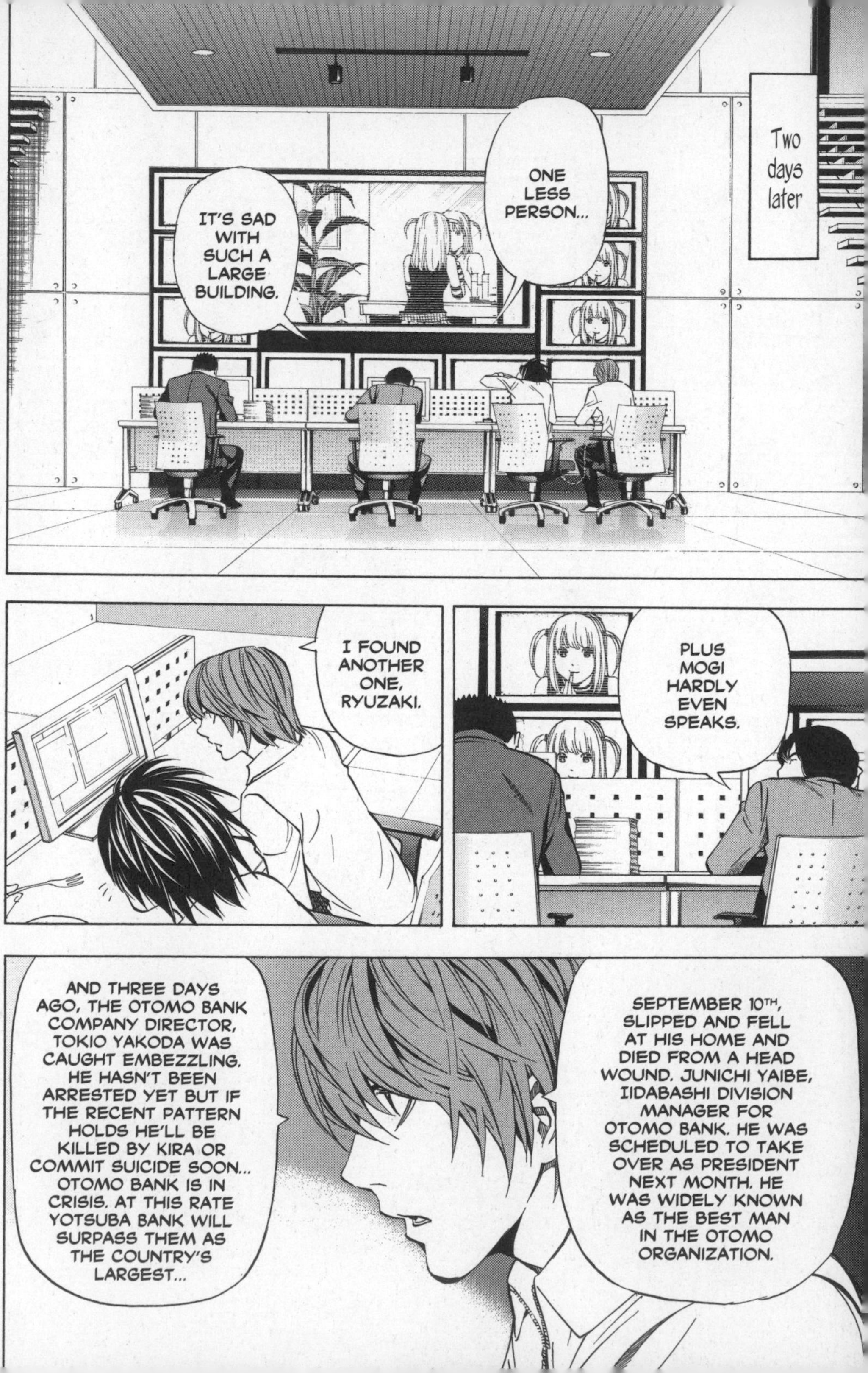
Two days later
ONE LESS PERSON...
IT'S SAD WITH SUCH A LARGE BUILDING.
PLUS MOGI HARDLY EVEN SPEAKS.
I FOUND ANOTHER ONE, RYUZAKI.
SEPTEMBER 10TH, SLIPPED AND FELL AT HIS HOME AND DIED FROM A HEAD WOUND. JUNICHI YAIBE, IIDABASHI DIVISION MANAGER FOR OTOMO BANK. HE WAS SCHEDULED TO TAKE OVER AS PRESIDENT NEXT MONTH. HE WAS WIDELY KNOWN AS THE BEST MAN IN THE OTOMO ORGANIZATION.
AND THREE DAYS AGO, THE OTOMO BANK COMPANY DIRECTOR, TOKIO YAKODA WAS CAUGHT EMBEZZLING. HE HASN'T BEEN ARRESTED YET BUT IF THE RECENT PATTERN HOLDS HE'LL BE KILLED BY KIRA OR COMMIT SUICIDE SOON... OTOMO BANK IS IN CRISIS. AT THIS RATE YOTSUBA BANK WILL SURPASS THEM AS THE COUNTRY'S LARGEST...

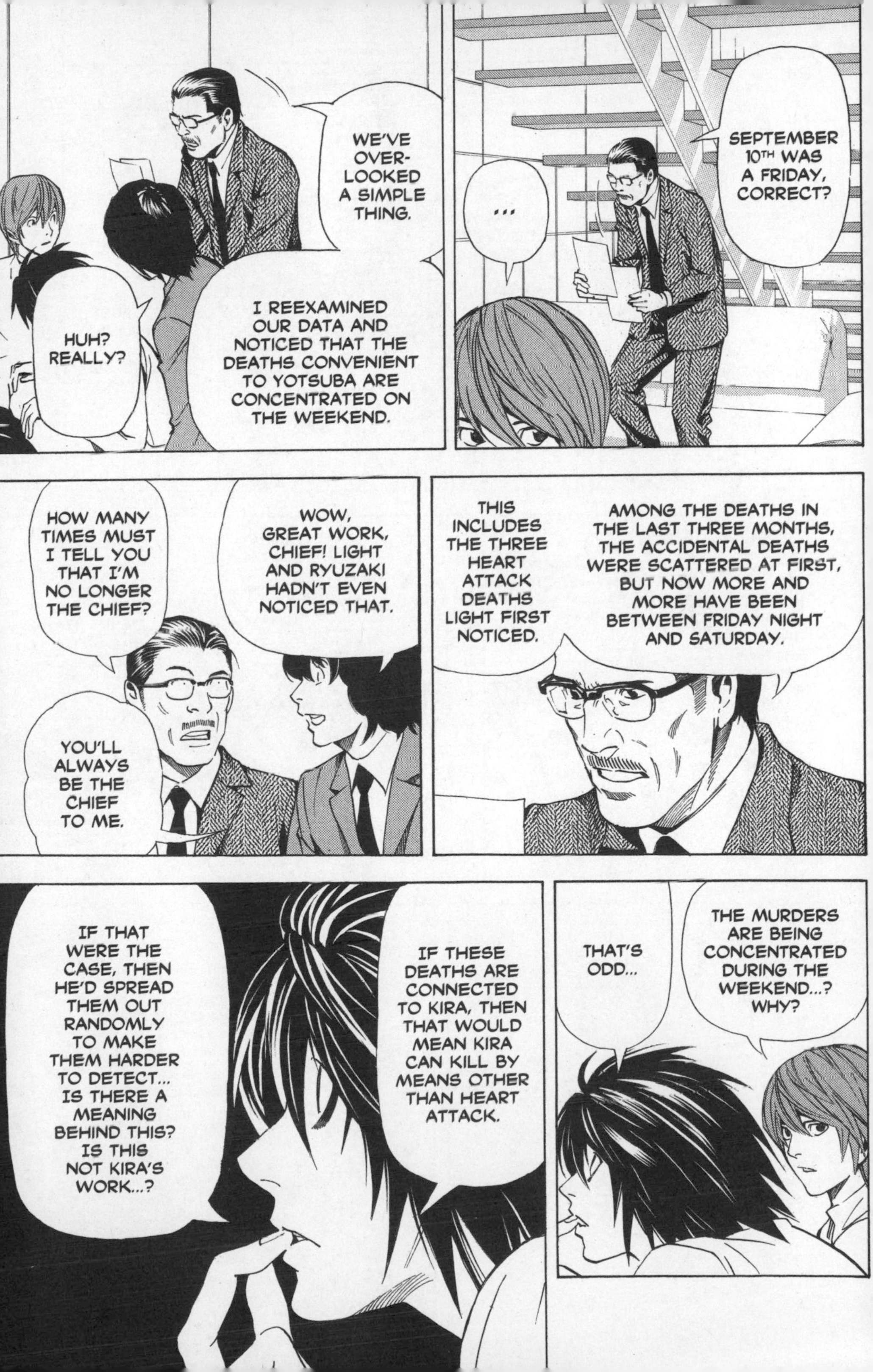
SEPTEMBER 10TH WAS A FRIDAY, CORRECT?
...
WE'VE OVER-LOOKED A SIMPLE THING.
I REEXAMINED OUR DATA AND NOTICED THAT THE DEATHS CONVENIENT TO YOTSUBA ARE CONCENTRATED ON THE WEEKEND.
HUH? REALLY?
AMONG THE DEATHS IN THE LAST THREE MONTHS, THE ACCIDENTAL DEATHS WERE SCATTERED AT FIRST, BUT NOW MORE AND MORE HAVE BEEN BETWEEN FRIDAY NIGHT AND SATURDAY.
THIS INCLUDES THE THREE HEART ATTACK DEATHS LIGHT FIRST NOTICED.
WOW, GREAT WORK, CHIEF! LIGHT AND RYUZAKI HADN'T EVEN NOTICED THAT.
HOW MANY TIMES MUST I TELL YOU THAT I'M NO LONGER THE CHIEF?
YOU'LL ALWAYS BE THE CHIEF TO ME.
THE MURDERS ARE BEING CONCENTRATED DURING THE WEEKEND...? WHY?
THAT'S ODD...
IF THESE DEATHS ARE CONNECTED TO KIRA, THEN THAT WOULD MEAN KIRA CAN KILL BY MEANS OTHER THAN HEART ATTACK.
IF THAT WERE THE CASE, THEN HE'D SPREAD THEM OUT RANDOMLY TO MAKE THEM HARDER TO DETECT... IS THERE A MEANING BEHIND THIS? IS THIS NOT KIRA'S WORK...?

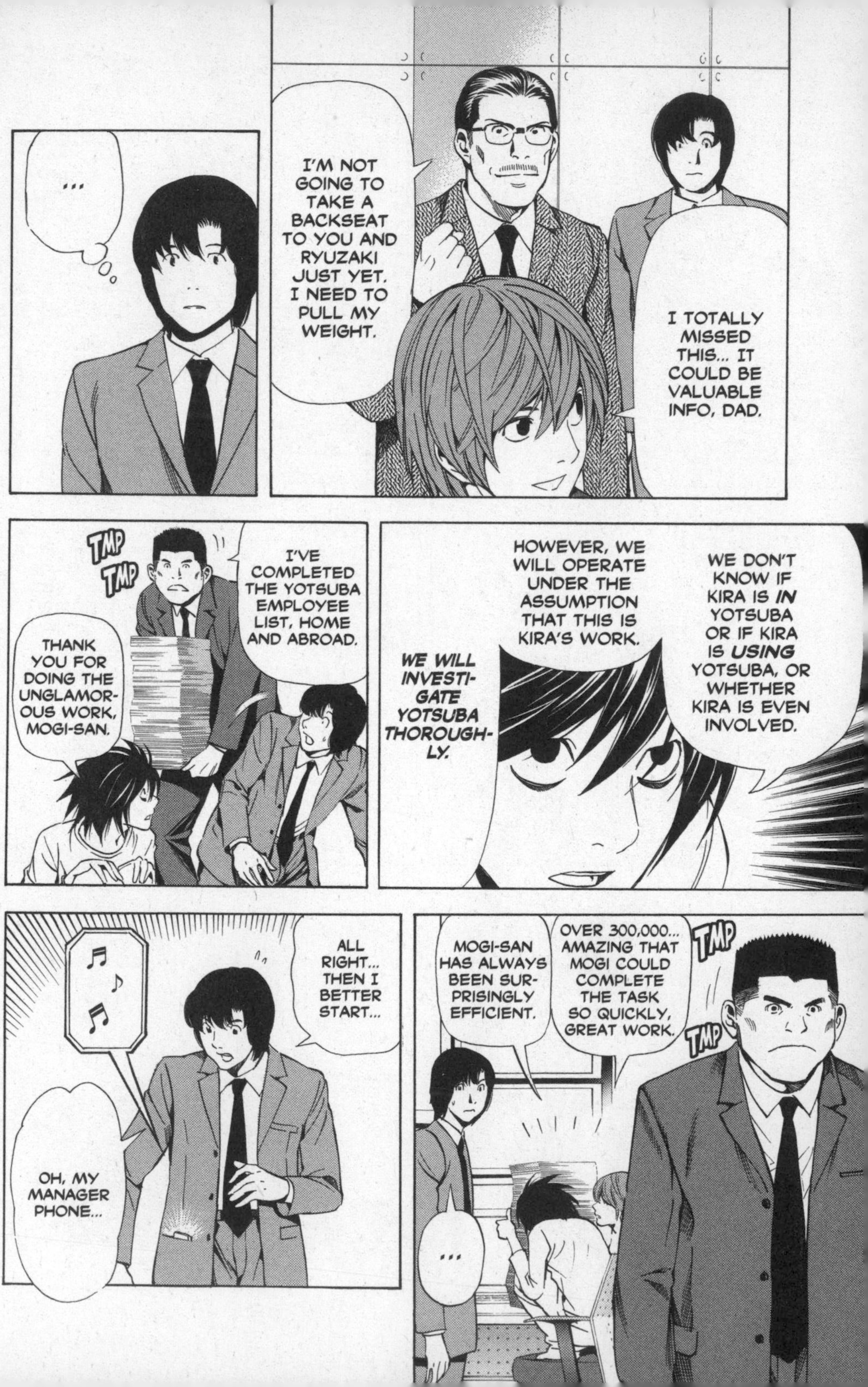
I TOTALLY MISSED THIS... IT COULD BE VALUABLE INFO, DAD.
I'M NOT GOING TO TAKE A BACKSEAT TO YOU AND RYUZAKI JUST YET. I NEED TO PULL MY WEIGHT.
...
WE DON'T KNOW IF KIRA IS *IN* YOTSUBA OR IF KIRA IS *USING* YOTSUBA, OR WHETHER KIRA IS EVEN INVOLVED.
HOWEVER, WE WILL OPERATE UNDER THE ASSUMPTION THAT THIS IS KIRA'S WORK.
WE WILL INVESTIGATE YOTSUBA THOROUGHLY.
TMP
TMP
I'VE COMPLETED THE YOTSUBA EMPLOYEE LIST, HOME AND ABROAD.
THANK YOU FOR DOING THE UNGLAMOROUS WORK, MOGI-SAN.
TMP
OVER 300,000... AMAZING THAT MOGI COULD COMPLETE THE TASK SO QUICKLY, GREAT WORK.
MOGI-SAN HAS ALWAYS BEEN SURPRISINGLY EFFICIENT.
TMP
...
ALL RIGHT... THEN I BETTER START...
OH, MY MANAGER PHONE...

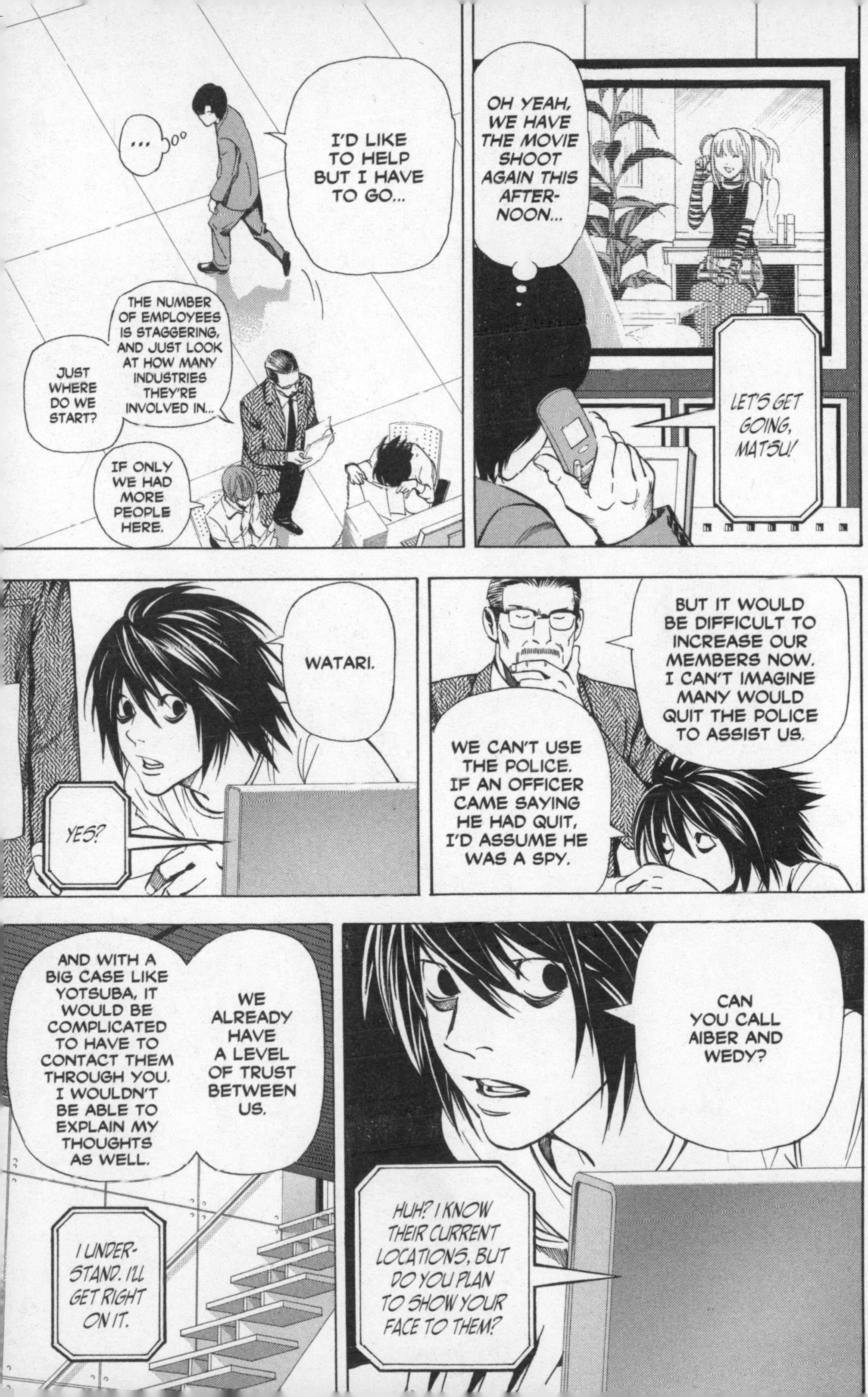
OH YEAH, WE HAVE THE MOVIE SHOOT AGAIN THIS AFTERNOON...
LET'S GET GOING, MATSU!
I'D LIKE TO HELP BUT I HAVE TO GO...
...
THE NUMBER OF EMPLOYEES IS STAGGERING, AND JUST LOOK AT HOW MANY INDUSTRIES THEY'RE INVOLVED IN...
JUST WHERE DO WE START?
IF ONLY WE HAD MORE PEOPLE HERE.
BUT IT WOULD BE DIFFICULT TO INCREASE OUR MEMBERS NOW. I CAN'T IMAGINE MANY WOULD QUIT THE POLICE TO ASSIST US.
WE CAN'T USE THE POLICE. IF AN OFFICER CAME SAYING HE HAD QUIT, I'D ASSUME HE WAS A SPY.
WATARI.
YES?
CAN YOU CALL AIBER AND WEDY?
HUH? I KNOW THEIR CURRENT LOCATIONS, BUT DO YOU PLAN TO SHOW YOUR FACE TO THEM?
WE ALREADY HAVE A LEVEL OF TRUST BETWEEN US.
AND WITH A BIG CASE LIKE YOTSUBA, IT WOULD BE COMPLICATED TO HAVE TO CONTACT THEM THROUGH YOU. I WOULDN'T BE ABLE TO EXPLAIN MY THOUGHTS AS WELL.
I UNDER-STAND. I'LL GET RIGHT ON IT.

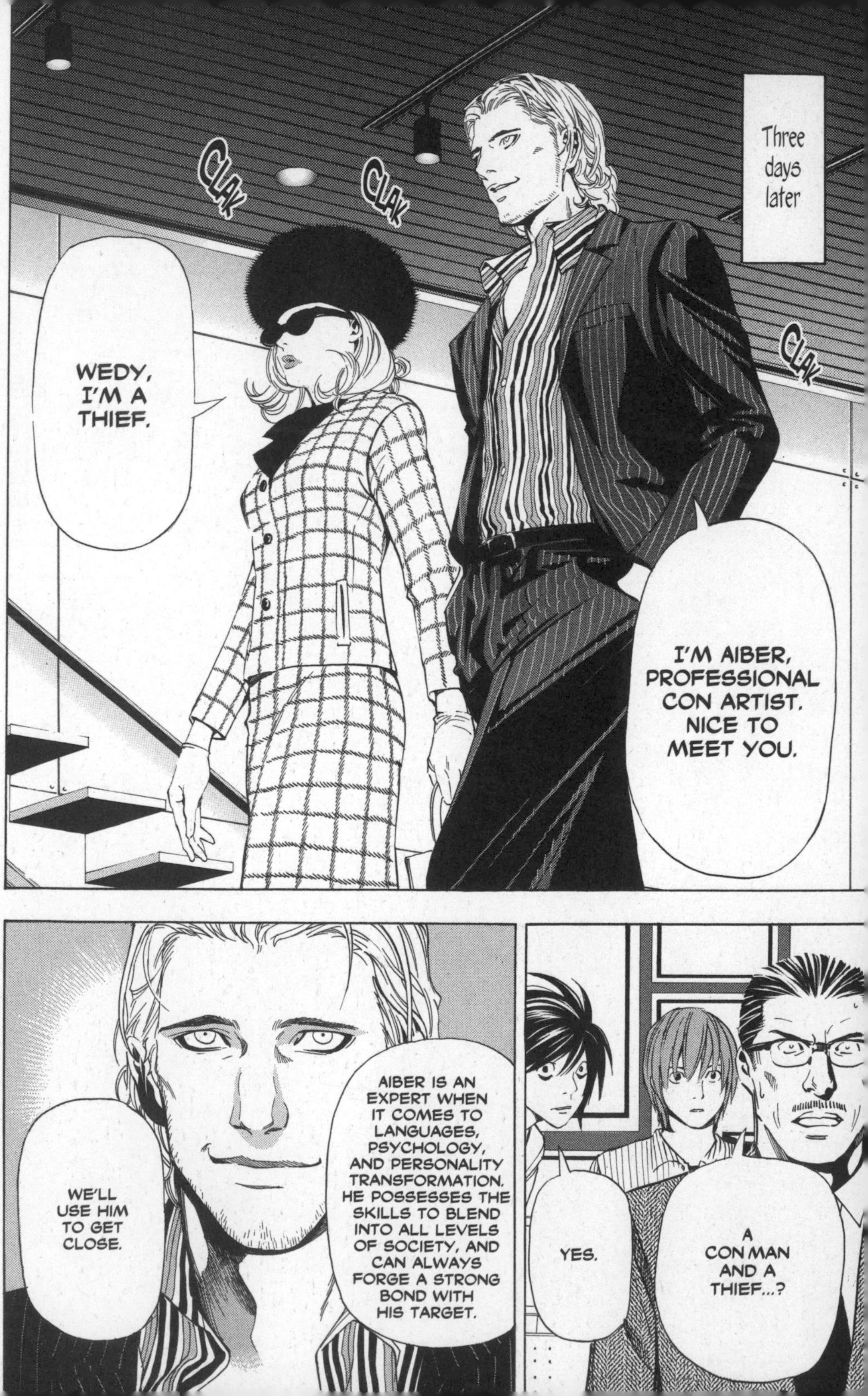
Three days later
CLAK
CLAK
CLAK
I'M AIBER, PROFESSIONAL CON ARTIST. NICE TO MEET YOU.
WEDY, I'M A THIEF.
A CON MAN AND A THIEF...?
YES.
AIBER IS AN EXPERT WHEN IT COMES TO LANGUAGES, PSYCHOLOGY, AND PERSONALITY TRANSFORMATION. HE POSSESSES THE SKILLS TO BLEND INTO ALL LEVELS OF SOCIETY, AND CAN ALWAYS FORGE A STRONG BOND WITH HIS TARGET.
WE'LL USE HIM TO GET CLOSE.

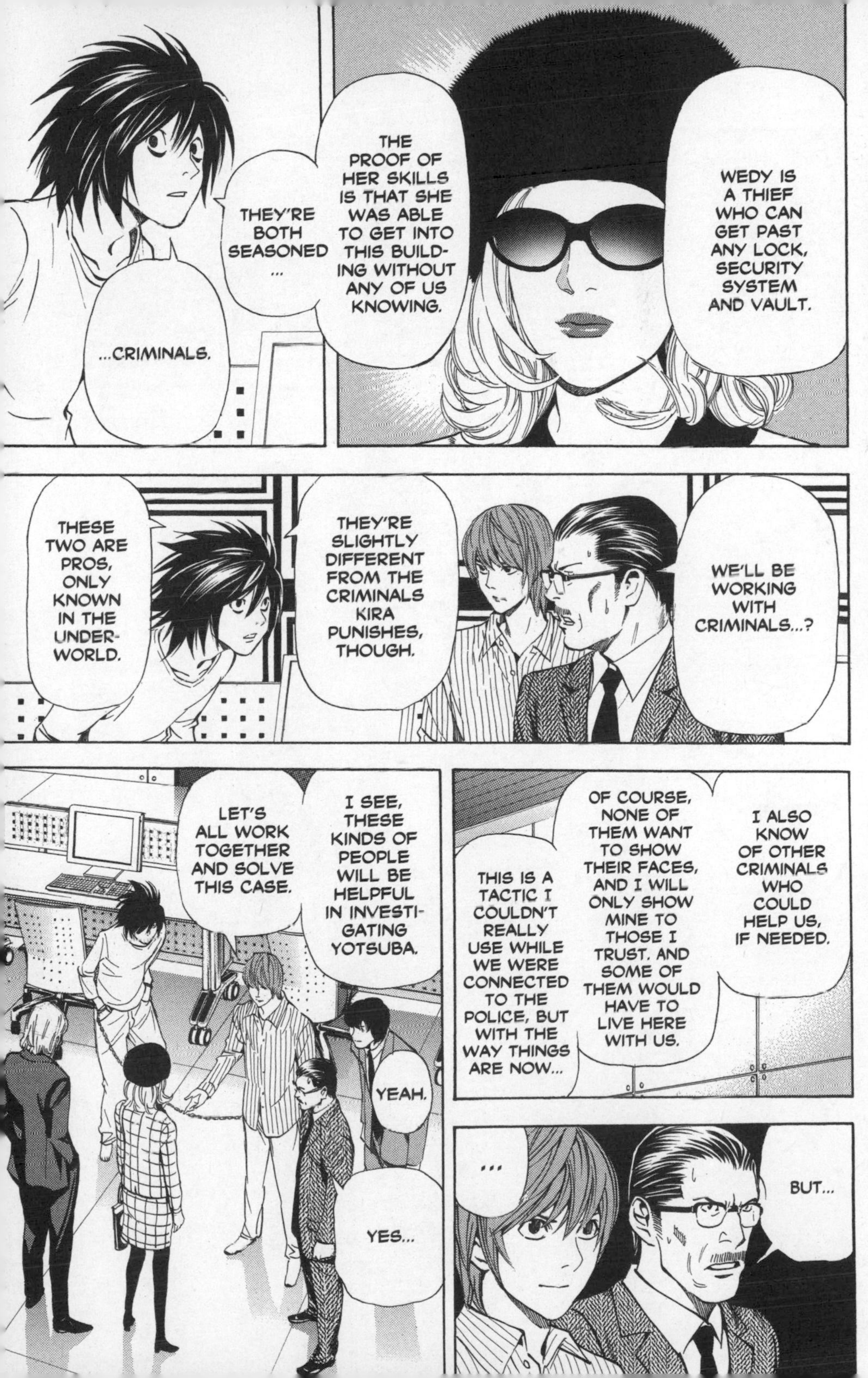
WEDY IS A THIEF WHO CAN GET PAST ANY LOCK, SECURITY SYSTEM AND VAULT.
THE PROOF OF HER SKILLS IS THAT SHE WAS ABLE TO GET INTO THIS BUILDING WITHOUT ANY OF US KNOWING.
THEY'RE BOTH SEASONED...
...CRIMINALS.
WE'LL BE WORKING WITH CRIMINALS...?
THEY'RE SLIGHTLY DIFFERENT FROM THE CRIMINALS KIRA PUNISHES, THOUGH.
THESE TWO ARE PROS, ONLY KNOWN IN THE UNDERWORLD.
I ALSO KNOW OF OTHER CRIMINALS WHO COULD HELP US, IF NEEDED.
OF COURSE, NONE OF THEM WANT TO SHOW THEIR FACES, AND I WILL ONLY SHOW MINE TO THOSE I TRUST. AND SOME OF THEM WOULD HAVE TO LIVE HERE WITH US.
THIS IS A TACTIC I COULDN'T REALLY USE WHILE WE WERE CONNECTED TO THE POLICE, BUT WITH THE WAY THINGS ARE NOW...
BUT...
...
I SEE, THESE KINDS OF PEOPLE WILL BE HELPFUL IN INVESTIGATING YOTSUBA.
LET'S ALL WORK TOGETHER AND SOLVE THIS CASE.
YEAH.
YES...

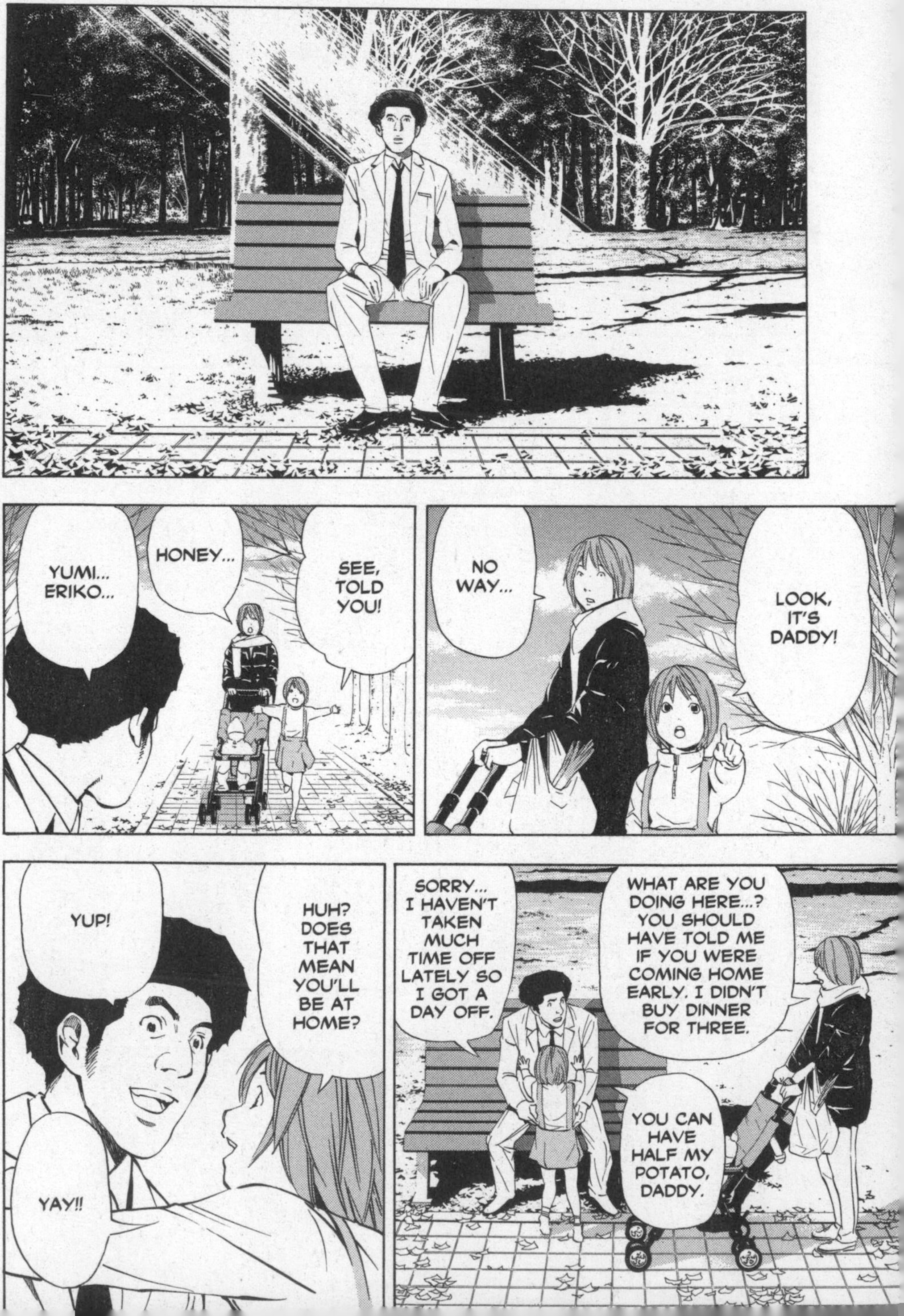
LOOK, IT'S DADDY!
NO WAY...
SEE, TOLD YOU!
HONEY...
YUMI... ERIKO...
WHAT ARE YOU DOING HERE...? YOU SHOULD HAVE TOLD ME IF YOU WERE COMING HOME EARLY. I DIDN'T BUY DINNER FOR THREE.
SORRY... I HAVEN'T TAKEN MUCH TIME OFF LATELY SO I GOT A DAY OFF.
YOU CAN HAVE HALF MY POTATO, DADDY.
HUH? DOES THAT MEAN YOU'LL BE AT HOME?
YUP!
YAY!!

READ THIS WAY

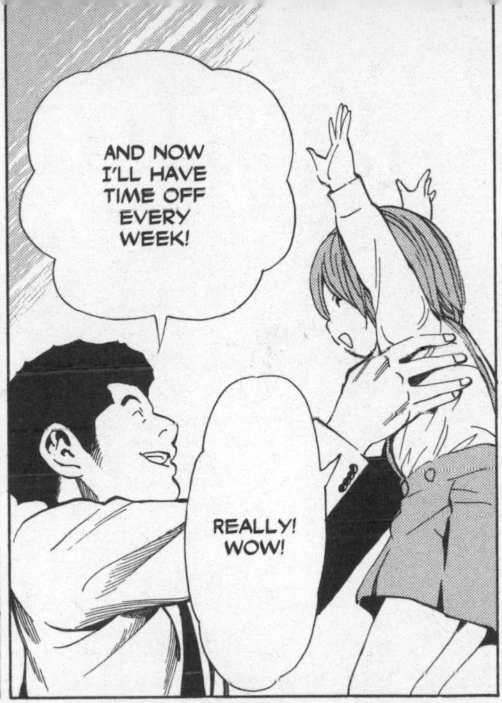
AND NOW I'LL HAVE TIME OFF EVERY WEEK!
REALLY! WOW!

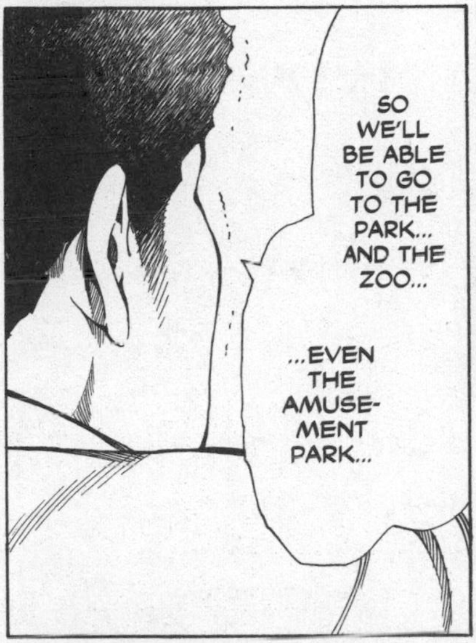
SO WE'LL BE ABLE TO GO TO THE PARK... AND THE ZOO...
...EVEN THE AMUSEMENT PARK...

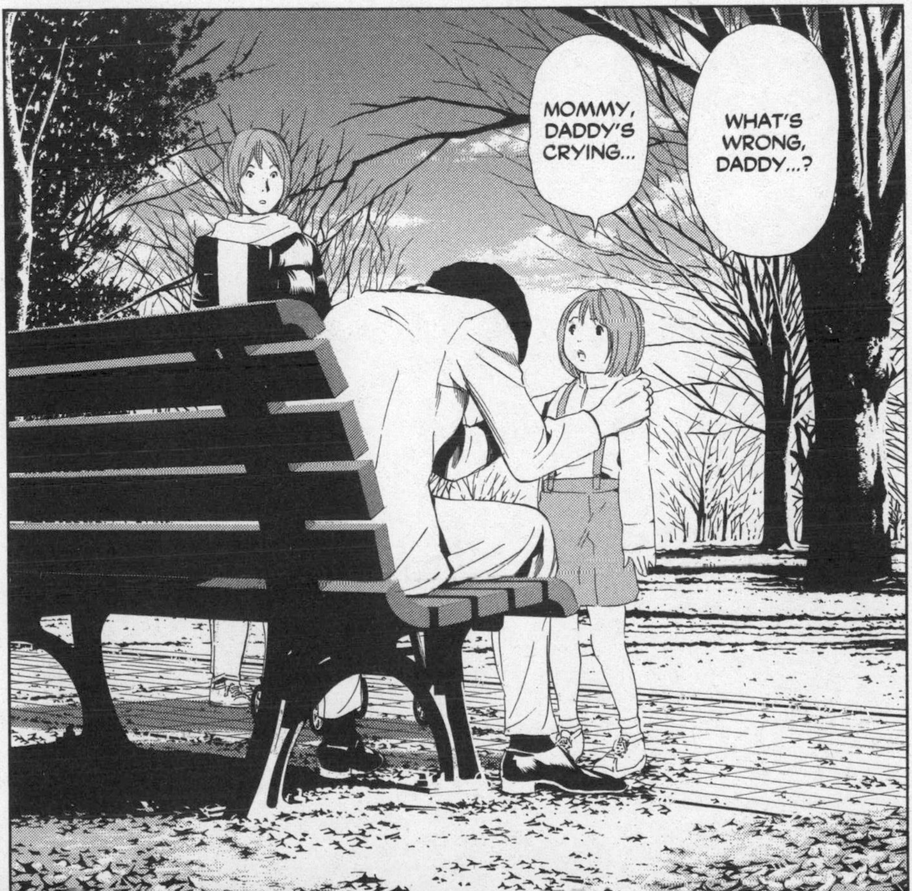
WHAT'S WRONG, DADDY...?
MOMMY, DADDY'S CRYING...

DEATH NOTE
How to use it
XXVIII

O If you write, "die of disease" like before with a specific disease's name, but without a specific time, if it takes more than 24 days for the human to die the 23-day rule will not take effect and the human will die at an adequate time depending on the disease.

病死とし、病名は書き死の時間指定をしない場合、
その病気で死ぬのに24日間以上かかる時は
「死の時間を操れるのは23日間」は適用されず、
その病気で死ぬのに適した時に死ぬ。

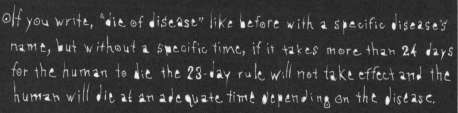

O When rewriting the cause and/or details of death it must be done within 6 minutes and 40 seconds. You cannot change the victim's time of death, however soon it may be.

上記の場合でも、死因や死の状況等を書き直せるのは6分40秒以内であり、
どんなに先の死であろうとその死の時間を動かす事はできない。

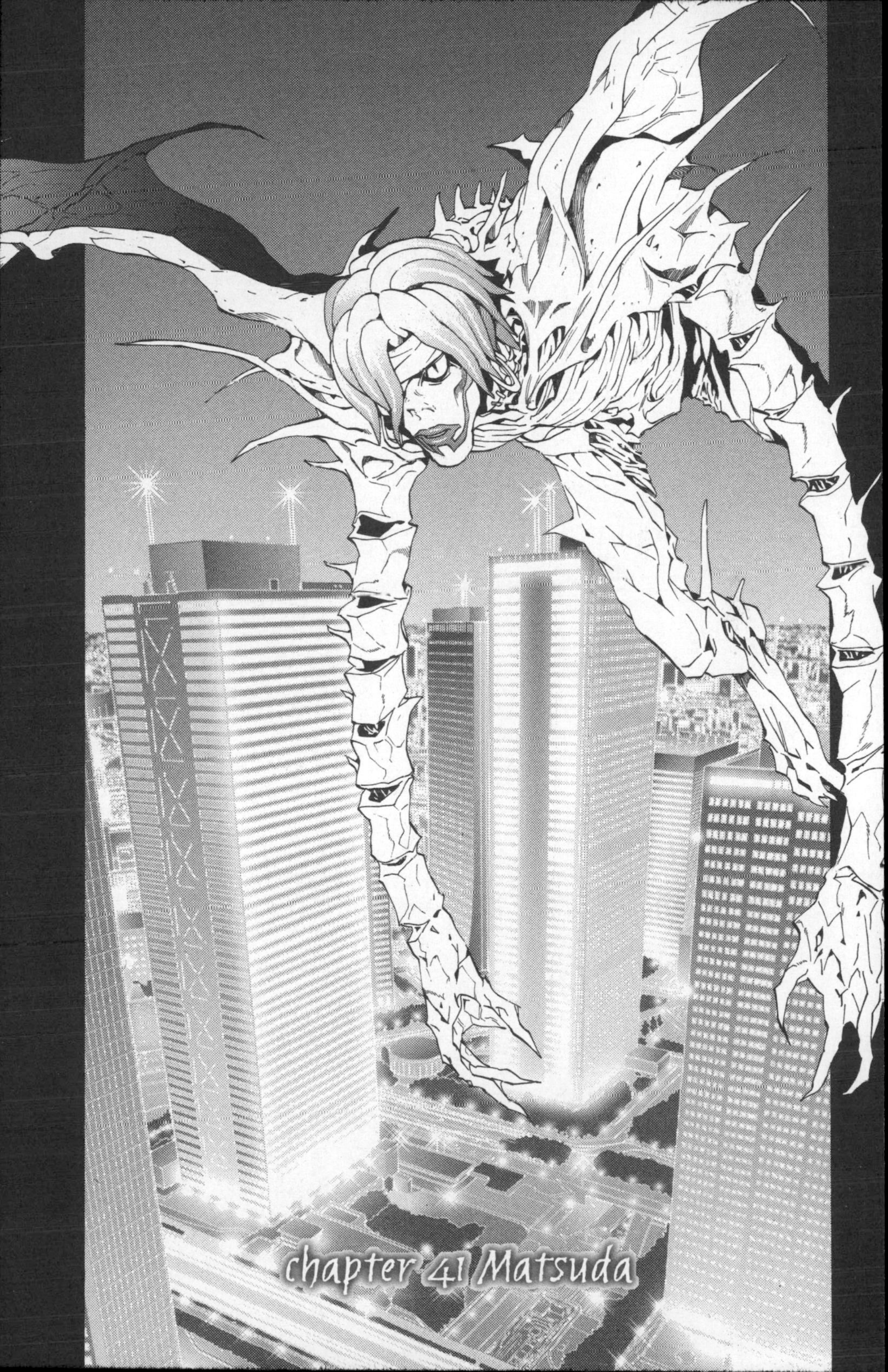
chapter 41 Matsuda

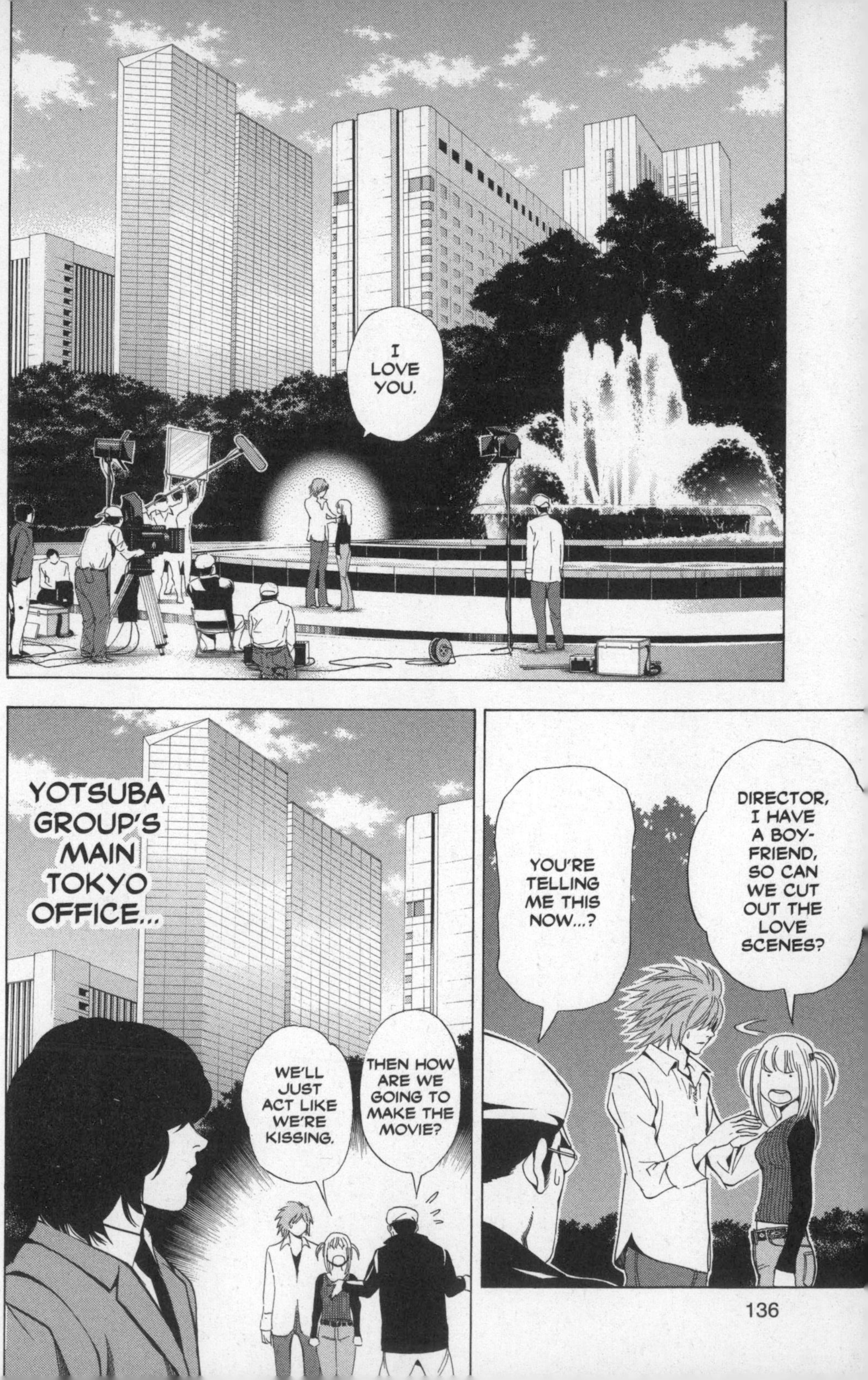
I LOVE YOU.
DIRECTOR, I HAVE A BOY-FRIEND, SO CAN WE CUT OUT THE LOVE SCENES?
YOU'RE TELLING ME THIS NOW...?
YOTSUBA GROUP'S MAIN TOKYO OFFICE...
THEN HOW ARE WE GOING TO MAKE THE MOVIE?
WE'LL JUST ACT LIKE WE'RE KISSING.

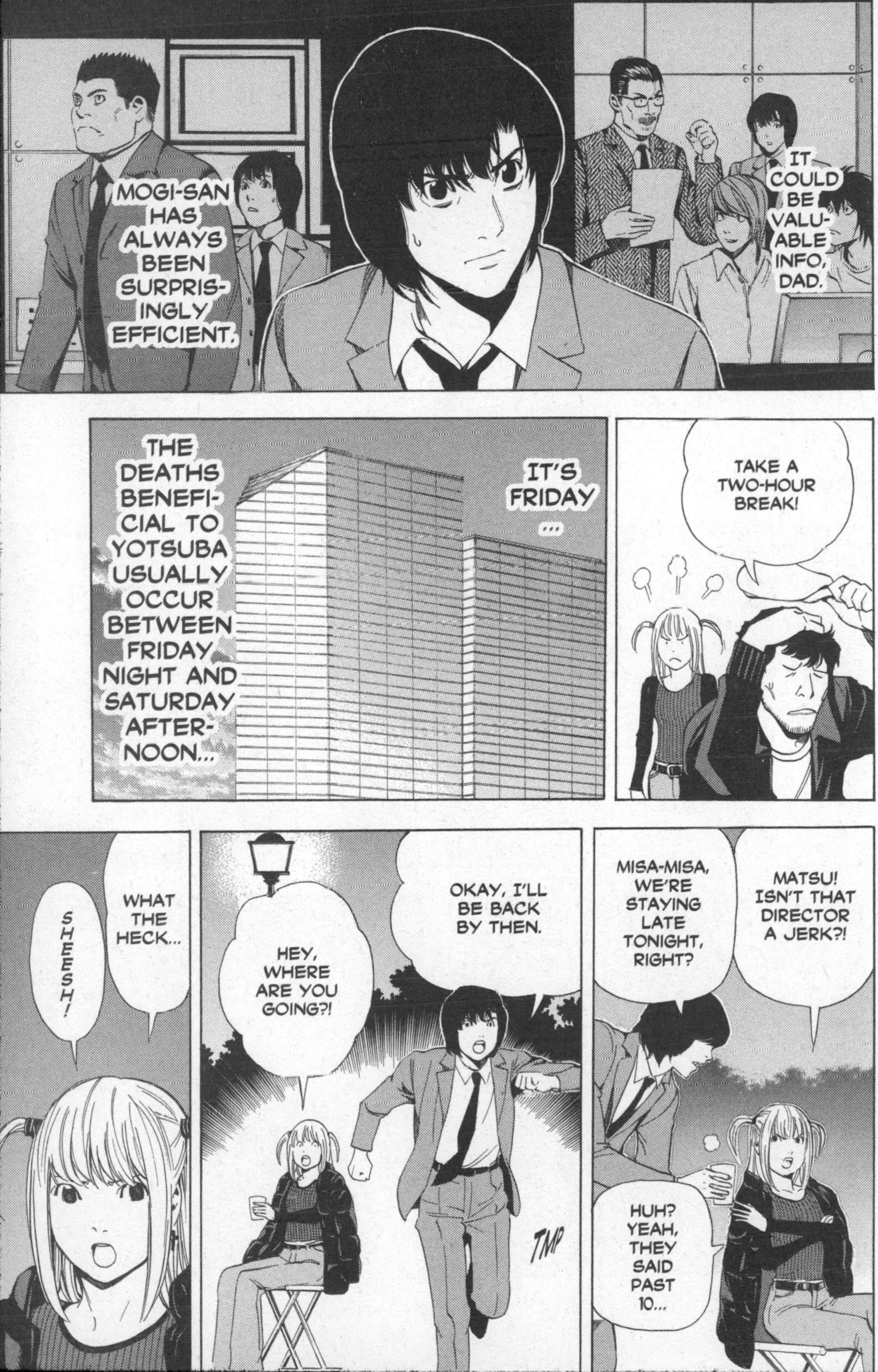
IT COULD BE VALUABLE INFO, DAD.
MOGI-SAN HAS ALWAYS BEEN SURPRISINGLY EFFICIENT.
TAKE A TWO-HOUR BREAK!
IT'S FRIDAY ...
THE DEATHS BENEFICIAL TO YOTSUBA USUALLY OCCUR BETWEEN FRIDAY NIGHT AND SATURDAY AFTERNOON...
MATSU! ISN'T THAT DIRECTOR A JERK?!
MISA-MISA, WE'RE STAYING LATE TONIGHT, RIGHT?
HUH? YEAH, THEY SAID PAST 10...
OKAY, I'LL BE BACK BY THEN.
HEY, WHERE ARE YOU GOING?!
TMP
WHAT THE HECK...
SHEESH!

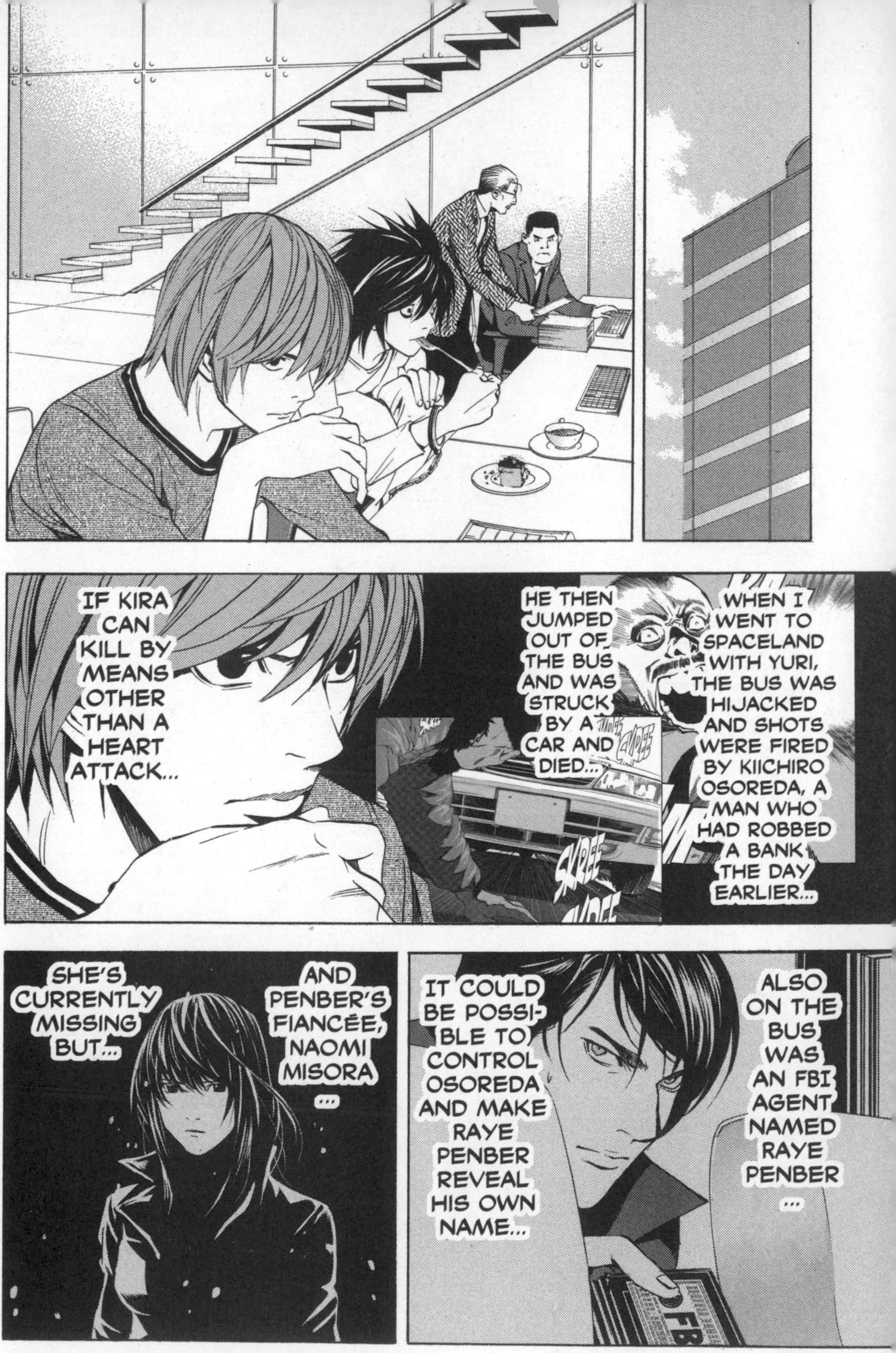
WHEN I WENT TO SPACELAND WITH YURI, THE BUS WAS HIJACKED AND SHOTS WERE FIRED BY KIICHIRO OSOREDA, A MAN WHO HAD ROBBED A BANK THE DAY EARLIER...
HE THEN JUMPED OUT OF THE BUS AND WAS STRUCK BY A CAR AND DIED...
IF KIRA CAN KILL BY MEANS OTHER THAN A HEART ATTACK...
ALSO ON THE BUS WAS AN FBI AGENT NAMED RAYE PENBER ...
IT COULD BE POSSIBLE TO CONTROL OSOREDA AND MAKE RAYE PENBER REVEAL HIS OWN NAME...
AND PENBER'S FIANCÉE, NAOMI MISORA ...
SHE'S CURRENTLY MISSING BUT...

READ THIS WAY

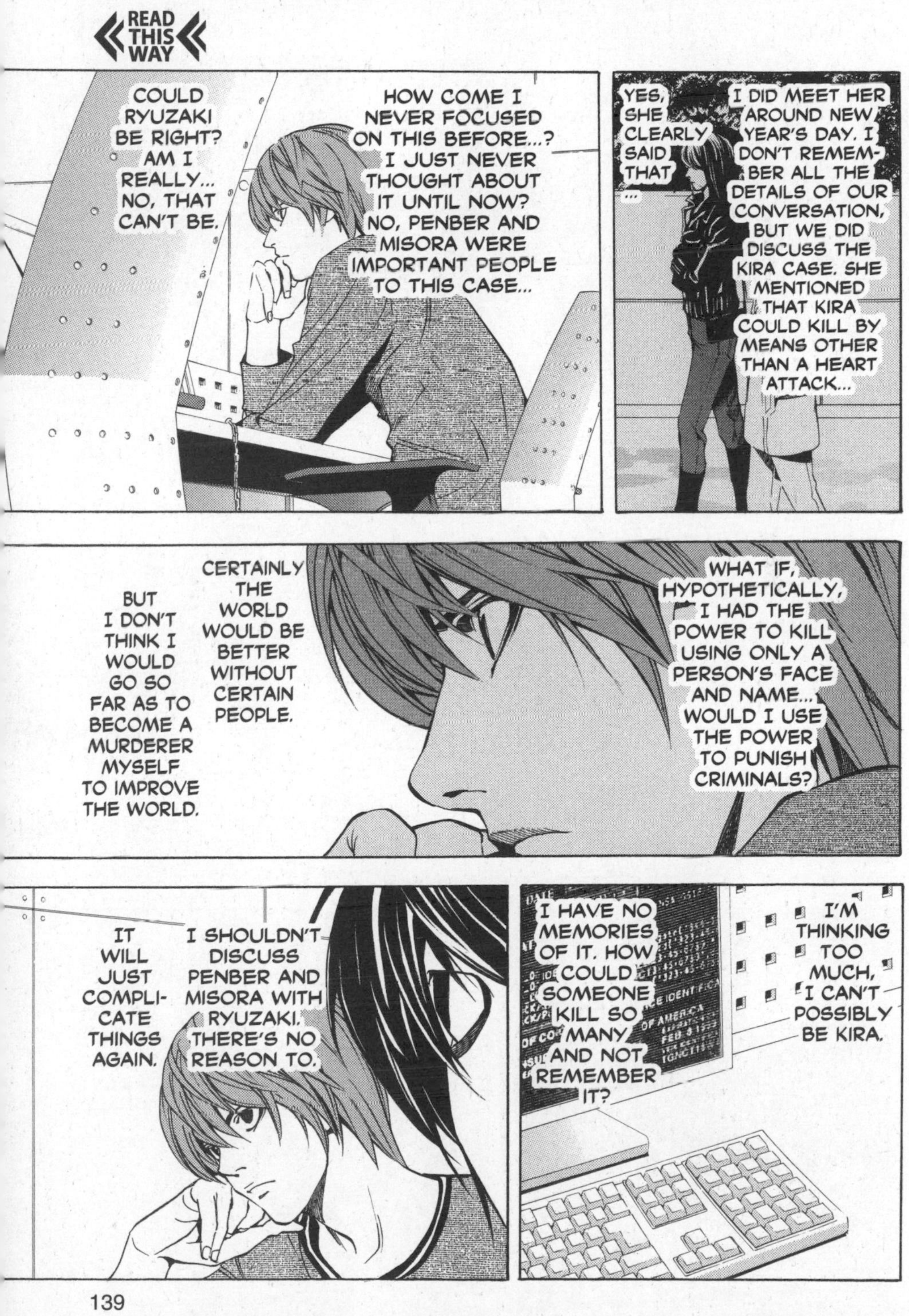

I DID MEET HER AROUND NEW YEAR'S DAY. I DON'T REMEMBER ALL THE DETAILS OF OUR CONVERSATION, BUT WE DID DISCUSS THE KIRA CASE. SHE MENTIONED THAT KIRA COULD KILL BY MEANS OTHER THAN A HEART ATTACK...
YES, SHE CLEARLY SAID THAT...
HOW COME I NEVER FOCUSED ON THIS BEFORE...? I JUST NEVER THOUGHT ABOUT IT UNTIL NOW? NO, PENBER AND MISORA WERE IMPORTANT PEOPLE TO THIS CASE...
COULD RYUZAKI BE RIGHT? AM I REALLY... NO, THAT CAN'T BE.
WHAT IF, HYPOTHETICALLY, I HAD THE POWER TO KILL USING ONLY A PERSON'S FACE AND NAME... WOULD I USE THE POWER TO PUNISH CRIMINALS?
CERTAINLY THE WORLD WOULD BE BETTER WITHOUT CERTAIN PEOPLE.
BUT I DON'T THINK I WOULD GO SO FAR AS TO BECOME A MURDERER MYSELF TO IMPROVE THE WORLD.
I'M THINKING TOO MUCH, I CAN'T POSSIBLY BE KIRA.
I HAVE NO MEMORIES OF IT. HOW COULD SOMEONE KILL SO MANY AND NOT REMEMBER IT?
I SHOULDN'T DISCUSS PENBER AND MISORA WITH RYUZAKI. THERE'S NO REASON TO.
IT WILL JUST COMPLICATE THINGS AGAIN.

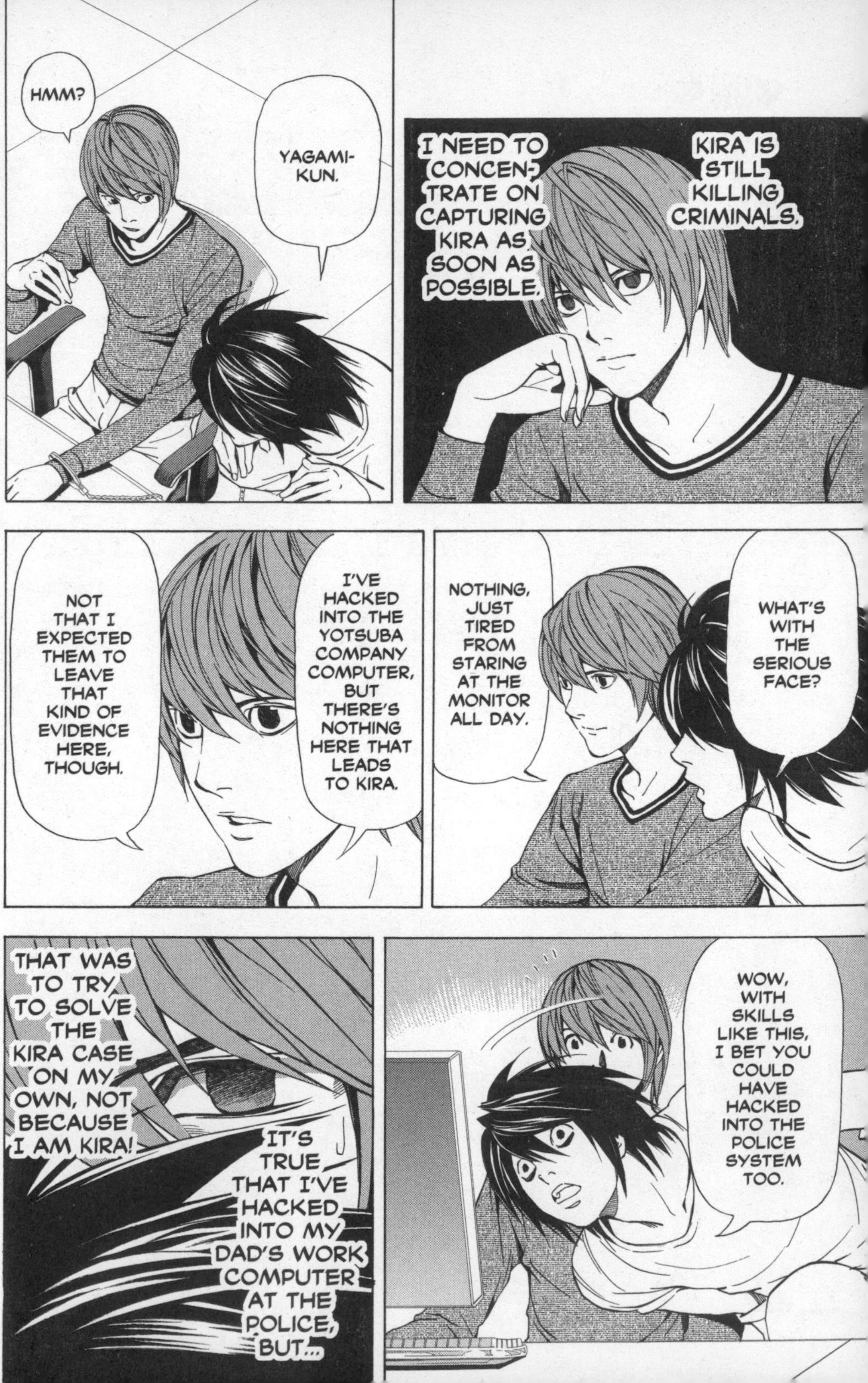
KIRA IS STILL KILLING CRIMINALS.
I NEED TO CONCENTRATE ON CAPTURING KIRA AS SOON AS POSSIBLE.
YAGAMI-KUN.
HMM?
WHAT'S WITH THE SERIOUS FACE?
NOTHING, JUST TIRED FROM STARING AT THE MONITOR ALL DAY.
I'VE HACKED INTO THE YOTSUBA COMPANY COMPUTER, BUT THERE'S NOTHING HERE THAT LEADS TO KIRA.
NOT THAT I EXPECTED THEM TO LEAVE THAT KIND OF EVIDENCE HERE, THOUGH.
WOW, WITH SKILLS LIKE THIS, I BET YOU COULD HAVE HACKED INTO THE POLICE SYSTEM TOO.
IT'S TRUE THAT I'VE HACKED INTO MY DAD'S WORK COMPUTER AT THE POLICE, BUT...
THAT WAS TO TRY TO SOLVE THE KIRA CASE ON MY OWN, NOT BECAUSE I AM KIRA!

READ THIS WAY

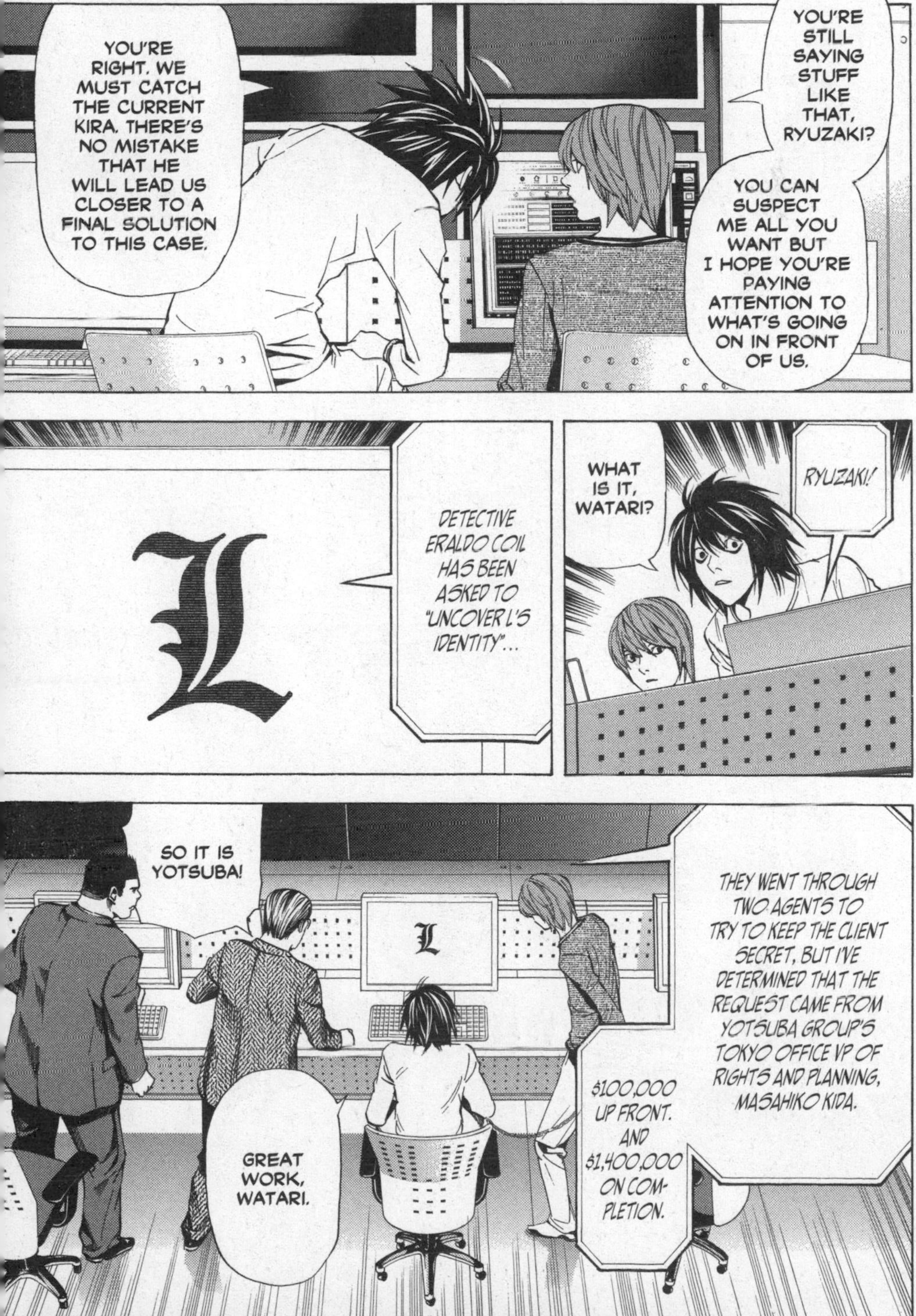
YOU'RE STILL SAYING STUFF LIKE THAT, RYUZAKI?
YOU CAN SUSPECT ME ALL YOU WANT BUT I HOPE YOU'RE PAYING ATTENTION TO WHAT'S GOING ON IN FRONT OF US.
YOU'RE RIGHT. WE MUST CATCH THE CURRENT KIRA. THERE'S NO MISTAKE THAT HE WILL LEAD US CLOSER TO A FINAL SOLUTION TO THIS CASE.
RYUZAKI!
WHAT IS IT, WATARI?
DETECTIVE ERALDO COIL HAS BEEN ASKED TO "UNCOVER L'S IDENTITY"...
THEY WENT THROUGH TWO AGENTS TO TRY TO KEEP THE CLIENT SECRET, BUT I'VE DETERMINED THAT THE REQUEST CAME FROM YOTSUBA GROUP'S TOKYO OFFICE VP OF RIGHTS AND PLANNING, MASAHIKO KIDA.
$100,000 UP FRONT. AND $1,400,000 ON COM-PLETION.
SO IT IS YOTSUBA!
GREAT WORK, WATARI.

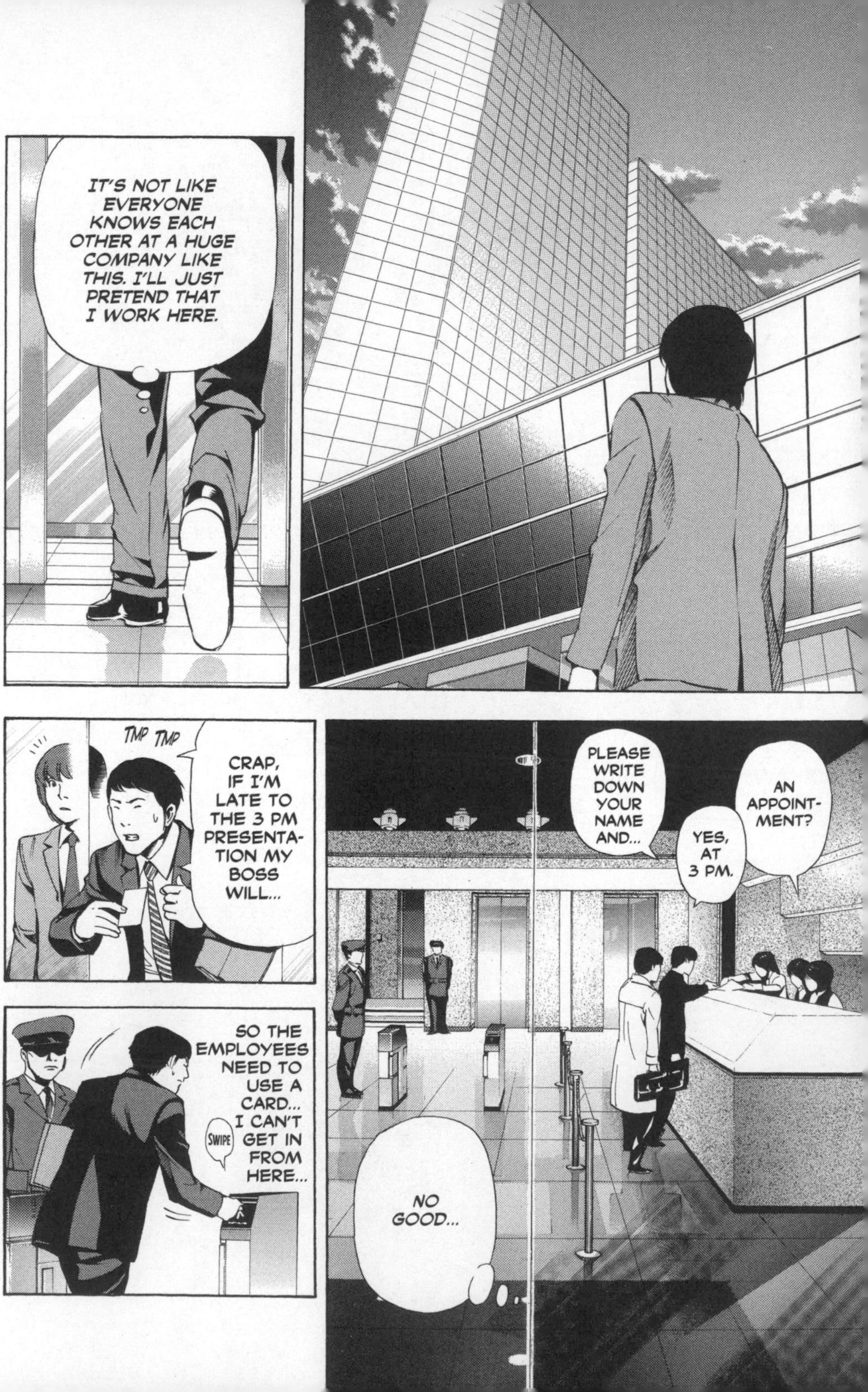
IT'S NOT LIKE EVERYONE KNOWS EACH OTHER AT A HUGE COMPANY LIKE THIS. I'LL JUST PRETEND THAT I WORK HERE.
AN APPOINTMENT?
YES, AT 3 PM.
PLEASE WRITE DOWN YOUR NAME AND...
NO GOOD...
TMP TMP
CRAP, IF I'M LATE TO THE 3 PM PRESENTATION MY BOSS WILL...
SO THE EMPLOYEES NEED TO USE A CARD... I CAN'T GET IN FROM HERE...
SWIPE

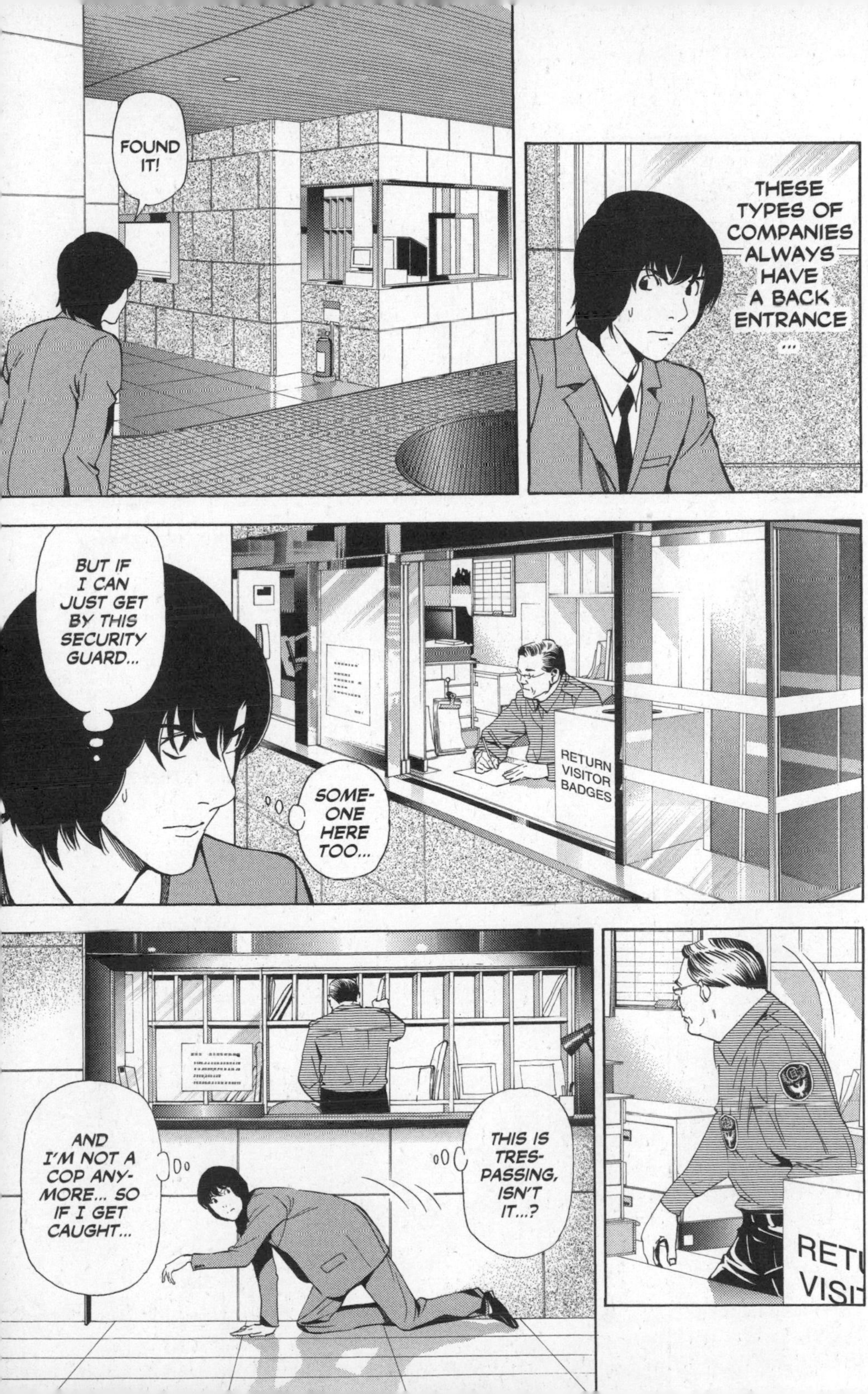
THESE TYPES OF COMPANIES ALWAYS HAVE A BACK ENTRANCE ...
FOUND IT!
SOME-ONE HERE TOO...
BUT IF I CAN JUST GET BY THIS SECURITY GUARD...
RETURN VISITOR BADGES
RETU VISIT
THIS IS TRES-PASSING, ISN'T IT...?
AND I'M NOT A COP ANY-MORE... SO IF I GET CAUGHT...

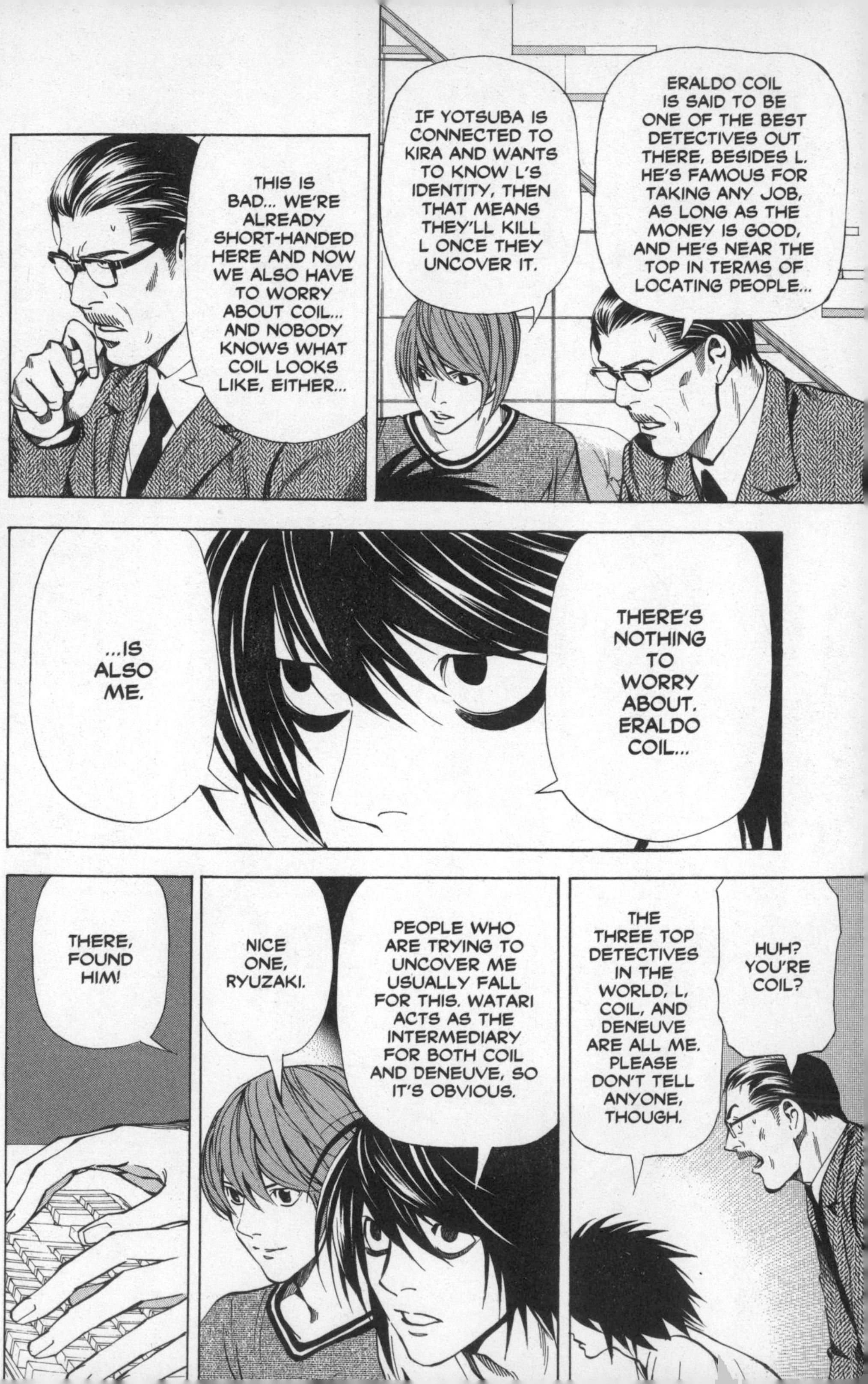
ERALDO COIL IS SAID TO BE ONE OF THE BEST DETECTIVES OUT THERE, BESIDES L. HE'S FAMOUS FOR TAKING ANY JOB, AS LONG AS THE MONEY IS GOOD, AND HE'S NEAR THE TOP IN TERMS OF LOCATING PEOPLE...
IF YOTSUBA IS CONNECTED TO KIRA AND WANTS TO KNOW L'S IDENTITY, THEN THAT MEANS THEY'LL KILL L ONCE THEY UNCOVER IT.
THIS IS BAD... WE'RE ALREADY SHORT-HANDED HERE AND NOW WE ALSO HAVE TO WORRY ABOUT COIL... AND NOBODY KNOWS WHAT COIL LOOKS LIKE, EITHER...
THERE'S NOTHING TO WORRY ABOUT. ERALDO COIL...
...IS ALSO ME.
HUH? YOU'RE COIL?
THE THREE TOP DETECTIVES IN THE WORLD, L, COIL, AND DENEUVE ARE ALL ME. PLEASE DON'T TELL ANYONE, THOUGH.
PEOPLE WHO ARE TRYING TO UNCOVER ME USUALLY FALL FOR THIS. WATARI ACTS AS THE INTERMEDIARY FOR BOTH COIL AND DENEUVE, SO IT'S OBVIOUS.
NICE ONE, RYUZAKI.
THERE, FOUND HIM!

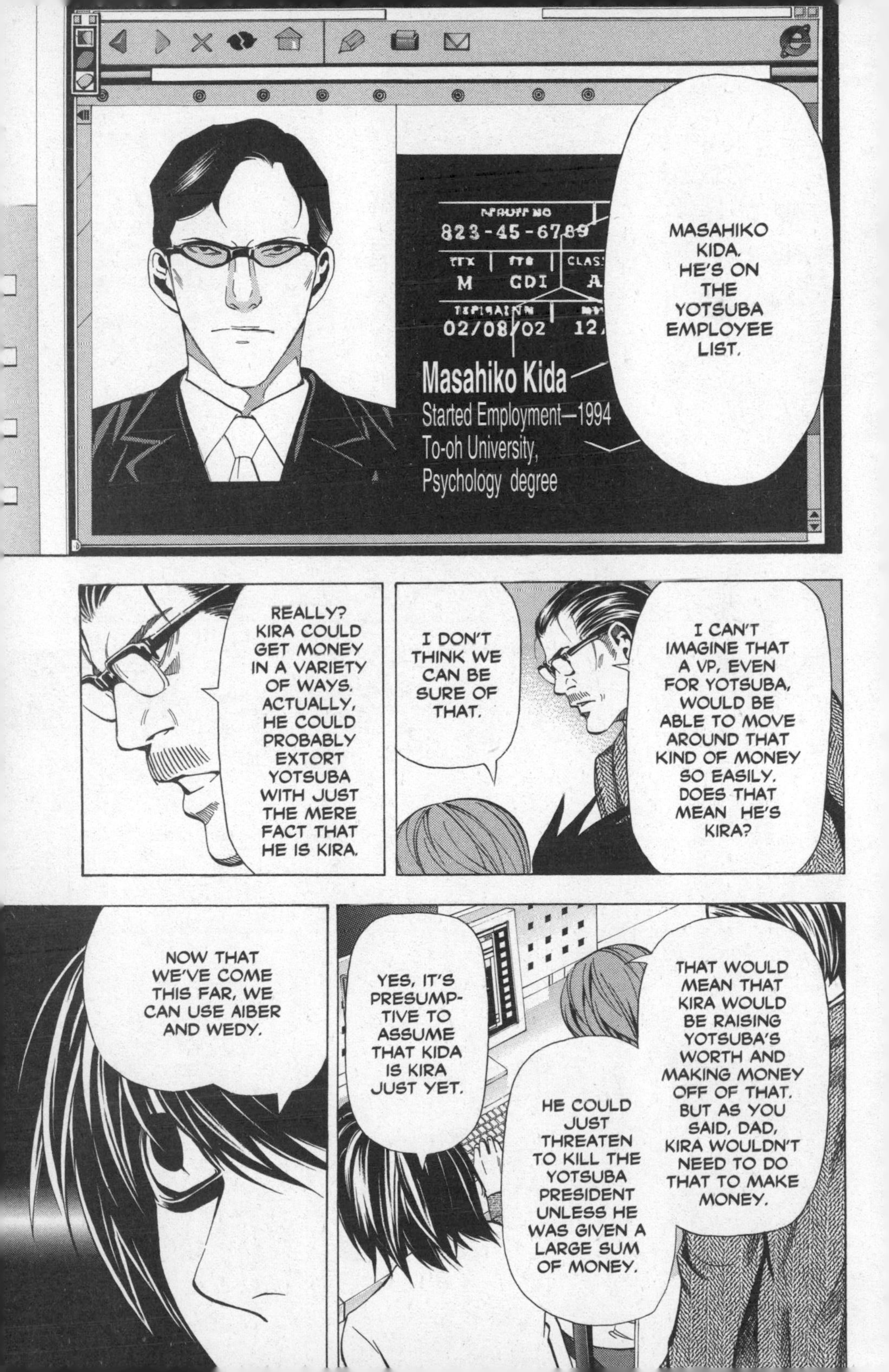
823-45-6789
M
GDI
02/08/02
Masahiko Kida
Started Employment—1994
To-oh University,
Psychology degree
MASAHIKO KIDA. HE'S ON THE YOTSUBA EMPLOYEE LIST.
I CAN'T IMAGINE THAT A VP, EVEN FOR YOTSUBA, WOULD BE ABLE TO MOVE AROUND THAT KIND OF MONEY SO EASILY. DOES THAT MEAN HE'S KIRA?
I DON'T THINK WE CAN BE SURE OF THAT.
REALLY? KIRA COULD GET MONEY IN A VARIETY OF WAYS. ACTUALLY, HE COULD PROBABLY EXTORT YOTSUBA WITH JUST THE MERE FACT THAT HE IS KIRA.
THAT WOULD MEAN THAT KIRA WOULD BE RAISING YOTSUBA'S WORTH AND MAKING MONEY OFF OF THAT. BUT AS YOU SAID, DAD, KIRA WOULDN'T NEED TO DO THAT TO MAKE MONEY.
HE COULD JUST THREATEN TO KILL THE YOTSUBA PRESIDENT UNLESS HE WAS GIVEN A LARGE SUM OF MONEY.
YES, IT'S PRESUMP-TIVE TO ASSUME THAT KIDA IS KIRA JUST YET.
NOW THAT WE'VE COME THIS FAR, WE CAN USE AIBER AND WEDY.

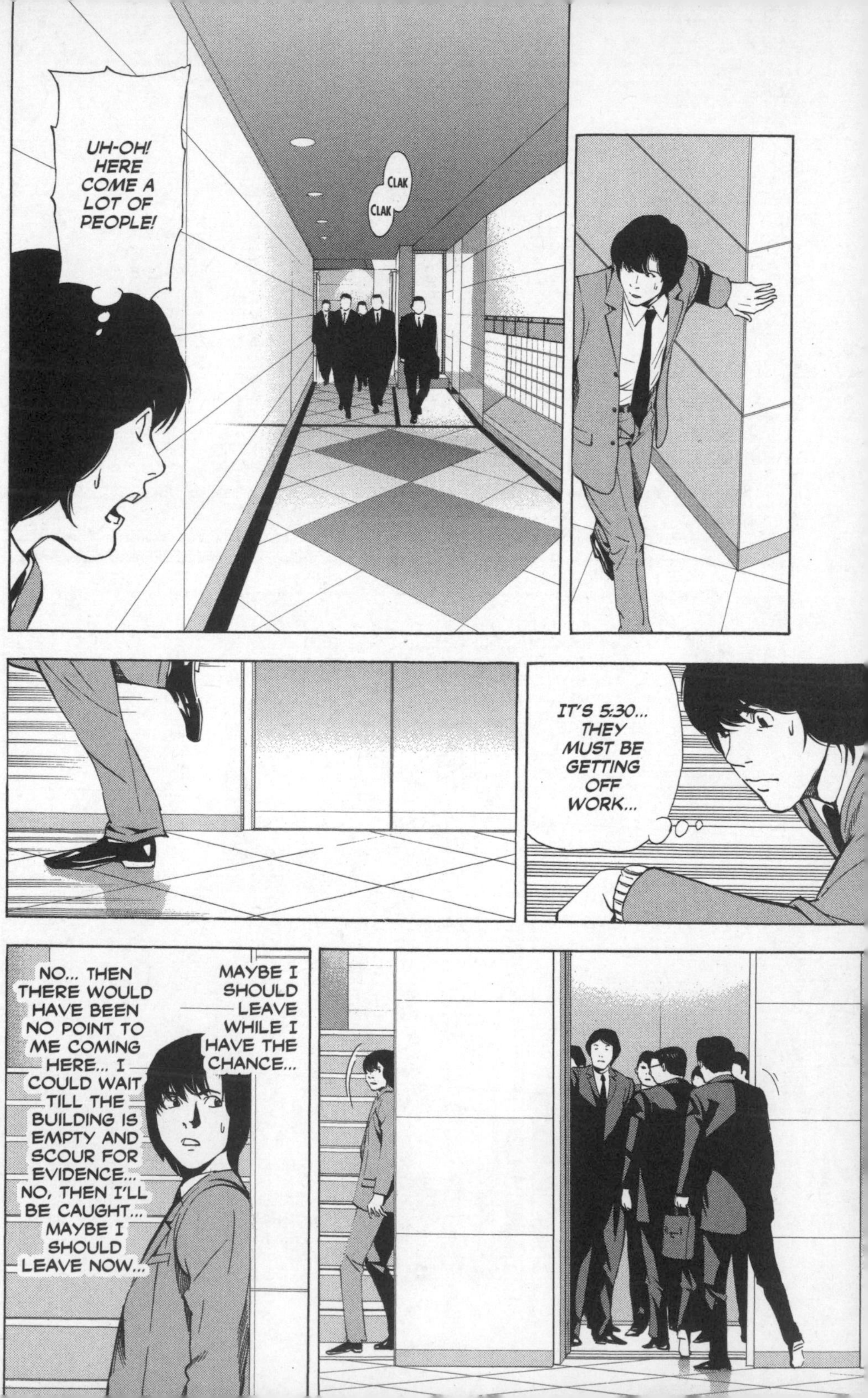
CLAK
CLAK
UH-OH! HERE COME A LOT OF PEOPLE!
IT'S 5:30... THEY MUST BE GETTING OFF WORK...
MAYBE I SHOULD LEAVE WHILE I HAVE THE CHANCE...
NO... THEN THERE WOULD HAVE BEEN NO POINT TO ME COMING HERE... I COULD WAIT TILL THE BUILDING IS EMPTY AND SCOUR FOR EVIDENCE... NO, THEN I'LL BE CAUGHT... MAYBE I SHOULD LEAVE NOW...

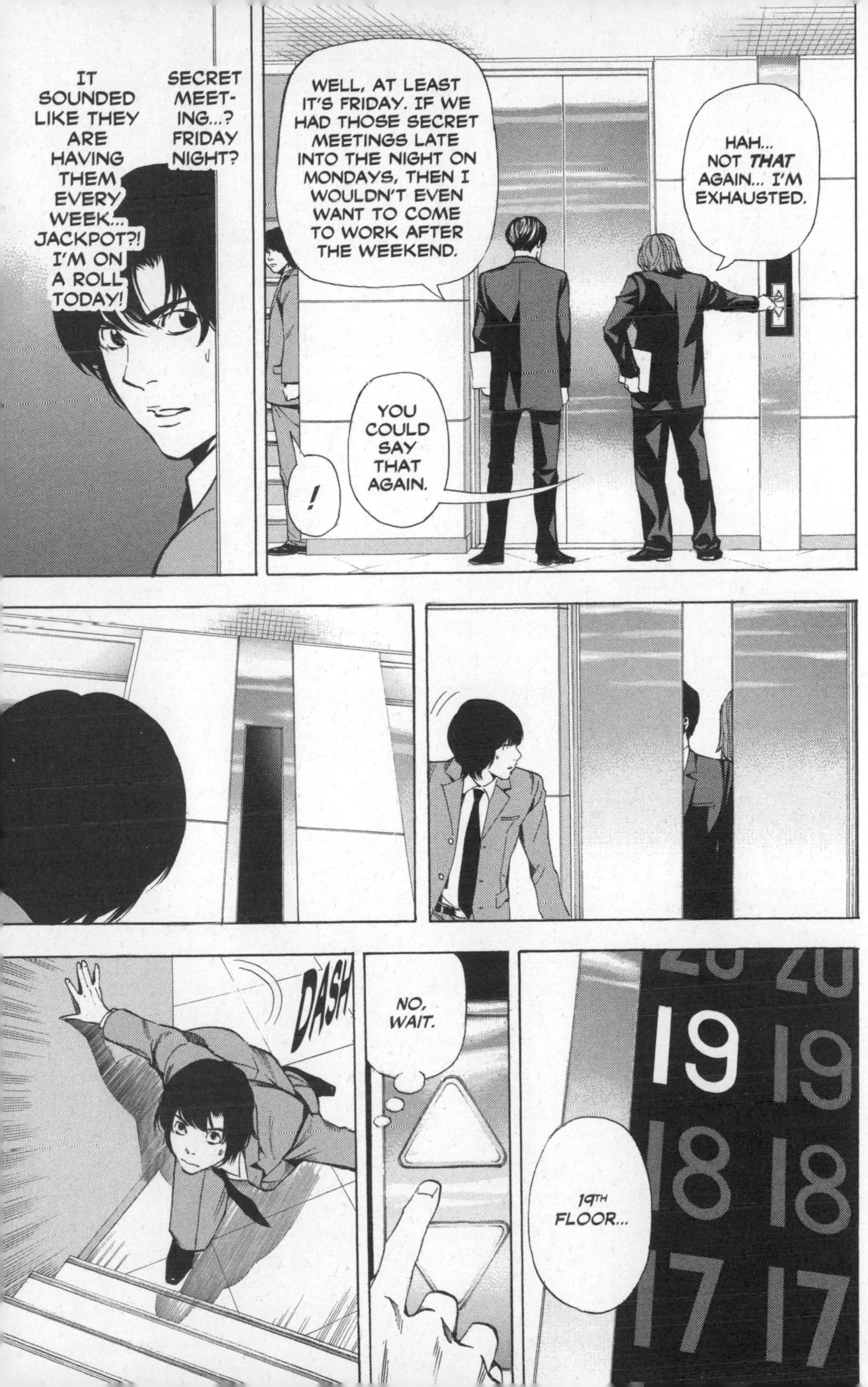
HAH... NOT THAT AGAIN... I'M EXHAUSTED.
WELL, AT LEAST IT'S FRIDAY. IF WE HAD THOSE SECRET MEETINGS LATE INTO THE NIGHT ON MONDAYS, THEN I WOULDN'T EVEN WANT TO COME TO WORK AFTER THE WEEKEND.
YOU COULD SAY THAT AGAIN.
!
SECRET MEETING...? FRIDAY NIGHT?
IT SOUNDED LIKE THEY ARE HAVING THEM EVERY WEEK... JACKPOT?! I'M ON A ROLL TODAY!
19TH FLOOR...
NO, WAIT.
DASH

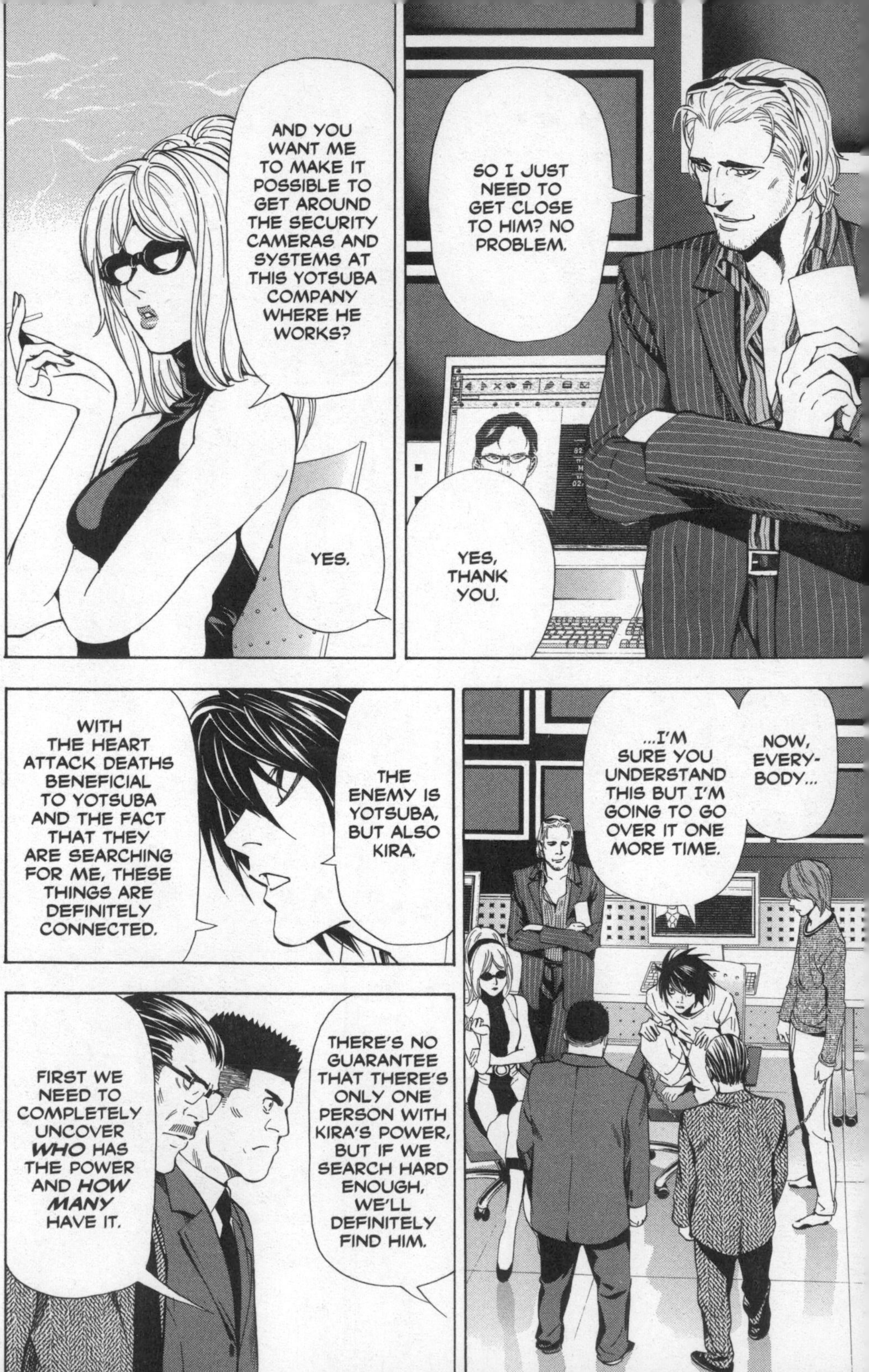

SO I JUST NEED TO GET CLOSE TO HIM? NO PROBLEM.
YES, THANK YOU.
AND YOU WANT ME TO MAKE IT POSSIBLE TO GET AROUND THE SECURITY CAMERAS AND SYSTEMS AT THIS YOTSUBA COMPANY WHERE HE WORKS?
YES.
NOW, EVERY-BODY...
...I'M SURE YOU UNDERSTAND THIS BUT I'M GOING TO GO OVER IT ONE MORE TIME.
THE ENEMY IS YOTSUBA, BUT ALSO KIRA.
WITH THE HEART ATTACK DEATHS BENEFICIAL TO YOTSUBA AND THE FACT THAT THEY ARE SEARCHING FOR ME, THESE THINGS ARE DEFINITELY CONNECTED.
THERE'S NO GUARANTEE THAT THERE'S ONLY ONE PERSON WITH KIRA'S POWER, BUT IF WE SEARCH HARD ENOUGH, WE'LL DEFINITELY FIND HIM.
FIRST WE NEED TO COMPLETELY UNCOVER *WHO* HAS THE POWER AND *HOW MANY* HAVE IT.

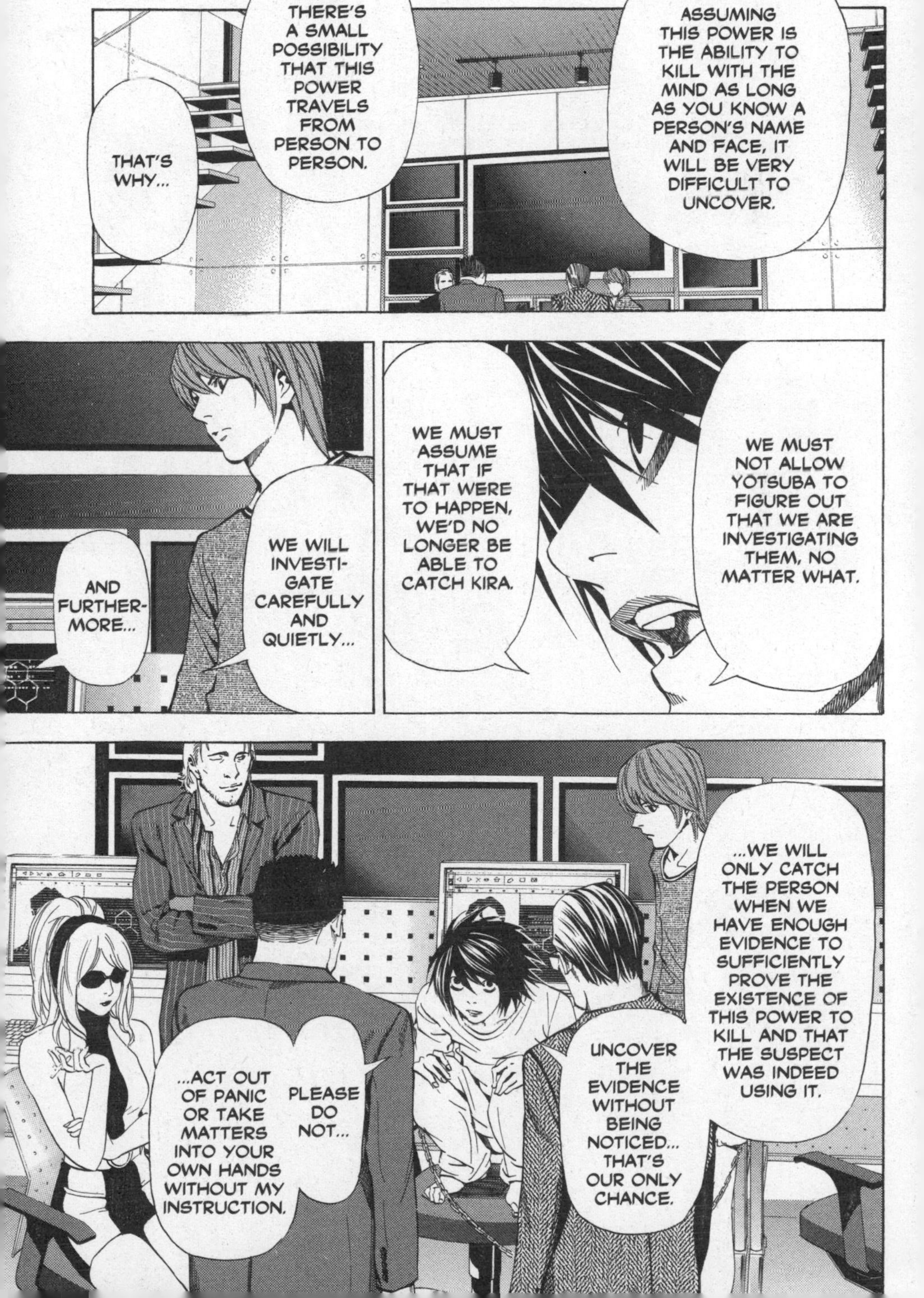
ASSUMING THIS POWER IS THE ABILITY TO KILL WITH THE MIND AS LONG AS YOU KNOW A PERSON'S NAME AND FACE, IT WILL BE VERY DIFFICULT TO UNCOVER.
AND THERE'S A SMALL POSSIBILITY THAT THIS POWER TRAVELS FROM PERSON TO PERSON.
THAT'S WHY...
WE MUST NOT ALLOW YOTSUBA TO FIGURE OUT THAT WE ARE INVESTIGATING THEM, NO MATTER WHAT.
WE MUST ASSUME THAT IF THAT WERE TO HAPPEN, WE'D NO LONGER BE ABLE TO CATCH KIRA.
WE WILL INVESTI-GATE CAREFULLY AND QUIETLY...
AND FURTHER-MORE...
...WE WILL ONLY CATCH THE PERSON WHEN WE HAVE ENOUGH EVIDENCE TO SUFFICIENTLY PROVE THE EXISTENCE OF THIS POWER TO KILL AND THAT THE SUSPECT WAS INDEED USING IT.
UNCOVER THE EVIDENCE WITHOUT BEING NOTICED... THAT'S OUR ONLY CHANCE.
PLEASE DO NOT...
...ACT OUT OF PANIC OR TAKE MATTERS INTO YOUR OWN HANDS WITHOUT MY INSTRUCTION.

HUFF

HUFF

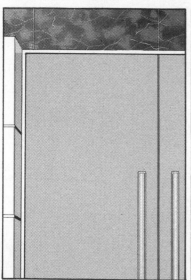

THAT MUST BE THE ROOM!

SOO...

READ THIS WAY

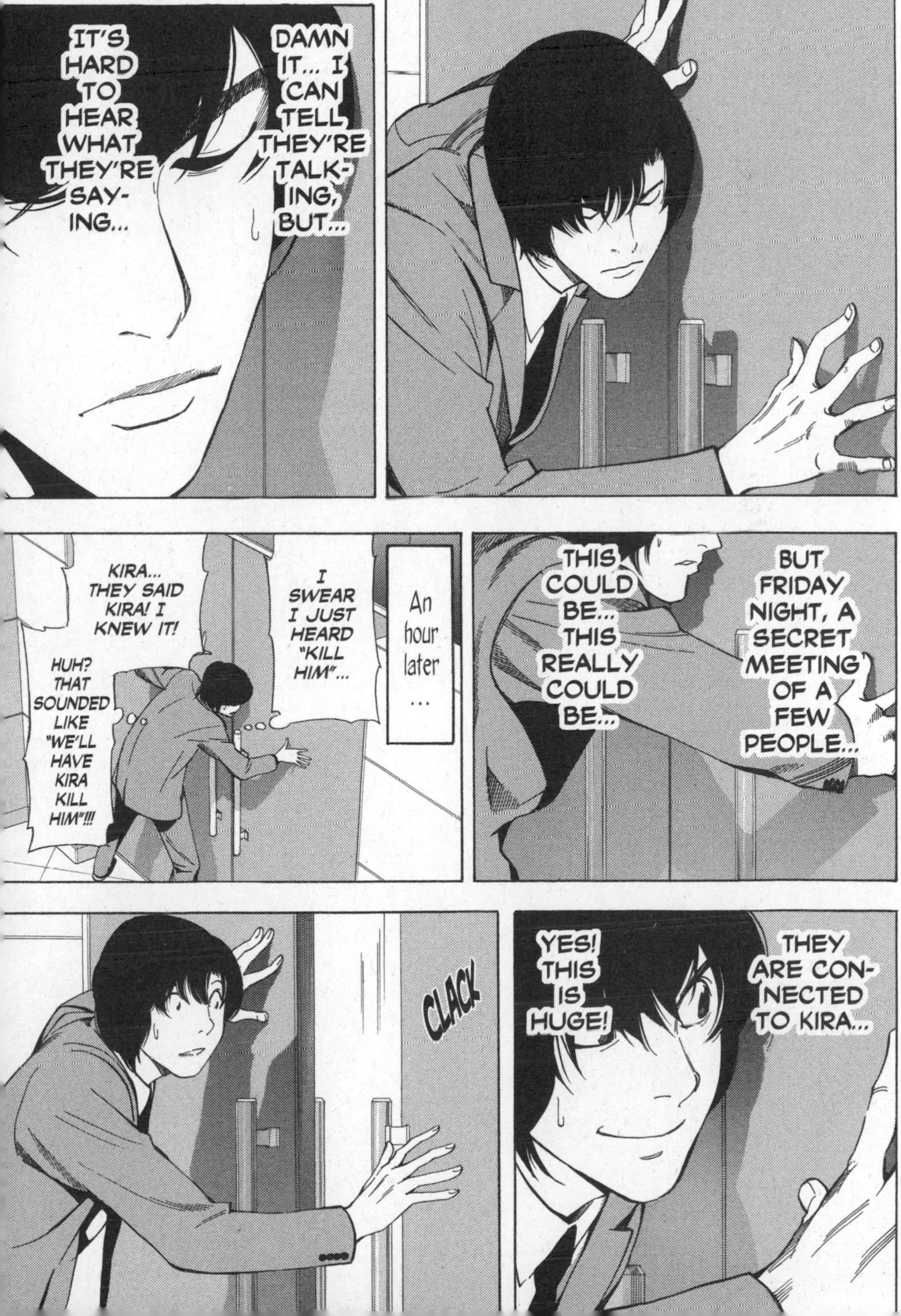
DAMN IT... I CAN TELL THEY'RE TALKING, BUT...
IT'S HARD TO HEAR WHAT THEY'RE SAYING...
BUT FRIDAY NIGHT, A SECRET MEETING OF A FEW PEOPLE...
THIS COULD BE... THIS REALLY COULD BE...
An hour later...
I SWEAR I JUST HEARD "KILL HIM"...
KIRA... THEY SAID KIRA! I KNEW IT!
HUH? THAT SOUNDED LIKE "WE'LL HAVE KIRA KILL HIM"!!!
THEY ARE CONNECTED TO KIRA...
YES! THIS IS HUGE!
CLACK

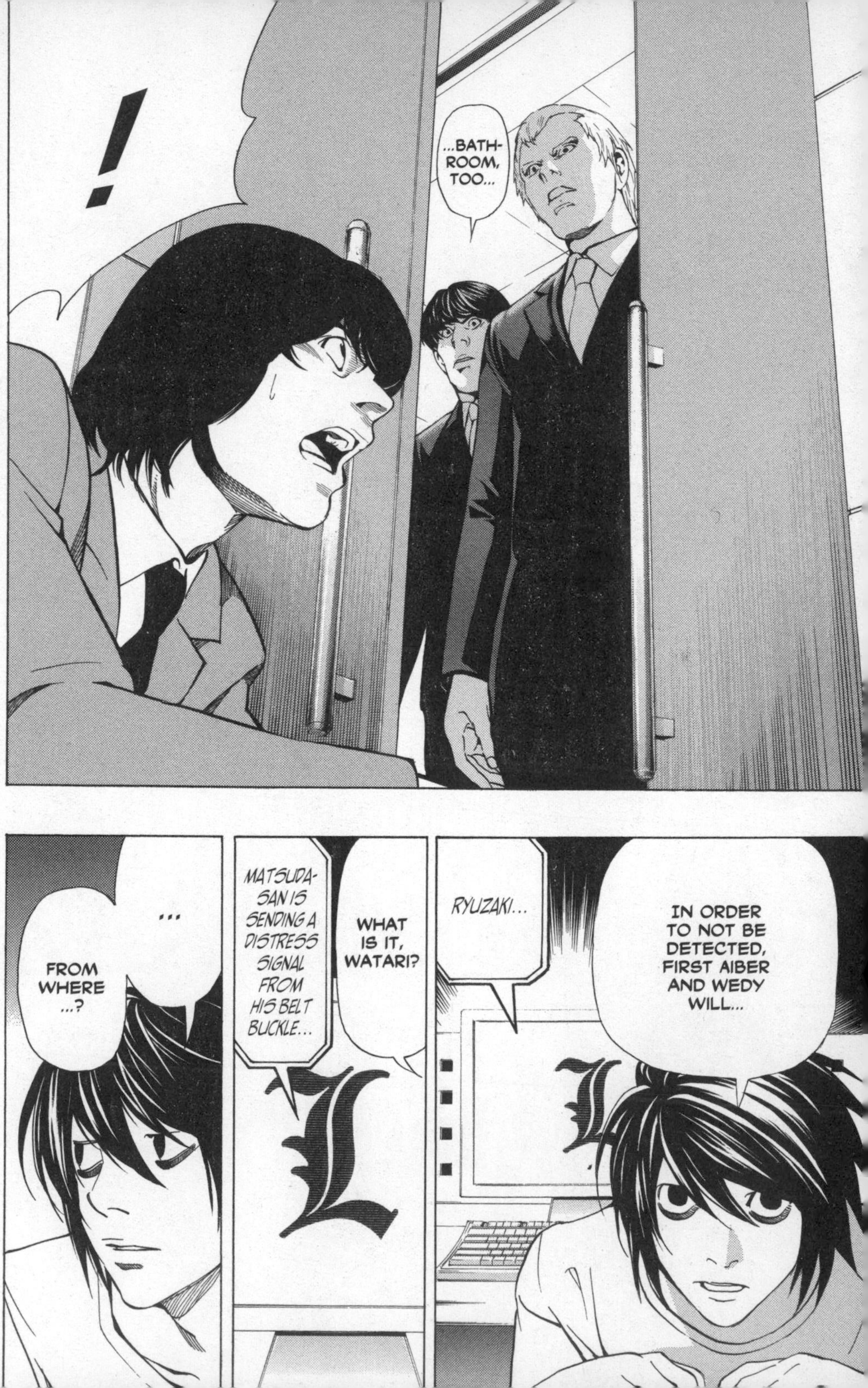
...BATH-
ROOM,
TOO...
!
IN ORDER TO NOT BE DETECTED, FIRST AIBER AND WEDY WILL...
RYUZAKI...
WHAT IS IT, WATARI?
MATSUDA-SAN IS SENDING A DISTRESS SIGNAL FROM HIS BELT BUCKLE...
...
FROM WHERE ...?

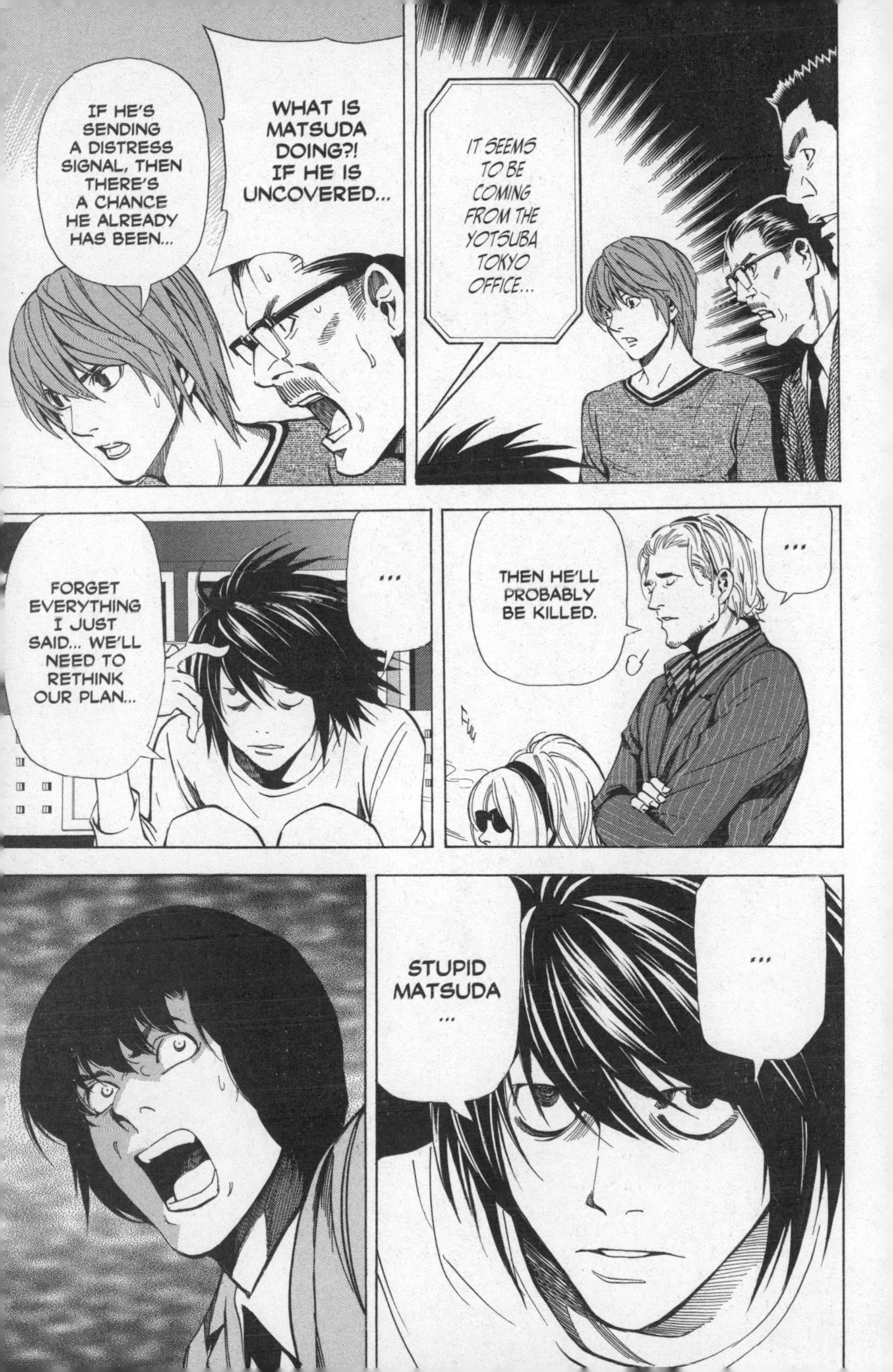
IT SEEMS TO BE COMING FROM THE YOTSUBA TOKYO OFFICE...
WHAT IS MATSUDA DOING?! IF HE IS UNCOVERED...
IF HE'S SENDING A DISTRESS SIGNAL, THEN THERE'S A CHANCE HE ALREADY HAS BEEN...
...
THEN HE'LL PROBABLY BE KILLED.
Fuu
...
FORGET EVERYTHING I JUST SAID... WE'LL NEED TO RETHINK OUR PLAN...
...
STUPID MATSUDA ...

DEATH NOTE
HOW to USE it
XXIX

⊙ You cannot kill humans at the age of 124 and over with the DEATH NOTE.

にんげんかいたんい さいいじょう にんげん ころ こと
人間界単位で124歳以上の人間をデスノートで殺す事はできない。

⊙ You cannot kill humans with less than 12 minutes of life left
(in human calculations).

のこ じゅみょう にんげんかいたんい ふんいか にんげん ころ こと
残りの寿命が人間界単位で12分以下の人間はデスノートで殺す事はできない。

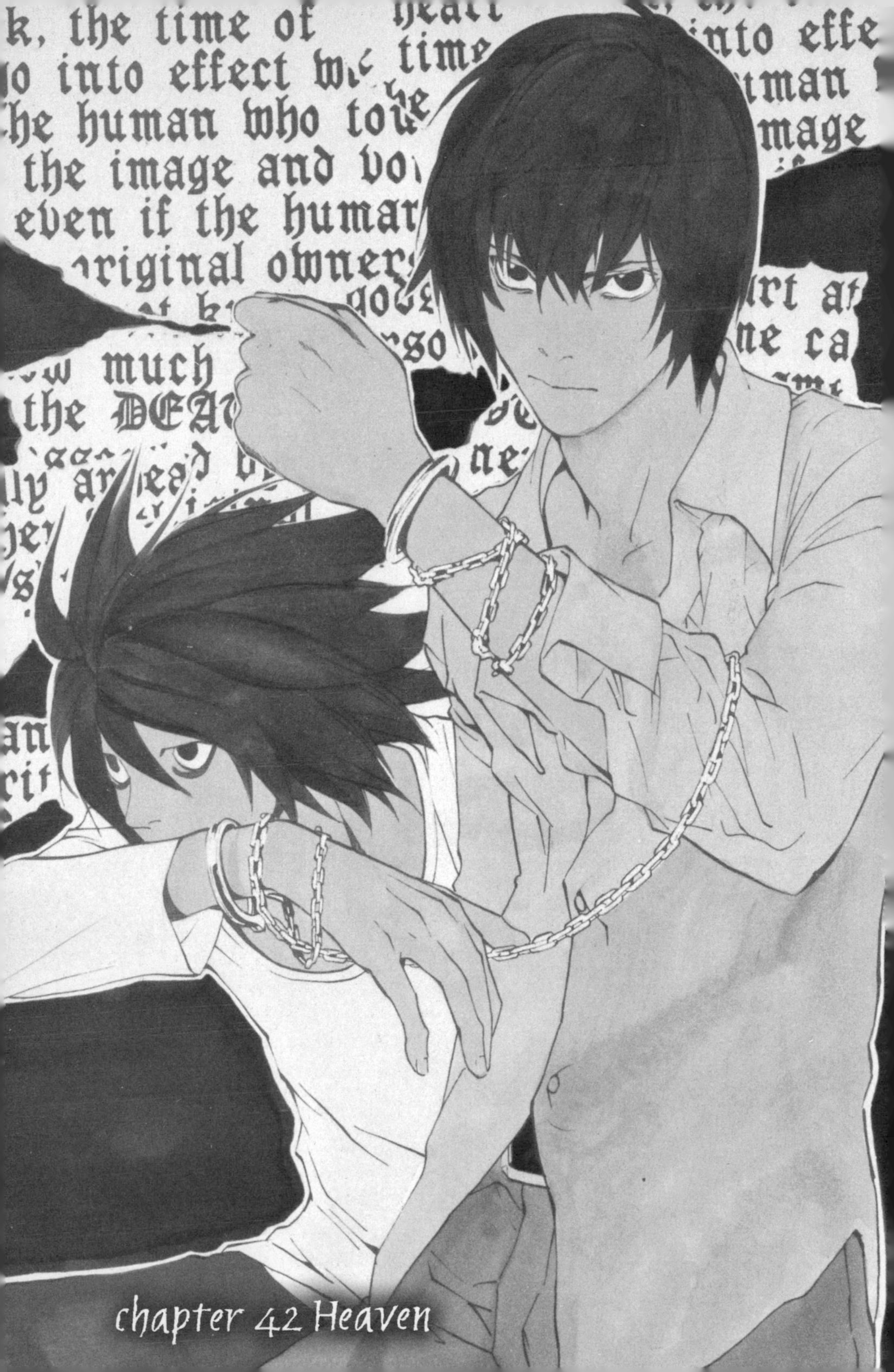

chapter 42 Heaven

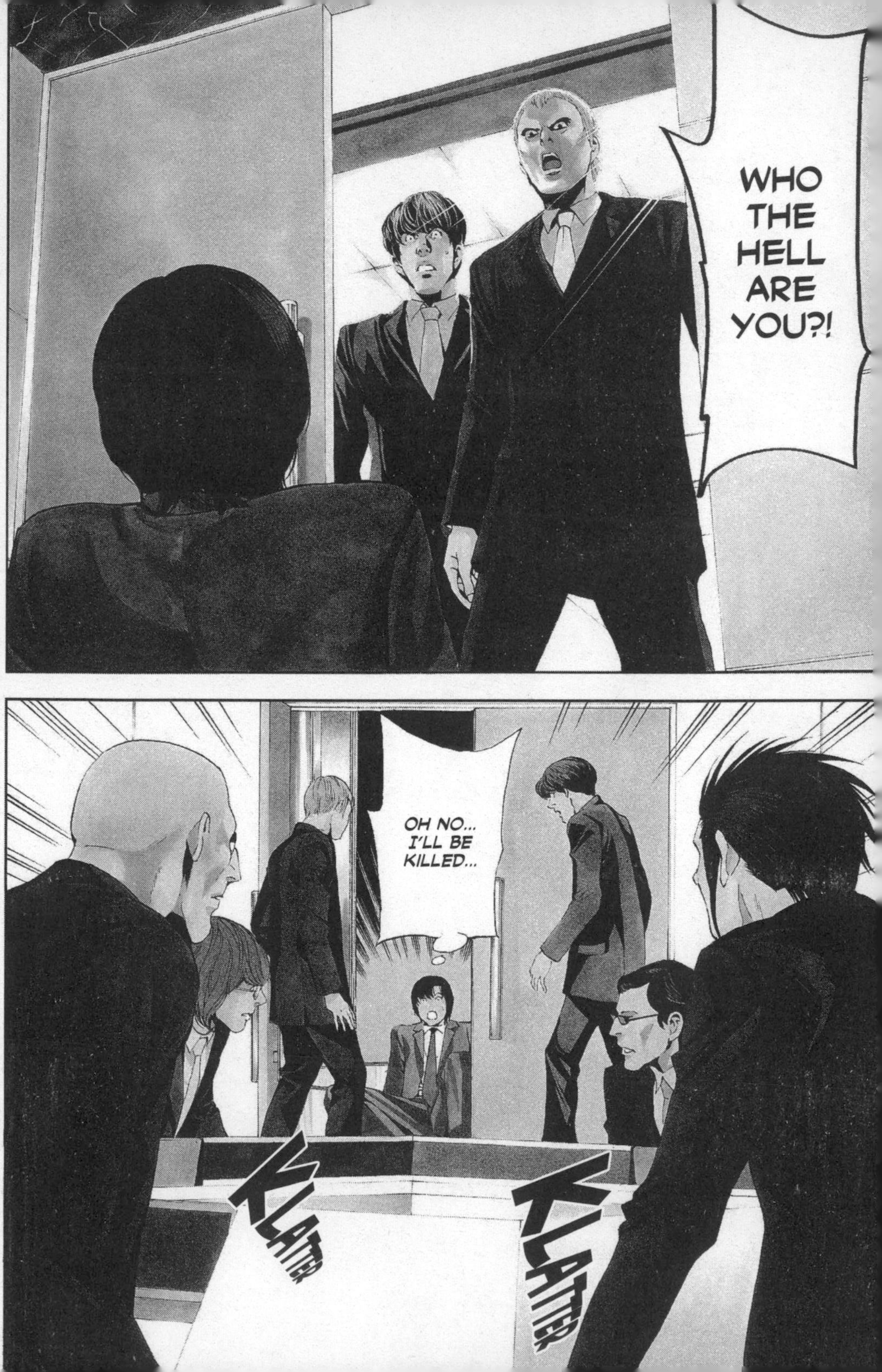
WHO THE HELL ARE YOU?!
OH NO... I'LL BE KILLED...
KLATTER
KLATTER

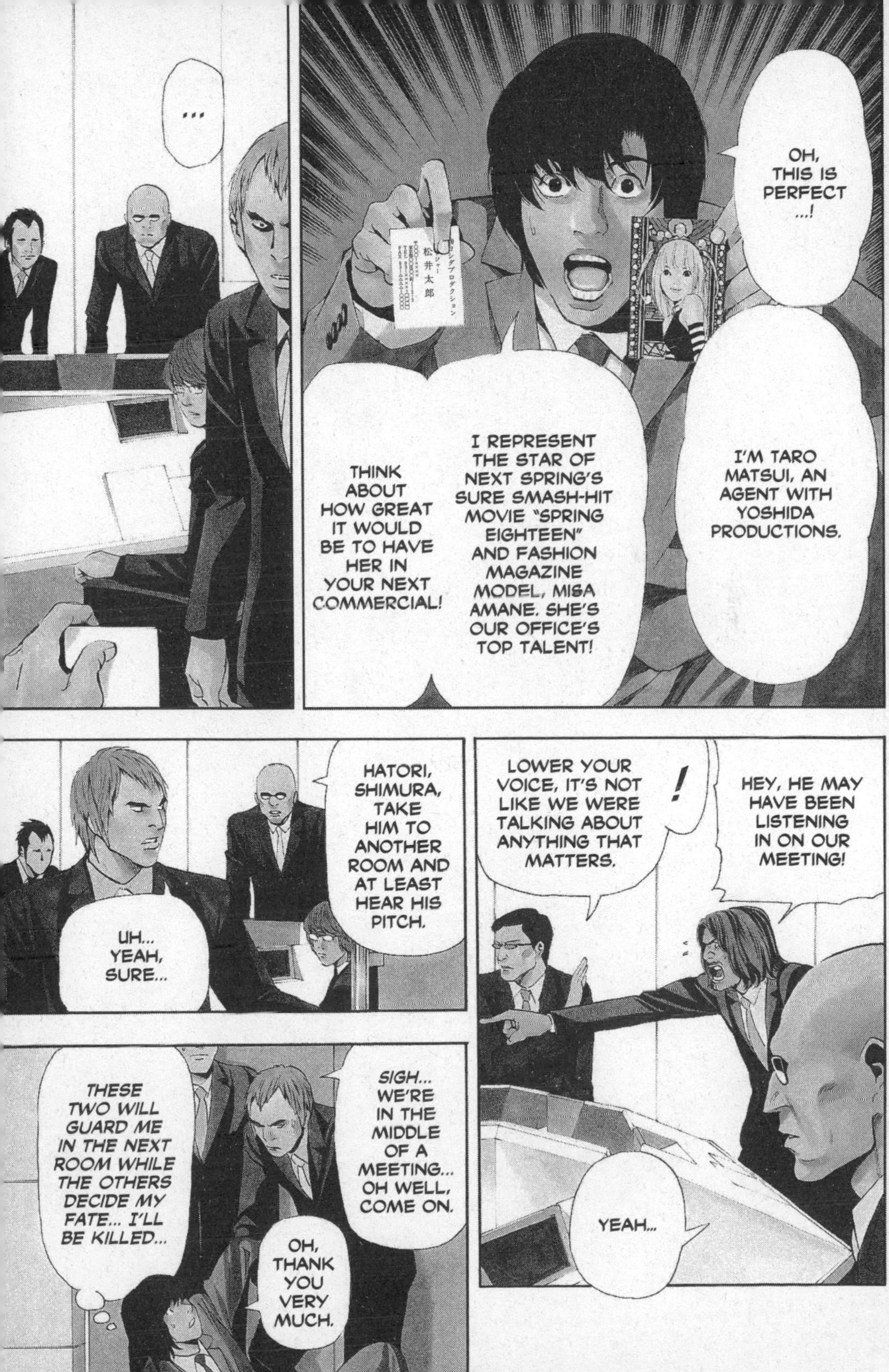
OH, THIS IS PERFECT ...!
I'M TARO MATSUI, AN AGENT WITH YOSHIDA PRODUCTIONS.
松井太郎
I REPRESENT THE STAR OF NEXT SPRING'S SURE SMASH-HIT MOVIE "SPRING EIGHTEEN" AND FASHION MAGAZINE MODEL, MISA AMANE. SHE'S OUR OFFICE'S TOP TALENT!
THINK ABOUT HOW GREAT IT WOULD BE TO HAVE HER IN YOUR NEXT COMMERCIAL!
...
HEY, HE MAY HAVE BEEN LISTENING IN ON OUR MEETING!
!
LOWER YOUR VOICE, IT'S NOT LIKE WE WERE TALKING ABOUT ANYTHING THAT MATTERS.
YEAH...
HATORI, SHIMURA, TAKE HIM TO ANOTHER ROOM AND AT LEAST HEAR HIS PITCH.
UH... YEAH, SURE...
SIGH... WE'RE IN THE MIDDLE OF A MEETING... OH WELL, COME ON.
THESE TWO WILL GUARD ME IN THE NEXT ROOM WHILE THE OTHERS DECIDE MY FATE... I'LL BE KILLED...
OH, THANK YOU VERY MUCH.

READ THIS WAY

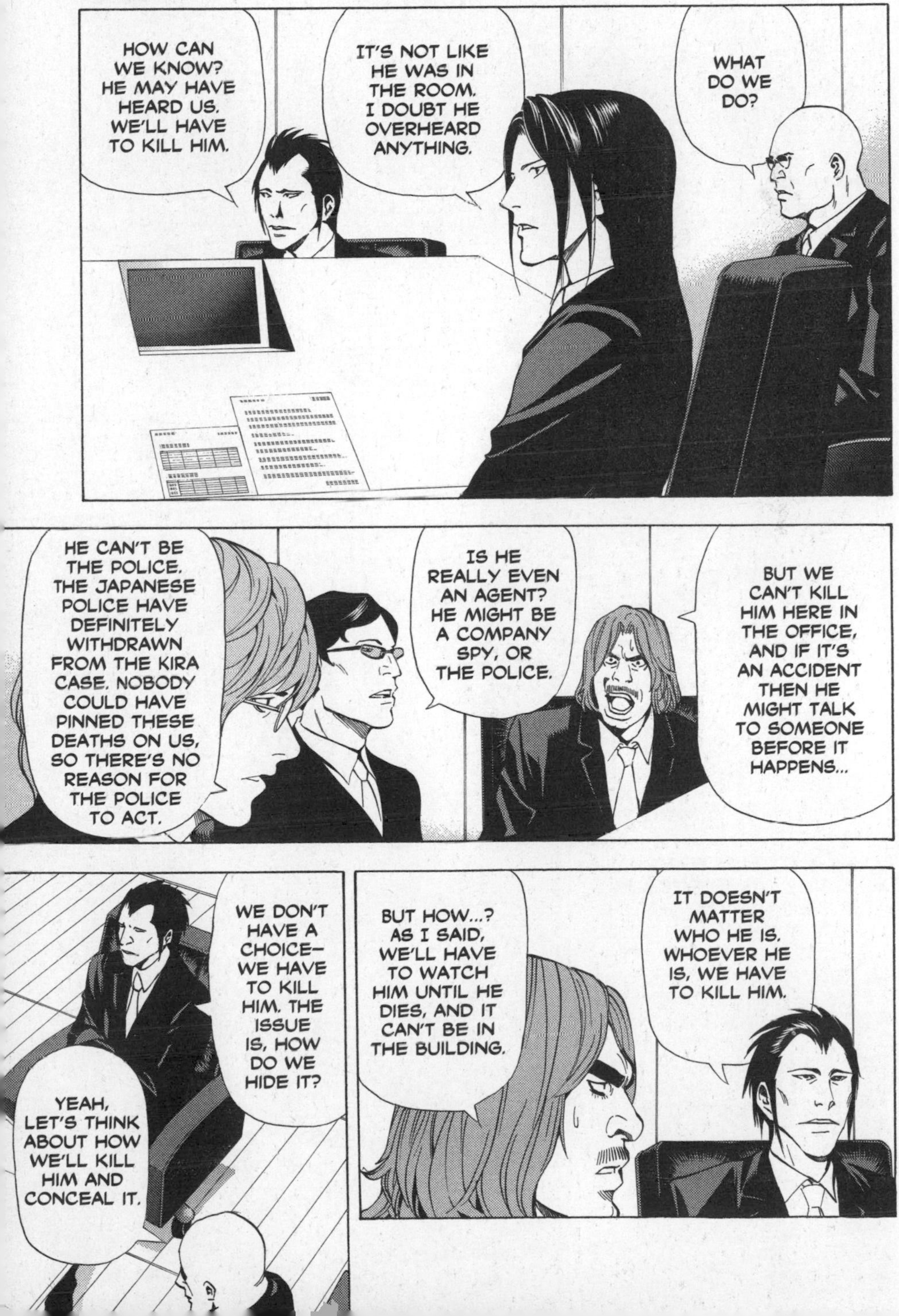
WHAT DO WE DO?
IT'S NOT LIKE HE WAS IN THE ROOM. I DOUBT HE OVERHEARD ANYTHING.
HOW CAN WE KNOW? HE MAY HAVE HEARD US. WE'LL HAVE TO KILL HIM.
BUT WE CAN'T KILL HIM HERE IN THE OFFICE, AND IF IT'S AN ACCIDENT THEN HE MIGHT TALK TO SOMEONE BEFORE IT HAPPENS...
IS HE REALLY EVEN AN AGENT? HE MIGHT BE A COMPANY SPY, OR THE POLICE.
HE CAN'T BE THE POLICE. THE JAPANESE POLICE HAVE DEFINITELY WITHDRAWN FROM THE KIRA CASE. NOBODY COULD HAVE PINNED THESE DEATHS ON US, SO THERE'S NO REASON FOR THE POLICE TO ACT.
IT DOESN'T MATTER WHO HE IS. WHOEVER HE IS, WE HAVE TO KILL HIM.
BUT HOW...? AS I SAID, WE'LL HAVE TO WATCH HIM UNTIL HE DIES, AND IT CAN'T BE IN THE BUILDING.
WE DON'T HAVE A CHOICE— WE HAVE TO KILL HIM. THE ISSUE IS, HOW DO WE HIDE IT?
YEAH, LET'S THINK ABOUT HOW WE'LL KILL HIM AND CONCEAL IT.

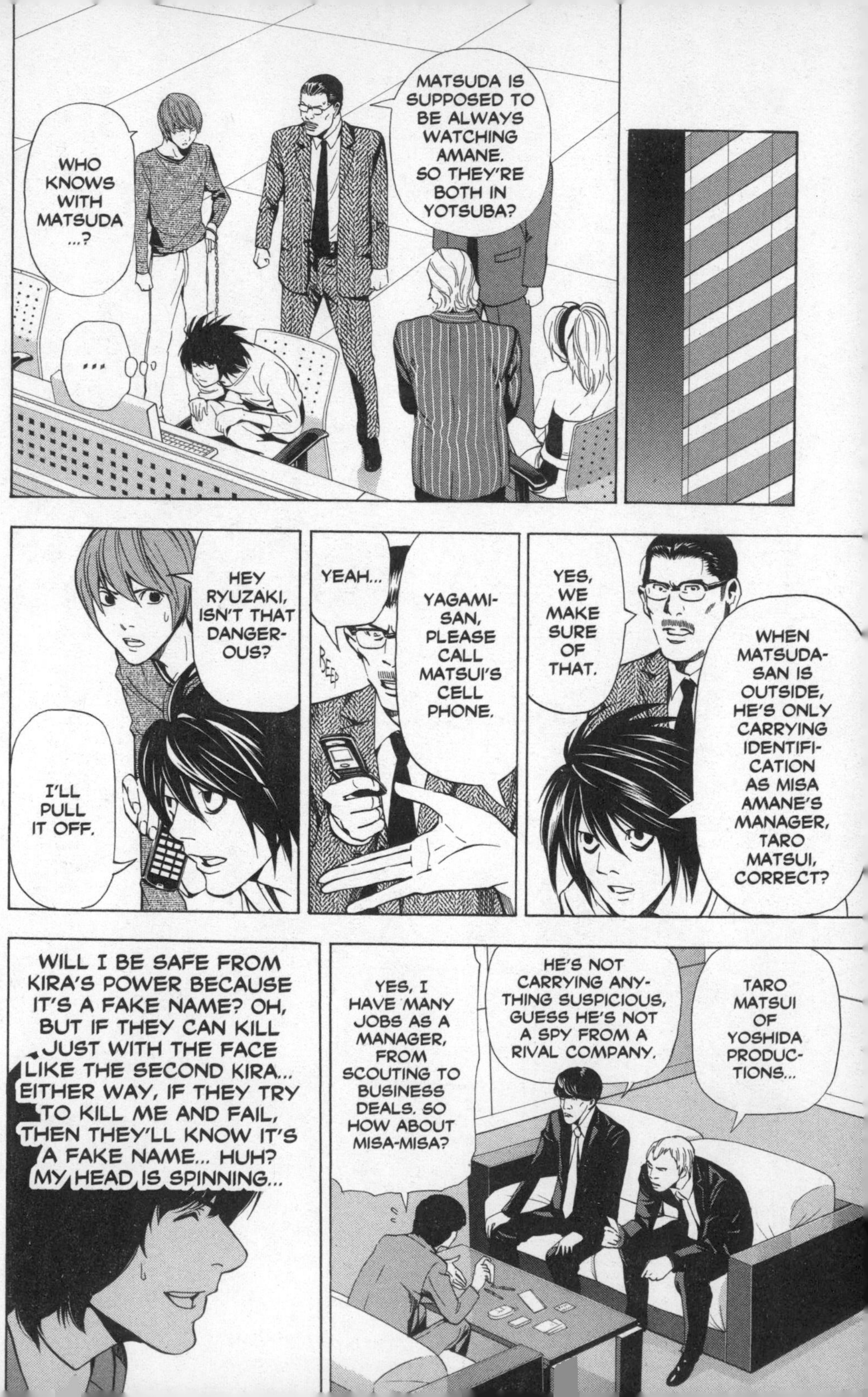
MATSUDA IS SUPPOSED TO BE ALWAYS WATCHING AMANE. SO THEY'RE BOTH IN YOTSUBA?
WHO KNOWS WITH MATSUDA ...?
...
WHEN MATSUDA-SAN IS OUTSIDE, HE'S ONLY CARRYING IDENTIFICATION AS MISA AMANE'S MANAGER, TARO MATSUI, CORRECT?
YES, WE MAKE SURE OF THAT.
YAGAMI-SAN, PLEASE CALL MATSUI'S CELL PHONE.
YEAH...
BEEP
HEY RYUZAKI, ISN'T THAT DANGEROUS?
I'LL PULL IT OFF.
TARO MATSUI OF YOSHIDA PRODUCTIONS...
HE'S NOT CARRYING ANYTHING SUSPICIOUS, GUESS HE'S NOT A SPY FROM A RIVAL COMPANY.
YES, I HAVE MANY JOBS AS A MANAGER, FROM SCOUTING TO BUSINESS DEALS. SO HOW ABOUT MISA-MISA?
WILL I BE SAFE FROM KIRA'S POWER BECAUSE IT'S A FAKE NAME? OH, BUT IF THEY CAN KILL JUST WITH THE FACE LIKE THE SECOND KIRA... EITHER WAY, IF THEY TRY TO KILL ME AND FAIL, THEN THEY'LL KNOW IT'S A FAKE NAME... HUH? MY HEAD IS SPINNING...

READ THIS WAY

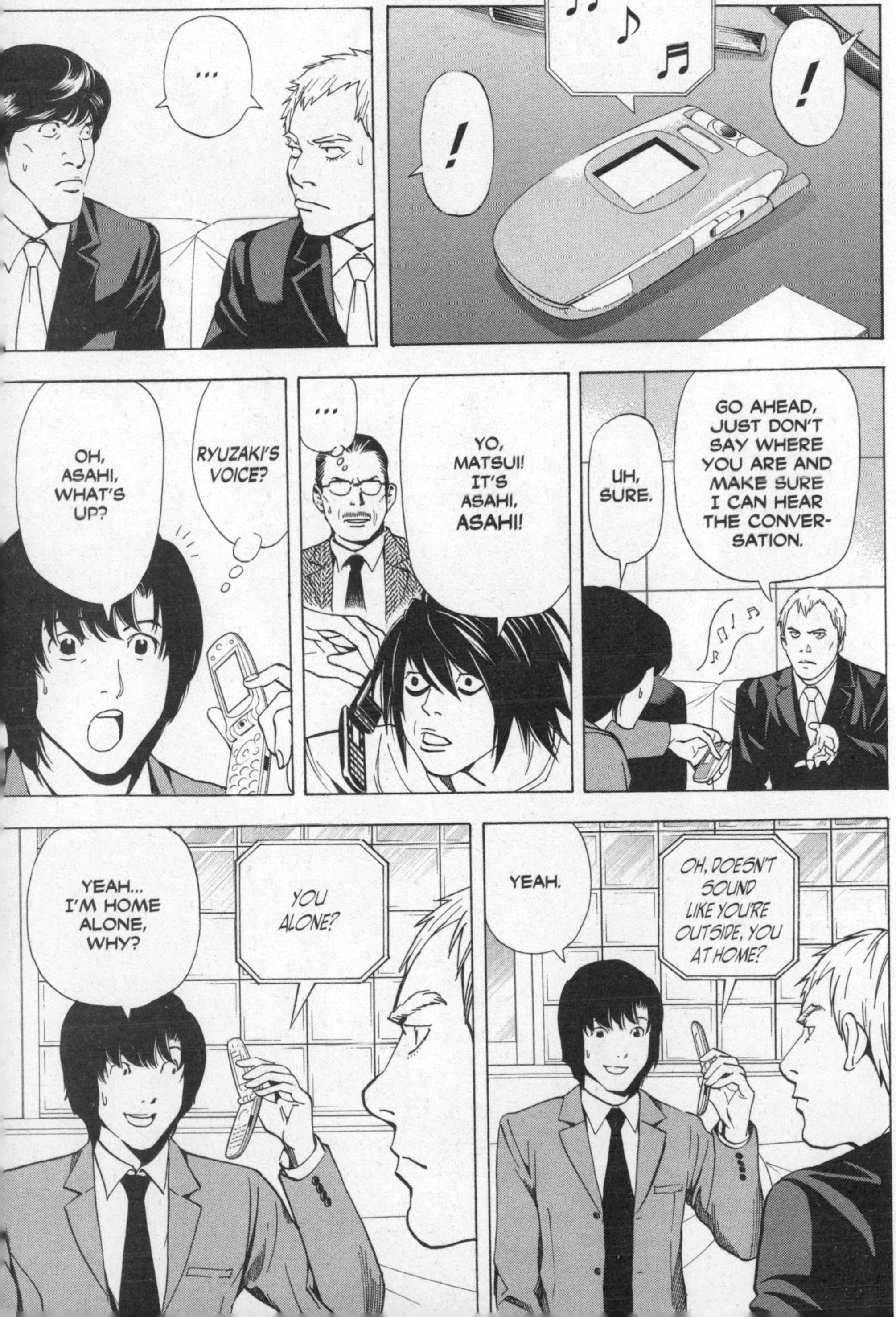
!
!
...
GO AHEAD, JUST DON'T SAY WHERE YOU ARE AND MAKE SURE I CAN HEAR THE CONVER-SATION.
UH, SURE.
YO, MATSUI! IT'S ASAHI, ASAHI!
...
RYUZAKI'S VOICE?
OH, ASAHI, WHAT'S UP?
OH, DOESN'T SOUND LIKE YOU'RE OUTSIDE, YOU AT HOME?
YEAH.
YOU ALONE?
YEAH... I'M HOME ALONE, WHY?

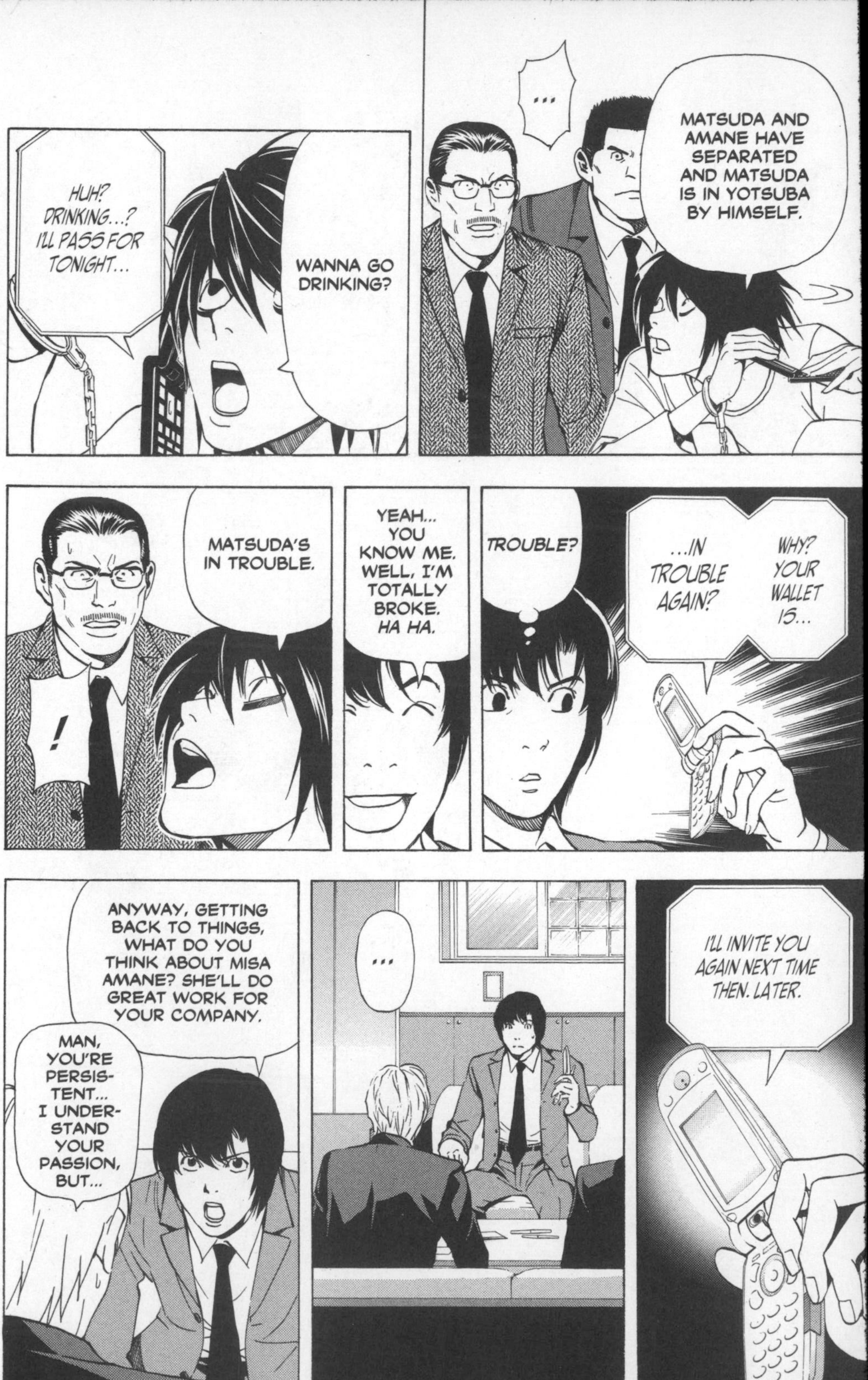
MATSUDA AND AMANE HAVE SEPARATED AND MATSUDA IS IN YOTSUBA BY HIMSELF.
...
WANNA GO DRINKING?
HUH? DRINKING...? I'LL PASS FOR TONIGHT...
WHY? YOUR WALLET IS...
...IN TROUBLE AGAIN?
TROUBLE?
YEAH... YOU KNOW ME. WELL, I'M TOTALLY BROKE. HA HA.
MATSUDA'S IN TROUBLE.
!
I'LL INVITE YOU AGAIN NEXT TIME THEN. LATER.
...
ANYWAY, GETTING BACK TO THINGS, WHAT DO YOU THINK ABOUT MISA AMANE? SHE'LL DO GREAT WORK FOR YOUR COMPANY.
MAN, YOU'RE PERSIS-TENT... I UNDER-STAND YOUR PASSION, BUT...

READ THIS WAY

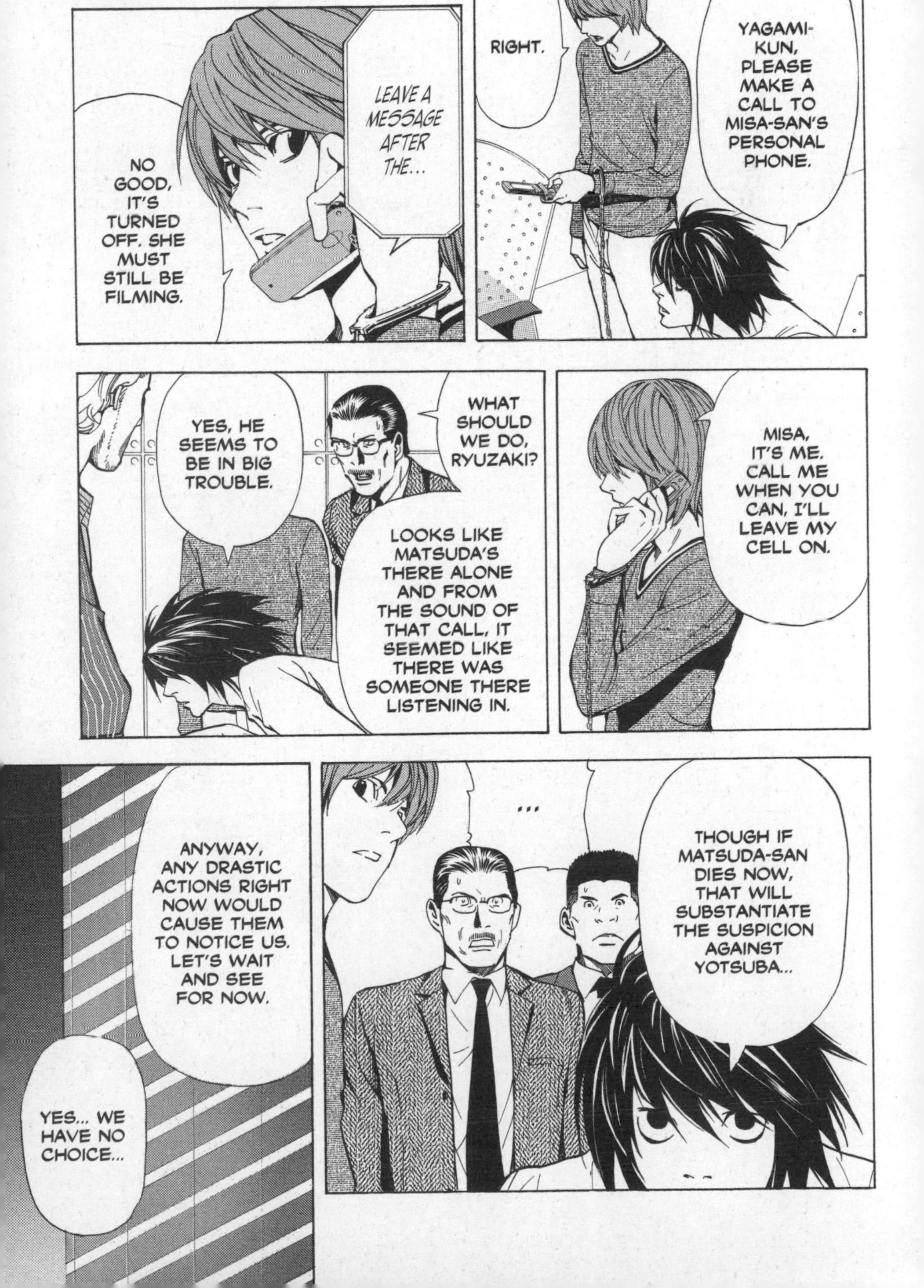
YAGAMI-KUN, PLEASE MAKE A CALL TO MISA-SAN'S PERSONAL PHONE.
RIGHT.
LEAVE A MESSAGE AFTER THE...
NO GOOD, IT'S TURNED OFF. SHE MUST STILL BE FILMING.
MISA, IT'S ME. CALL ME WHEN YOU CAN, I'LL LEAVE MY CELL ON.
WHAT SHOULD WE DO, RYUZAKI?
YES, HE SEEMS TO BE IN BIG TROUBLE.
LOOKS LIKE MATSUDA'S THERE ALONE AND FROM THE SOUND OF THAT CALL, IT SEEMED LIKE THERE WAS SOMEONE THERE LISTENING IN.
THOUGH IF MATSUDA-SAN DIES NOW, THAT WILL SUBSTANTIATE THE SUSPICION AGAINST YOTSUBA...
...
ANYWAY, ANY DRASTIC ACTIONS RIGHT NOW WOULD CAUSE THEM TO NOTICE US. LET'S WAIT AND SEE FOR NOW.
YES... WE HAVE NO CHOICE...

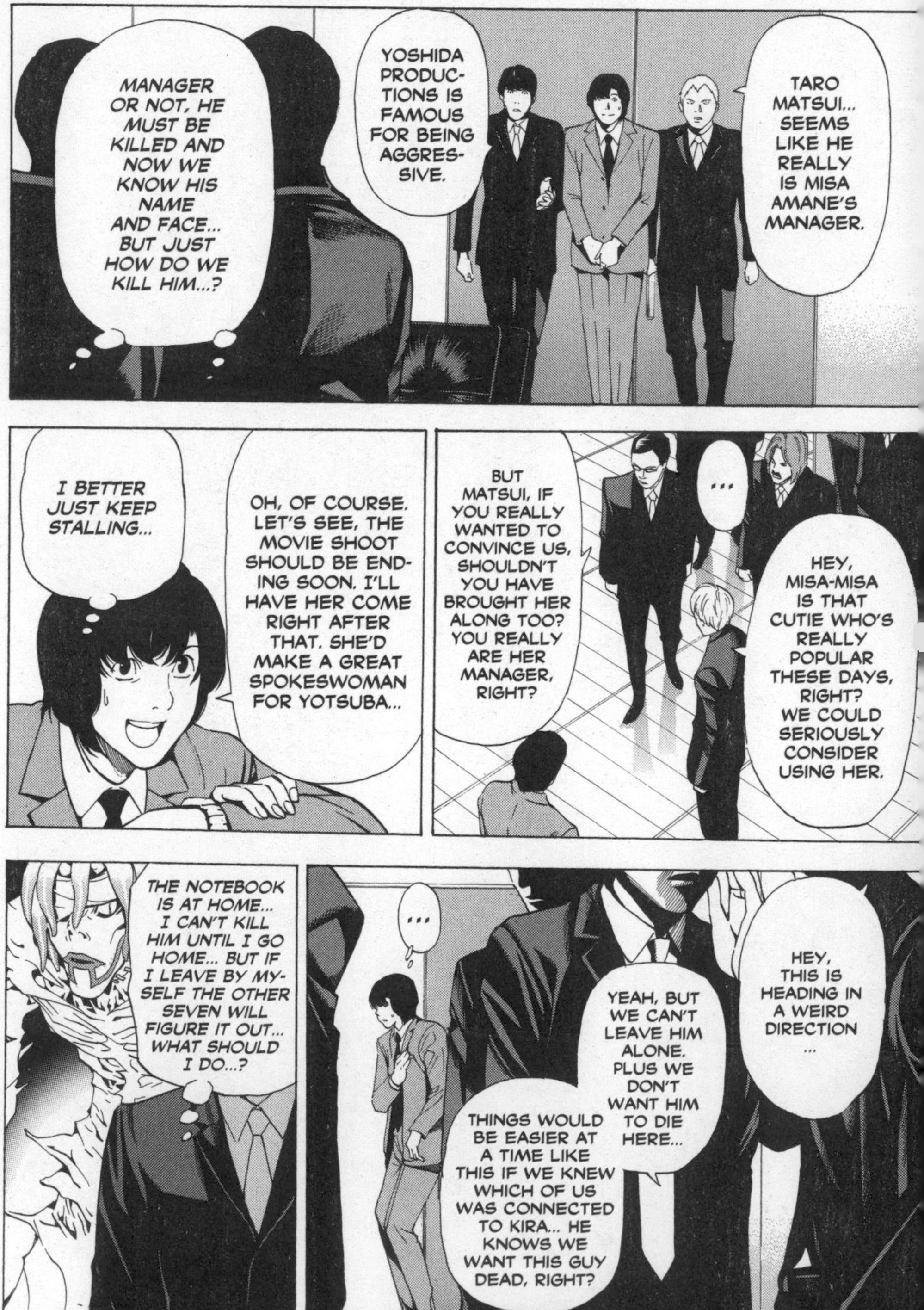
TARO MATSUI... SEEMS LIKE HE REALLY IS MISA AMANE'S MANAGER.
YOSHIDA PRODUCTIONS IS FAMOUS FOR BEING AGGRESSIVE.
MANAGER OR NOT, HE MUST BE KILLED AND NOW WE KNOW HIS NAME AND FACE... BUT JUST HOW DO WE KILL HIM...?
HEY, MISA-MISA IS THAT CUTIE WHO'S REALLY POPULAR THESE DAYS, RIGHT? WE COULD SERIOUSLY CONSIDER USING HER.
...
BUT MATSUI, IF YOU REALLY WANTED TO CONVINCE US, SHOULDN'T YOU HAVE BROUGHT HER ALONG TOO? YOU REALLY ARE HER MANAGER, RIGHT?
OH, OF COURSE. LET'S SEE, THE MOVIE SHOOT SHOULD BE ENDING SOON. I'LL HAVE HER COME RIGHT AFTER THAT. SHE'D MAKE A GREAT SPOKESWOMAN FOR YOTSUBA...
I BETTER JUST KEEP STALLING...
HEY, THIS IS HEADING IN A WEIRD DIRECTION ...
YEAH, BUT WE CAN'T LEAVE HIM ALONE. PLUS WE DON'T WANT HIM TO DIE HERE...
...
THINGS WOULD BE EASIER AT A TIME LIKE THIS IF WE KNEW WHICH OF US WAS CONNECTED TO KIRA... HE KNOWS WE WANT THIS GUY DEAD, RIGHT?
THE NOTEBOOK IS AT HOME... I CAN'T KILL HIM UNTIL I GO HOME... BUT IF I LEAVE BY MYSELF THE OTHER SEVEN WILL FIGURE IT OUT... WHAT SHOULD I DO...?

READ THIS WAY

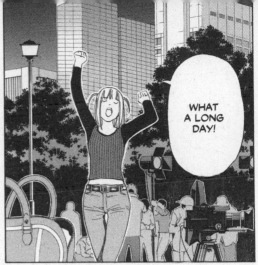

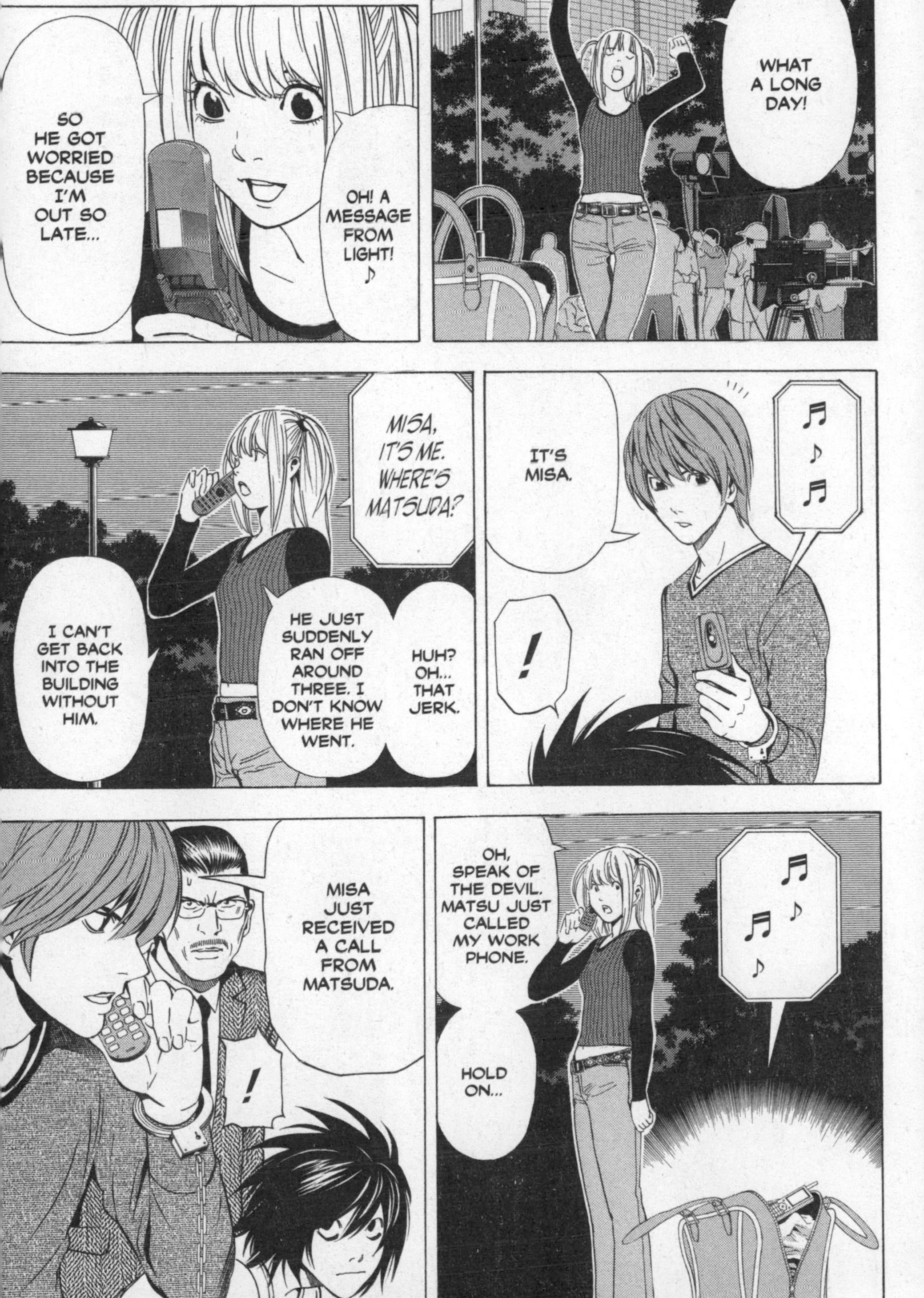
WHAT A LONG DAY!
OH! A MESSAGE FROM LIGHT! ♪
SO HE GOT WORRIED BECAUSE I'M OUT SO LATE...
♬ ♪ ♬
IT'S MISA.
!
MISA, IT'S ME. WHERE'S MATSUDA?
HUH? OH... THAT JERK.
HE JUST SUDDENLY RAN OFF AROUND THREE. I DON'T KNOW WHERE HE WENT.
I CAN'T GET BACK INTO THE BUILDING WITHOUT HIM.
♬ ♪ ♬ ♪
OH, SPEAK OF THE DEVIL. MATSU JUST CALLED MY WORK PHONE.
HOLD ON...
MISA JUST RECEIVED A CALL FROM MATSUDA.
!

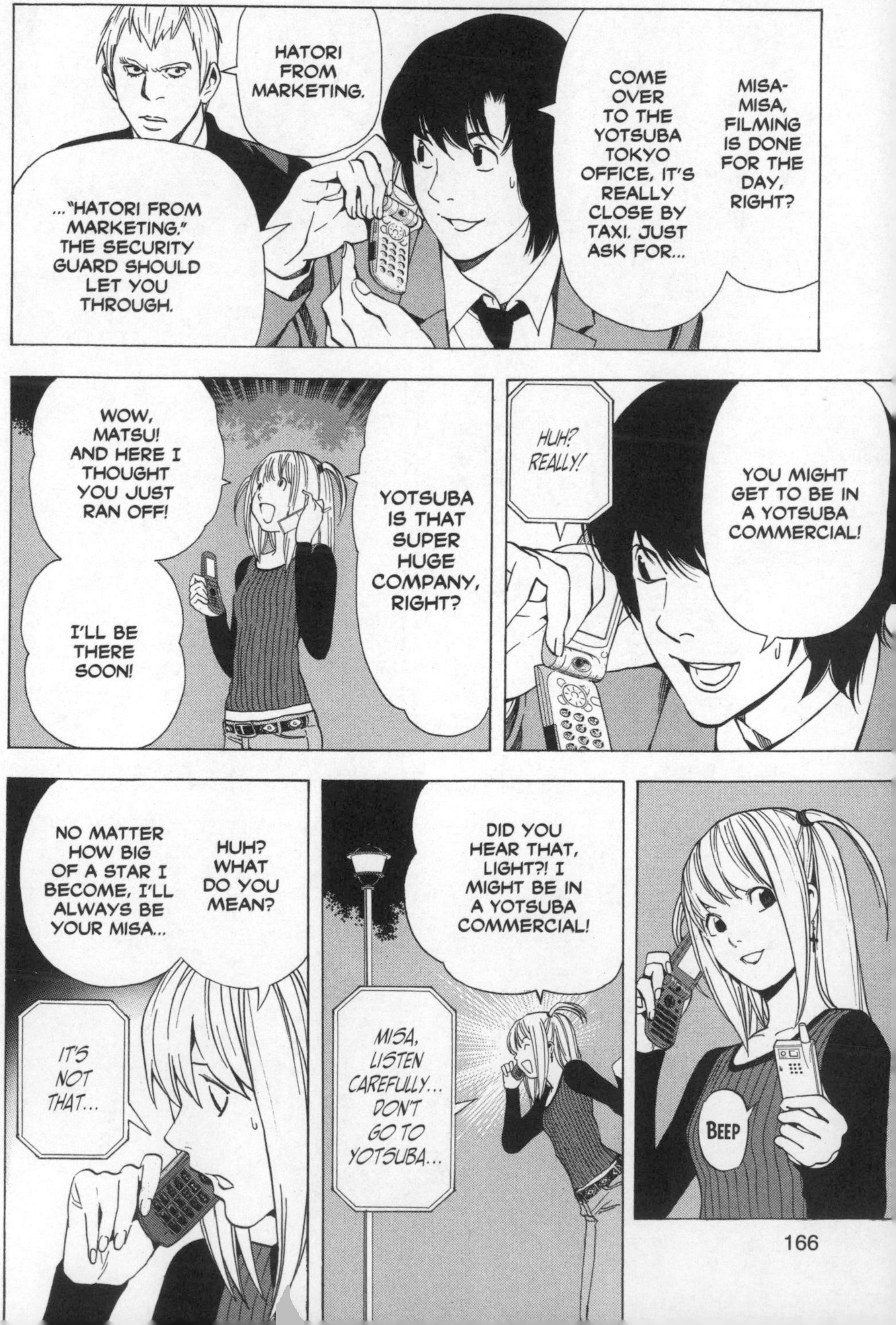
MISA-MISA, FILMING IS DONE FOR THE DAY, RIGHT?
COME OVER TO THE YOTSUBA TOKYO OFFICE, IT'S REALLY CLOSE BY TAXI. JUST ASK FOR...
HATORI FROM MARKETING.
..."HATORI FROM MARKETING." THE SECURITY GUARD SHOULD LET YOU THROUGH.
YOU MIGHT GET TO BE IN A YOTSUBA COMMERCIAL!
HUH? REALLY!
YOTSUBA IS THAT SUPER HUGE COMPANY, RIGHT?
WOW, MATSU! AND HERE I THOUGHT YOU JUST RAN OFF!
I'LL BE THERE SOON!
BEEP
DID YOU HEAR THAT, LIGHT?! I MIGHT BE IN A YOTSUBA COMMERCIAL!
MISA, LISTEN CAREFULLY... DON'T GO TO YOTSUBA...
HUH? WHAT DO YOU MEAN?
NO MATTER HOW BIG OF A STAR I BECOME, I'LL ALWAYS BE YOUR MISA...
IT'S NOT THAT...

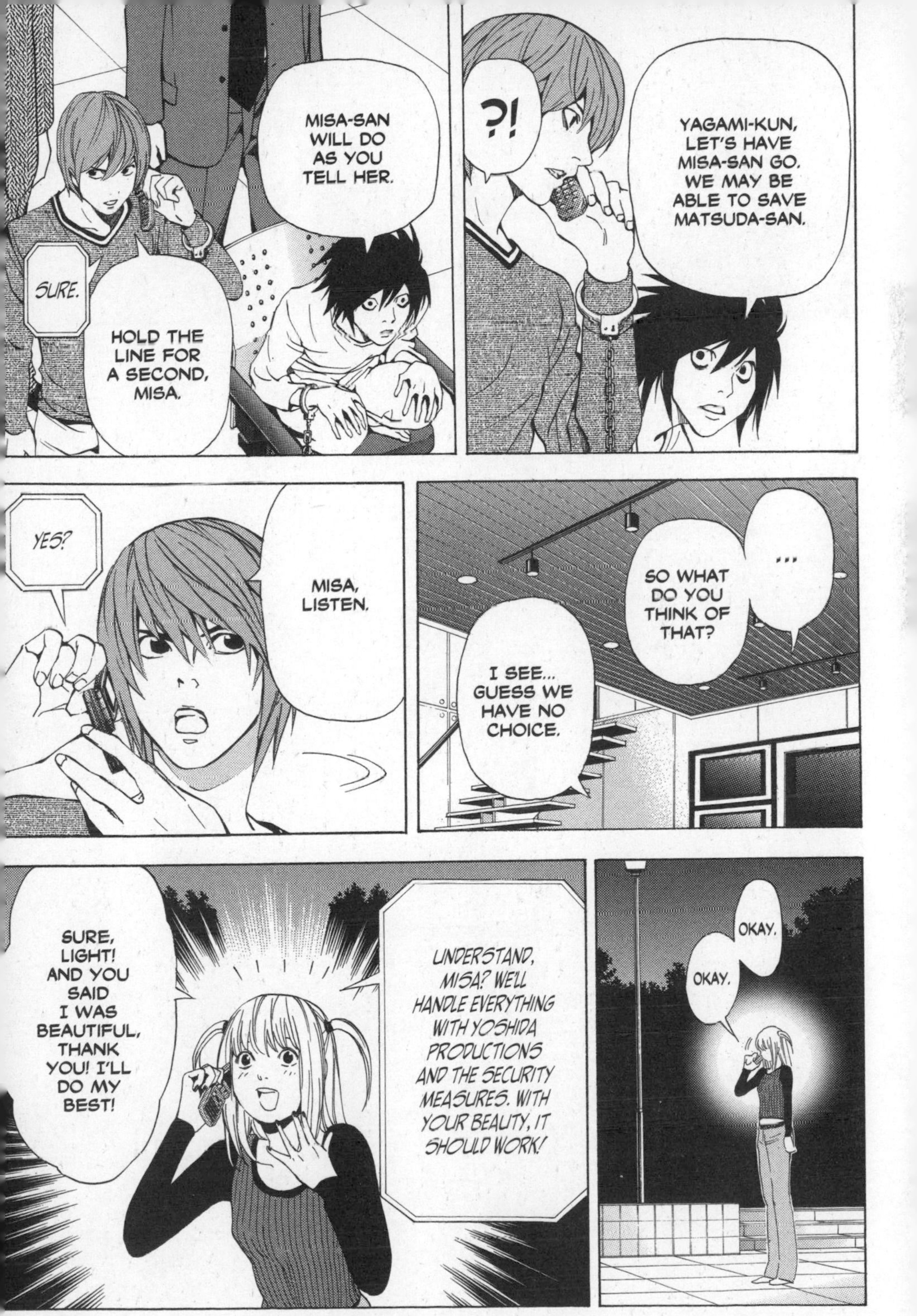
YAGAMI-KUN, LET'S HAVE MISA-SAN GO. WE MAY BE ABLE TO SAVE MATSUDA-SAN.
?!
MISA-SAN WILL DO AS YOU TELL HER.
SURE.
HOLD THE LINE FOR A SECOND, MISA.
...
SO WHAT DO YOU THINK OF THAT?
I SEE... GUESS WE HAVE NO CHOICE.
MISA, LISTEN.
YES?
OKAY.
OKAY.
UNDERSTAND, MISA? WE'LL HANDLE EVERYTHING WITH YOSHIDA PRODUCTIONS AND THE SECURITY MEASURES. WITH YOUR BEAUTY, IT SHOULD WORK!
SURE, LIGHT! AND YOU SAID I WAS BEAUTIFUL, THANK YOU! I'LL DO MY BEST!

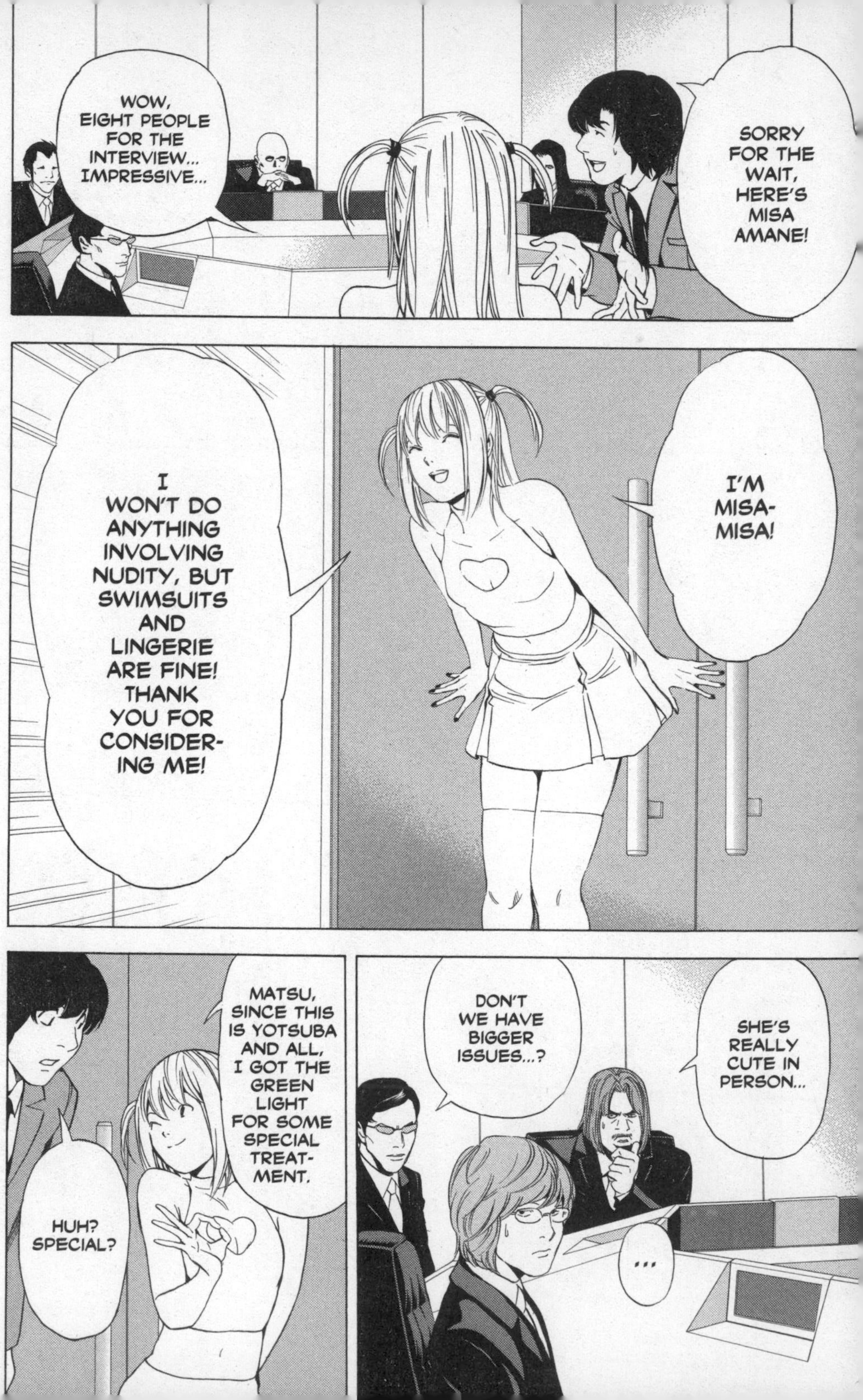
SORRY FOR THE WAIT, HERE'S MISA AMANE!
WOW, EIGHT PEOPLE FOR THE INTERVIEW... IMPRESSIVE...
I'M MISA-MISA!
I WON'T DO ANYTHING INVOLVING NUDITY, BUT SWIMSUITS AND LINGERIE ARE FINE! THANK YOU FOR CONSIDERING ME!
SHE'S REALLY CUTE IN PERSON...
DON'T WE HAVE BIGGER ISSUES...?
...
MATSU, SINCE THIS IS YOTSUBA AND ALL, I GOT THE GREEN LIGHT FOR SOME SPECIAL TREATMENT.
HUH? SPECIAL?

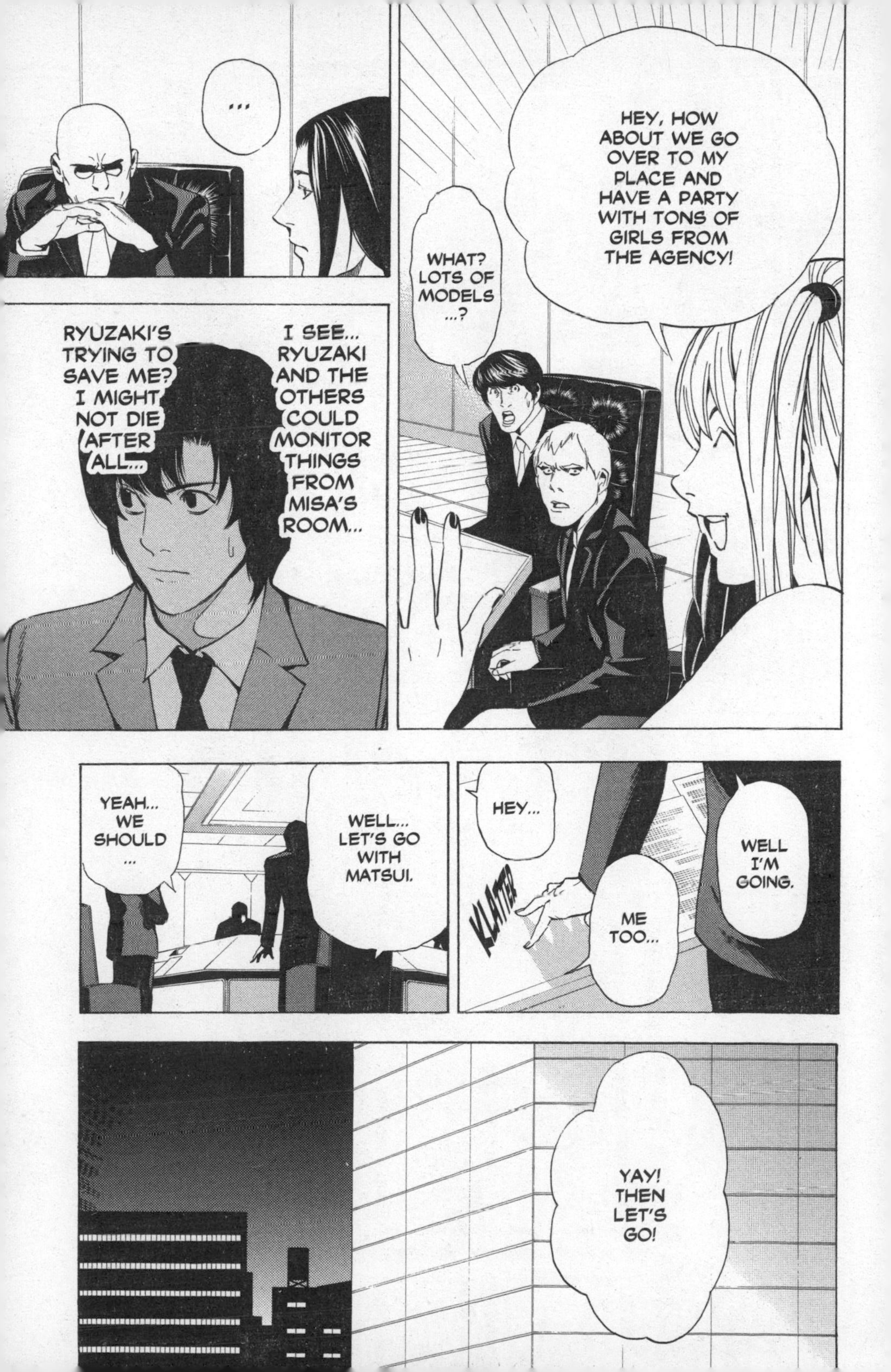

HEY, HOW ABOUT WE GO OVER TO MY PLACE AND HAVE A PARTY WITH TONS OF GIRLS FROM THE AGENCY!
WHAT? LOTS OF MODELS ...?
...
I SEE... RYUZAKI AND THE OTHERS COULD MONITOR THINGS FROM MISA'S ROOM...
RYUZAKI'S TRYING TO SAVE ME? I MIGHT NOT DIE AFTER ALL...
WELL I'M GOING.
HEY...
ME TOO...
KLATTER
WELL... LET'S GO WITH MATSUI.
YEAH... WE SHOULD ...
YAY! THEN LET'S GO!

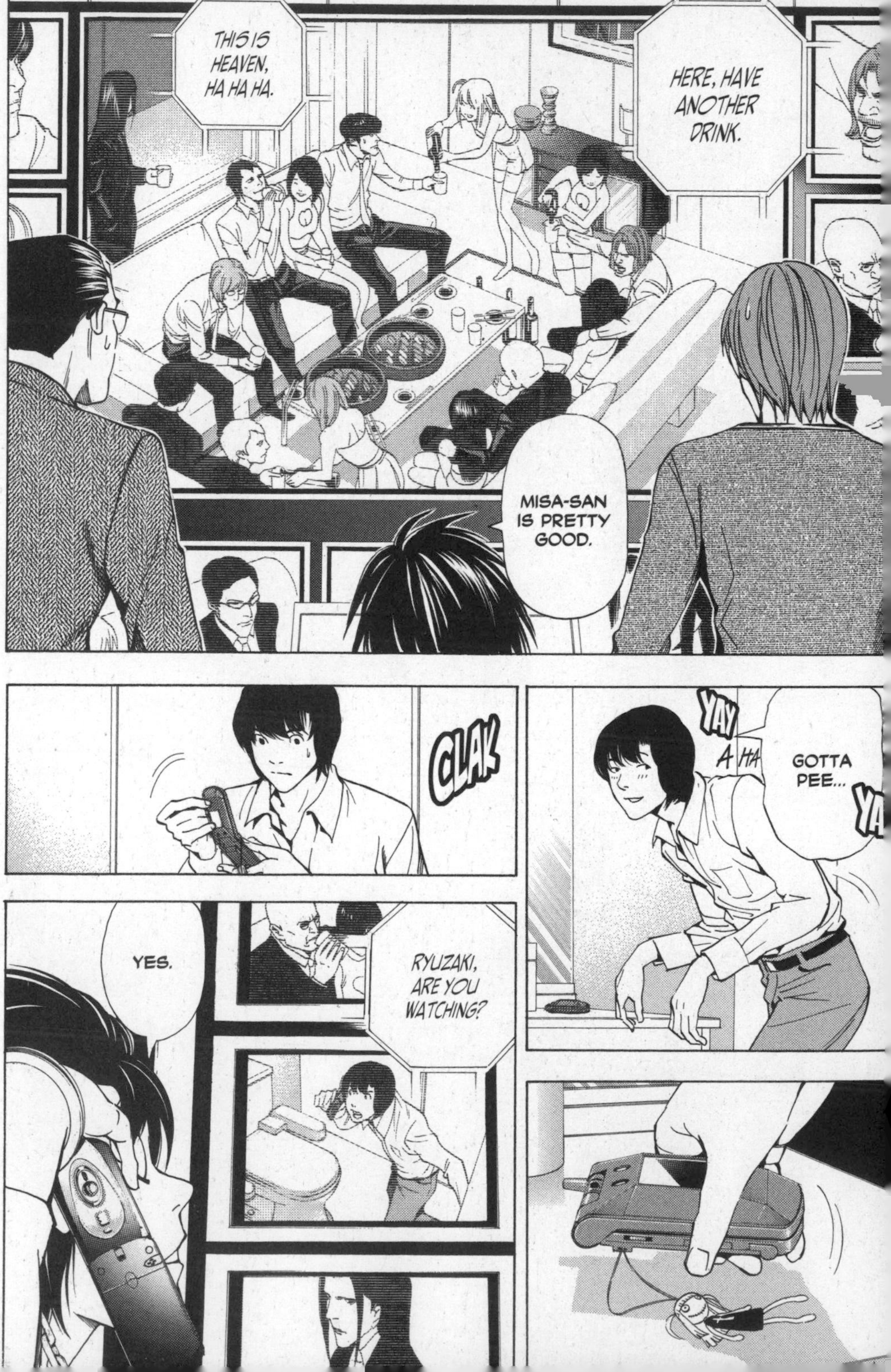
HERE, HAVE ANOTHER DRINK.
THIS IS HEAVEN, HA HA HA.
MISA-SAN IS PRETTY GOOD.
YAY
A HA
GOTTA PEE...
YA
CLAK
RYUZAKI, ARE YOU WATCHING?
YES.

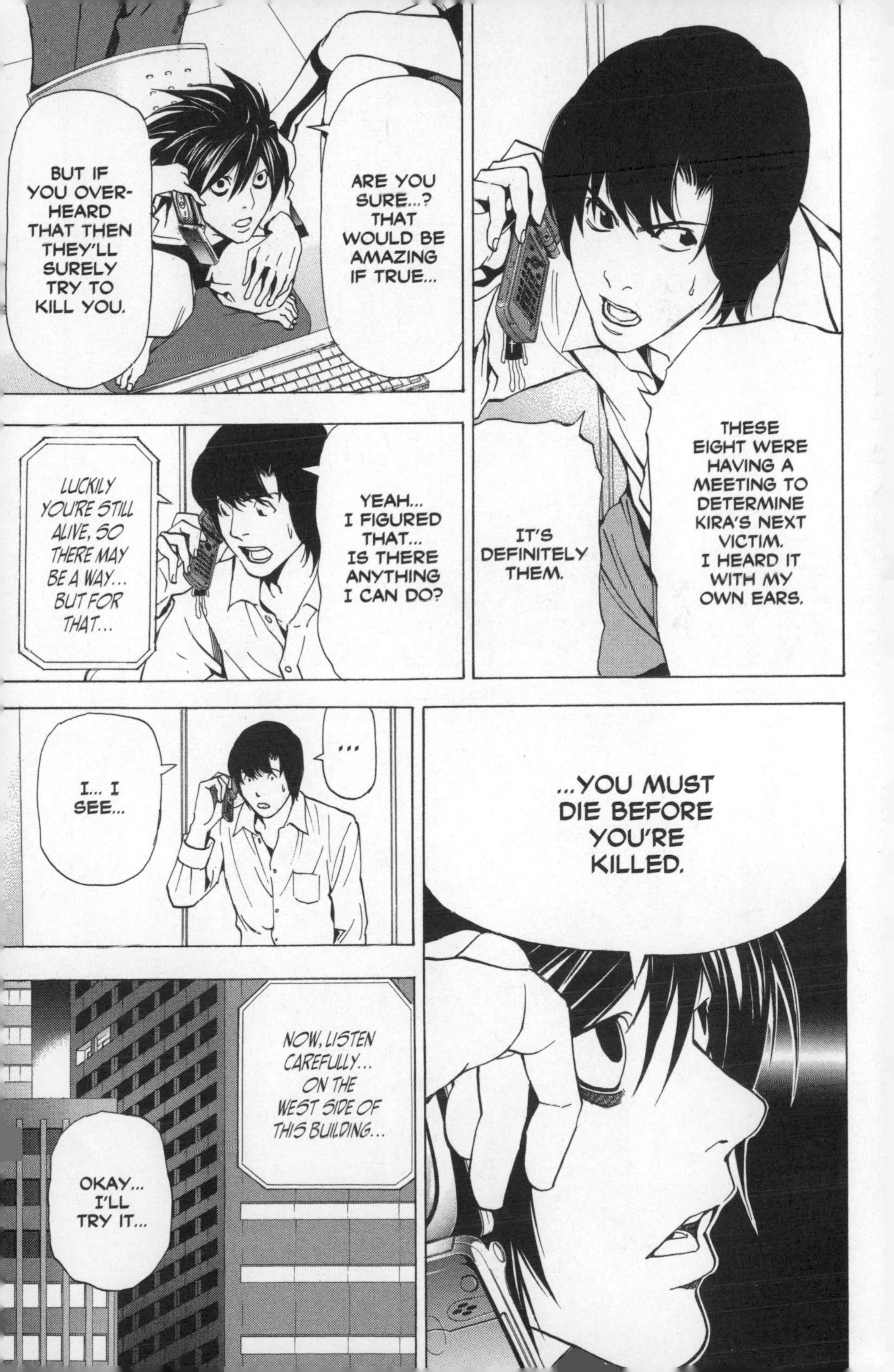
ARE YOU SURE...? THAT WOULD BE AMAZING IF TRUE...
BUT IF YOU OVER-HEARD THAT THEN THEY'LL SURELY TRY TO KILL YOU.
THESE EIGHT WERE HAVING A MEETING TO DETERMINE KIRA'S NEXT VICTIM. I HEARD IT WITH MY OWN EARS.
IT'S DEFINITELY THEM.
YEAH... I FIGURED THAT... IS THERE ANYTHING I CAN DO?
LUCKILY YOU'RE STILL ALIVE, SO THERE MAY BE A WAY... BUT FOR THAT...
...YOU MUST DIE BEFORE YOU'RE KILLED.
...
I... I SEE...
NOW, LISTEN CAREFULLY... ON THE WEST SIDE OF THIS BUILDING...
OKAY... I'LL TRY IT...

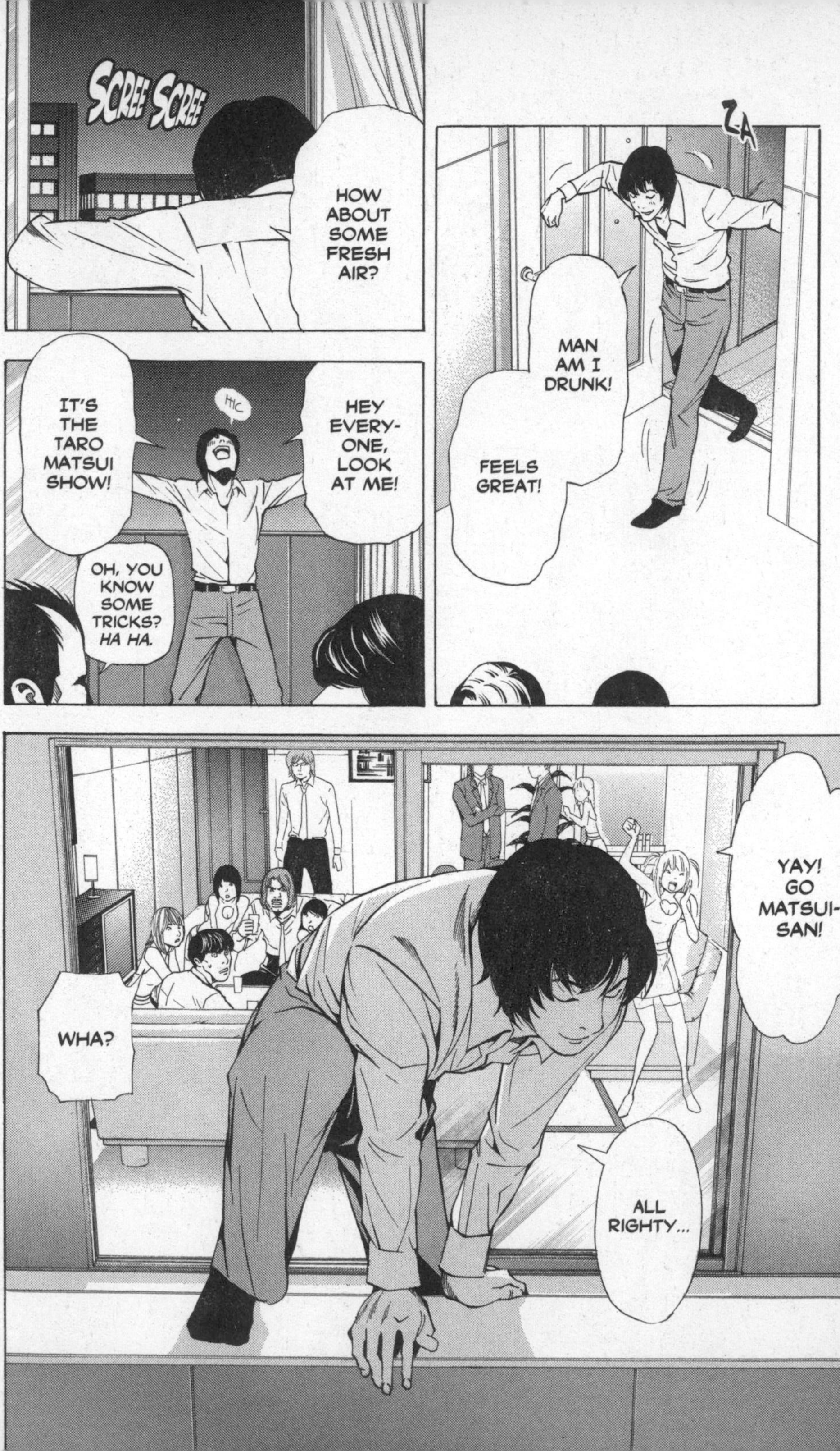
Z-A
MAN AM I DRUNK!
FEELS GREAT!
SCREE SCREE
HOW ABOUT SOME FRESH AIR?
HEY EVERYONE, LOOK AT ME!
HIC
IT'S THE TARO MATSUI SHOW!
OH, YOU KNOW SOME TRICKS? *HA HA.*
YAY! GO MATSUI-SAN!
WHA?
ALL RIGHTY...

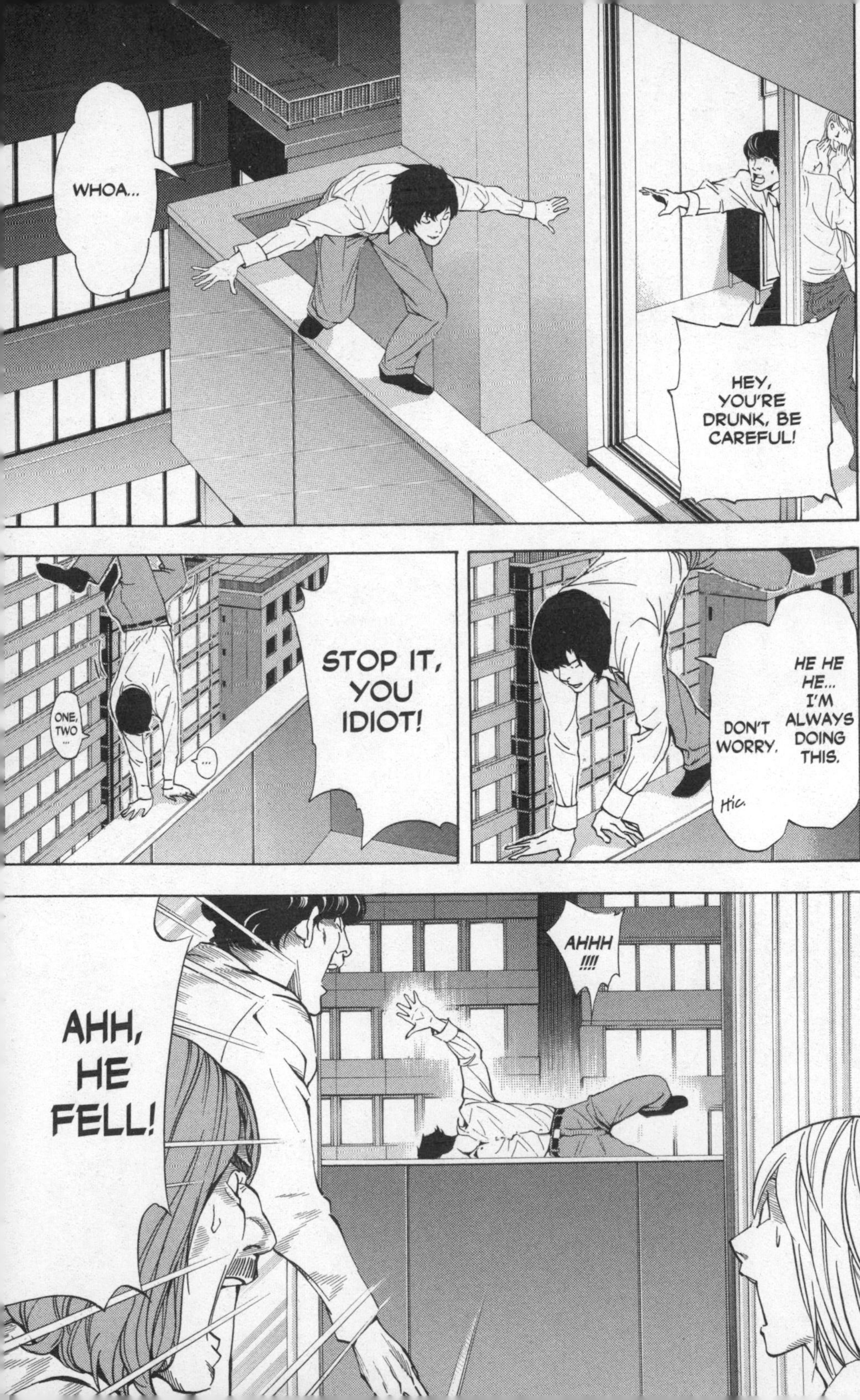

HEY, YOU'RE DRUNK, BE CAREFUL!
WHOA...
HE HE HE... I'M ALWAYS DOING THIS.
DON'T WORRY.
Hic.
STOP IT, YOU IDIOT!
ONE, TWO ...
...
AHHH !!!!
AHH, HE FELL!

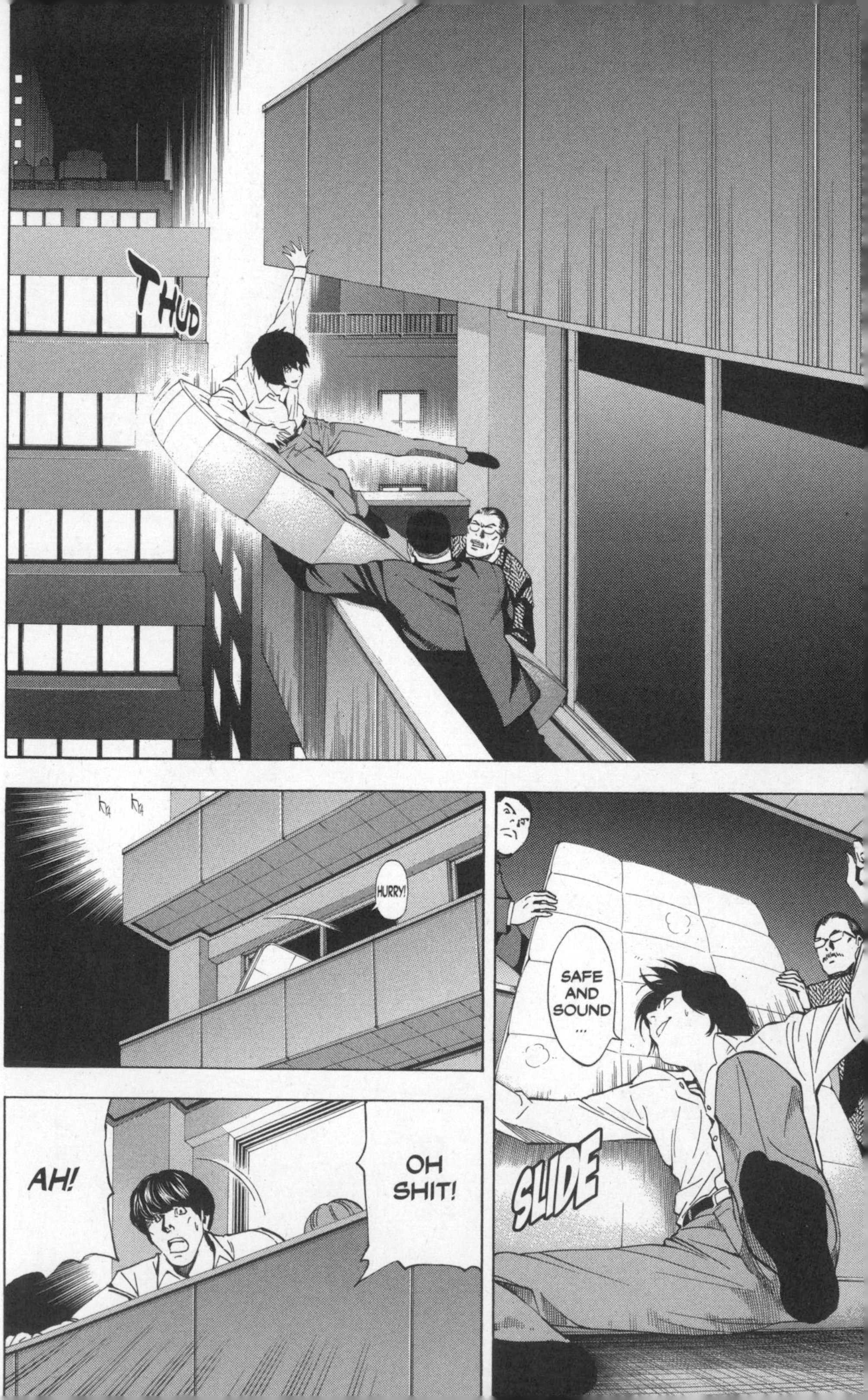
THUD
SAFE AND SOUND ...
SLIDE
HURRY!
OH SHIT!
AH!

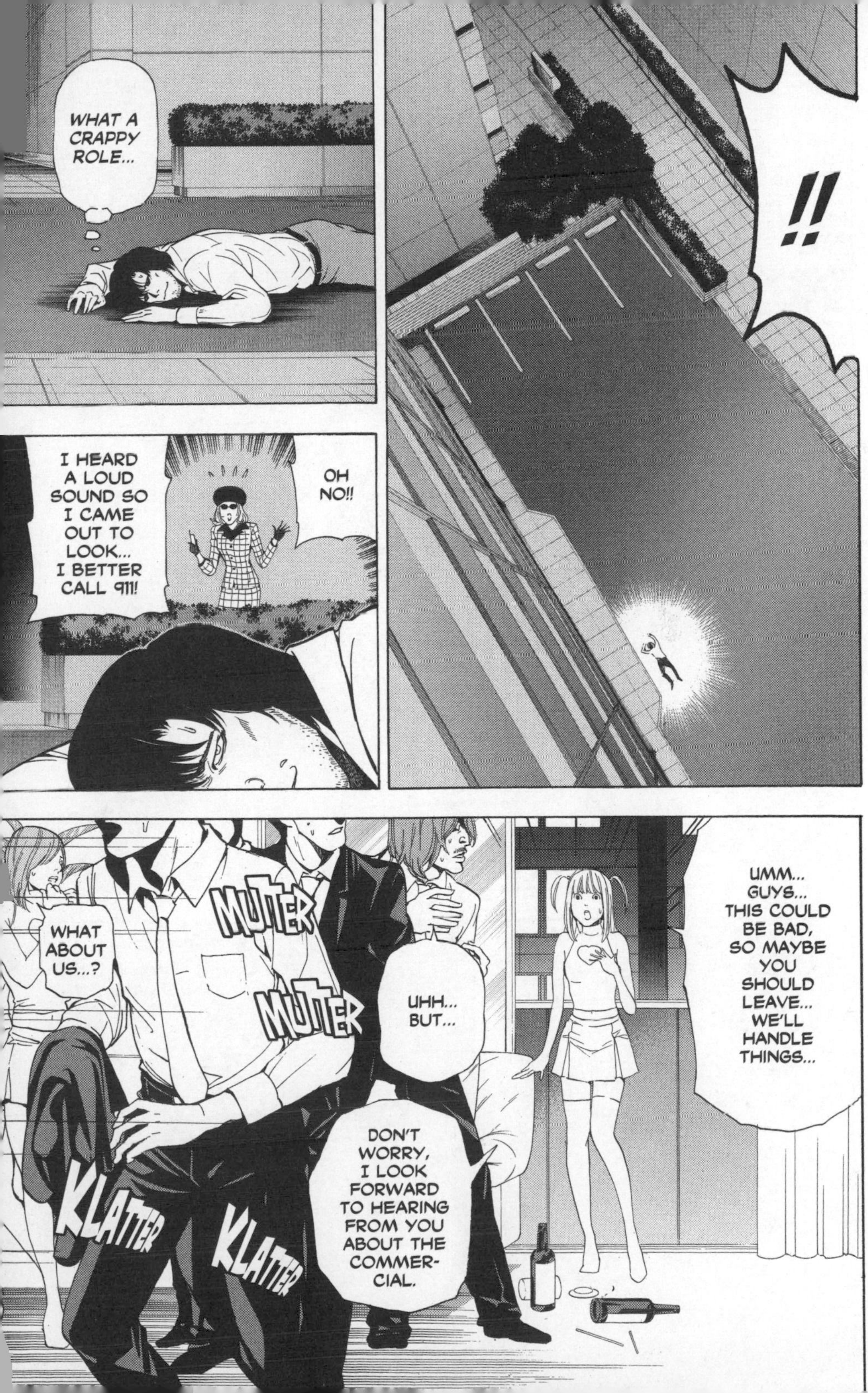
!!
WHAT A CRAPPY ROLE...
OH NO!!
I HEARD A LOUD SOUND SO I CAME OUT TO LOOK... I BETTER CALL 911!
UMM... GUYS... THIS COULD BE BAD, SO MAYBE YOU SHOULD LEAVE... WE'LL HANDLE THINGS...
UHH... BUT...
MUTTER
MUTTER
WHAT ABOUT US...?
DON'T WORRY, I LOOK FORWARD TO HEARING FROM YOU ABOUT THE COMMERCIAL.
KLATTER
KLATTER

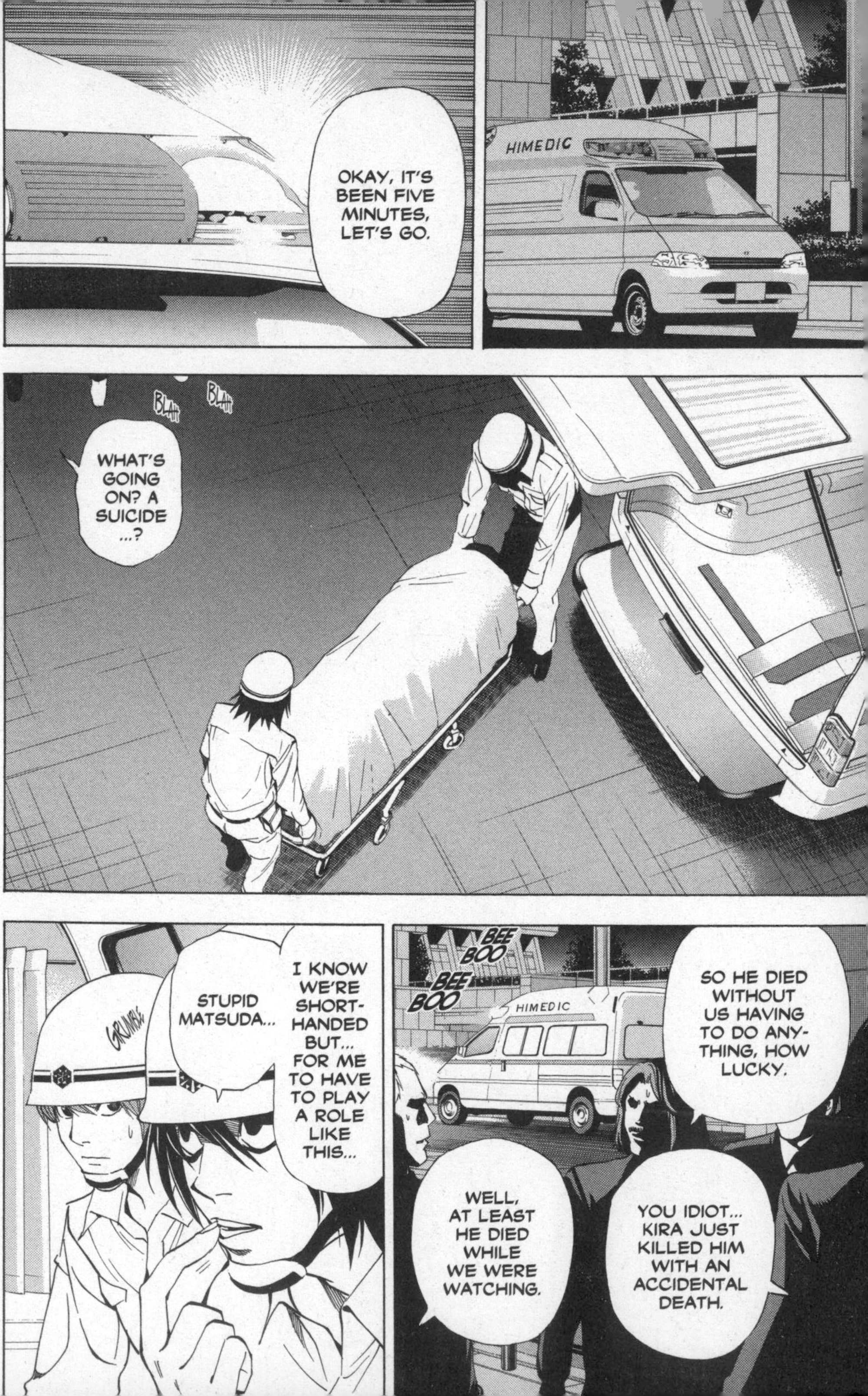
HIMEDIC
OKAY, IT'S BEEN FIVE MINUTES, LET'S GO.
BLAH
BLAH
WHAT'S GOING ON? A SUICIDE ...?
BEE BOO
BEE BOO
HIMEDIC
SO HE DIED WITHOUT US HAVING TO DO ANY-THING, HOW LUCKY.
WELL, AT LEAST HE DIED WHILE WE WERE WATCHING.
YOU IDIOT... KIRA JUST KILLED HIM WITH AN ACCIDENTAL DEATH.
I KNOW WE'RE SHORT-HANDED BUT... FOR ME TO HAVE TO PLAY A ROLE LIKE THIS...
STUPID MATSUDA...
GRUMBLE

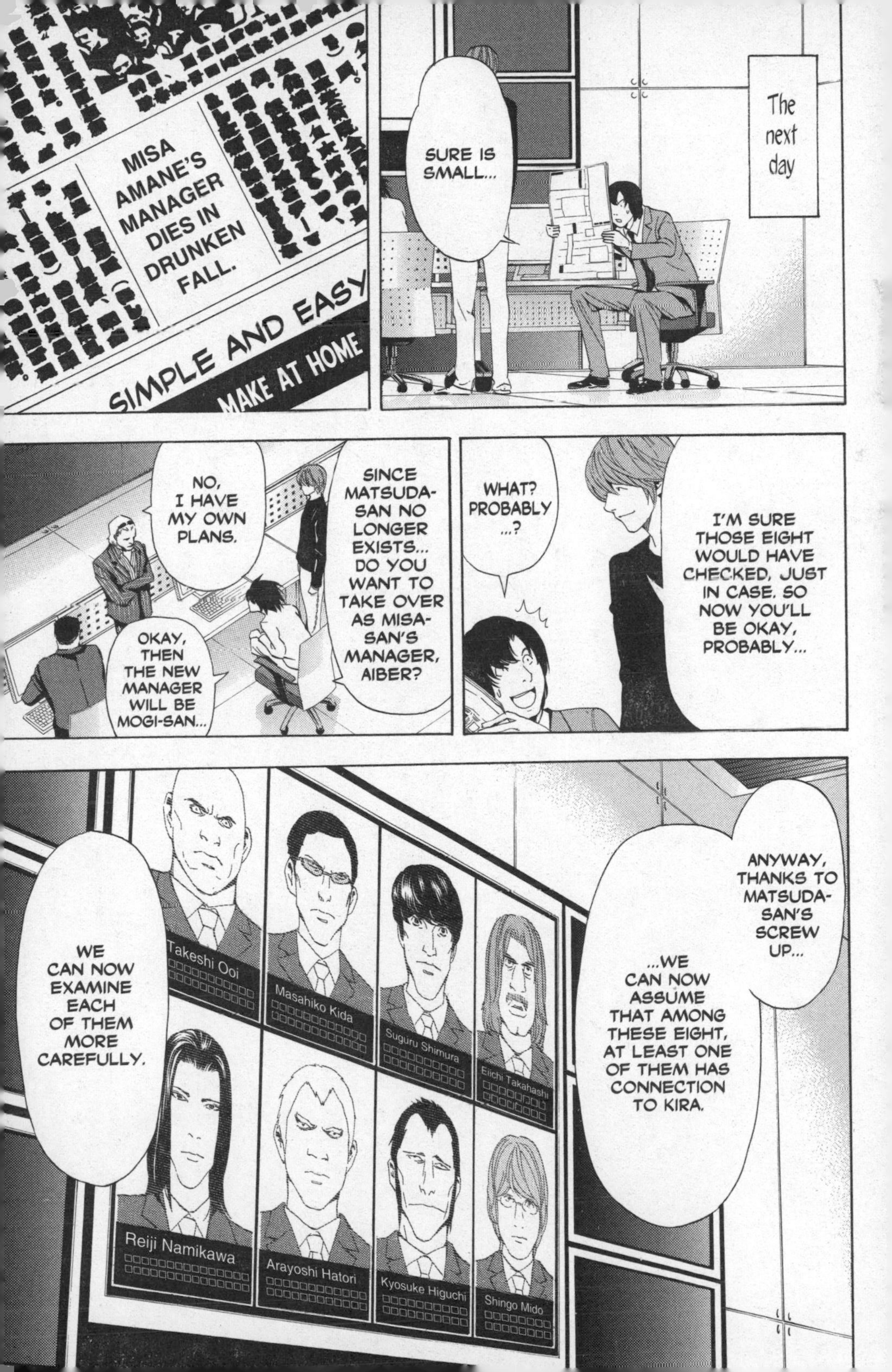

The next day
SURE IS SMALL...
MISA AMANE'S MANAGER DIES IN DRUNKEN FALL.
SIMPLE AND EASY
MAKE AT HOME
I'M SURE THOSE EIGHT WOULD HAVE CHECKED, JUST IN CASE. SO NOW YOU'LL BE OKAY, PROBABLY...
WHAT? PROBABLY ...?
SINCE MATSUDA-SAN NO LONGER EXISTS... DO YOU WANT TO TAKE OVER AS MISA-SAN'S MANAGER, AIBER?
NO, I HAVE MY OWN PLANS.
OKAY, THEN THE NEW MANAGER WILL BE MOGI-SAN...
ANYWAY, THANKS TO MATSUDA-SAN'S SCREW UP...
...WE CAN NOW ASSUME THAT AMONG THESE EIGHT, AT LEAST ONE OF THEM HAS CONNECTION TO KIRA.
WE CAN NOW EXAMINE EACH OF THEM MORE CAREFULLY.
Takeshi Ooi
Masahiko Kida
Suguru Shimura
Eiichi Takahashi
Reiji Namikawa
Arayoshi Hatori
Kyosuke Higuchi
Shingo Mido

DEATH NOTE
How to use it
XXX

○ If you have traded the eye power of a god of death, you will see a person's primary life span in the human world.

死神と眼球の取引をし、その目で見える人間の寿命は
人間界にあるデスノートに関わっていない人間界での本来の寿命である。

○ The names you see with the eye power of a god of death are the names needed to kill that person. You will be able to see the names even if that person isn't registered in the family registration.

また、死神の目で見る事のできる人間の名前は
「その人間を殺すのに必要な名前」であり、たとえ戸籍等に
名前がなくとも殺すのに必要な名前は見える。

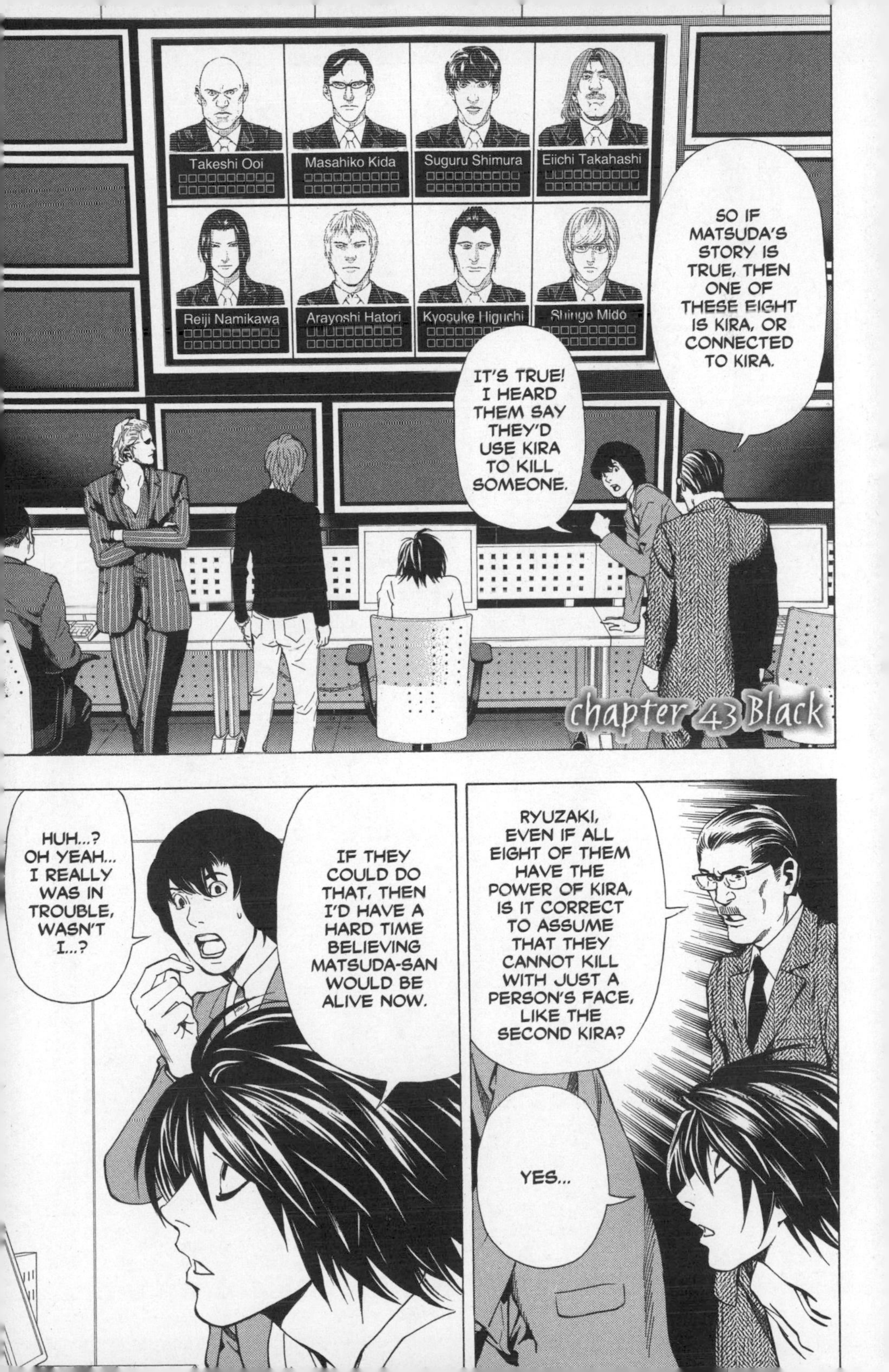
Takeshi Ooi
Masahiko Kida
Suguru Shimura
Eiichi Takahashi
Reiji Namikawa
Arayoshi Hatori
Kyosuke Higuchi
Shingo Mido
SO IF MATSUDA'S STORY IS TRUE, THEN ONE OF THESE EIGHT IS KIRA, OR CONNECTED TO KIRA.
IT'S TRUE! I HEARD THEM SAY THEY'D USE KIRA TO KILL SOMEONE.
chapter 43 Black
RYUZAKI, EVEN IF ALL EIGHT OF THEM HAVE THE POWER OF KIRA, IS IT CORRECT TO ASSUME THAT THEY CANNOT KILL WITH JUST A PERSON'S FACE, LIKE THE SECOND KIRA?
YES...
IF THEY COULD DO THAT, THEN I'D HAVE A HARD TIME BELIEVING MATSUDA-SAN WOULD BE ALIVE NOW.
HUH...? OH YEAH... I REALLY WAS IN TROUBLE, WASN'T I...?

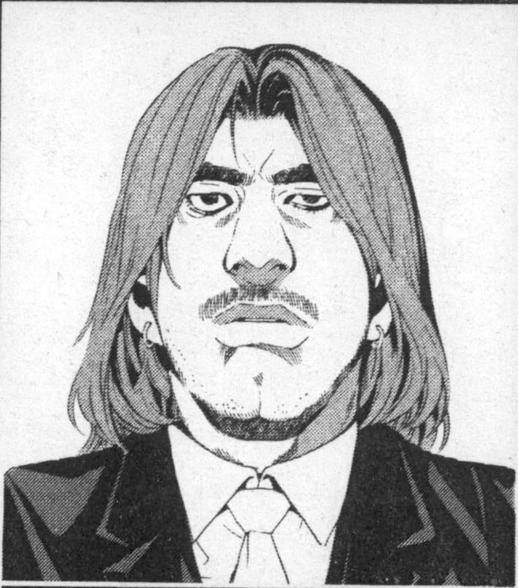

Eiichi Takahashi

Age 40, married with child.
VP of Material Planning Division and Yotsuba Homes.
Graduate of Keiyo Business School.
His hobby is surfing. The son of Karazo Takahashi, president of the Japan Financial Times.

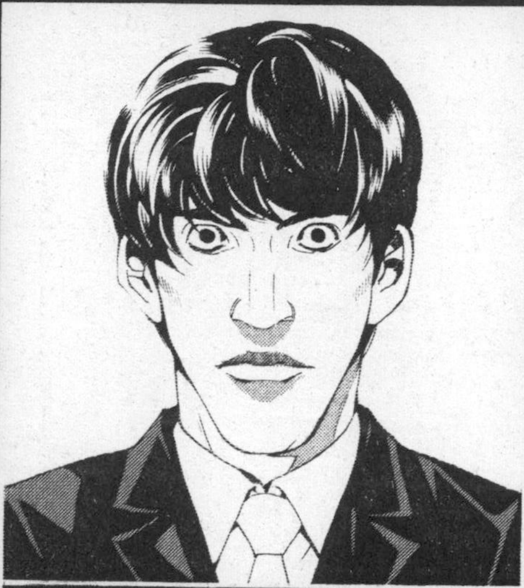

Suguru Shimura

Age 36, single.
Head of Personnel.
Graduate of Kyodo University Law department.
High school rugby star, was chosen as a member of the National team. Raised by a single mom.

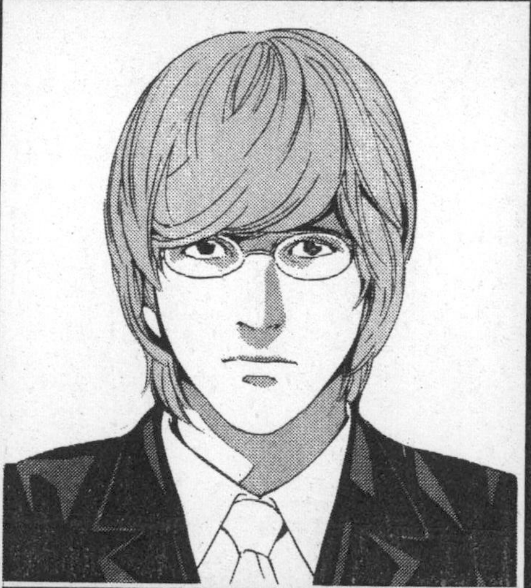

Shingo Mido

Age 32, single.
VP of Corporate Strategy and Director of Financial Planning
Graduate of To-oh University Law department.
His hobby is fencing. Son of Eigo Mido, member of the House of Councilors.

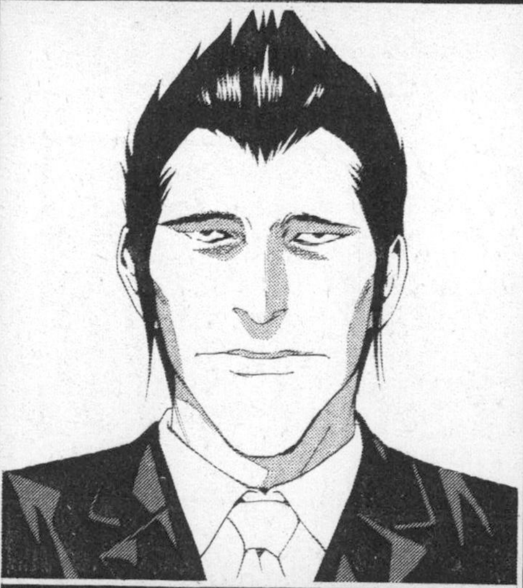

Kyosuke Higuchi

Age 32, single.
Head of Technological Development
Graduate of Wasegi University Political Science department. A Five-Dan in Kendo.
Son of Jiro Higuchi, President of Yotsuba Heavy Industrial.

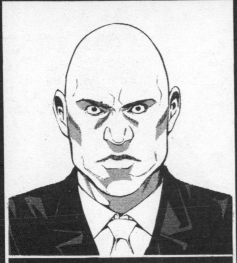

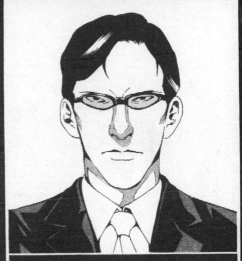

Masahiko Kida

Age 32, married.
VP of Rights and Planning.
Graduate of To-oh University Science department. His hobby is collecting eye glasses. Both his parents are professors of biology.

Takeshi Ooi

Age 43, single.
Vice-president of VT Enterprise. Graduate of Wasegi University Law department. A weapon enthusiast whose father works for the Ministry of Defense.

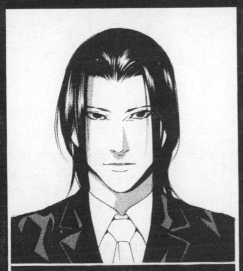

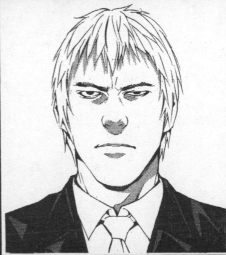

Arayoshi Hatori

Age 33, married with children.
VP of Marketing.
Graduate of Futatsubashi University Literature department. His hobby is ceramics. The illegitimate son of current Yotsuba President, Dainosuke Yotsuba.

Reiji Namikawa

Age 30, single.
VP of Sales.
Graduate of Harvard University Business department. His Shogi level is that of a professional 4-dan. Son of the President of the Yotsuba American division. He's lived in America for 6 years.

chapter 43 Black

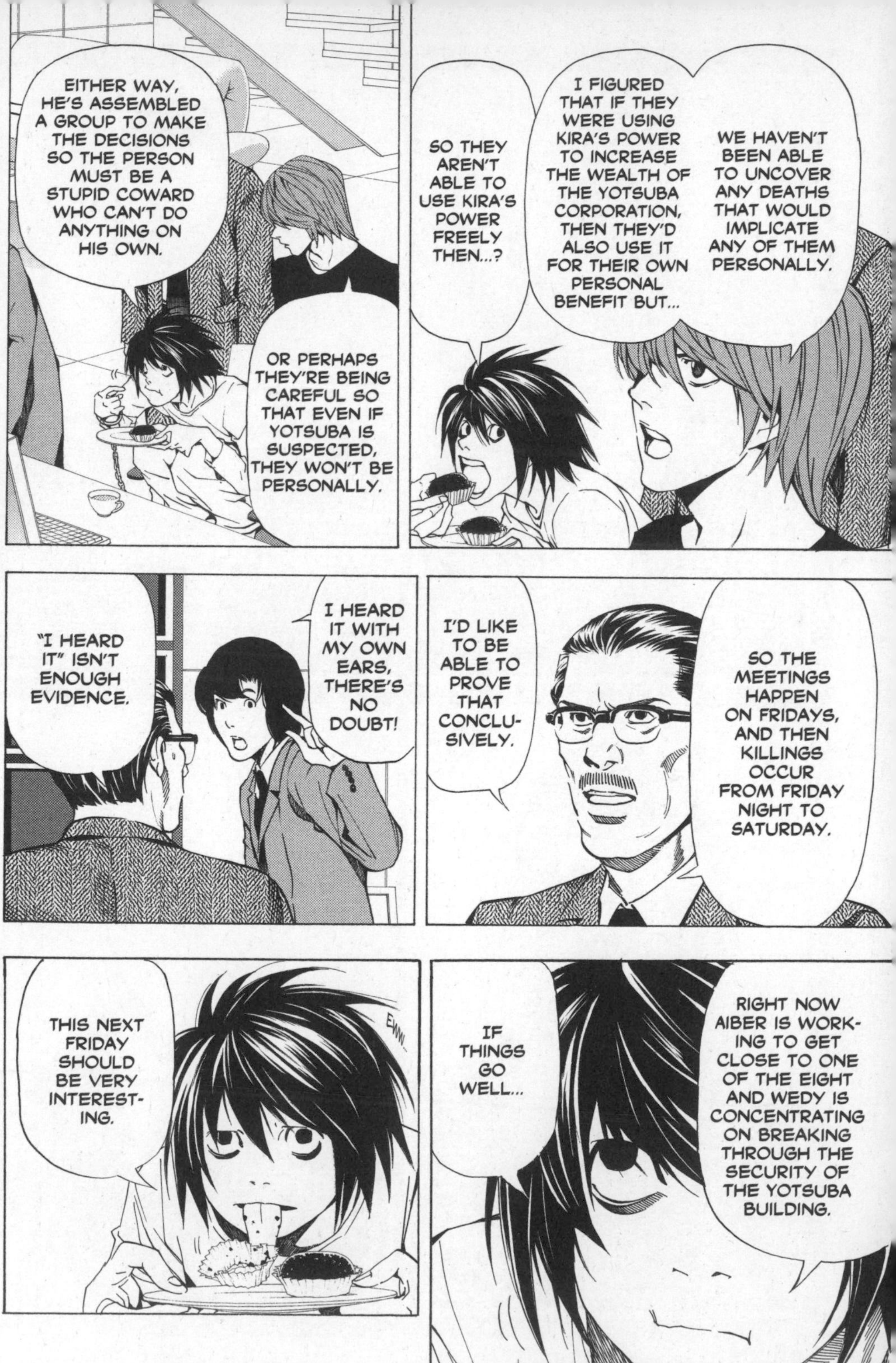
WE HAVEN'T BEEN ABLE TO UNCOVER ANY DEATHS THAT WOULD IMPLICATE ANY OF THEM PERSONALLY.
I FIGURED THAT IF THEY WERE USING KIRA'S POWER TO INCREASE THE WEALTH OF THE YOTSUBA CORPORATION, THEN THEY'D ALSO USE IT FOR THEIR OWN PERSONAL BENEFIT BUT...
SO THEY AREN'T ABLE TO USE KIRA'S POWER FREELY THEN...?
EITHER WAY, HE'S ASSEMBLED A GROUP TO MAKE THE DECISIONS SO THE PERSON MUST BE A STUPID COWARD WHO CAN'T DO ANYTHING ON HIS OWN.
OR PERHAPS THEY'RE BEING CAREFUL SO THAT EVEN IF YOTSUBA IS SUSPECTED, THEY WON'T BE PERSONALLY.
SO THE MEETINGS HAPPEN ON FRIDAYS, AND THEN KILLINGS OCCUR FROM FRIDAY NIGHT TO SATURDAY.
I'D LIKE TO BE ABLE TO PROVE THAT CONCLU-SIVELY.
I HEARD IT WITH MY OWN EARS, THERE'S NO DOUBT!
"I HEARD IT" ISN'T ENOUGH EVIDENCE.
RIGHT NOW AIBER IS WORK-ING TO GET CLOSE TO ONE OF THE EIGHT AND WEDY IS CONCENTRATING ON BREAKING THROUGH THE SECURITY OF THE YOTSUBA BUILDING.
IF THINGS GO WELL...
EWW...
THIS NEXT FRIDAY SHOULD BE VERY INTEREST-ING.

READ THIS WAY

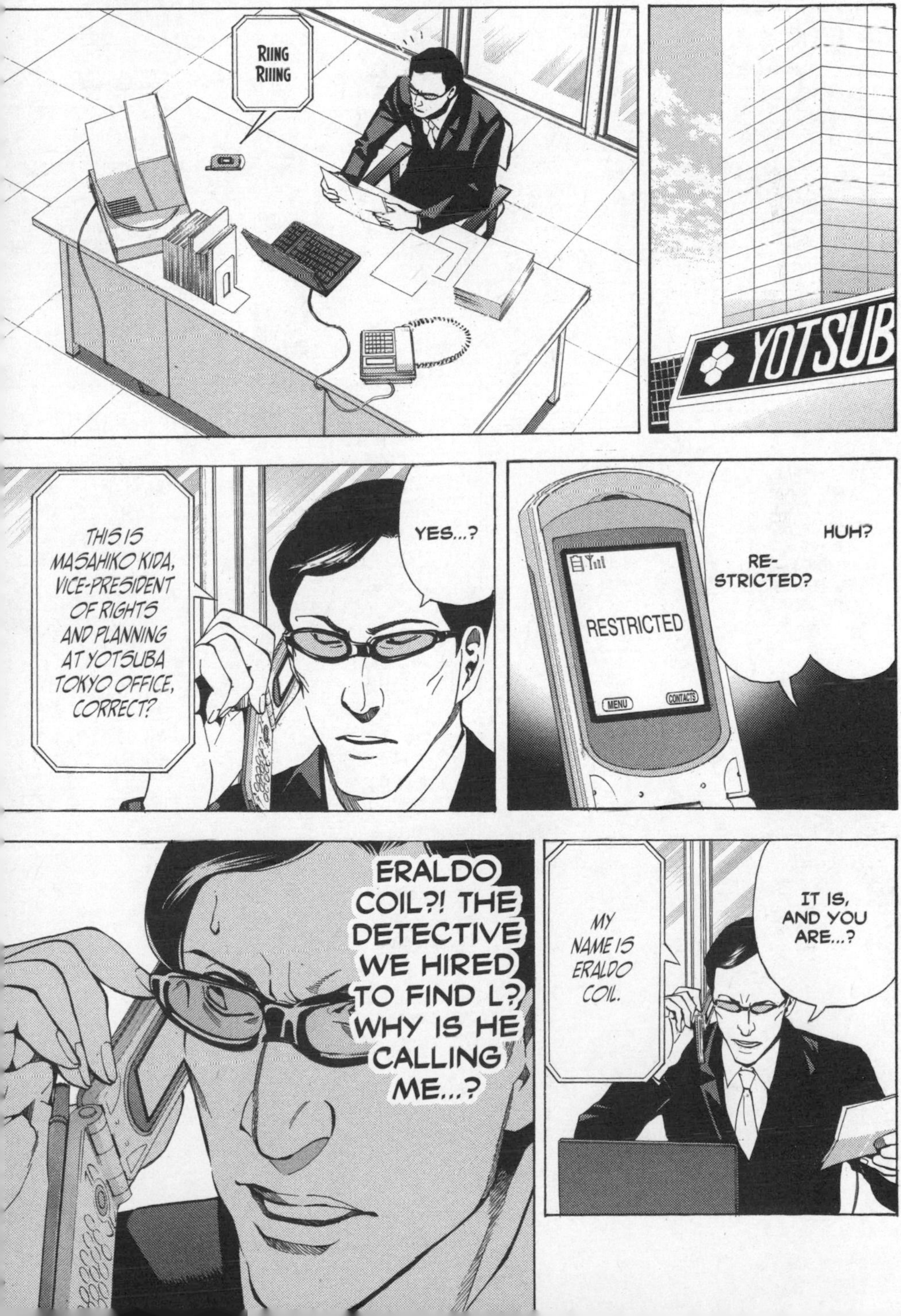
YOTSUB
RIING RIIING
HUH?
RE-STRICTED?
RESTRICTED
MENU
CONTACTS
YES...?
THIS IS MASAHIKO KIDA, VICE-PRESIDENT OF RIGHTS AND PLANNING AT YOTSUBA TOKYO OFFICE, CORRECT?
IT IS, AND YOU ARE...?
MY NAME IS ERALDO COIL.
ERALDO COIL?! THE DETECTIVE WE HIRED TO FIND L? WHY IS HE CALLING ME...?

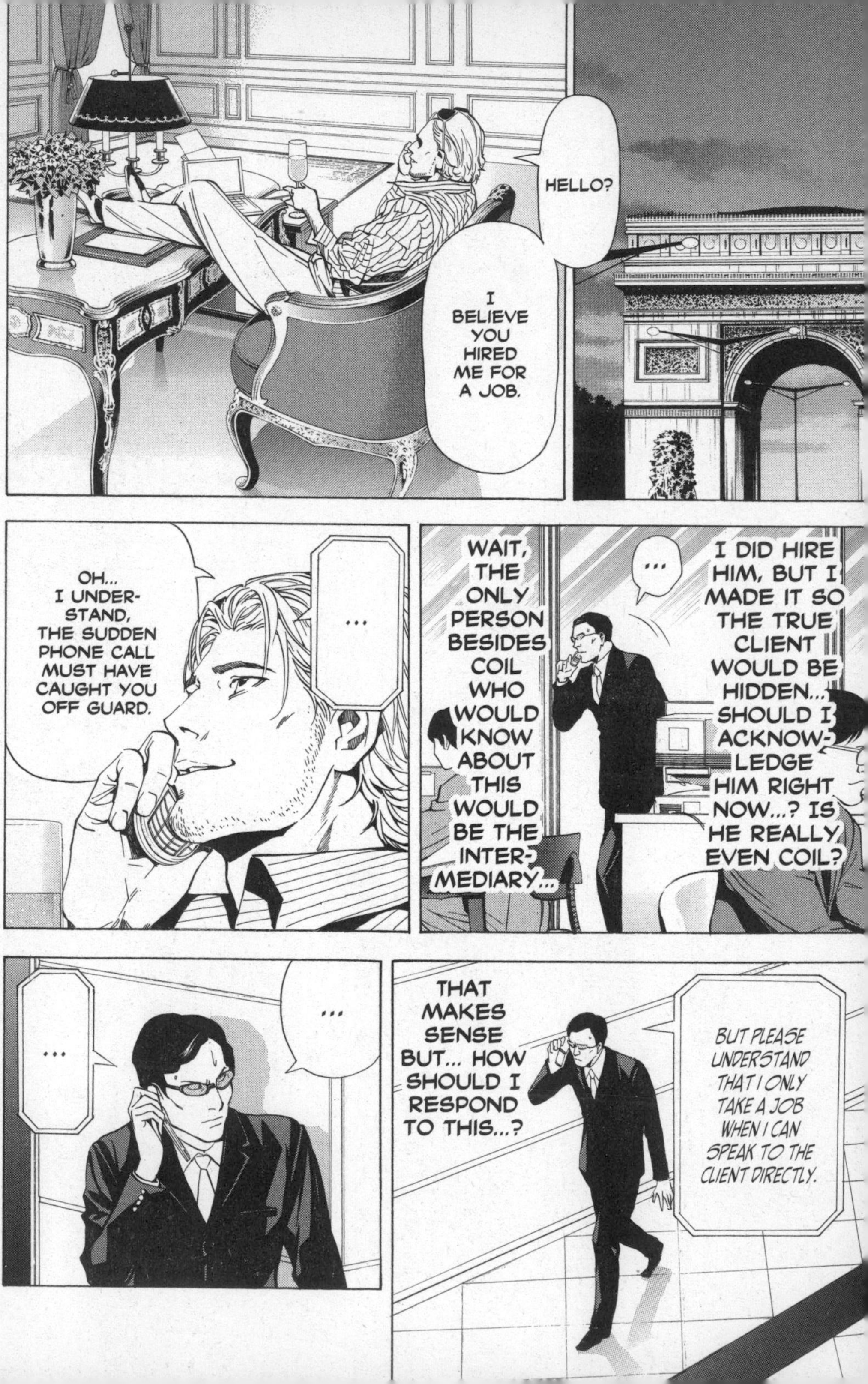

HELLO?
I BELIEVE YOU HIRED ME FOR A JOB.
I DID HIRE HIM, BUT I MADE IT SO THE TRUE CLIENT WOULD BE HIDDEN... SHOULD I ACKNOWLEDGE HIM RIGHT NOW...? IS HE REALLY EVEN COIL?
...
WAIT, THE ONLY PERSON BESIDES COIL WHO WOULD KNOW ABOUT THIS WOULD BE THE INTERMEDIARY...
...
OH... I UNDERSTAND, THE SUDDEN PHONE CALL MUST HAVE CAUGHT YOU OFF GUARD.
BUT PLEASE UNDERSTAND THAT I ONLY TAKE A JOB WHEN I CAN SPEAK TO THE CLIENT DIRECTLY.
THAT MAKES SENSE BUT... HOW SHOULD I RESPOND TO THIS...?
...
...

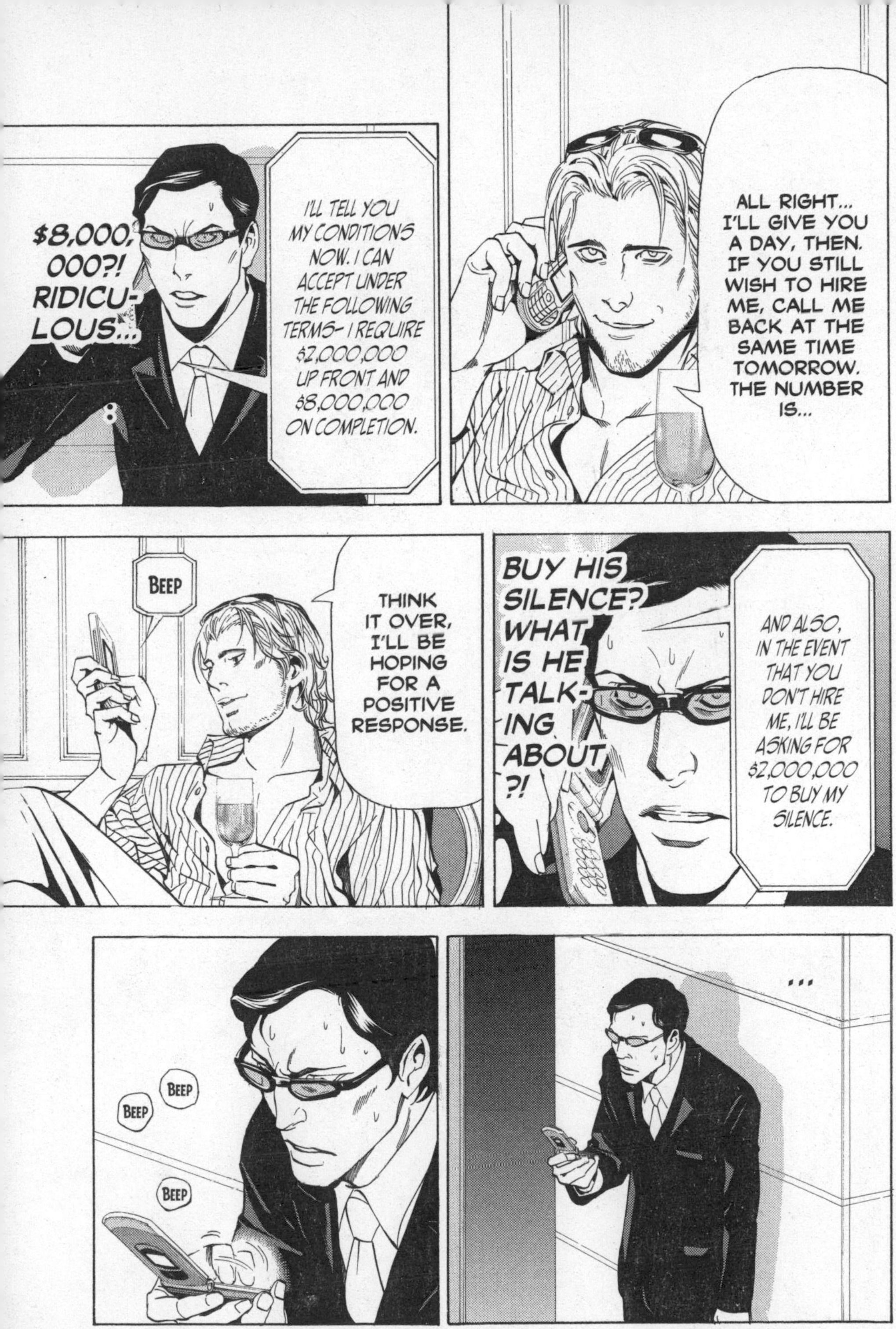
ALL RIGHT... I'LL GIVE YOU A DAY, THEN. IF YOU STILL WISH TO HIRE ME, CALL ME BACK AT THE SAME TIME TOMORROW. THE NUMBER IS...
I'LL TELL YOU MY CONDITIONS NOW. I CAN ACCEPT UNDER THE FOLLOWING TERMS- I REQUIRE $2,000,000 UP FRONT AND $8,000,000 ON COMPLETION.
$8,000,000?! RIDICULOUS...
AND ALSO, IN THE EVENT THAT YOU DON'T HIRE ME, I'LL BE ASKING FOR $2,000,000 TO BUY MY SILENCE.
BUY HIS SILENCE? WHAT IS HE TALKING ABOUT?!
THINK IT OVER, I'LL BE HOPING FOR A POSITIVE RESPONSE.
BEEP
...
BEEP
BEEP
BEEP

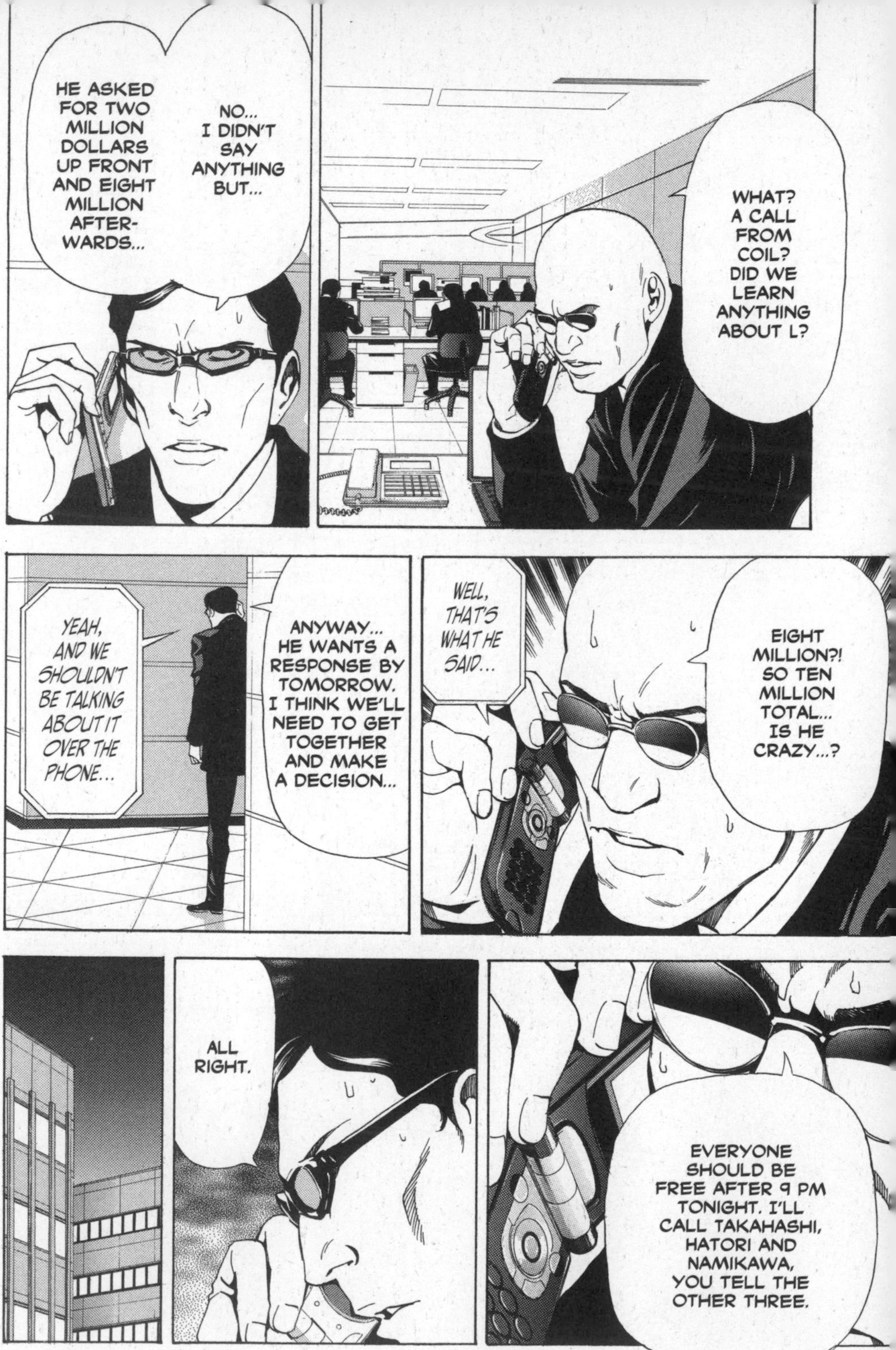
WHAT? A CALL FROM COIL? DID WE LEARN ANYTHING ABOUT L?
NO... I DIDN'T SAY ANYTHING BUT...
HE ASKED FOR TWO MILLION DOLLARS UP FRONT AND EIGHT MILLION AFTER-WARDS...
EIGHT MILLION?! SO TEN MILLION TOTAL... IS HE CRAZY...?
WELL, THAT'S WHAT HE SAID...
ANYWAY... HE WANTS A RESPONSE BY TOMORROW. I THINK WE'LL NEED TO GET TOGETHER AND MAKE A DECISION...
YEAH, AND WE SHOULDN'T BE TALKING ABOUT IT OVER THE PHONE...
EVERYONE SHOULD BE FREE AFTER 9 PM TONIGHT. I'LL CALL TAKAHASHI, HATORI AND NAMIKAWA, YOU TELL THE OTHER THREE.
ALL RIGHT.

READ THIS WAY

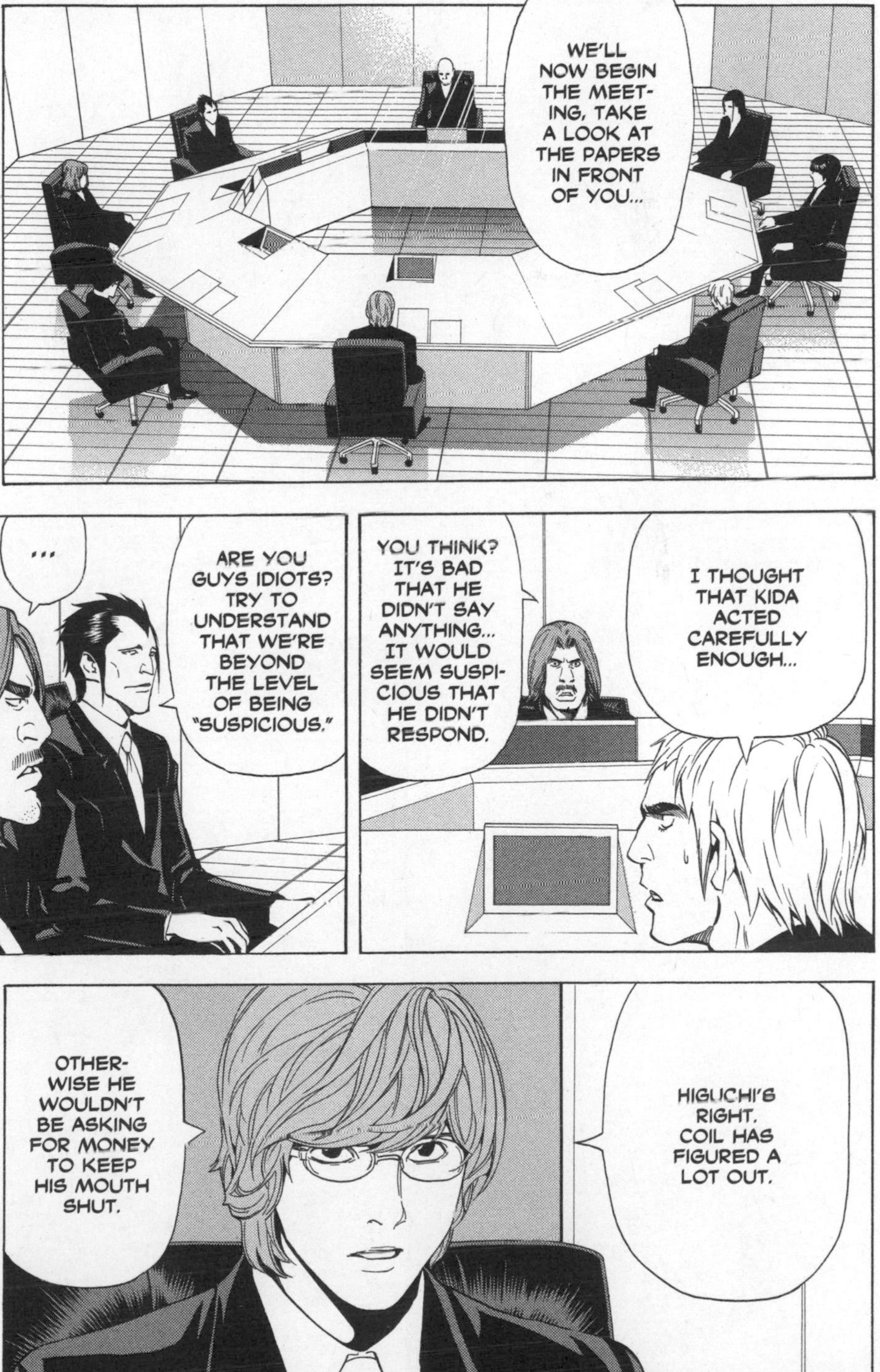
WE'LL NOW BEGIN THE MEETING, TAKE A LOOK AT THE PAPERS IN FRONT OF YOU...
I THOUGHT THAT KIDA ACTED CAREFULLY ENOUGH...
YOU THINK? IT'S BAD THAT HE DIDN'T SAY ANYTHING... IT WOULD SEEM SUSPICIOUS THAT HE DIDN'T RESPOND.
ARE YOU GUYS IDIOTS? TRY TO UNDERSTAND THAT WE'RE BEYOND THE LEVEL OF BEING "SUSPICIOUS."
...
HIGUCHI'S RIGHT. COIL HAS FIGURED A LOT OUT.
OTHERWISE HE WOULDN'T BE ASKING FOR MONEY TO KEEP HIS MOUTH SHUT.

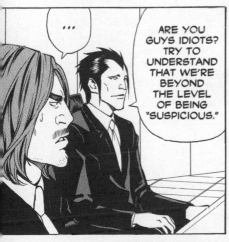

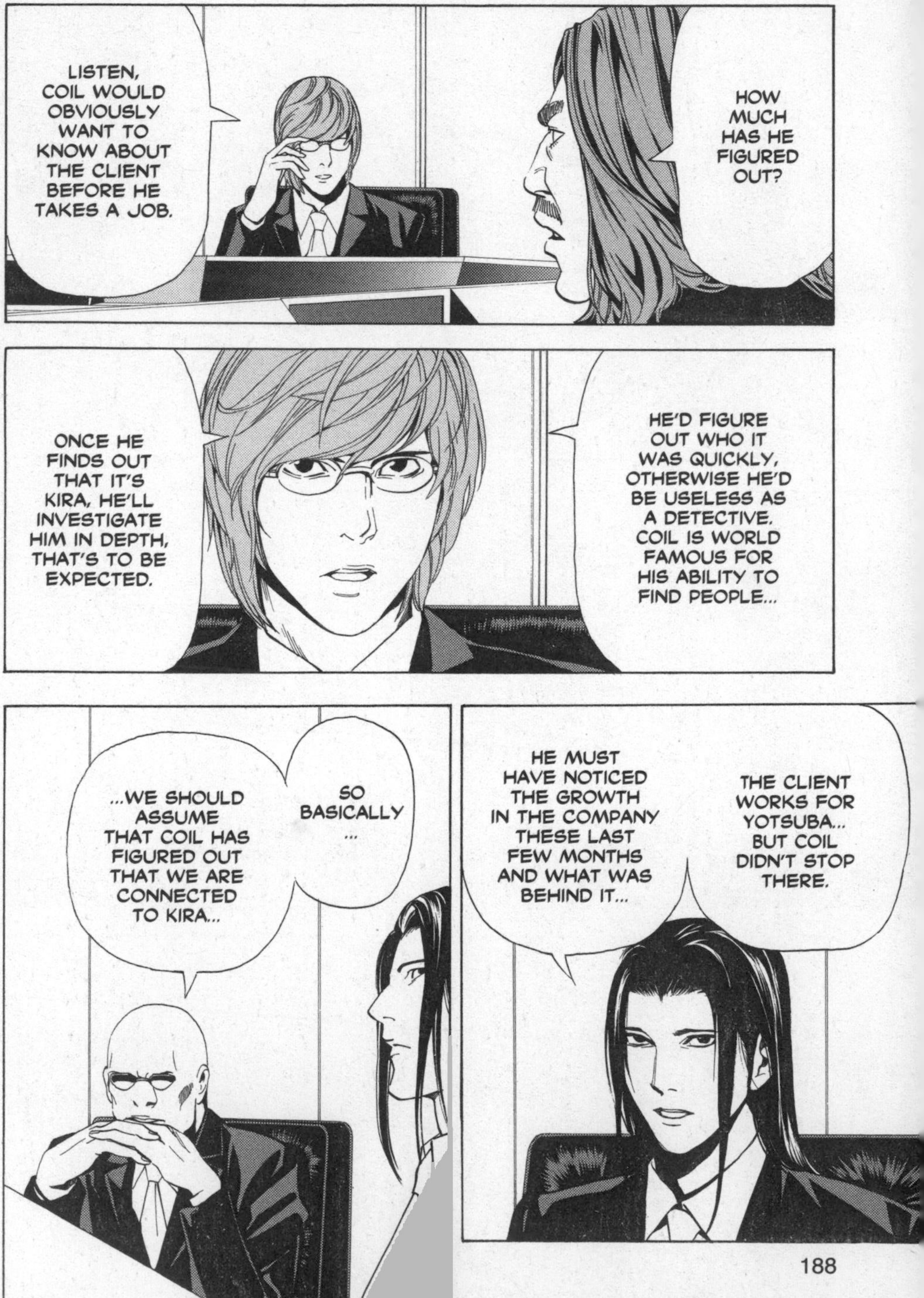
HOW MUCH HAS HE FIGURED OUT?
LISTEN, COIL WOULD OBVIOUSLY WANT TO KNOW ABOUT THE CLIENT BEFORE HE TAKES A JOB.
HE'D FIGURE OUT WHO IT WAS QUICKLY, OTHERWISE HE'D BE USELESS AS A DETECTIVE. COIL IS WORLD FAMOUS FOR HIS ABILITY TO FIND PEOPLE...
ONCE HE FINDS OUT THAT IT'S KIRA, HE'LL INVESTIGATE HIM IN DEPTH, THAT'S TO BE EXPECTED.
THE CLIENT WORKS FOR YOTSUBA... BUT COIL DIDN'T STOP THERE.
HE MUST HAVE NOTICED THE GROWTH IN THE COMPANY THESE LAST FEW MONTHS AND WHAT WAS BEHIND IT...
SO BASICALLY ...
...WE SHOULD ASSUME THAT COIL HAS FIGURED OUT THAT WE ARE CONNECTED TO KIRA...

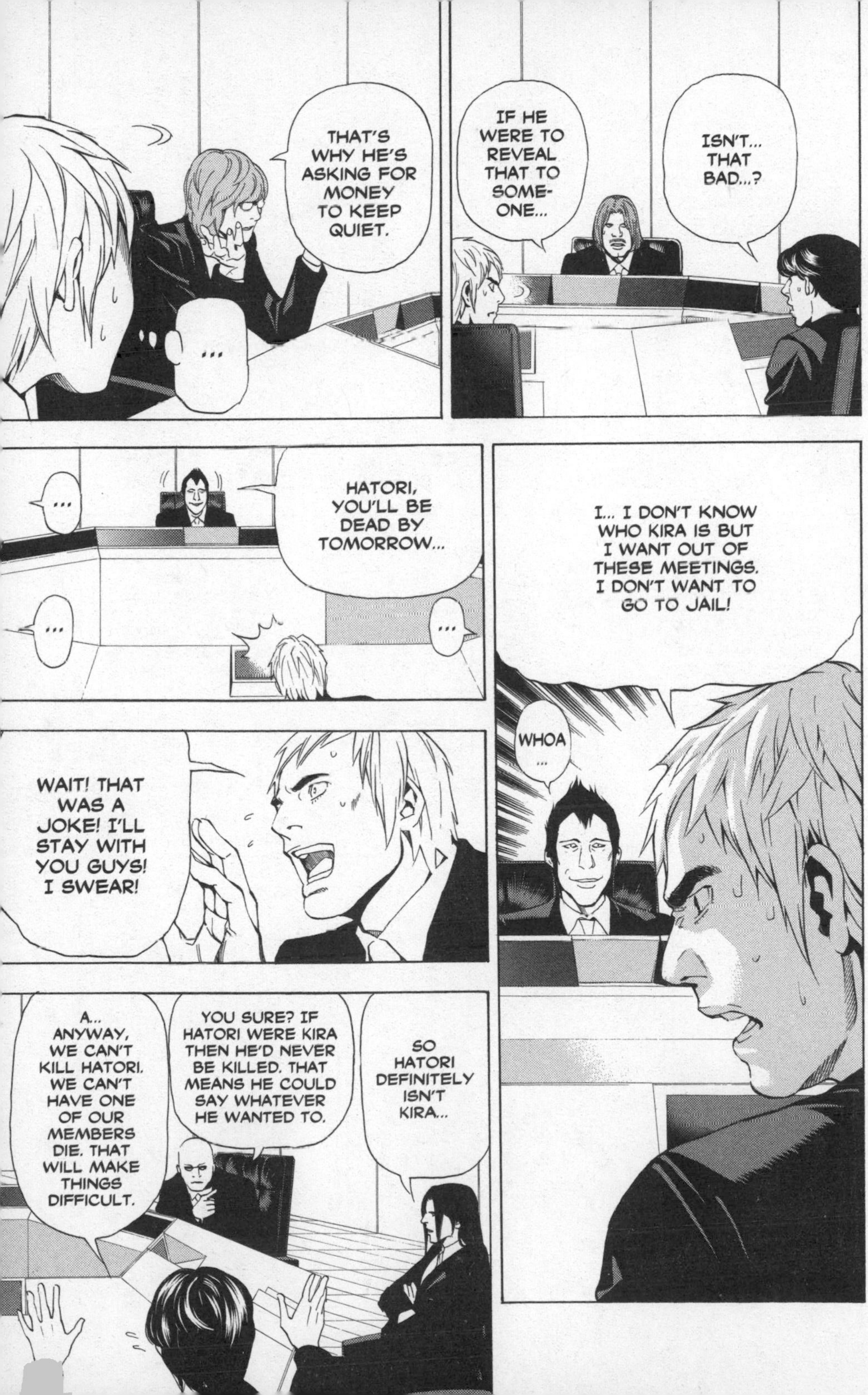
ISN'T... THAT BAD...?
IF HE WERE TO REVEAL THAT TO SOME-ONE...
THAT'S WHY HE'S ASKING FOR MONEY TO KEEP QUIET.
...
I... I DON'T KNOW WHO KIRA IS BUT I WANT OUT OF THESE MEETINGS. I DON'T WANT TO GO TO JAIL!
WHOA ...
HATORI, YOU'LL BE DEAD BY TOMORROW...
...
...
...
WAIT! THAT WAS A JOKE! I'LL STAY WITH YOU GUYS! I SWEAR!
SO HATORI DEFINITELY ISN'T KIRA...
YOU SURE? IF HATORI WERE KIRA THEN HE'D NEVER BE KILLED. THAT MEANS HE COULD SAY WHATEVER HE WANTED TO.
A... ANYWAY, WE CAN'T KILL HATORI. WE CAN'T HAVE ONE OF OUR MEMBERS DIE. THAT WILL MAKE THINGS DIFFICULT.

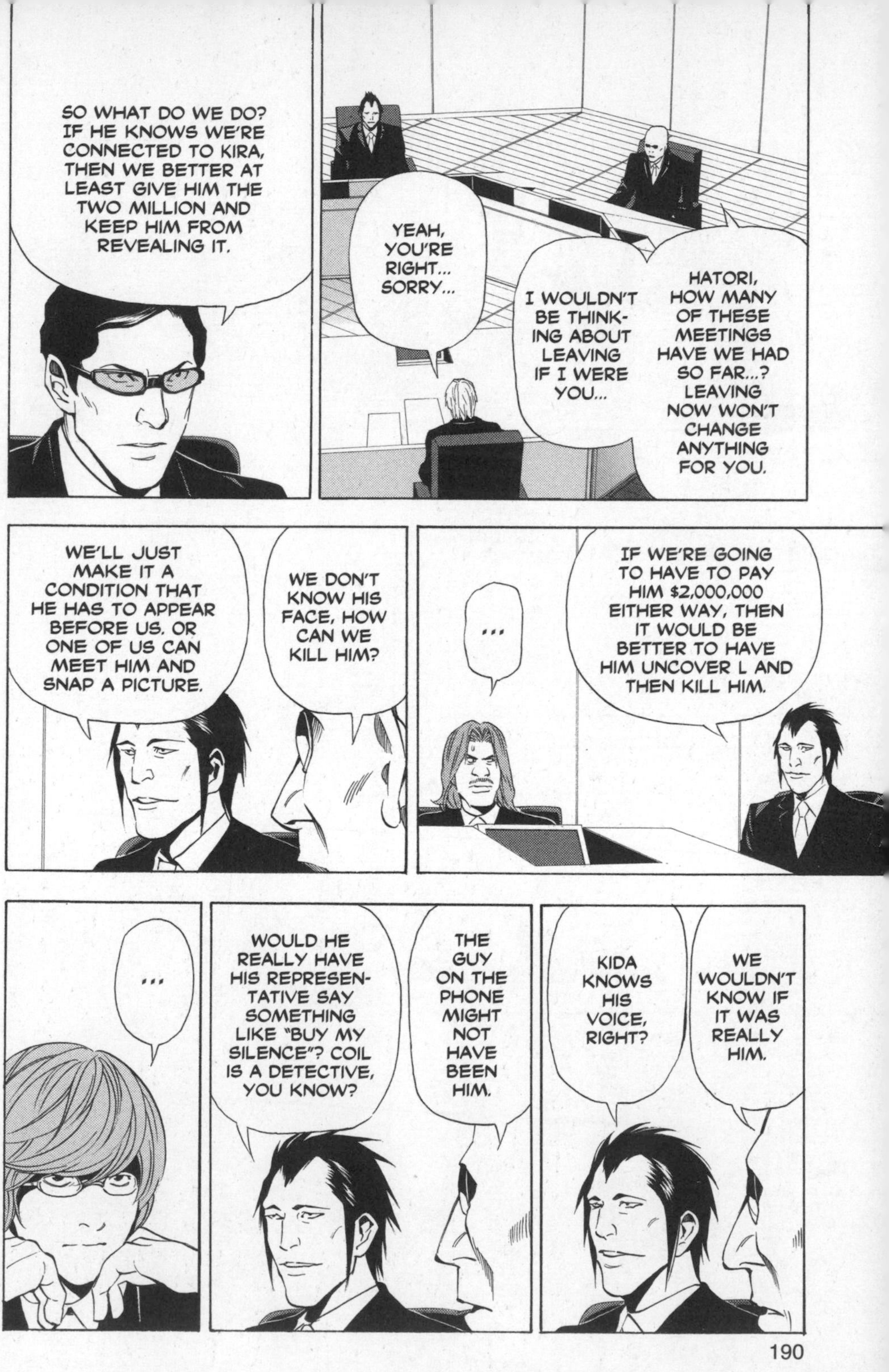
HATORI, HOW MANY OF THESE MEETINGS HAVE WE HAD SO FAR...? LEAVING NOW WON'T CHANGE ANYTHING FOR YOU.
I WOULDN'T BE THINKING ABOUT LEAVING IF I WERE YOU...
YEAH, YOU'RE RIGHT... SORRY...
SO WHAT DO WE DO? IF HE KNOWS WE'RE CONNECTED TO KIRA, THEN WE BETTER AT LEAST GIVE HIM THE TWO MILLION AND KEEP HIM FROM REVEALING IT.
IF WE'RE GOING TO HAVE TO PAY HIM $2,000,000 EITHER WAY, THEN IT WOULD BE BETTER TO HAVE HIM UNCOVER L AND THEN KILL HIM.
...
WE DON'T KNOW HIS FACE, HOW CAN WE KILL HIM?
WE'LL JUST MAKE IT A CONDITION THAT HE HAS TO APPEAR BEFORE US. OR ONE OF US CAN MEET HIM AND SNAP A PICTURE.
WE WOULDN'T KNOW IF IT WAS REALLY HIM.
KIDA KNOWS HIS VOICE, RIGHT?
THE GUY ON THE PHONE MIGHT NOT HAVE BEEN HIM.
WOULD HE REALLY HAVE HIS REPRESENTATIVE SAY SOMETHING LIKE "BUY MY SILENCE"? COIL IS A DETECTIVE, YOU KNOW?
...

READ THIS WAY

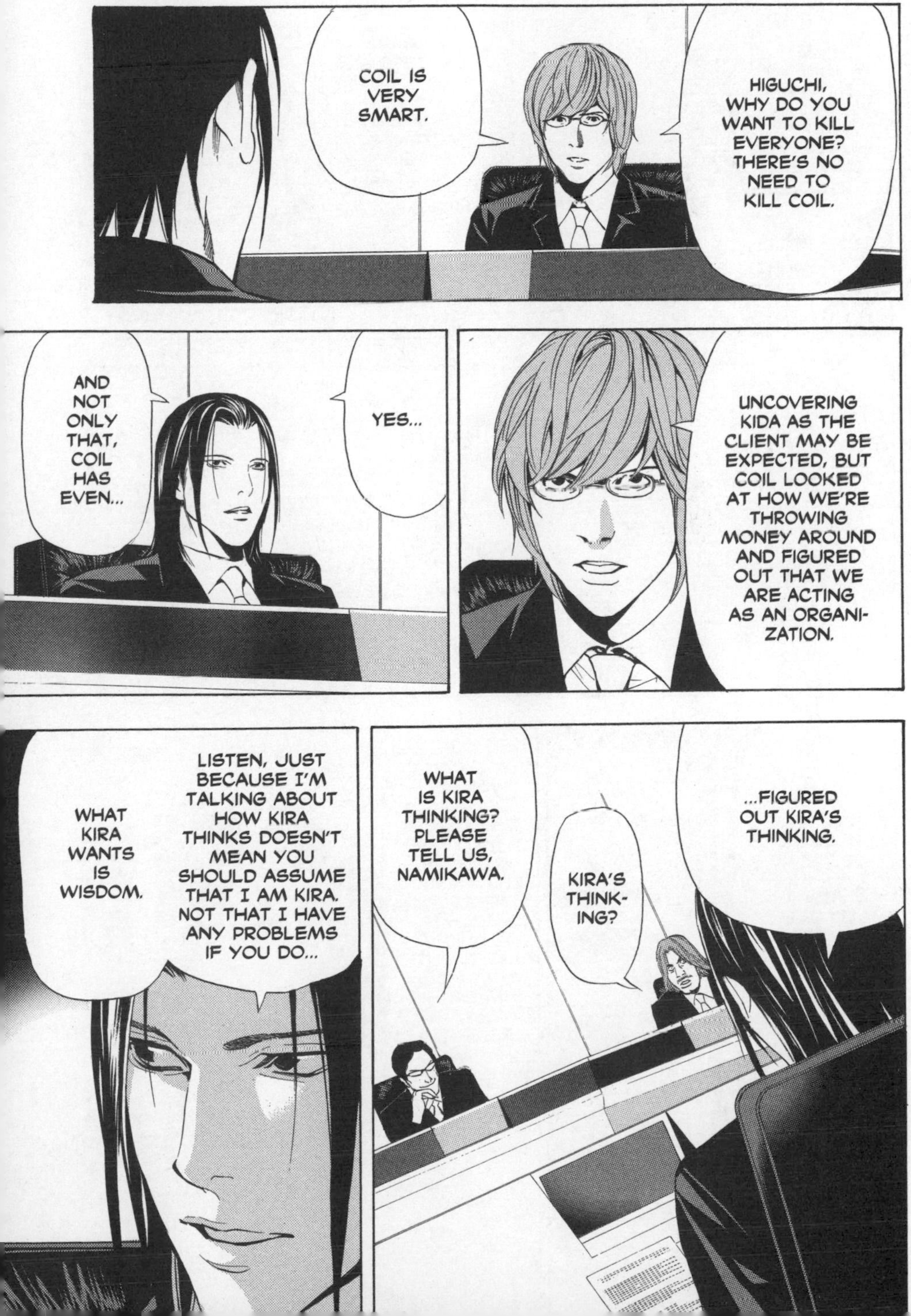
HIGUCHI, WHY DO YOU WANT TO KILL EVERYONE? THERE'S NO NEED TO KILL COIL.
COIL IS VERY SMART.
UNCOVERING KIDA AS THE CLIENT MAY BE EXPECTED, BUT COIL LOOKED AT HOW WE'RE THROWING MONEY AROUND AND FIGURED OUT THAT WE ARE ACTING AS AN ORGANI-ZATION.
YES...
AND NOT ONLY THAT, COIL HAS EVEN...
...FIGURED OUT KIRA'S THINKING.
KIRA'S THINK-ING?
WHAT IS KIRA THINKING? PLEASE TELL US, NAMIKAWA.
LISTEN, JUST BECAUSE I'M TALKING ABOUT HOW KIRA THINKS DOESN'T MEAN YOU SHOULD ASSUME THAT I AM KIRA. NOT THAT I HAVE ANY PROBLEMS IF YOU DO...
WHAT KIRA WANTS IS WISDOM.

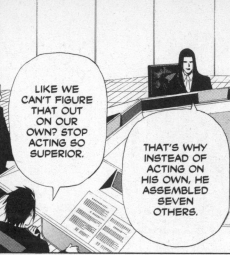

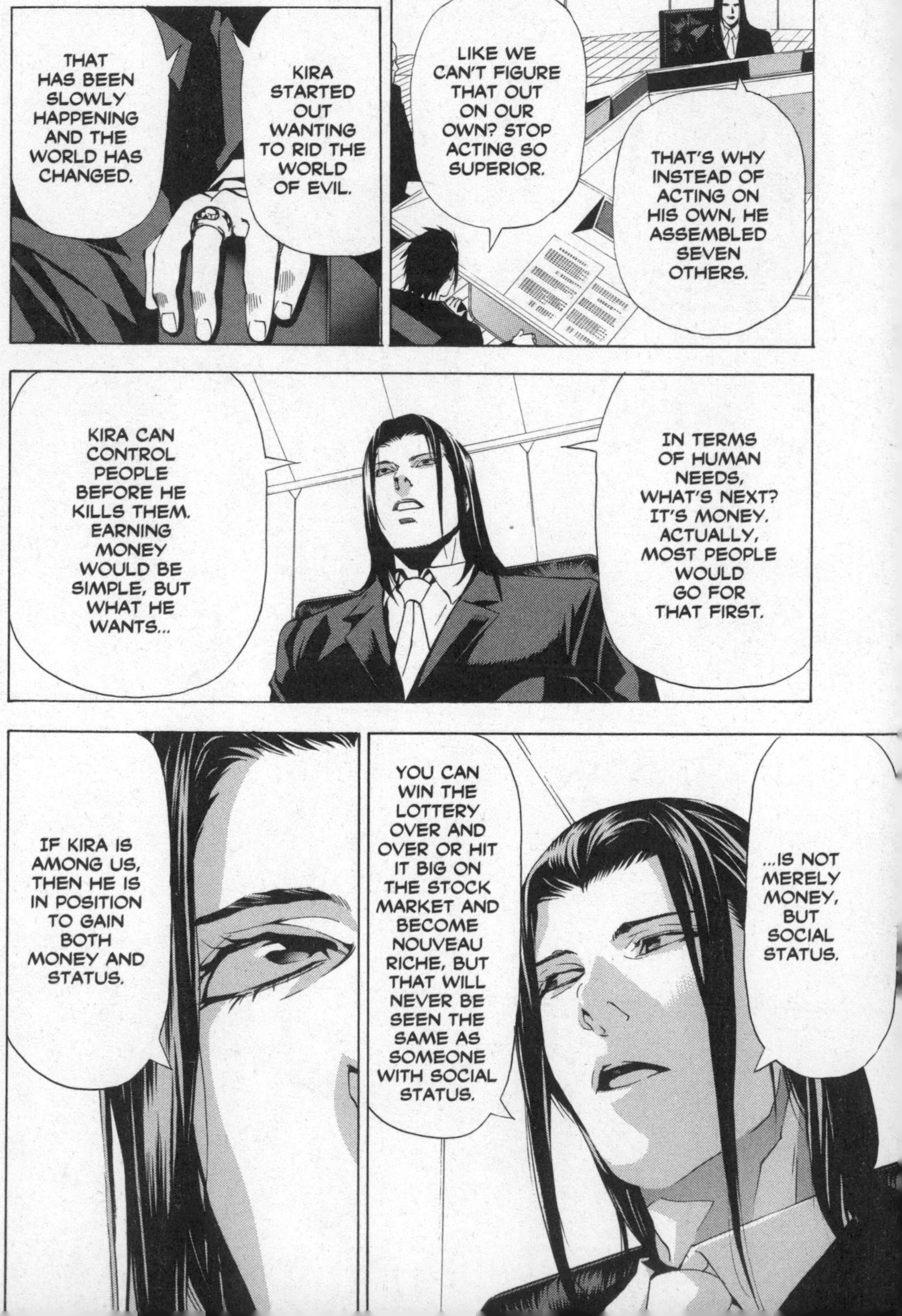
THAT'S WHY INSTEAD OF ACTING ON HIS OWN, HE ASSEMBLED SEVEN OTHERS.
LIKE WE CAN'T FIGURE THAT OUT ON OUR OWN? STOP ACTING SO SUPERIOR.
KIRA STARTED OUT WANTING TO RID THE WORLD OF EVIL.
THAT HAS BEEN SLOWLY HAPPENING AND THE WORLD HAS CHANGED.
IN TERMS OF HUMAN NEEDS, WHAT'S NEXT? IT'S MONEY. ACTUALLY, MOST PEOPLE WOULD GO FOR THAT FIRST.
KIRA CAN CONTROL PEOPLE BEFORE HE KILLS THEM. EARNING MONEY WOULD BE SIMPLE, BUT WHAT HE WANTS...
...IS NOT MERELY MONEY, BUT SOCIAL STATUS.
YOU CAN WIN THE LOTTERY OVER AND OVER OR HIT IT BIG ON THE STOCK MARKET AND BECOME NOUVEAU RICHE, BUT THAT WILL NEVER BE SEEN THE SAME AS SOMEONE WITH SOCIAL STATUS.
IF KIRA IS AMONG US, THEN HE IS IN POSITION TO GAIN BOTH MONEY AND STATUS.

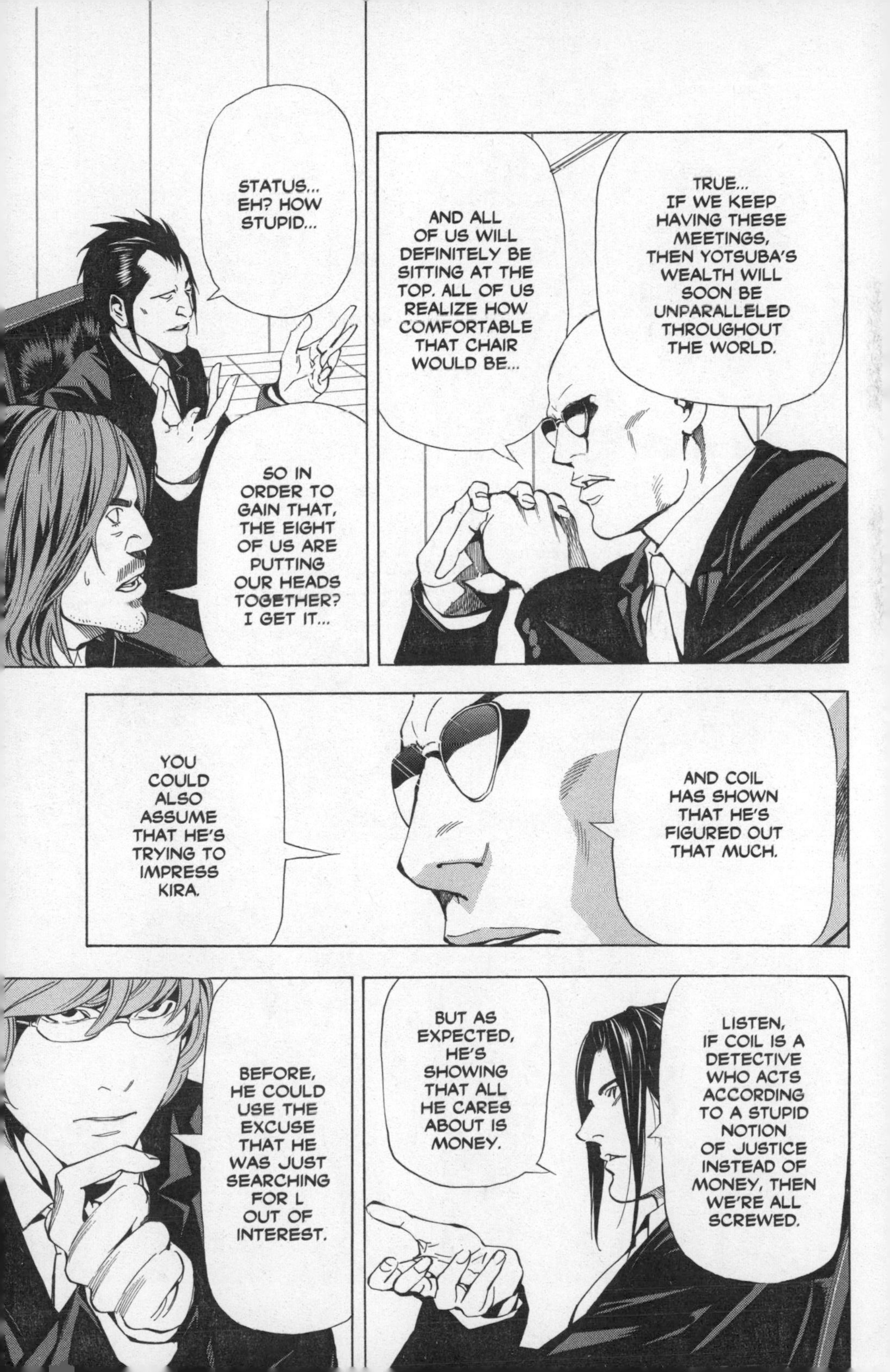
TRUE... IF WE KEEP HAVING THESE MEETINGS, THEN YOTSUBA'S WEALTH WILL SOON BE UNPARALLELED THROUGHOUT THE WORLD.
AND ALL OF US WILL DEFINITELY BE SITTING AT THE TOP. ALL OF US REALIZE HOW COMFORTABLE THAT CHAIR WOULD BE...
STATUS... EH? HOW STUPID...
SO IN ORDER TO GAIN THAT, THE EIGHT OF US ARE PUTTING OUR HEADS TOGETHER? I GET IT...
AND COIL HAS SHOWN THAT HE'S FIGURED OUT THAT MUCH.
YOU COULD ALSO ASSUME THAT HE'S TRYING TO IMPRESS KIRA.
LISTEN, IF COIL IS A DETECTIVE WHO ACTS ACCORDING TO A STUPID NOTION OF JUSTICE INSTEAD OF MONEY, THEN WE'RE ALL SCREWED.
BUT AS EXPECTED, HE'S SHOWING THAT ALL HE CARES ABOUT IS MONEY.
BEFORE, HE COULD USE THE EXCUSE THAT HE WAS JUST SEARCHING FOR L OUT OF INTEREST.

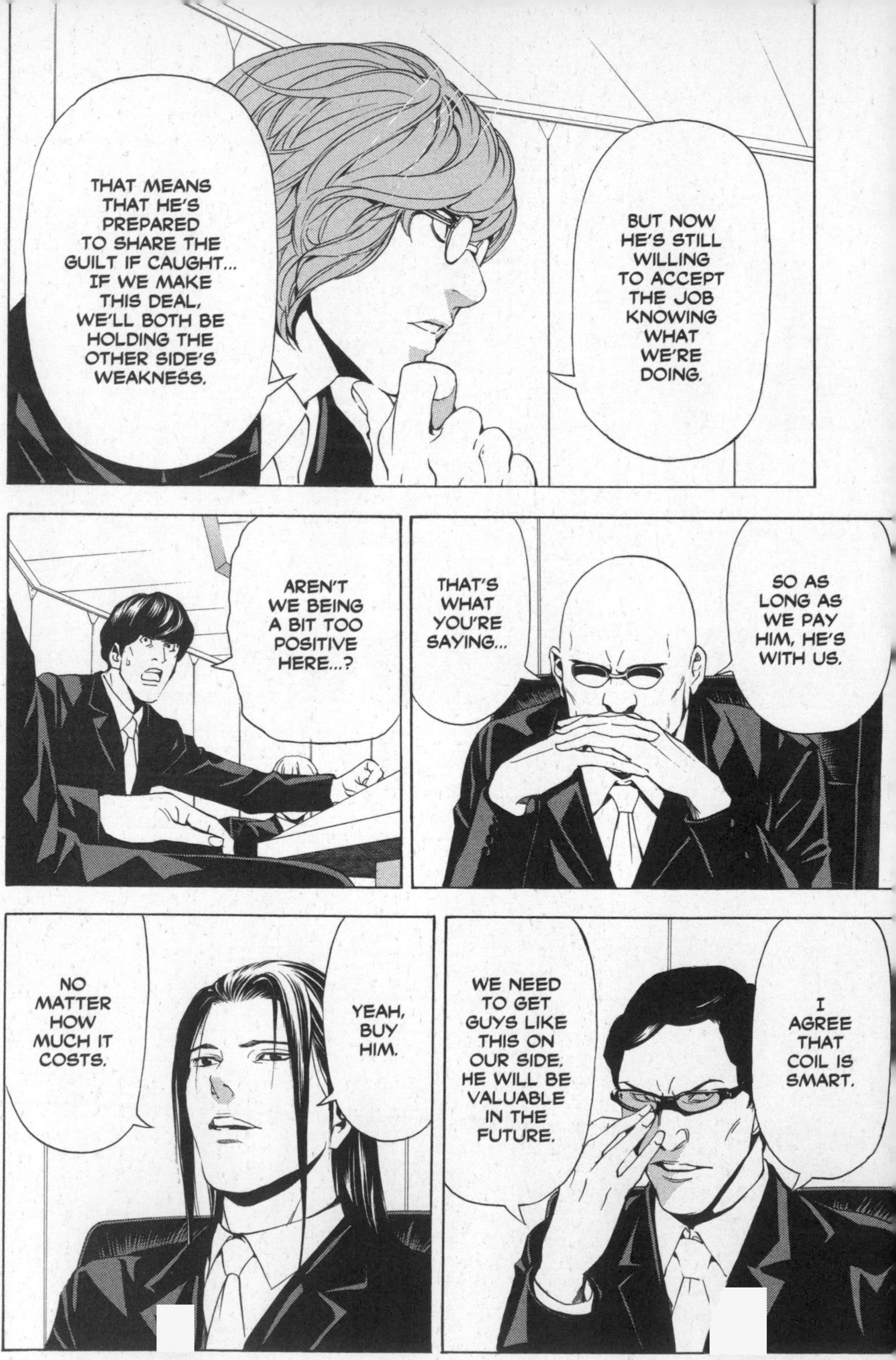
BUT NOW HE'S STILL WILLING TO ACCEPT THE JOB KNOWING WHAT WE'RE DOING.
THAT MEANS THAT HE'S PREPARED TO SHARE THE GUILT IF CAUGHT... IF WE MAKE THIS DEAL, WE'LL BOTH BE HOLDING THE OTHER SIDE'S WEAKNESS.
SO AS LONG AS WE PAY HIM, HE'S WITH US.
THAT'S WHAT YOU'RE SAYING...
AREN'T WE BEING A BIT TOO POSITIVE HERE...?
I AGREE THAT COIL IS SMART.
WE NEED TO GET GUYS LIKE THIS ON OUR SIDE. HE WILL BE VALUABLE IN THE FUTURE.
YEAH, BUY HIM.
NO MATTER HOW MUCH IT COSTS.

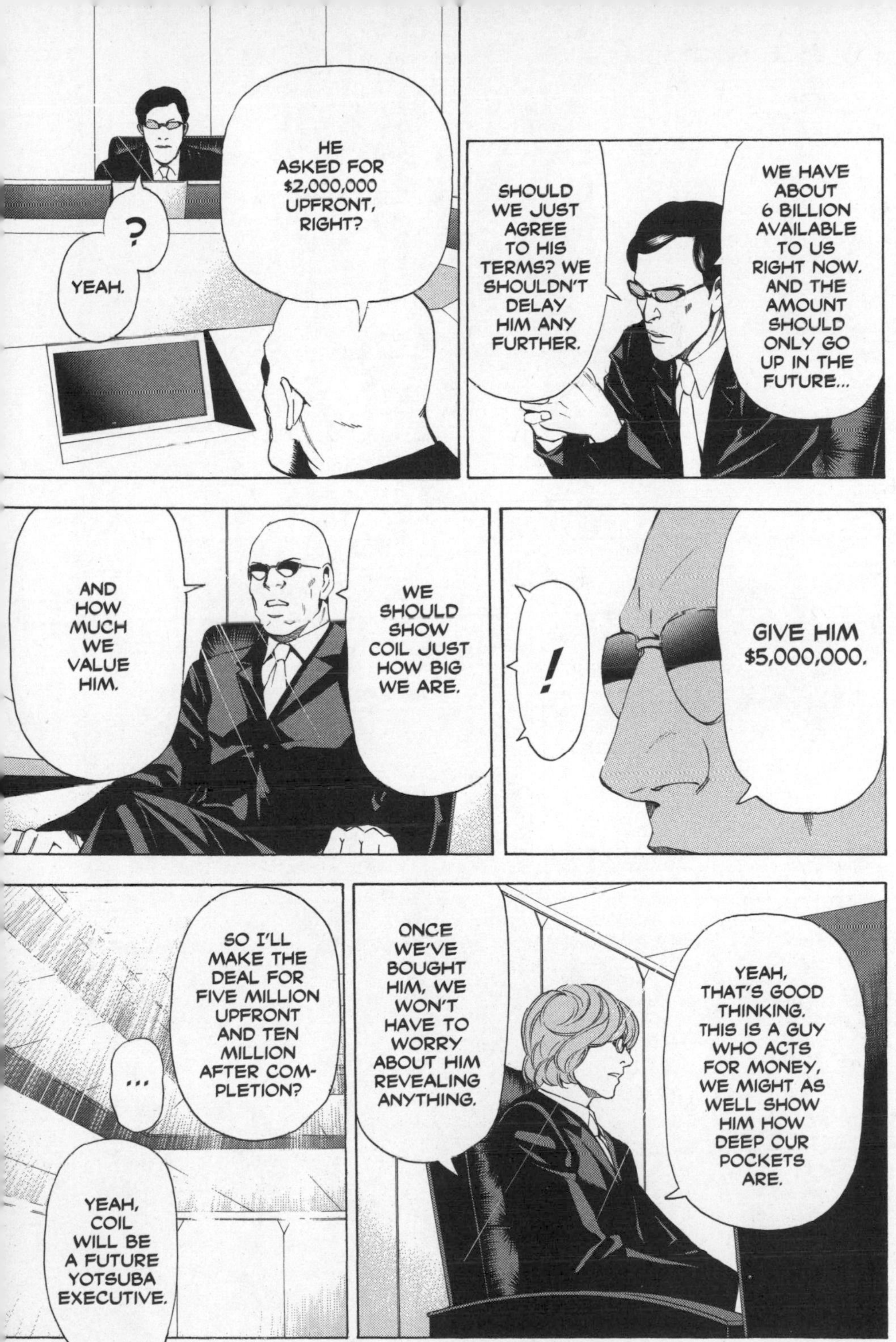
WE HAVE ABOUT 6 BILLION AVAILABLE TO US RIGHT NOW. AND THE AMOUNT SHOULD ONLY GO UP IN THE FUTURE...
SHOULD WE JUST AGREE TO HIS TERMS? WE SHOULDN'T DELAY HIM ANY FURTHER.
HE ASKED FOR $2,000,000 UPFRONT, RIGHT?
?
YEAH.
GIVE HIM $5,000,000.
!
WE SHOULD SHOW COIL JUST HOW BIG WE ARE.
AND HOW MUCH WE VALUE HIM.
YEAH, THAT'S GOOD THINKING. THIS IS A GUY WHO ACTS FOR MONEY, WE MIGHT AS WELL SHOW HIM HOW DEEP OUR POCKETS ARE.
ONCE WE'VE BOUGHT HIM, WE WON'T HAVE TO WORRY ABOUT HIM REVEALING ANYTHING.
SO I'LL MAKE THE DEAL FOR FIVE MILLION UPFRONT AND TEN MILLION AFTER COMPLETION?
...
YEAH, COIL WILL BE A FUTURE YOTSUBA EXECUTIVE.

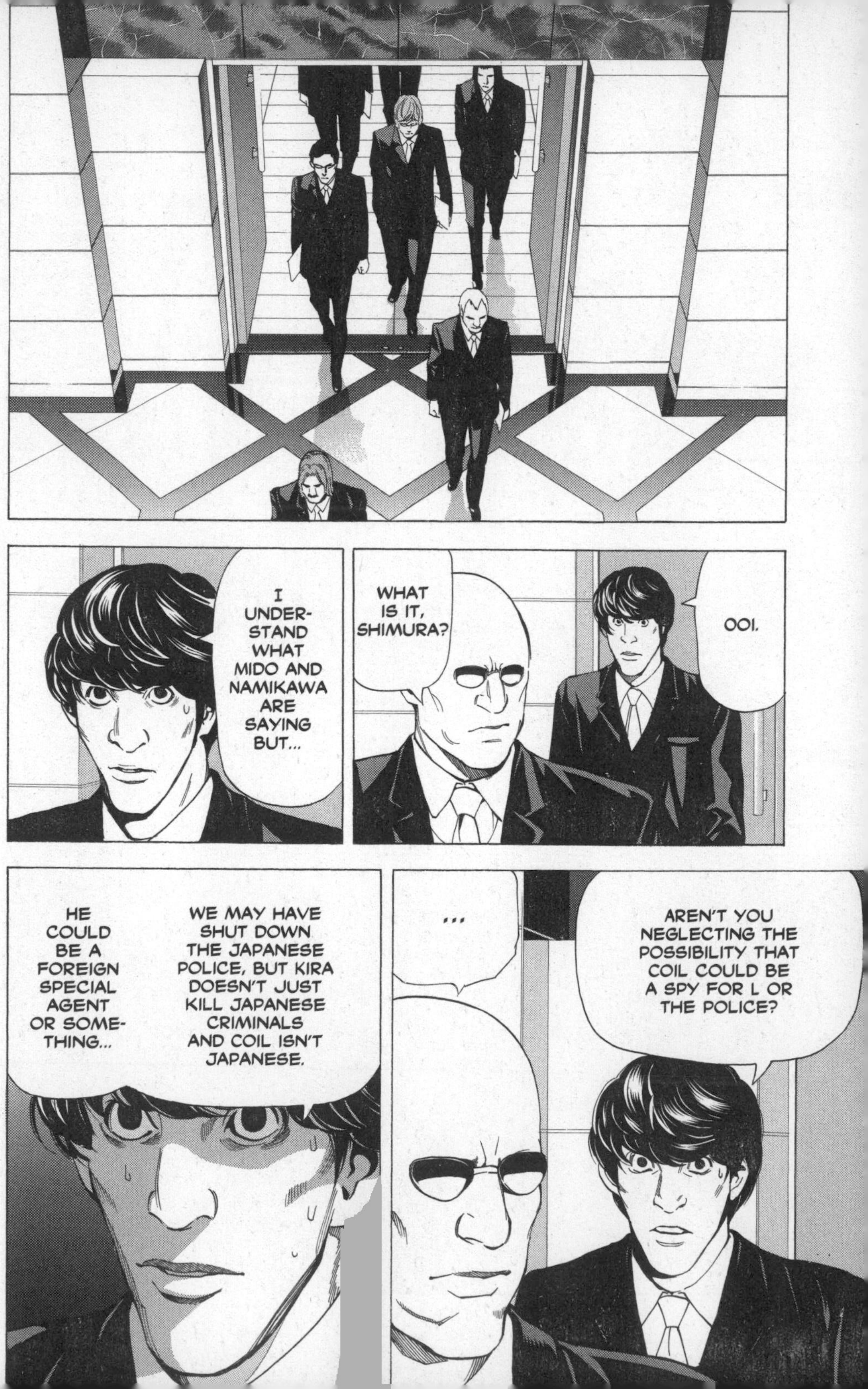

OOI.
WHAT IS IT, SHIMURA?
I UNDERSTAND WHAT MIDO AND NAMIKAWA ARE SAYING BUT...
AREN'T YOU NEGLECTING THE POSSIBILITY THAT COIL COULD BE A SPY FOR L OR THE POLICE?
...
WE MAY HAVE SHUT DOWN THE JAPANESE POLICE, BUT KIRA DOESN'T JUST KILL JAPANESE CRIMINALS AND COIL ISN'T JAPANESE.
HE COULD BE A FOREIGN SPECIAL AGENT OR SOMETHING...

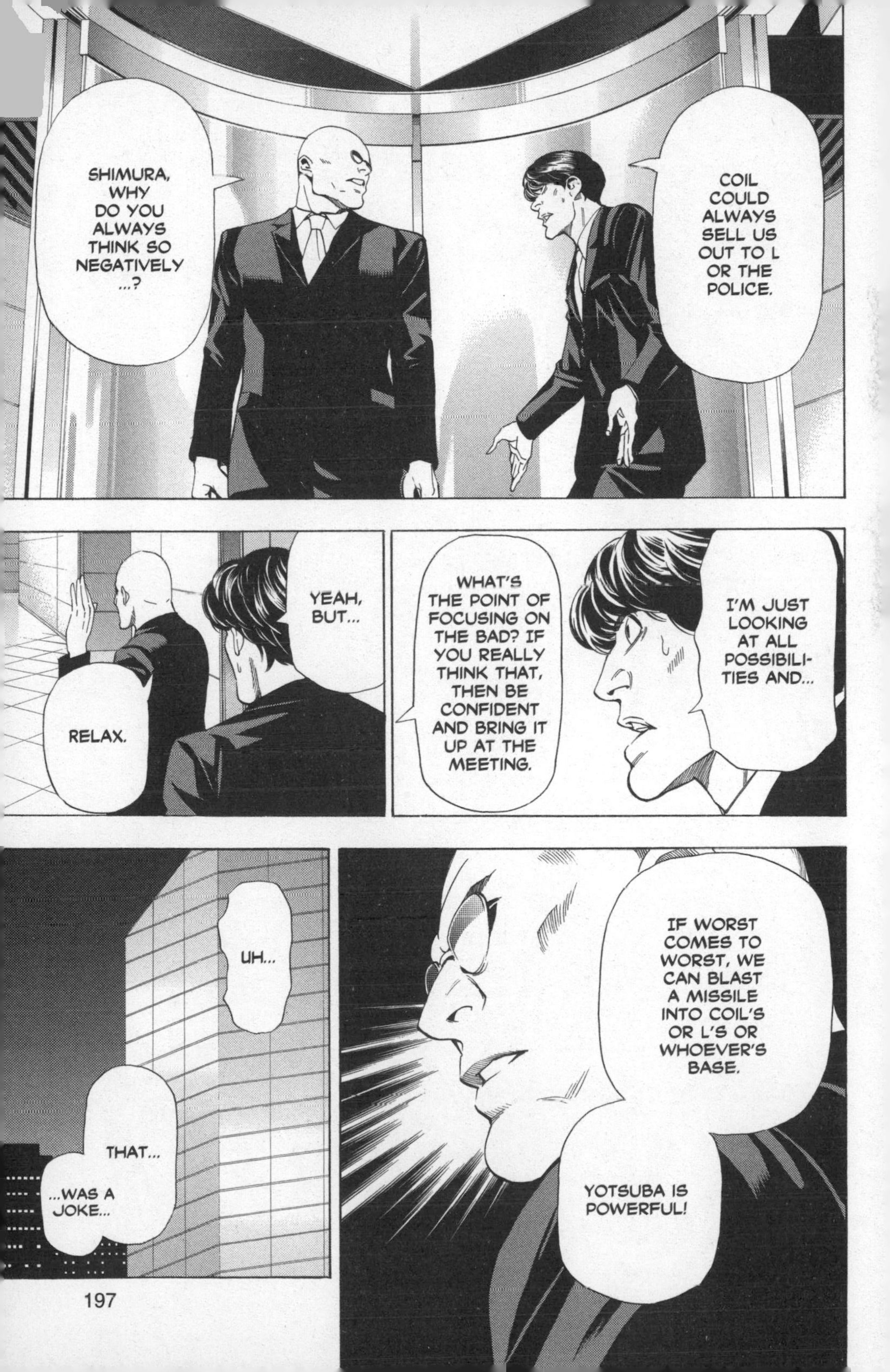
COIL COULD ALWAYS SELL US OUT TO L OR THE POLICE.
SHIMURA, WHY DO YOU ALWAYS THINK SO NEGATIVELY ...?
I'M JUST LOOKING AT ALL POSSIBILITIES AND...
WHAT'S THE POINT OF FOCUSING ON THE BAD? IF YOU REALLY THINK THAT, THEN BE CONFIDENT AND BRING IT UP AT THE MEETING.
YEAH, BUT...
RELAX.
IF WORST COMES TO WORST, WE CAN BLAST A MISSILE INTO COIL'S OR L'S OR WHOEVER'S BASE.
YOTSUBA IS POWERFUL!
UH...
THAT...
...WAS A JOKE...

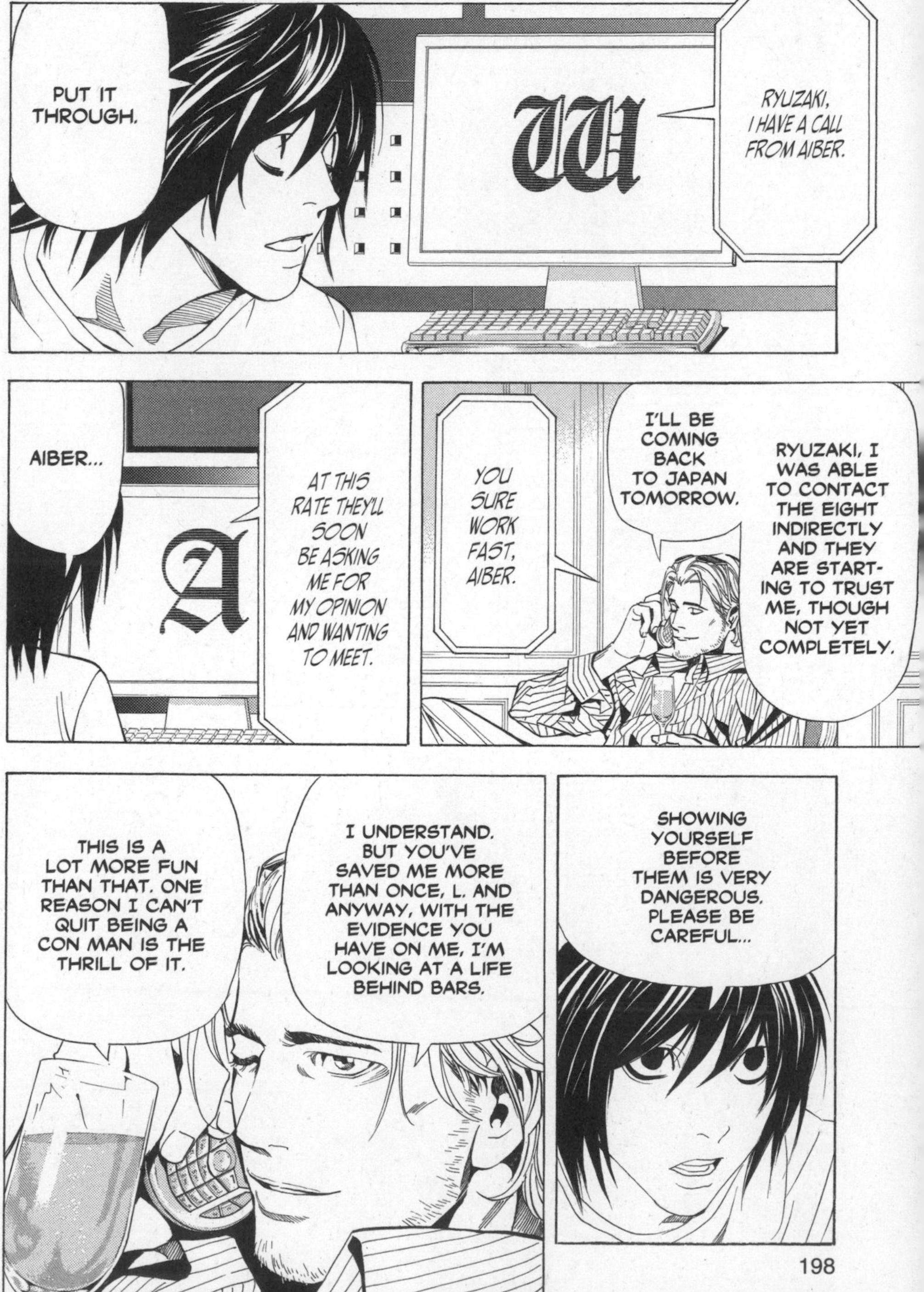
RYUZAKI, I HAVE A CALL FROM AIBER.
PUT IT THROUGH.
RYUZAKI, I WAS ABLE TO CONTACT THE EIGHT INDIRECTLY AND THEY ARE STARTING TO TRUST ME, THOUGH NOT YET COMPLETELY.
I'LL BE COMING BACK TO JAPAN TOMORROW.
YOU SURE WORK FAST, AIBER.
AT THIS RATE THEY'LL SOON BE ASKING ME FOR MY OPINION AND WANTING TO MEET.
AIBER...
SHOWING YOURSELF BEFORE THEM IS VERY DANGEROUS. PLEASE BE CAREFUL...
I UNDERSTAND. BUT YOU'VE SAVED ME MORE THAN ONCE, L. AND ANYWAY, WITH THE EVIDENCE YOU HAVE ON ME, I'M LOOKING AT A LIFE BEHIND BARS.
THIS IS A LOT MORE FUN THAN THAT. ONE REASON I CAN'T QUIT BEING A CON MAN IS THE THRILL OF IT.

READ THIS WAY

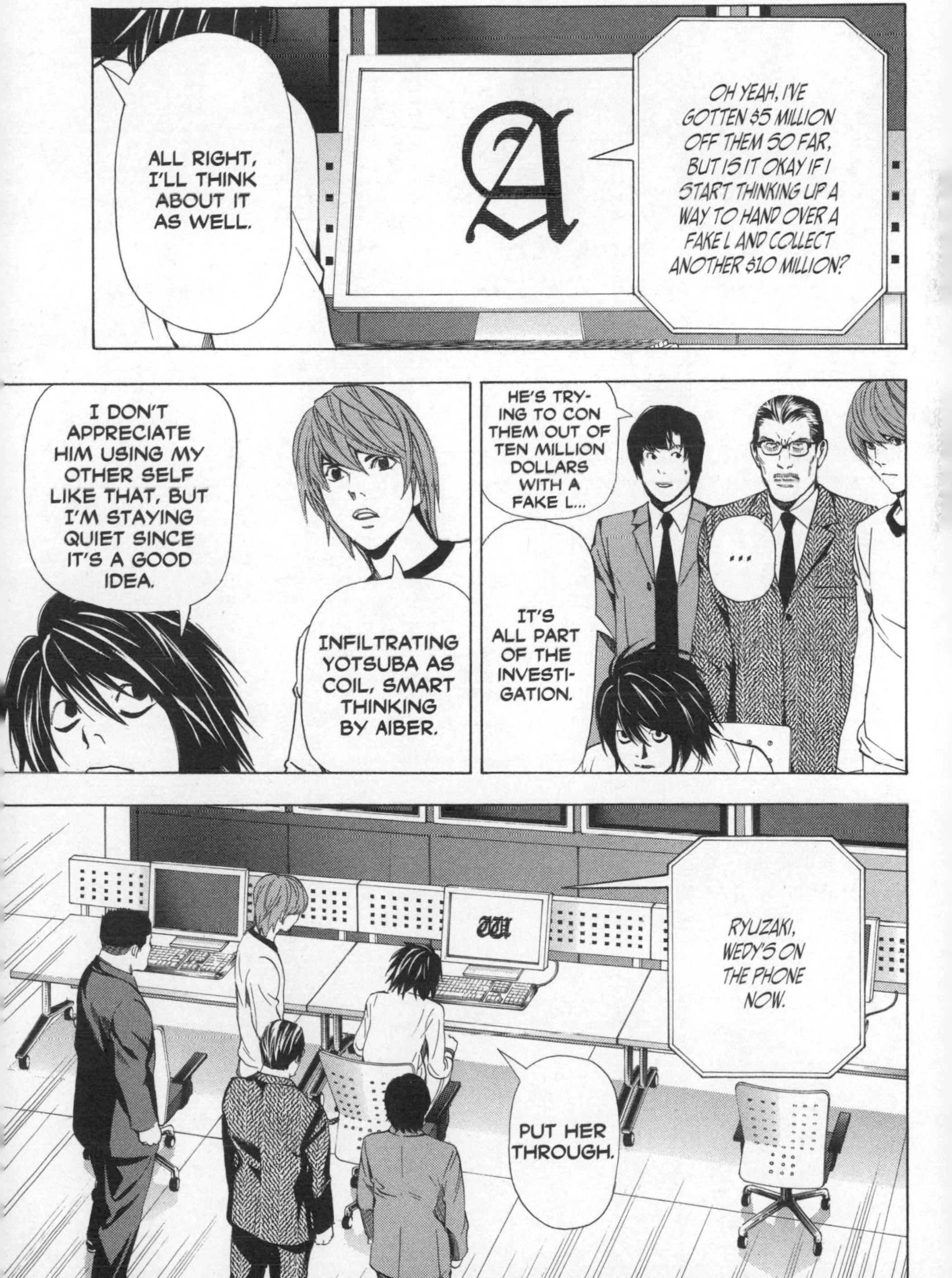
OH YEAH, I'VE GOTTEN $5 MILLION OFF THEM SO FAR, BUT IS IT OKAY IF I START THINKING UP A WAY TO HAND OVER A FAKE L AND COLLECT ANOTHER $10 MILLION?
ALL RIGHT, I'LL THINK ABOUT IT AS WELL.
HE'S TRYING TO CON THEM OUT OF TEN MILLION DOLLARS WITH A FAKE L...
...
IT'S ALL PART OF THE INVESTIGATION.
INFILTRATING YOTSUBA AS COIL, SMART THINKING BY AIBER.
I DON'T APPRECIATE HIM USING MY OTHER SELF LIKE THAT, BUT I'M STAYING QUIET SINCE IT'S A GOOD IDEA.
RYUZAKI, WEDY'S ON THE PHONE NOW.
PUT HER THROUGH.

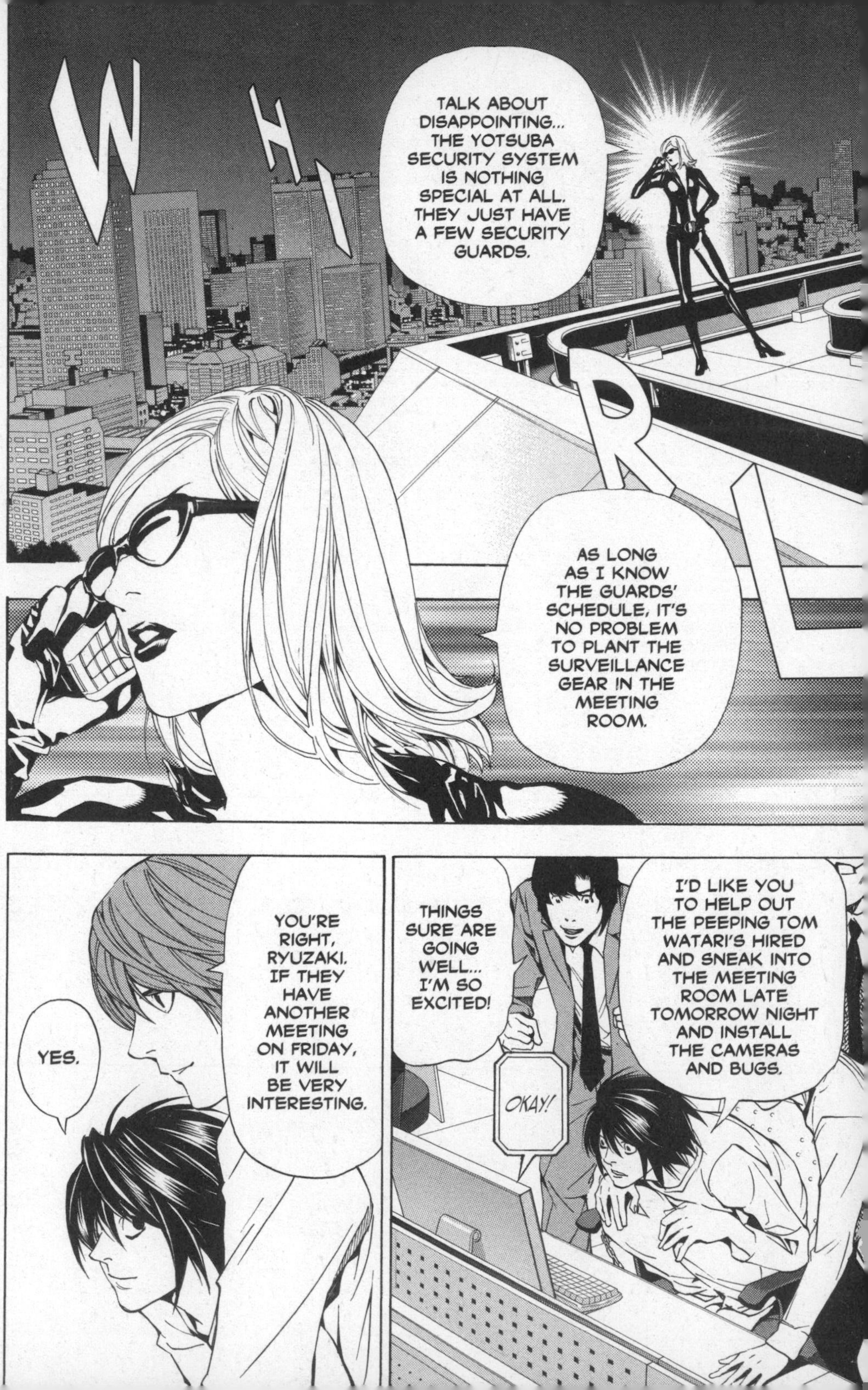
WHIRL
TALK ABOUT DISAPPOINTING... THE YOTSUBA SECURITY SYSTEM IS NOTHING SPECIAL AT ALL. THEY JUST HAVE A FEW SECURITY GUARDS.
AS LONG AS I KNOW THE GUARDS' SCHEDULE, IT'S NO PROBLEM TO PLANT THE SURVEILLANCE GEAR IN THE MEETING ROOM.
I'D LIKE YOU TO HELP OUT THE PEEPING TOM WATARI'S HIRED AND SNEAK INTO THE MEETING ROOM LATE TOMORROW NIGHT AND INSTALL THE CAMERAS AND BUGS.
THINGS SURE ARE GOING WELL... I'M SO EXCITED!
OKAY!
YOU'RE RIGHT, RYUZAKI. IF THEY HAVE ANOTHER MEETING ON FRIDAY, IT WILL BE VERY INTERESTING.
YES.

READ THIS WAY

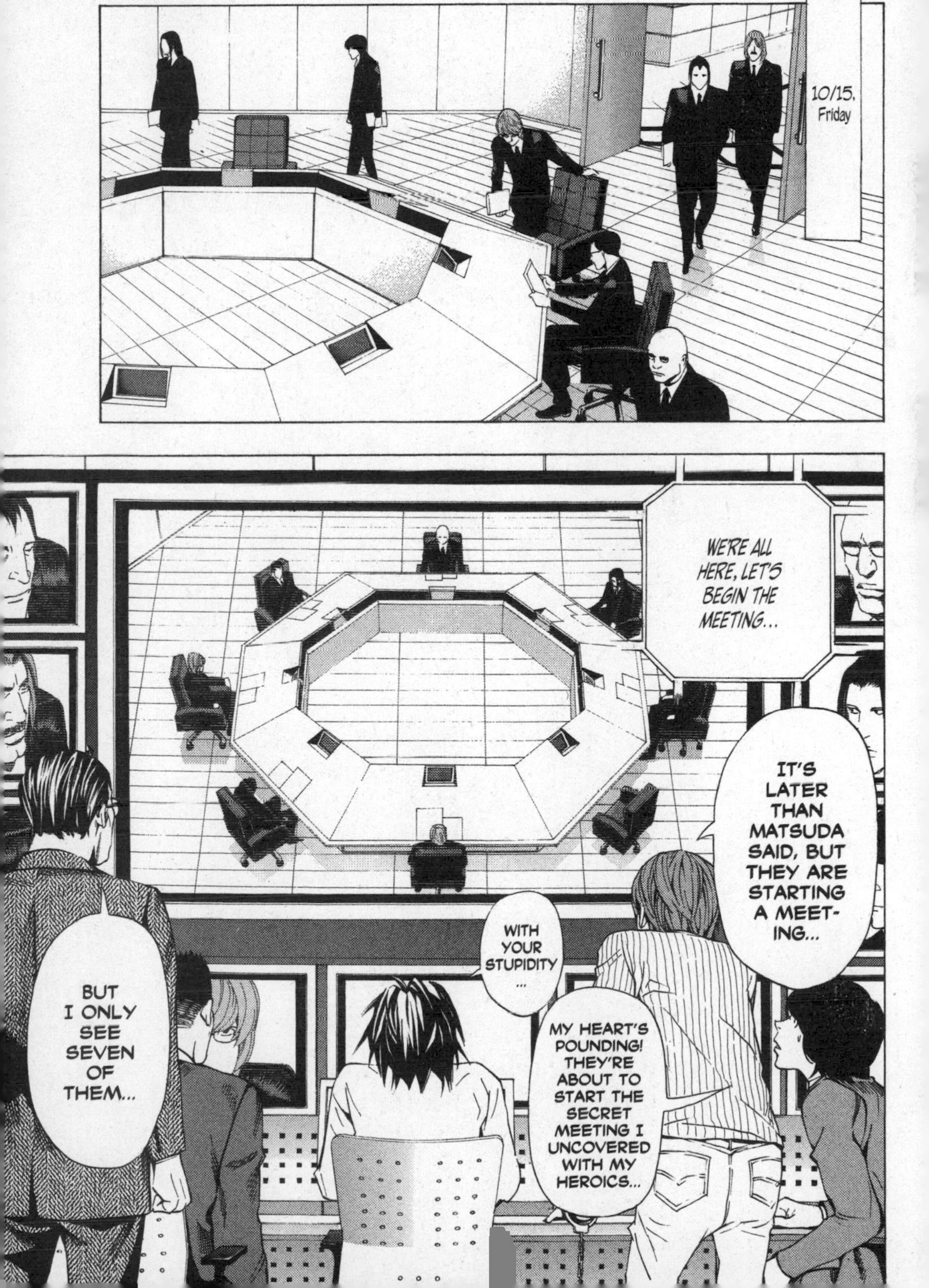
10/15, Friday
WE'RE ALL HERE, LET'S BEGIN THE MEETING...
IT'S LATER THAN MATSUDA SAID, BUT THEY ARE STARTING A MEET-ING...
MY HEART'S POUNDING! THEY'RE ABOUT TO START THE SECRET MEETING I UNCOVERED WITH MY HEROICS...
WITH YOUR STUPIDITY ...
BUT I ONLY SEE SEVEN OF THEM...

DEATH NOTE
HOW TO USE IT
XXXI

○The number of pages of the DEATH NOTE will never run out.

デスノートは、いくら名前を書いてもページがなくならない。

I figured I'd at least try hard to not be so wordy here.
I'm tired and I'm working hard.

-Tsugumi Ohba

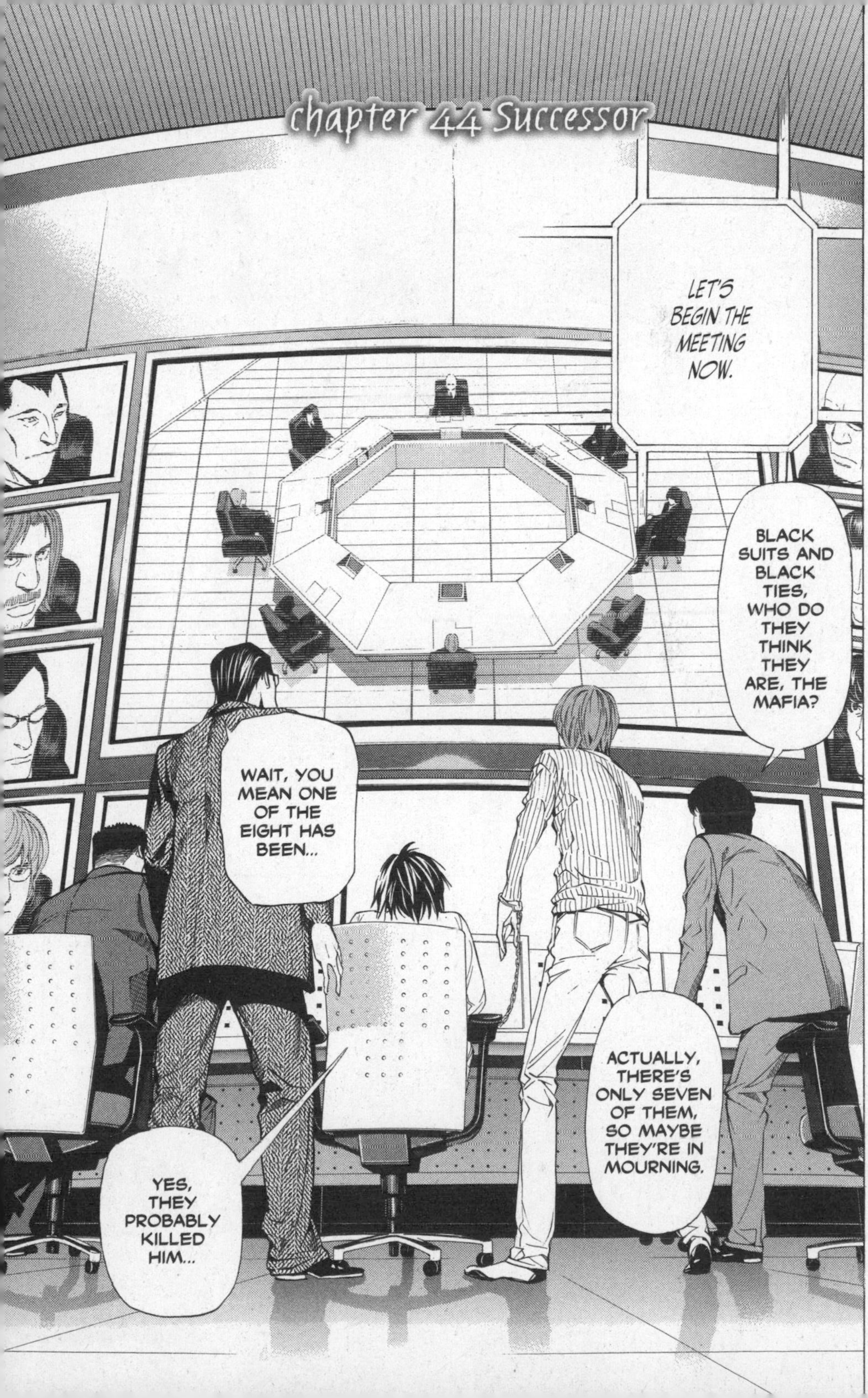
chapter 44 Successor
LET'S BEGIN THE MEETING NOW.
BLACK SUITS AND BLACK TIES, WHO DO THEY THINK THEY ARE, THE MAFIA?
ACTUALLY, THERE'S ONLY SEVEN OF THEM, SO MAYBE THEY'RE IN MOURNING.
WAIT, YOU MEAN ONE OF THE EIGHT HAS BEEN...
YES, THEY PROBABLY KILLED HIM...

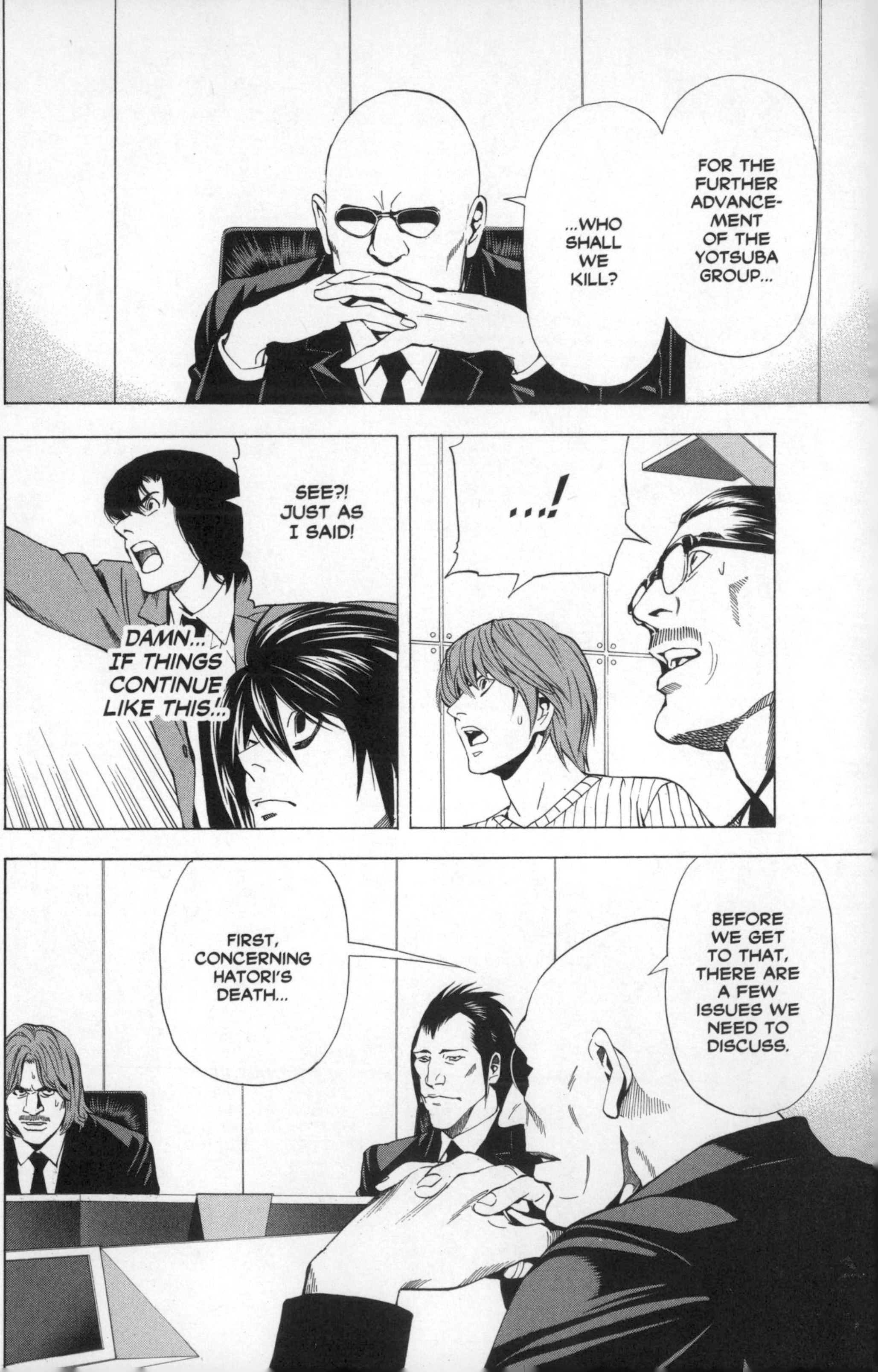
FOR THE FURTHER ADVANCE-MENT OF THE YOTSUBA GROUP...
...WHO SHALL WE KILL?
...!
SEE?! JUST AS I SAID!
DAMN... IF THINGS CONTINUE LIKE THIS...
BEFORE WE GET TO THAT, THERE ARE A FEW ISSUES WE NEED TO DISCUSS.
FIRST, CONCERNING HATORI'S DEATH...

READ THIS WAY

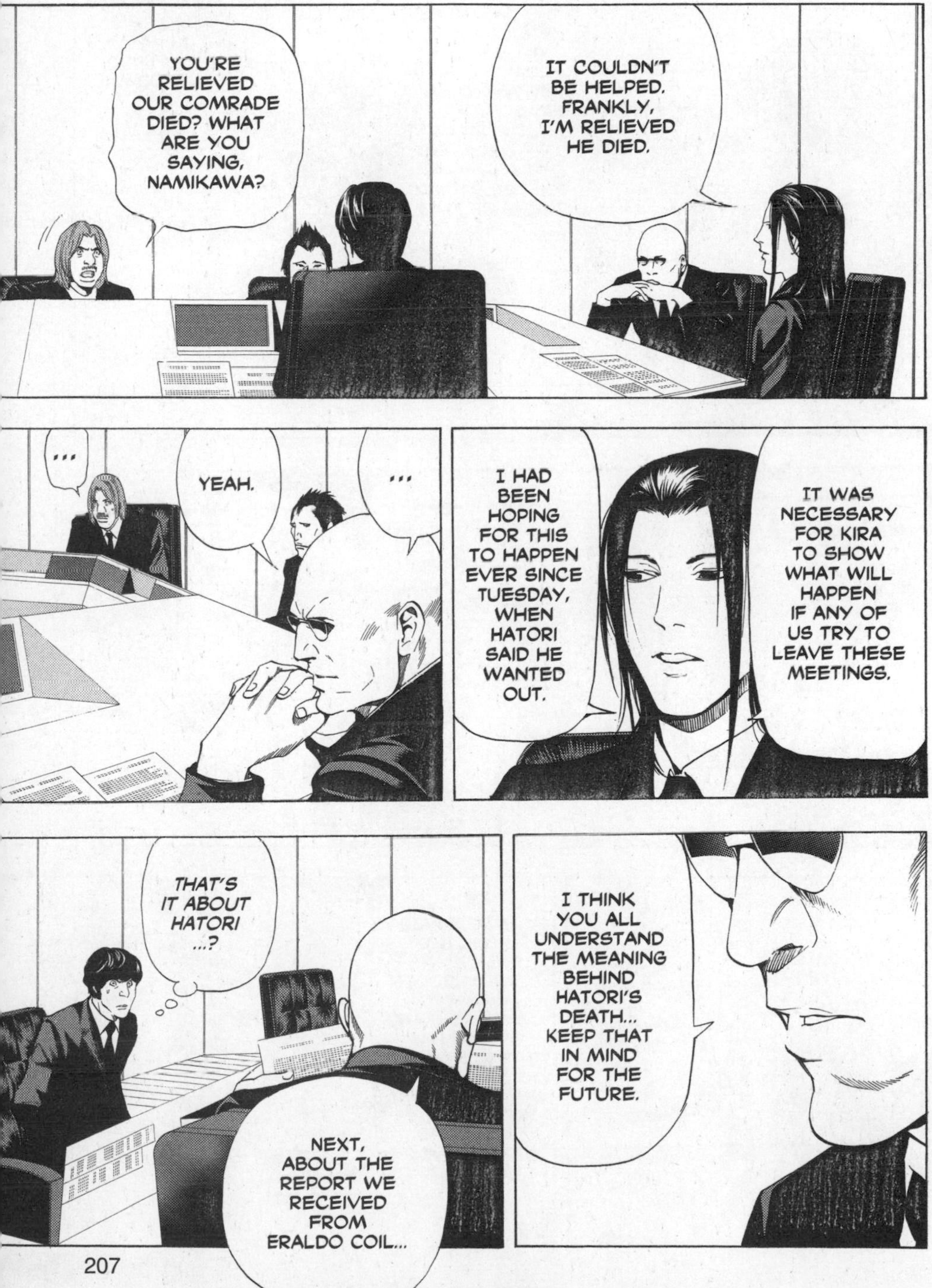
IT COULDN'T BE HELPED. FRANKLY, I'M RELIEVED HE DIED.
YOU'RE RELIEVED OUR COMRADE DIED? WHAT ARE YOU SAYING, NAMIKAWA?
IT WAS NECESSARY FOR KIRA TO SHOW WHAT WILL HAPPEN IF ANY OF US TRY TO LEAVE THESE MEETINGS.
I HAD BEEN HOPING FOR THIS TO HAPPEN EVER SINCE TUESDAY, WHEN HATORI SAID HE WANTED OUT.
...
YEAH.
...
I THINK YOU ALL UNDERSTAND THE MEANING BEHIND HATORI'S DEATH... KEEP THAT IN MIND FOR THE FUTURE.
THAT'S IT ABOUT HATORI ...?
NEXT, ABOUT THE REPORT WE RECEIVED FROM ERALDO COIL...

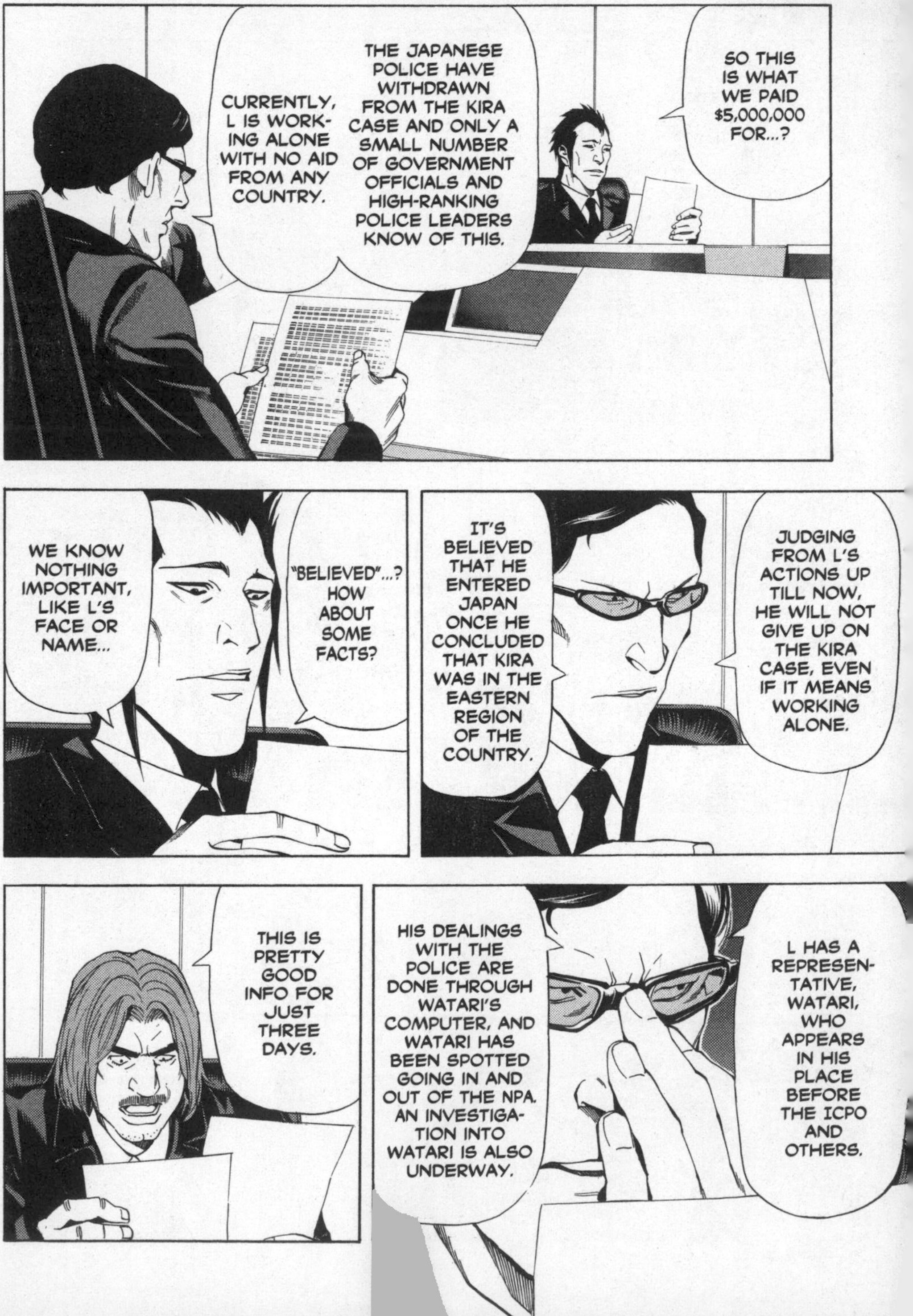
SO THIS IS WHAT WE PAID $5,000,000 FOR...?
THE JAPANESE POLICE HAVE WITHDRAWN FROM THE KIRA CASE AND ONLY A SMALL NUMBER OF GOVERNMENT OFFICIALS AND HIGH-RANKING POLICE LEADERS KNOW OF THIS.
CURRENTLY, L IS WORK-ING ALONE WITH NO AID FROM ANY COUNTRY.
JUDGING FROM L'S ACTIONS UP TILL NOW, HE WILL NOT GIVE UP ON THE KIRA CASE, EVEN IF IT MEANS WORKING ALONE.
IT'S BELIEVED THAT HE ENTERED JAPAN ONCE HE CONCLUDED THAT KIRA WAS IN THE EASTERN REGION OF THE COUNTRY.
"BELIEVED"...? HOW ABOUT SOME FACTS?
WE KNOW NOTHING IMPORTANT, LIKE L'S FACE OR NAME...
L HAS A REPRESEN-TATIVE, WATARI, WHO APPEARS IN HIS PLACE BEFORE THE ICPO AND OTHERS.
HIS DEALINGS WITH THE POLICE ARE DONE THROUGH WATARI'S COMPUTER, AND WATARI HAS BEEN SPOTTED GOING IN AND OUT OF THE NPA. AN INVESTIGA-TION INTO WATARI IS ALSO UNDERWAY.
THIS IS PRETTY GOOD INFO FOR JUST THREE DAYS.

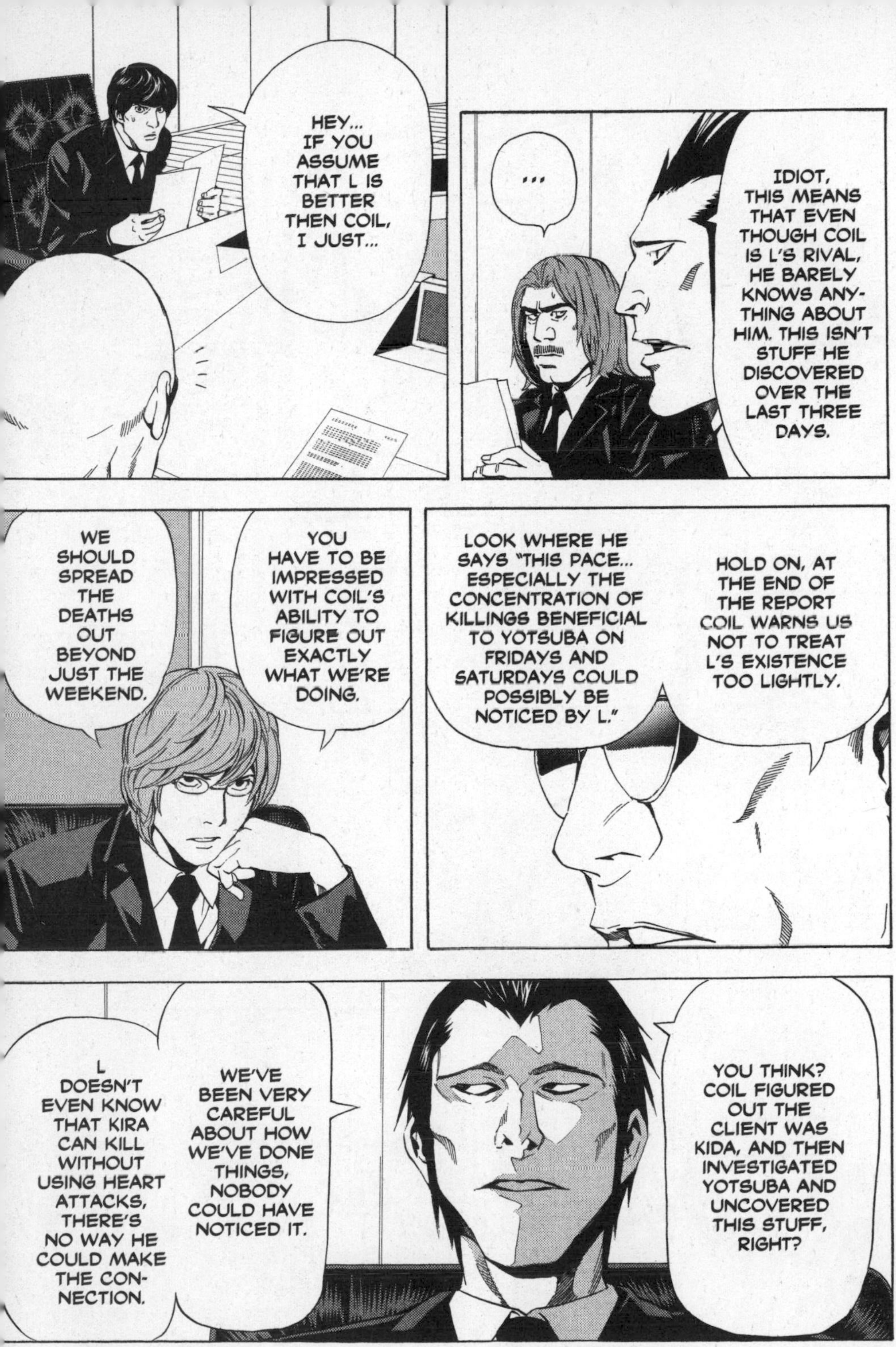
IDIOT, THIS MEANS THAT EVEN THOUGH COIL IS L'S RIVAL, HE BARELY KNOWS ANY-THING ABOUT HIM. THIS ISN'T STUFF HE DISCOVERED OVER THE LAST THREE DAYS.
...
HEY... IF YOU ASSUME THAT L IS BETTER THEN COIL, I JUST...
HOLD ON, AT THE END OF THE REPORT COIL WARNS US NOT TO TREAT L'S EXISTENCE TOO LIGHTLY.
LOOK WHERE HE SAYS "THIS PACE... ESPECIALLY THE CONCENTRATION OF KILLINGS BENEFICIAL TO YOTSUBA ON FRIDAYS AND SATURDAYS COULD POSSIBLY BE NOTICED BY L."
YOU HAVE TO BE IMPRESSED WITH COIL'S ABILITY TO FIGURE OUT EXACTLY WHAT WE'RE DOING.
WE SHOULD SPREAD THE DEATHS OUT BEYOND JUST THE WEEKEND.
YOU THINK? COIL FIGURED OUT THE CLIENT WAS KIDA, AND THEN INVESTIGATED YOTSUBA AND UNCOVERED THIS STUFF, RIGHT?
WE'VE BEEN VERY CAREFUL ABOUT HOW WE'VE DONE THINGS, NOBODY COULD HAVE NOTICED IT.
L DOESN'T EVEN KNOW THAT KIRA CAN KILL WITHOUT USING HEART ATTACKS, THERE'S NO WAY HE COULD MAKE THE CON-NECTION.

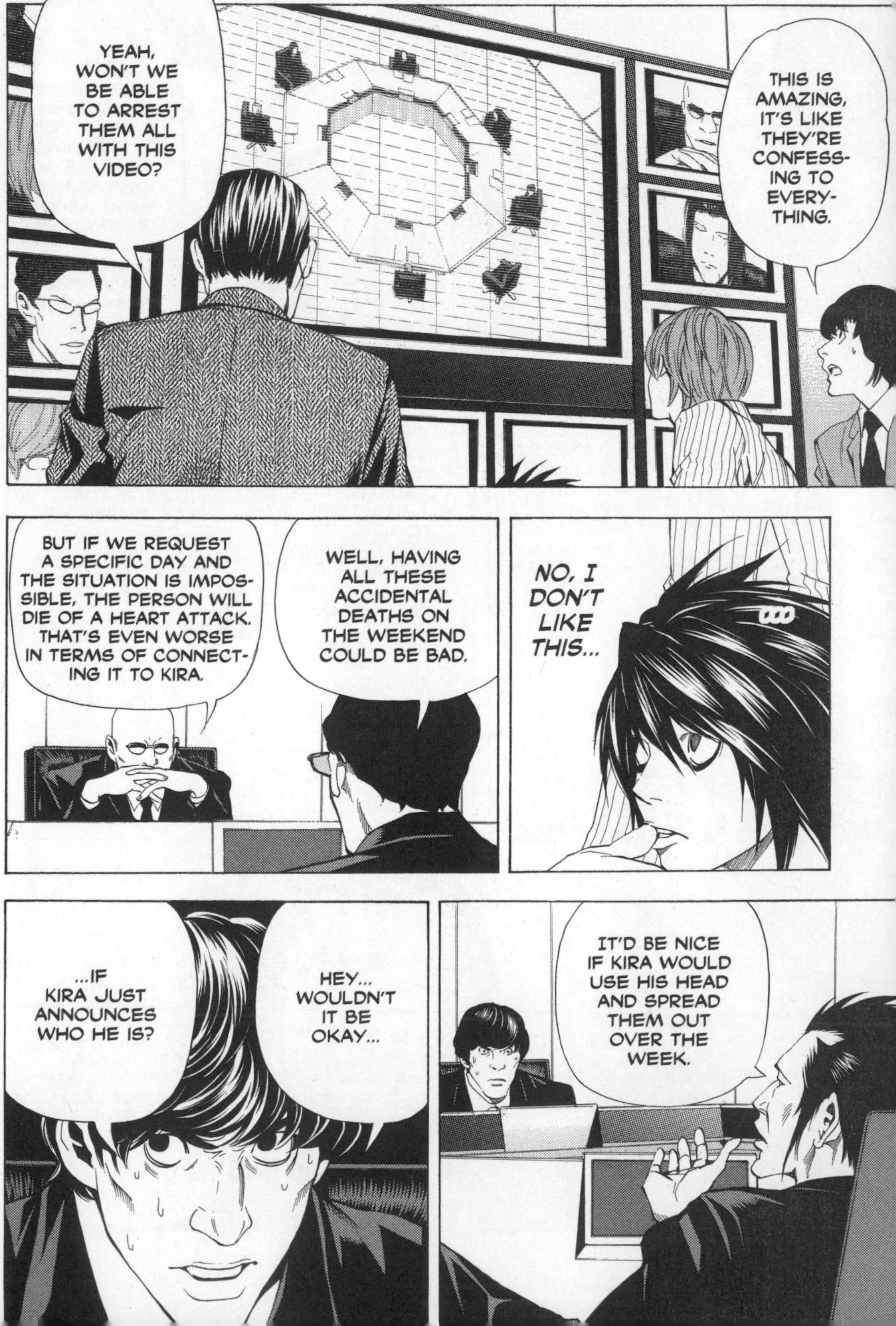
THIS IS AMAZING, IT'S LIKE THEY'RE CONFESSING TO EVERYTHING.
YEAH, WON'T WE BE ABLE TO ARREST THEM ALL WITH THIS VIDEO?
NO, I DON'T LIKE THIS...
WELL, HAVING ALL THESE ACCIDENTAL DEATHS ON THE WEEKEND COULD BE BAD.
BUT IF WE REQUEST A SPECIFIC DAY AND THE SITUATION IS IMPOSSIBLE, THE PERSON WILL DIE OF A HEART ATTACK. THAT'S EVEN WORSE IN TERMS OF CONNECTING IT TO KIRA.
IT'D BE NICE IF KIRA WOULD USE HIS HEAD AND SPREAD THEM OUT OVER THE WEEK.
HEY... WOULDN'T IT BE OKAY...
...IF KIRA JUST ANNOUNCES WHO HE IS?

READ THIS WAY

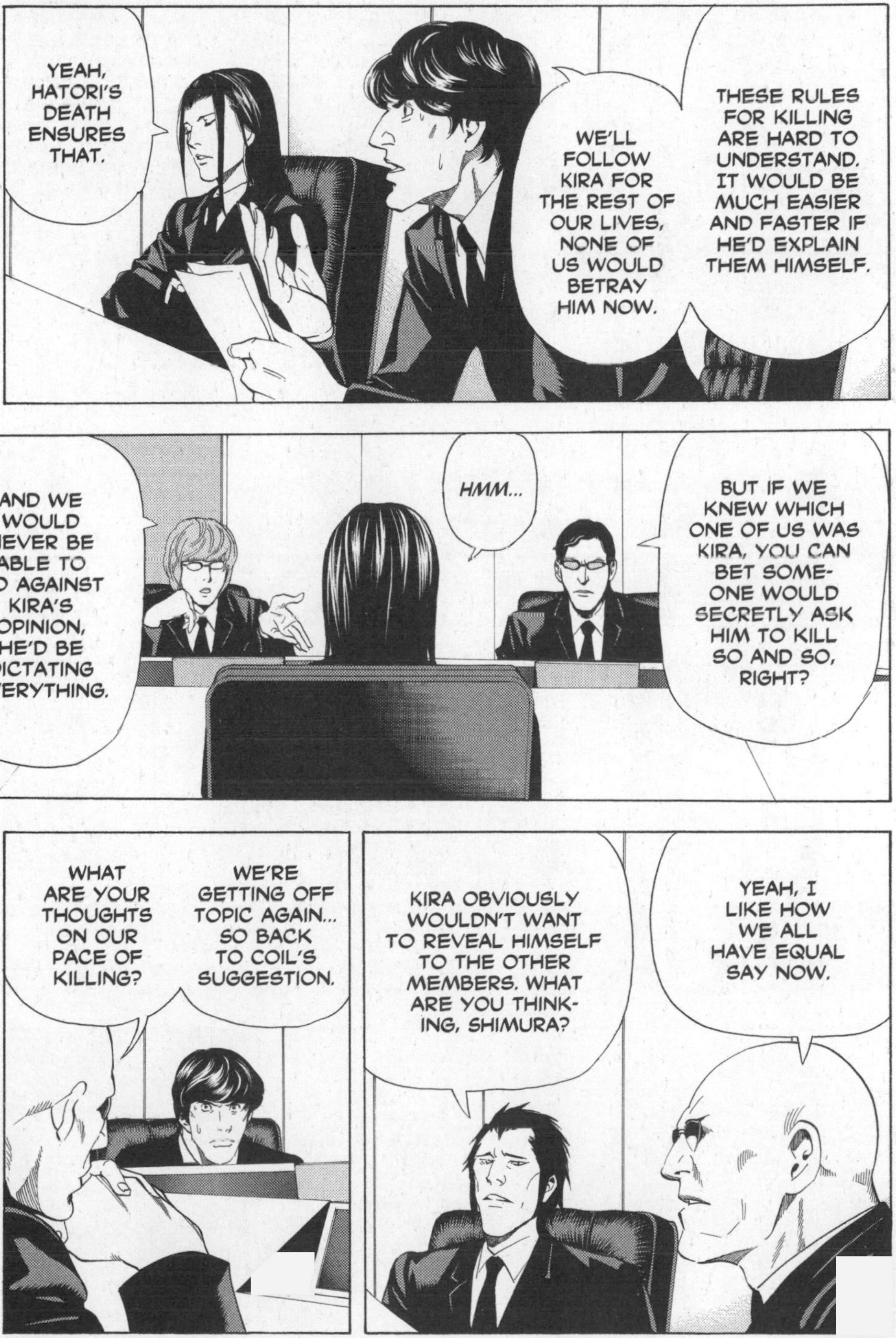
THESE RULES FOR KILLING ARE HARD TO UNDERSTAND. IT WOULD BE MUCH EASIER AND FASTER IF HE'D EXPLAIN THEM HIMSELF.
WE'LL FOLLOW KIRA FOR THE REST OF OUR LIVES, NONE OF US WOULD BETRAY HIM NOW.
YEAH, HATORI'S DEATH ENSURES THAT.
BUT IF WE KNEW WHICH ONE OF US WAS KIRA, YOU CAN BET SOME-ONE WOULD SECRETLY ASK HIM TO KILL SO AND SO, RIGHT?
HMM...
AND WE WOULD NEVER BE ABLE TO GO AGAINST KIRA'S OPINION, HE'D BE DICTATING EVERYTHING.
YEAH, I LIKE HOW WE ALL HAVE EQUAL SAY NOW.
KIRA OBVIOUSLY WOULDN'T WANT TO REVEAL HIMSELF TO THE OTHER MEMBERS. WHAT ARE YOU THINK-ING, SHIMURA?
WE'RE GETTING OFF TOPIC AGAIN... SO BACK TO COIL'S SUGGESTION.
WHAT ARE YOUR THOUGHTS ON OUR PACE OF KILLING?

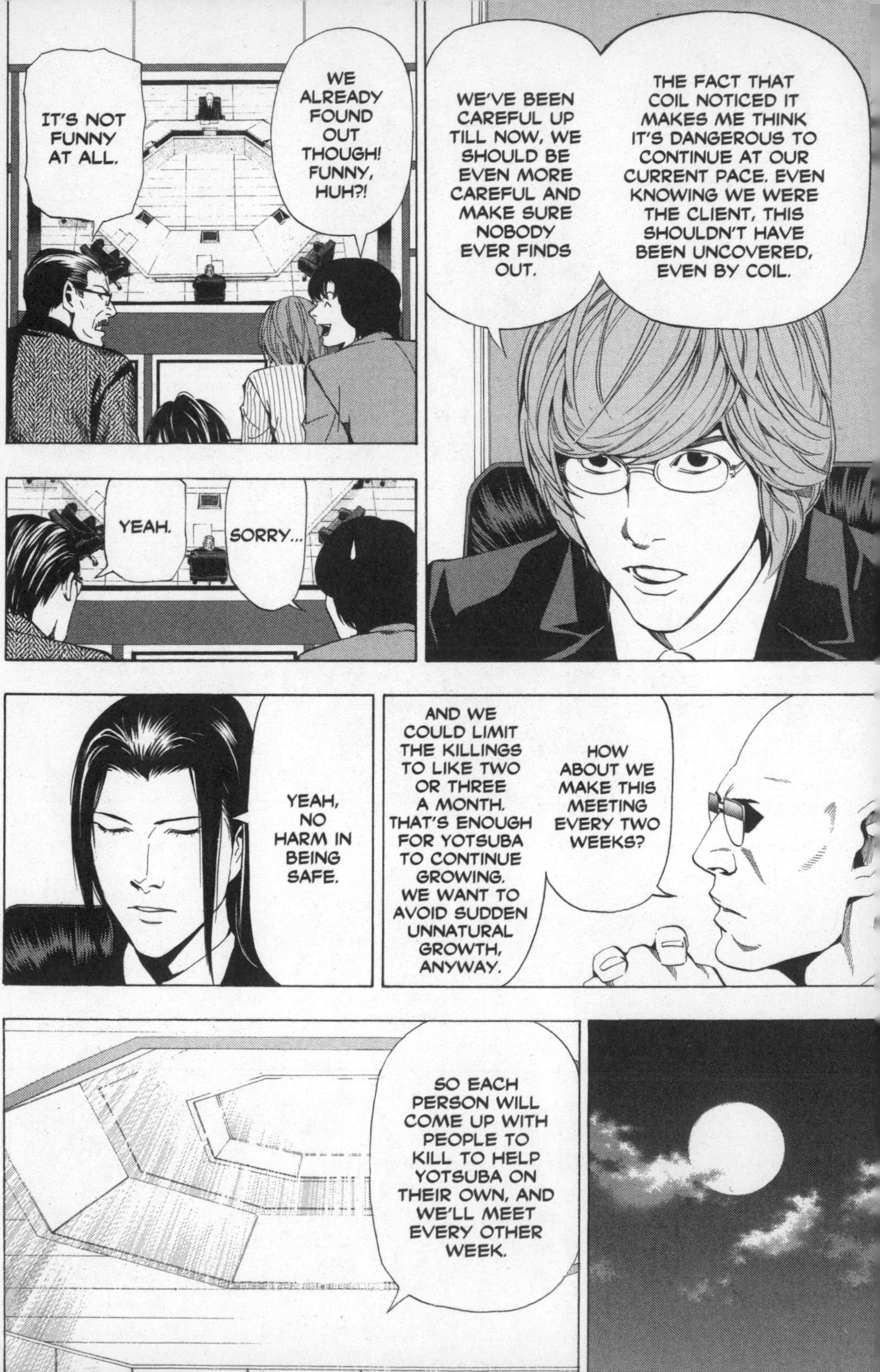
THE FACT THAT COIL NOTICED IT MAKES ME THINK IT'S DANGEROUS TO CONTINUE AT OUR CURRENT PACE. EVEN KNOWING WE WERE THE CLIENT, THIS SHOULDN'T HAVE BEEN UNCOVERED, EVEN BY COIL.
WE'VE BEEN CAREFUL UP TILL NOW, WE SHOULD BE EVEN MORE CAREFUL AND MAKE SURE NOBODY EVER FINDS OUT.
WE ALREADY FOUND OUT THOUGH! FUNNY, HUH?!
IT'S NOT FUNNY AT ALL.
SORRY...
YEAH.
HOW ABOUT WE MAKE THIS MEETING EVERY TWO WEEKS?
AND WE COULD LIMIT THE KILLINGS TO LIKE TWO OR THREE A MONTH. THAT'S ENOUGH FOR YOTSUBA TO CONTINUE GROWING. WE WANT TO AVOID SUDDEN UNNATURAL GROWTH, ANYWAY.
YEAH, NO HARM IN BEING SAFE.
SO EACH PERSON WILL COME UP WITH PEOPLE TO KILL TO HELP YOTSUBA ON THEIR OWN, AND WE'LL MEET EVERY OTHER WEEK.

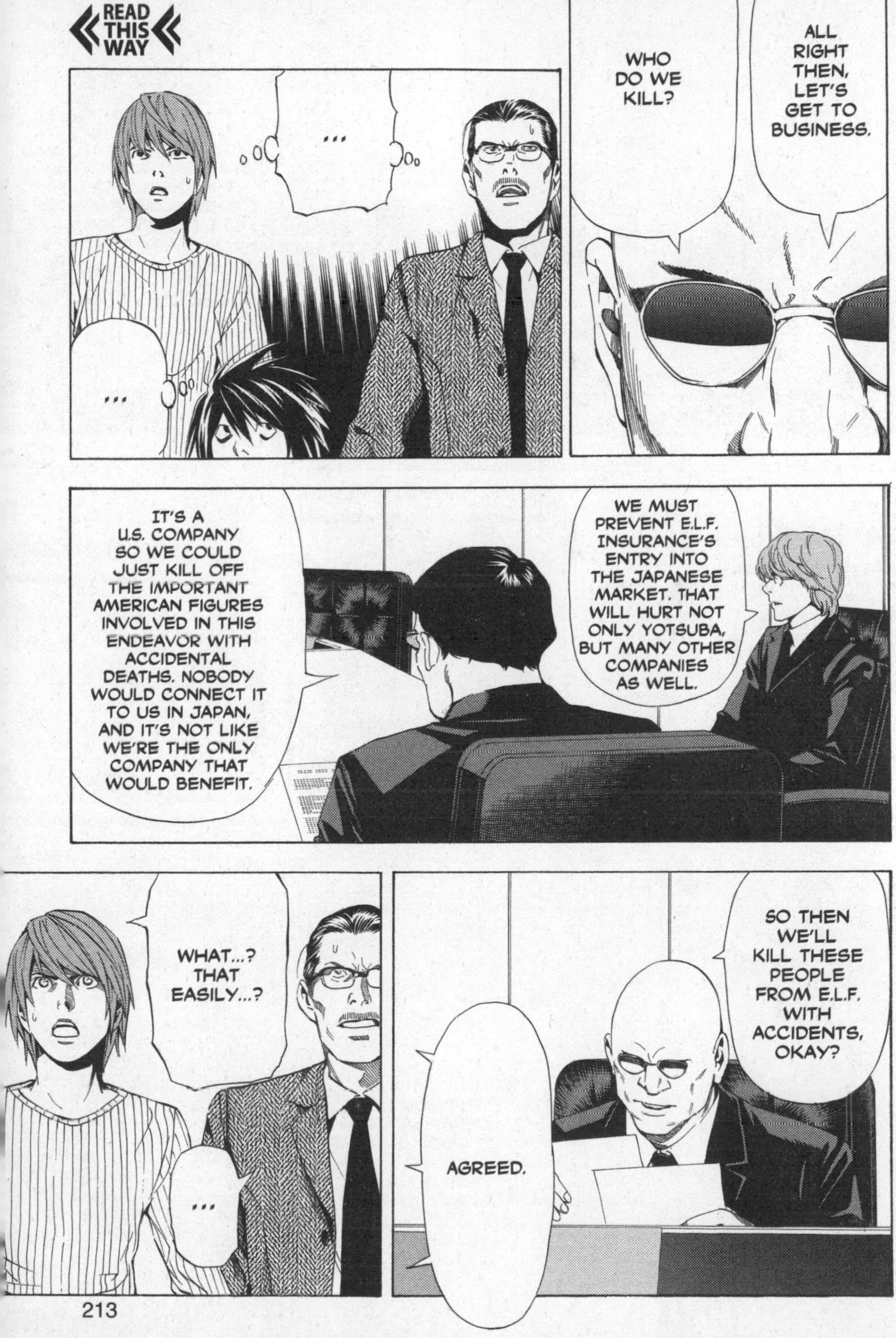
READ THIS WAY
ALL RIGHT THEN, LET'S GET TO BUSINESS.
WHO DO WE KILL?
...
...
WE MUST PREVENT E.L.F. INSURANCE'S ENTRY INTO THE JAPANESE MARKET. THAT WILL HURT NOT ONLY YOTSUBA, BUT MANY OTHER COMPANIES AS WELL.
IT'S A U.S. COMPANY SO WE COULD JUST KILL OFF THE IMPORTANT AMERICAN FIGURES INVOLVED IN THIS ENDEAVOR WITH ACCIDENTAL DEATHS. NOBODY WOULD CONNECT IT TO US IN JAPAN, AND IT'S NOT LIKE WE'RE THE ONLY COMPANY THAT WOULD BENEFIT.
SO THEN WE'LL KILL THESE PEOPLE FROM E.L.F. WITH ACCIDENTS, OKAY?
AGREED.
WHAT...? THAT EASILY...?
...

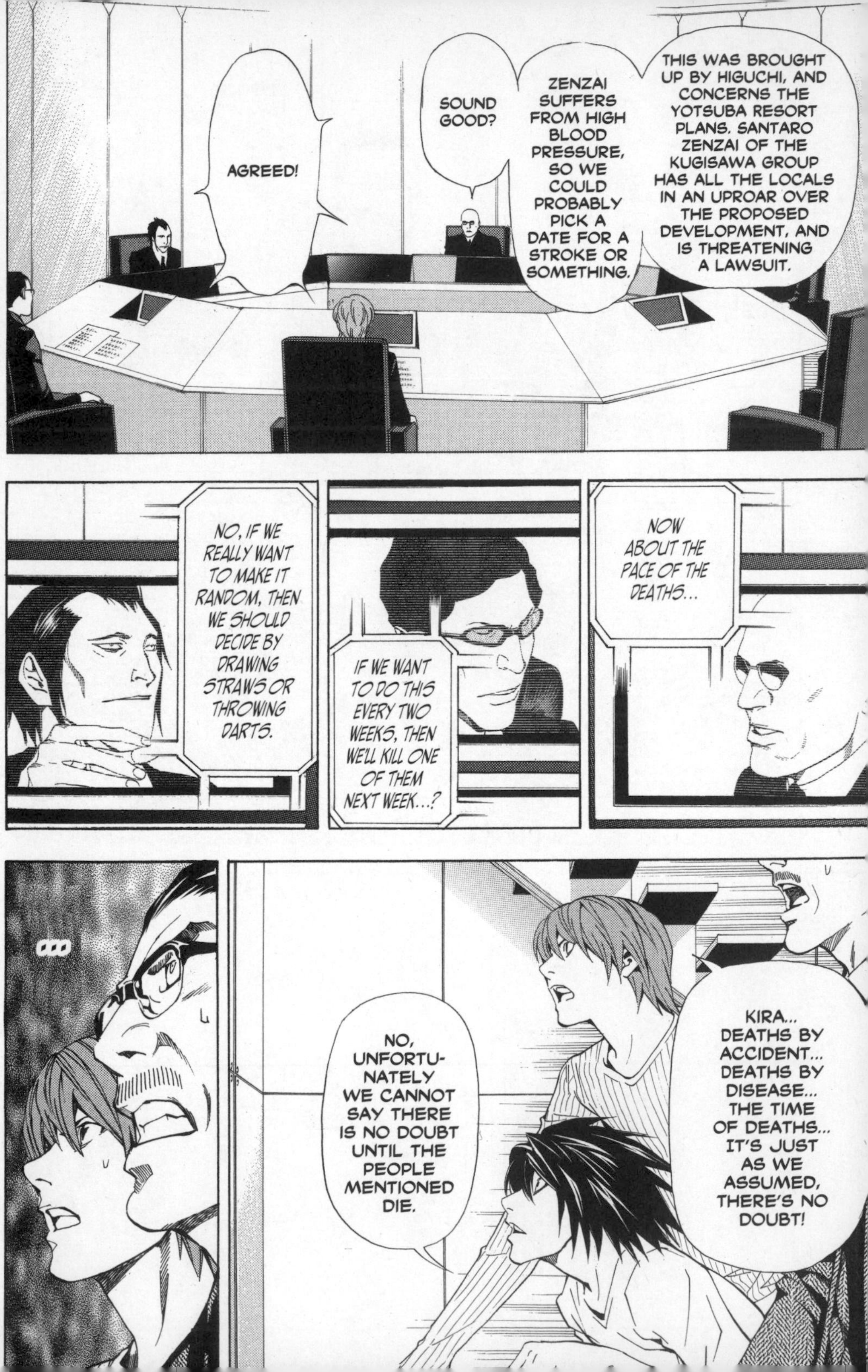
THIS WAS BROUGHT UP BY HIGUCHI, AND CONCERNS THE YOTSUBA RESORT PLANS. SANTARO ZENZAI OF THE KUGISAWA GROUP HAS ALL THE LOCALS IN AN UPROAR OVER THE PROPOSED DEVELOPMENT, AND IS THREATENING A LAWSUIT.
ZENZAI SUFFERS FROM HIGH BLOOD PRESSURE, SO WE COULD PROBABLY PICK A DATE FOR A STROKE OR SOMETHING.
SOUND GOOD?
AGREED!
NOW ABOUT THE PACE OF THE DEATHS...
IF WE WANT TO DO THIS EVERY TWO WEEKS, THEN WE'LL KILL ONE OF THEM NEXT WEEK...?
NO, IF WE REALLY WANT TO MAKE IT RANDOM, THEN WE SHOULD DECIDE BY DRAWING STRAWS OR THROWING DARTS.
KIRA... DEATHS BY ACCIDENT... DEATHS BY DISEASE... THE TIME OF DEATHS... IT'S JUST AS WE ASSUMED, THERE'S NO DOUBT!
NO, UNFORTU-NATELY WE CANNOT SAY THERE IS NO DOUBT UNTIL THE PEOPLE MENTIONED DIE.
...

READ THIS WAY

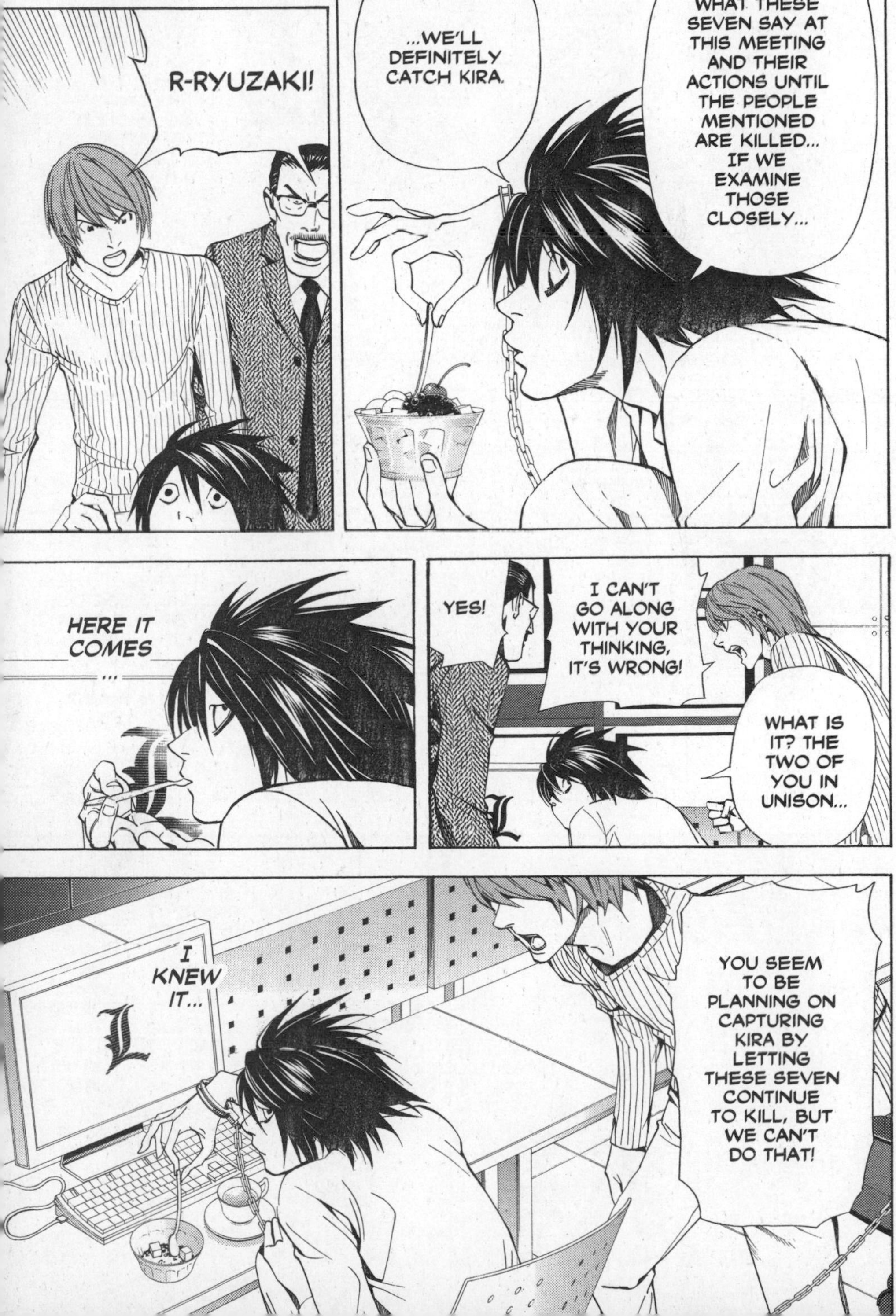
WHAT THESE SEVEN SAY AT THIS MEETING AND THEIR ACTIONS UNTIL THE PEOPLE MENTIONED ARE KILLED... IF WE EXAMINE THOSE CLOSELY...
...WE'LL DEFINITELY CATCH KIRA.
R-RYUZAKI!
I CAN'T GO ALONG WITH YOUR THINKING, IT'S WRONG!
YES!
WHAT IS IT? THE TWO OF YOU IN UNISON...
HERE IT COMES...
YOU SEEM TO BE PLANNING ON CAPTURING KIRA BY LETTING THESE SEVEN CONTINUE TO KILL, BUT WE CAN'T DO THAT!
I KNEW IT...

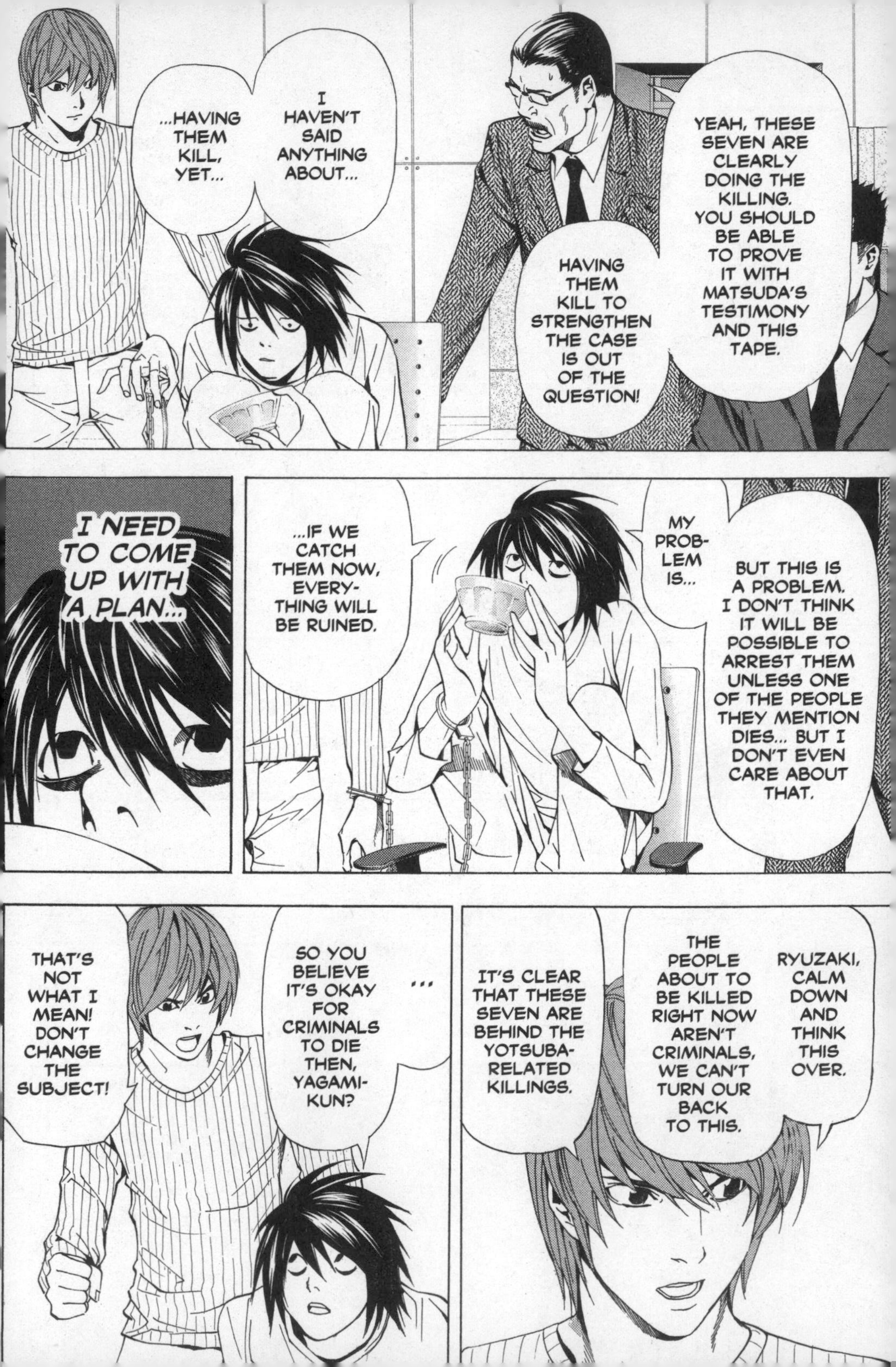
YEAH, THESE SEVEN ARE CLEARLY DOING THE KILLING. YOU SHOULD BE ABLE TO PROVE IT WITH MATSUDA'S TESTIMONY AND THIS TAPE.
HAVING THEM KILL TO STRENGTHEN THE CASE IS OUT OF THE QUESTION!
I HAVEN'T SAID ANYTHING ABOUT...
...HAVING THEM KILL, YET...
BUT THIS IS A PROBLEM. I DON'T THINK IT WILL BE POSSIBLE TO ARREST THEM UNLESS ONE OF THE PEOPLE THEY MENTION DIES... BUT I DON'T EVEN CARE ABOUT THAT.
MY PROBLEM IS...
...IF WE CATCH THEM NOW, EVERYTHING WILL BE RUINED.
I NEED TO COME UP WITH A PLAN...
RYUZAKI, CALM DOWN AND THINK THIS OVER.
THE PEOPLE ABOUT TO BE KILLED RIGHT NOW AREN'T CRIMINALS, WE CAN'T TURN OUR BACK TO THIS.
IT'S CLEAR THAT THESE SEVEN ARE BEHIND THE YOTSUBA-RELATED KILLINGS.
...
SO YOU BELIEVE IT'S OKAY FOR CRIMINALS TO DIE THEN, YAGAMI-KUN?
THAT'S NOT WHAT I MEAN! DON'T CHANGE THE SUBJECT!

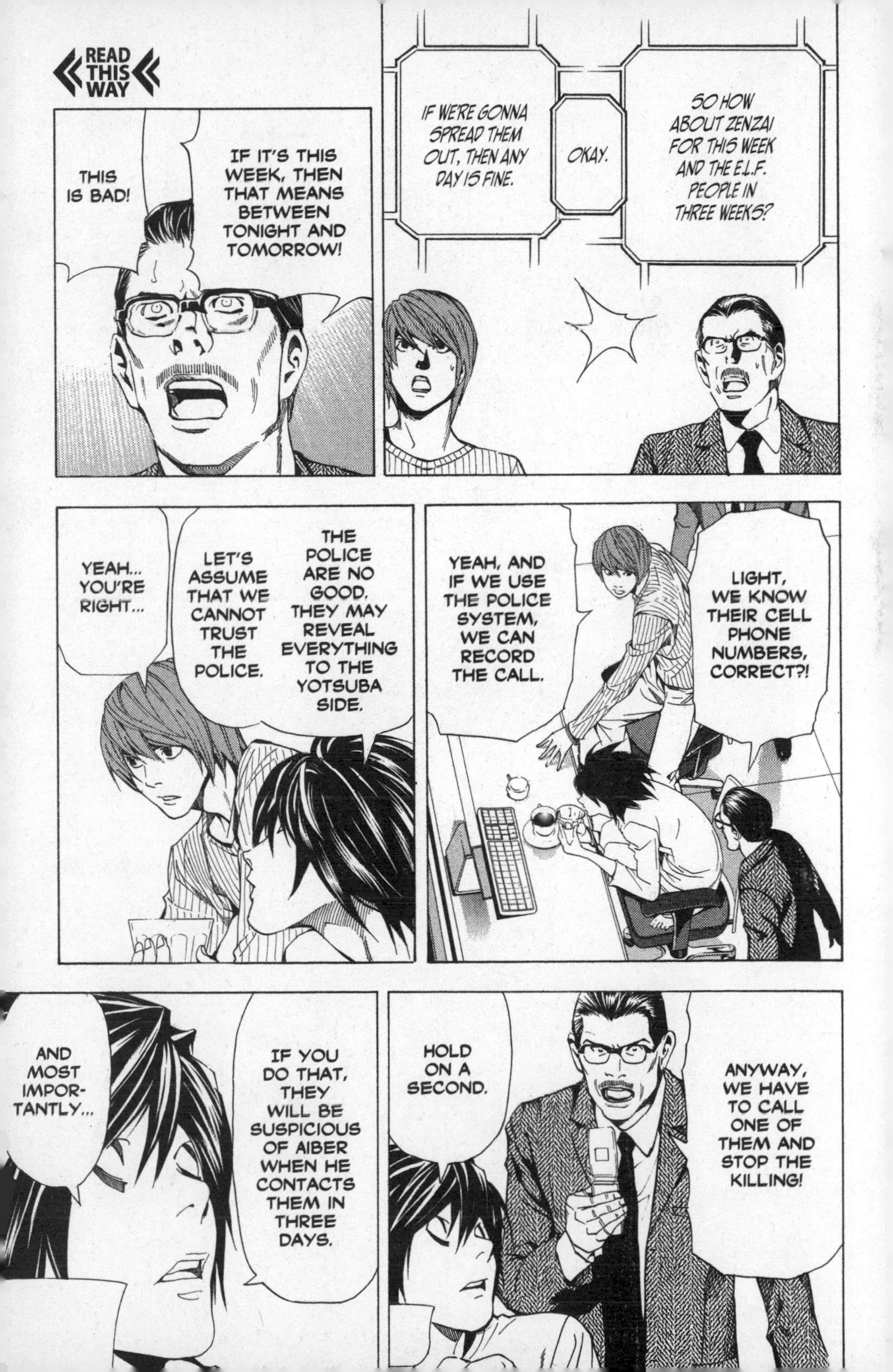
READ THIS WAY
SO HOW ABOUT ZENZAI FOR THIS WEEK AND THE E.L.F. PEOPLE IN THREE WEEKS?
OKAY.
IF WE'RE GONNA SPREAD THEM OUT, THEN ANY DAY IS FINE.
THIS IS BAD!
IF IT'S THIS WEEK, THEN THAT MEANS BETWEEN TONIGHT AND TOMORROW!
LIGHT, WE KNOW THEIR CELL PHONE NUMBERS, CORRECT?!
YEAH, AND IF WE USE THE POLICE SYSTEM, WE CAN RECORD THE CALL.
THE POLICE ARE NO GOOD. THEY MAY REVEAL EVERYTHING TO THE YOTSUBA SIDE.
LET'S ASSUME THAT WE CANNOT TRUST THE POLICE.
YEAH... YOU'RE RIGHT...
ANYWAY, WE HAVE TO CALL ONE OF THEM AND STOP THE KILLING!
HOLD ON A SECOND.
IF YOU DO THAT, THEY WILL BE SUSPICIOUS OF AIBER WHEN HE CONTACTS THEM IN THREE DAYS.
AND MOST IMPOR-TANTLY...

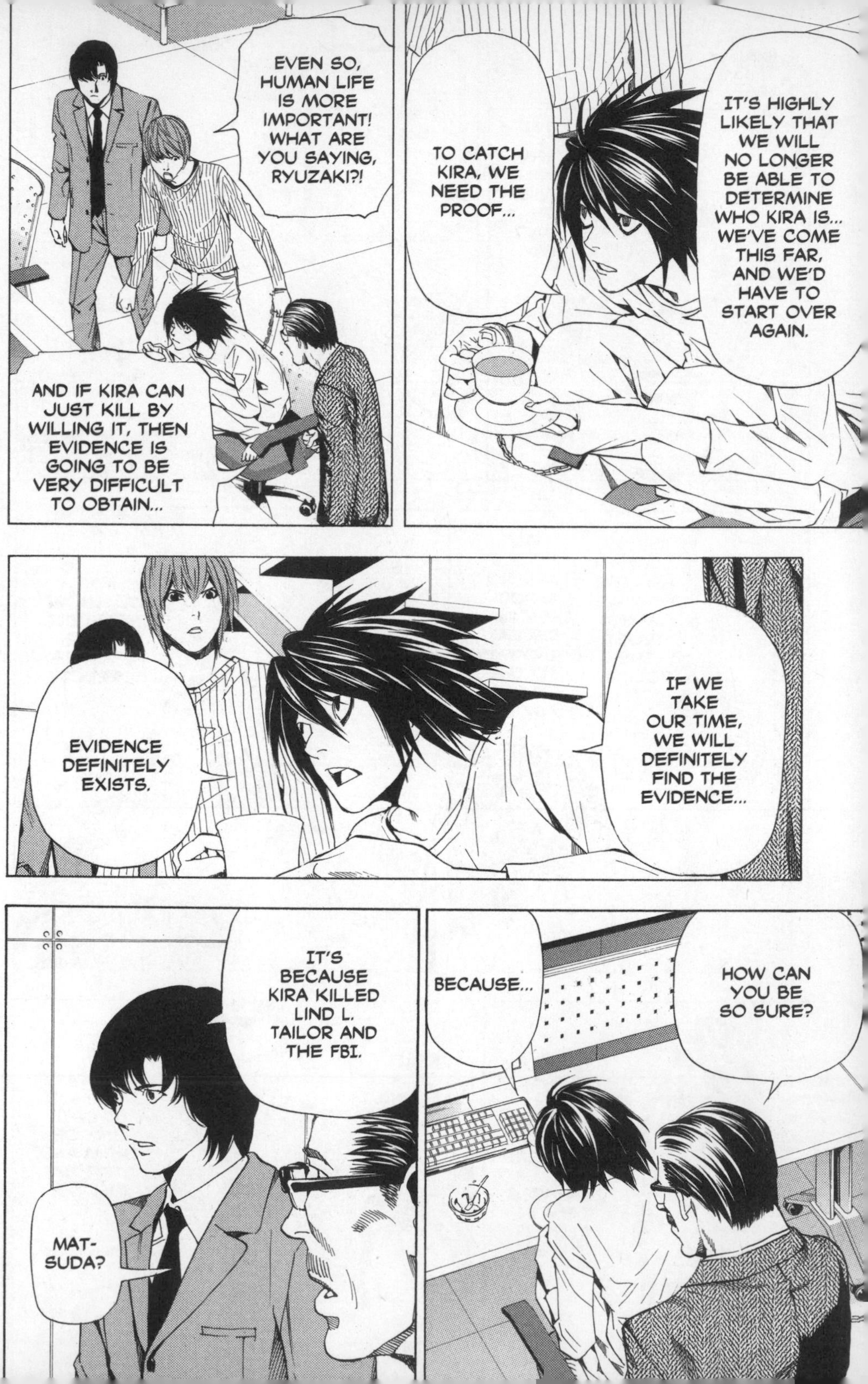
IT'S HIGHLY LIKELY THAT WE WILL NO LONGER BE ABLE TO DETERMINE WHO KIRA IS... WE'VE COME THIS FAR, AND WE'D HAVE TO START OVER AGAIN.
TO CATCH KIRA, WE NEED THE PROOF...
EVEN SO, HUMAN LIFE IS MORE IMPORTANT! WHAT ARE YOU SAYING, RYUZAKI?!
AND IF KIRA CAN JUST KILL BY WILLING IT, THEN EVIDENCE IS GOING TO BE VERY DIFFICULT TO OBTAIN...
IF WE TAKE OUR TIME, WE WILL DEFINITELY FIND THE EVIDENCE...
EVIDENCE DEFINITELY EXISTS.
HOW CAN YOU BE SO SURE?
BECAUSE...
IT'S BECAUSE KIRA KILLED LIND L. TAILOR AND THE FBI.
MAT-SUDA?

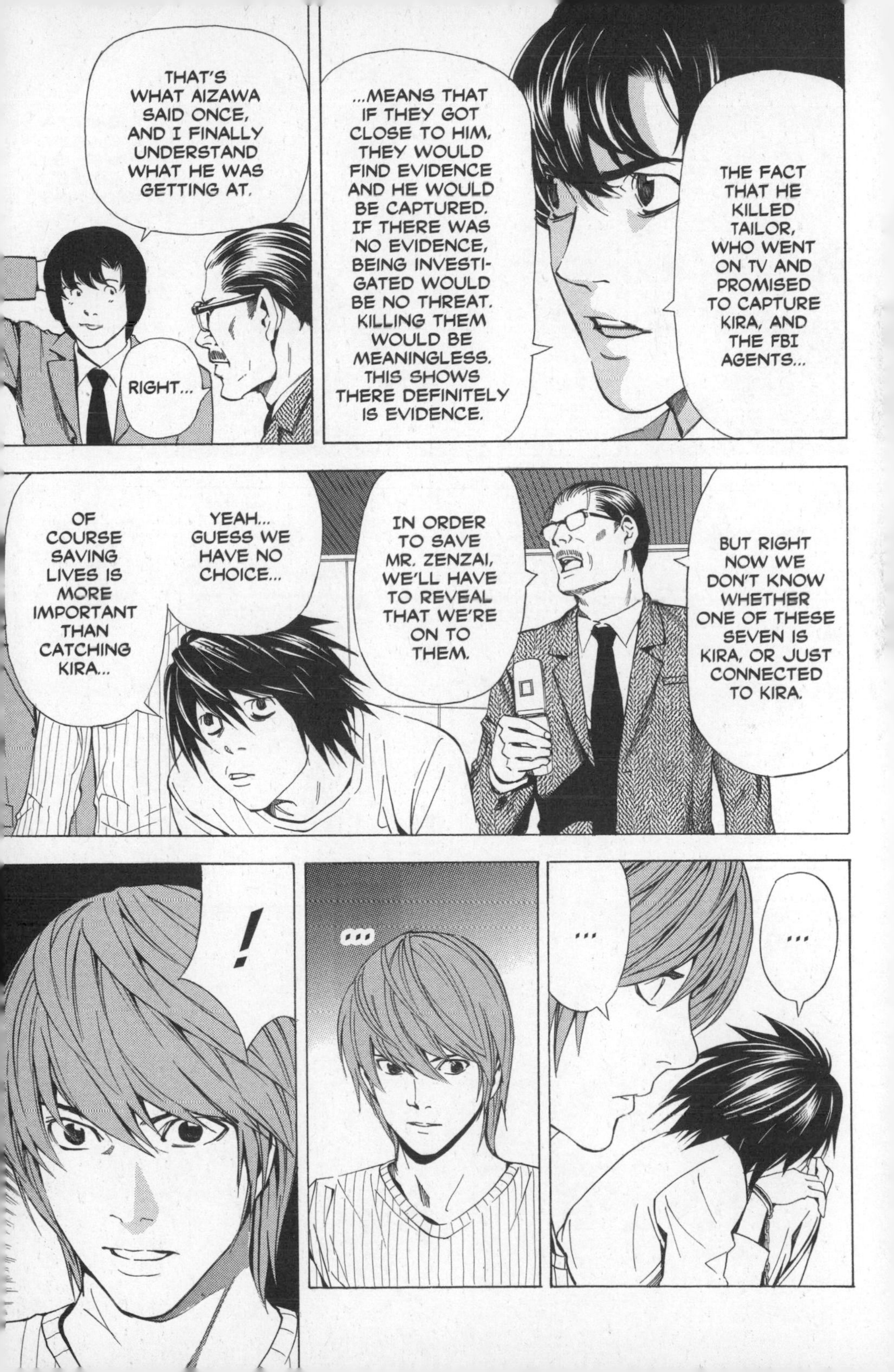
THE FACT THAT HE KILLED TAILOR, WHO WENT ON TV AND PROMISED TO CAPTURE KIRA, AND THE FBI AGENTS...
...MEANS THAT IF THEY GOT CLOSE TO HIM, THEY WOULD FIND EVIDENCE AND HE WOULD BE CAPTURED. IF THERE WAS NO EVIDENCE, BEING INVESTIGATED WOULD BE NO THREAT. KILLING THEM WOULD BE MEANINGLESS. THIS SHOWS THERE DEFINITELY IS EVIDENCE.
THAT'S WHAT AIZAWA SAID ONCE, AND I FINALLY UNDERSTAND WHAT HE WAS GETTING AT.
RIGHT...
BUT RIGHT NOW WE DON'T KNOW WHETHER ONE OF THESE SEVEN IS KIRA, OR JUST CONNECTED TO KIRA.
IN ORDER TO SAVE MR. ZENZAI, WE'LL HAVE TO REVEAL THAT WE'RE ON TO THEM.
YEAH... GUESS WE HAVE NO CHOICE...
OF COURSE SAVING LIVES IS MORE IMPORTANT THAN CATCHING KIRA...
...
...
...
!

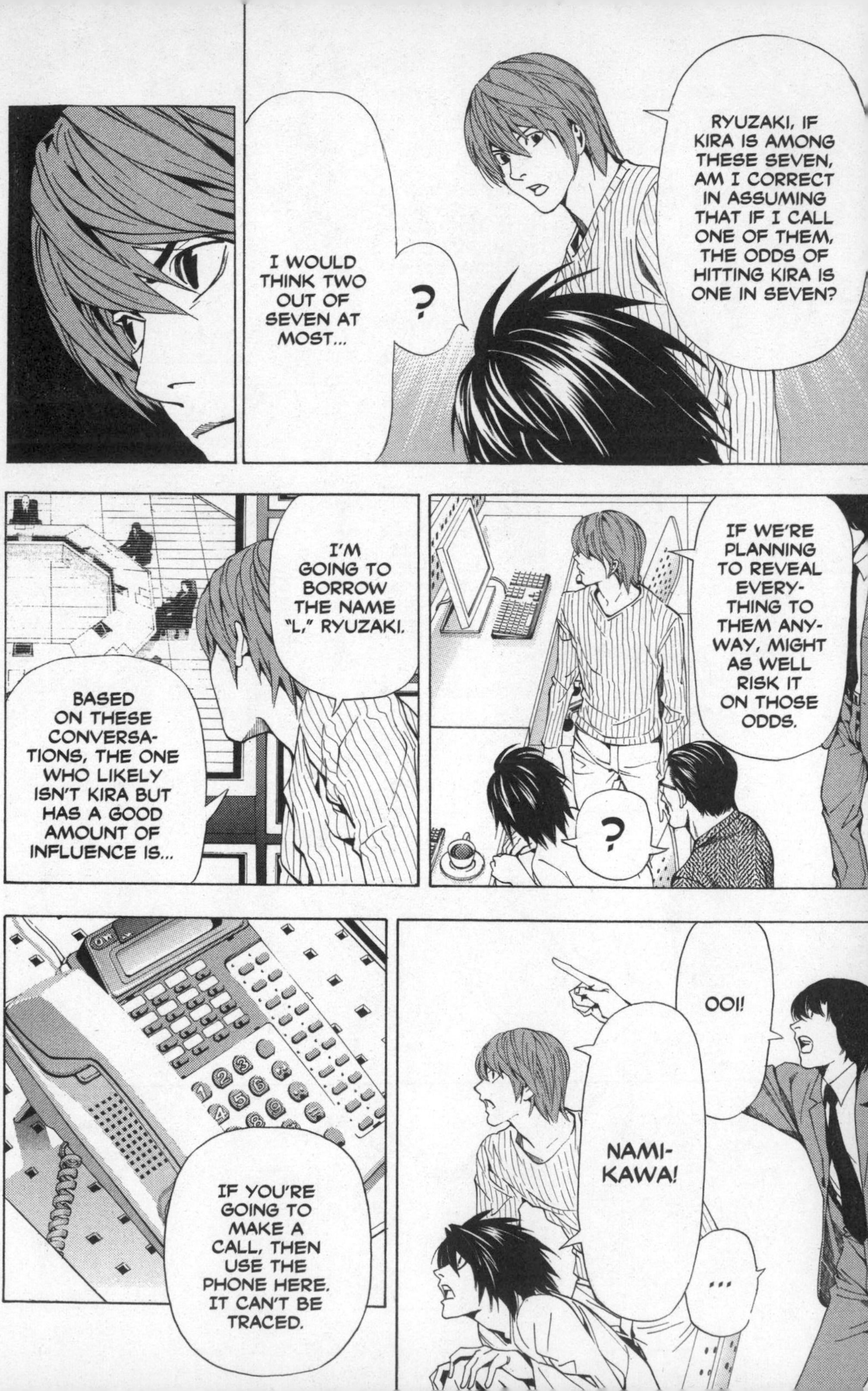
RYUZAKI, IF KIRA IS AMONG THESE SEVEN, AM I CORRECT IN ASSUMING THAT IF I CALL ONE OF THEM, THE ODDS OF HITTING KIRA IS ONE IN SEVEN?
?
I WOULD THINK TWO OUT OF SEVEN AT MOST...
IF WE'RE PLANNING TO REVEAL EVERY-THING TO THEM ANY-WAY, MIGHT AS WELL RISK IT ON THOSE ODDS.
?
I'M GOING TO BORROW THE NAME "L," RYUZAKI.
BASED ON THESE CONVERSA-TIONS, THE ONE WHO LIKELY ISN'T KIRA BUT HAS A GOOD AMOUNT OF INFLUENCE IS...
OOI!
NAMI-KAWA!
...
IF YOU'RE GOING TO MAKE A CALL, THEN USE THE PHONE HERE. IT CAN'T BE TRACED.

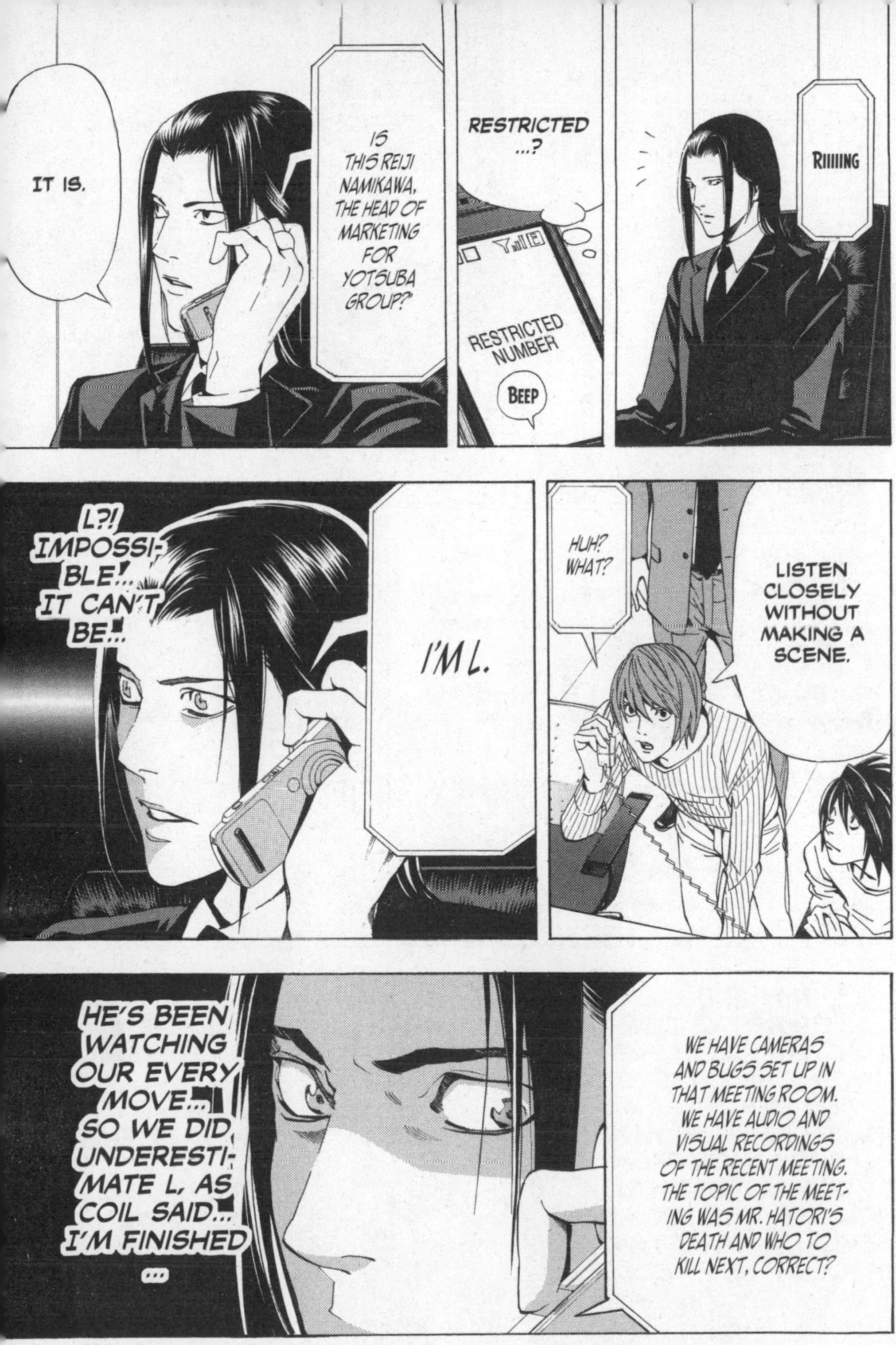
RIIIING
RESTRICTED ...?
RESTRICTED NUMBER
BEEP
IS THIS REIJI NAMIKAWA, THE HEAD OF MARKETING FOR YOTSUBA GROUP?
IT IS.
LISTEN CLOSELY WITHOUT MAKING A SCENE.
HUH? WHAT?
I'M L.
L?! IMPOSSIBLE... IT CAN'T BE...
WE HAVE CAMERAS AND BUGS SET UP IN THAT MEETING ROOM. WE HAVE AUDIO AND VISUAL RECORDINGS OF THE RECENT MEETING. THE TOPIC OF THE MEETING WAS MR. HATORI'S DEATH AND WHO TO KILL NEXT, CORRECT?
HE'S BEEN WATCHING OUR EVERY MOVE... SO WE DID UNDERESTIMATE L, AS COIL SAID... I'M FINISHED ...

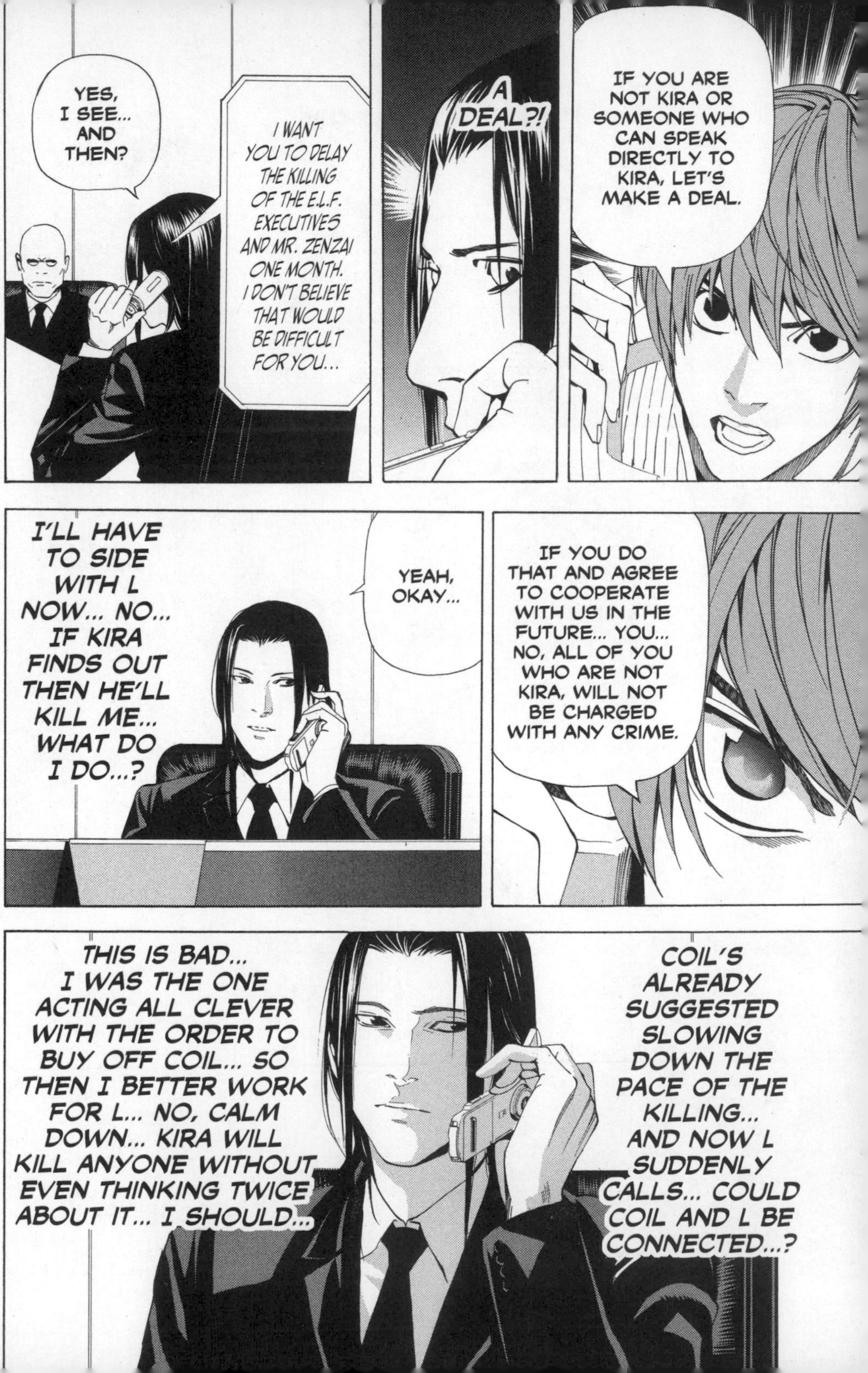

IF YOU ARE NOT KIRA OR SOMEONE WHO CAN SPEAK DIRECTLY TO KIRA, LET'S MAKE A DEAL.
A DEAL?!
I WANT YOU TO DELAY THE KILLING OF THE E.L.F. EXECUTIVES AND MR. ZENZAI ONE MONTH. I DON'T BELIEVE THAT WOULD BE DIFFICULT FOR YOU...
YES, I SEE... AND THEN?
IF YOU DO THAT AND AGREE TO COOPERATE WITH US IN THE FUTURE... YOU... NO, ALL OF YOU WHO ARE NOT KIRA, WILL NOT BE CHARGED WITH ANY CRIME.
YEAH, OKAY...
I'LL HAVE TO SIDE WITH L NOW... NO... IF KIRA FINDS OUT THEN HE'LL KILL ME... WHAT DO I DO...?
COIL'S ALREADY SUGGESTED SLOWING DOWN THE PACE OF THE KILLING... AND NOW L SUDDENLY CALLS... COULD COIL AND L BE CONNECTED...?
THIS IS BAD... I WAS THE ONE ACTING ALL CLEVER WITH THE ORDER TO BUY OFF COIL... SO THEN I BETTER WORK FOR L... NO, CALM DOWN... KIRA WILL KILL ANYONE WITHOUT EVEN THINKING TWICE ABOUT IT... I SHOULD...

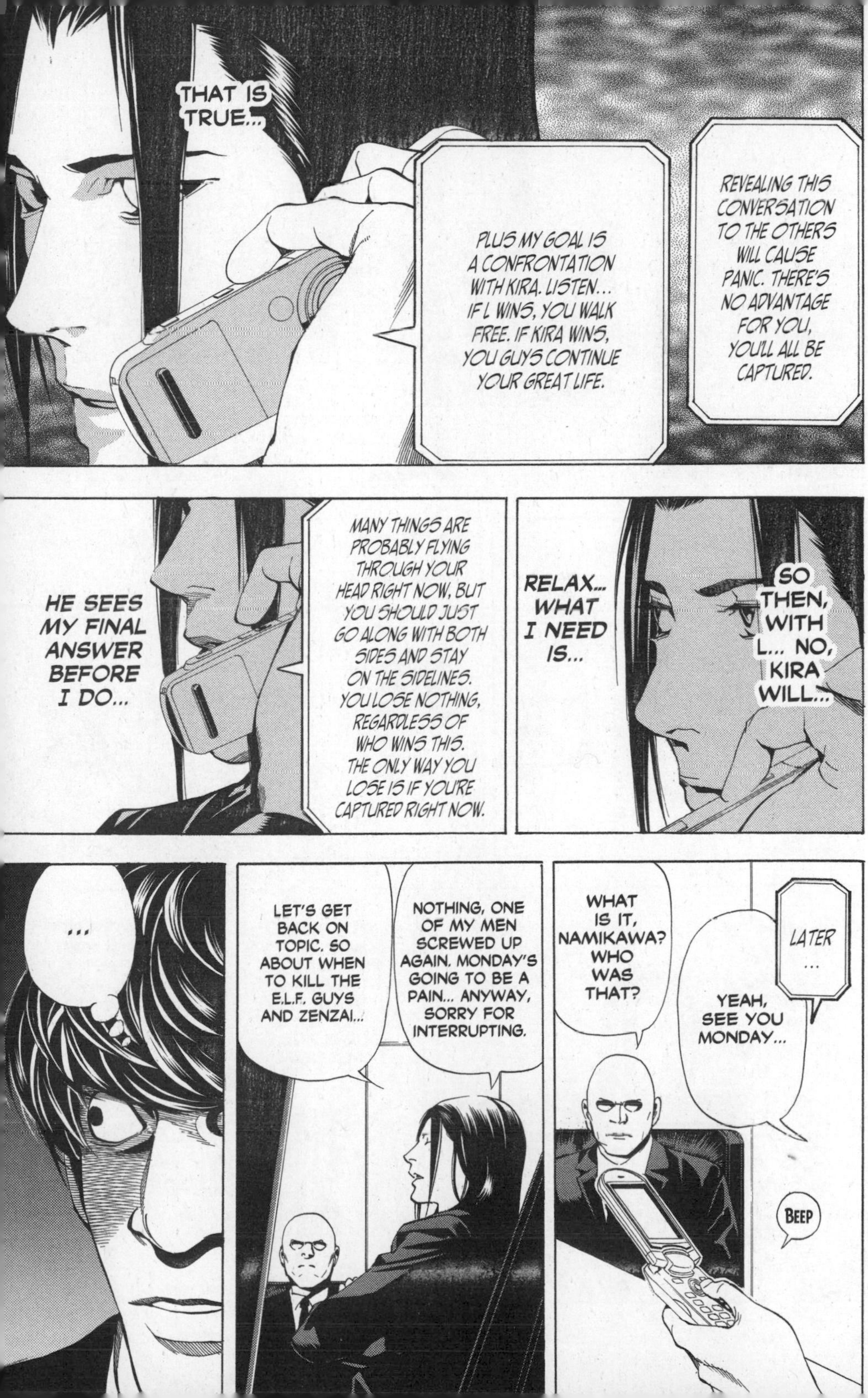
REVEALING THIS CONVERSATION TO THE OTHERS WILL CAUSE PANIC. THERE'S NO ADVANTAGE FOR YOU, YOU'LL ALL BE CAPTURED.
PLUS MY GOAL IS A CONFRONTATION WITH KIRA. LISTEN... IF L WINS, YOU WALK FREE. IF KIRA WINS, YOU GUYS CONTINUE YOUR GREAT LIFE.
THAT IS TRUE...
SO THEN, WITH L... NO, KIRA WILL...
RELAX... WHAT I NEED IS...
MANY THINGS ARE PROBABLY FLYING THROUGH YOUR HEAD RIGHT NOW, BUT YOU SHOULD JUST GO ALONG WITH BOTH SIDES AND STAY ON THE SIDELINES. YOU LOSE NOTHING, REGARDLESS OF WHO WINS THIS. THE ONLY WAY YOU LOSE IS IF YOU'RE CAPTURED RIGHT NOW.
HE SEES MY FINAL ANSWER BEFORE I DO...
LATER ...
YEAH, SEE YOU MONDAY...
BEEP
WHAT IS IT, NAMIKAWA? WHO WAS THAT?
NOTHING, ONE OF MY MEN SCREWED UP AGAIN. MONDAY'S GOING TO BE A PAIN... ANYWAY, SORRY FOR INTERRUPTING.
LET'S GET BACK ON TOPIC. SO ABOUT WHEN TO KILL THE E.L.F. GUYS AND ZENZAI...
...

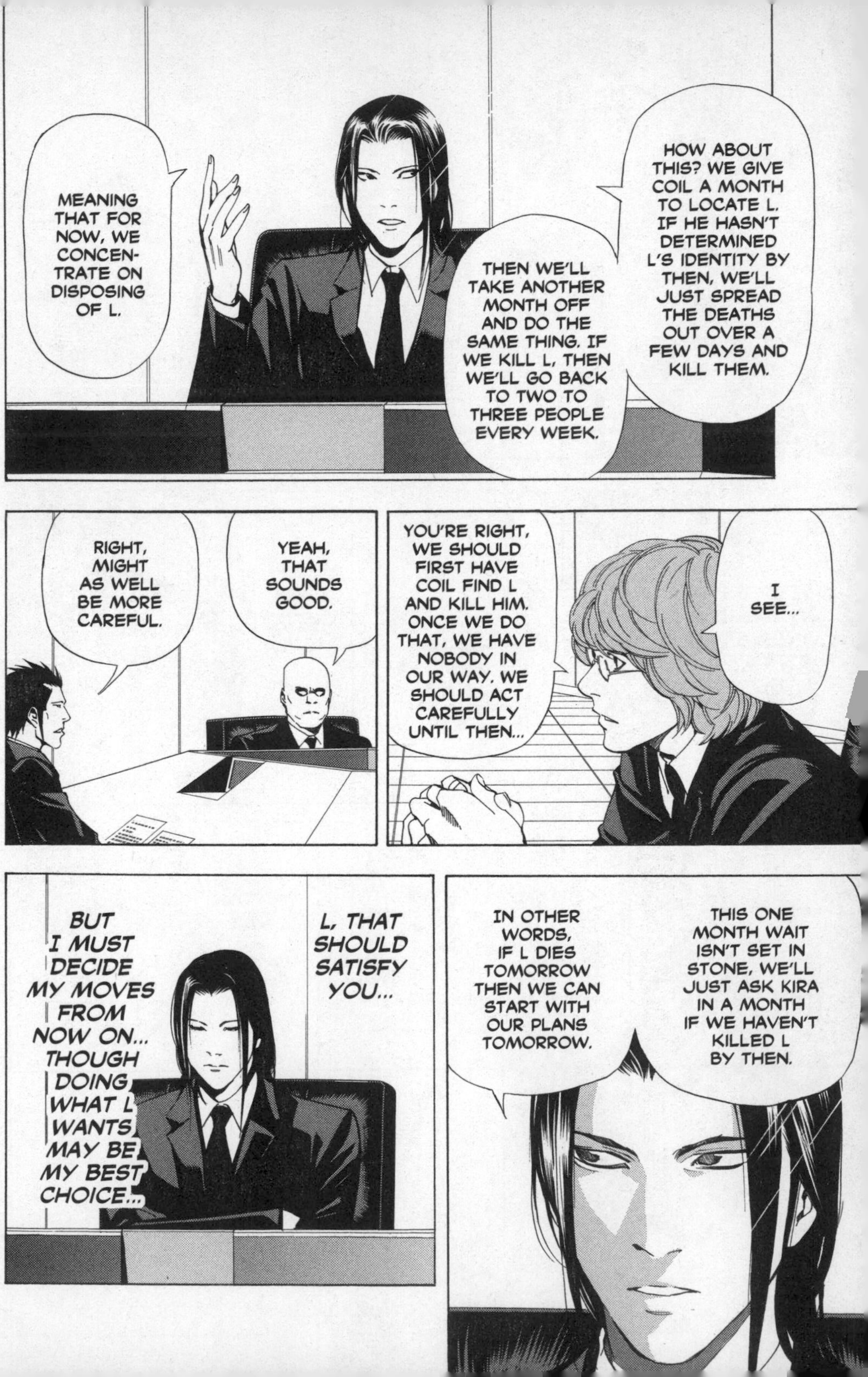
HOW ABOUT THIS? WE GIVE COIL A MONTH TO LOCATE L. IF HE HASN'T DETERMINED L'S IDENTITY BY THEN, WE'LL JUST SPREAD THE DEATHS OUT OVER A FEW DAYS AND KILL THEM.
THEN WE'LL TAKE ANOTHER MONTH OFF AND DO THE SAME THING. IF WE KILL L, THEN WE'LL GO BACK TO TWO TO THREE PEOPLE EVERY WEEK.
MEANING THAT FOR NOW, WE CONCEN-TRATE ON DISPOSING OF L.
I SEE...
YOU'RE RIGHT, WE SHOULD FIRST HAVE COIL FIND L AND KILL HIM. ONCE WE DO THAT, WE HAVE NOBODY IN OUR WAY. WE SHOULD ACT CAREFULLY UNTIL THEN...
YEAH, THAT SOUNDS GOOD.
RIGHT, MIGHT AS WELL BE MORE CAREFUL.
THIS ONE MONTH WAIT ISN'T SET IN STONE, WE'LL JUST ASK KIRA IN A MONTH IF WE HAVEN'T KILLED L BY THEN.
IN OTHER WORDS, IF L DIES TOMORROW THEN WE CAN START WITH OUR PLANS TOMORROW.
L, THAT SHOULD SATISFY YOU...
BUT I MUST DECIDE MY MOVES FROM NOW ON... THOUGH DOING WHAT L WANTS MAY BE MY BEST CHOICE...

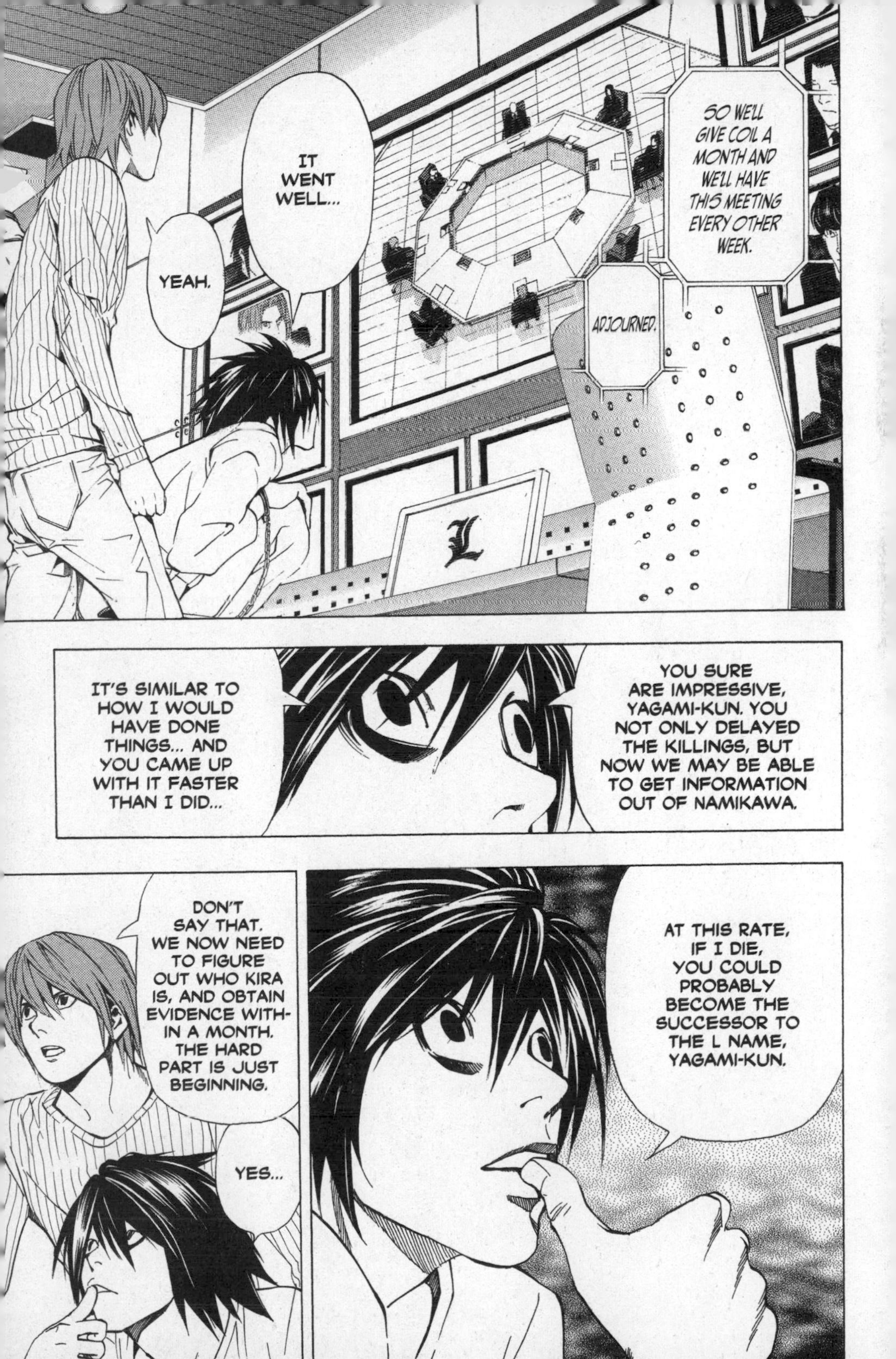
SO WE'LL GIVE COIL A MONTH AND WE'LL HAVE THIS MEETING EVERY OTHER WEEK.
ADJOURNED.
IT WENT WELL...
YEAH.
YOU SURE ARE IMPRESSIVE, YAGAMI-KUN. YOU NOT ONLY DELAYED THE KILLINGS, BUT NOW WE MAY BE ABLE TO GET INFORMATION OUT OF NAMIKAWA.
IT'S SIMILAR TO HOW I WOULD HAVE DONE THINGS... AND YOU CAME UP WITH IT FASTER THAN I DID...
AT THIS RATE, IF I DIE, YOU COULD PROBABLY BECOME THE SUCCESSOR TO THE L NAME, YAGAMI-KUN.
DON'T SAY THAT. WE NOW NEED TO FIGURE OUT WHO KIRA IS, AND OBTAIN EVIDENCE WITH-IN A MONTH. THE HARD PART IS JUST BEGINNING.
YES...

DEATH NOTE
How to use it
XXXII

⊙ If someone possesses more than one DEATH NOTE, by visualizing the victim, then writing down the name in one of the DEATH NOTES and the cause of death in the other, it will take effect.

The order however, is unimportant, if you write down the cause of death in one DEATH NOTE and afterwards, write the name in the other, it will still take effect.

二冊以上のデスノートを所有した場合、
同じ人間の顔を思い浮かべて書き込めば、一冊に名前、
もう一冊に死因・死の状況を書いても、その通りになる。
ゆえに、一冊に死因・死の状況を書き、後からもう一冊に名前というのも有効。

⊙ This can also be accomplished by two DEATH NOTE owners working together. In this case, it's necessary that the two touch each other's DEATH NOTES.

上記を所有権の異なる二人の人間が共同でする事も、
互いのノートに触れ合っていれば可能である。

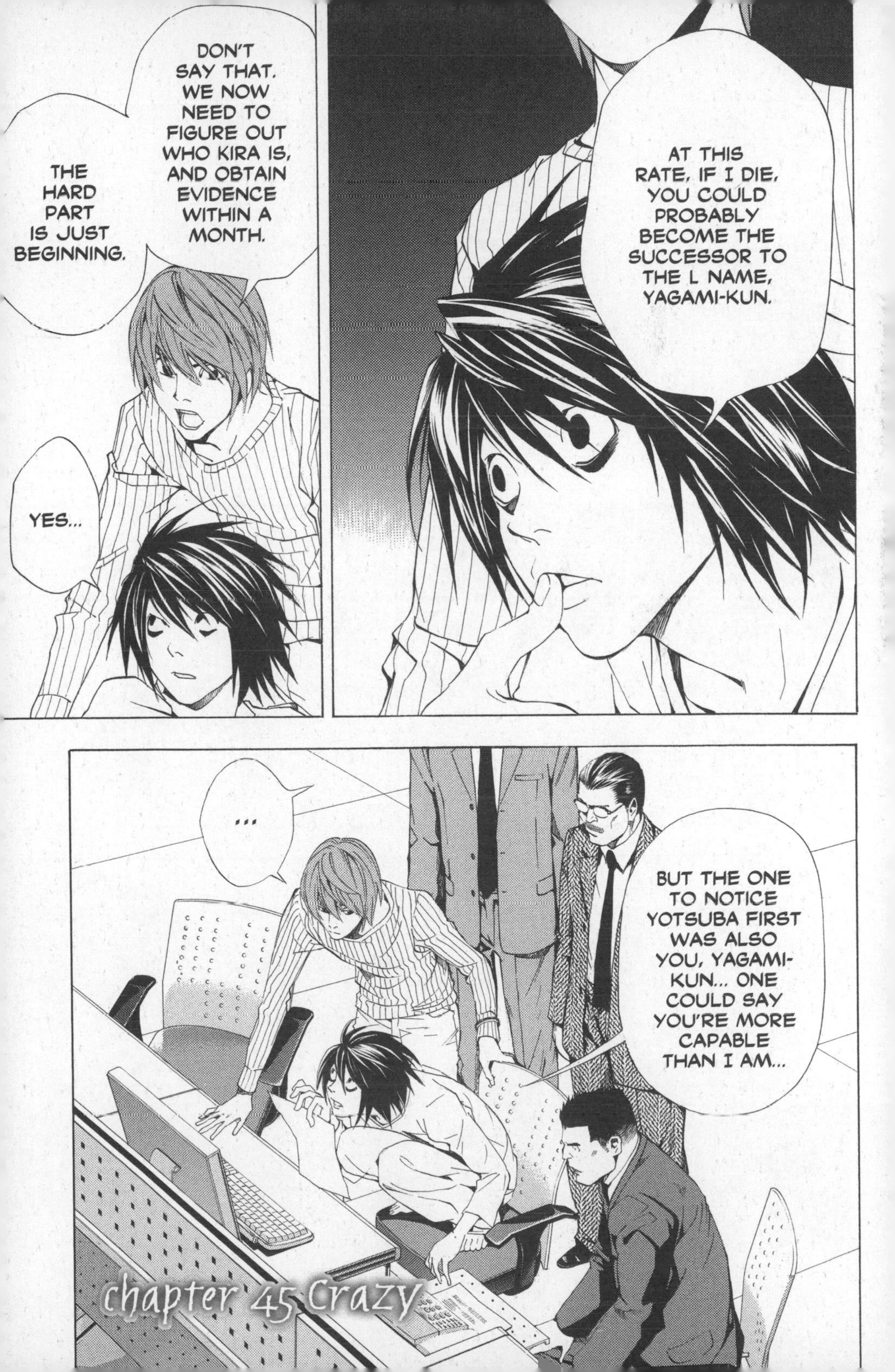
AT THIS RATE, IF I DIE, YOU COULD PROBABLY BECOME THE SUCCESSOR TO THE L NAME, YAGAMI-KUN.
DON'T SAY THAT. WE NOW NEED TO FIGURE OUT WHO KIRA IS, AND OBTAIN EVIDENCE WITHIN A MONTH.
THE HARD PART IS JUST BEGINNING.
YES...
BUT THE ONE TO NOTICE YOTSUBA FIRST WAS ALSO YOU, YAGAMI-KUN... ONE COULD SAY YOU'RE MORE CAPABLE THAN I AM...
...
chapter 45 Crazy

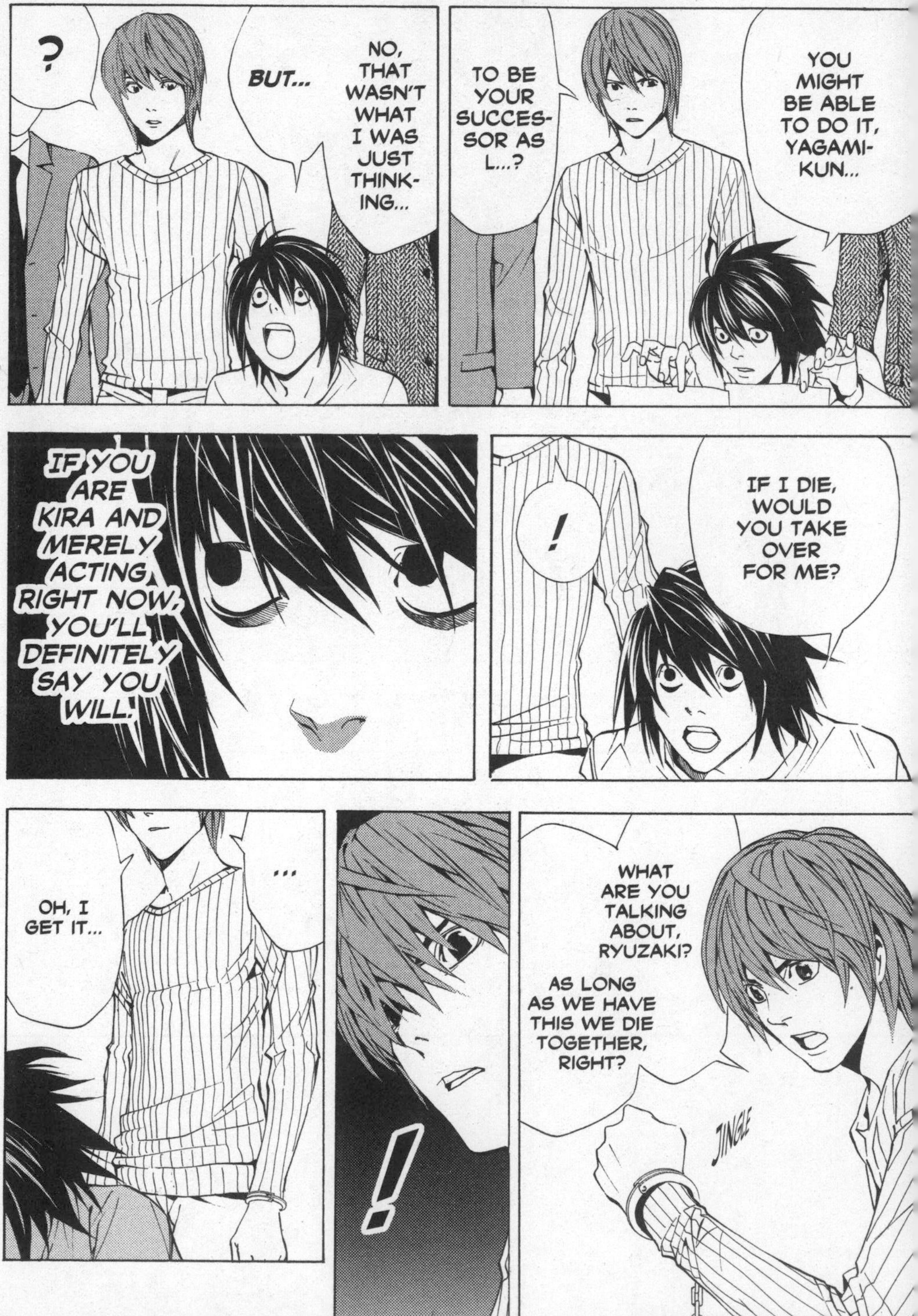
YOU MIGHT BE ABLE TO DO IT, YAGAMI-KUN...
TO BE YOUR SUCCESSOR AS L...?
NO, THAT WASN'T WHAT I WAS JUST THINKING...
BUT...
?
IF I DIE, WOULD YOU TAKE OVER FOR ME?
!
IF YOU ARE KIRA AND MERELY ACTING RIGHT NOW, YOU'LL DEFINITELY SAY YOU WILL.
WHAT ARE YOU TALKING ABOUT, RYUZAKI?
AS LONG AS WE HAVE THIS WE DIE TOGETHER, RIGHT?
JINGLE
!
...
OH, I GET IT...

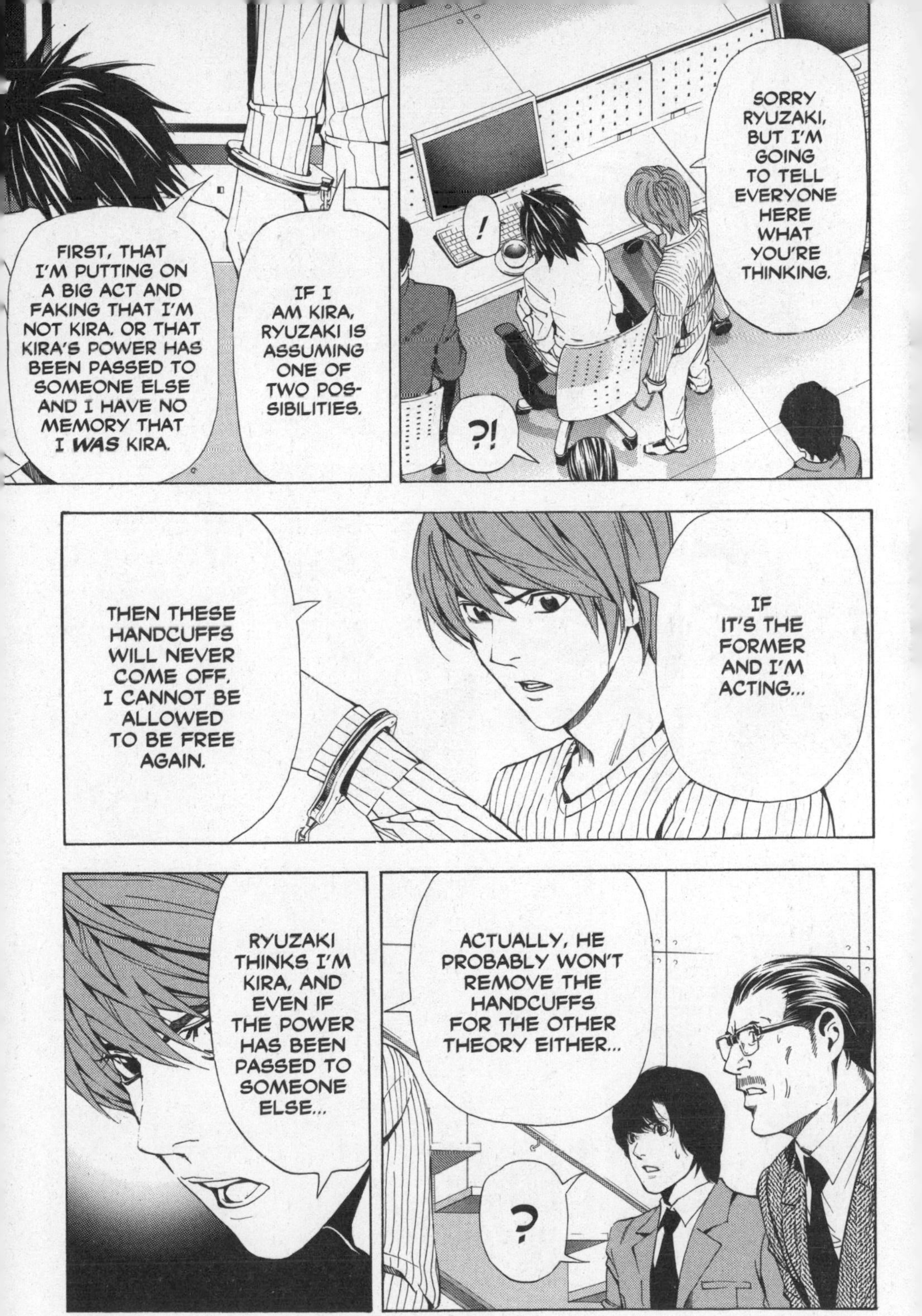
SORRY RYUZAKI, BUT I'M GOING TO TELL EVERYONE HERE WHAT YOU'RE THINKING.
!
?!
IF I AM KIRA, RYUZAKI IS ASSUMING ONE OF TWO POSSIBILITIES.
FIRST, THAT I'M PUTTING ON A BIG ACT AND FAKING THAT I'M NOT KIRA. OR THAT KIRA'S POWER HAS BEEN PASSED TO SOMEONE ELSE AND I HAVE NO MEMORY THAT I *WAS* KIRA.
IF IT'S THE FORMER AND I'M ACTING...
THEN THESE HANDCUFFS WILL NEVER COME OFF. I CANNOT BE ALLOWED TO BE FREE AGAIN.
ACTUALLY, HE PROBABLY WON'T REMOVE THE HANDCUFFS FOR THE OTHER THEORY EITHER...
?
RYUZAKI THINKS I'M KIRA, AND EVEN IF THE POWER HAS BEEN PASSED TO SOMEONE ELSE...

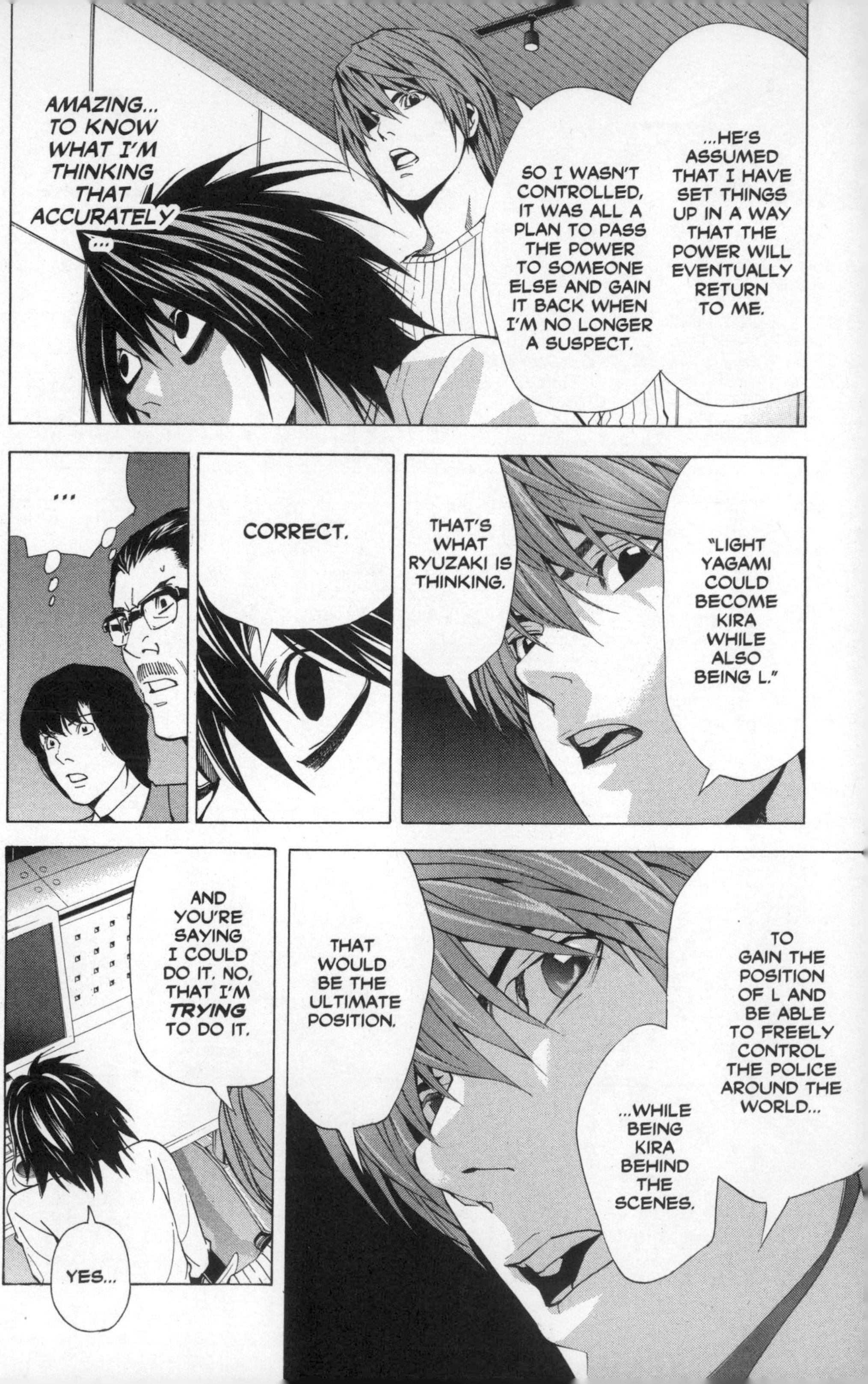
...HE'S ASSUMED THAT I HAVE SET THINGS UP IN A WAY THAT THE POWER WILL EVENTUALLY RETURN TO ME.
SO I WASN'T CONTROLLED, IT WAS ALL A PLAN TO PASS THE POWER TO SOMEONE ELSE AND GAIN IT BACK WHEN I'M NO LONGER A SUSPECT.
AMAZING... TO KNOW WHAT I'M THINKING THAT ACCURATELY...
"LIGHT YAGAMI COULD BECOME KIRA WHILE ALSO BEING L."
THAT'S WHAT RYUZAKI IS THINKING.
CORRECT.
...
TO GAIN THE POSITION OF L AND BE ABLE TO FREELY CONTROL THE POLICE AROUND THE WORLD...
...WHILE BEING KIRA BEHIND THE SCENES.
THAT WOULD BE THE ULTIMATE POSITION.
AND YOU'RE SAYING I COULD DO IT. NO, THAT I'M *TRYING* TO DO IT.
YES...

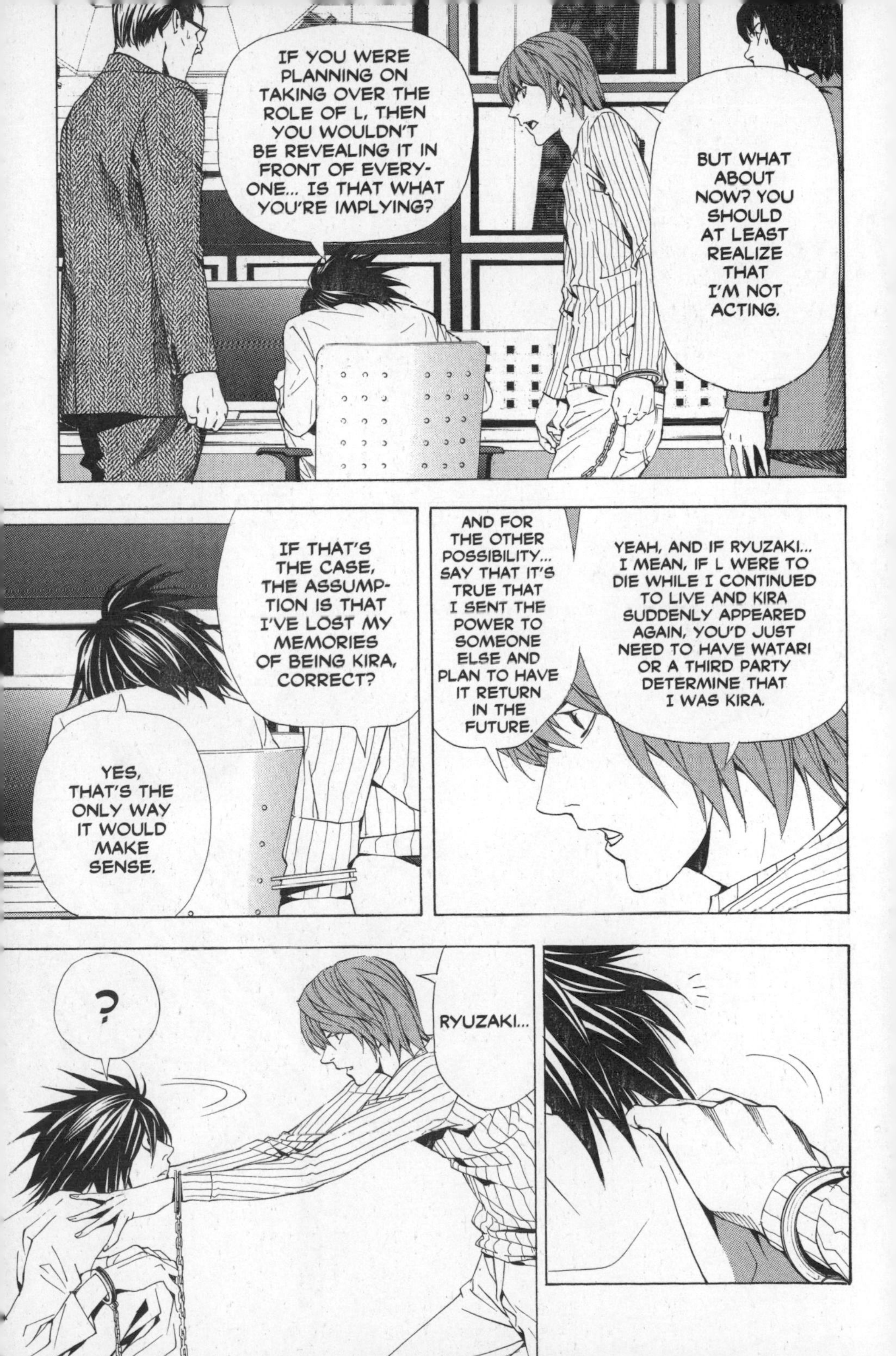
IF YOU WERE PLANNING ON TAKING OVER THE ROLE OF L, THEN YOU WOULDN'T BE REVEALING IT IN FRONT OF EVERY-ONE... IS THAT WHAT YOU'RE IMPLYING?
BUT WHAT ABOUT NOW? YOU SHOULD AT LEAST REALIZE THAT I'M NOT ACTING.
YEAH, AND IF RYUZAKI... I MEAN, IF L WERE TO DIE WHILE I CONTINUED TO LIVE AND KIRA SUDDENLY APPEARED AGAIN, YOU'D JUST NEED TO HAVE WATARI OR A THIRD PARTY DETERMINE THAT I WAS KIRA.
AND FOR THE OTHER POSSIBILITY... SAY THAT IT'S TRUE THAT I SENT THE POWER TO SOMEONE ELSE AND PLAN TO HAVE IT RETURN IN THE FUTURE.
IF THAT'S THE CASE, THE ASSUMP-TION IS THAT I'VE LOST MY MEMORIES OF BEING KIRA, CORRECT?
YES, THAT'S THE ONLY WAY IT WOULD MAKE SENSE.
RYUZAKI...
?

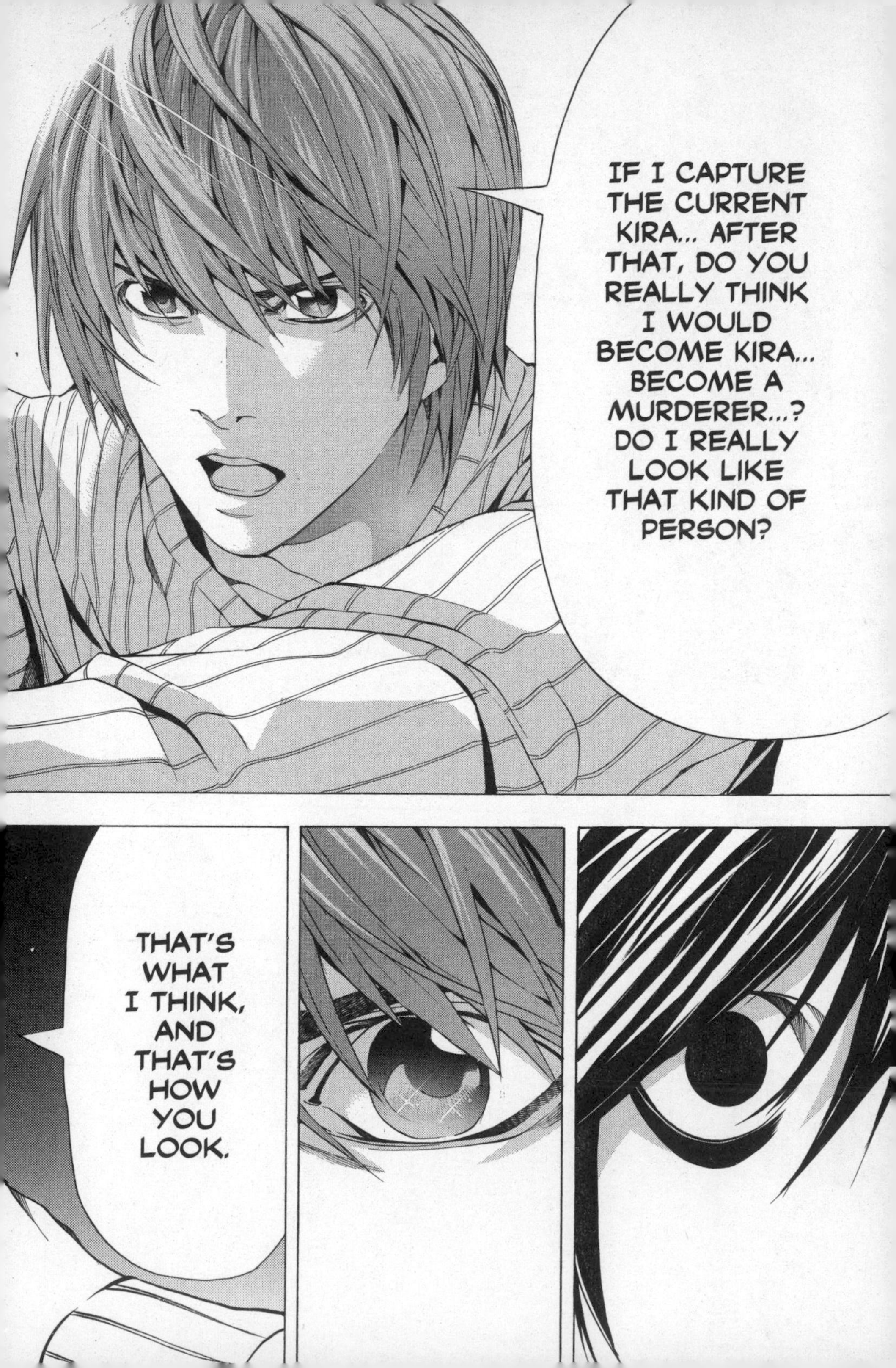
IF I CAPTURE THE CURRENT KIRA... AFTER THAT, DO YOU REALLY THINK I WOULD BECOME KIRA... BECOME A MURDERER...? DO I REALLY LOOK LIKE THAT KIND OF PERSON?
THAT'S WHAT I THINK, AND THAT'S HOW YOU LOOK.

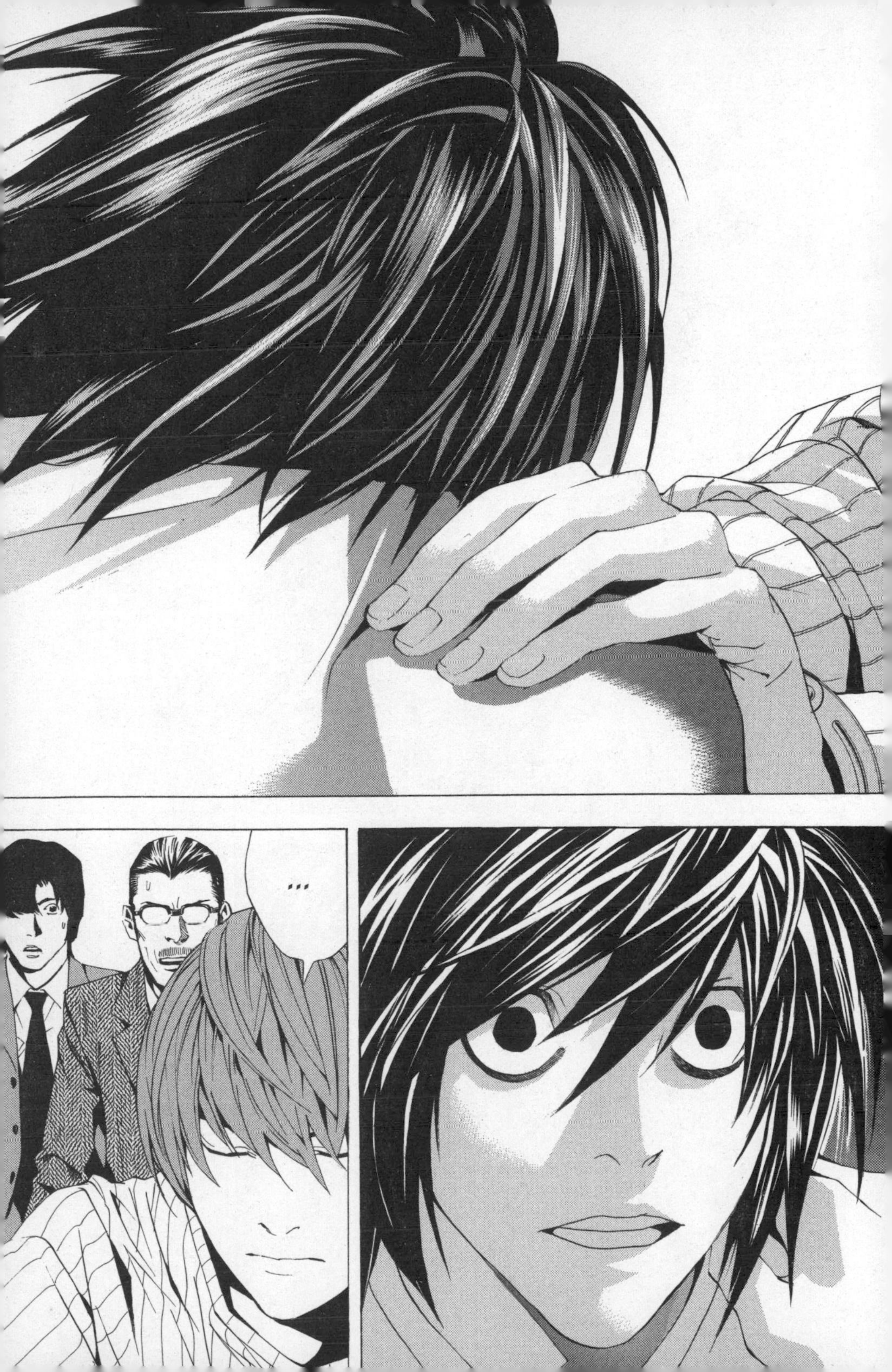
...

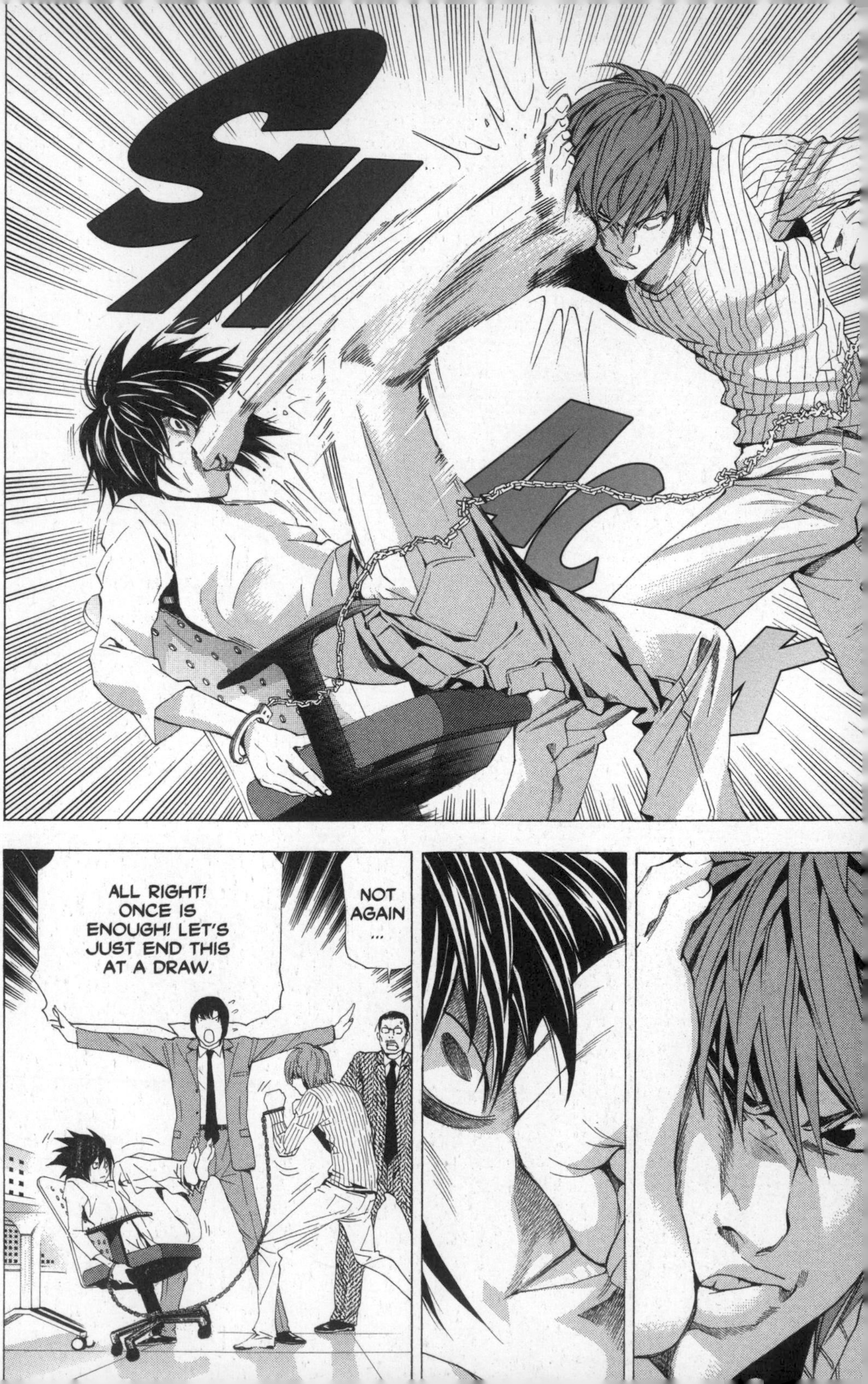
NOT AGAIN ...
ALL RIGHT! ONCE IS ENOUGH! LET'S JUST END THIS AT A DRAW.

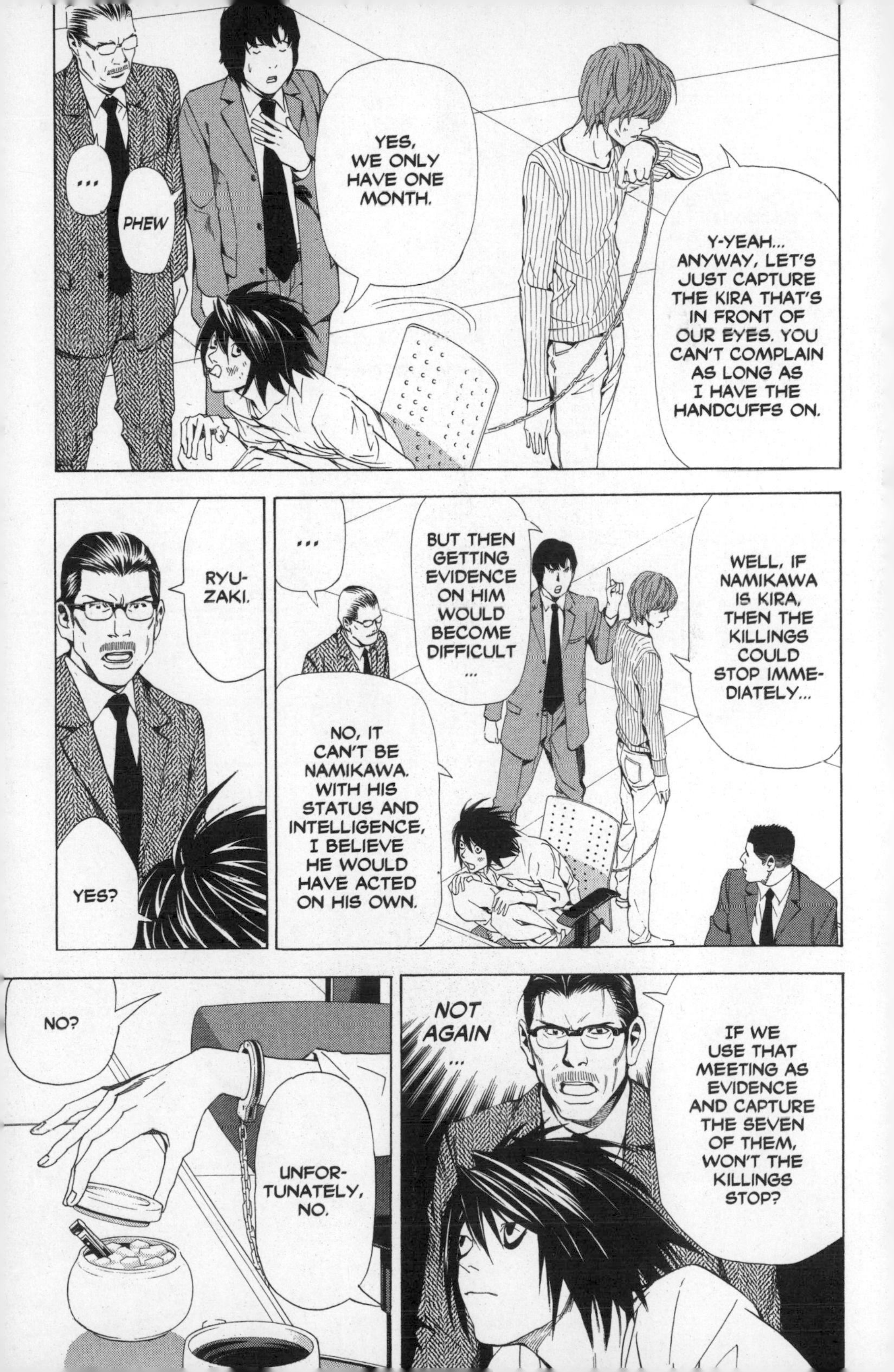
Y-YEAH... ANYWAY, LET'S JUST CAPTURE THE KIRA THAT'S IN FRONT OF OUR EYES. YOU CAN'T COMPLAIN AS LONG AS I HAVE THE HANDCUFFS ON.
YES, WE ONLY HAVE ONE MONTH.
...
PHEW
WELL, IF NAMIKAWA IS KIRA, THEN THE KILLINGS COULD STOP IMMEDIATELY...
BUT THEN GETTING EVIDENCE ON HIM WOULD BECOME DIFFICULT ...
...
NO, IT CAN'T BE NAMIKAWA. WITH HIS STATUS AND INTELLIGENCE, I BELIEVE HE WOULD HAVE ACTED ON HIS OWN.
RYU-ZAKI.
YES?
IF WE USE THAT MEETING AS EVIDENCE AND CAPTURE THE SEVEN OF THEM, WON'T THE KILLINGS STOP?
NOT AGAIN ...
NO?
UNFORTUNATELY, NO.

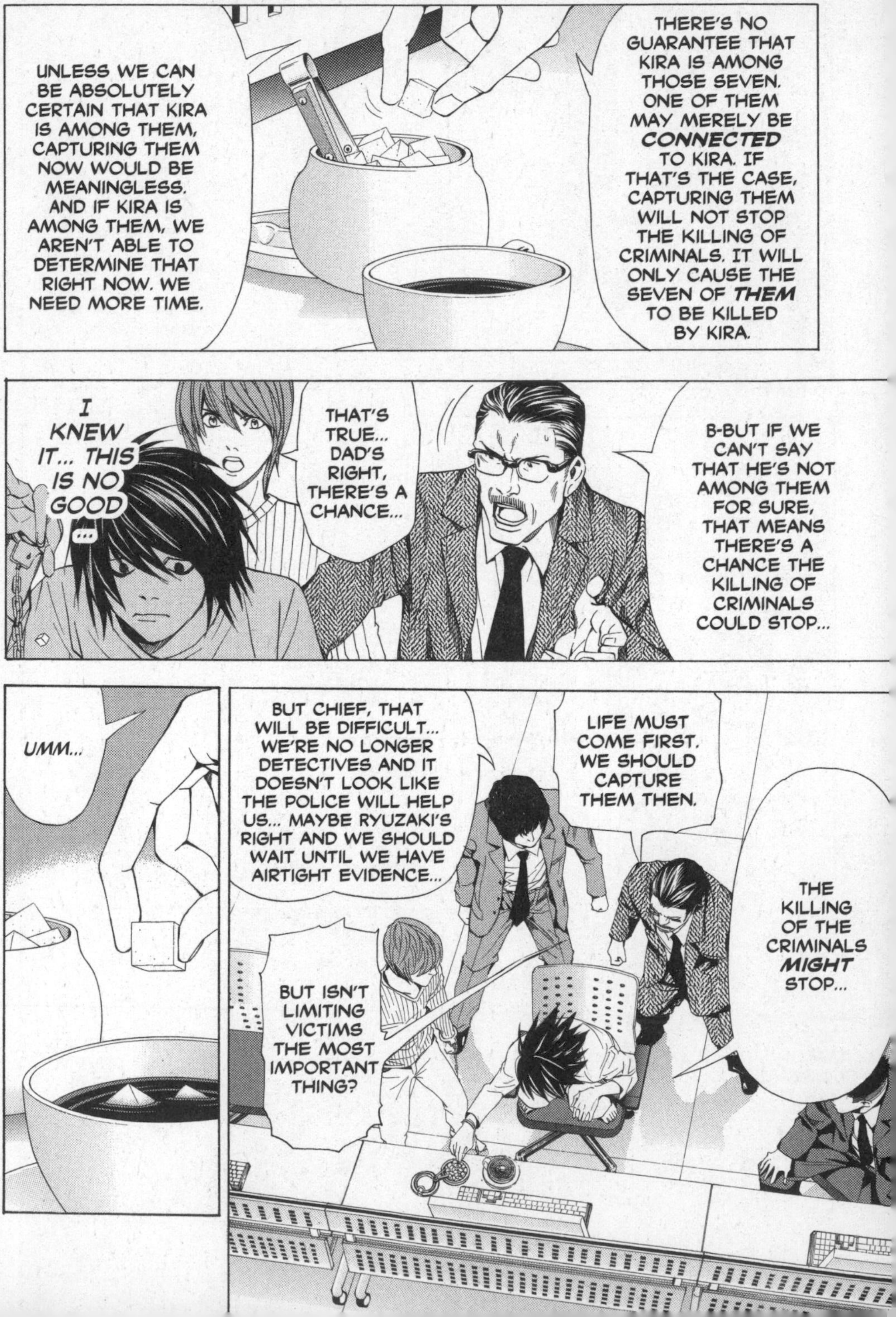
THERE'S NO GUARANTEE THAT KIRA IS AMONG THOSE SEVEN. ONE OF THEM MAY MERELY BE ***CONNECTED*** TO KIRA. IF THAT'S THE CASE, CAPTURING THEM WILL NOT STOP THE KILLING OF CRIMINALS. IT WILL ONLY CAUSE THE SEVEN OF ***THEM*** TO BE KILLED BY KIRA.
UNLESS WE CAN BE ABSOLUTELY CERTAIN THAT KIRA IS AMONG THEM, CAPTURING THEM NOW WOULD BE MEANINGLESS. AND IF KIRA IS AMONG THEM, WE AREN'T ABLE TO DETERMINE THAT RIGHT NOW. WE NEED MORE TIME.
B-BUT IF WE CAN'T SAY THAT HE'S NOT AMONG THEM FOR SURE, THAT MEANS THERE'S A CHANCE THE KILLING OF CRIMINALS COULD STOP...
THAT'S TRUE... DAD'S RIGHT, THERE'S A CHANCE...
I KNEW IT... THIS IS NO GOOD...
THE KILLING OF THE CRIMINALS ***MIGHT*** STOP...
LIFE MUST COME FIRST. WE SHOULD CAPTURE THEM THEN.
BUT CHIEF, THAT WILL BE DIFFICULT... WE'RE NO LONGER DETECTIVES AND IT DOESN'T LOOK LIKE THE POLICE WILL HELP US... MAYBE RYUZAKI'S RIGHT AND WE SHOULD WAIT UNTIL WE HAVE AIRTIGHT EVIDENCE...
BUT ISN'T LIMITING VICTIMS THE MOST IMPORTANT THING?
UMM...

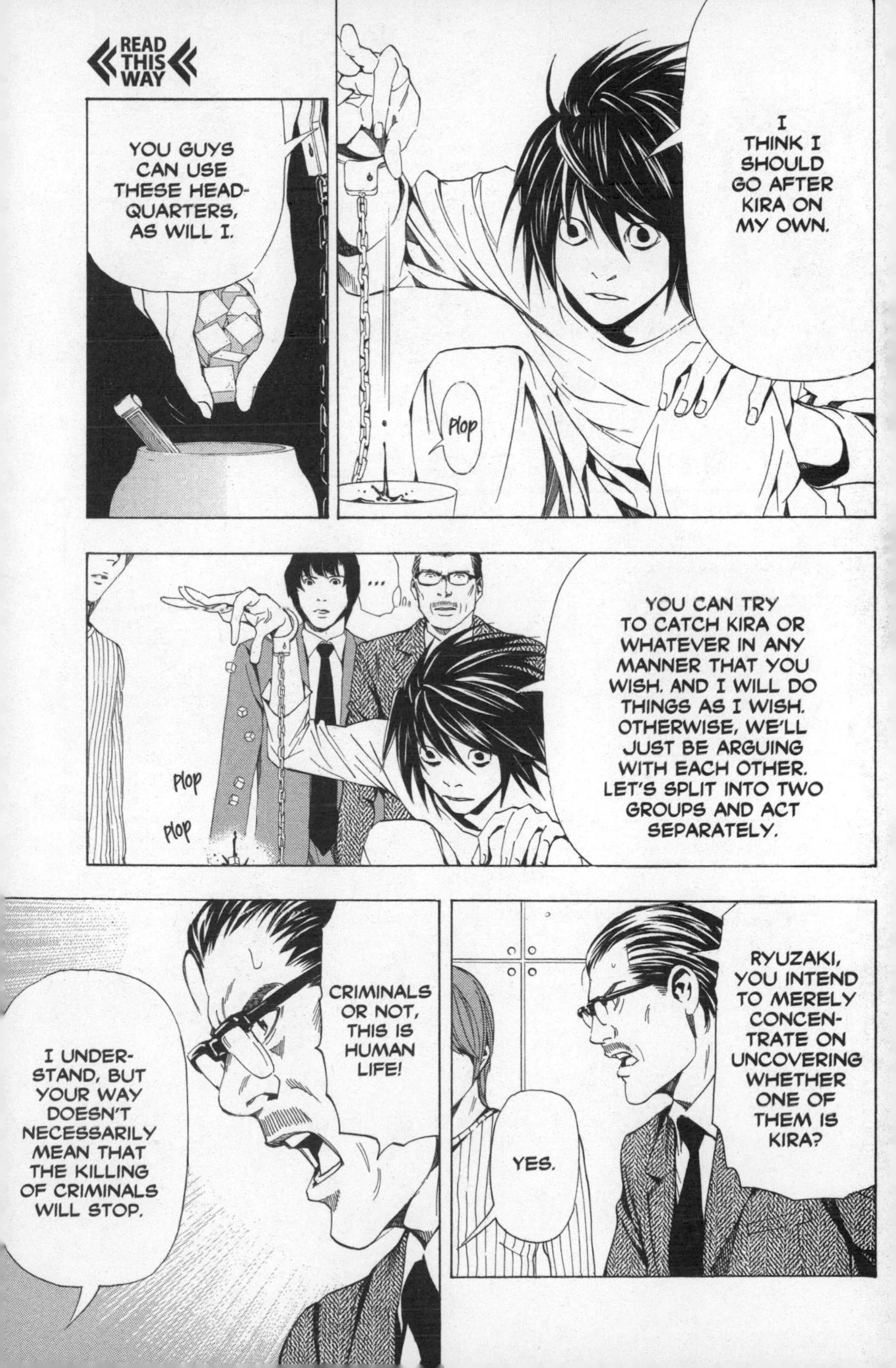
READ THIS WAY
I THINK I SHOULD GO AFTER KIRA ON MY OWN.
plop
YOU GUYS CAN USE THESE HEAD-QUARTERS, AS WILL I.
YOU CAN TRY TO CATCH KIRA OR WHATEVER IN ANY MANNER THAT YOU WISH. AND I WILL DO THINGS AS I WISH. OTHERWISE, WE'LL JUST BE ARGUING WITH EACH OTHER. LET'S SPLIT INTO TWO GROUPS AND ACT SEPARATELY.
...
plop
plop
RYUZAKI, YOU INTEND TO MERELY CONCEN-TRATE ON UNCOVERING WHETHER ONE OF THEM IS KIRA?
YES.
CRIMINALS OR NOT, THIS IS HUMAN LIFE!
I UNDER-STAND, BUT YOUR WAY DOESN'T NECESSARILY MEAN THAT THE KILLING OF CRIMINALS WILL STOP.

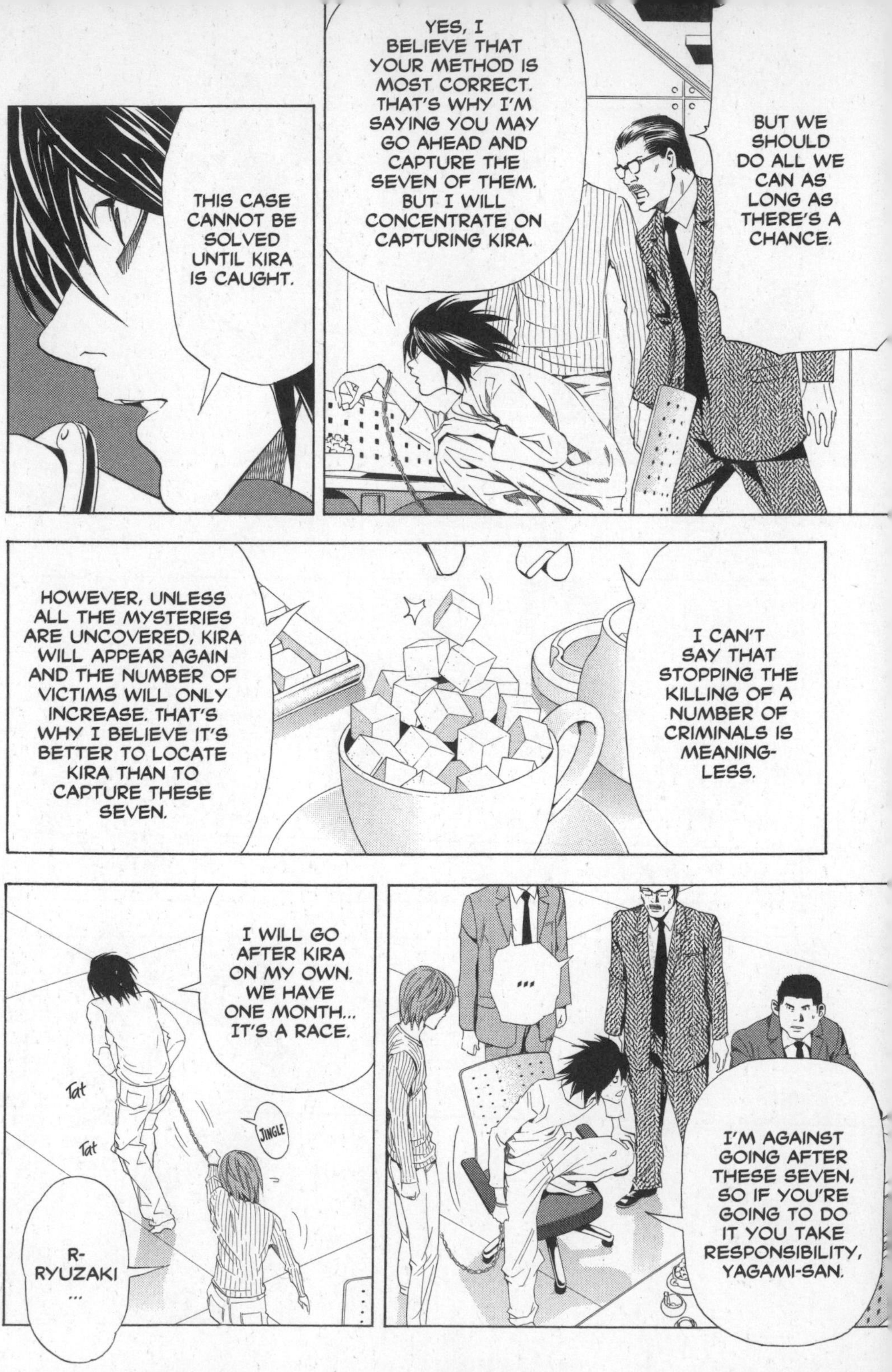
BUT WE SHOULD DO ALL WE CAN AS LONG AS THERE'S A CHANCE.
YES, I BELIEVE THAT YOUR METHOD IS MOST CORRECT. THAT'S WHY I'M SAYING YOU MAY GO AHEAD AND CAPTURE THE SEVEN OF THEM. BUT I WILL CONCENTRATE ON CAPTURING KIRA.
THIS CASE CANNOT BE SOLVED UNTIL KIRA IS CAUGHT.
I CAN'T SAY THAT STOPPING THE KILLING OF A NUMBER OF CRIMINALS IS MEANING-LESS.
HOWEVER, UNLESS ALL THE MYSTERIES ARE UNCOVERED, KIRA WILL APPEAR AGAIN AND THE NUMBER OF VICTIMS WILL ONLY INCREASE. THAT'S WHY I BELIEVE IT'S BETTER TO LOCATE KIRA THAN TO CAPTURE THESE SEVEN.
I'M AGAINST GOING AFTER THESE SEVEN, SO IF YOU'RE GOING TO DO IT YOU TAKE RESPONSIBILITY, YAGAMI-SAN.
...
I WILL GO AFTER KIRA ON MY OWN. WE HAVE ONE MONTH... IT'S A RACE.
Tat
Tat
JINGLE
R-RYUZAKI ...

READ THIS WAY

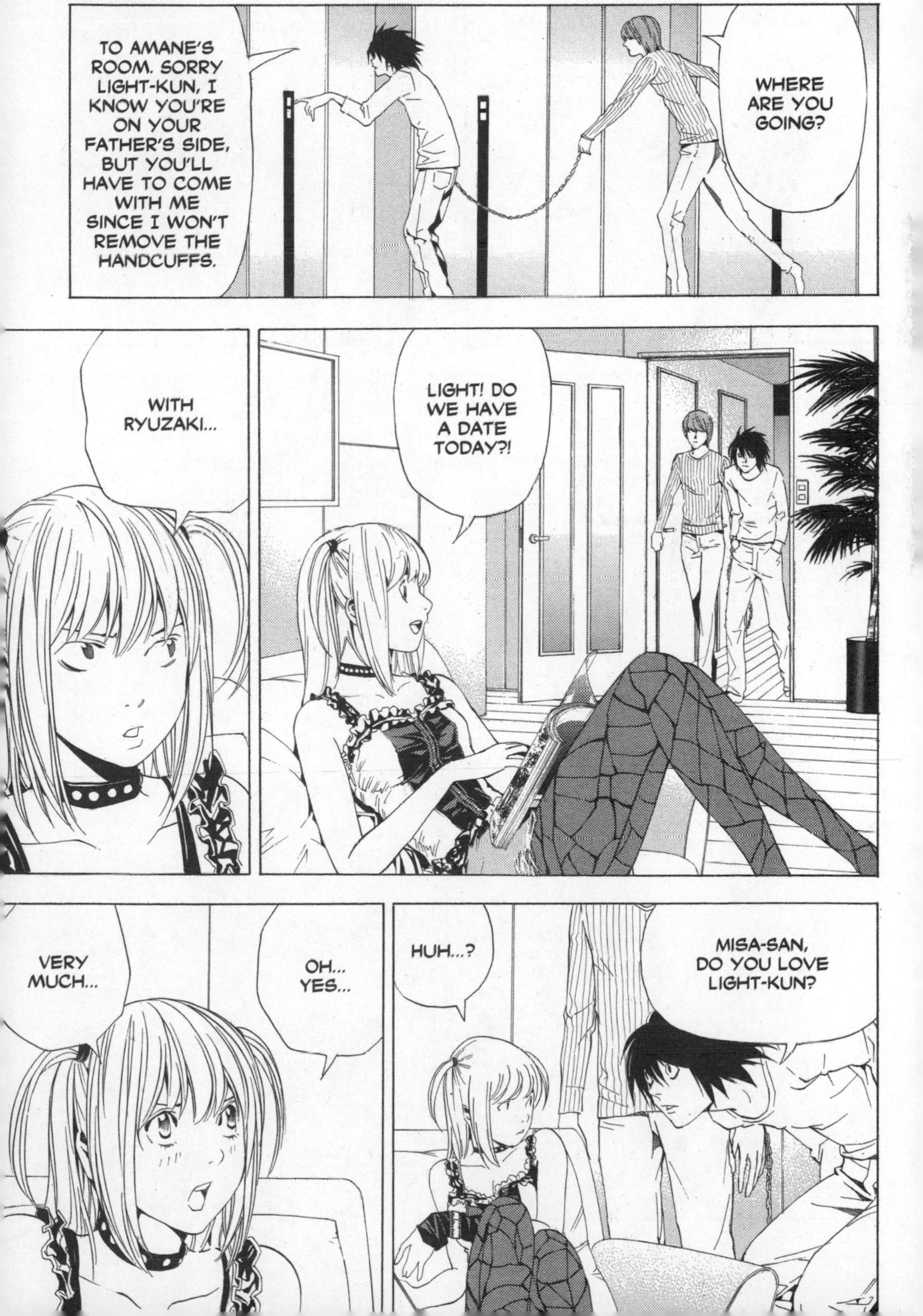
WHERE ARE YOU GOING?
TO AMANE'S ROOM. SORRY LIGHT-KUN, I KNOW YOU'RE ON YOUR FATHER'S SIDE, BUT YOU'LL HAVE TO COME WITH ME SINCE I WON'T REMOVE THE HANDCUFFS.
LIGHT! DO WE HAVE A DATE TODAY?!
WITH RYUZAKI...
MISA-SAN, DO YOU LOVE LIGHT-KUN?
HUH...?
OH... YES...
VERY MUCH...

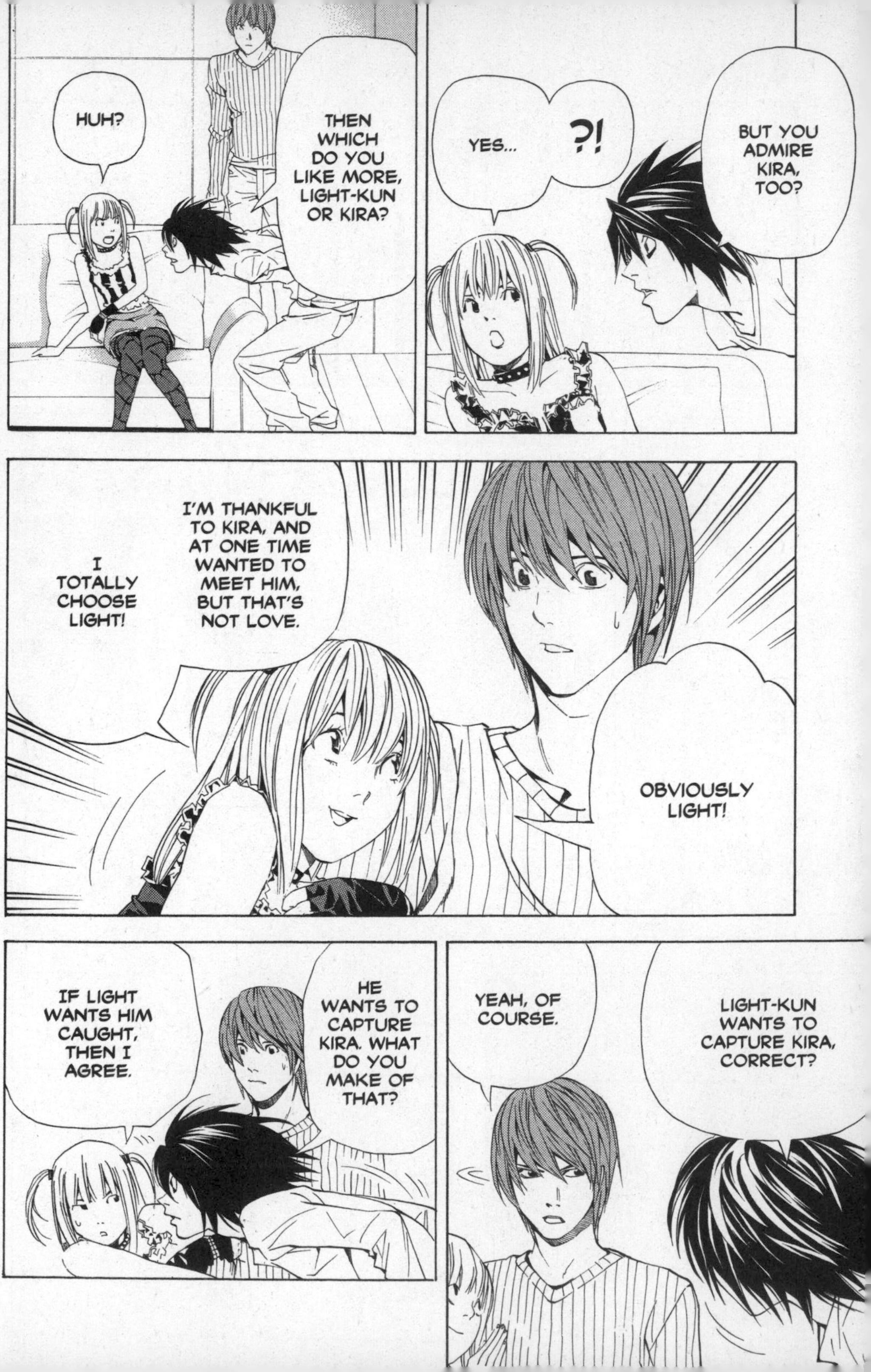
BUT YOU ADMIRE KIRA, TOO?
YES... ?!
THEN WHICH DO YOU LIKE MORE, LIGHT-KUN OR KIRA?
HUH?
OBVIOUSLY LIGHT!
I'M THANKFUL TO KIRA, AND AT ONE TIME WANTED TO MEET HIM, BUT THAT'S NOT LOVE.
I TOTALLY CHOOSE LIGHT!
LIGHT-KUN WANTS TO CAPTURE KIRA, CORRECT?
YEAH, OF COURSE.
HE WANTS TO CAPTURE KIRA. WHAT DO YOU MAKE OF THAT?
IF LIGHT WANTS HIM CAUGHT, THEN I AGREE.

READ THIS WAY

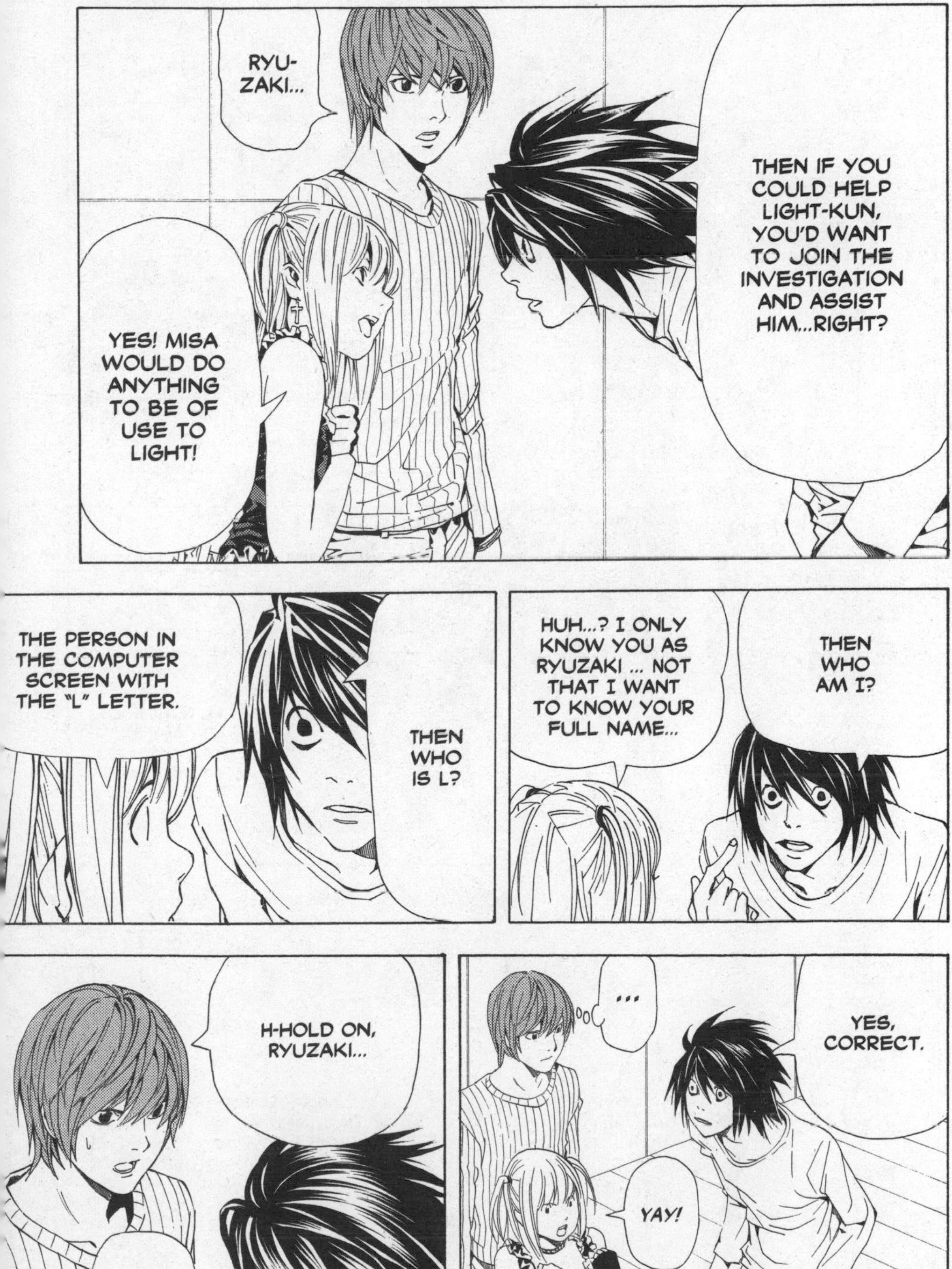
THEN IF YOU COULD HELP LIGHT-KUN, YOU'D WANT TO JOIN THE INVESTIGATION AND ASSIST HIM...RIGHT?
RYU-ZAKI...
YES! MISA WOULD DO ANYTHING TO BE OF USE TO LIGHT!
THEN WHO AM I?
HUH...? I ONLY KNOW YOU AS RYUZAKI ... NOT THAT I WANT TO KNOW YOUR FULL NAME...
THEN WHO IS L?
THE PERSON IN THE COMPUTER SCREEN WITH THE "L" LETTER.
YES, CORRECT.
...
YAY!
H-HOLD ON, RYUZAKI...
YES?

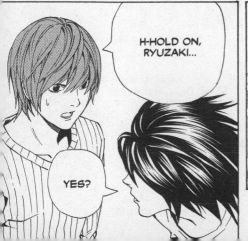

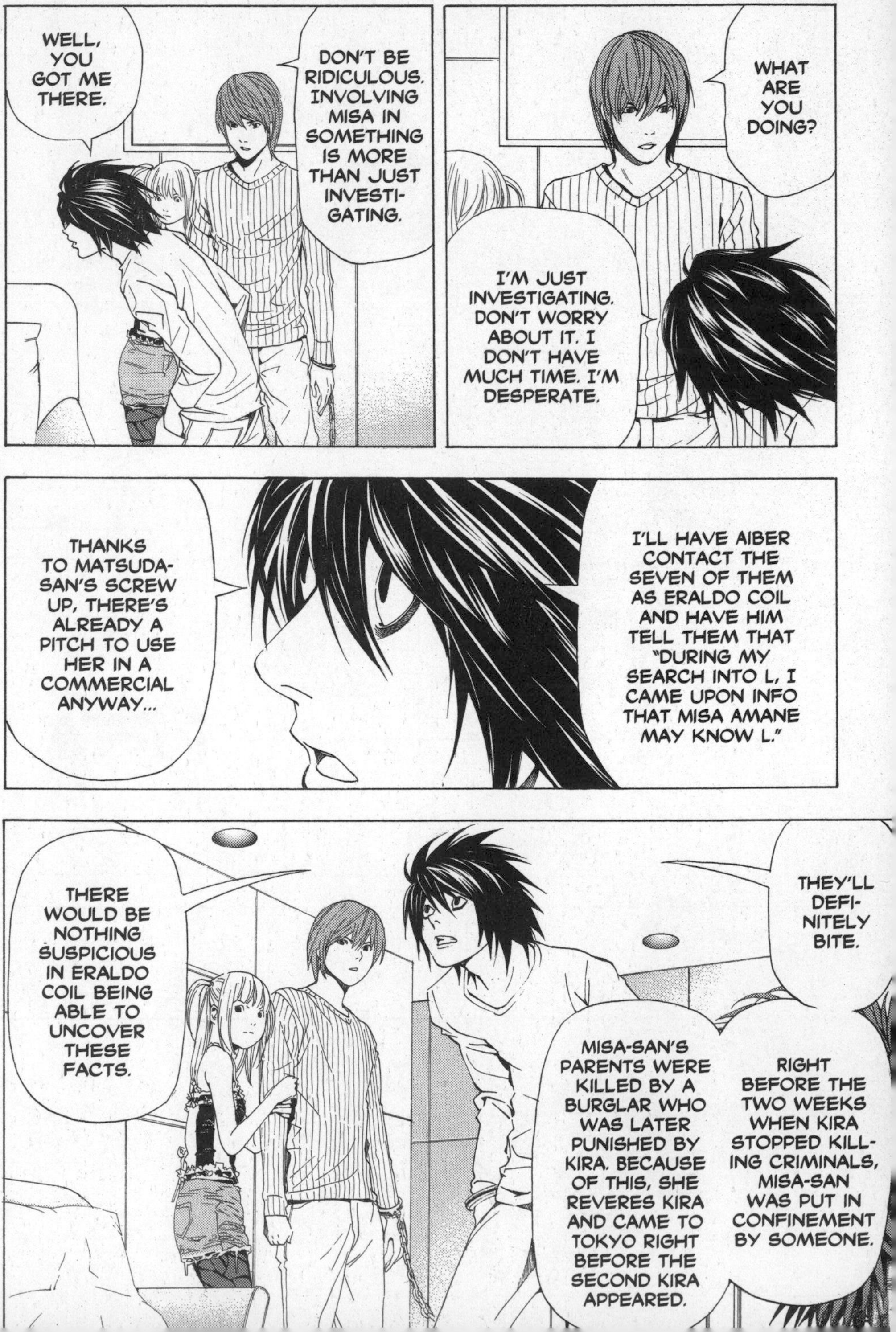
WHAT ARE YOU DOING?
I'M JUST INVESTIGATING. DON'T WORRY ABOUT IT. I DON'T HAVE MUCH TIME. I'M DESPERATE.
DON'T BE RIDICULOUS. INVOLVING MISA IN SOMETHING IS MORE THAN JUST INVESTIGATING.
WELL, YOU GOT ME THERE.
I'LL HAVE AIBER CONTACT THE SEVEN OF THEM AS ERALDO COIL AND HAVE HIM TELL THEM THAT "DURING MY SEARCH INTO L, I CAME UPON INFO THAT MISA AMANE MAY KNOW L."
THANKS TO MATSUDA-SAN'S SCREW UP, THERE'S ALREADY A PITCH TO USE HER IN A COMMERCIAL ANYWAY...
THEY'LL DEFINITELY BITE.
RIGHT BEFORE THE TWO WEEKS WHEN KIRA STOPPED KILLING CRIMINALS, MISA-SAN WAS PUT IN CONFINEMENT BY SOMEONE.
MISA-SAN'S PARENTS WERE KILLED BY A BURGLAR WHO WAS LATER PUNISHED BY KIRA. BECAUSE OF THIS, SHE REVERES KIRA AND CAME TO TOKYO RIGHT BEFORE THE SECOND KIRA APPEARED.
THERE WOULD BE NOTHING SUSPICIOUS IN ERALDO COIL BEING ABLE TO UNCOVER THESE FACTS.

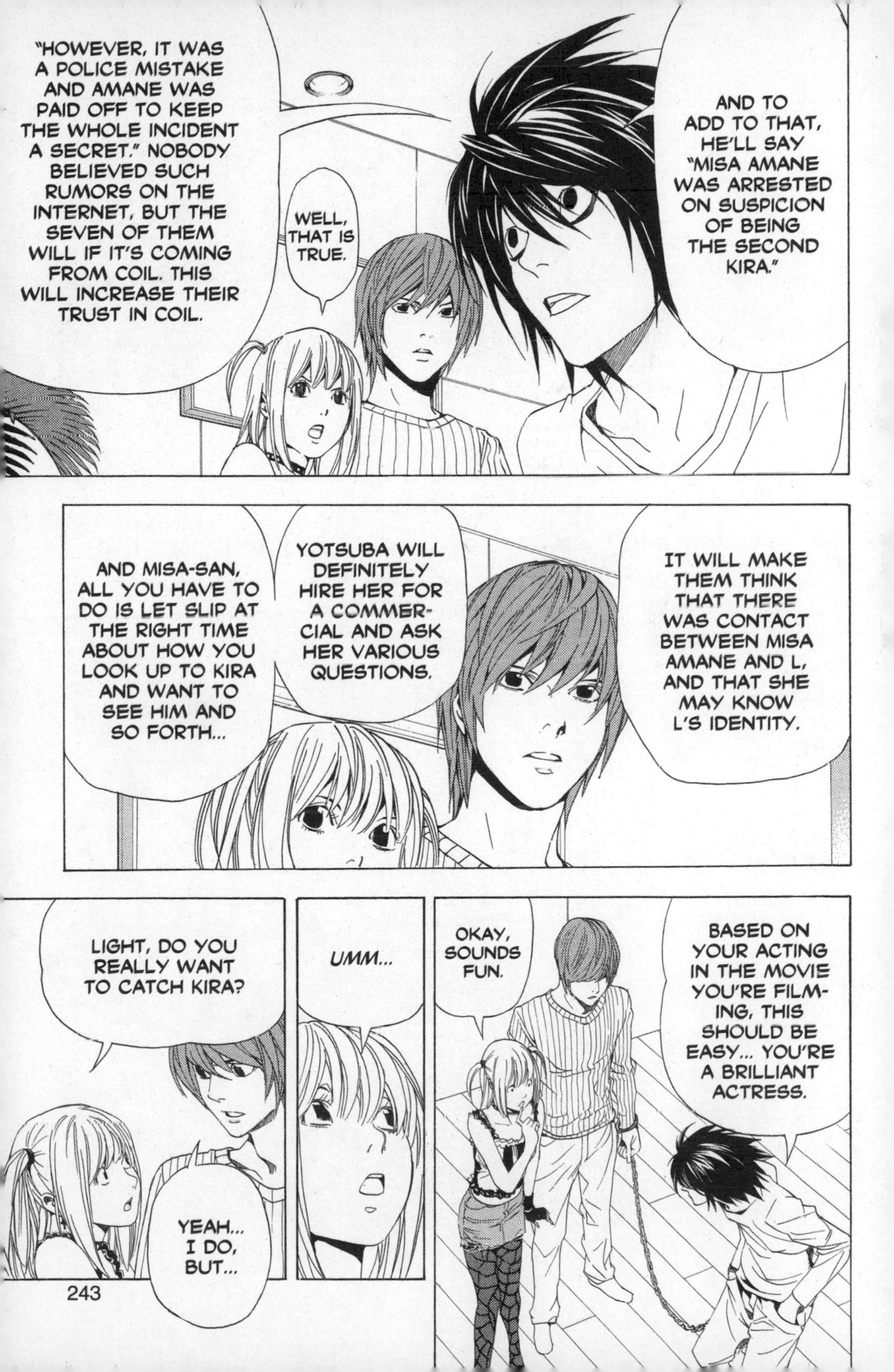
AND TO ADD TO THAT, HE'LL SAY "MISA AMANE WAS ARRESTED ON SUSPICION OF BEING THE SECOND KIRA."
"HOWEVER, IT WAS A POLICE MISTAKE AND AMANE WAS PAID OFF TO KEEP THE WHOLE INCIDENT A SECRET." NOBODY BELIEVED SUCH RUMORS ON THE INTERNET, BUT THE SEVEN OF THEM WILL IF IT'S COMING FROM COIL. THIS WILL INCREASE THEIR TRUST IN COIL.
WELL, THAT IS TRUE.
IT WILL MAKE THEM THINK THAT THERE WAS CONTACT BETWEEN MISA AMANE AND L, AND THAT SHE MAY KNOW L'S IDENTITY.
YOTSUBA WILL DEFINITELY HIRE HER FOR A COMMERCIAL AND ASK HER VARIOUS QUESTIONS.
AND MISA-SAN, ALL YOU HAVE TO DO IS LET SLIP AT THE RIGHT TIME ABOUT HOW YOU LOOK UP TO KIRA AND WANT TO SEE HIM AND SO FORTH...
BASED ON YOUR ACTING IN THE MOVIE YOU'RE FILMING, THIS SHOULD BE EASY... YOU'RE A BRILLIANT ACTRESS.
OKAY, SOUNDS FUN.
UMM...
LIGHT, DO YOU REALLY WANT TO CATCH KIRA?
YEAH... I DO, BUT...

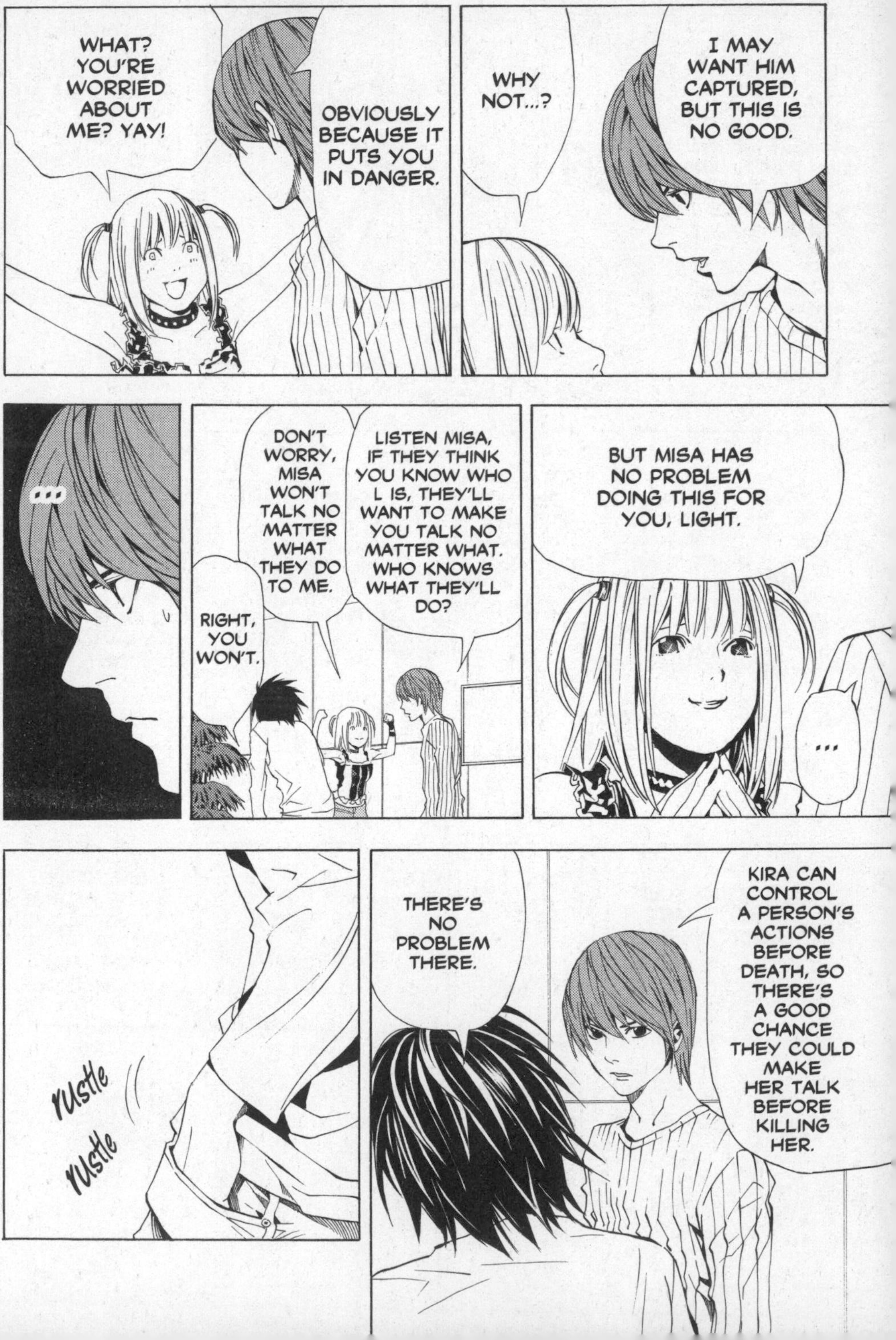
I MAY WANT HIM CAPTURED, BUT THIS IS NO GOOD.
WHY NOT...?
OBVIOUSLY BECAUSE IT PUTS YOU IN DANGER.
WHAT? YOU'RE WORRIED ABOUT ME? YAY!
BUT MISA HAS NO PROBLEM DOING THIS FOR YOU, LIGHT.
...
LISTEN MISA, IF THEY THINK YOU KNOW WHO L IS, THEY'LL WANT TO MAKE YOU TALK NO MATTER WHAT. WHO KNOWS WHAT THEY'LL DO?
DON'T WORRY, MISA WON'T TALK NO MATTER WHAT THEY DO TO ME.
RIGHT, YOU WON'T.
...
KIRA CAN CONTROL A PERSON'S ACTIONS BEFORE DEATH, SO THERE'S A GOOD CHANCE THEY COULD MAKE HER TALK BEFORE KILLING HER.
THERE'S NO PROBLEM THERE.
rustle
rustle

READ THIS WAY

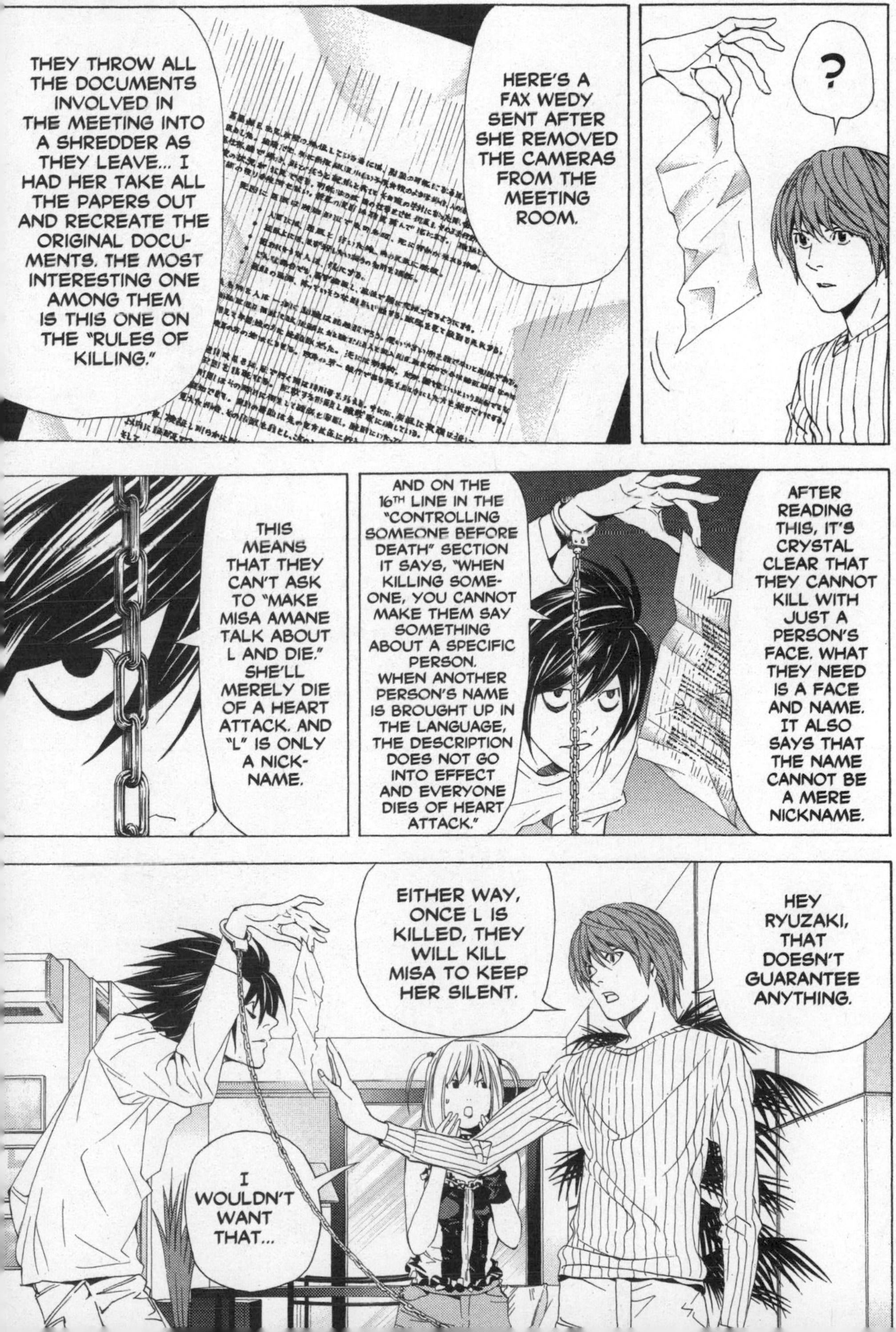
?
HERE'S A FAX WEDY SENT AFTER SHE REMOVED THE CAMERAS FROM THE MEETING ROOM.
THEY THROW ALL THE DOCUMENTS INVOLVED IN THE MEETING INTO A SHREDDER AS THEY LEAVE... I HAD HER TAKE ALL THE PAPERS OUT AND RECREATE THE ORIGINAL DOCU-MENTS. THE MOST INTERESTING ONE AMONG THEM IS THIS ONE ON THE "RULES OF KILLING."
AFTER READING THIS, IT'S CRYSTAL CLEAR THAT THEY CANNOT KILL WITH JUST A PERSON'S FACE. WHAT THEY NEED IS A FACE AND NAME. IT ALSO SAYS THAT THE NAME CANNOT BE A MERE NICKNAME.
AND ON THE 16TH LINE IN THE "CONTROLLING SOMEONE BEFORE DEATH" SECTION IT SAYS, "WHEN KILLING SOME-ONE, YOU CANNOT MAKE THEM SAY SOMETHING ABOUT A SPECIFIC PERSON. WHEN ANOTHER PERSON'S NAME IS BROUGHT UP IN THE LANGUAGE, THE DESCRIPTION DOES NOT GO INTO EFFECT AND EVERYONE DIES OF HEART ATTACK."
THIS MEANS THAT THEY CAN'T ASK TO "MAKE MISA AMANE TALK ABOUT L AND DIE." SHE'LL MERELY DIE OF A HEART ATTACK. AND "L" IS ONLY A NICK-NAME.
HEY RYUZAKI, THAT DOESN'T GUARANTEE ANYTHING.
EITHER WAY, ONCE L IS KILLED, THEY WILL KILL MISA TO KEEP HER SILENT.
I WOULDN'T WANT THAT...

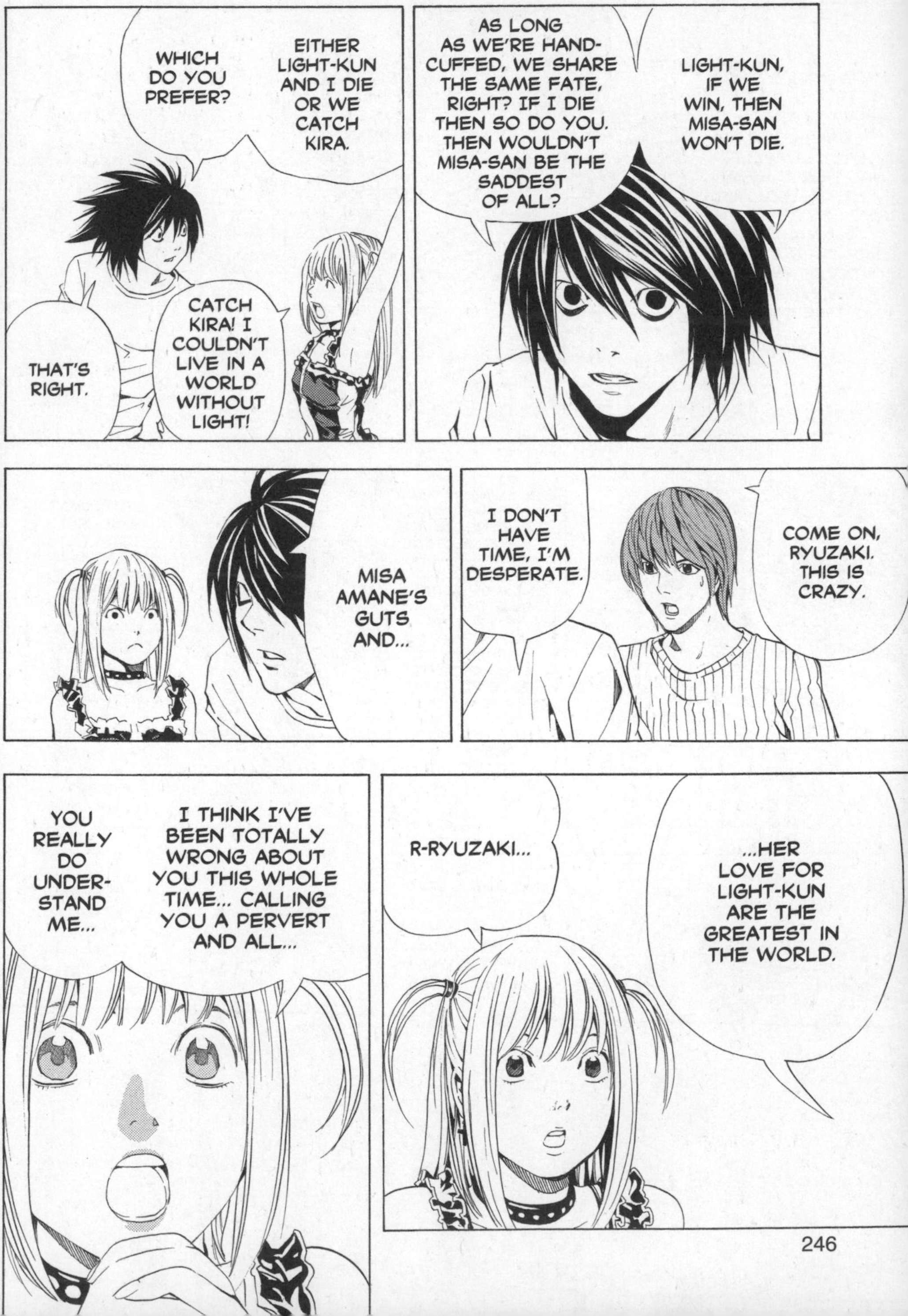
LIGHT-KUN, IF WE WIN, THEN MISA-SAN WON'T DIE.
AS LONG AS WE'RE HAND-CUFFED, WE SHARE THE SAME FATE, RIGHT? IF I DIE THEN SO DO YOU. THEN WOULDN'T MISA-SAN BE THE SADDEST OF ALL?
EITHER LIGHT-KUN AND I DIE OR WE CATCH KIRA.
WHICH DO YOU PREFER?
CATCH KIRA! I COULDN'T LIVE IN A WORLD WITHOUT LIGHT!
THAT'S RIGHT.
COME ON, RYUZAKI. THIS IS CRAZY.
I DON'T HAVE TIME, I'M DESPERATE.
MISA AMANE'S GUTS AND...
...HER LOVE FOR LIGHT-KUN ARE THE GREATEST IN THE WORLD.
R-RYUZAKI...
I THINK I'VE BEEN TOTALLY WRONG ABOUT YOU THIS WHOLE TIME... CALLING YOU A PERVERT AND ALL...
YOU REALLY DO UNDER-STAND ME...

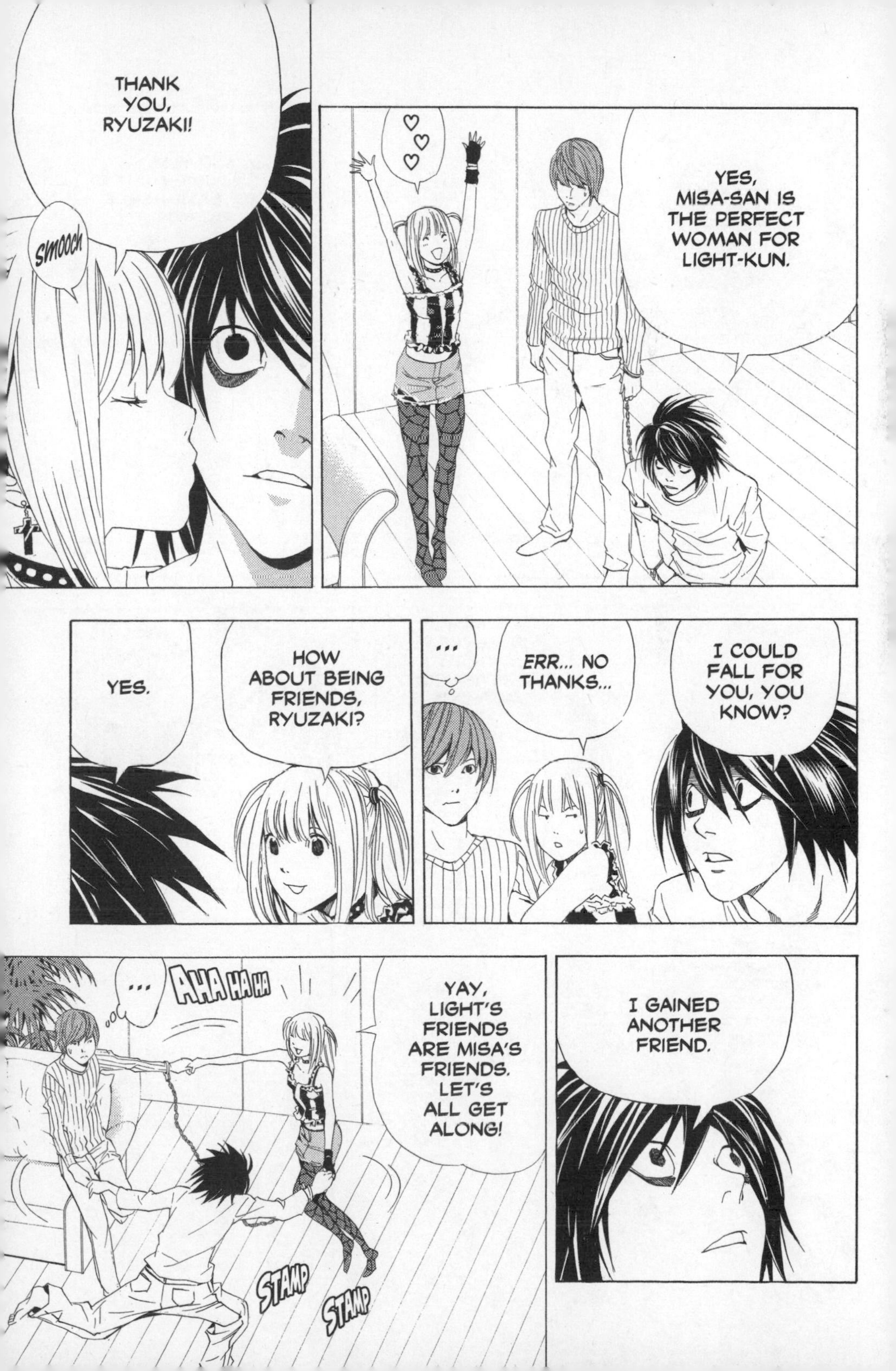
YES, MISA-SAN IS THE PERFECT WOMAN FOR LIGHT-KUN.
THANK YOU, RYUZAKI!
SMOOCH
I COULD FALL FOR YOU, YOU KNOW?
ERR... NO THANKS...
...
HOW ABOUT BEING FRIENDS, RYUZAKI?
YES.
I GAINED ANOTHER FRIEND.
YAY, LIGHT'S FRIENDS ARE MISA'S FRIENDS. LET'S ALL GET ALONG!
AHAHAHA
...
STAMP
STAMP

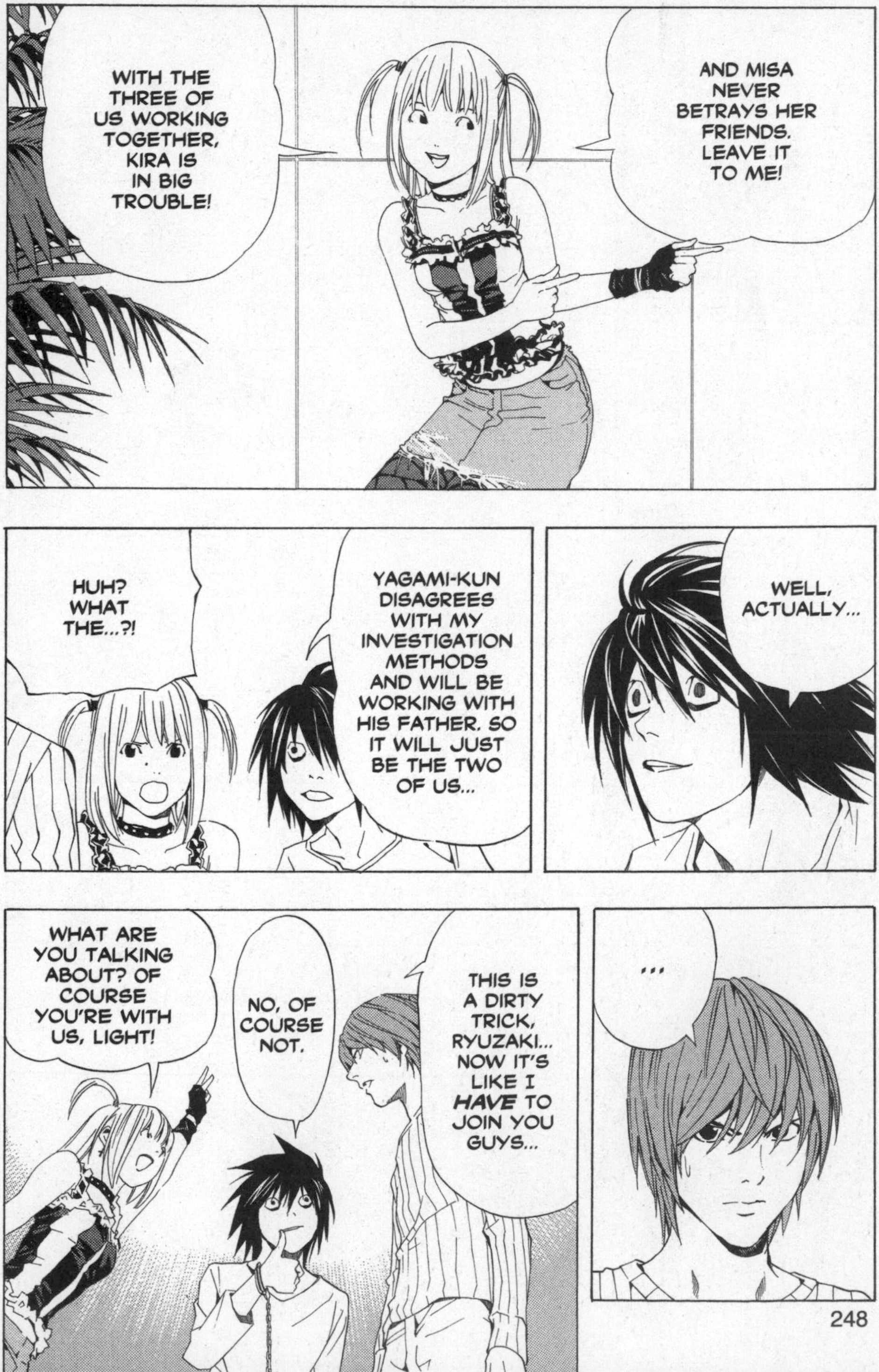
AND MISA NEVER BETRAYS HER FRIENDS. LEAVE IT TO ME!
WITH THE THREE OF US WORKING TOGETHER, KIRA IS IN BIG TROUBLE!
WELL, ACTUALLY...
YAGAMI-KUN DISAGREES WITH MY INVESTIGATION METHODS AND WILL BE WORKING WITH HIS FATHER. SO IT WILL JUST BE THE TWO OF US...
HUH? WHAT THE...?!
...
THIS IS A DIRTY TRICK, RYUZAKI... NOW IT'S LIKE I *HAVE* TO JOIN YOU GUYS...
NO, OF COURSE NOT.
WHAT ARE YOU TALKING ABOUT? OF COURSE YOU'RE WITH US, LIGHT!

READ THIS WAY

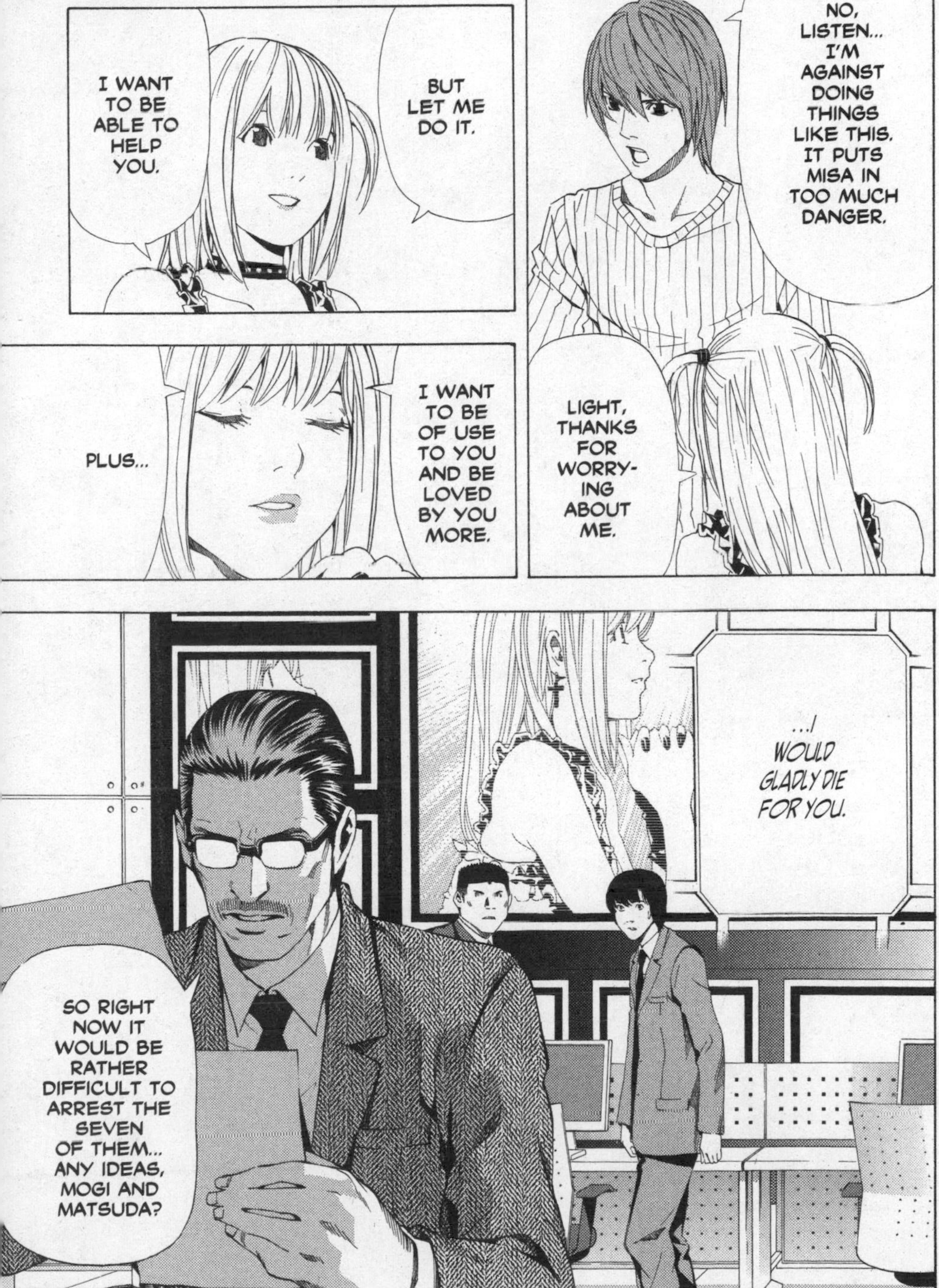
NO, LISTEN... I'M AGAINST DOING THINGS LIKE THIS. IT PUTS MISA IN TOO MUCH DANGER.
LIGHT, THANKS FOR WORRYING ABOUT ME.
BUT LET ME DO IT.
I WANT TO BE ABLE TO HELP YOU.
I WANT TO BE OF USE TO YOU AND BE LOVED BY YOU MORE.
PLUS...
...I WOULD GLADLY DIE FOR YOU.
SO RIGHT NOW IT WOULD BE RATHER DIFFICULT TO ARREST THE SEVEN OF THEM... ANY IDEAS, MOGI AND MATSUDA?

DEATH NOTE
HOW to USE it
XXXII

○ If a person loses possession of a DEATH NOTE, they will not recognize the gods of death by sight or voice any more. If however, the owner lets someone else touch his DEATH NOTE, from that time on, that person will recognize the god of death.

デスノートの所有権を失うと、そのデスノートに憑いていた死神の姿や声は認知できなくなるが、所有者でないノートに触れた人間には、その持ち主の死神の姿や声が認知され続ける。

○ In accordance with the above, the human who touched the DEATH NOTE and began to recognize the gods of death's sight and voice, will continue to recognize it until that human actually owns the DEATH NOTE and subsequently loses possession of it.

よって、ノートの所有権のない人間がノートに触れる事で認知した死神は、そのノートの所有権を得て所有権を失わない限り、認知される事になる。

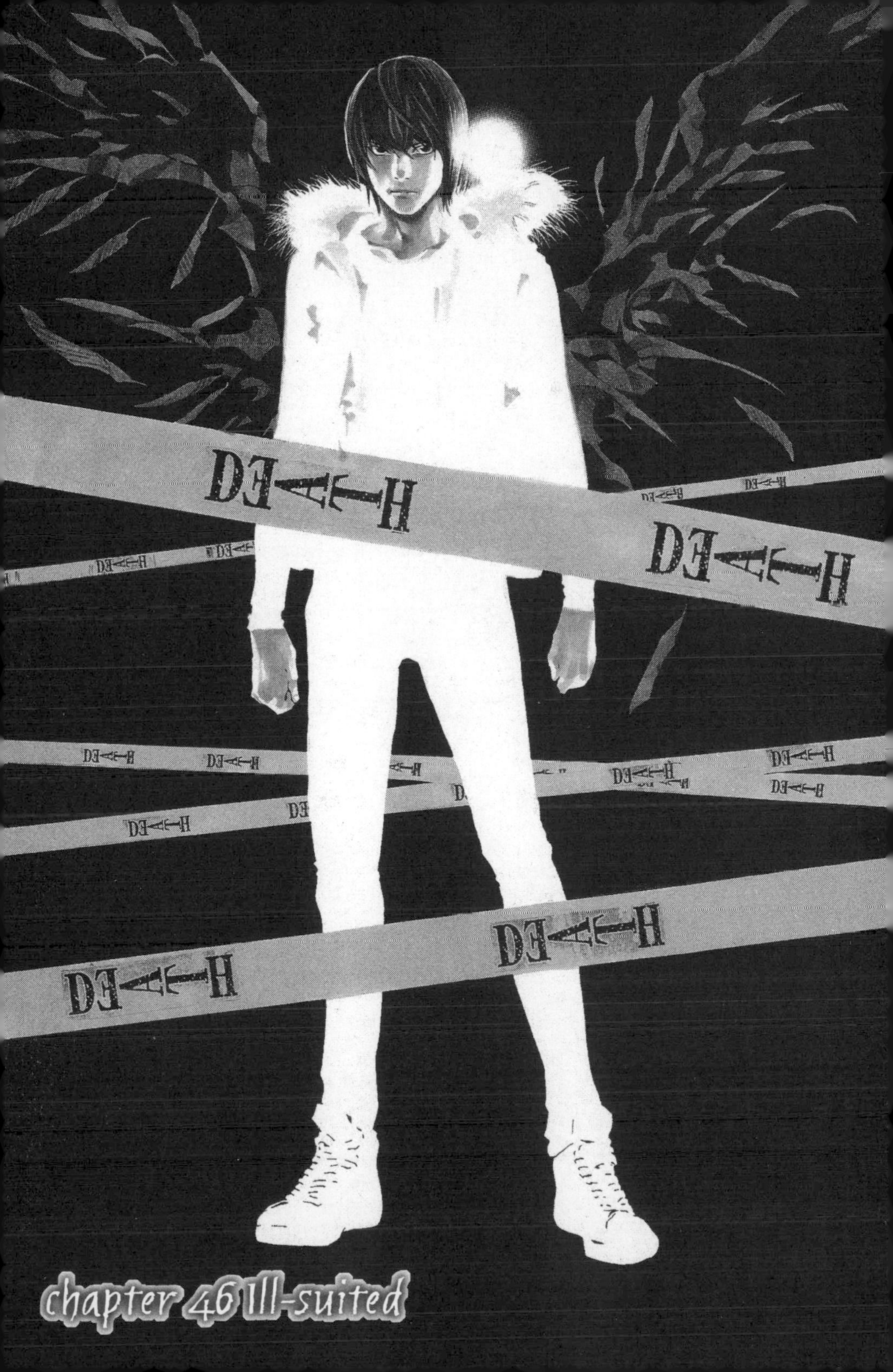
DEATH

chapter 46 Ill-suited

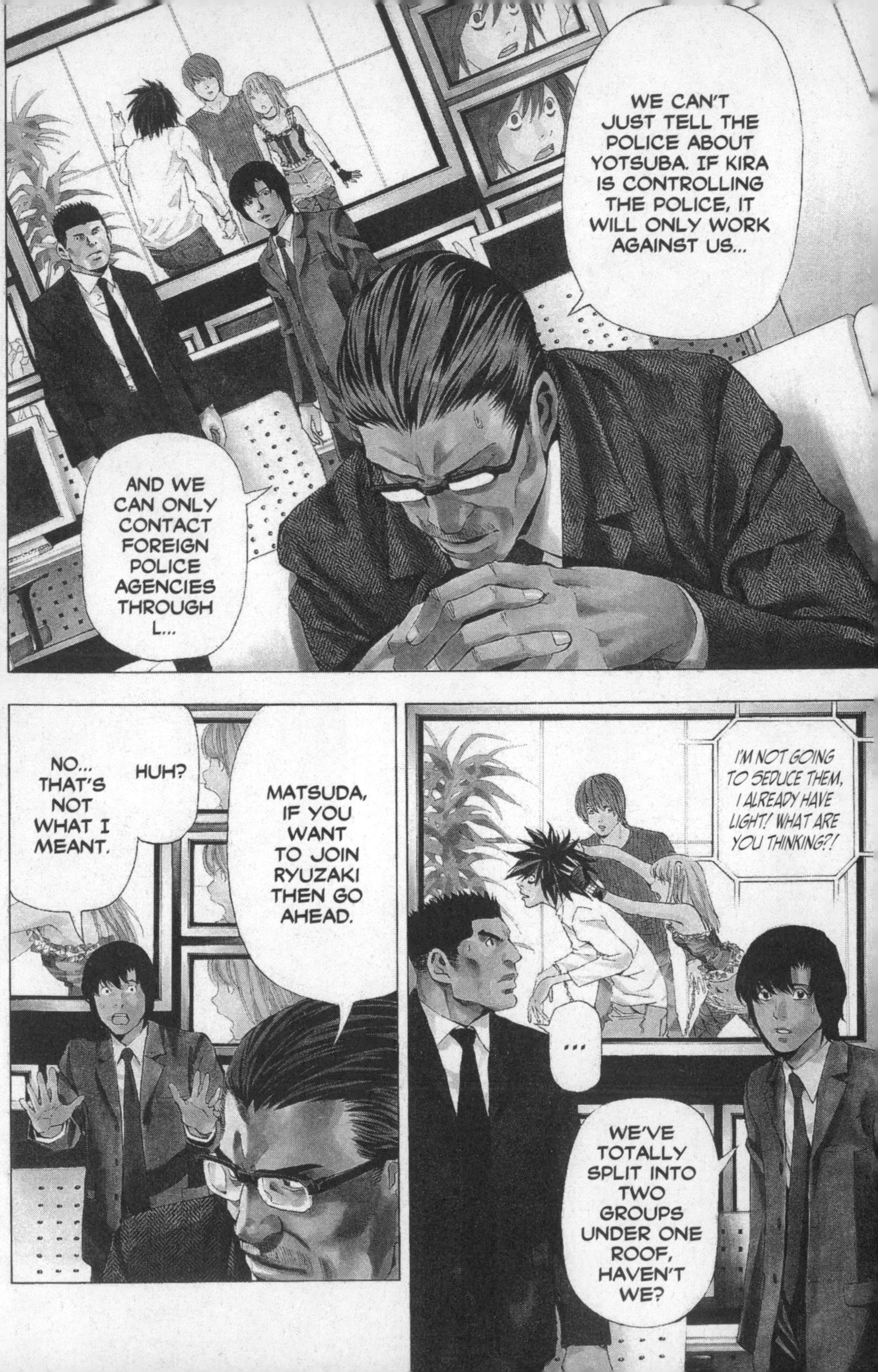
WE CAN'T JUST TELL THE POLICE ABOUT YOTSUBA. IF KIRA IS CONTROLLING THE POLICE, IT WILL ONLY WORK AGAINST US...
AND WE CAN ONLY CONTACT FOREIGN POLICE AGENCIES THROUGH L...
I'M NOT GOING TO SEDUCE THEM, I ALREADY HAVE LIGHT! WHAT ARE YOU THINKING?!
...
WE'VE TOTALLY SPLIT INTO TWO GROUPS UNDER ONE ROOF, HAVEN'T WE?
MATSUDA, IF YOU WANT TO JOIN RYUZAKI THEN GO AHEAD.
HUH?
NO... THAT'S NOT WHAT I MEANT.

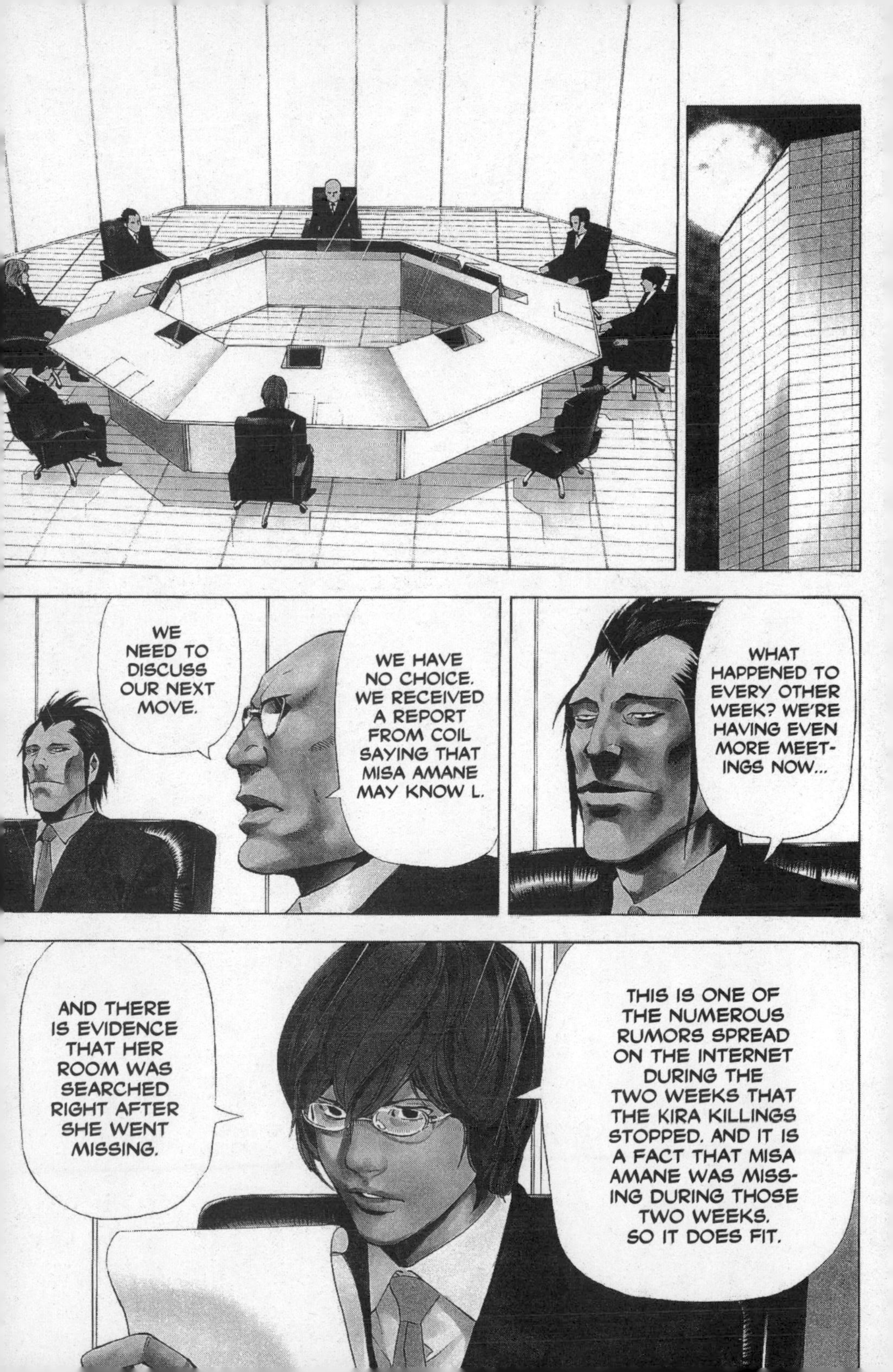
WHAT HAPPENED TO EVERY OTHER WEEK? WE'RE HAVING EVEN MORE MEETINGS NOW...
WE HAVE NO CHOICE. WE RECEIVED A REPORT FROM COIL SAYING THAT MISA AMANE MAY KNOW L.
WE NEED TO DISCUSS OUR NEXT MOVE.
THIS IS ONE OF THE NUMEROUS RUMORS SPREAD ON THE INTERNET DURING THE TWO WEEKS THAT THE KIRA KILLINGS STOPPED. AND IT IS A FACT THAT MISA AMANE WAS MISSING DURING THOSE TWO WEEKS. SO IT DOES FIT.
AND THERE IS EVIDENCE THAT HER ROOM WAS SEARCHED RIGHT AFTER SHE WENT MISSING.

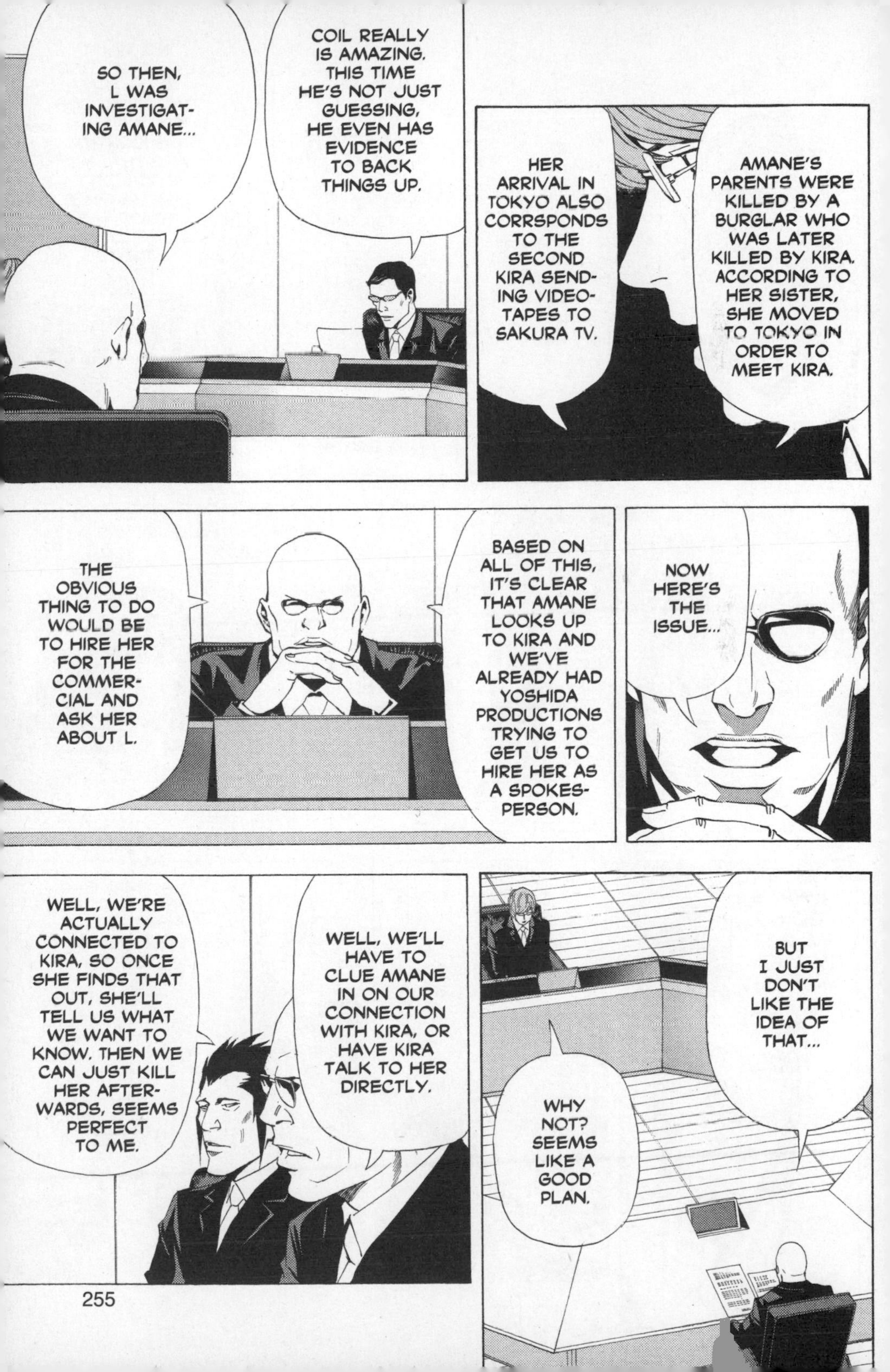
AMANE'S PARENTS WERE KILLED BY A BURGLAR WHO WAS LATER KILLED BY KIRA. ACCORDING TO HER SISTER, SHE MOVED TO TOKYO IN ORDER TO MEET KIRA.
HER ARRIVAL IN TOKYO ALSO CORRSPONDS TO THE SECOND KIRA SENDING VIDEOTAPES TO SAKURA TV.
COIL REALLY IS AMAZING. THIS TIME HE'S NOT JUST GUESSING, HE EVEN HAS EVIDENCE TO BACK THINGS UP.
SO THEN, L WAS INVESTIGATING AMANE...
NOW HERE'S THE ISSUE...
BASED ON ALL OF THIS, IT'S CLEAR THAT AMANE LOOKS UP TO KIRA AND WE'VE ALREADY HAD YOSHIDA PRODUCTIONS TRYING TO GET US TO HIRE HER AS A SPOKESPERSON.
THE OBVIOUS THING TO DO WOULD BE TO HIRE HER FOR THE COMMERCIAL AND ASK HER ABOUT L.
BUT I JUST DON'T LIKE THE IDEA OF THAT...
WHY NOT? SEEMS LIKE A GOOD PLAN.
WELL, WE'LL HAVE TO CLUE AMANE IN ON OUR CONNECTION WITH KIRA, OR HAVE KIRA TALK TO HER DIRECTLY.
WELL, WE'RE ACTUALLY CONNECTED TO KIRA, SO ONCE SHE FINDS THAT OUT, SHE'LL TELL US WHAT WE WANT TO KNOW. THEN WE CAN JUST KILL HER AFTERWARDS, SEEMS PERFECT TO ME.

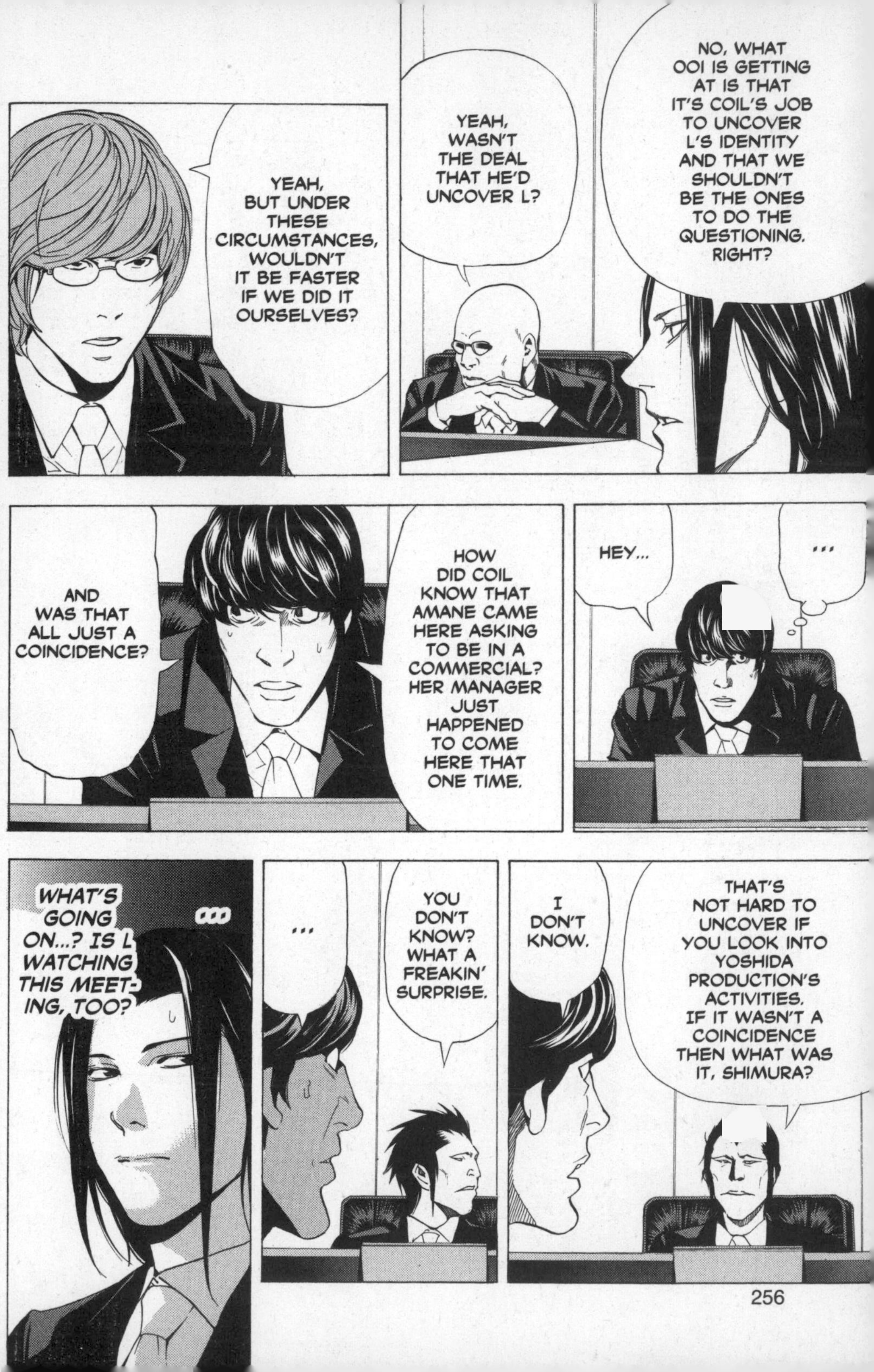
NO, WHAT OOI IS GETTING AT IS THAT IT'S COIL'S JOB TO UNCOVER L'S IDENTITY AND THAT WE SHOULDN'T BE THE ONES TO DO THE QUESTIONING. RIGHT?
YEAH, WASN'T THE DEAL THAT HE'D UNCOVER L?
YEAH, BUT UNDER THESE CIRCUMSTANCES, WOULDN'T IT BE FASTER IF WE DID IT OURSELVES?
...
HEY...
HOW DID COIL KNOW THAT AMANE CAME HERE ASKING TO BE IN A COMMERCIAL? HER MANAGER JUST HAPPENED TO COME HERE THAT ONE TIME.
AND WAS THAT ALL JUST A COINCIDENCE?
THAT'S NOT HARD TO UNCOVER IF YOU LOOK INTO YOSHIDA PRODUCTION'S ACTIVITIES. IF IT WASN'T A COINCIDENCE THEN WHAT WAS IT, SHIMURA?
I DON'T KNOW.
YOU DON'T KNOW? WHAT A FREAKIN' SURPRISE.
...
...
WHAT'S GOING ON...? IS L WATCHING THIS MEETING, TOO?

READ THIS WAY

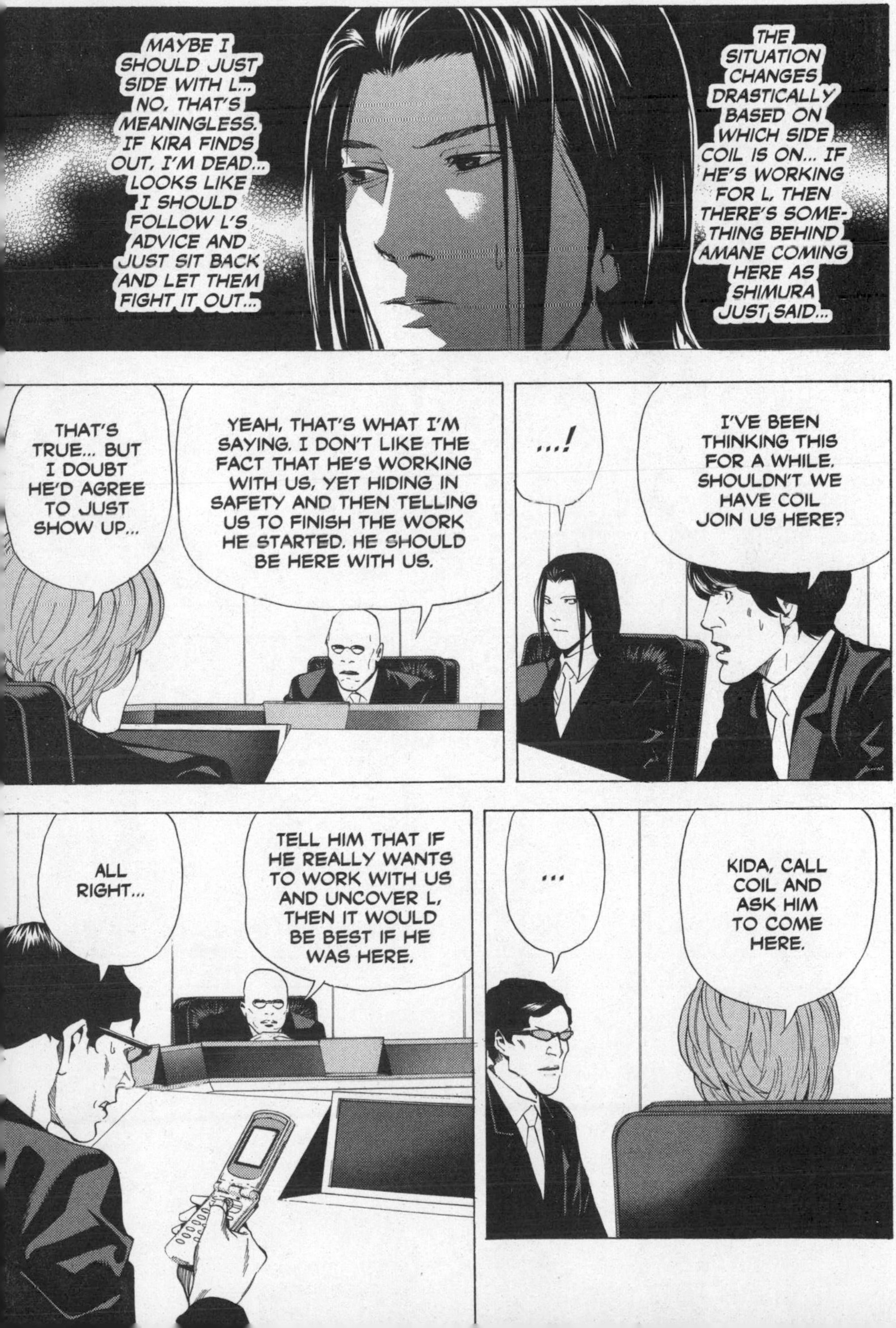
THE SITUATION CHANGES DRASTICALLY BASED ON WHICH SIDE COIL IS ON... IF HE'S WORKING FOR L, THEN THERE'S SOME-THING BEHIND AMANE COMING HERE AS SHIMURA JUST SAID...
MAYBE I SHOULD JUST SIDE WITH L... NO. THAT'S MEANINGLESS. IF KIRA FINDS OUT, I'M DEAD... LOOKS LIKE I SHOULD FOLLOW L'S ADVICE AND JUST SIT BACK AND LET THEM FIGHT IT OUT...
I'VE BEEN THINKING THIS FOR A WHILE. SHOULDN'T WE HAVE COIL JOIN US HERE?
...!
YEAH, THAT'S WHAT I'M SAYING. I DON'T LIKE THE FACT THAT HE'S WORKING WITH US, YET HIDING IN SAFETY AND THEN TELLING US TO FINISH THE WORK HE STARTED. HE SHOULD BE HERE WITH US.
THAT'S TRUE... BUT I DOUBT HE'D AGREE TO JUST SHOW UP...
KIDA, CALL COIL AND ASK HIM TO COME HERE.
...
TELL HIM THAT IF HE REALLY WANTS TO WORK WITH US AND UNCOVER L, THEN IT WOULD BE BEST IF HE WAS HERE.
ALL RIGHT...

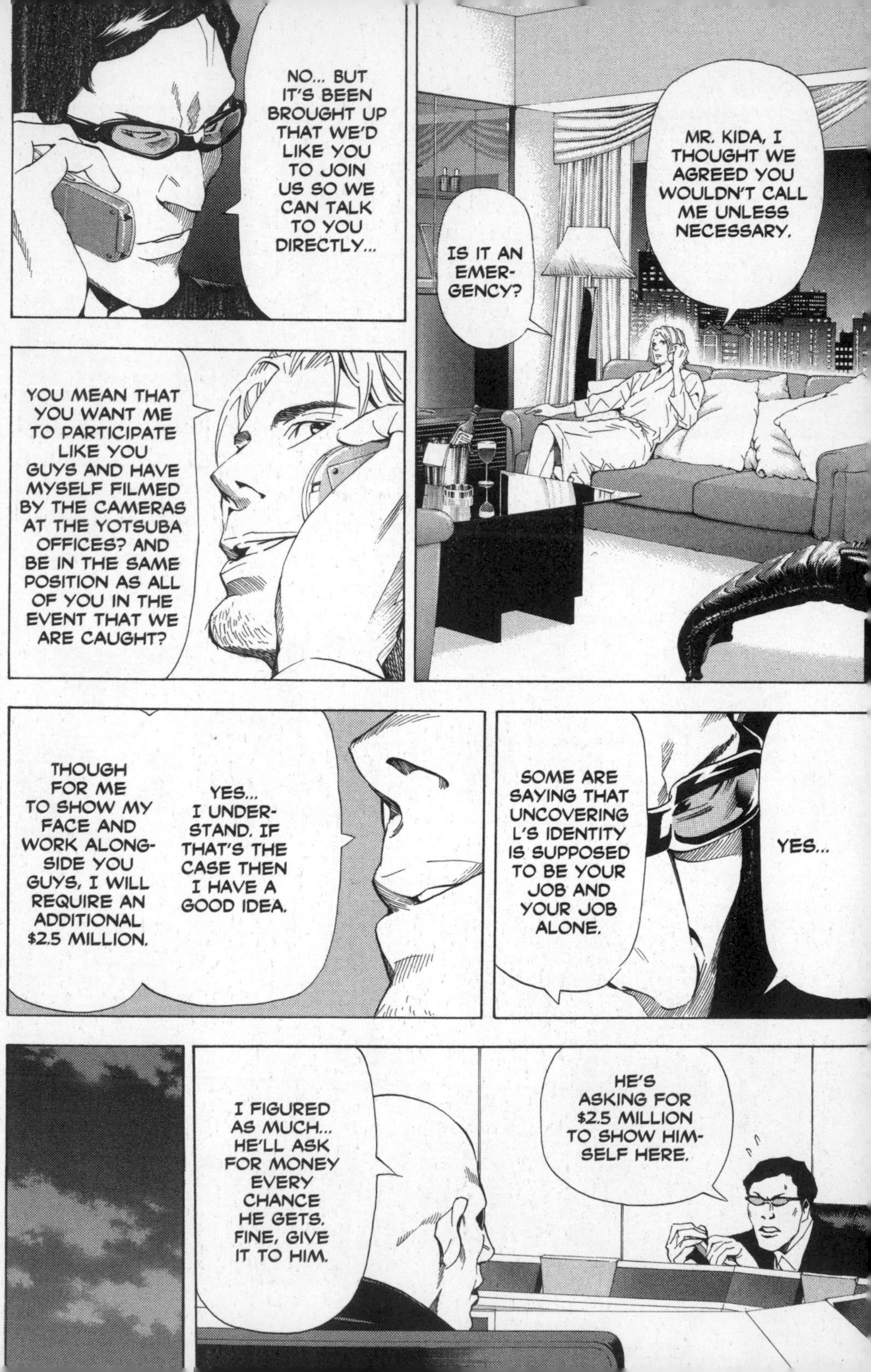
MR. KIDA, I THOUGHT WE AGREED YOU WOULDN'T CALL ME UNLESS NECESSARY.
IS IT AN EMERGENCY?
NO... BUT IT'S BEEN BROUGHT UP THAT WE'D LIKE YOU TO JOIN US SO WE CAN TALK TO YOU DIRECTLY...
YOU MEAN THAT YOU WANT ME TO PARTICIPATE LIKE YOU GUYS AND HAVE MYSELF FILMED BY THE CAMERAS AT THE YOTSUBA OFFICES? AND BE IN THE SAME POSITION AS ALL OF YOU IN THE EVENT THAT WE ARE CAUGHT?
YES...
SOME ARE SAYING THAT UNCOVERING L'S IDENTITY IS SUPPOSED TO BE YOUR JOB AND YOUR JOB ALONE.
YES... I UNDERSTAND. IF THAT'S THE CASE THEN I HAVE A GOOD IDEA.
THOUGH FOR ME TO SHOW MY FACE AND WORK ALONGSIDE YOU GUYS, I WILL REQUIRE AN ADDITIONAL $2.5 MILLION.
HE'S ASKING FOR $2.5 MILLION TO SHOW HIMSELF HERE.
I FIGURED AS MUCH... HE'LL ASK FOR MONEY EVERY CHANCE HE GETS. FINE, GIVE IT TO HIM.

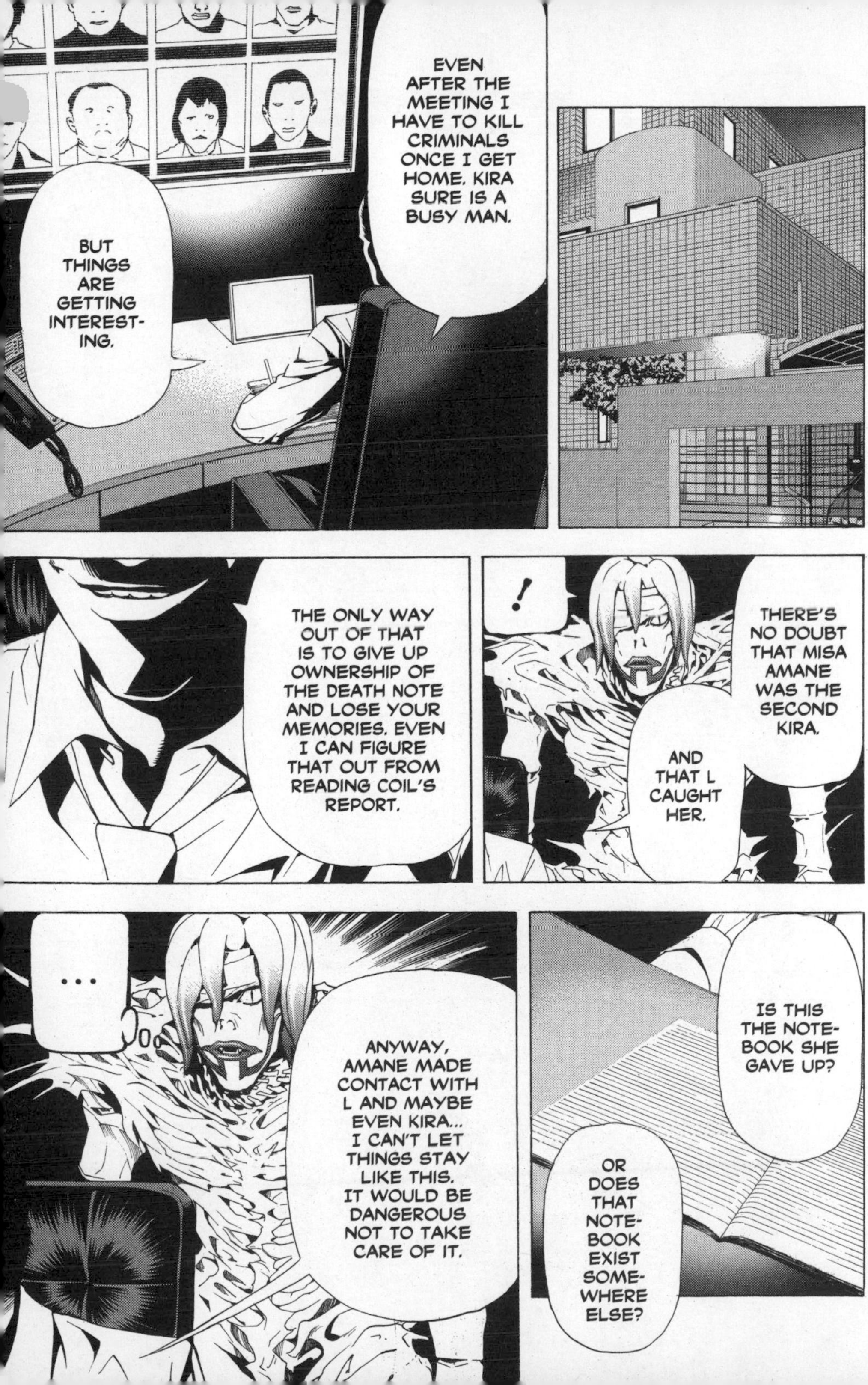

EVEN AFTER THE MEETING I HAVE TO KILL CRIMINALS ONCE I GET HOME. KIRA SURE IS A BUSY MAN.
BUT THINGS ARE GETTING INTEREST-ING.
THERE'S NO DOUBT THAT MISA AMANE WAS THE SECOND KIRA.
!
AND THAT L CAUGHT HER.
THE ONLY WAY OUT OF THAT IS TO GIVE UP OWNERSHIP OF THE DEATH NOTE AND LOSE YOUR MEMORIES. EVEN I CAN FIGURE THAT OUT FROM READING COIL'S REPORT.
IS THIS THE NOTE-BOOK SHE GAVE UP?
OR DOES THAT NOTE-BOOK EXIST SOME-WHERE ELSE?
...
ANYWAY, AMANE MADE CONTACT WITH L AND MAYBE EVEN KIRA... I CAN'T LET THINGS STAY LIKE THIS. IT WOULD BE DANGEROUS NOT TO TAKE CARE OF IT.

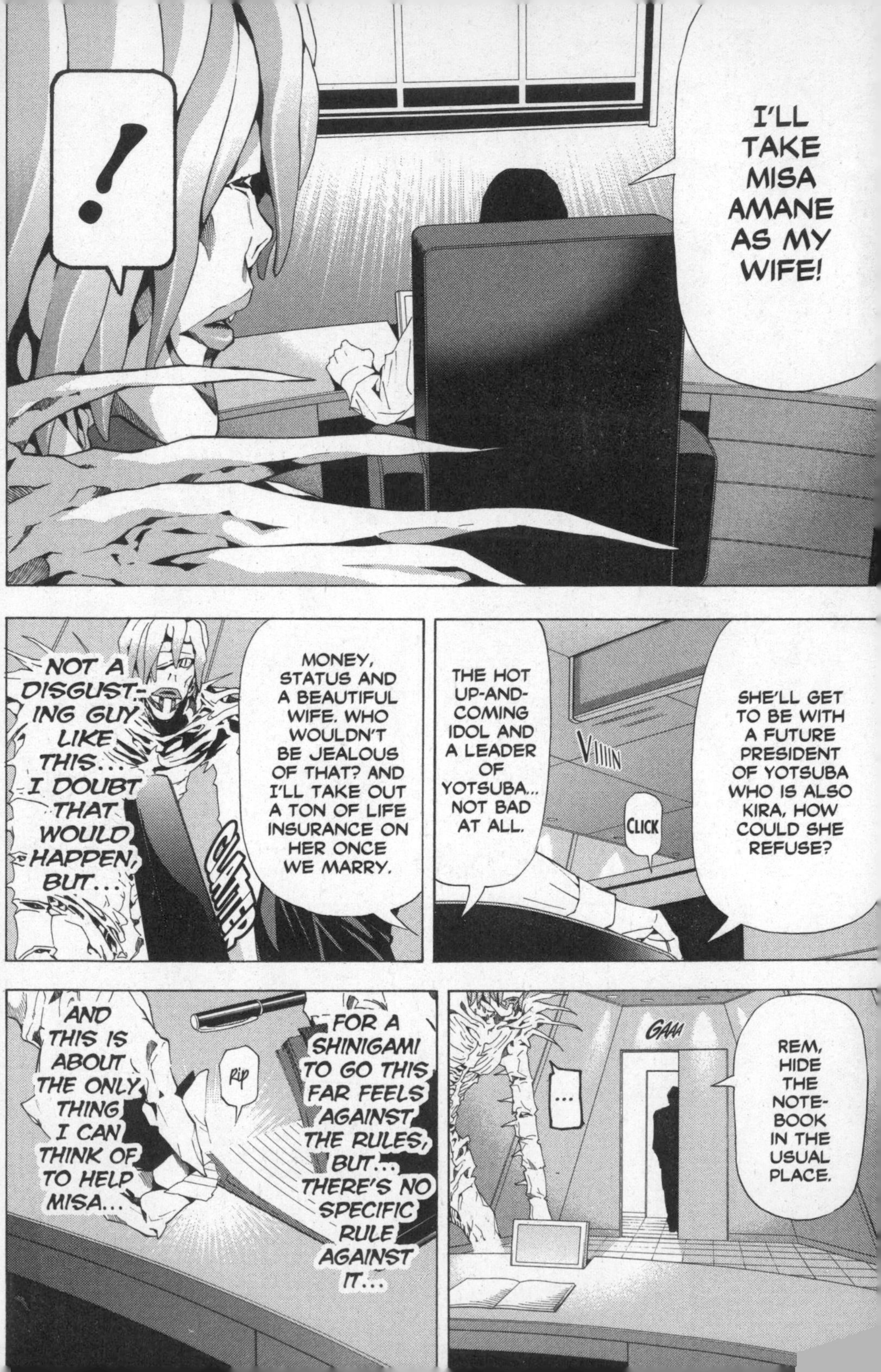
I'LL TAKE MISA AMANE AS MY WIFE!
!
SHE'LL GET TO BE WITH A FUTURE PRESIDENT OF YOTSUBA WHO IS ALSO KIRA, HOW COULD SHE REFUSE?
VIIIIN
CLICK
THE HOT UP-AND-COMING IDOL AND A LEADER OF YOTSUBA... NOT BAD AT ALL.
MONEY, STATUS AND A BEAUTIFUL WIFE. WHO WOULDN'T BE JEALOUS OF THAT? AND I'LL TAKE OUT A TON OF LIFE INSURANCE ON HER ONCE WE MARRY.
NOT A DISGUSTING GUY LIKE THIS... I DOUBT THAT WOULD HAPPEN, BUT...
REM, HIDE THE NOTEBOOK IN THE USUAL PLACE.
GAAA
...
FOR A SHINIGAMI TO GO THIS FAR FEELS AGAINST THE RULES, BUT... THERE'S NO SPECIFIC RULE AGAINST IT...
Rip
AND THIS IS ABOUT THE ONLY THING I CAN THINK OF TO HELP MISA...

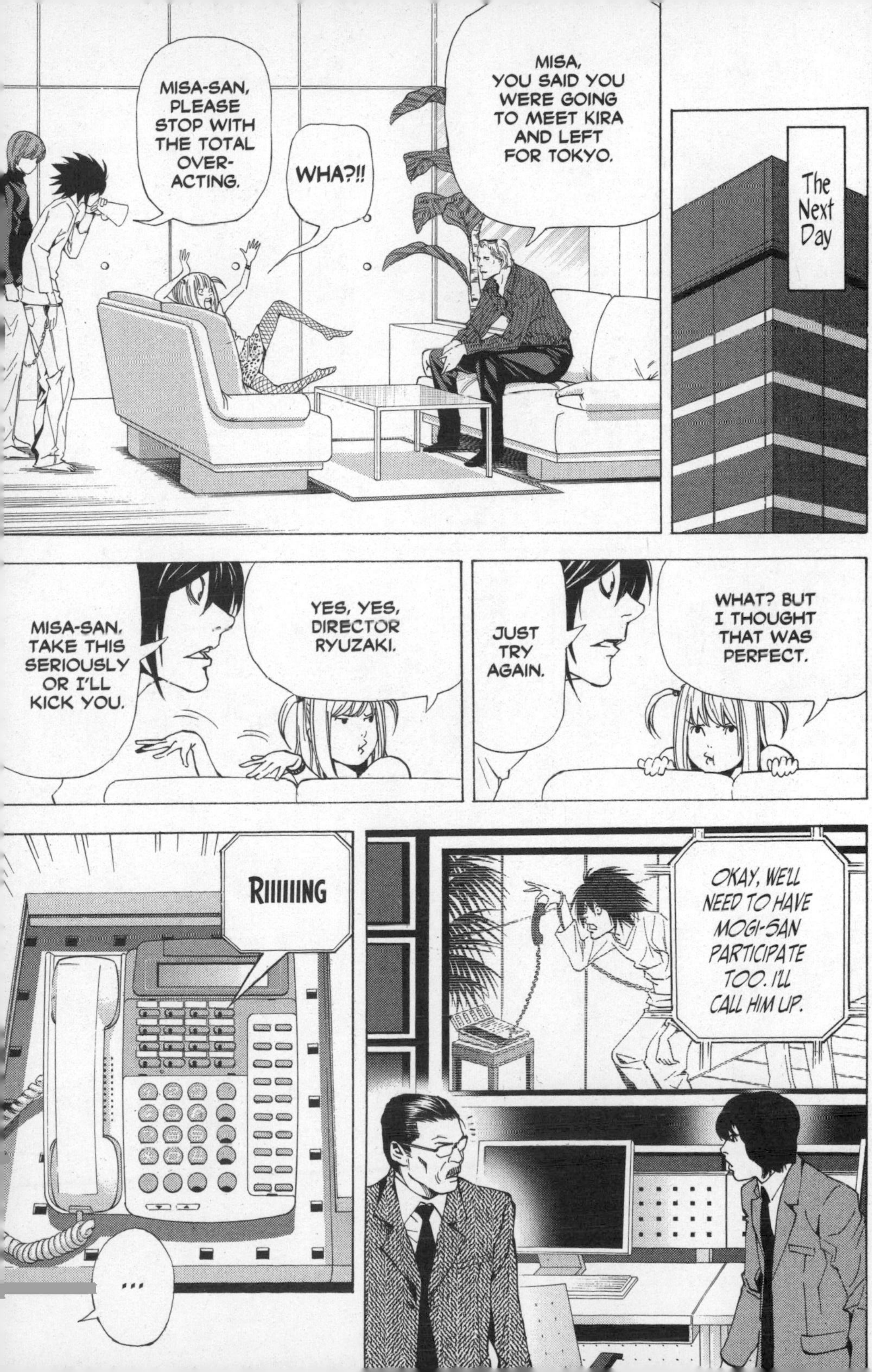
The Next Day
MISA, YOU SAID YOU WERE GOING TO MEET KIRA AND LEFT FOR TOKYO.
WHA?!!
MISA-SAN, PLEASE STOP WITH THE TOTAL OVER-ACTING.
WHAT? BUT I THOUGHT THAT WAS PERFECT.
JUST TRY AGAIN.
YES, YES, DIRECTOR RYUZAKI.
MISA-SAN. TAKE THIS SERIOUSLY OR I'LL KICK YOU.
OKAY, WE'LL NEED TO HAVE MOGI-SAN PARTICIPATE TOO. I'LL CALL HIM UP.
RIIIIIING
...

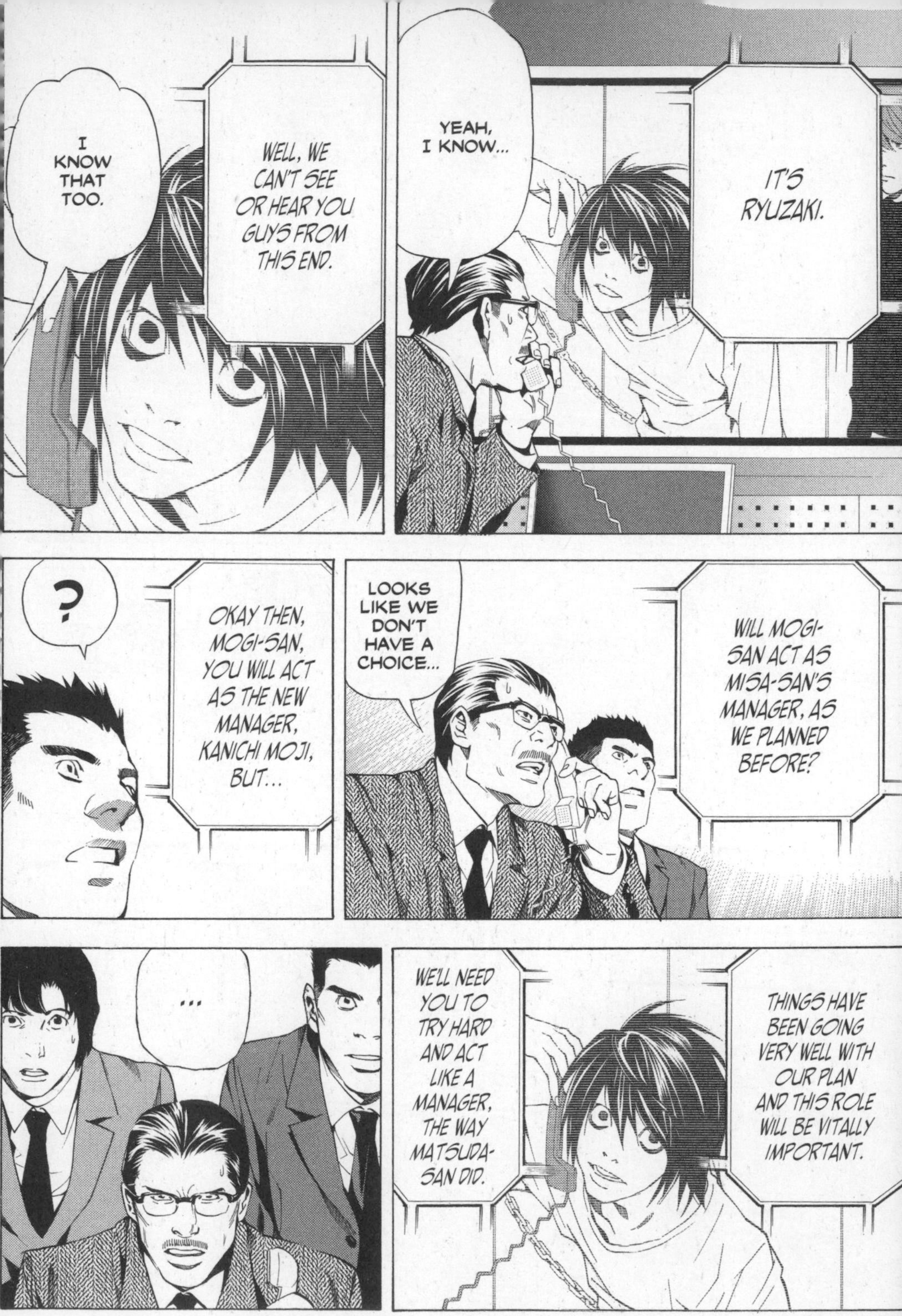
IT'S RYUZAKI.
YEAH, I KNOW...
WELL, WE CAN'T SEE OR HEAR YOU GUYS FROM THIS END.
I KNOW THAT TOO.
WILL MOGI-SAN ACT AS MISA-SAN'S MANAGER, AS WE PLANNED BEFORE?
LOOKS LIKE WE DON'T HAVE A CHOICE...
OKAY THEN, MOGI-SAN, YOU WILL ACT AS THE NEW MANAGER, KANICHI MOJI, BUT...
?
THINGS HAVE BEEN GOING VERY WELL WITH OUR PLAN AND THIS ROLE WILL BE VITALLY IMPORTANT.
WE'LL NEED YOU TO TRY HARD AND ACT LIKE A MANAGER, THE WAY MATSUDA-SAN DID.
...

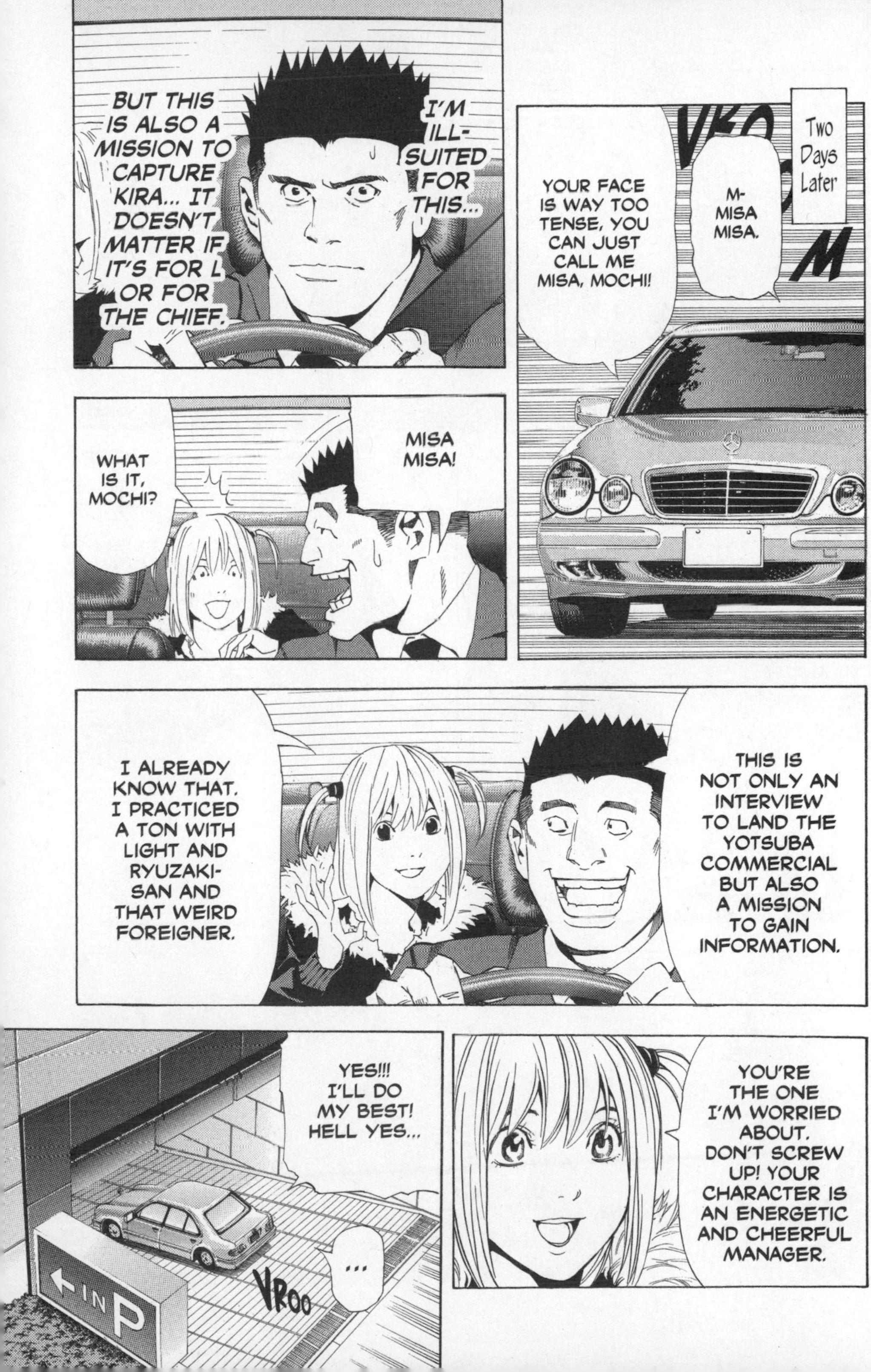
Two Days Later
VROOM
M-MISA MISA.
YOUR FACE IS WAY TOO TENSE, YOU CAN JUST CALL ME MISA, MOCHI!
I'M ILL-SUITED FOR THIS...
BUT THIS IS ALSO A MISSION TO CAPTURE KIRA... IT DOESN'T MATTER IF IT'S FOR L OR FOR THE CHIEF.
MISA MISA!
WHAT IS IT, MOCHI?
THIS IS NOT ONLY AN INTERVIEW TO LAND THE YOTSUBA COMMERCIAL BUT ALSO A MISSION TO GAIN INFORMATION.
I ALREADY KNOW THAT. I PRACTICED A TON WITH LIGHT AND RYUZAKI-SAN AND THAT WEIRD FOREIGNER.
YOU'RE THE ONE I'M WORRIED ABOUT. DON'T SCREW UP! YOUR CHARACTER IS AN ENERGETIC AND CHEERFUL MANAGER.
YES!!! I'LL DO MY BEST! HELL YES...
...
VROO
IN P

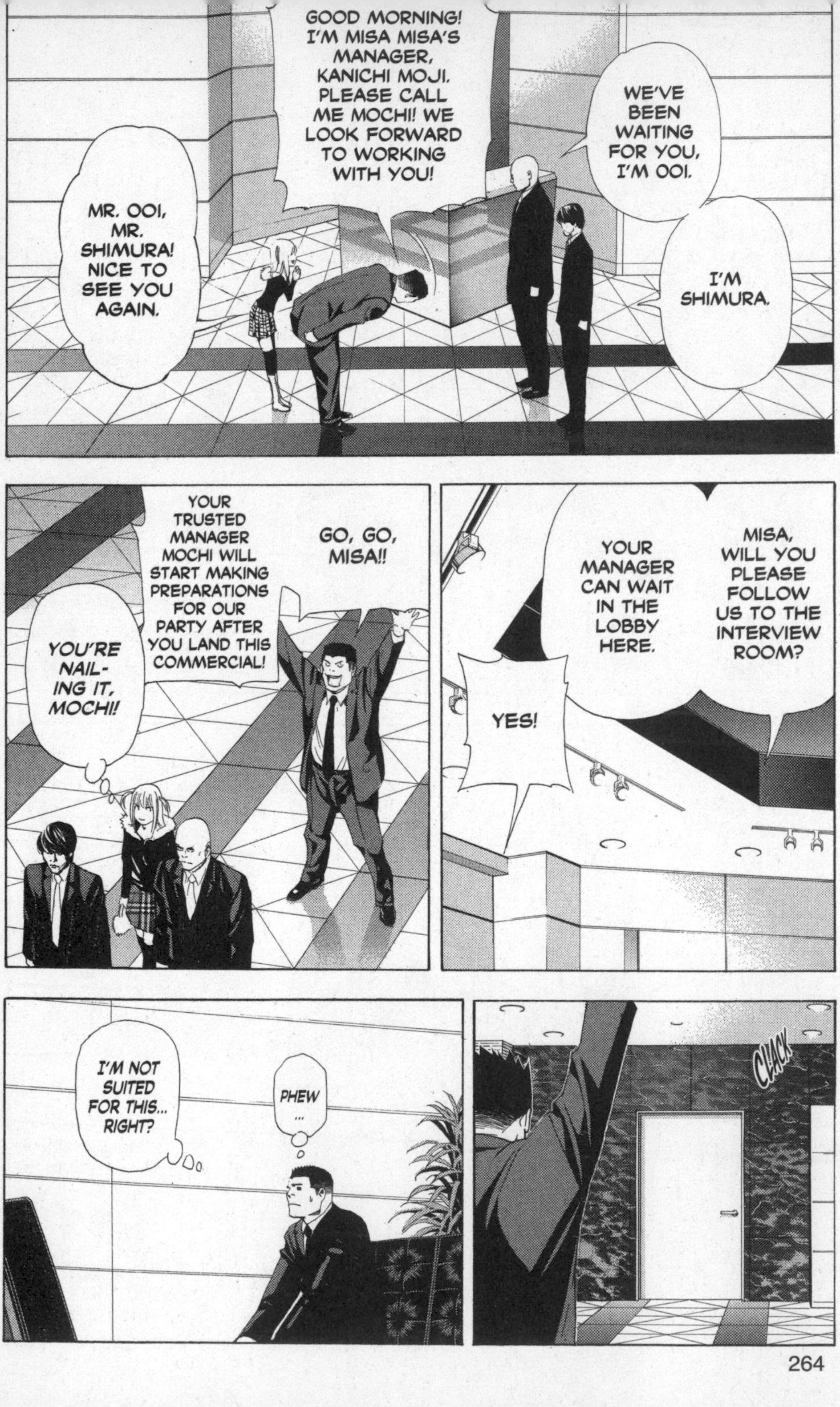
WE'VE BEEN WAITING FOR YOU, I'M OOI.
I'M SHIMURA.
GOOD MORNING! I'M MISA MISA'S MANAGER, KANICHI MOJI. PLEASE CALL ME MOCHI! WE LOOK FORWARD TO WORKING WITH YOU!
MR. OOI, MR. SHIMURA! NICE TO SEE YOU AGAIN.
MISA, WILL YOU PLEASE FOLLOW US TO THE INTERVIEW ROOM?
YOUR MANAGER CAN WAIT IN THE LOBBY HERE.
YES!
GO, GO, MISA!!
YOUR TRUSTED MANAGER MOCHI WILL START MAKING PREPARATIONS FOR OUR PARTY AFTER YOU LAND THIS COMMERCIAL!
YOU'RE NAIL-ING IT, MOCHI!
CLACK
PHEW ...
I'M NOT SUITED FOR THIS... RIGHT?

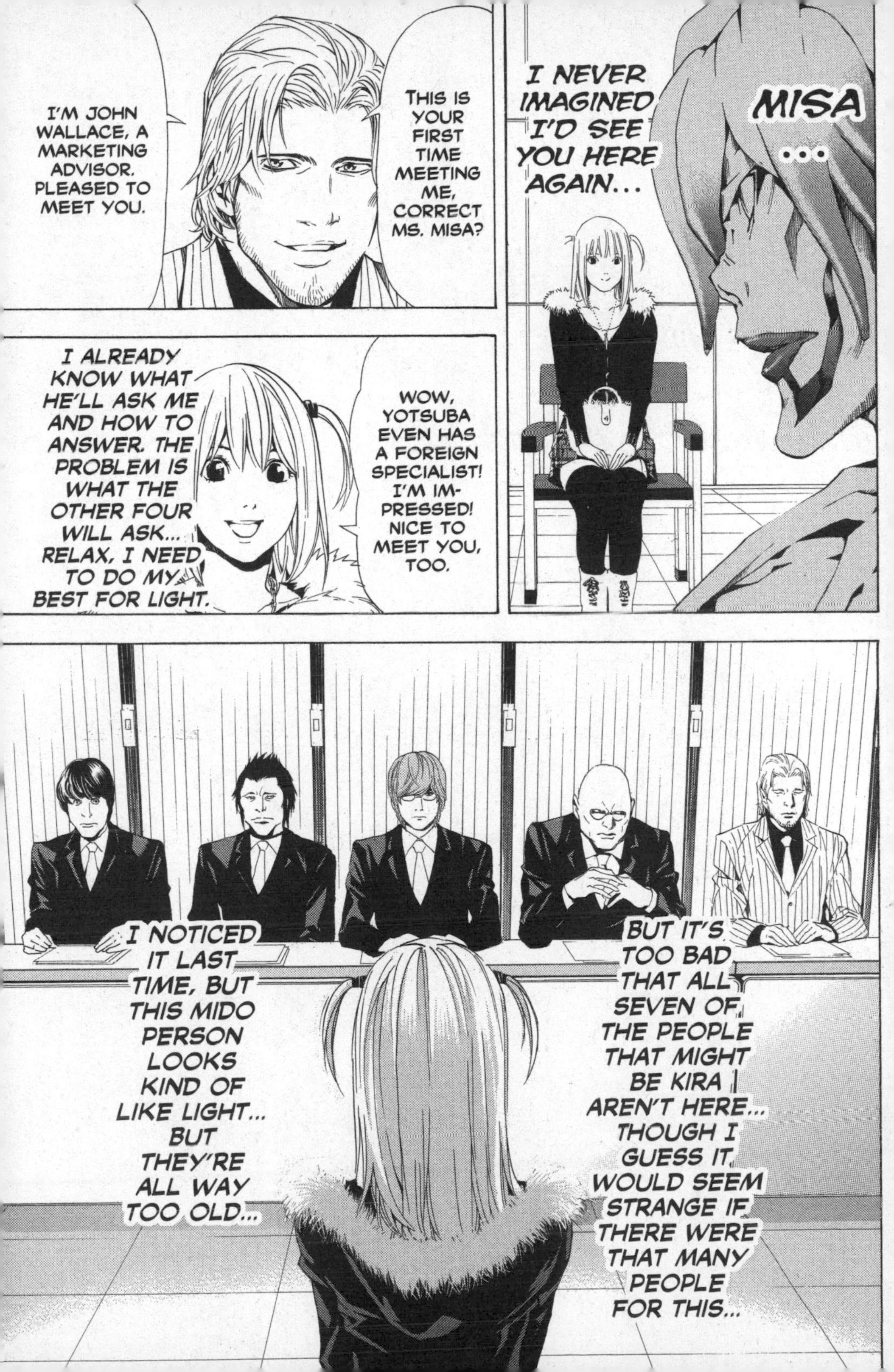
MISA ...
I NEVER IMAGINED I'D SEE YOU HERE AGAIN...
THIS IS YOUR FIRST TIME MEETING ME, CORRECT MS. MISA?
I'M JOHN WALLACE, A MARKETING ADVISOR. PLEASED TO MEET YOU.
WOW, YOTSUBA EVEN HAS A FOREIGN SPECIALIST! I'M IM-PRESSED! NICE TO MEET YOU, TOO.
I ALREADY KNOW WHAT HE'LL ASK ME AND HOW TO ANSWER. THE PROBLEM IS WHAT THE OTHER FOUR WILL ASK... RELAX, I NEED TO DO MY BEST FOR LIGHT.
BUT IT'S TOO BAD THAT ALL SEVEN OF THE PEOPLE THAT MIGHT BE KIRA AREN'T HERE... THOUGH I GUESS IT WOULD SEEM STRANGE IF THERE WERE THAT MANY PEOPLE FOR THIS...
I NOTICED IT LAST TIME, BUT THIS MIDO PERSON LOOKS KIND OF LIKE LIGHT... BUT THEY'RE ALL WAY TOO OLD...

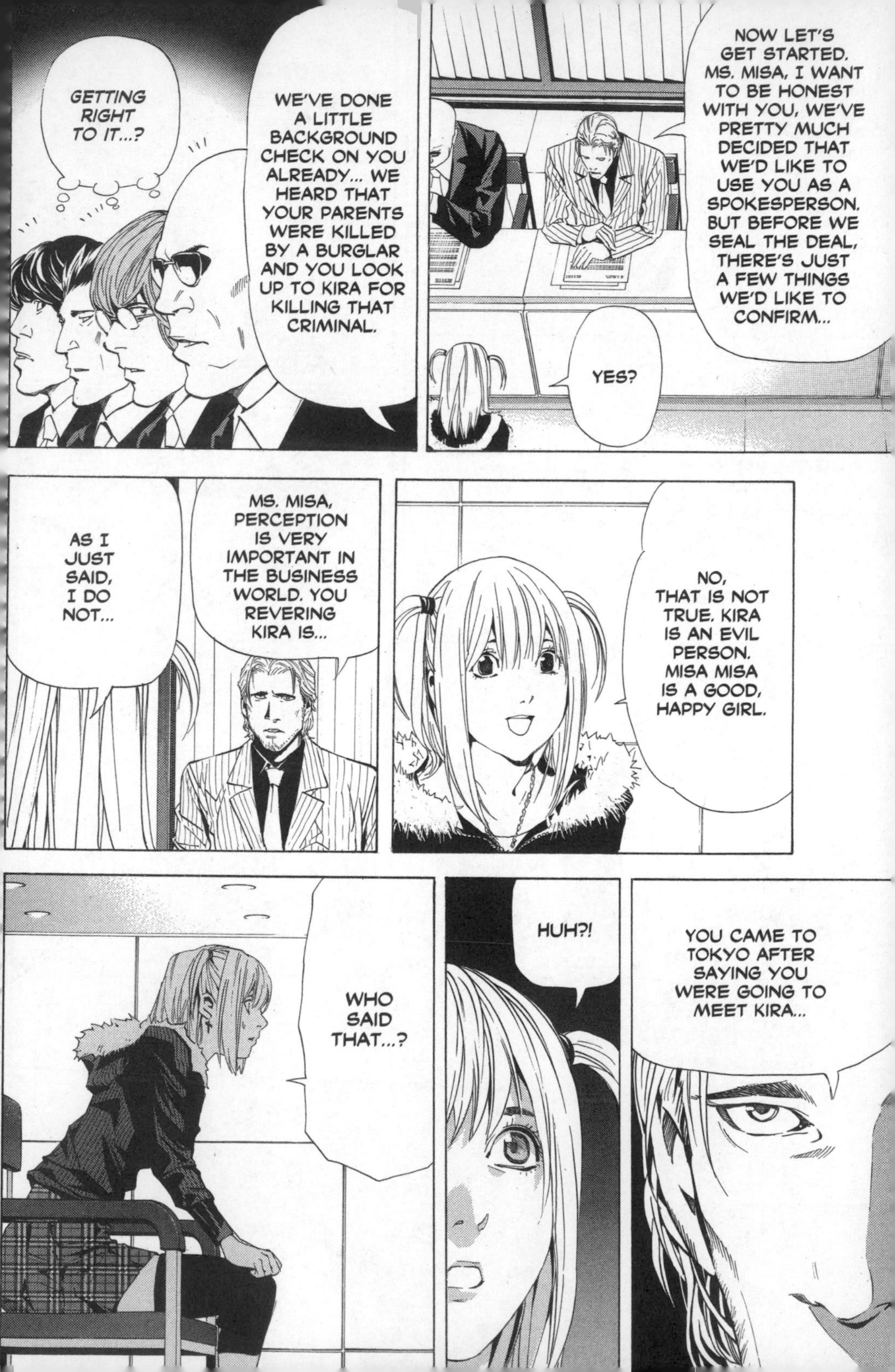
NOW LET'S GET STARTED. MS. MISA, I WANT TO BE HONEST WITH YOU, WE'VE PRETTY MUCH DECIDED THAT WE'D LIKE TO USE YOU AS A SPOKESPERSON. BUT BEFORE WE SEAL THE DEAL, THERE'S JUST A FEW THINGS WE'D LIKE TO CONFIRM...
YES?
WE'VE DONE A LITTLE BACKGROUND CHECK ON YOU ALREADY... WE HEARD THAT YOUR PARENTS WERE KILLED BY A BURGLAR AND YOU LOOK UP TO KIRA FOR KILLING THAT CRIMINAL.
GETTING RIGHT TO IT...?
NO, THAT IS NOT TRUE. KIRA IS AN EVIL PERSON. MISA MISA IS A GOOD, HAPPY GIRL.
MS. MISA, PERCEPTION IS VERY IMPORTANT IN THE BUSINESS WORLD. YOU REVERING KIRA IS...
AS I JUST SAID, I DO NOT...
YOU CAME TO TOKYO AFTER SAYING YOU WERE GOING TO MEET KIRA...
HUH?!
WHO SAID THAT...?

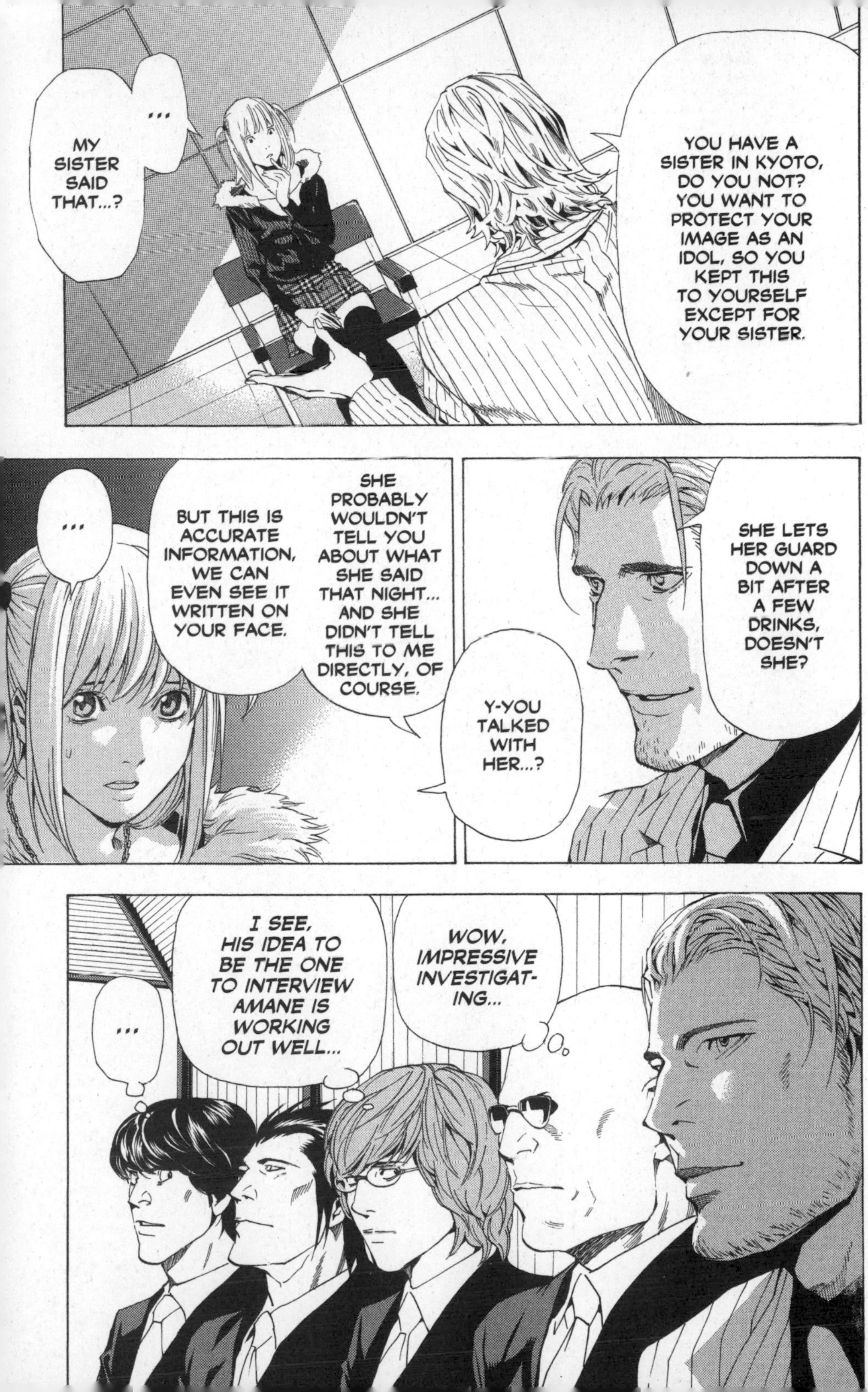
YOU HAVE A SISTER IN KYOTO, DO YOU NOT? YOU WANT TO PROTECT YOUR IMAGE AS AN IDOL, SO YOU KEPT THIS TO YOURSELF EXCEPT FOR YOUR SISTER.
...
MY SISTER SAID THAT...?
SHE LETS HER GUARD DOWN A BIT AFTER A FEW DRINKS, DOESN'T SHE?
Y-YOU TALKED WITH HER...?
SHE PROBABLY WOULDN'T TELL YOU ABOUT WHAT SHE SAID THAT NIGHT... AND SHE DIDN'T TELL THIS TO ME DIRECTLY, OF COURSE.
BUT THIS IS ACCURATE INFORMATION, WE CAN EVEN SEE IT WRITTEN ON YOUR FACE.
...
WOW. IMPRESSIVE INVESTIGATING...
I SEE, HIS IDEA TO BE THE ONE TO INTERVIEW AMANE IS WORKING OUT WELL...
...

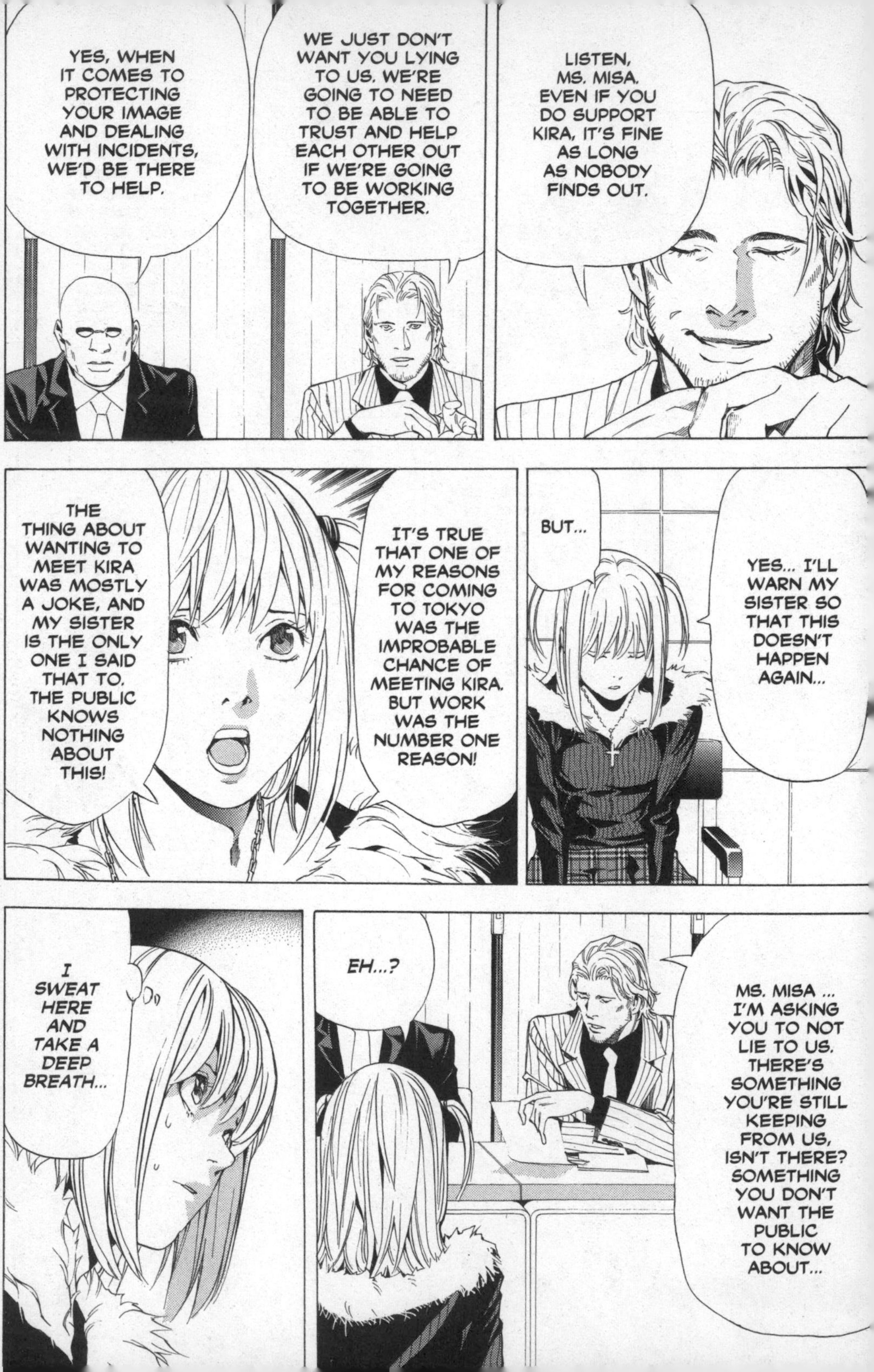
LISTEN, MS. MISA. EVEN IF YOU DO SUPPORT KIRA, IT'S FINE AS LONG AS NOBODY FINDS OUT.
WE JUST DON'T WANT YOU LYING TO US. WE'RE GOING TO NEED TO BE ABLE TO TRUST AND HELP EACH OTHER OUT IF WE'RE GOING TO BE WORKING TOGETHER.
YES, WHEN IT COMES TO PROTECTING YOUR IMAGE AND DEALING WITH INCIDENTS, WE'D BE THERE TO HELP.
YES... I'LL WARN MY SISTER SO THAT THIS DOESN'T HAPPEN AGAIN...
BUT...
IT'S TRUE THAT ONE OF MY REASONS FOR COMING TO TOKYO WAS THE IMPROBABLE CHANCE OF MEETING KIRA. BUT WORK WAS THE NUMBER ONE REASON!
THE THING ABOUT WANTING TO MEET KIRA WAS MOSTLY A JOKE, AND MY SISTER IS THE ONLY ONE I SAID THAT TO. THE PUBLIC KNOWS NOTHING ABOUT THIS!
MS. MISA ... I'M ASKING YOU TO NOT LIE TO US. THERE'S SOMETHING YOU'RE STILL KEEPING FROM US, ISN'T THERE? SOMETHING YOU DON'T WANT THE PUBLIC TO KNOW ABOUT...
EH...?
I SWEAT HERE AND TAKE A DEEP BREATH...

READ THIS WAY

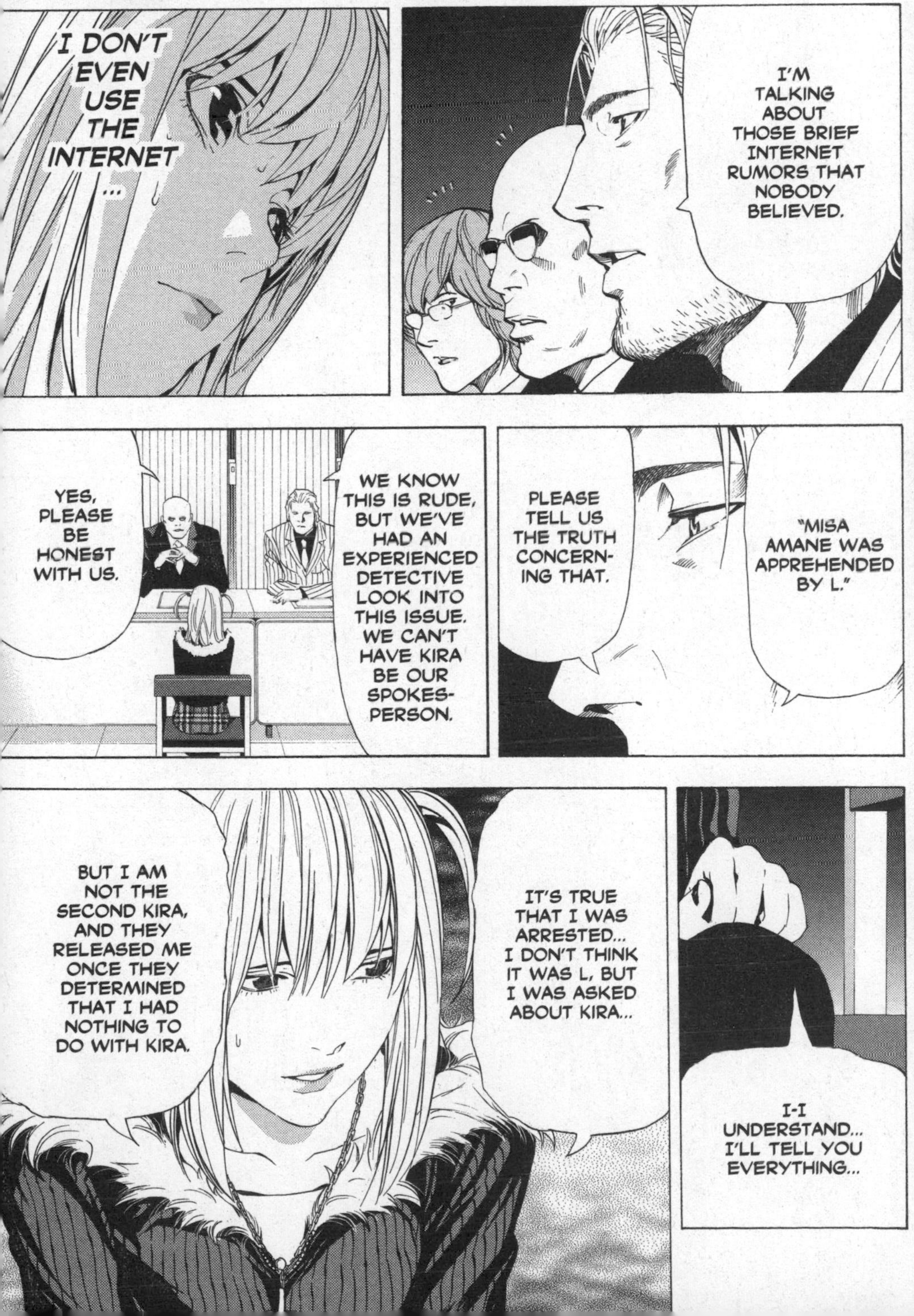

I'M TALKING ABOUT THOSE BRIEF INTERNET RUMORS THAT NOBODY BELIEVED.
I DON'T EVEN USE THE INTERNET ...
"MISA AMANE WAS APPREHENDED BY L."
PLEASE TELL US THE TRUTH CONCERNING THAT.
WE KNOW THIS IS RUDE, BUT WE'VE HAD AN EXPERIENCED DETECTIVE LOOK INTO THIS ISSUE. WE CAN'T HAVE KIRA BE OUR SPOKES-PERSON.
YES, PLEASE BE HONEST WITH US.
I-I UNDERSTAND... I'LL TELL YOU EVERYTHING...
IT'S TRUE THAT I WAS ARRESTED... I DON'T THINK IT WAS L, BUT I WAS ASKED ABOUT KIRA...
BUT I AM NOT THE SECOND KIRA, AND THEY RELEASED ME ONCE THEY DETERMINED THAT I HAD NOTHING TO DO WITH KIRA.

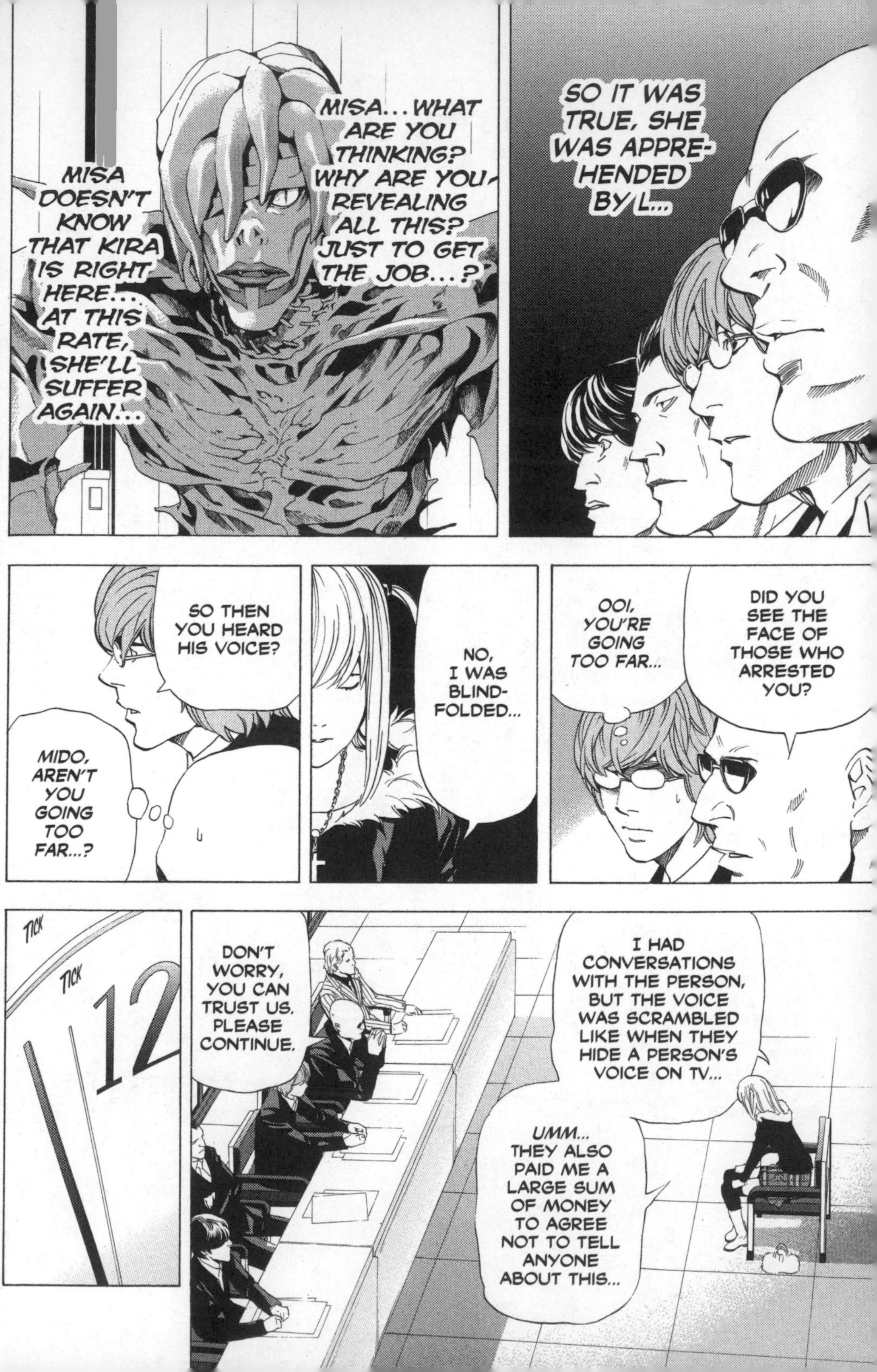
SO IT WAS TRUE, SHE WAS APPRE-HENDED BY L...
MISA...WHAT ARE YOU THINKING? WHY ARE YOU REVEALING ALL THIS? JUST TO GET THE JOB...?
MISA DOESN'T KNOW THAT KIRA IS RIGHT HERE... AT THIS RATE, SHE'LL SUFFER AGAIN...
DID YOU SEE THE FACE OF THOSE WHO ARRESTED YOU?
OOI, YOU'RE GOING TOO FAR...
NO, I WAS BLIND-FOLDED...
SO THEN YOU HEARD HIS VOICE?
MIDO, AREN'T YOU GOING TOO FAR...?
I HAD CONVERSATIONS WITH THE PERSON, BUT THE VOICE WAS SCRAMBLED LIKE WHEN THEY HIDE A PERSON'S VOICE ON TV...
UMM... THEY ALSO PAID ME A LARGE SUM OF MONEY TO AGREE NOT TO TELL ANYONE ABOUT THIS...
DON'T WORRY, YOU CAN TRUST US. PLEASE CONTINUE.
TICK
TICK
12

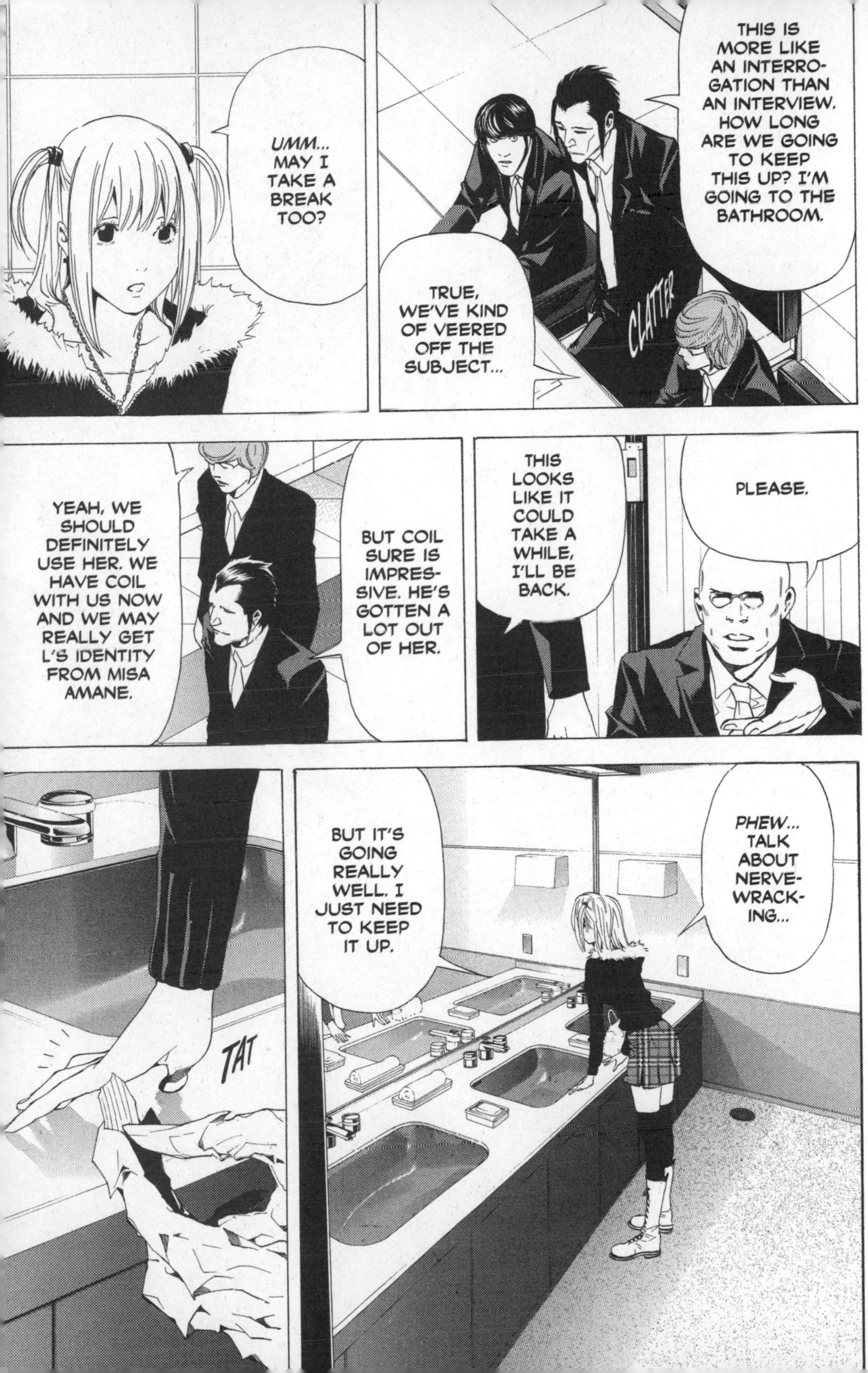
THIS IS MORE LIKE AN INTERROGATION THAN AN INTERVIEW. HOW LONG ARE WE GOING TO KEEP THIS UP? I'M GOING TO THE BATHROOM.
TRUE, WE'VE KIND OF VEERED OFF THE SUBJECT...
CLATTER
UMM... MAY I TAKE A BREAK TOO?
PLEASE.
THIS LOOKS LIKE IT COULD TAKE A WHILE, I'LL BE BACK.
BUT COIL SURE IS IMPRESSIVE. HE'S GOTTEN A LOT OUT OF HER.
YEAH, WE SHOULD DEFINITELY USE HER. WE HAVE COIL WITH US NOW AND WE MAY REALLY GET L'S IDENTITY FROM MISA AMANE.
PHEW... TALK ABOUT NERVE-WRACKING...
BUT IT'S GOING REALLY WELL. I JUST NEED TO KEEP IT UP.
TAT

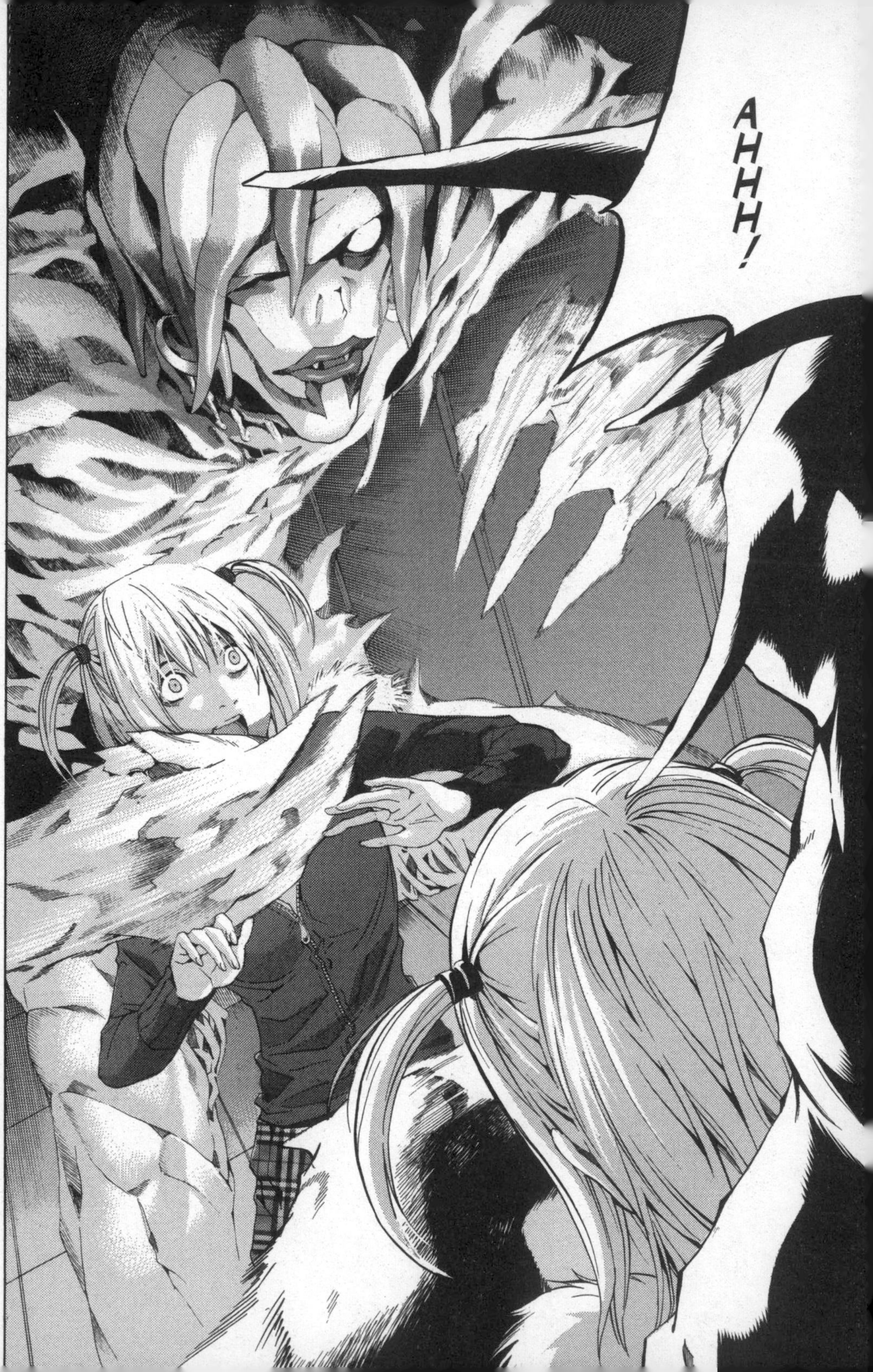
AHHH!

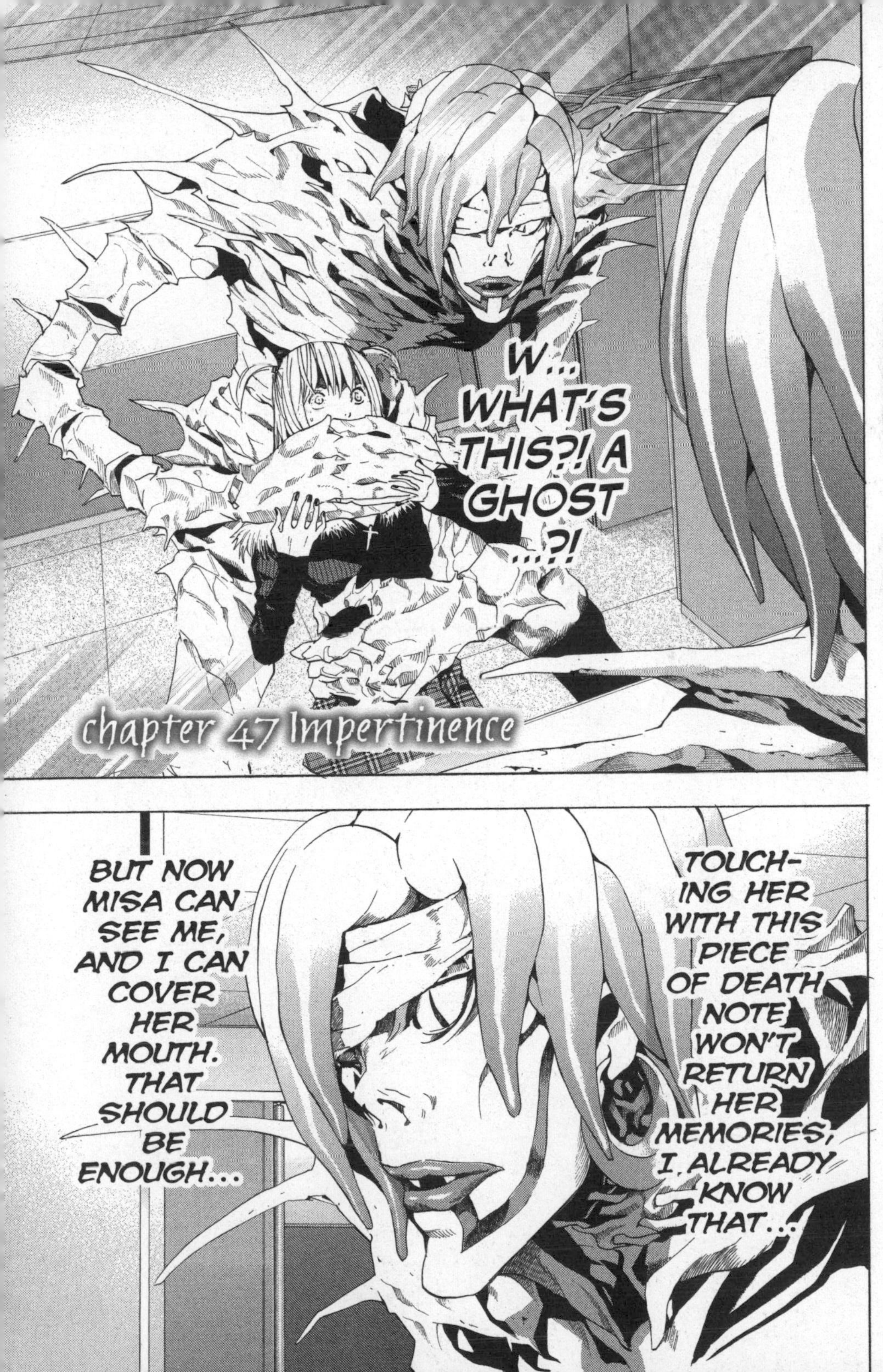
W... WHAT'S THIS?! A GHOST ...?!
chapter 47 Impertinence
TOUCHING HER WITH THIS PIECE OF DEATH NOTE WON'T RETURN HER MEMORIES, I ALREADY KNOW THAT...
BUT NOW MISA CAN SEE ME, AND I CAN COVER HER MOUTH. THAT SHOULD BE ENOUGH...

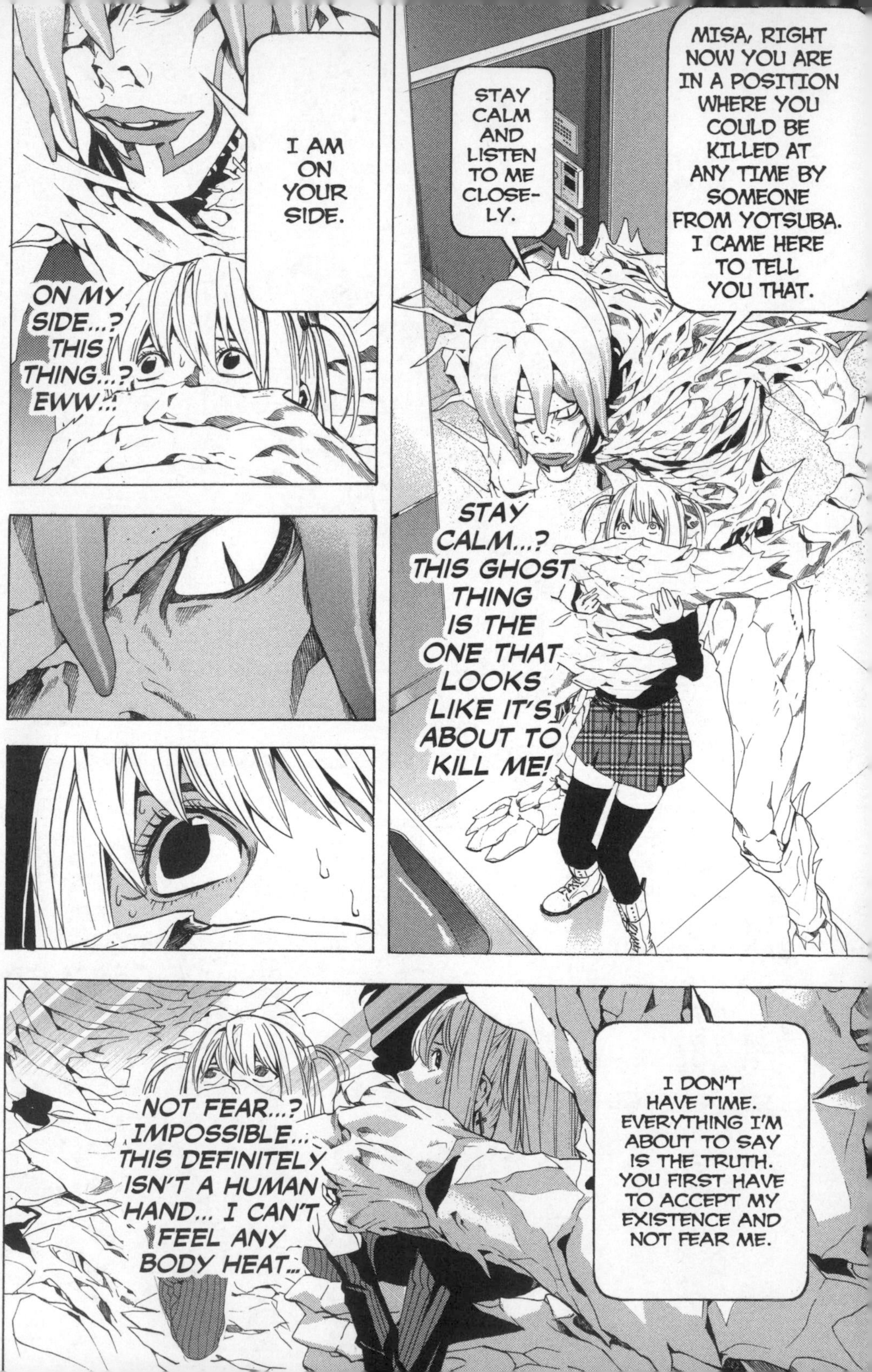
MISA, RIGHT NOW YOU ARE IN A POSITION WHERE YOU COULD BE KILLED AT ANY TIME BY SOMEONE FROM YOTSUBA. I CAME HERE TO TELL YOU THAT.
STAY CALM AND LISTEN TO ME CLOSE-LY.
STAY CALM...? THIS GHOST THING IS THE ONE THAT LOOKS LIKE IT'S ABOUT TO KILL ME!
I AM ON YOUR SIDE.
ON MY SIDE...? THIS THING...? EWW...
I DON'T HAVE TIME. EVERYTHING I'M ABOUT TO SAY IS THE TRUTH. YOU FIRST HAVE TO ACCEPT MY EXISTENCE AND NOT FEAR ME.
NOT FEAR...? IMPOSSIBLE... THIS DEFINITELY ISN'T A HUMAN HAND... I CAN'T FEEL ANY BODY HEAT...

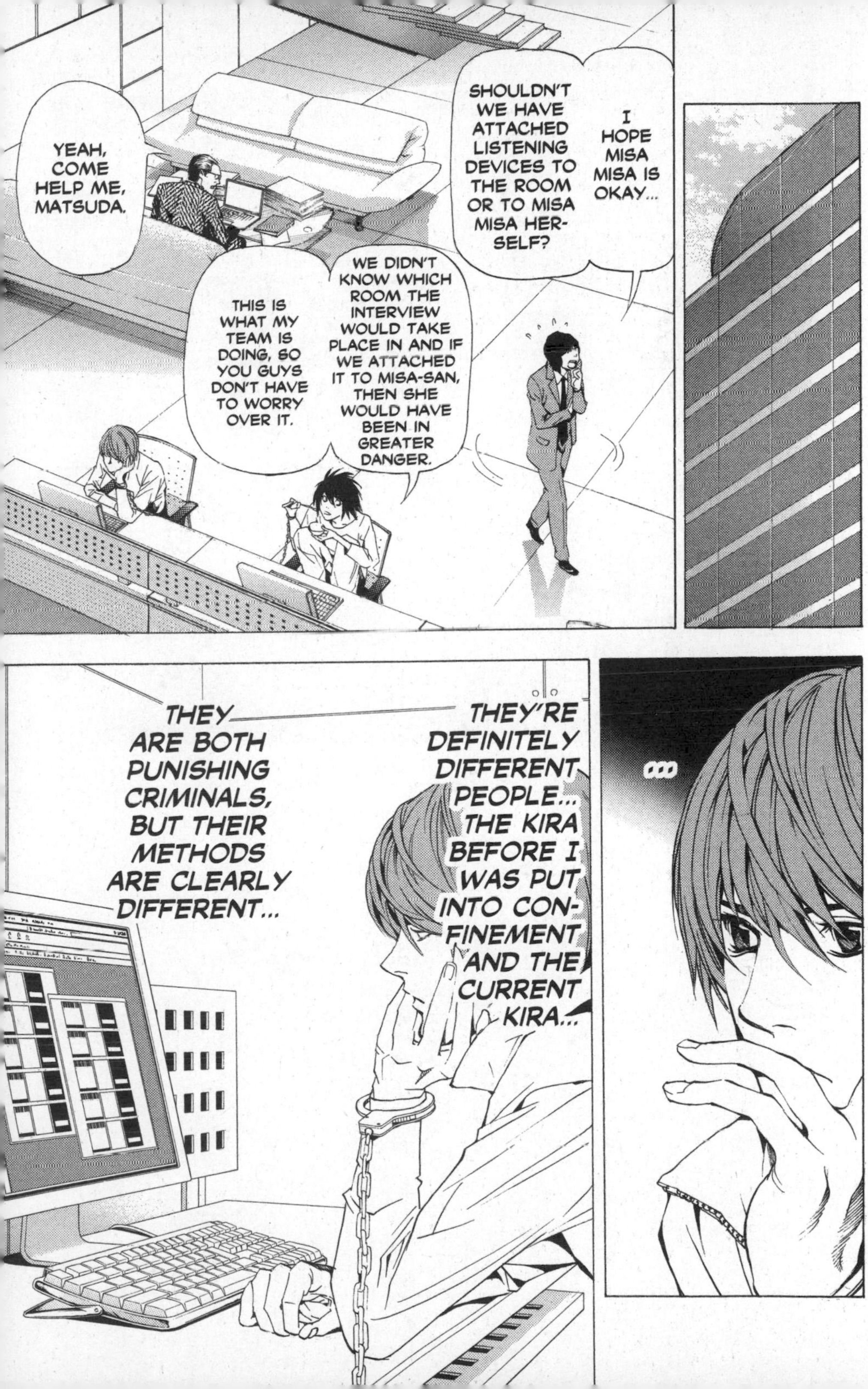
I HOPE MISA MISA IS OKAY...
SHOULDN'T WE HAVE ATTACHED LISTENING DEVICES TO THE ROOM OR TO MISA MISA HER-SELF?
WE DIDN'T KNOW WHICH ROOM THE INTERVIEW WOULD TAKE PLACE IN AND IF WE ATTACHED IT TO MISA-SAN, THEN SHE WOULD HAVE BEEN IN GREATER DANGER.
THIS IS WHAT MY TEAM IS DOING, SO YOU GUYS DON'T HAVE TO WORRY OVER IT.
YEAH, COME HELP ME, MATSUDA.
...
THEY'RE DEFINITELY DIFFERENT PEOPLE... THE KIRA BEFORE I WAS PUT INTO CON-FINEMENT AND THE CURRENT KIRA...
THEY ARE BOTH PUNISHING CRIMINALS, BUT THEIR METHODS ARE CLEARLY DIFFERENT...

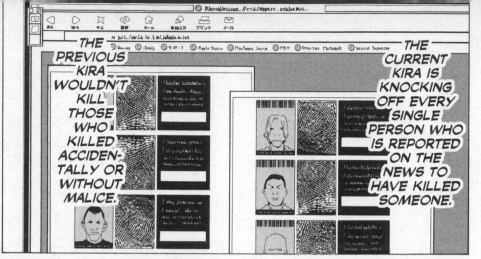

THE CURRENT KIRA IS KNOCKING OFF EVERY SINGLE PERSON WHO IS REPORTED ON THE NEWS TO HAVE KILLED SOMEONE.
THE PREVIOUS KIRA WOULDN'T KILL THOSE WHO KILLED ACCIDEN-TALLY OR WITHOUT MALICE.
LIKE CAR ACCIDENT DEATHS, FOR EXAMPLE.
UNLESS THAT PERSON CAUSED AN ACCIDENT THROUGH SOME EXTREMELY MALICIOUS CIRCUMSTANCE, KIRA WOULDN'T PUNISH HIM.
IF THE ORIGINAL KIRA DETERMINED THAT THE PERSON MURDERED DESERVED WHAT HE GOT, THE KILLER WAS NOT PUNISHED...
IF I WAS KIRA, I'D PROBABLY OPERATE LIKE THAT...
IN COMPARI-SON, I FEEL NO HUMAN EMOTIONS COMING FROM THE ACTIONS OF THIS CURRENT KIRA...

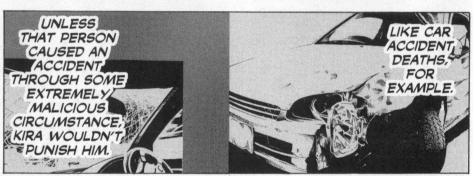

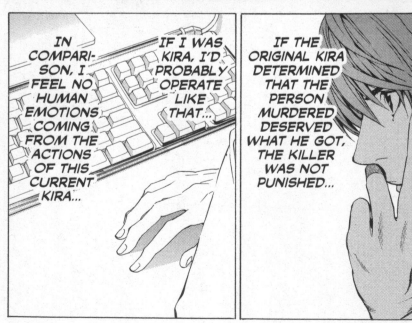

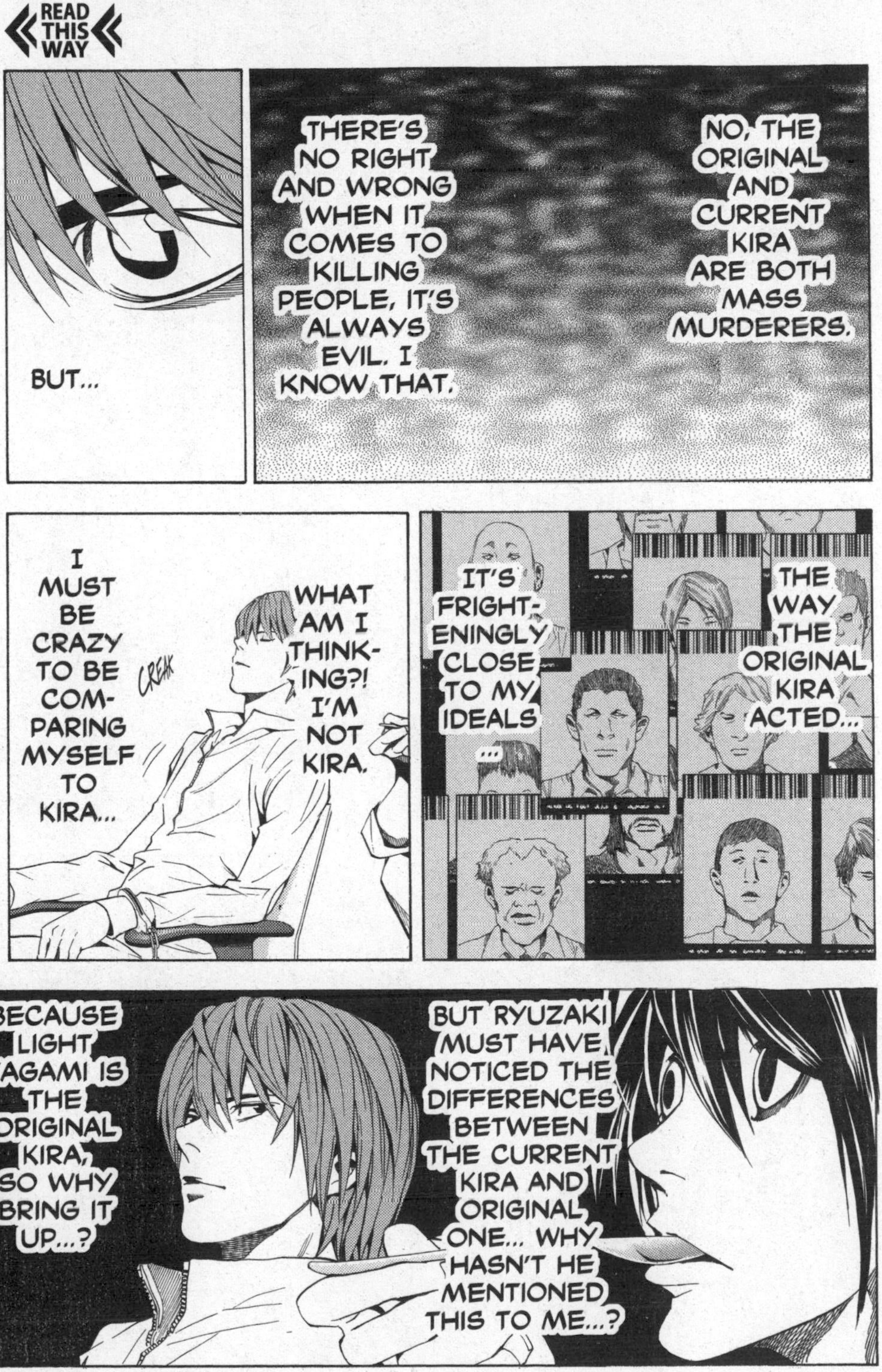
READ THIS WAY
NO, THE ORIGINAL AND CURRENT KIRA ARE BOTH MASS MURDERERS.
THERE'S NO RIGHT AND WRONG WHEN IT COMES TO KILLING PEOPLE, IT'S ALWAYS EVIL. I KNOW THAT.
BUT...
THE WAY THE ORIGINAL KIRA ACTED...
IT'S FRIGHTENINGLY CLOSE TO MY IDEALS...
WHAT AM I THINKING?! I'M NOT KIRA.
I MUST BE CRAZY TO BE COMPARING MYSELF TO KIRA...
CREAK
BUT RYUZAKI MUST HAVE NOTICED THE DIFFERENCES BETWEEN THE CURRENT KIRA AND ORIGINAL ONE... WHY HASN'T HE MENTIONED THIS TO ME...?
BECAUSE LIGHT YAGAMI IS THE ORIGINAL KIRA, SO WHY BRING IT UP...?

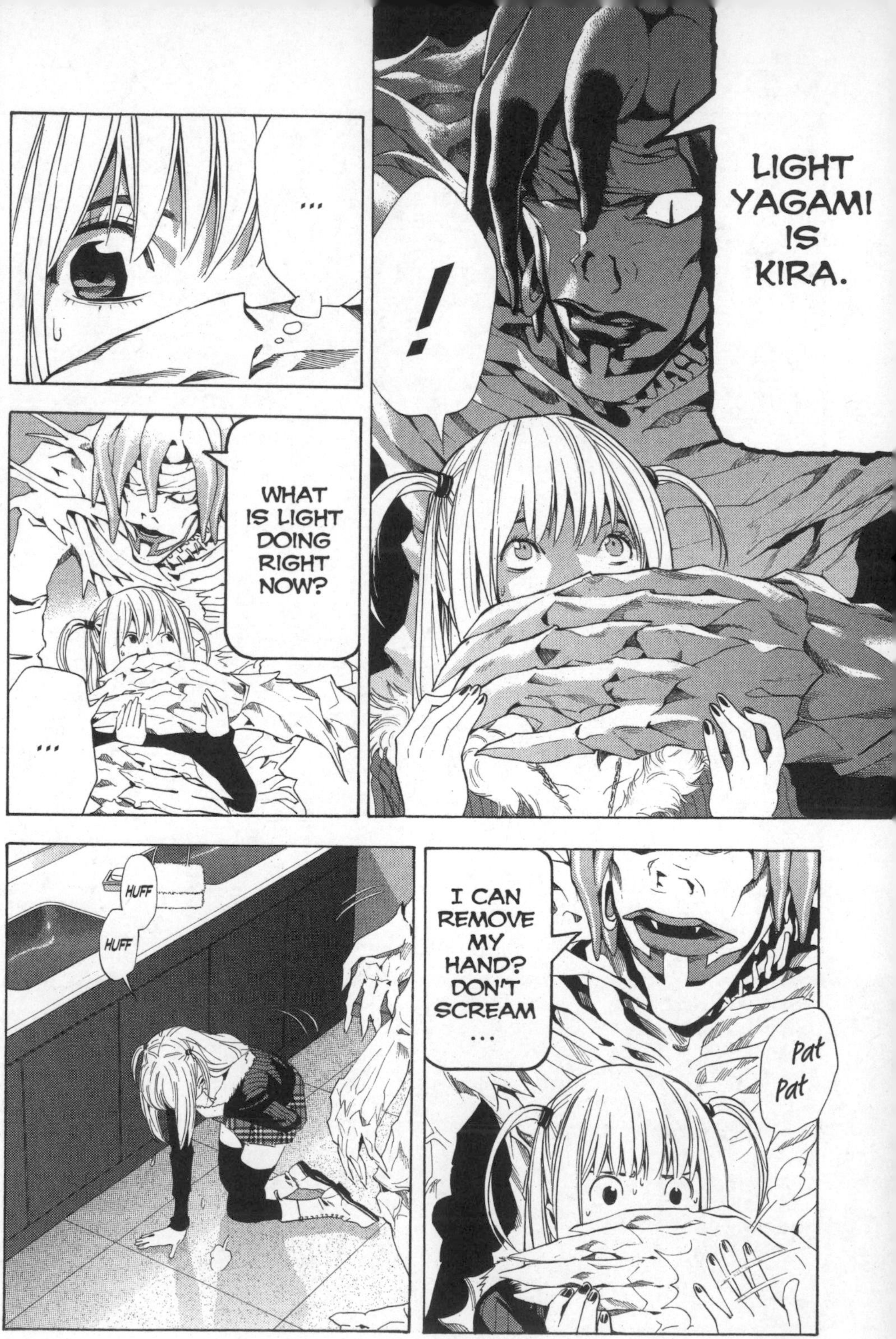

LIGHT YAGAMI IS KIRA.
!
...
WHAT IS LIGHT DOING RIGHT NOW?
...
I CAN REMOVE MY HAND? DON'T SCREAM ...
Pat Pat
HUFF
HUFF

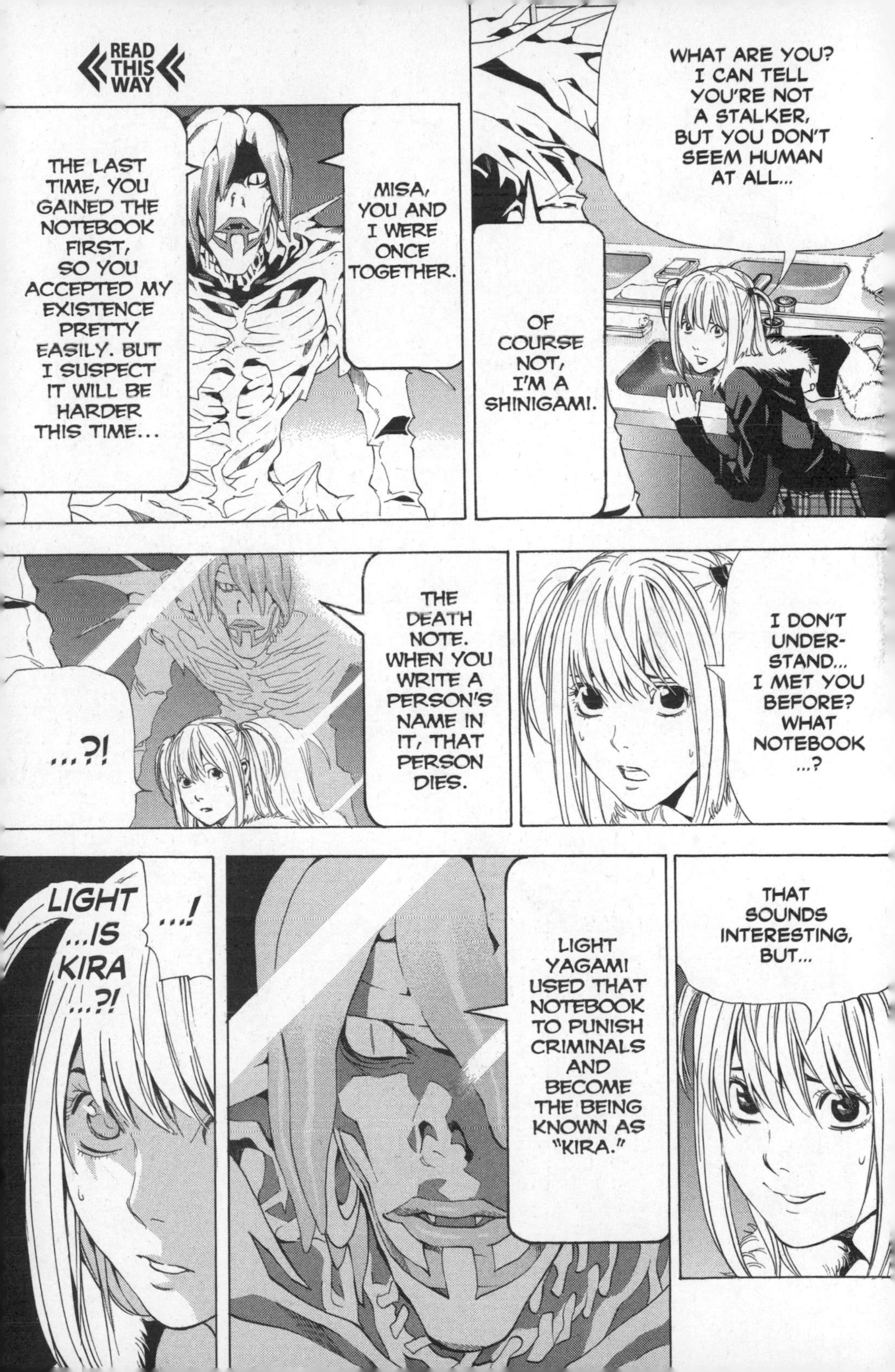
READ THIS WAY
WHAT ARE YOU? I CAN TELL YOU'RE NOT A STALKER, BUT YOU DON'T SEEM HUMAN AT ALL...
OF COURSE NOT, I'M A SHINIGAMI.
MISA, YOU AND I WERE ONCE TOGETHER.
THE LAST TIME, YOU GAINED THE NOTEBOOK FIRST, SO YOU ACCEPTED MY EXISTENCE PRETTY EASILY. BUT I SUSPECT IT WILL BE HARDER THIS TIME...
I DON'T UNDER-STAND... I MET YOU BEFORE? WHAT NOTEBOOK ...?
THE DEATH NOTE. WHEN YOU WRITE A PERSON'S NAME IN IT, THAT PERSON DIES.
...?!
THAT SOUNDS INTERESTING, BUT...
LIGHT YAGAMI USED THAT NOTEBOOK TO PUNISH CRIMINALS AND BECOME THE BEING KNOWN AS "KIRA."
...!
LIGHT ...IS KIRA ...?!

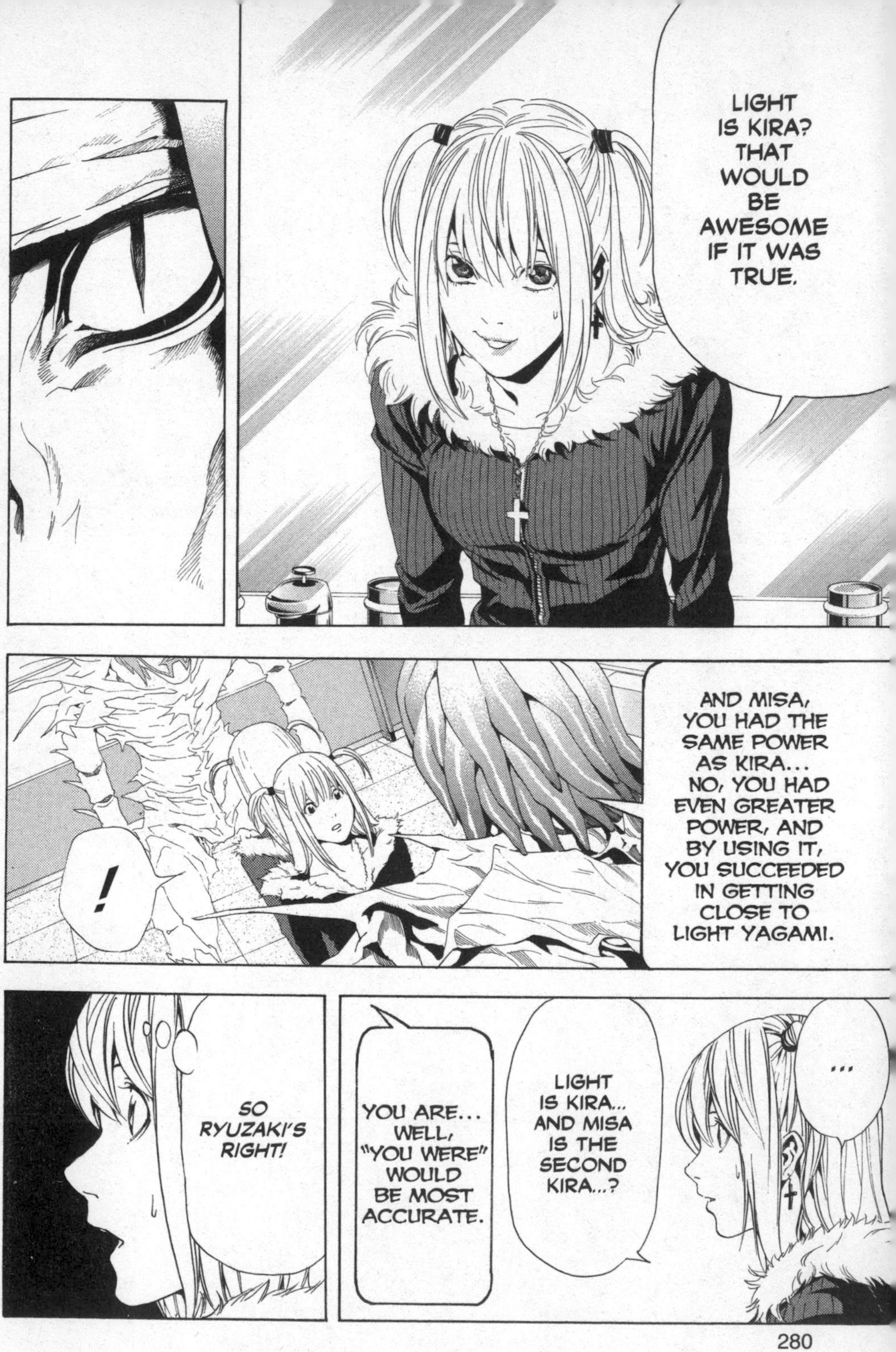
LIGHT IS KIRA? THAT WOULD BE AWESOME IF IT WAS TRUE.
AND MISA, YOU HAD THE SAME POWER AS KIRA... NO, YOU HAD EVEN GREATER POWER, AND BY USING IT, YOU SUCCEEDED IN GETTING CLOSE TO LIGHT YAGAMI.
!
...
LIGHT IS KIRA... AND MISA IS THE SECOND KIRA...?
YOU ARE... WELL, "YOU WERE" WOULD BE MOST ACCURATE.
SO RYUZAKI'S RIGHT!

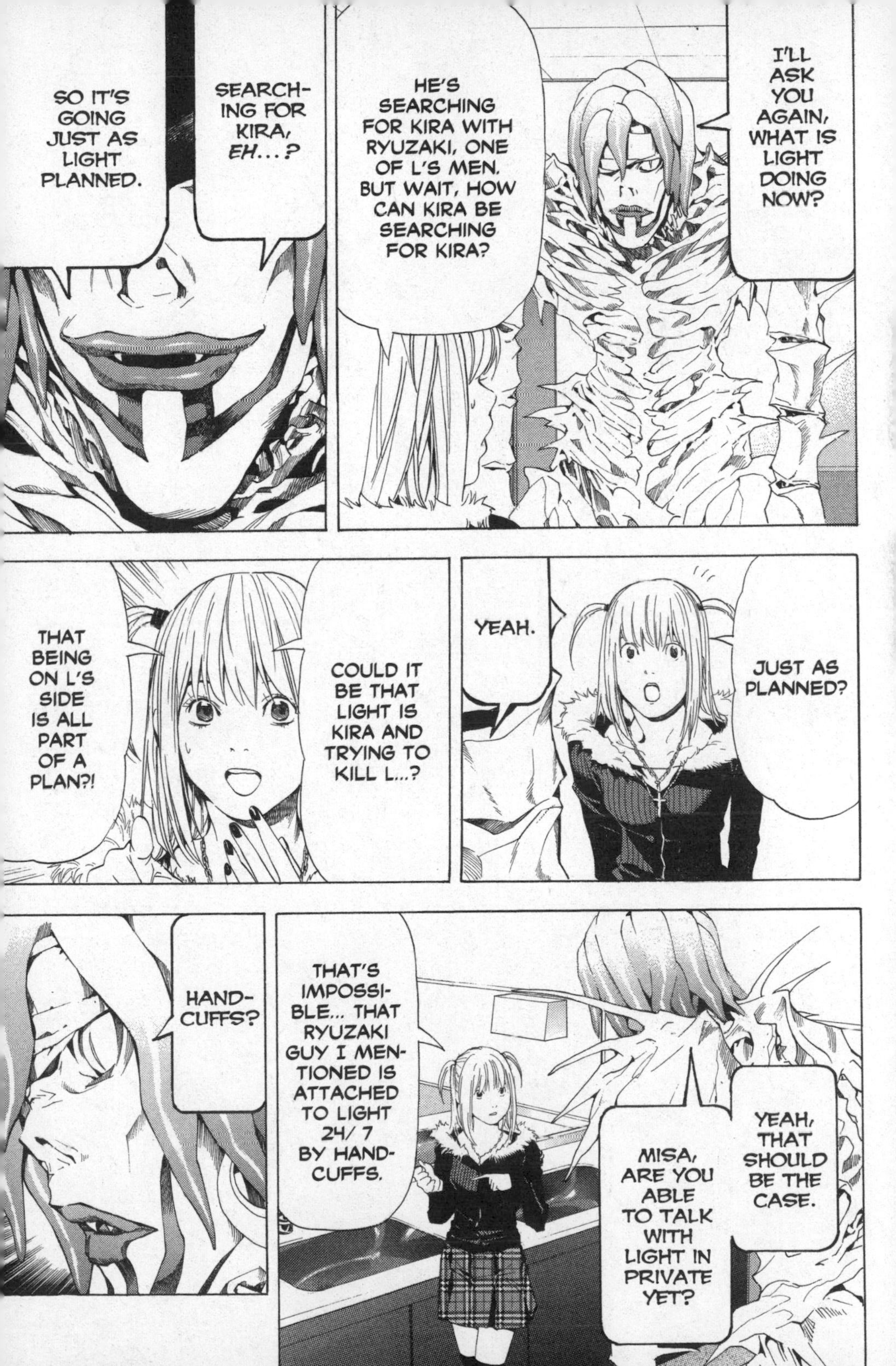
I'LL ASK YOU AGAIN, WHAT IS LIGHT DOING NOW?
HE'S SEARCHING FOR KIRA WITH RYUZAKI, ONE OF L'S MEN. BUT WAIT, HOW CAN KIRA BE SEARCHING FOR KIRA?
SEARCH-ING FOR KIRA, *EH...?*
SO IT'S GOING JUST AS LIGHT PLANNED.
JUST AS PLANNED?
YEAH.
COULD IT BE THAT LIGHT IS KIRA AND TRYING TO KILL L...?
THAT BEING ON L'S SIDE IS ALL PART OF A PLAN?!
YEAH, THAT SHOULD BE THE CASE.
MISA, ARE YOU ABLE TO TALK WITH LIGHT IN PRIVATE YET?
THAT'S IMPOSSI-BLE... THAT RYUZAKI GUY I MEN-TIONED IS ATTACHED TO LIGHT 24/ 7 BY HAND-CUFFS.
HAND-CUFFS?

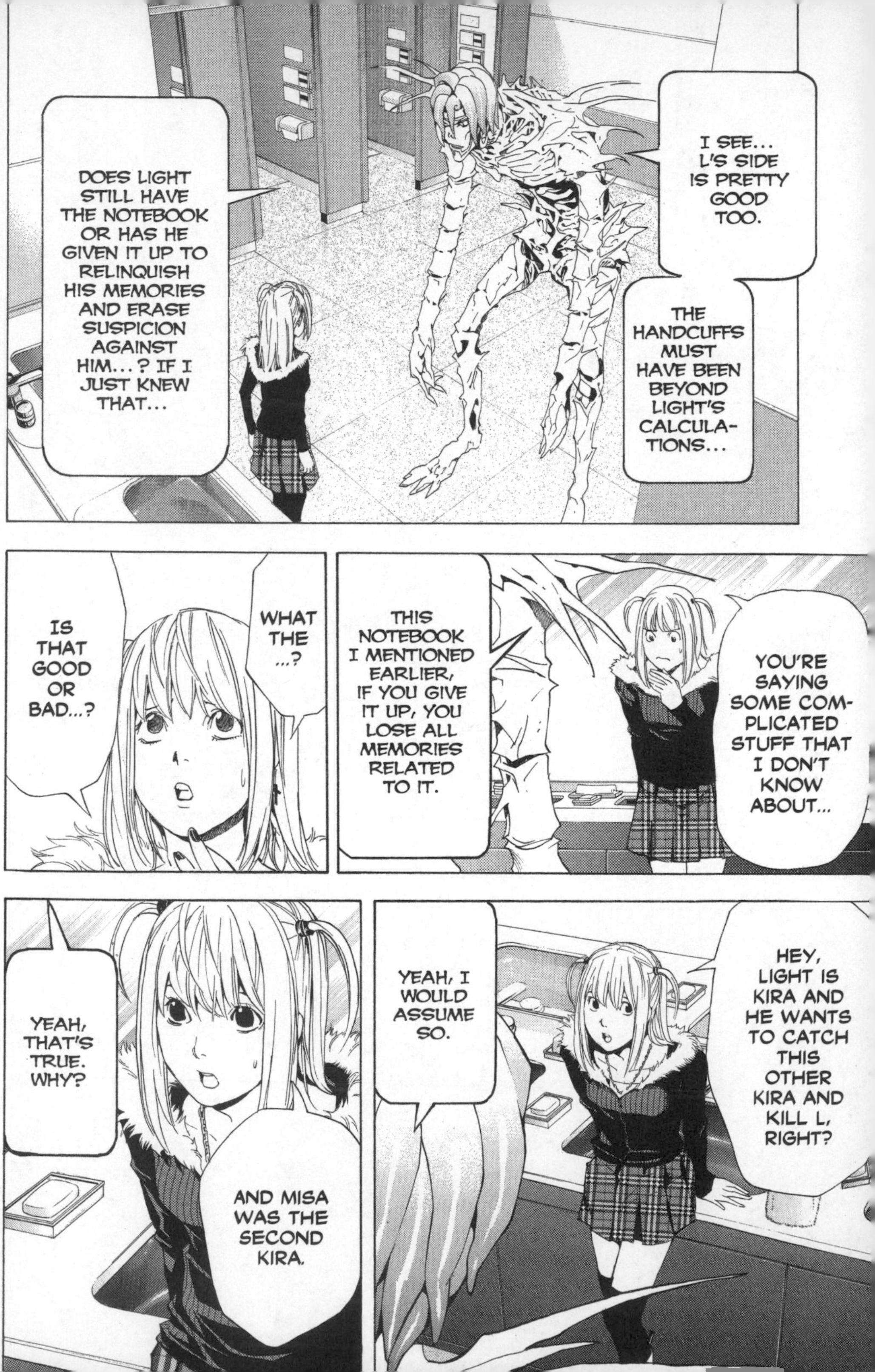
I SEE... L'S SIDE IS PRETTY GOOD TOO.
THE HANDCUFFS MUST HAVE BEEN BEYOND LIGHT'S CALCULA-TIONS...
DOES LIGHT STILL HAVE THE NOTEBOOK OR HAS HE GIVEN IT UP TO RELINQUISH HIS MEMORIES AND ERASE SUSPICION AGAINST HIM...? IF I JUST KNEW THAT...
YOU'RE SAYING SOME COM-PLICATED STUFF THAT I DON'T KNOW ABOUT...
THIS NOTEBOOK I MENTIONED EARLIER, IF YOU GIVE IT UP, YOU LOSE ALL MEMORIES RELATED TO IT.
WHAT THE ...?
IS THAT GOOD OR BAD...?
HEY, LIGHT IS KIRA AND HE WANTS TO CATCH THIS OTHER KIRA AND KILL L, RIGHT?
YEAH, I WOULD ASSUME SO.
AND MISA WAS THE SECOND KIRA.
YEAH, THAT'S TRUE. WHY?

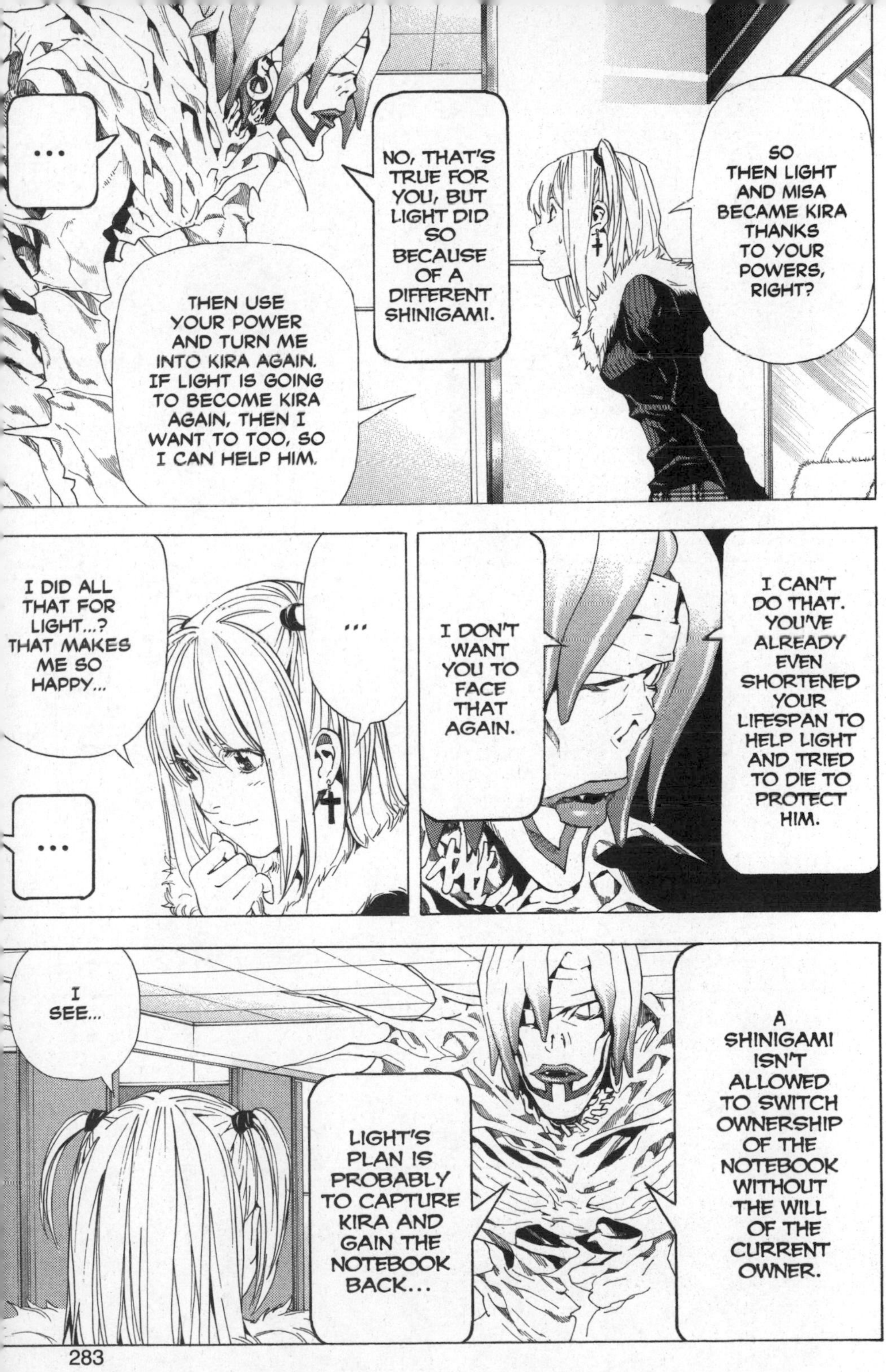
SO THEN LIGHT AND MISA BECAME KIRA THANKS TO YOUR POWERS, RIGHT?
NO, THAT'S TRUE FOR YOU, BUT LIGHT DID SO BECAUSE OF A DIFFERENT SHINIGAMI.
...
THEN USE YOUR POWER AND TURN ME INTO KIRA AGAIN. IF LIGHT IS GOING TO BECOME KIRA AGAIN, THEN I WANT TO TOO, SO I CAN HELP HIM.
I CAN'T DO THAT. YOU'VE ALREADY EVEN SHORTENED YOUR LIFESPAN TO HELP LIGHT AND TRIED TO DIE TO PROTECT HIM.
I DON'T WANT YOU TO FACE THAT AGAIN.
...
I DID ALL THAT FOR LIGHT...? THAT MAKES ME SO HAPPY...
...
A SHINIGAMI ISN'T ALLOWED TO SWITCH OWNERSHIP OF THE NOTEBOOK WITHOUT THE WILL OF THE CURRENT OWNER.
I SEE...
LIGHT'S PLAN IS PROBABLY TO CAPTURE KIRA AND GAIN THE NOTEBOOK BACK...

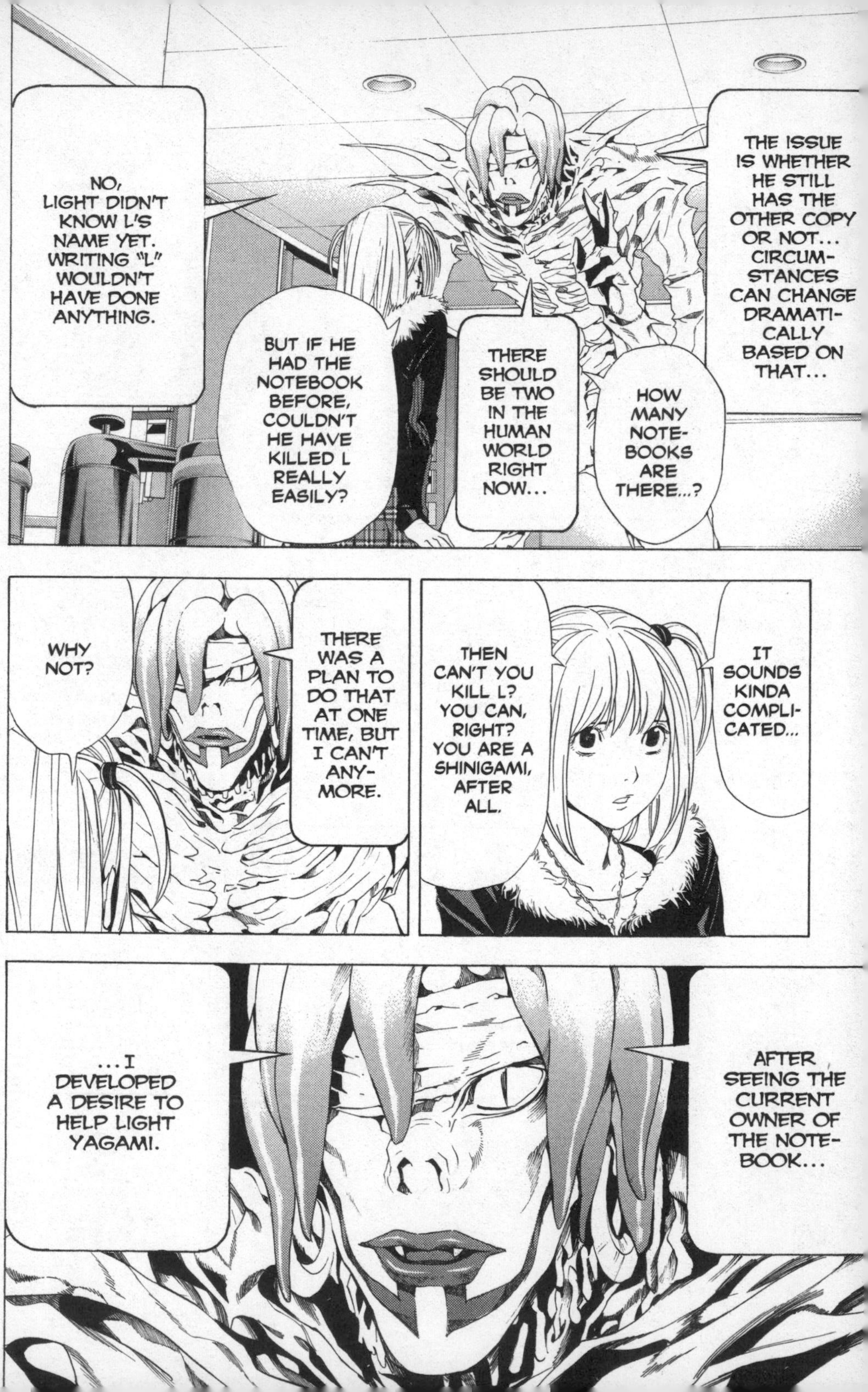
THE ISSUE IS WHETHER HE STILL HAS THE OTHER COPY OR NOT... CIRCUM-STANCES CAN CHANGE DRAMATI-CALLY BASED ON THAT...
HOW MANY NOTE-BOOKS ARE THERE...?
THERE SHOULD BE TWO IN THE HUMAN WORLD RIGHT NOW...
BUT IF HE HAD THE NOTEBOOK BEFORE, COULDN'T HE HAVE KILLED L REALLY EASILY?
NO, LIGHT DIDN'T KNOW L'S NAME YET. WRITING "L" WOULDN'T HAVE DONE ANYTHING.
IT SOUNDS KINDA COMPLI-CATED...
THEN CAN'T YOU KILL L? YOU CAN, RIGHT? YOU ARE A SHINIGAMI, AFTER ALL.
THERE WAS A PLAN TO DO THAT AT ONE TIME, BUT I CAN'T ANY-MORE.
WHY NOT?
AFTER SEEING THE CURRENT OWNER OF THE NOTE-BOOK...
...I DEVELOPED A DESIRE TO HELP LIGHT YAGAMI.

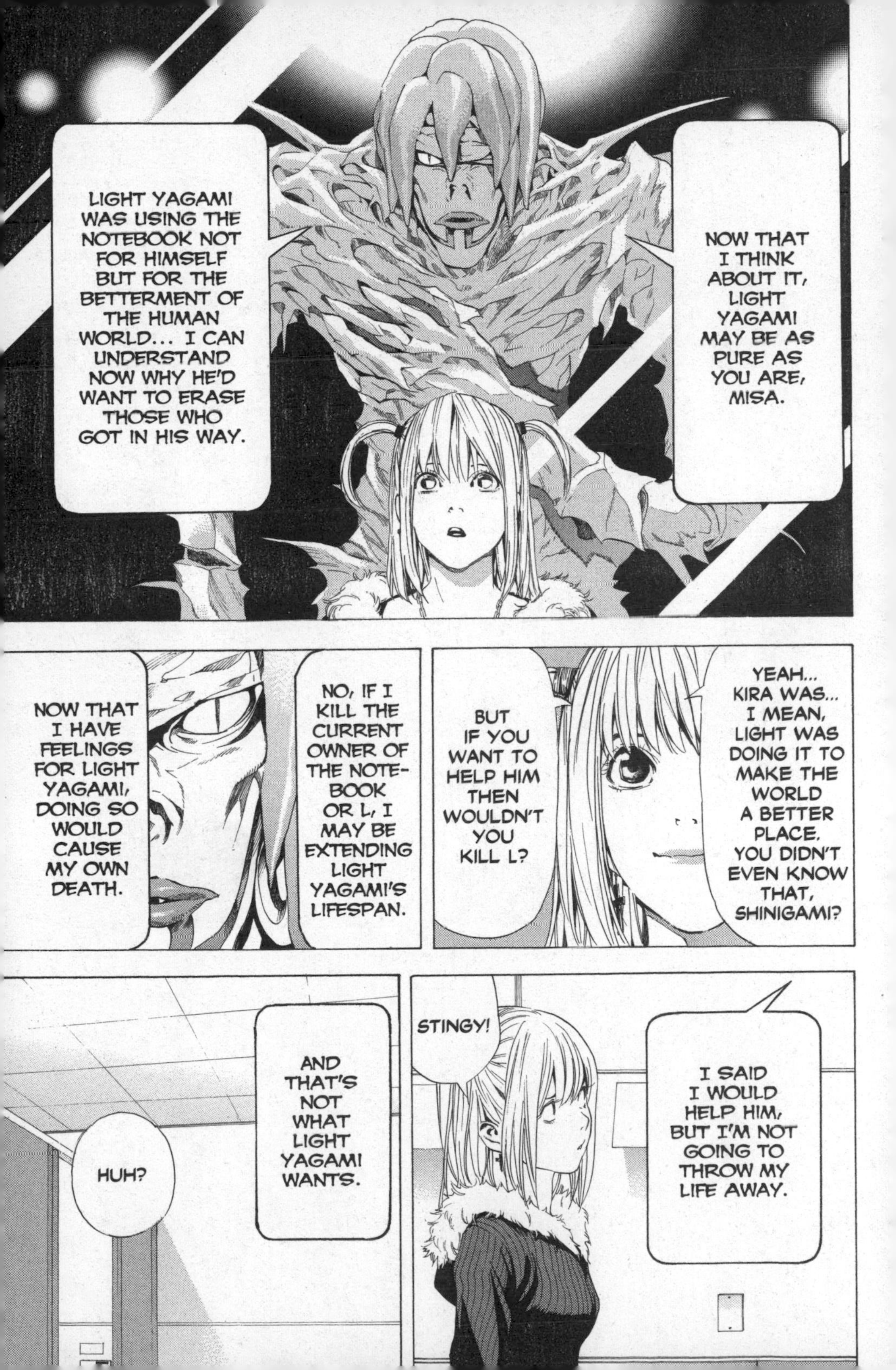
NOW THAT I THINK ABOUT IT, LIGHT YAGAMI MAY BE AS PURE AS YOU ARE, MISA.
LIGHT YAGAMI WAS USING THE NOTEBOOK NOT FOR HIMSELF BUT FOR THE BETTERMENT OF THE HUMAN WORLD... I CAN UNDERSTAND NOW WHY HE'D WANT TO ERASE THOSE WHO GOT IN HIS WAY.
YEAH... KIRA WAS... I MEAN, LIGHT WAS DOING IT TO MAKE THE WORLD A BETTER PLACE. YOU DIDN'T EVEN KNOW THAT, SHINIGAMI?
BUT IF YOU WANT TO HELP HIM THEN WOULDN'T YOU KILL L?
NO, IF I KILL THE CURRENT OWNER OF THE NOTE-BOOK OR L, I MAY BE EXTENDING LIGHT YAGAMI'S LIFESPAN.
NOW THAT I HAVE FEELINGS FOR LIGHT YAGAMI, DOING SO WOULD CAUSE MY OWN DEATH.
I SAID I WOULD HELP HIM, BUT I'M NOT GOING TO THROW MY LIFE AWAY.
STINGY!
AND THAT'S NOT WHAT LIGHT YAGAMI WANTS.
HUH?

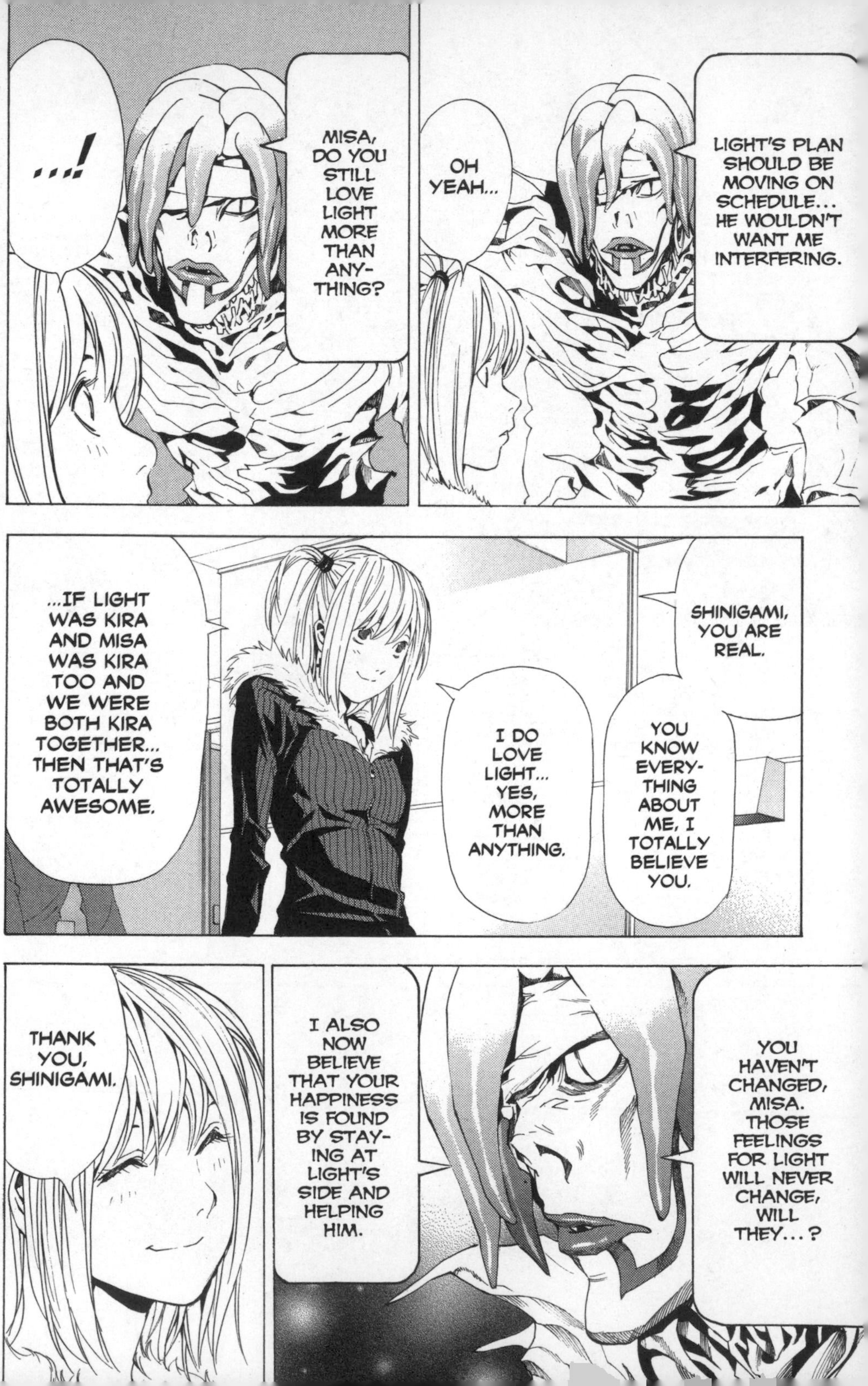
LIGHT'S PLAN SHOULD BE MOVING ON SCHEDULE... HE WOULDN'T WANT ME INTERFERING.
OH YEAH...
MISA, DO YOU STILL LOVE LIGHT MORE THAN ANY-THING?
...!
SHINIGAMI, YOU ARE REAL.
YOU KNOW EVERY-THING ABOUT ME, I TOTALLY BELIEVE YOU.
I DO LOVE LIGHT... YES, MORE THAN ANYTHING.
...IF LIGHT WAS KIRA AND MISA WAS KIRA TOO AND WE WERE BOTH KIRA TOGETHER... THEN THAT'S TOTALLY AWESOME.
YOU HAVEN'T CHANGED, MISA. THOSE FEELINGS FOR LIGHT WILL NEVER CHANGE, WILL THEY...?
I ALSO NOW BELIEVE THAT YOUR HAPPINESS IS FOUND BY STAY-ING AT LIGHT'S SIDE AND HELPING HIM.
THANK YOU, SHINIGAMI.

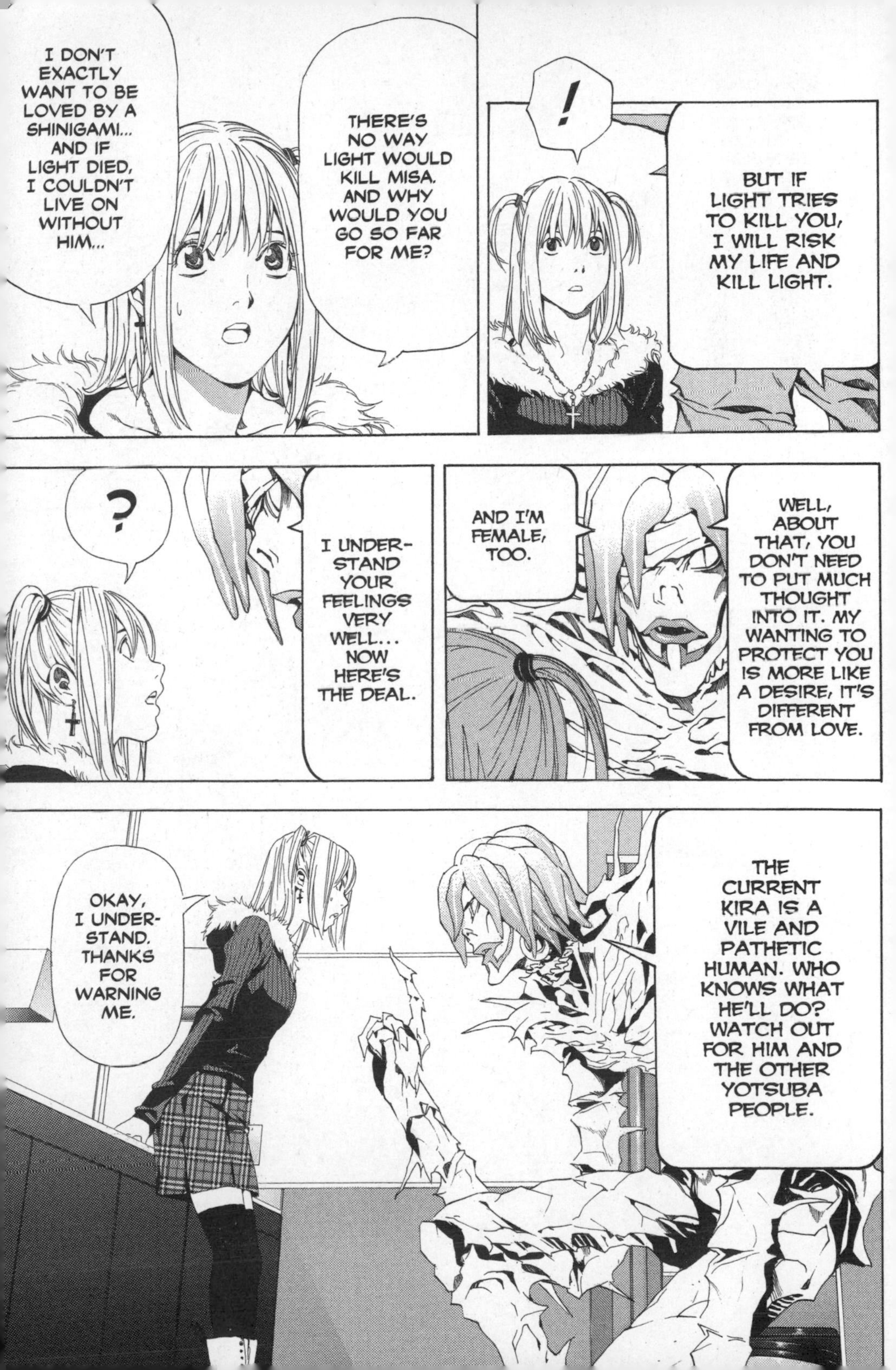
BUT IF LIGHT TRIES TO KILL YOU, I WILL RISK MY LIFE AND KILL LIGHT.
!
THERE'S NO WAY LIGHT WOULD KILL MISA. AND WHY WOULD YOU GO SO FAR FOR ME?
I DON'T EXACTLY WANT TO BE LOVED BY A SHINIGAMI... AND IF LIGHT DIED, I COULDN'T LIVE ON WITHOUT HIM...
WELL, ABOUT THAT, YOU DON'T NEED TO PUT MUCH THOUGHT INTO IT. MY WANTING TO PROTECT YOU IS MORE LIKE A DESIRE, IT'S DIFFERENT FROM LOVE.
AND I'M FEMALE, TOO.
I UNDER-STAND YOUR FEELINGS VERY WELL... NOW HERE'S THE DEAL.
?
THE CURRENT KIRA IS A VILE AND PATHETIC HUMAN. WHO KNOWS WHAT HE'LL DO? WATCH OUT FOR HIM AND THE OTHER YOTSUBA PEOPLE.
OKAY, I UNDER-STAND. THANKS FOR WARNING ME.

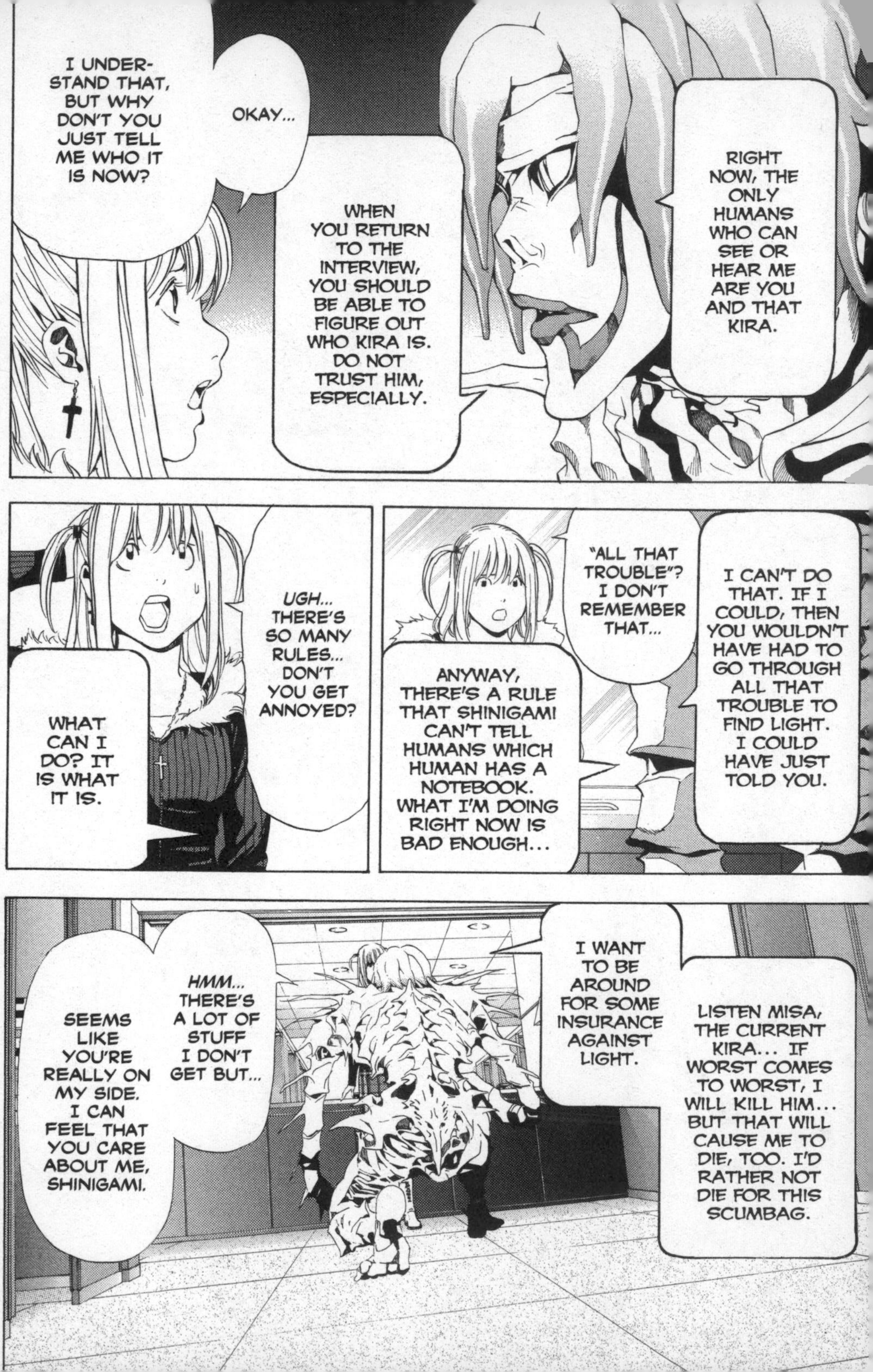
RIGHT NOW, THE ONLY HUMANS WHO CAN SEE OR HEAR ME ARE YOU AND THAT KIRA.
WHEN YOU RETURN TO THE INTERVIEW, YOU SHOULD BE ABLE TO FIGURE OUT WHO KIRA IS. DO NOT TRUST HIM, ESPECIALLY.
OKAY...
I UNDER-STAND THAT, BUT WHY DON'T YOU JUST TELL ME WHO IT IS NOW?
I CAN'T DO THAT. IF I COULD, THEN YOU WOULDN'T HAVE HAD TO GO THROUGH ALL THAT TROUBLE TO FIND LIGHT. I COULD HAVE JUST TOLD YOU.
"ALL THAT TROUBLE"? I DON'T REMEMBER THAT...
ANYWAY, THERE'S A RULE THAT SHINIGAMI CAN'T TELL HUMANS WHICH HUMAN HAS A NOTEBOOK. WHAT I'M DOING RIGHT NOW IS BAD ENOUGH...
UGH... THERE'S SO MANY RULES... DON'T YOU GET ANNOYED?
WHAT CAN I DO? IT IS WHAT IT IS.
LISTEN MISA, THE CURRENT KIRA... IF WORST COMES TO WORST, I WILL KILL HIM... BUT THAT WILL CAUSE ME TO DIE, TOO. I'D RATHER NOT DIE FOR THIS SCUMBAG.
I WANT TO BE AROUND FOR SOME INSURANCE AGAINST LIGHT.
HMM... THERE'S A LOT OF STUFF I DON'T GET BUT...
SEEMS LIKE YOU'RE REALLY ON MY SIDE. I CAN FEEL THAT YOU CARE ABOUT ME, SHINIGAMI.

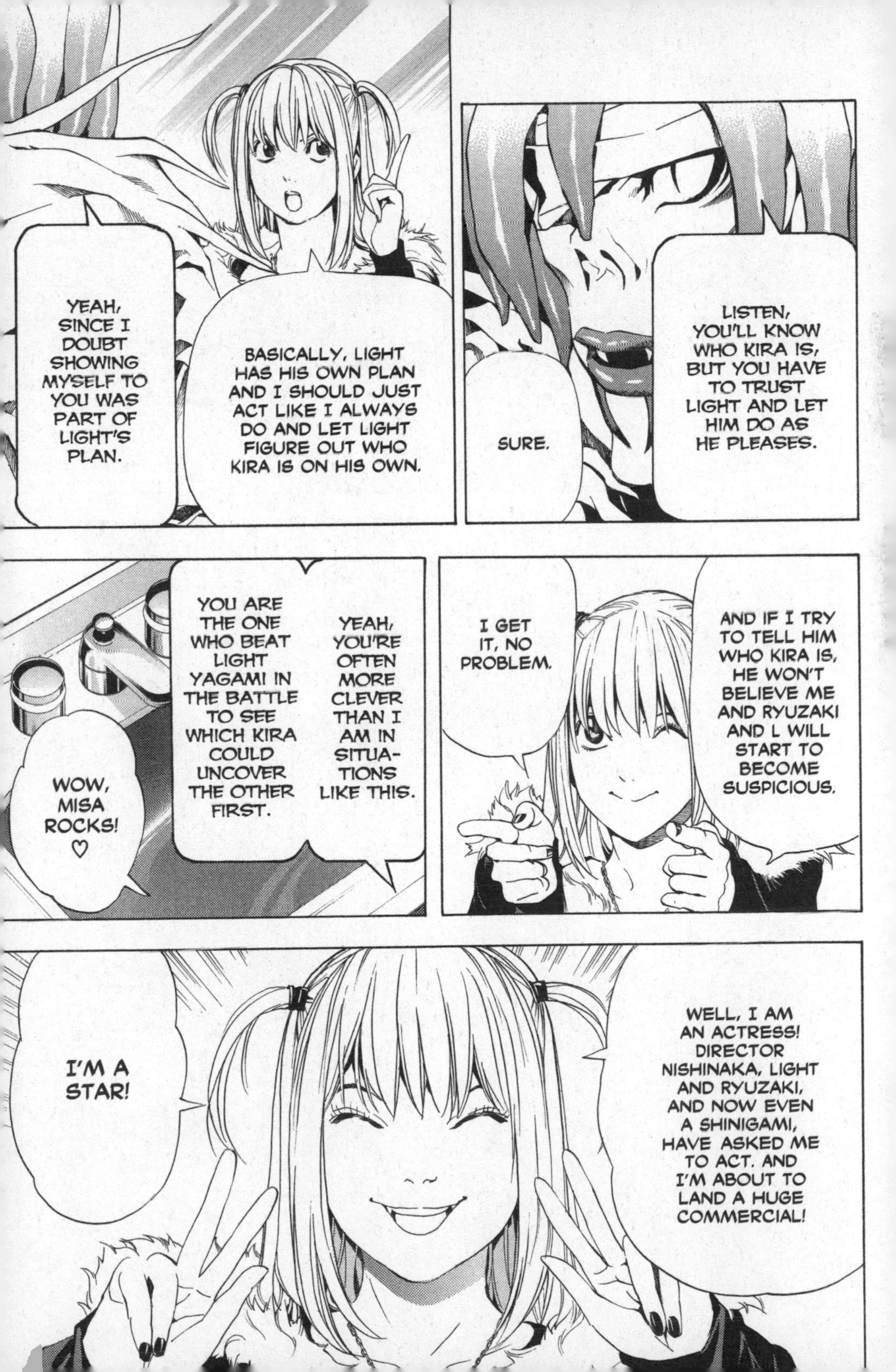

LISTEN, YOU'LL KNOW WHO KIRA IS, BUT YOU HAVE TO TRUST LIGHT AND LET HIM DO AS HE PLEASES.
SURE.
BASICALLY, LIGHT HAS HIS OWN PLAN AND I SHOULD JUST ACT LIKE I ALWAYS DO AND LET LIGHT FIGURE OUT WHO KIRA IS ON HIS OWN.
YEAH, SINCE I DOUBT SHOWING MYSELF TO YOU WAS PART OF LIGHT'S PLAN.
AND IF I TRY TO TELL HIM WHO KIRA IS, HE WON'T BELIEVE ME AND RYUZAKI AND L WILL START TO BECOME SUSPICIOUS.
I GET IT, NO PROBLEM.
YEAH, YOU'RE OFTEN MORE CLEVER THAN I AM IN SITUATIONS LIKE THIS.
YOU ARE THE ONE WHO BEAT LIGHT YAGAMI IN THE BATTLE TO SEE WHICH KIRA COULD UNCOVER THE OTHER FIRST.
WOW, MISA ROCKS! ♡
WELL, I AM AN ACTRESS! DIRECTOR NISHINAKA, LIGHT AND RYUZAKI, AND NOW EVEN A SHINIGAMI, HAVE ASKED ME TO ACT. AND I'M ABOUT TO LAND A HUGE COMMERCIAL!
I'M A STAR!

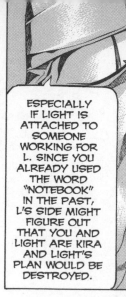

IT'S FUN TALKING TO YOU AND I'D LIKE TO ASK YOU MORE STUFF, BUT I SHOULD HEAD BACK SOON.
NOBODY THINKS IDOLS ACTUALLY GO TO THE BATHROOM.
YEAH...
LET ME TELL YOU ONE MORE IMPORTANT THING. NO MATTER HOW MUCH YOU WANT TO HELP LIGHT, YOU MUST NOT REVEAL THE EXISTENCE OF THE NOTEBOOK OR ME TO ANYONE.
ESPECIALLY IF LIGHT IS ATTACHED TO SOMEONE WORKING FOR L. SINCE YOU ALREADY USED THE WORD "NOTEBOOK" IN THE PAST, L'S SIDE MIGHT FIGURE OUT THAT YOU AND LIGHT ARE KIRA AND LIGHT'S PLAN WOULD BE DESTROYED.
OKAY, I UNDERSTAND.
WELL, I'LL BE GOING NOW. WATCH OUT FOR THE YOTSUBA PEOPLE, AND ESPECIALLY KIRA.
OH!
SHINIGAMI, WHAT'S YOUR NAME?
IT'S REM.
ZU...

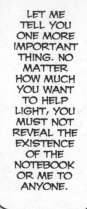

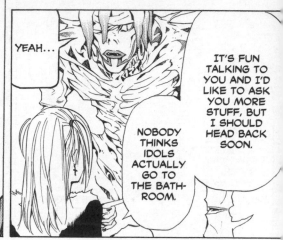

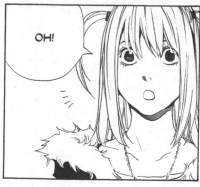

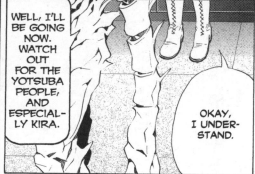

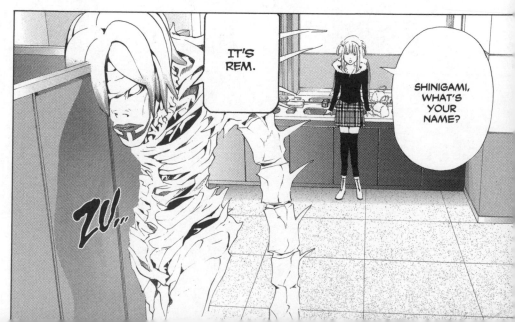

READ THIS WAY

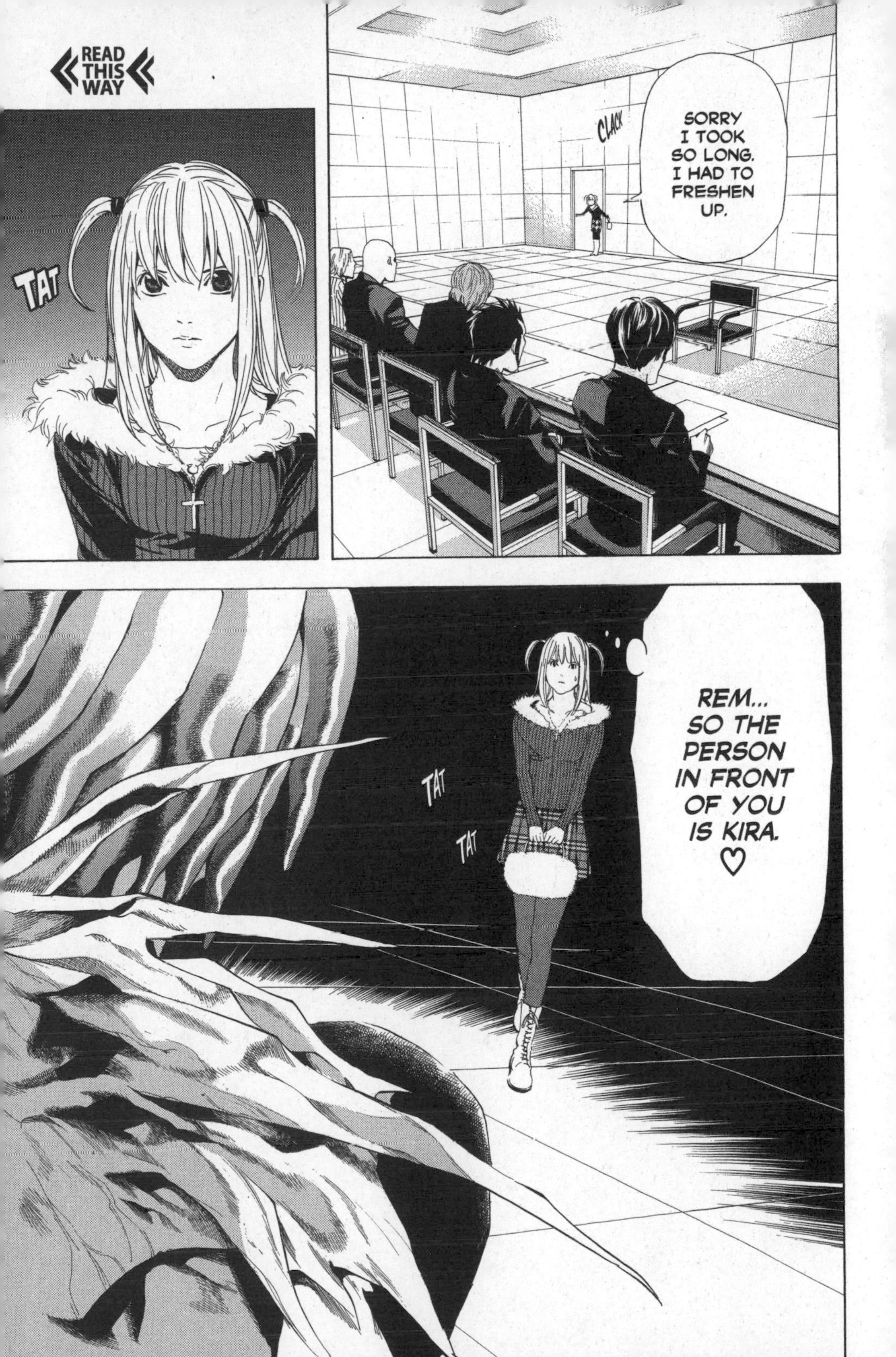
CLACK
SORRY I TOOK SO LONG. I HAD TO FRESHEN UP.
TAT
REM... SO THE PERSON IN FRONT OF YOU IS KIRA. ♡
TAT
TAT

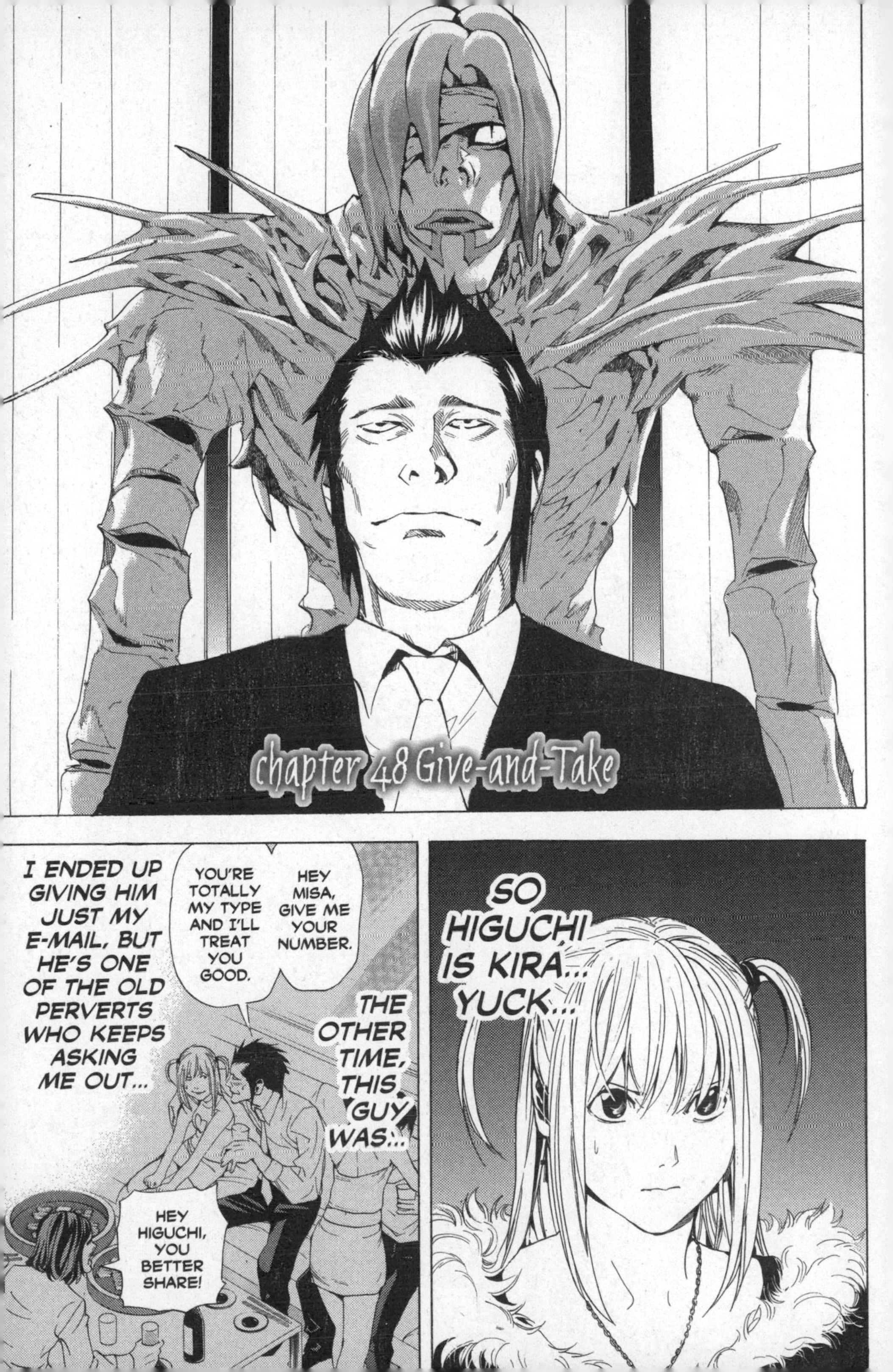
chapter 48 Give-and-Take
SO HIGUCHI IS KIRA... YUCK...
THE OTHER TIME, THIS GUY WAS...
HEY MISA, GIVE ME YOUR NUMBER.
YOU'RE TOTALLY MY TYPE AND I'LL TREAT YOU GOOD.
I ENDED UP GIVING HIM JUST MY E-MAIL, BUT HE'S ONE OF THE OLD PERVERTS WHO KEEPS ASKING ME OUT...
HEY HIGUCHI, YOU BETTER SHARE!

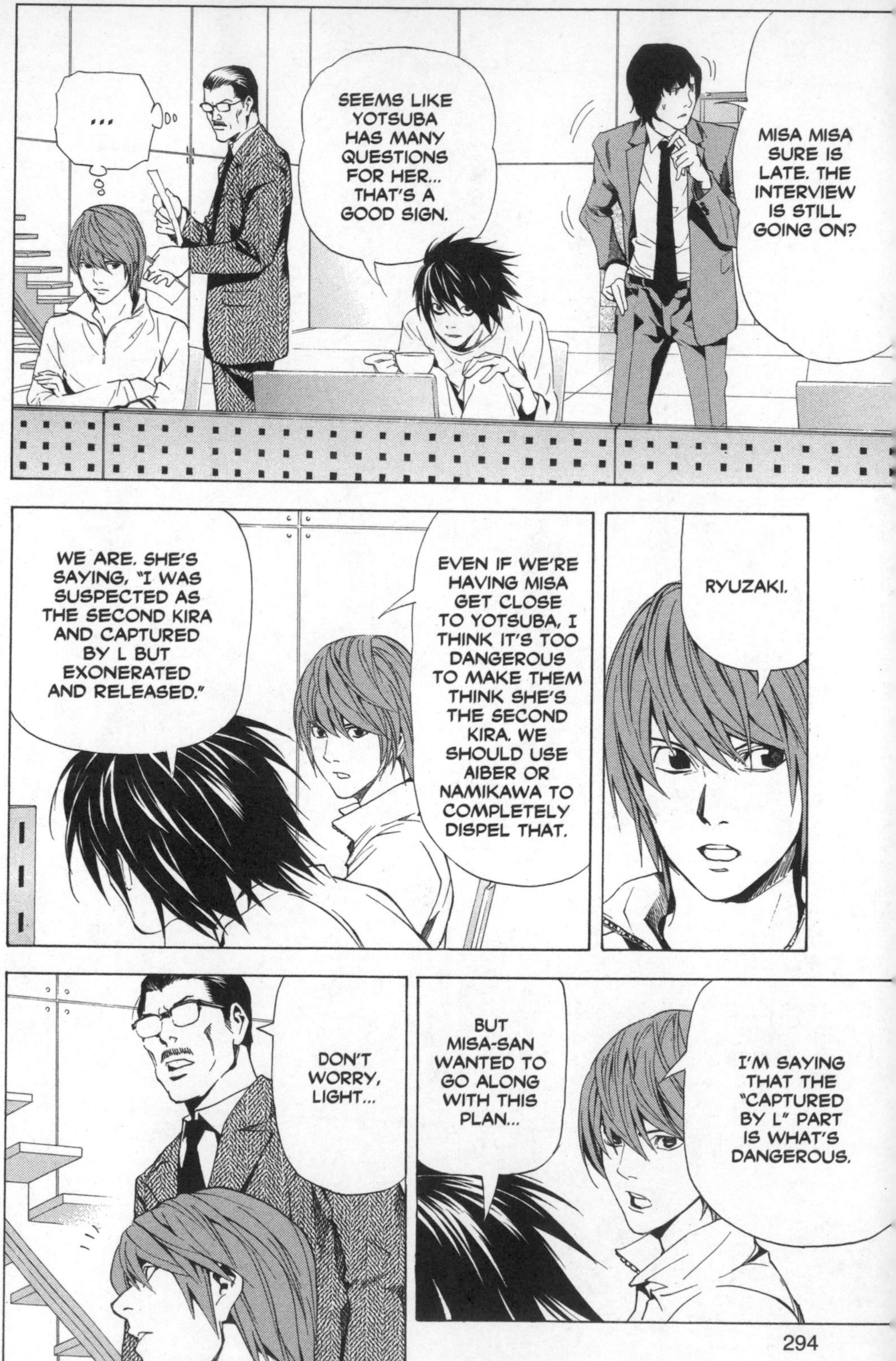
MISA MISA SURE IS LATE. THE INTERVIEW IS STILL GOING ON?
SEEMS LIKE YOTSUBA HAS MANY QUESTIONS FOR HER... THAT'S A GOOD SIGN.
...
RYUZAKI.
EVEN IF WE'RE HAVING MISA GET CLOSE TO YOTSUBA, I THINK IT'S TOO DANGEROUS TO MAKE THEM THINK SHE'S THE SECOND KIRA. WE SHOULD USE AIBER OR NAMIKAWA TO COMPLETELY DISPEL THAT.
WE ARE. SHE'S SAYING, "I WAS SUSPECTED AS THE SECOND KIRA AND CAPTURED BY L BUT EXONERATED AND RELEASED."
I'M SAYING THAT THE "CAPTURED BY L" PART IS WHAT'S DANGEROUS.
BUT MISA-SAN WANTED TO GO ALONG WITH THIS PLAN...
DON'T WORRY, LIGHT...

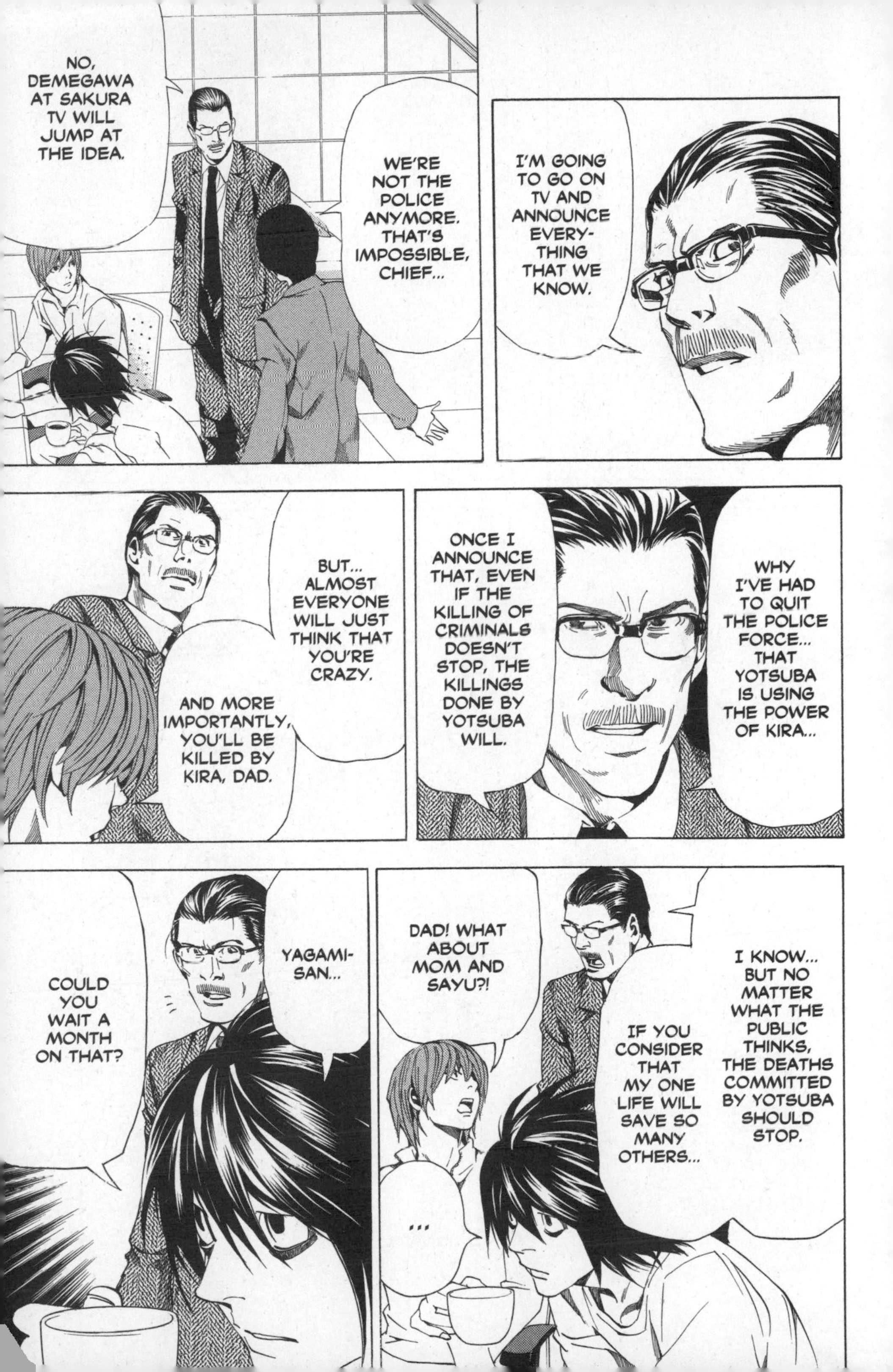
I'M GOING TO GO ON TV AND ANNOUNCE EVERYTHING THAT WE KNOW.
WE'RE NOT THE POLICE ANYMORE. THAT'S IMPOSSIBLE, CHIEF...
NO, DEMEGAWA AT SAKURA TV WILL JUMP AT THE IDEA.
WHY I'VE HAD TO QUIT THE POLICE FORCE... THAT YOTSUBA IS USING THE POWER OF KIRA...
ONCE I ANNOUNCE THAT, EVEN IF THE KILLING OF CRIMINALS DOESN'T STOP, THE KILLINGS DONE BY YOTSUBA WILL.
BUT... ALMOST EVERYONE WILL JUST THINK THAT YOU'RE CRAZY.
AND MORE IMPORTANTLY, YOU'LL BE KILLED BY KIRA, DAD.
I KNOW... BUT NO MATTER WHAT THE PUBLIC THINKS, THE DEATHS COMMITTED BY YOTSUBA SHOULD STOP.
IF YOU CONSIDER THAT MY ONE LIFE WILL SAVE SO MANY OTHERS...
DAD! WHAT ABOUT MOM AND SAYU?!
...
YAGAMI-SAN...
COULD YOU WAIT A MONTH ON THAT?

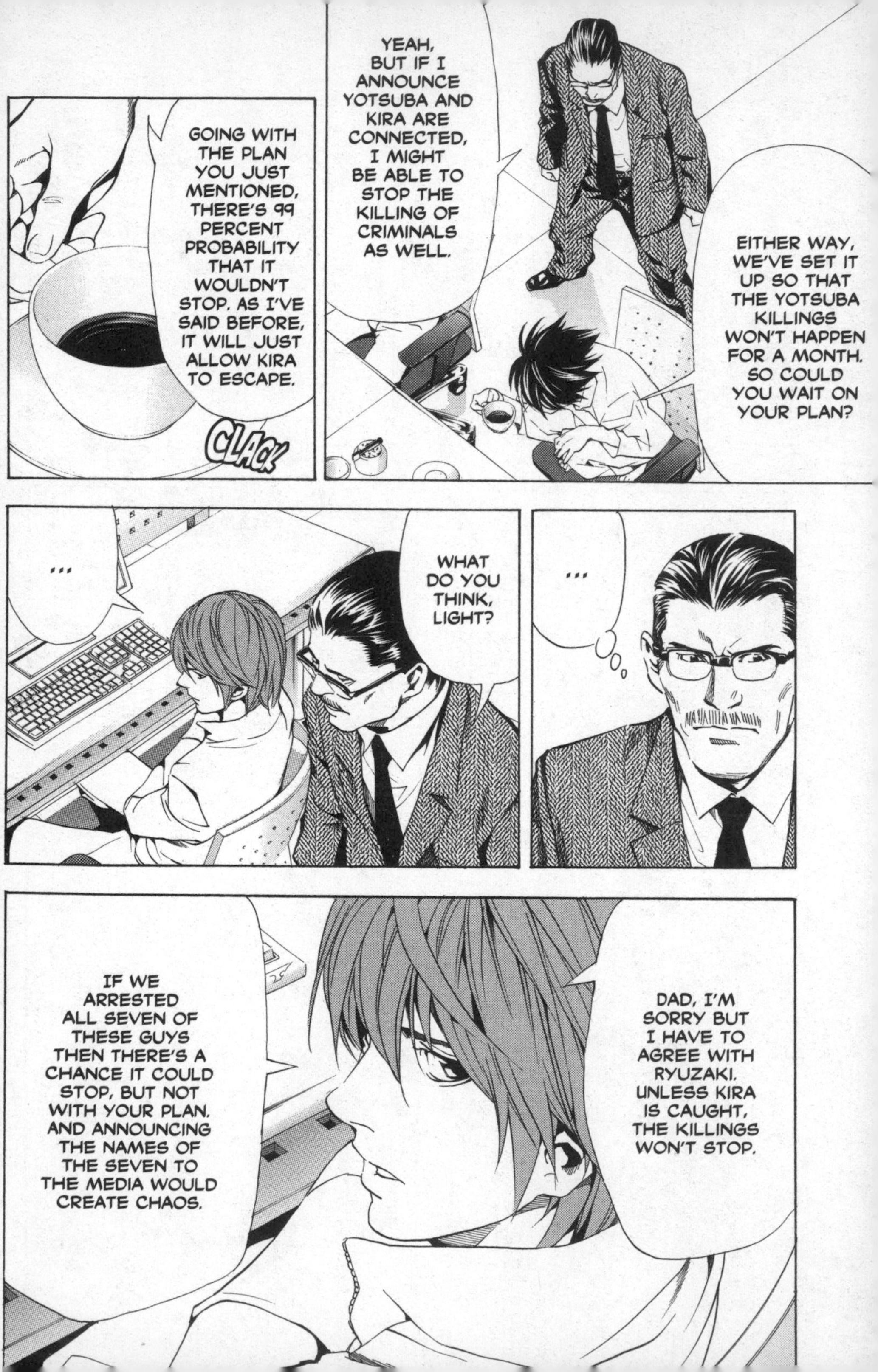
YEAH, BUT IF I ANNOUNCE YOTSUBA AND KIRA ARE CONNECTED, I MIGHT BE ABLE TO STOP THE KILLING OF CRIMINALS AS WELL.
EITHER WAY, WE'VE SET IT UP SO THAT THE YOTSUBA KILLINGS WON'T HAPPEN FOR A MONTH. SO COULD YOU WAIT ON YOUR PLAN?
GOING WITH THE PLAN YOU JUST MENTIONED, THERE'S 99 PERCENT PROBABILITY THAT IT WOULDN'T STOP. AS I'VE SAID BEFORE, IT WILL JUST ALLOW KIRA TO ESCAPE.
CLACK
...
WHAT DO YOU THINK, LIGHT?
...
DAD, I'M SORRY BUT I HAVE TO AGREE WITH RYUZAKI. UNLESS KIRA IS CAUGHT, THE KILLINGS WON'T STOP.
IF WE ARRESTED ALL SEVEN OF THESE GUYS THEN THERE'S A CHANCE IT COULD STOP, BUT NOT WITH YOUR PLAN. AND ANNOUNCING THE NAMES OF THE SEVEN TO THE MEDIA WOULD CREATE CHAOS.

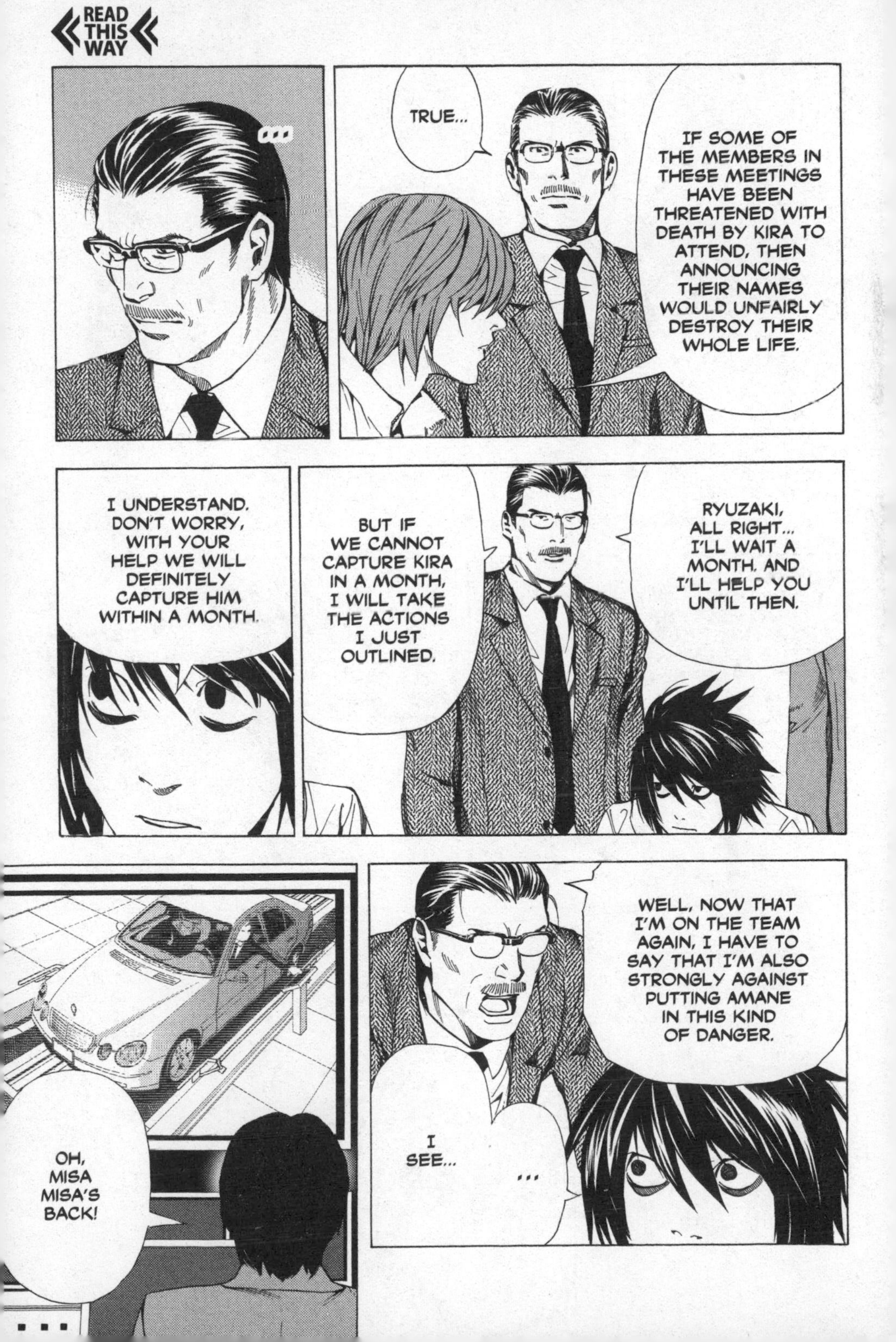
READ THIS WAY
IF SOME OF THE MEMBERS IN THESE MEETINGS HAVE BEEN THREATENED WITH DEATH BY KIRA TO ATTEND, THEN ANNOUNCING THEIR NAMES WOULD UNFAIRLY DESTROY THEIR WHOLE LIFE.
TRUE...
...
RYUZAKI, ALL RIGHT... I'LL WAIT A MONTH. AND I'LL HELP YOU UNTIL THEN.
BUT IF WE CANNOT CAPTURE KIRA IN A MONTH, I WILL TAKE THE ACTIONS I JUST OUTLINED.
I UNDERSTAND. DON'T WORRY, WITH YOUR HELP WE WILL DEFINITELY CAPTURE HIM WITHIN A MONTH.
WELL, NOW THAT I'M ON THE TEAM AGAIN, I HAVE TO SAY THAT I'M ALSO STRONGLY AGAINST PUTTING AMANE IN THIS KIND OF DANGER.
I SEE...
...
OH, MISA MISA'S BACK!
...

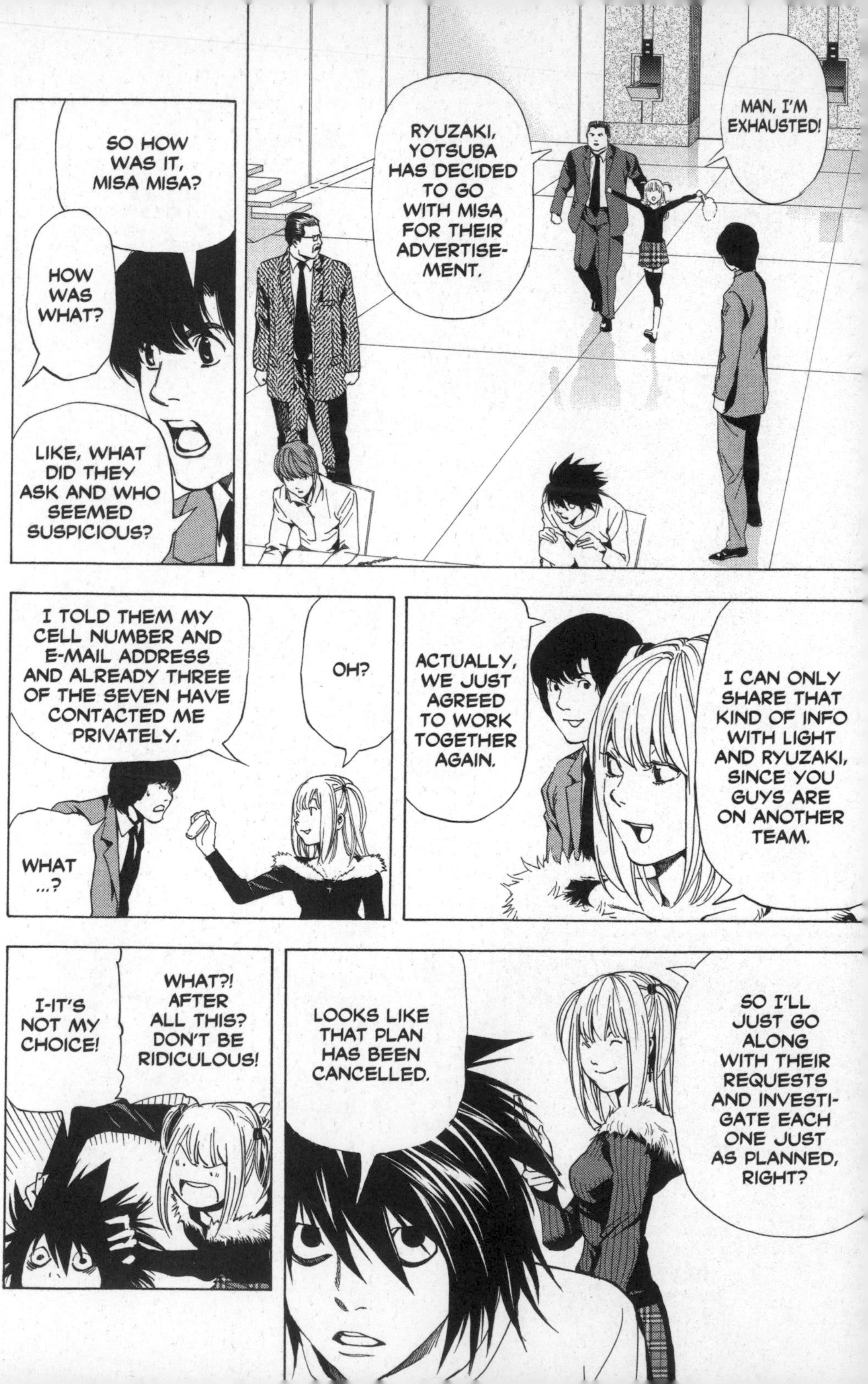
MAN, I'M EXHAUSTED!
RYUZAKI, YOTSUBA HAS DECIDED TO GO WITH MISA FOR THEIR ADVERTISE-MENT.
SO HOW WAS IT, MISA MISA?
HOW WAS WHAT?
LIKE, WHAT DID THEY ASK AND WHO SEEMED SUSPICIOUS?
I CAN ONLY SHARE THAT KIND OF INFO WITH LIGHT AND RYUZAKI, SINCE YOU GUYS ARE ON ANOTHER TEAM.
ACTUALLY, WE JUST AGREED TO WORK TOGETHER AGAIN.
OH?
I TOLD THEM MY CELL NUMBER AND E-MAIL ADDRESS AND ALREADY THREE OF THE SEVEN HAVE CONTACTED ME PRIVATELY.
WHAT ...?
SO I'LL JUST GO ALONG WITH THEIR REQUESTS AND INVESTI-GATE EACH ONE JUST AS PLANNED, RIGHT?
LOOKS LIKE THAT PLAN HAS BEEN CANCELLED.
WHAT?! AFTER ALL THIS? DON'T BE RIDICULOUS!
I-IT'S NOT MY CHOICE!

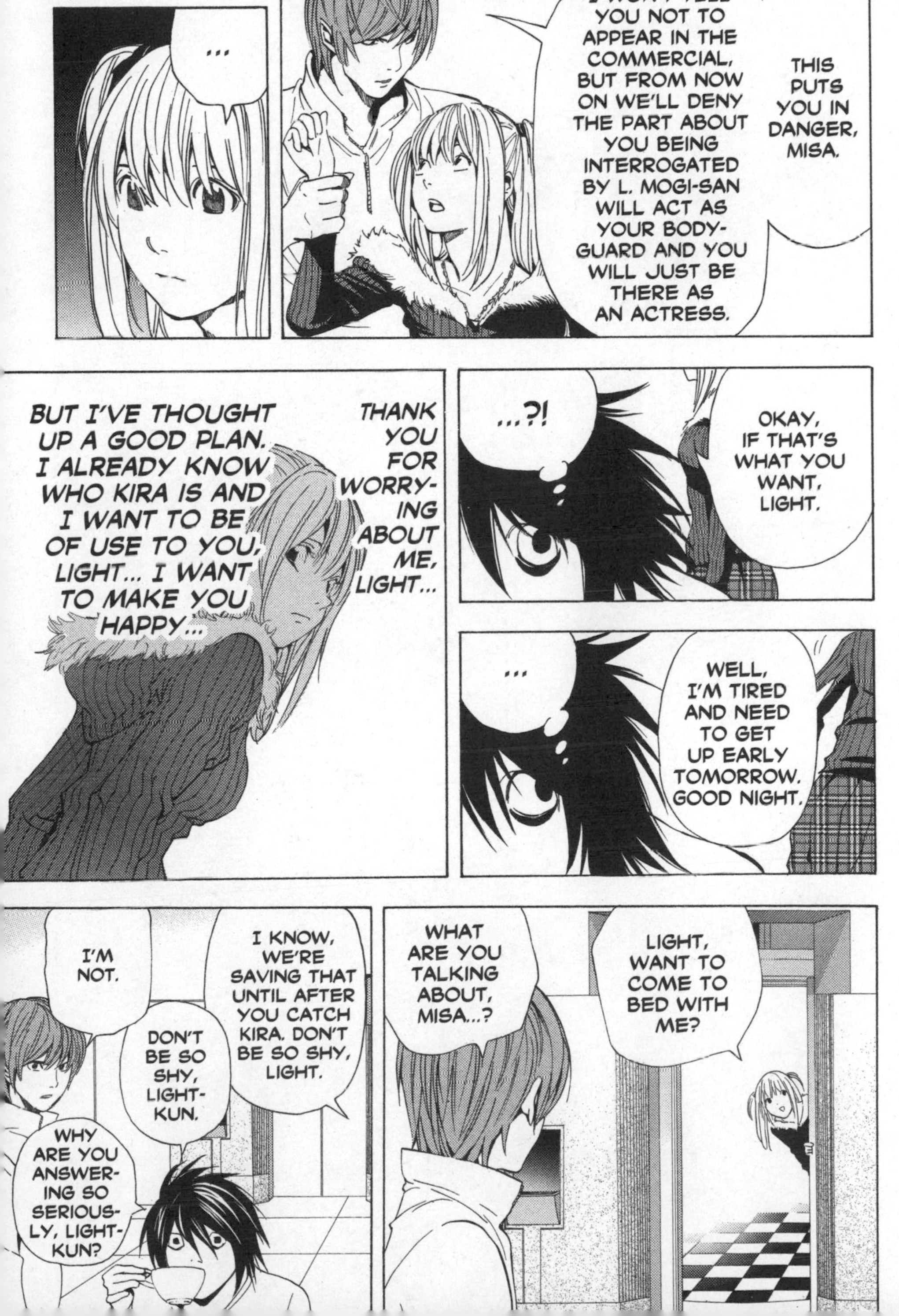
THIS PUTS YOU IN DANGER, MISA.
I WON'T TELL YOU NOT TO APPEAR IN THE COMMERCIAL, BUT FROM NOW ON WE'LL DENY THE PART ABOUT YOU BEING INTERROGATED BY L. MOGI-SAN WILL ACT AS YOUR BODY-GUARD AND YOU WILL JUST BE THERE AS AN ACTRESS.
...
OKAY, IF THAT'S WHAT YOU WANT, LIGHT.
...?!
WELL, I'M TIRED AND NEED TO GET UP EARLY TOMORROW. GOOD NIGHT.
...
THANK YOU FOR WORRY-ING ABOUT ME, LIGHT...
BUT I'VE THOUGHT UP A GOOD PLAN. I ALREADY KNOW WHO KIRA IS AND I WANT TO BE OF USE TO YOU, LIGHT... I WANT TO MAKE YOU HAPPY...
LIGHT, WANT TO COME TO BED WITH ME?
WHAT ARE YOU TALKING ABOUT, MISA...?
I KNOW, WE'RE SAVING THAT UNTIL AFTER YOU CATCH KIRA. DON'T BE SO SHY, LIGHT.
I'M NOT.
DON'T BE SO SHY, LIGHT-KUN.
WHY ARE YOU ANSWER-ING SO SERIOUS-LY, LIGHT-KUN?

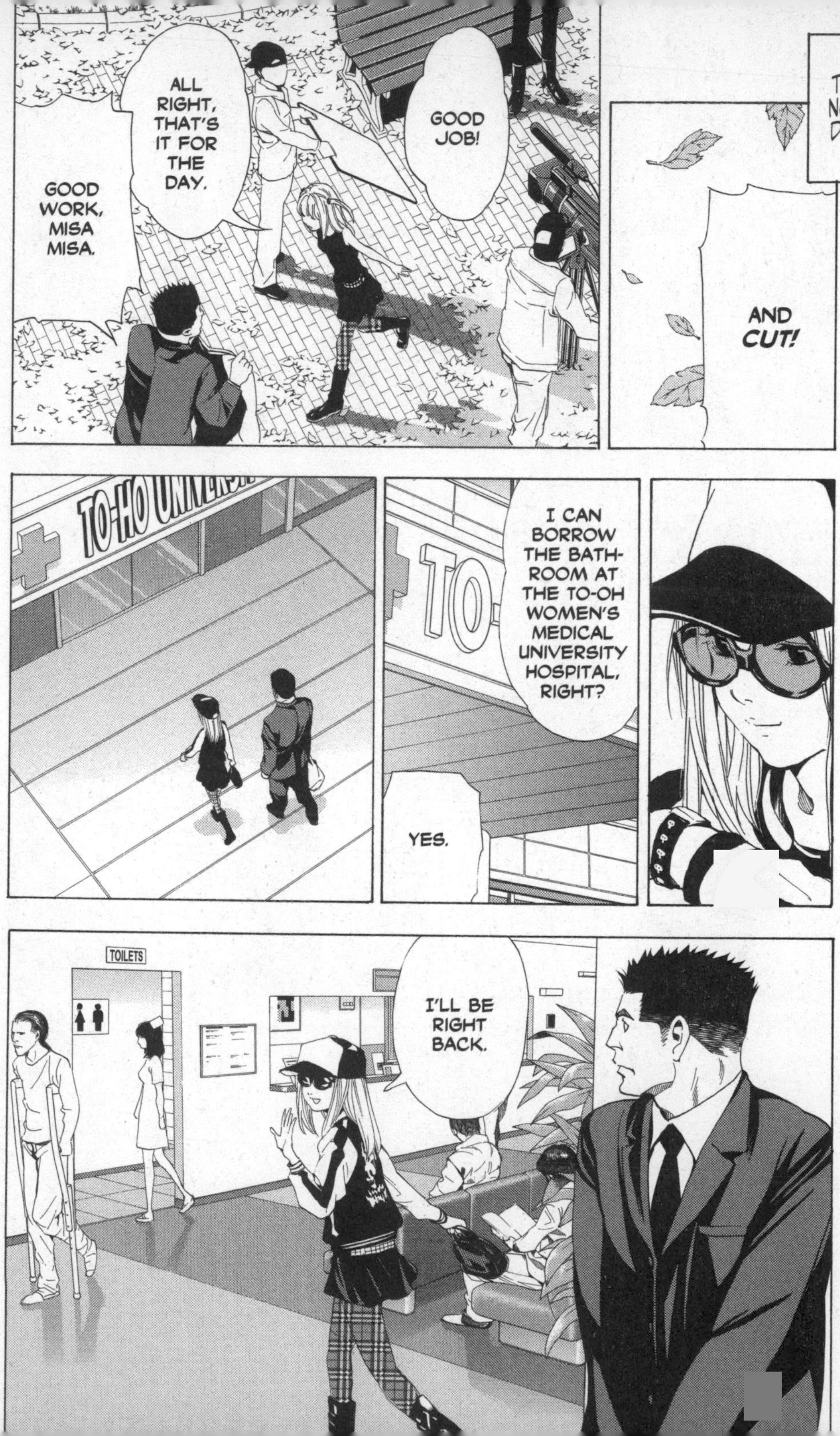
The Next Day
AND CUT!
GOOD JOB!
ALL RIGHT, THAT'S IT FOR THE DAY.
GOOD WORK, MISA MISA.
I CAN BORROW THE BATHROOM AT THE TO-OH WOMEN'S MEDICAL UNIVERSITY HOSPITAL, RIGHT?
YES.
TOILETS
I'LL BE RIGHT BACK.

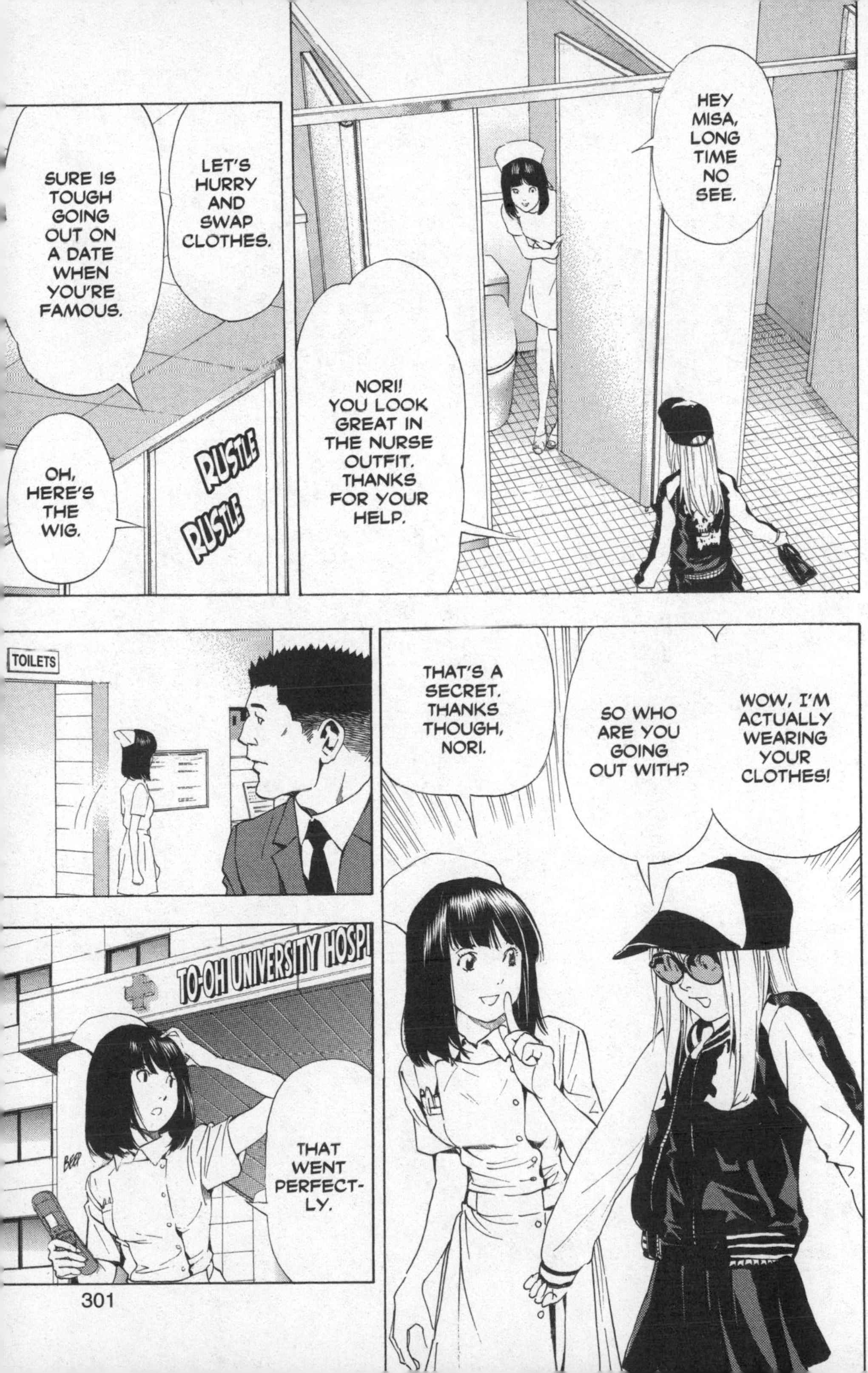
HEY MISA, LONG TIME NO SEE.
NORI! YOU LOOK GREAT IN THE NURSE OUTFIT. THANKS FOR YOUR HELP.
LET'S HURRY AND SWAP CLOTHES.
SURE IS TOUGH GOING OUT ON A DATE WHEN YOU'RE FAMOUS.
RUSTLE
RUSTLE
OH, HERE'S THE WIG.
WOW, I'M ACTUALLY WEARING YOUR CLOTHES!
SO WHO ARE YOU GOING OUT WITH?
THAT'S A SECRET. THANKS THOUGH, NORI.
TOILETS
TO-OH UNIVERSITY HOSPI
BEEP
THAT WENT PERFECT-LY.

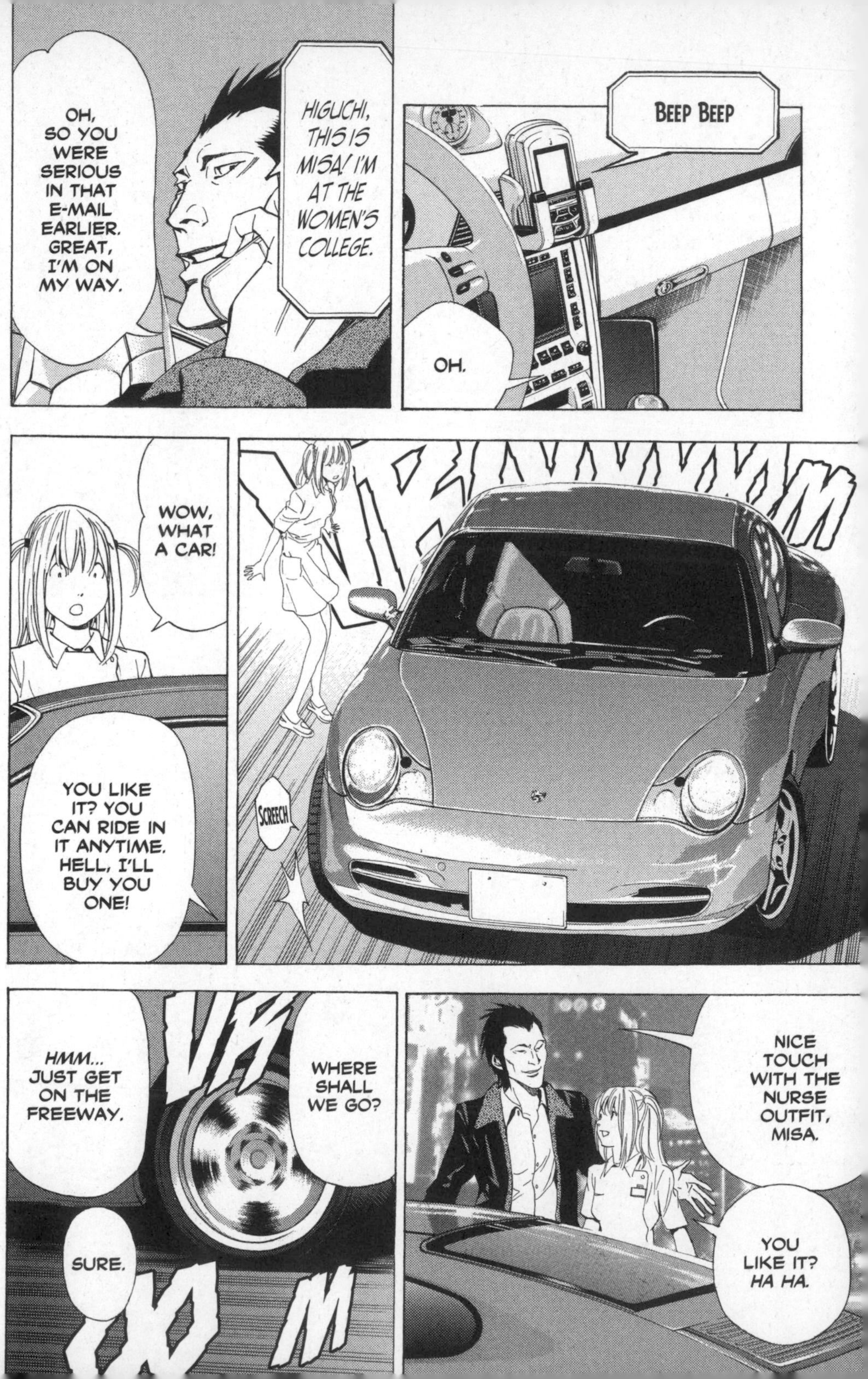
Beep Beep
OH.
HIGUCHI, THIS IS MISA! I'M AT THE WOMEN'S COLLEGE.
OH, SO YOU WERE SERIOUS IN THAT E-MAIL EARLIER. GREAT, I'M ON MY WAY.
SCREECH
WOW, WHAT A CAR!
YOU LIKE IT? YOU CAN RIDE IN IT ANYTIME. HELL, I'LL BUY YOU ONE!
NICE TOUCH WITH THE NURSE OUTFIT, MISA.
YOU LIKE IT? HA HA.
WHERE SHALL WE GO?
HMM... JUST GET ON THE FREEWAY.
SURE.

READ THIS WAY

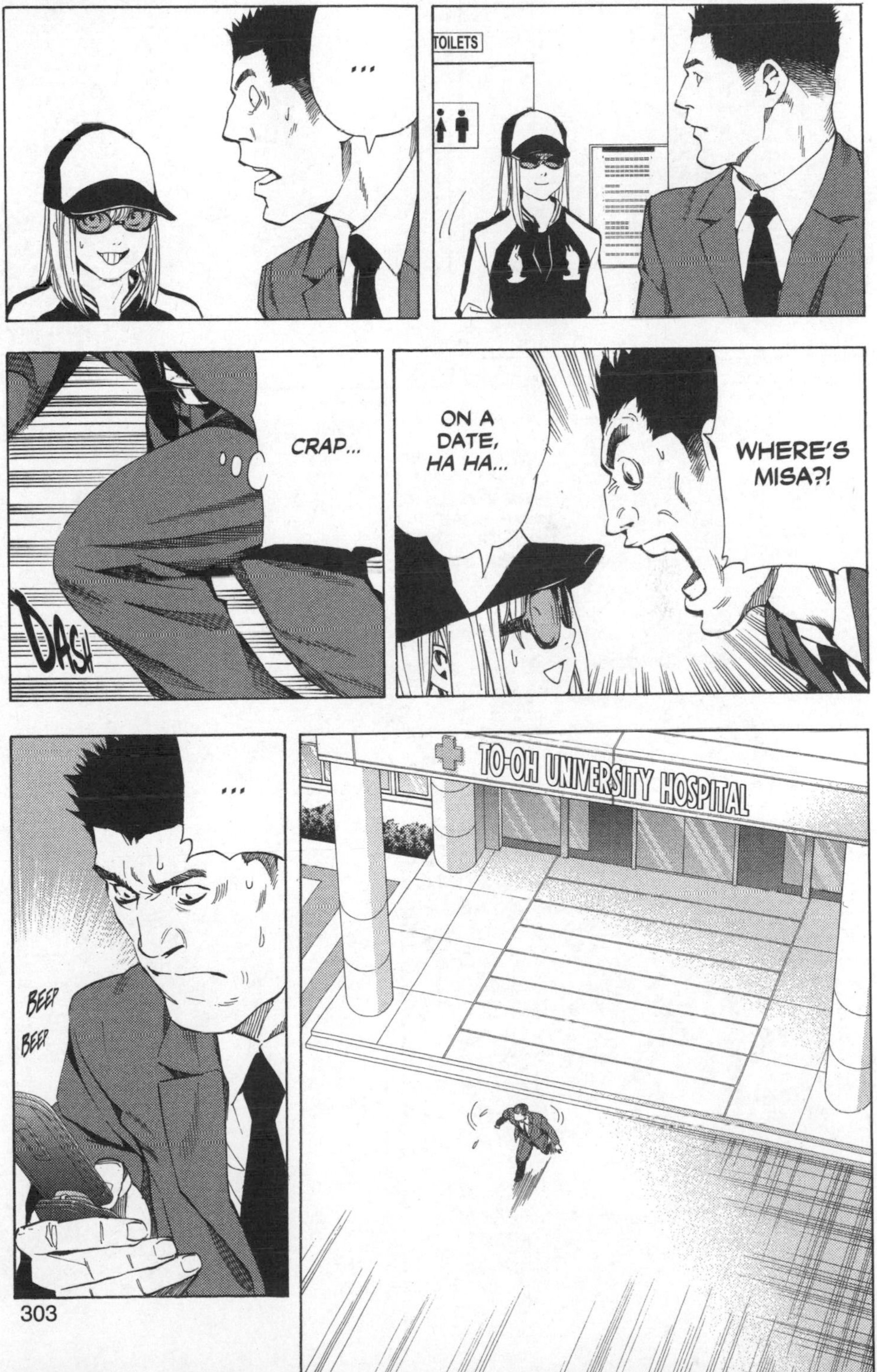
TOILETS
...
WHERE'S MISA?!
ON A DATE, HA HA...
CRAP...
DASH
TO-OH UNIVERSITY HOSPITAL
...
BEEP BEEP

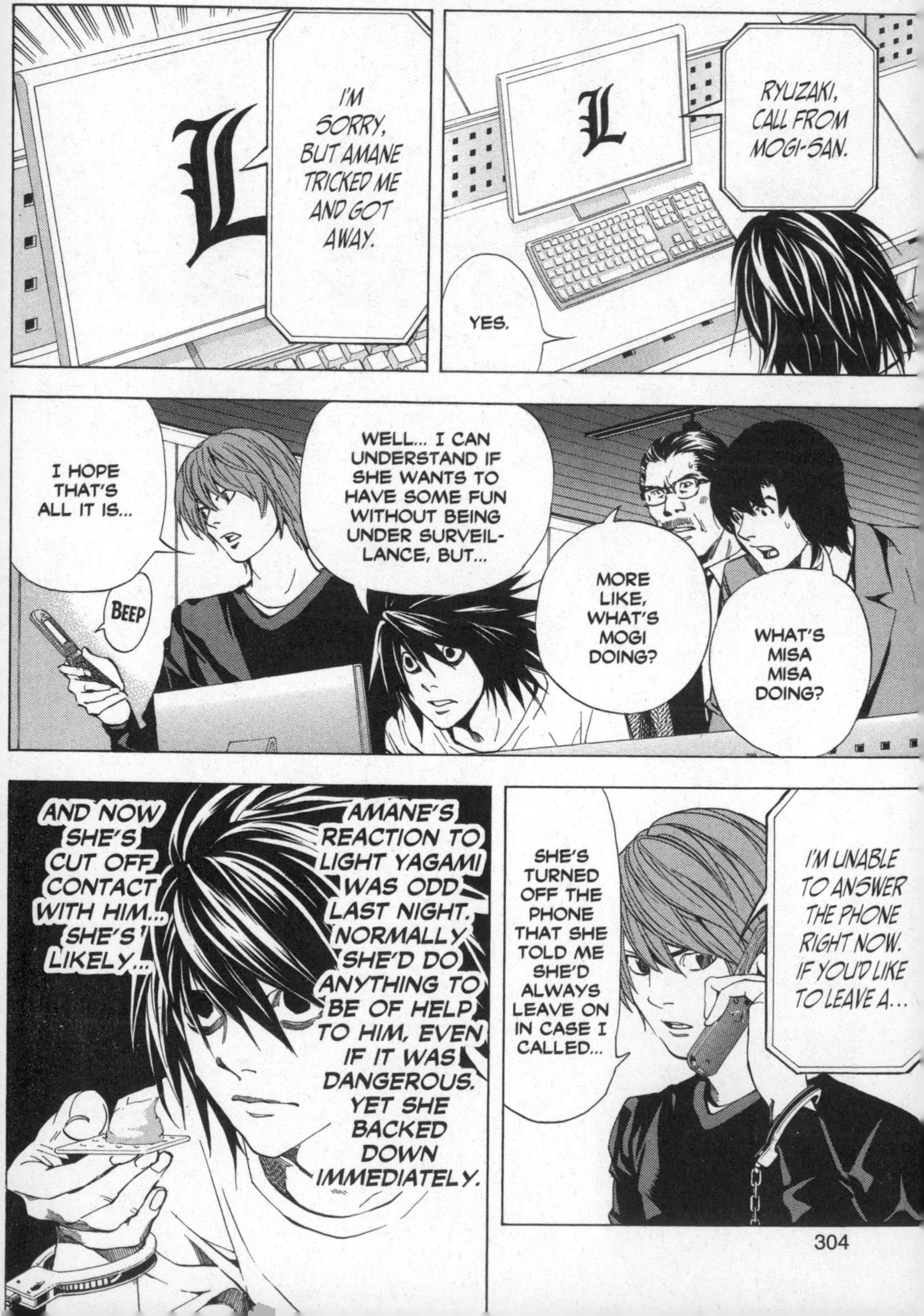
RYUZAKI, CALL FROM MOGI-SAN.
YES.
I'M SORRY, BUT AMANE TRICKED ME AND GOT AWAY.
WHAT'S MISA MISA DOING?
MORE LIKE, WHAT'S MOGI DOING?
WELL... I CAN UNDERSTAND IF SHE WANTS TO HAVE SOME FUN WITHOUT BEING UNDER SURVEIL-LANCE, BUT...
I HOPE THAT'S ALL IT IS...
BEEP
I'M UNABLE TO ANSWER THE PHONE RIGHT NOW. IF YOU'D LIKE TO LEAVE A...
SHE'S TURNED OFF THE PHONE THAT SHE TOLD ME SHE'D ALWAYS LEAVE ON IN CASE I CALLED...
AMANE'S REACTION TO LIGHT YAGAMI WAS ODD LAST NIGHT. NORMALLY SHE'D DO ANYTHING TO BE OF HELP TO HIM, EVEN IF IT WAS DANGEROUS. YET SHE BACKED DOWN IMMEDIATELY.
AND NOW SHE'S CUT OFF CONTACT WITH HIM... SHE'S LIKELY...

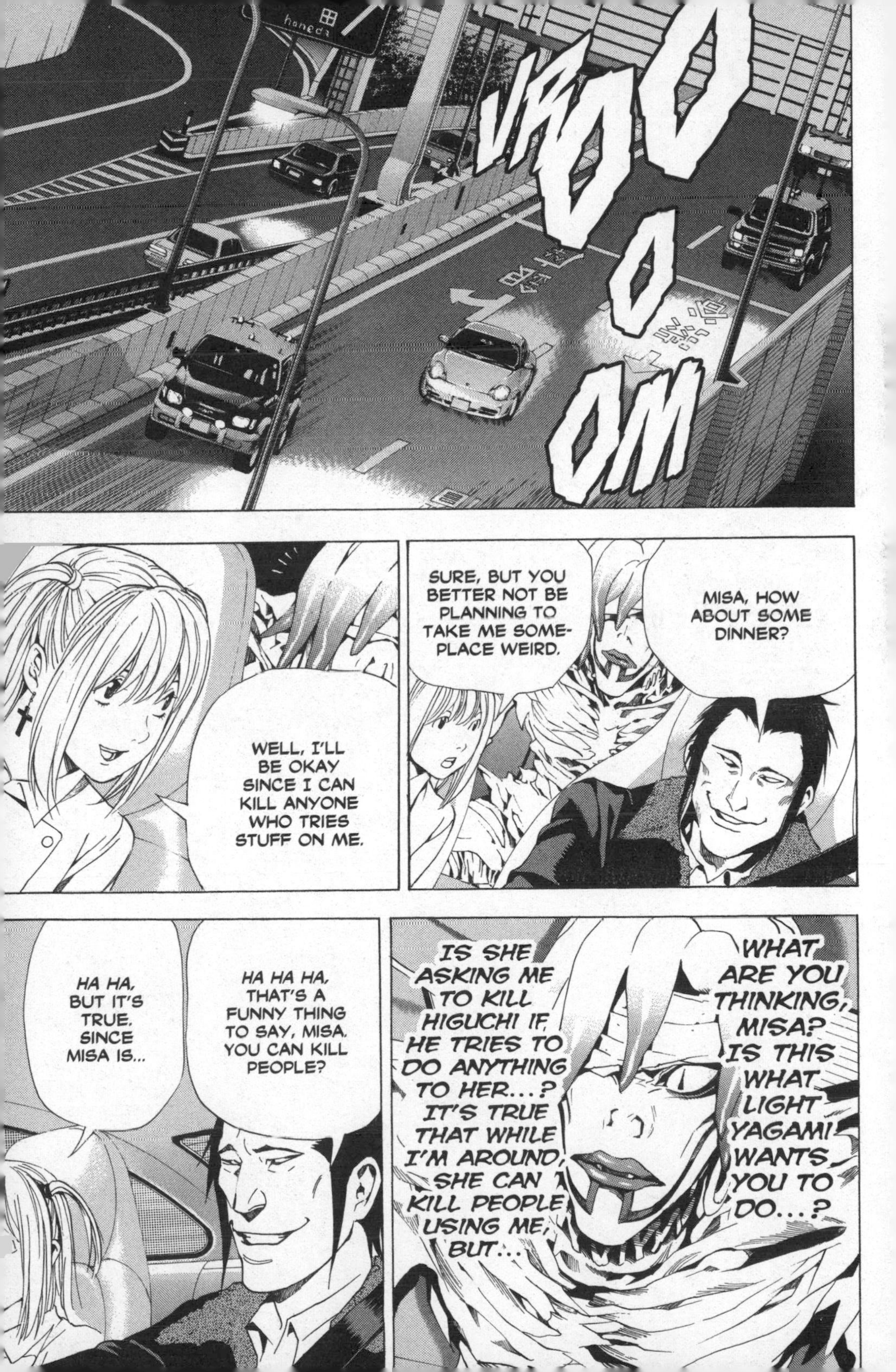
haneda
VROOOOOM
MISA, HOW ABOUT SOME DINNER?
SURE, BUT YOU BETTER NOT BE PLANNING TO TAKE ME SOME-PLACE WEIRD.
WELL, I'LL BE OKAY SINCE I CAN KILL ANYONE WHO TRIES STUFF ON ME.
WHAT ARE YOU THINKING, MISA? IS THIS WHAT LIGHT YAGAMI WANTS YOU TO DO...?
IS SHE ASKING ME TO KILL HIGUCHI IF HE TRIES TO DO ANYTHING TO HER...? IT'S TRUE THAT WHILE I'M AROUND, SHE CAN KILL PEOPLE USING ME, BUT...
HA HA HA, THAT'S A FUNNY THING TO SAY, MISA. YOU CAN KILL PEOPLE?
HA HA, BUT IT'S TRUE. SINCE MISA IS...

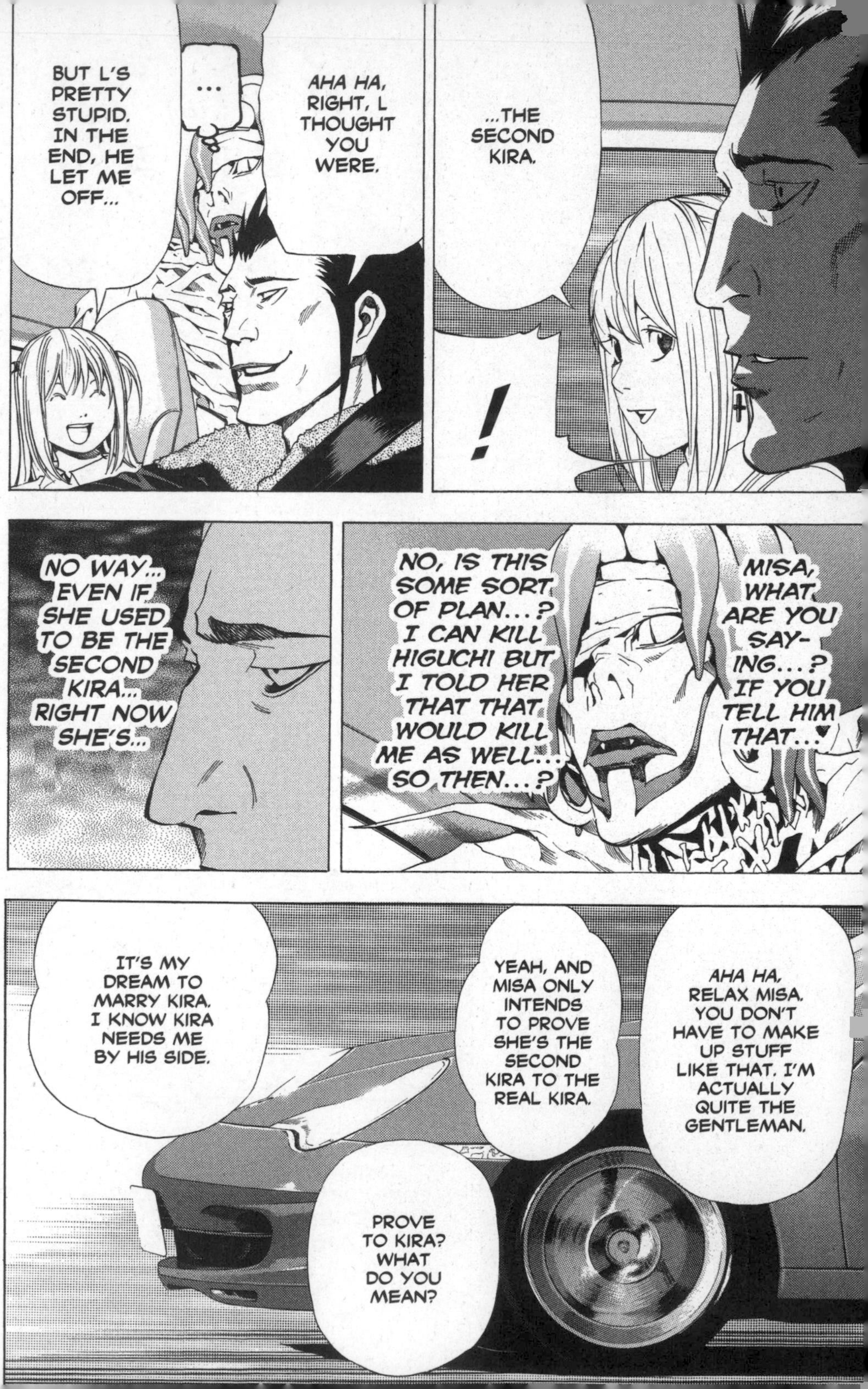
...THE SECOND KIRA.
!
AHA HA, RIGHT, L THOUGHT YOU WERE.
...
BUT L'S PRETTY STUPID. IN THE END, HE LET ME OFF...
MISA, WHAT ARE YOU SAYING...? IF YOU TELL HIM THAT...
NO, IS THIS SOME SORT OF PLAN...? I CAN KILL HIGUCHI BUT I TOLD HER THAT THAT WOULD KILL ME AS WELL... SO THEN...?
NO WAY... EVEN IF SHE USED TO BE THE SECOND KIRA... RIGHT NOW SHE'S...
AHA HA, RELAX MISA. YOU DON'T HAVE TO MAKE UP STUFF LIKE THAT. I'M ACTUALLY QUITE THE GENTLEMAN.
YEAH, AND MISA ONLY INTENDS TO PROVE SHE'S THE SECOND KIRA TO THE REAL KIRA.
PROVE TO KIRA? WHAT DO YOU MEAN?
IT'S MY DREAM TO MARRY KIRA. I KNOW KIRA NEEDS ME BY HIS SIDE.

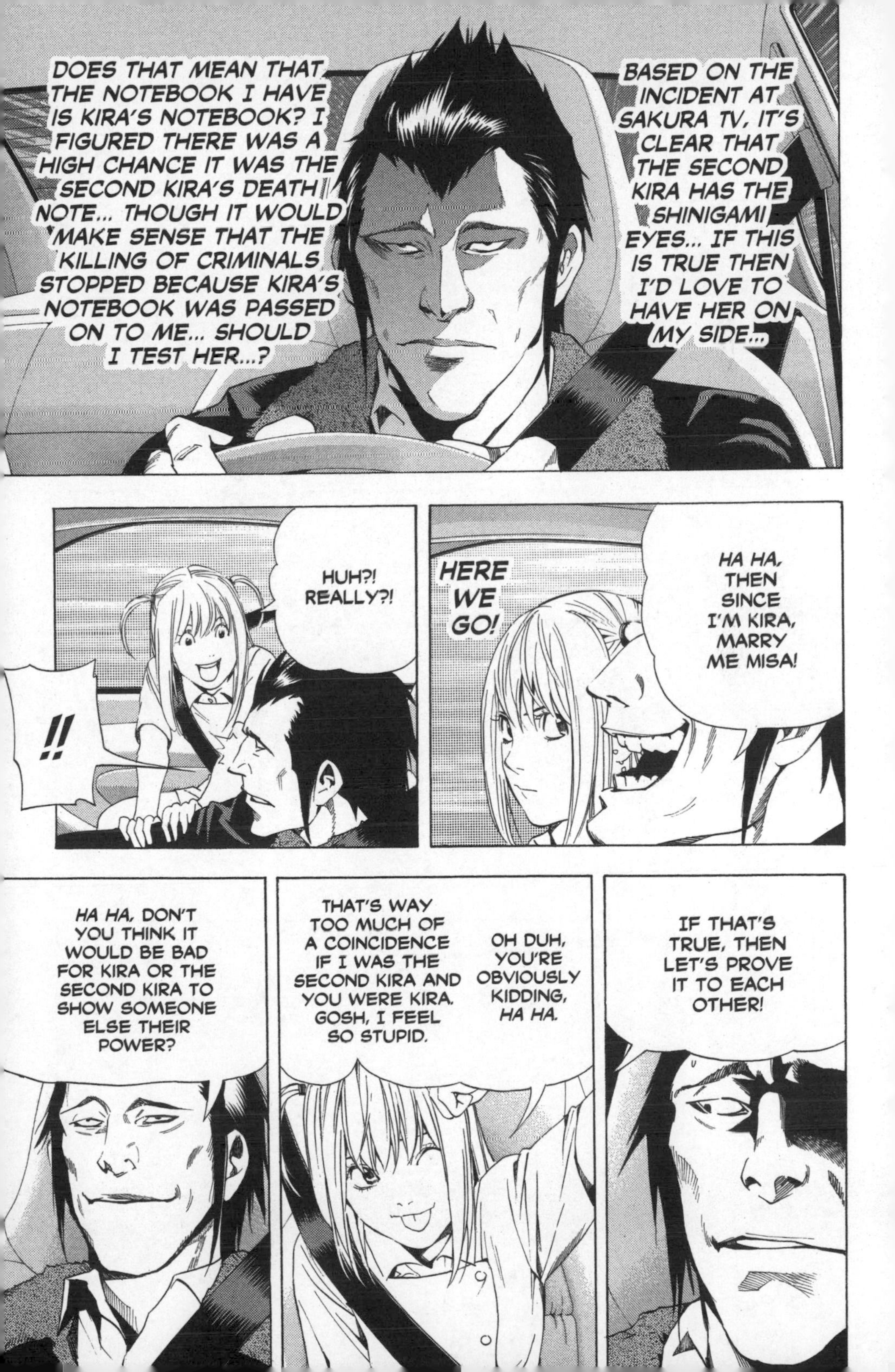
BASED ON THE INCIDENT AT SAKURA TV, IT'S CLEAR THAT THE SECOND KIRA HAS THE SHINIGAMI EYES... IF THIS IS TRUE THEN I'D LOVE TO HAVE HER ON MY SIDE...
DOES THAT MEAN THAT THE NOTEBOOK I HAVE IS KIRA'S NOTEBOOK? I FIGURED THERE WAS A HIGH CHANCE IT WAS THE SECOND KIRA'S DEATH NOTE... THOUGH IT WOULD MAKE SENSE THAT THE KILLING OF CRIMINALS STOPPED BECAUSE KIRA'S NOTEBOOK WAS PASSED ON TO ME... SHOULD I TEST HER...?
HA HA, THEN SINCE I'M KIRA, MARRY ME MISA!
HERE WE GO!
HUH?! REALLY?!
!!
IF THAT'S TRUE, THEN LET'S PROVE IT TO EACH OTHER!
OH DUH, YOU'RE OBVIOUSLY KIDDING, HA HA.
THAT'S WAY TOO MUCH OF A COINCIDENCE IF I WAS THE SECOND KIRA AND YOU WERE KIRA. GOSH, I FEEL SO STUPID.
HA HA, DON'T YOU THINK IT WOULD BE BAD FOR KIRA OR THE SECOND KIRA TO SHOW SOMEONE ELSE THEIR POWER?

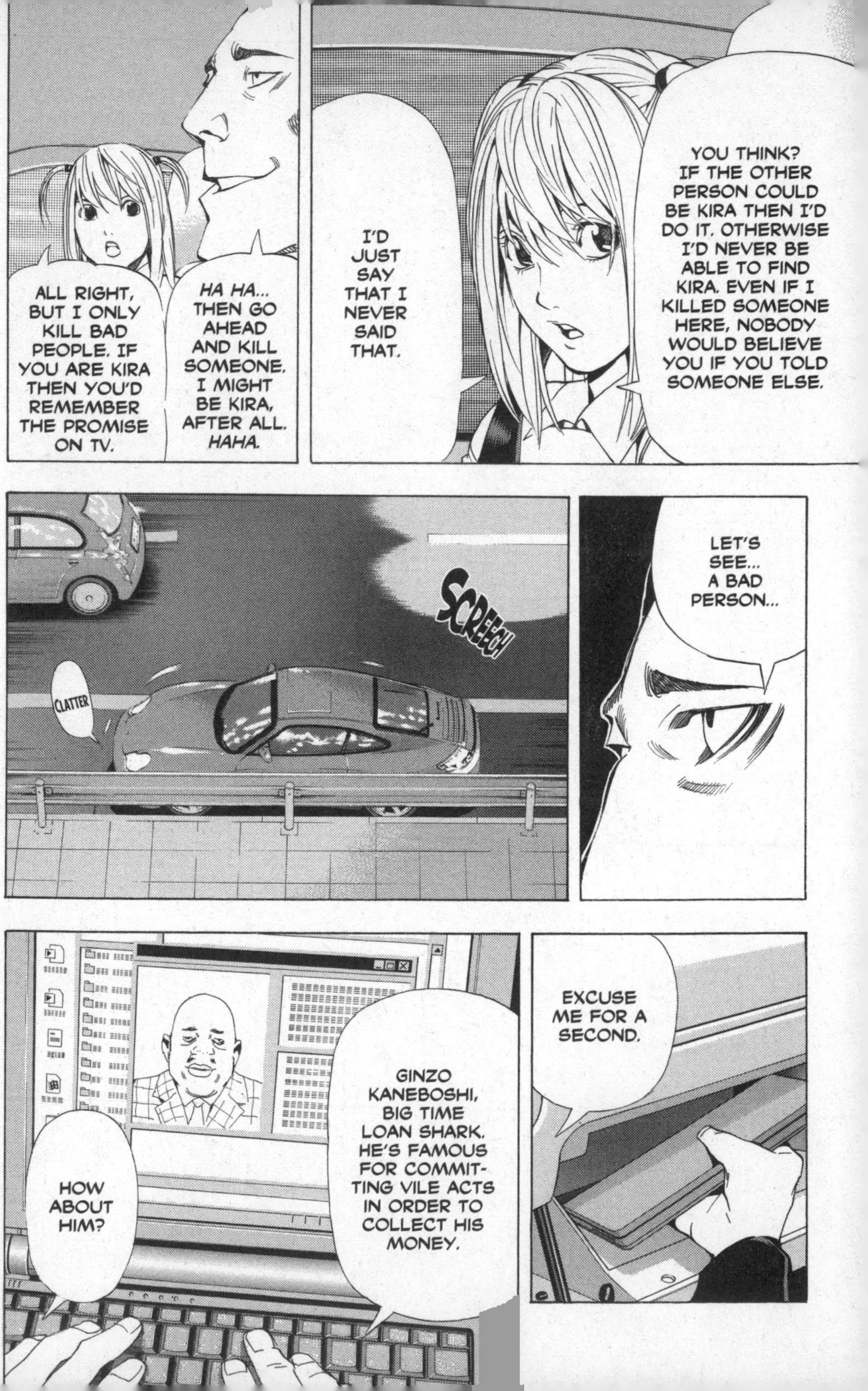
YOU THINK? IF THE OTHER PERSON COULD BE KIRA THEN I'D DO IT. OTHERWISE I'D NEVER BE ABLE TO FIND KIRA. EVEN IF I KILLED SOMEONE HERE, NOBODY WOULD BELIEVE YOU IF YOU TOLD SOMEONE ELSE.
I'D JUST SAY THAT I NEVER SAID THAT.
HA HA... THEN GO AHEAD AND KILL SOMEONE. I MIGHT BE KIRA, AFTER ALL. *HAHA*.
ALL RIGHT, BUT I ONLY KILL BAD PEOPLE. IF YOU ARE KIRA THEN YOU'D REMEMBER THE PROMISE ON TV.
LET'S SEE... A BAD PERSON...
SCREECH
CLATTER
EXCUSE ME FOR A SECOND.
GINZO KANEBOSHI, BIG TIME LOAN SHARK. HE'S FAMOUS FOR COMMIT-TING VILE ACTS IN ORDER TO COLLECT HIS MONEY.
HOW ABOUT HIM?

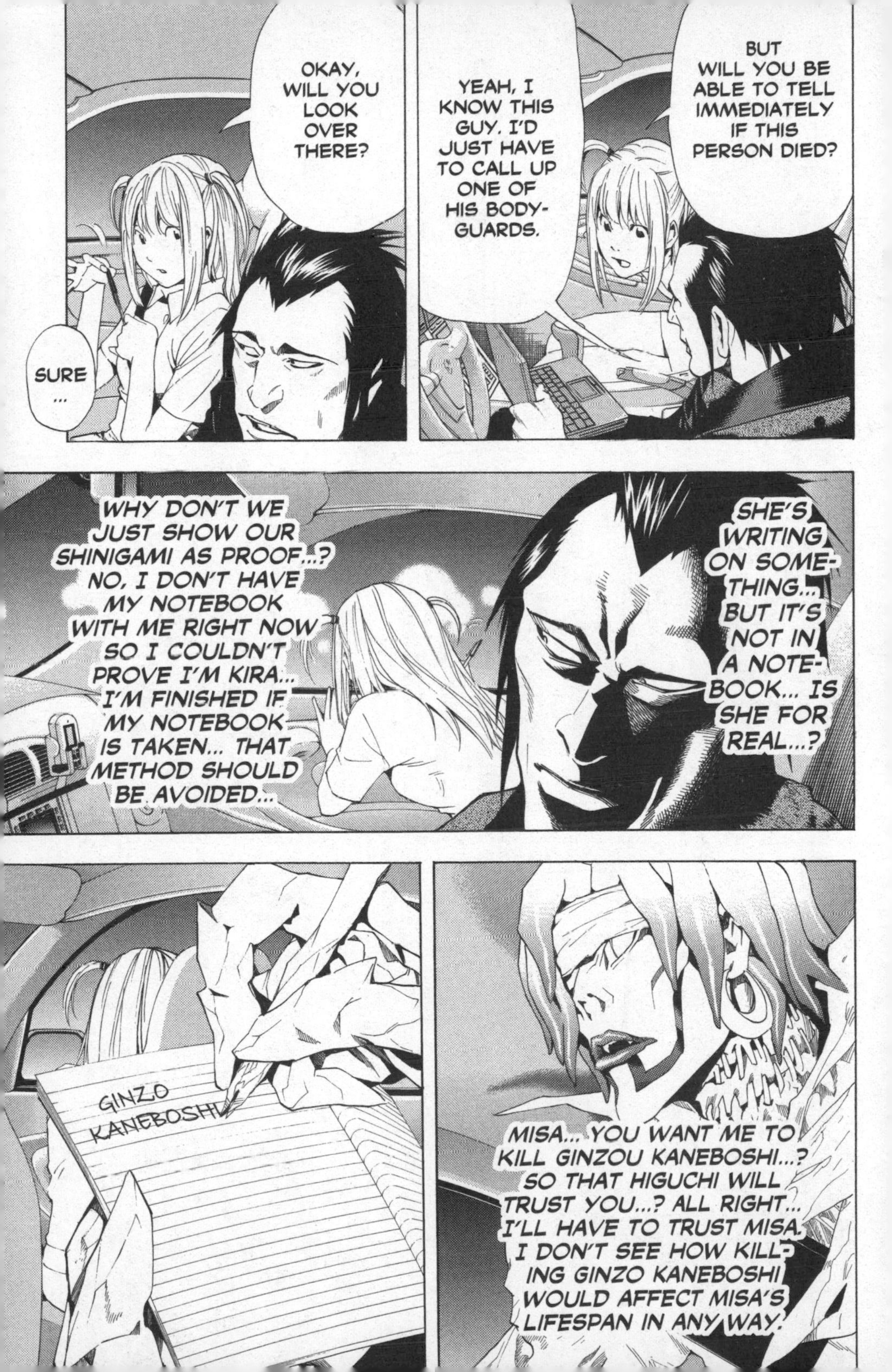
BUT WILL YOU BE ABLE TO TELL IMMEDIATELY IF THIS PERSON DIED?
YEAH, I KNOW THIS GUY. I'D JUST HAVE TO CALL UP ONE OF HIS BODY-GUARDS.
OKAY, WILL YOU LOOK OVER THERE?
SURE ...
SHE'S WRITING ON SOME-THING... BUT IT'S NOT IN A NOTE-BOOK... IS SHE FOR REAL...?
WHY DON'T WE JUST SHOW OUR SHINIGAMI AS PROOF...? NO, I DON'T HAVE MY NOTEBOOK WITH ME RIGHT NOW SO I COULDN'T PROVE I'M KIRA... I'M FINISHED IF MY NOTEBOOK IS TAKEN... THAT METHOD SHOULD BE AVOIDED...
MISA... YOU WANT ME TO KILL GINZOU KANEBOSHI...? SO THAT HIGUCHI WILL TRUST YOU...? ALL RIGHT... I'LL HAVE TO TRUST MISA. I DON'T SEE HOW KILL-ING GINZO KANEBOSHI WOULD AFFECT MISA'S LIFESPAN IN ANY WAY.
GINZO KANEBOSHI

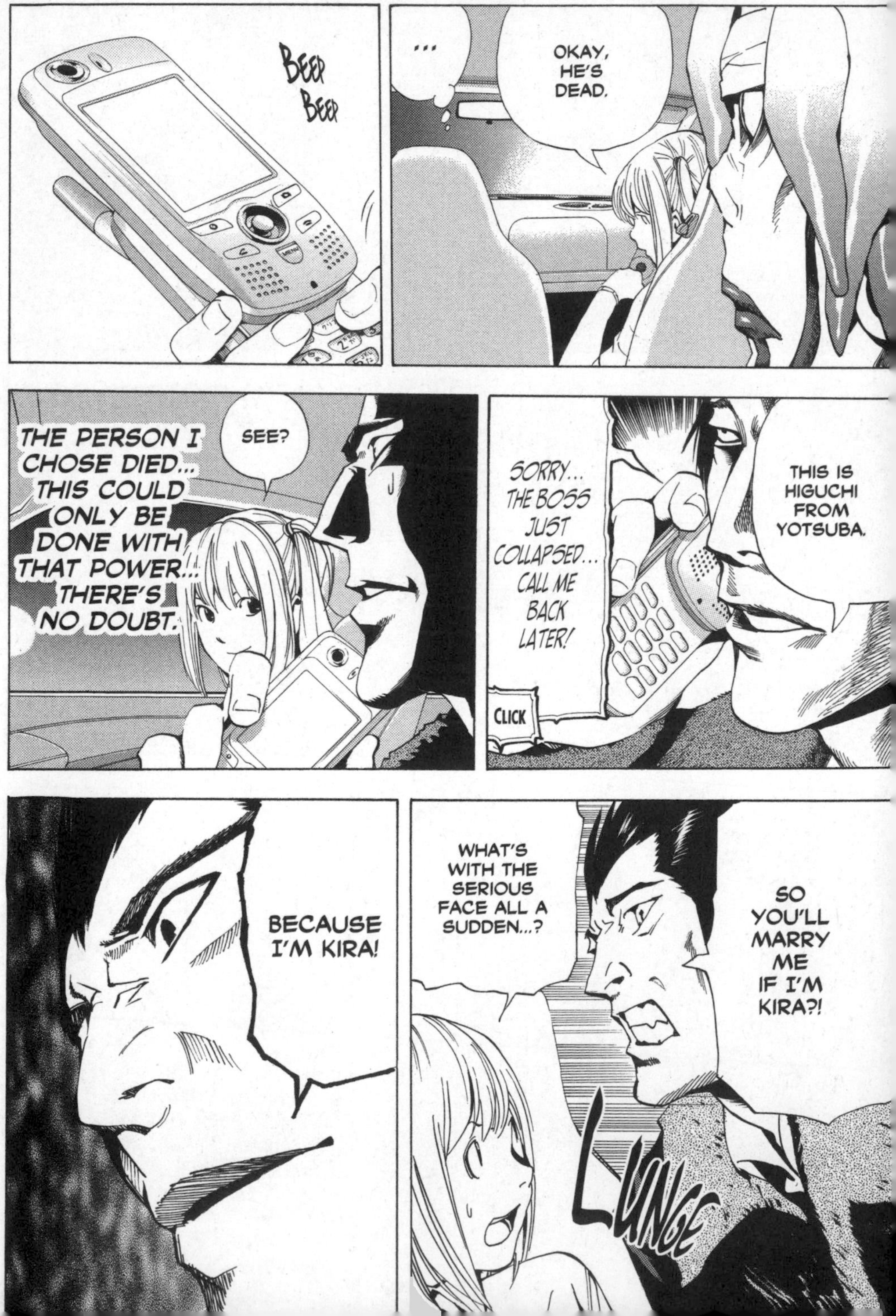
OKAY, HE'S DEAD.
...
BEEP BEEP
THIS IS HIGUCHI FROM YOTSUBA.
SORRY... THE BOSS JUST COLLAPSED... CALL ME BACK LATER!
CLICK
SEE?
THE PERSON I CHOSE DIED... THIS COULD ONLY BE DONE WITH THAT POWER... THERE'S NO DOUBT.
SO YOU'LL MARRY ME IF I'M KIRA?!
WHAT'S WITH THE SERIOUS FACE ALL A SUDDEN...?
LUNGE
BECAUSE I'M KIRA!

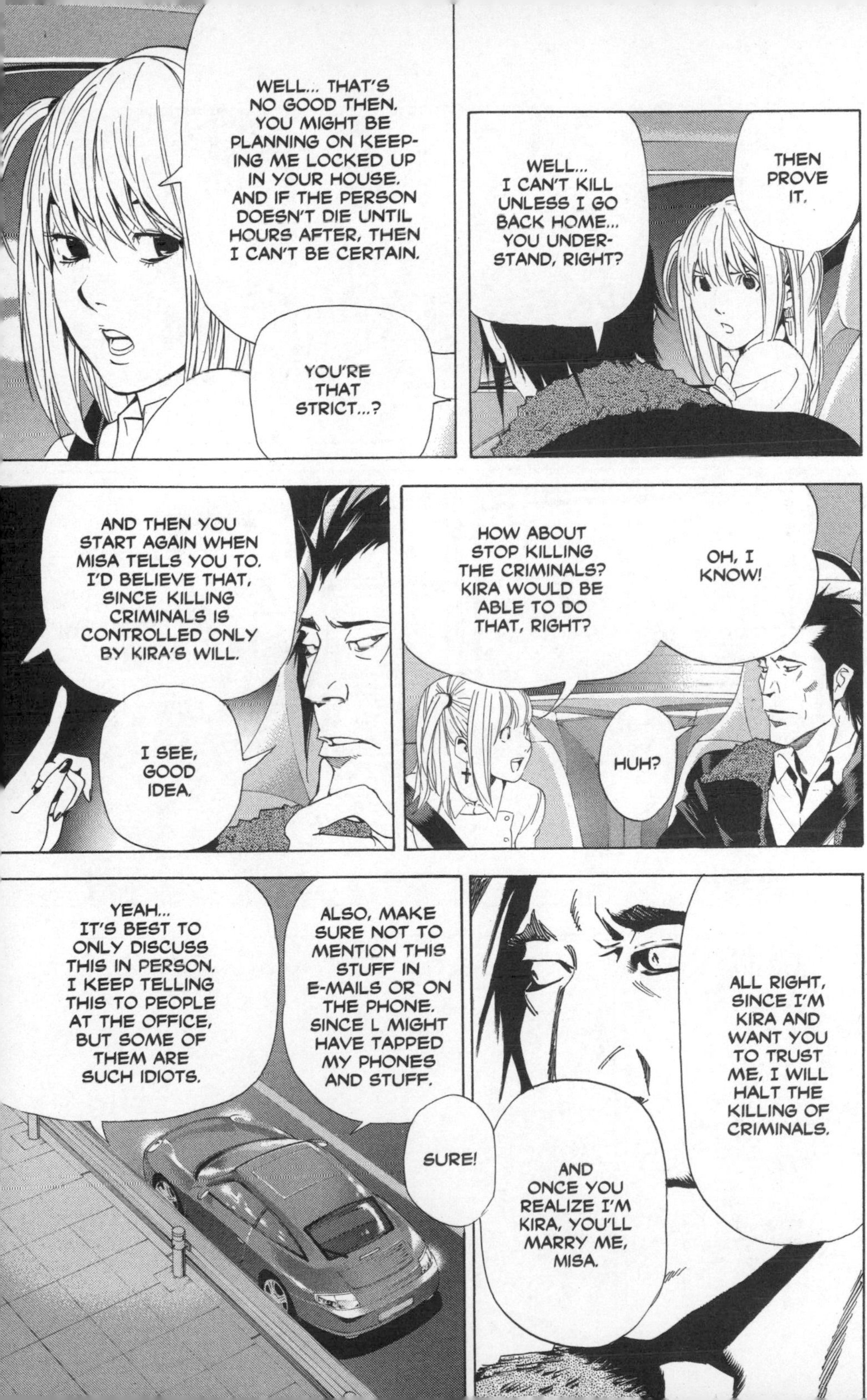

THEN PROVE IT.
WELL... I CAN'T KILL UNLESS I GO BACK HOME... YOU UNDER-STAND, RIGHT?
WELL... THAT'S NO GOOD THEN. YOU MIGHT BE PLANNING ON KEEP-ING ME LOCKED UP IN YOUR HOUSE. AND IF THE PERSON DOESN'T DIE UNTIL HOURS AFTER, THEN I CAN'T BE CERTAIN.
YOU'RE THAT STRICT...?
OH, I KNOW!
HOW ABOUT STOP KILLING THE CRIMINALS? KIRA WOULD BE ABLE TO DO THAT, RIGHT?
HUH?
AND THEN YOU START AGAIN WHEN MISA TELLS YOU TO. I'D BELIEVE THAT, SINCE KILLING CRIMINALS IS CONTROLLED ONLY BY KIRA'S WILL.
I SEE, GOOD IDEA.
ALL RIGHT, SINCE I'M KIRA AND WANT YOU TO TRUST ME, I WILL HALT THE KILLING OF CRIMINALS.
AND ONCE YOU REALIZE I'M KIRA, YOU'LL MARRY ME, MISA.
SURE!
ALSO, MAKE SURE NOT TO MENTION THIS STUFF IN E-MAILS OR ON THE PHONE. SINCE L MIGHT HAVE TAPPED MY PHONES AND STUFF.
YEAH... IT'S BEST TO ONLY DISCUSS THIS IN PERSON. I KEEP TELLING THIS TO PEOPLE AT THE OFFICE, BUT SOME OF THEM ARE SUCH IDIOTS.

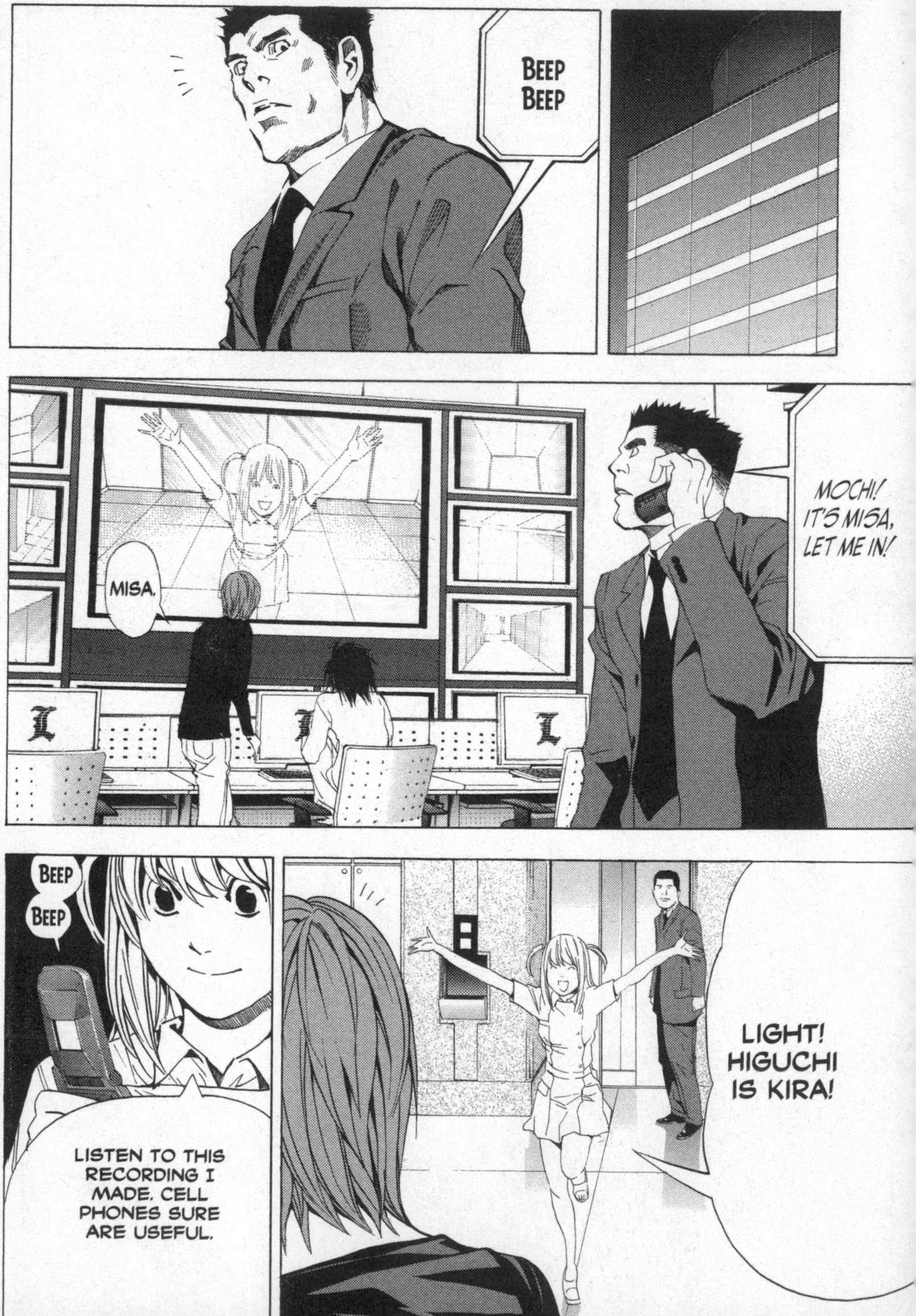
BEEP BEEP
MOCHI! IT'S MISA, LET ME IN!
MISA.
LIGHT! HIGUCHI IS KIRA!
BEEP BEEP
LISTEN TO THIS RECORDING I MADE. CELL PHONES SURE ARE USEFUL.

READ THIS WAY

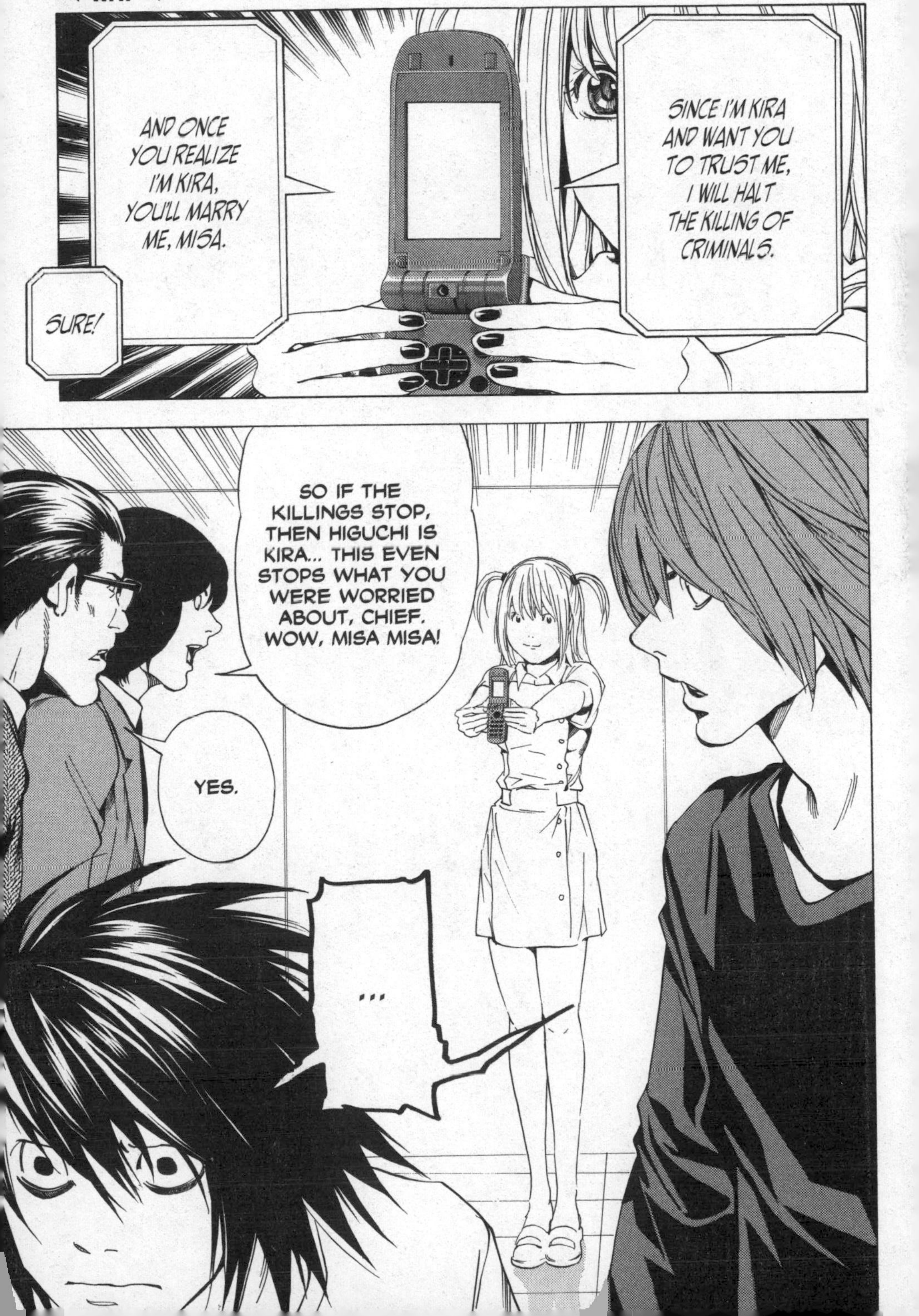

SINCE I'M KIRA AND WANT YOU TO TRUST ME, I WILL HALT THE KILLING OF CRIMINALS.
AND ONCE YOU REALIZE I'M KIRA, YOU'LL MARRY ME, MISA.
SURE!
SO IF THE KILLINGS STOP, THEN HIGUCHI IS KIRA... THIS EVEN STOPS WHAT YOU WERE WORRIED ABOUT, CHIEF. WOW, MISA MISA!
YES.
...

DEATH NOTE
How to use it
XXXIV

- The owner of the DEATH NOTE cannot be killed by a god of death who is living in the world of the gods of death.

  デスノートを持った人間を死神界にいる死神が殺す事はできない。

- Also, a god of death who comes to the human world, in the objective to kill the owner of the DEATH NOTE, will not be able to do so.

  デスノートを持った人間を殺す目的で、死神が人間界に下り、
  その人間を殺す事もできない。

- Only a god of death that has passed on their DEATH NOTE to a human is able to kill the owner of the DEATH NOTE.

  デスノートを持った人間を殺せるのは
  人間界にデスノートを譲渡している死神だけである。

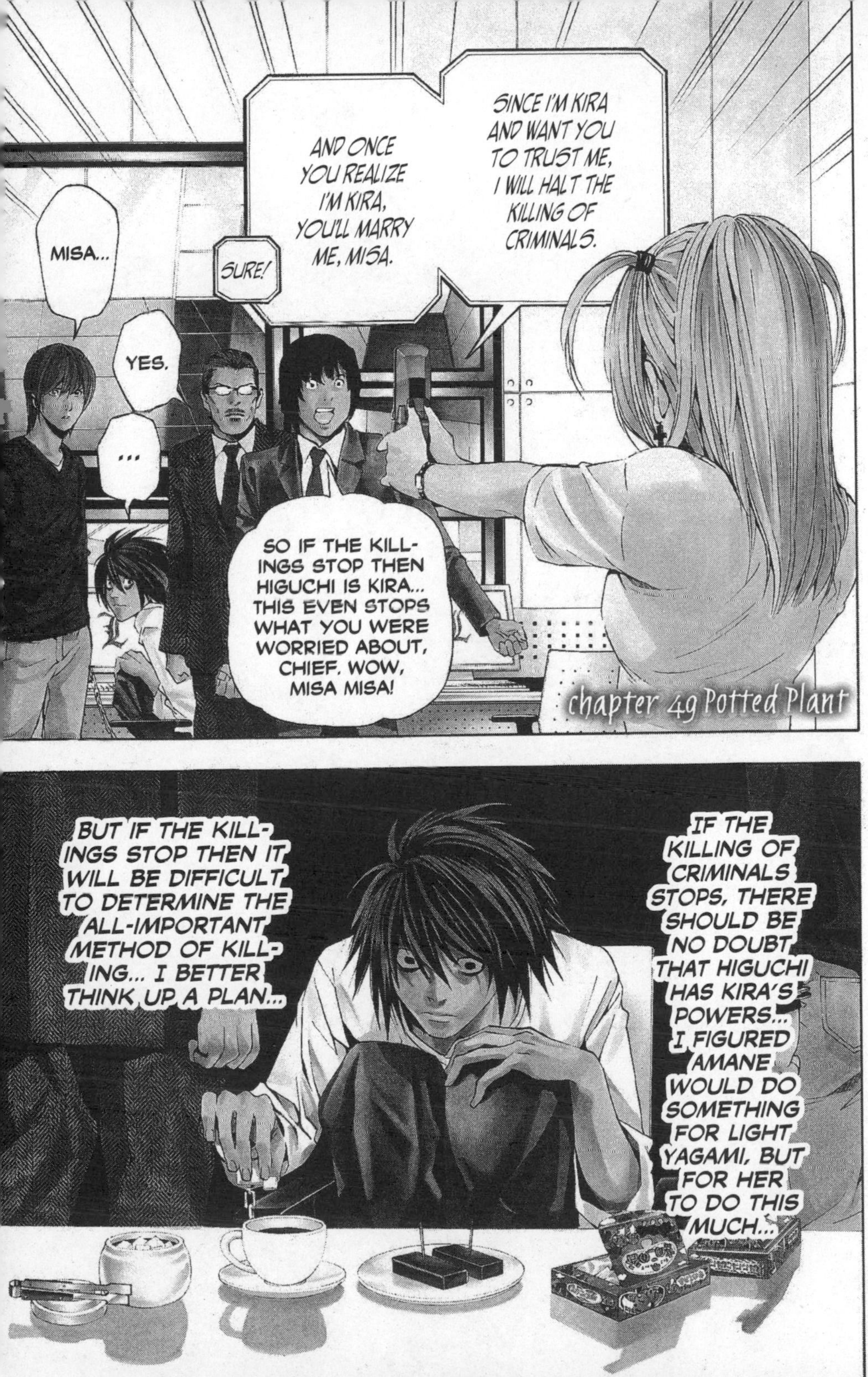
SINCE I'M KIRA AND WANT YOU TO TRUST ME, I WILL HALT THE KILLING OF CRIMINALS.
AND ONCE YOU REALIZE I'M KIRA, YOU'LL MARRY ME, MISA.
SURE!
MISA...
YES.
...
SO IF THE KILL-INGS STOP THEN HIGUCHI IS KIRA... THIS EVEN STOPS WHAT YOU WERE WORRIED ABOUT, CHIEF. WOW, MISA MISA!
chapter 49 Potted Plant
IF THE KILLING OF CRIMINALS STOPS, THERE SHOULD BE NO DOUBT THAT HIGUCHI HAS KIRA'S POWERS... I FIGURED AMANE WOULD DO SOMETHING FOR LIGHT YAGAMI, BUT FOR HER TO DO THIS MUCH...
BUT IF THE KILL-INGS STOP THEN IT WILL BE DIFFICULT TO DETERMINE THE ALL-IMPORTANT METHOD OF KILL-ING... I BETTER THINK UP A PLAN...

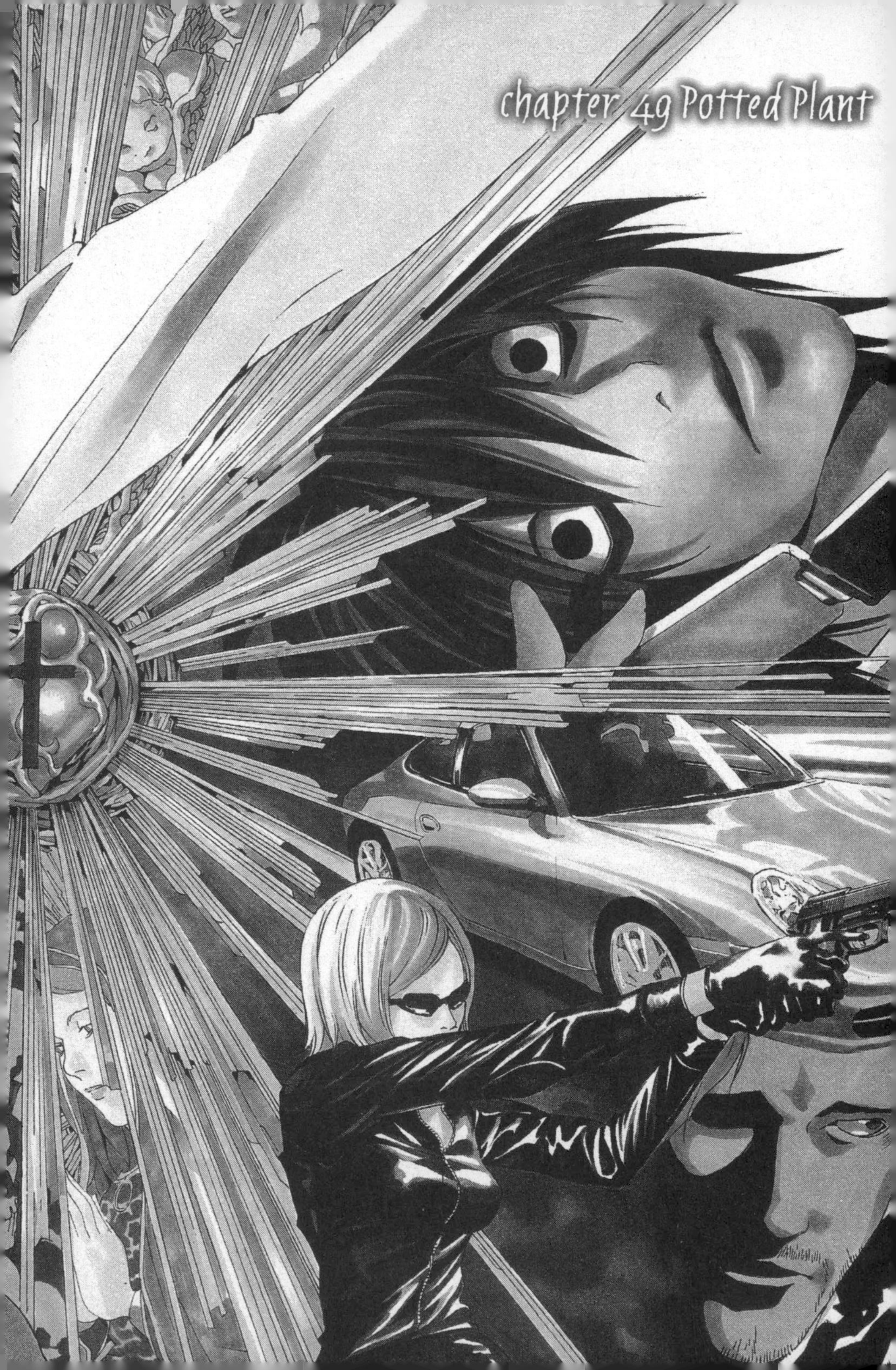
chapter 49 Potted Plant

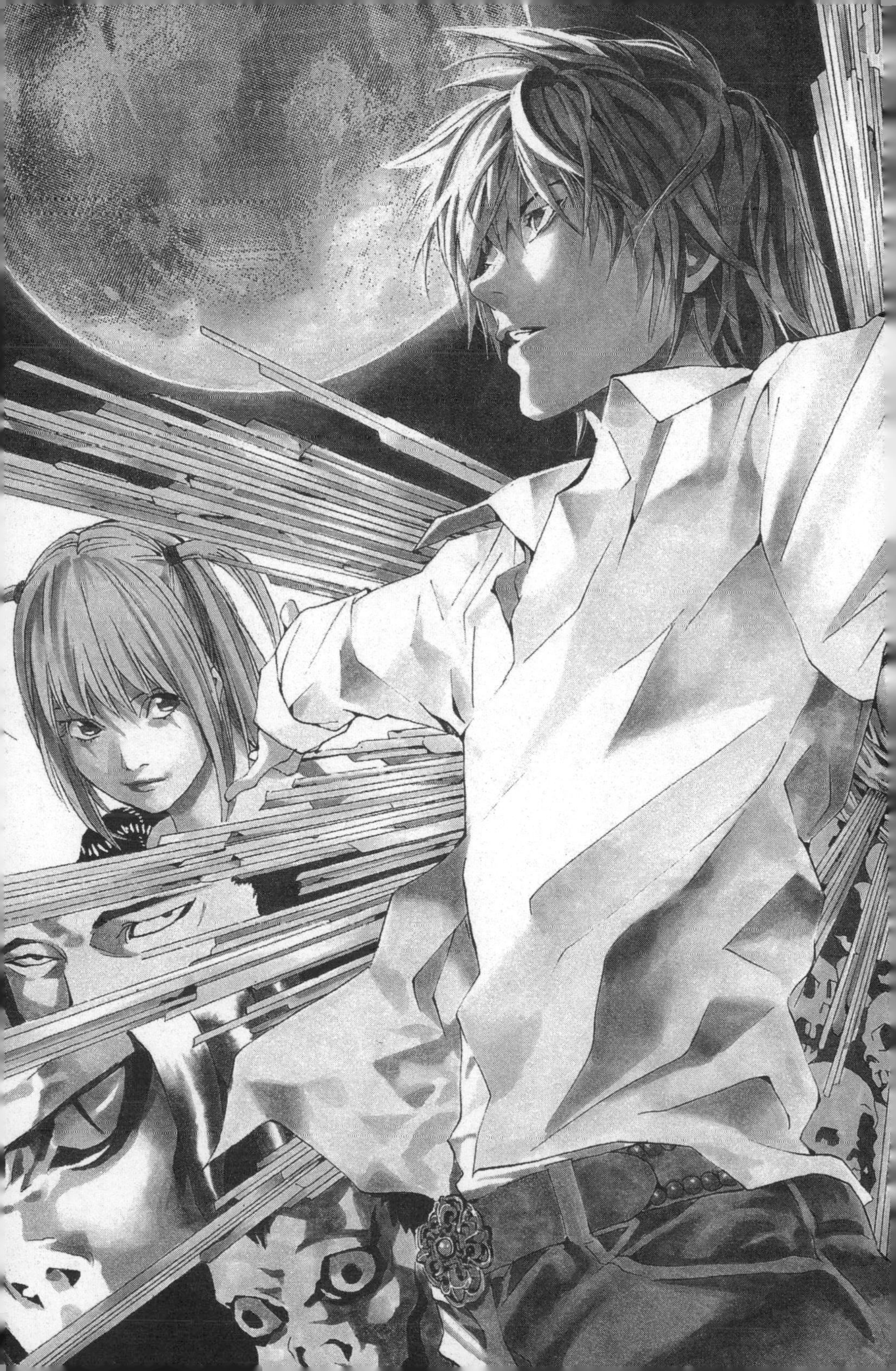

READ THIS WAY

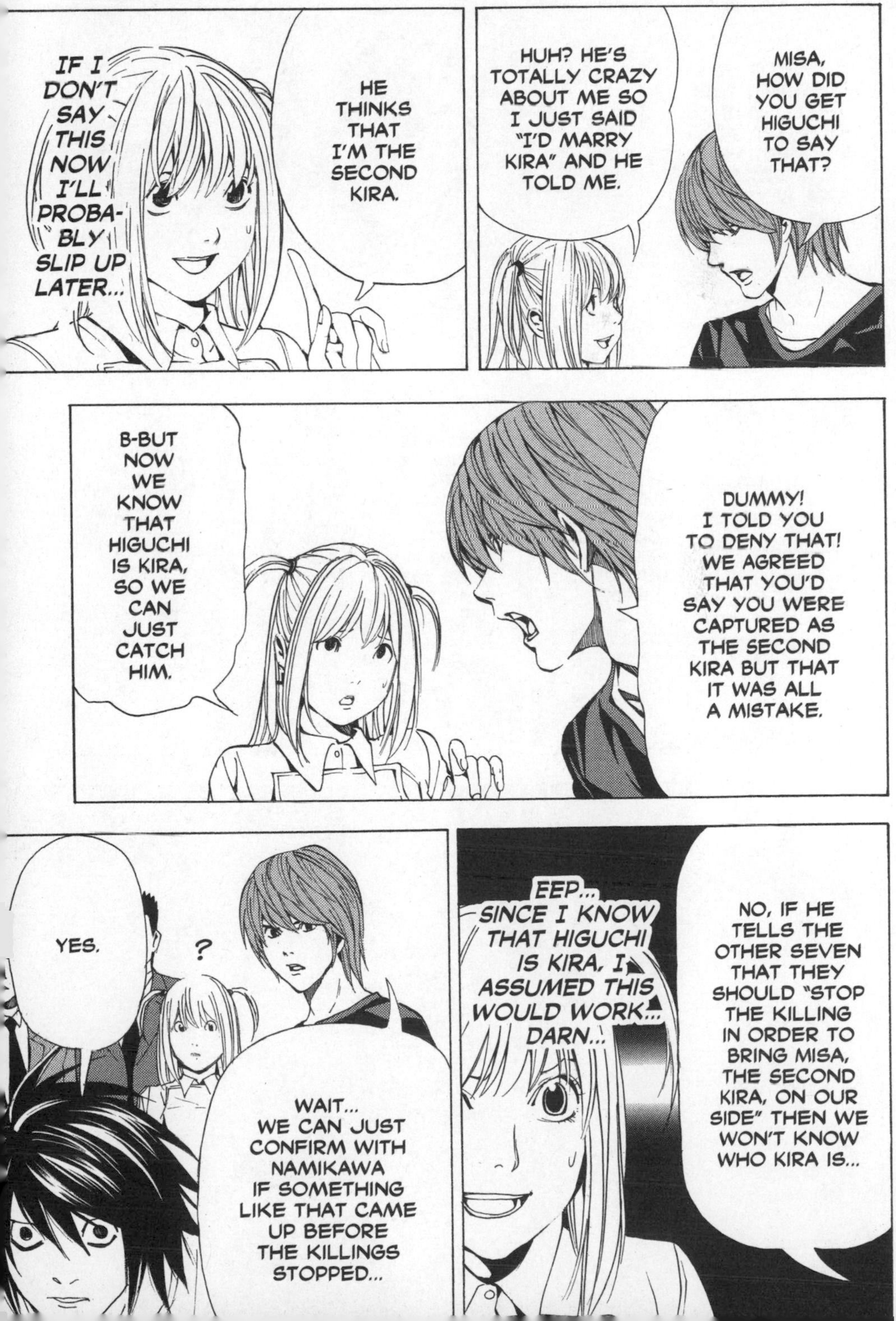
MISA, HOW DID YOU GET HIGUCHI TO SAY THAT?
HUH? HE'S TOTALLY CRAZY ABOUT ME SO I JUST SAID "I'D MARRY KIRA" AND HE TOLD ME.
HE THINKS THAT I'M THE SECOND KIRA.
IF I DON'T SAY THIS NOW I'LL PROBABLY SLIP UP LATER...
DUMMY! I TOLD YOU TO DENY THAT! WE AGREED THAT YOU'D SAY YOU WERE CAPTURED AS THE SECOND KIRA BUT THAT IT WAS ALL A MISTAKE.
B-BUT NOW WE KNOW THAT HIGUCHI IS KIRA, SO WE CAN JUST CATCH HIM.
NO, IF HE TELLS THE OTHER SEVEN THAT THEY SHOULD "STOP THE KILLING IN ORDER TO BRING MISA, THE SECOND KIRA, ON OUR SIDE" THEN WE WON'T KNOW WHO KIRA IS...
EEP... SINCE I KNOW THAT HIGUCHI IS KIRA, I ASSUMED THIS WOULD WORK... DARN...
YES.
?
WAIT... WE CAN JUST CONFIRM WITH NAMIKAWA IF SOMETHING LIKE THAT CAME UP BEFORE THE KILLINGS STOPPED...

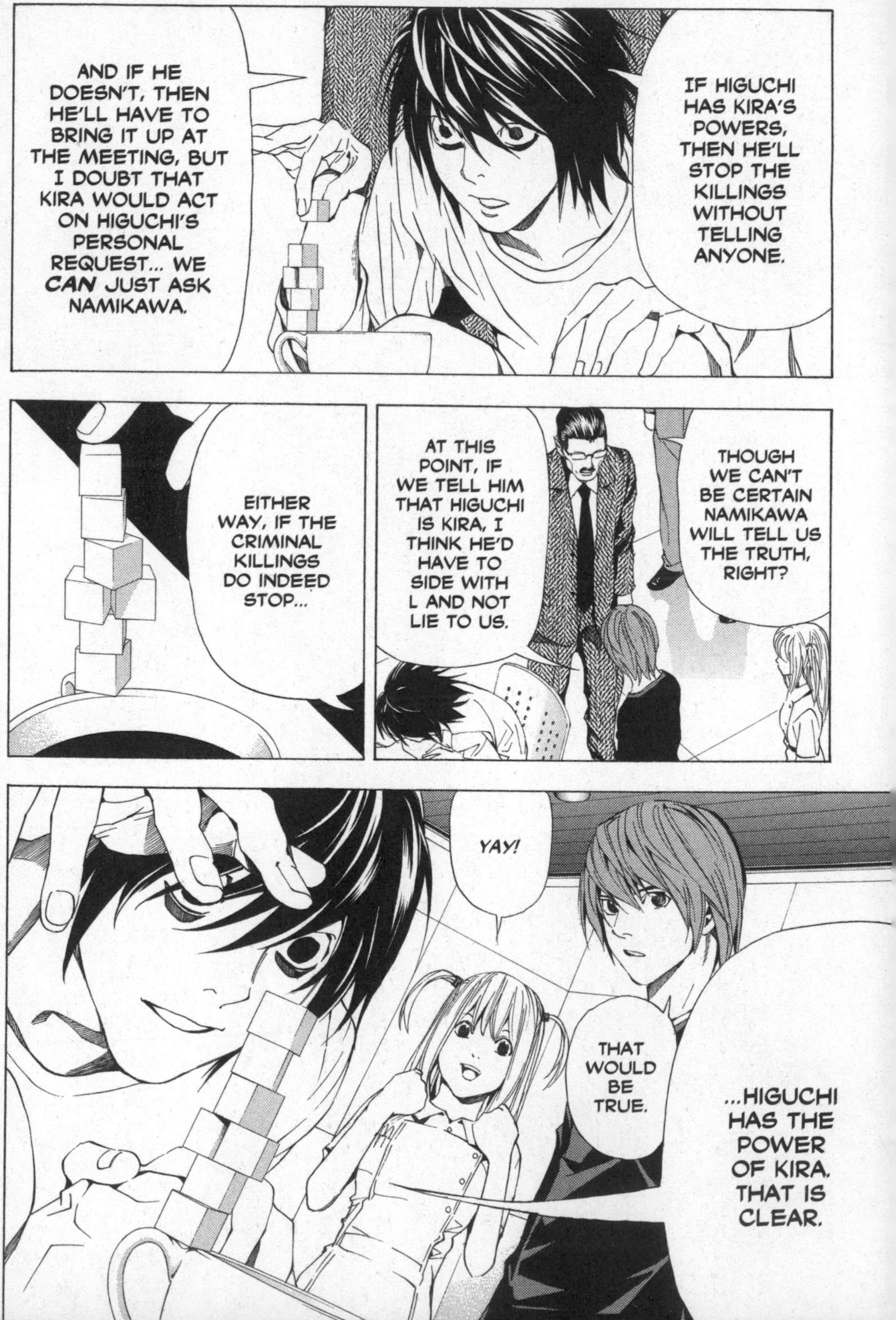
IF HIGUCHI HAS KIRA'S POWERS, THEN HE'LL STOP THE KILLINGS WITHOUT TELLING ANYONE.
AND IF HE DOESN'T, THEN HE'LL HAVE TO BRING IT UP AT THE MEETING, BUT I DOUBT THAT KIRA WOULD ACT ON HIGUCHI'S PERSONAL REQUEST... WE *CAN* JUST ASK NAMIKAWA.
THOUGH WE CAN'T BE CERTAIN NAMIKAWA WILL TELL US THE TRUTH, RIGHT?
AT THIS POINT, IF WE TELL HIM THAT HIGUCHI IS KIRA, I THINK HE'D HAVE TO SIDE WITH L AND NOT LIE TO US.
EITHER WAY, IF THE CRIMINAL KILLINGS DO INDEED STOP...
...HIGUCHI HAS THE POWER OF KIRA. THAT IS CLEAR.
THAT WOULD BE TRUE.
YAY!

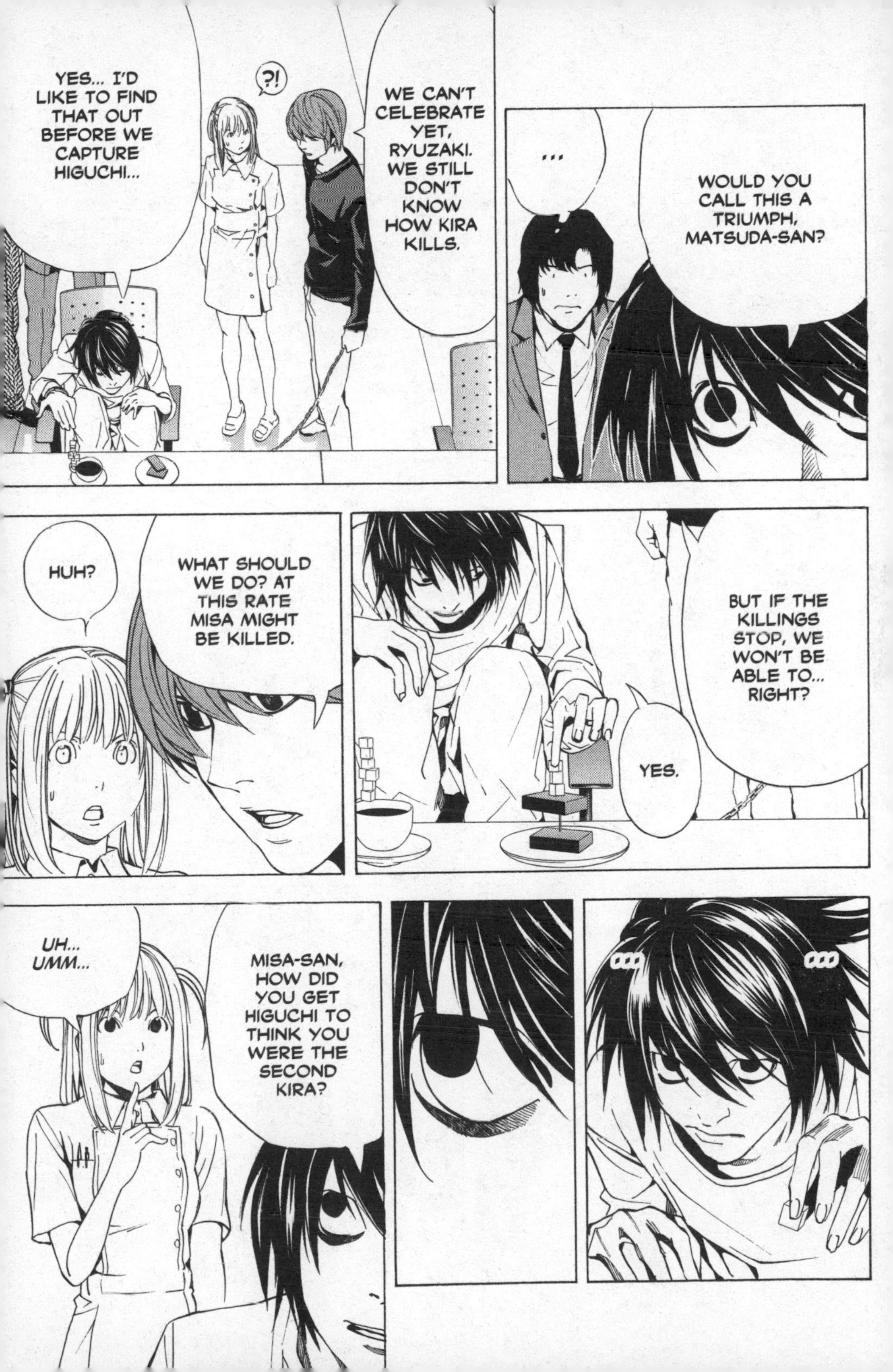

WOULD YOU CALL THIS A TRIUMPH, MATSUDA-SAN?
...
WE CAN'T CELEBRATE YET, RYUZAKI. WE STILL DON'T KNOW HOW KIRA KILLS.
?!
YES... I'D LIKE TO FIND THAT OUT BEFORE WE CAPTURE HIGUCHI...
BUT IF THE KILLINGS STOP, WE WON'T BE ABLE TO... RIGHT?
YES.
WHAT SHOULD WE DO? AT THIS RATE MISA MIGHT BE KILLED.
HUH?
MISA-SAN, HOW DID YOU GET HIGUCHI TO THINK YOU WERE THE SECOND KIRA?
UH... UMM...

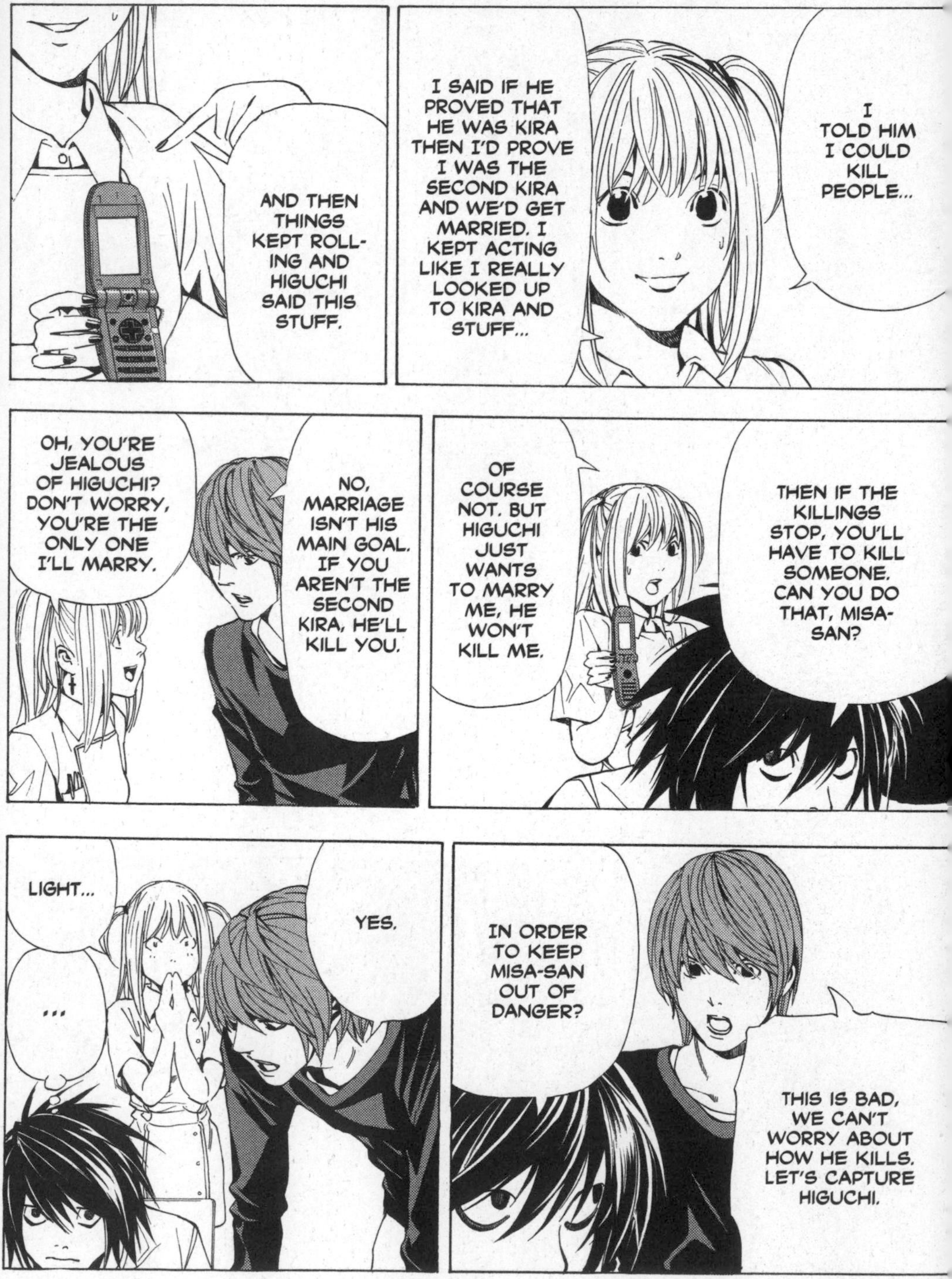
I TOLD HIM I COULD KILL PEOPLE...
I SAID IF HE PROVED THAT HE WAS KIRA THEN I'D PROVE I WAS THE SECOND KIRA AND WE'D GET MARRIED. I KEPT ACTING LIKE I REALLY LOOKED UP TO KIRA AND STUFF...
AND THEN THINGS KEPT ROLL-ING AND HIGUCHI SAID THIS STUFF.
THEN IF THE KILLINGS STOP, YOU'LL HAVE TO KILL SOMEONE. CAN YOU DO THAT, MISA-SAN?
OF COURSE NOT. BUT HIGUCHI JUST WANTS TO MARRY ME, HE WON'T KILL ME.
NO, MARRIAGE ISN'T HIS MAIN GOAL. IF YOU AREN'T THE SECOND KIRA, HE'LL KILL YOU.
OH, YOU'RE JEALOUS OF HIGUCHI? DON'T WORRY, YOU'RE THE ONLY ONE I'LL MARRY.
IN ORDER TO KEEP MISA-SAN OUT OF DANGER?
THIS IS BAD, WE CAN'T WORRY ABOUT HOW HE KILLS. LET'S CAPTURE HIGUCHI.
YES.
LIGHT...
...

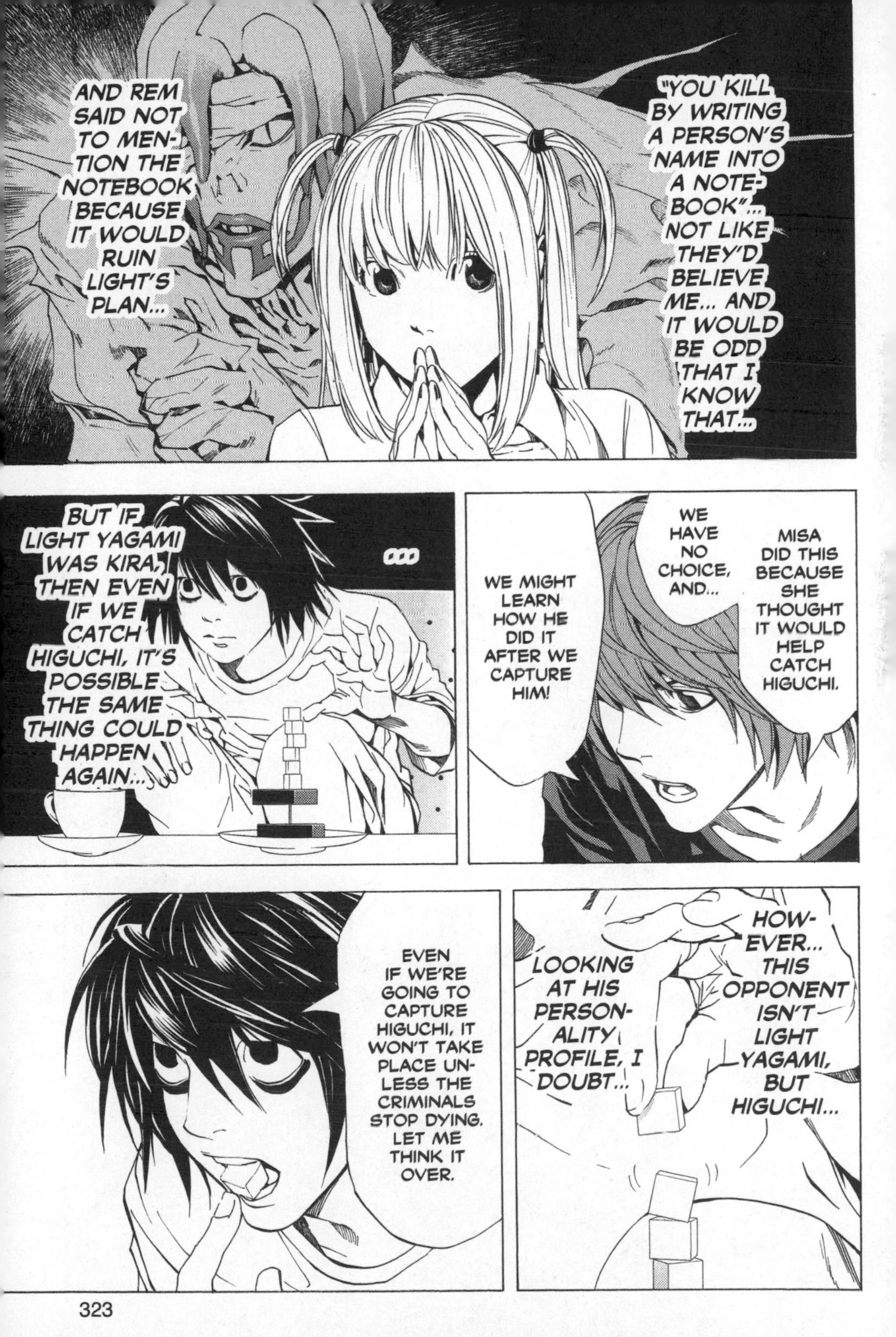
"YOU KILL BY WRITING A PERSON'S NAME INTO A NOTEBOOK"... NOT LIKE THEY'D BELIEVE ME... AND IT WOULD BE ODD THAT I KNOW THAT...
AND REM SAID NOT TO MENTION THE NOTEBOOK BECAUSE IT WOULD RUIN LIGHT'S PLAN...
MISA DID THIS BECAUSE SHE THOUGHT IT WOULD HELP CATCH HIGUCHI.
WE HAVE NO CHOICE, AND...
WE MIGHT LEARN HOW HE DID IT AFTER WE CAPTURE HIM!
...
BUT IF LIGHT YAGAMI WAS KIRA, THEN EVEN IF WE CATCH HIGUCHI, IT'S POSSIBLE THE SAME THING COULD HAPPEN AGAIN...
HOWEVER... THIS OPPONENT ISN'T LIGHT YAGAMI, BUT HIGUCHI...
LOOKING AT HIS PERSONALITY PROFILE, I DOUBT...
EVEN IF WE'RE GOING TO CAPTURE HIGUCHI, IT WON'T TAKE PLACE UNLESS THE CRIMINALS STOP DYING. LET ME THINK IT OVER.

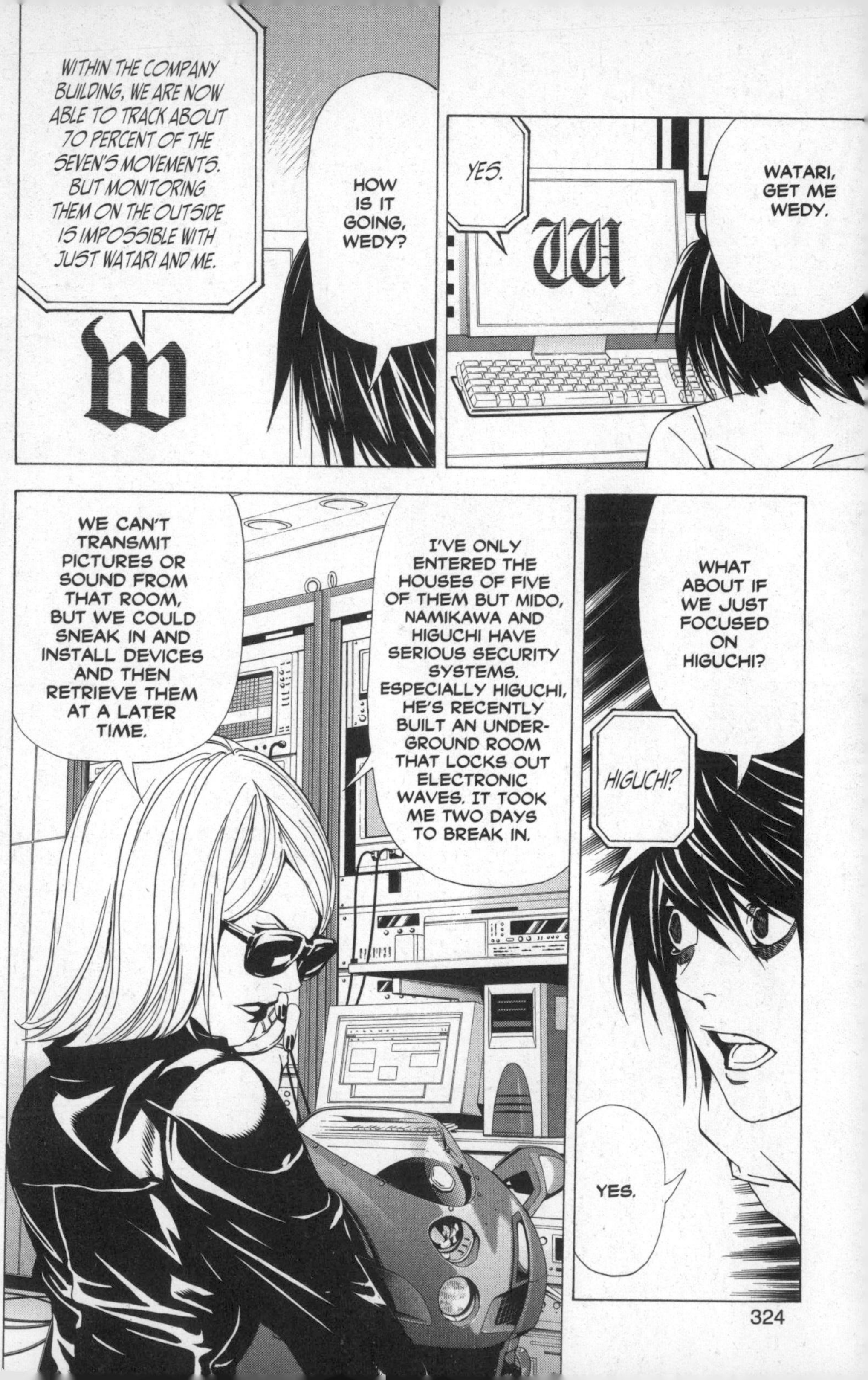
WATARI, GET ME WEDY.
YES.
HOW IS IT GOING, WEDY?
WITHIN THE COMPANY BUILDING, WE ARE NOW ABLE TO TRACK ABOUT 70 PERCENT OF THE SEVEN'S MOVEMENTS. BUT MONITORING THEM ON THE OUTSIDE IS IMPOSSIBLE WITH JUST WATARI AND ME.
WHAT ABOUT IF WE JUST FOCUSED ON HIGUCHI?
HIGUCHI?
YES.
I'VE ONLY ENTERED THE HOUSES OF FIVE OF THEM BUT MIDO, NAMIKAWA AND HIGUCHI HAVE SERIOUS SECURITY SYSTEMS. ESPECIALLY HIGUCHI, HE'S RECENTLY BUILT AN UNDER-GROUND ROOM THAT LOCKS OUT ELECTRONIC WAVES. IT TOOK ME TWO DAYS TO BREAK IN.
WE CAN'T TRANSMIT PICTURES OR SOUND FROM THAT ROOM, BUT WE COULD SNEAK IN AND INSTALL DEVICES AND THEN RETRIEVE THEM AT A LATER TIME.

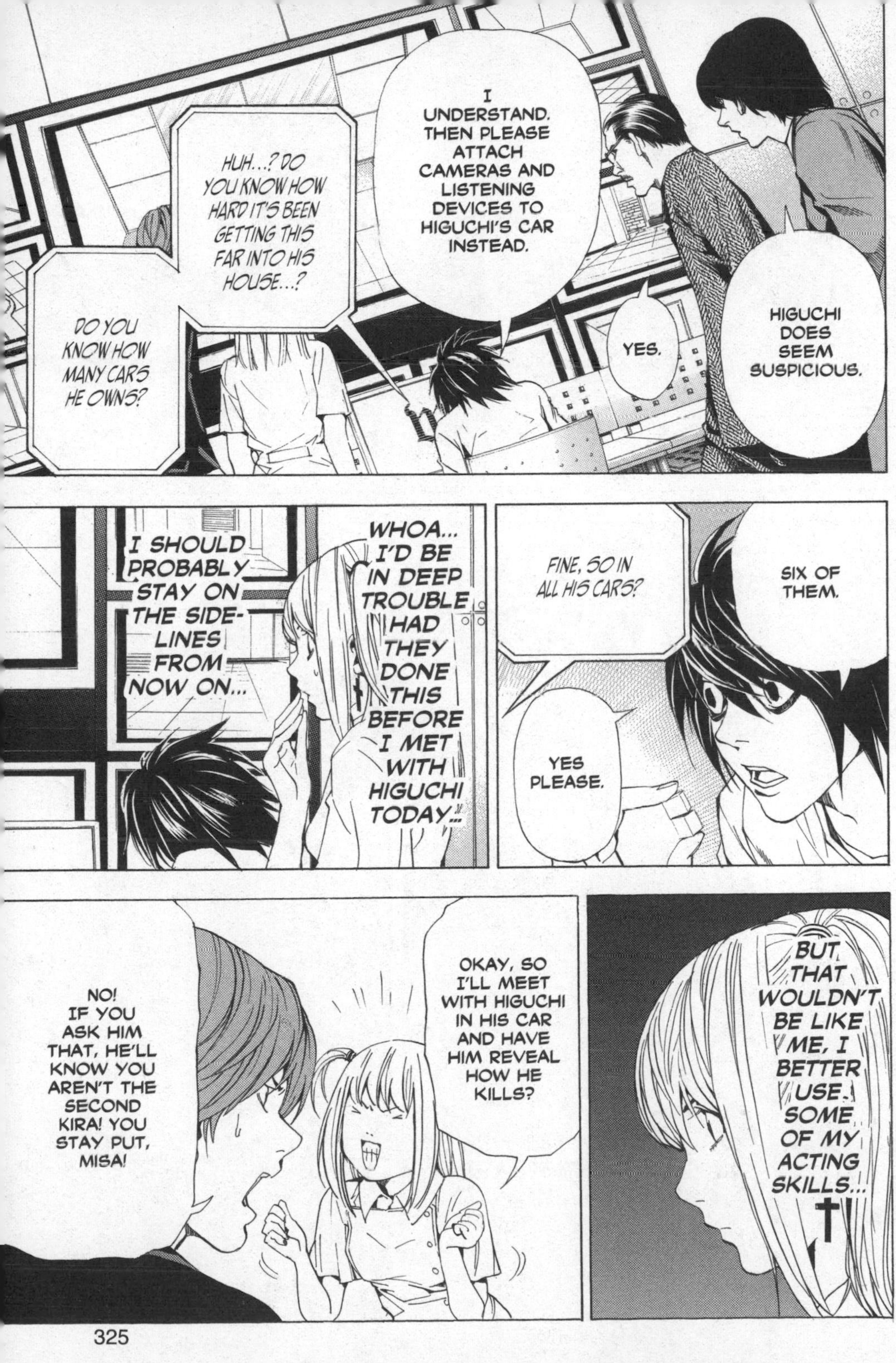
HIGUCHI DOES SEEM SUSPICIOUS.
YES.
I UNDERSTAND. THEN PLEASE ATTACH CAMERAS AND LISTENING DEVICES TO HIGUCHI'S CAR INSTEAD.
HUH...? DO YOU KNOW HOW HARD IT'S BEEN GETTING THIS FAR INTO HIS HOUSE...?
DO YOU KNOW HOW MANY CARS HE OWNS?
SIX OF THEM.
FINE, SO IN ALL HIS CARS?
YES PLEASE.
WHOA... I'D BE IN DEEP TROUBLE HAD THEY DONE THIS BEFORE I MET WITH HIGUCHI TODAY...
I SHOULD PROBABLY STAY ON THE SIDE-LINES FROM NOW ON...
BUT THAT WOULDN'T BE LIKE ME, I BETTER USE SOME OF MY ACTING SKILLS...
OKAY, SO I'LL MEET WITH HIGUCHI IN HIS CAR AND HAVE HIM REVEAL HOW HE KILLS?
NO! IF YOU ASK HIM THAT, HE'LL KNOW YOU AREN'T THE SECOND KIRA! YOU STAY PUT, MISA!

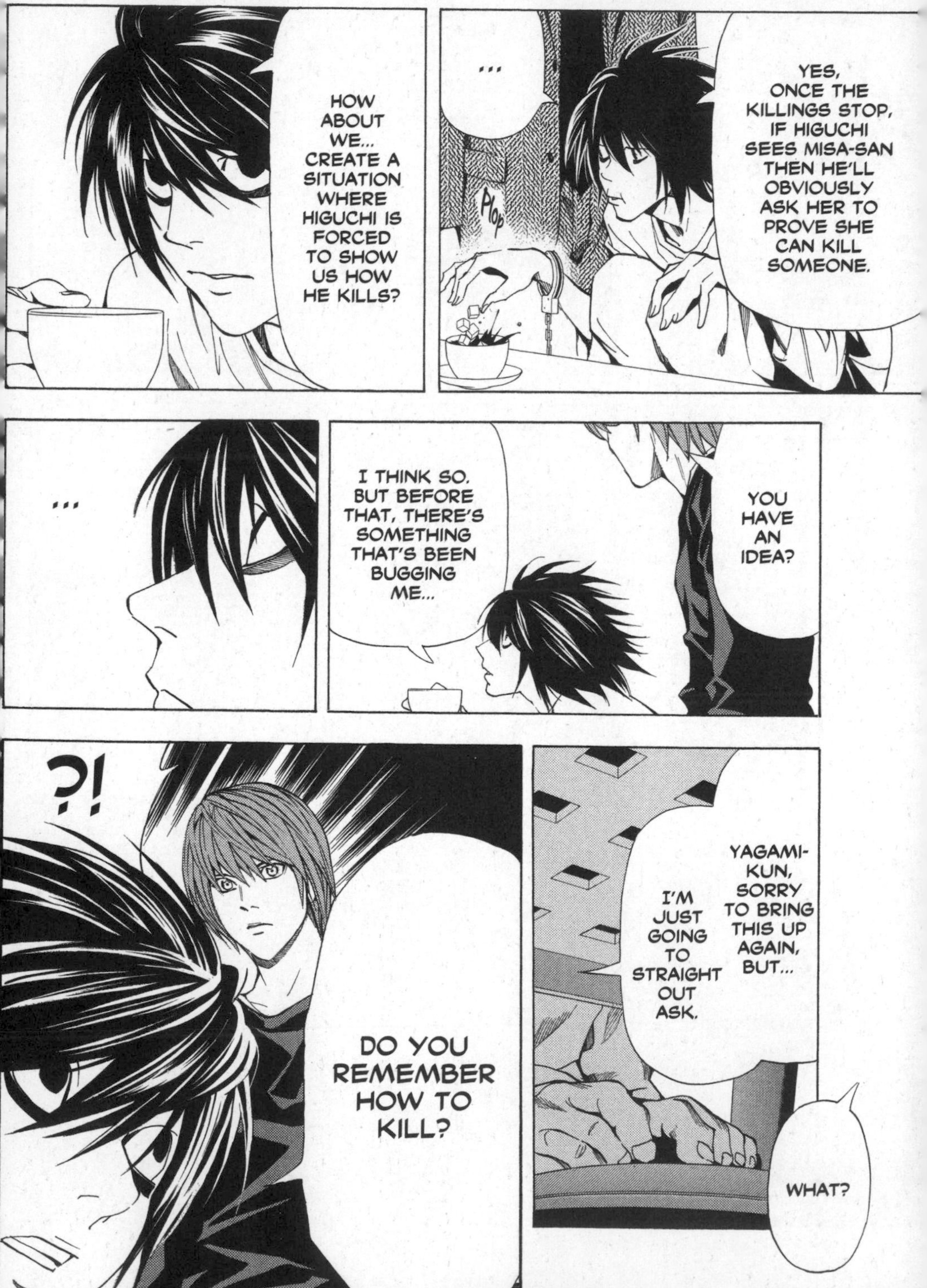
YES, ONCE THE KILLINGS STOP, IF HIGUCHI SEES MISA-SAN THEN HE'LL OBVIOUSLY ASK HER TO PROVE SHE CAN KILL SOMEONE.
...
Plop
HOW ABOUT WE... CREATE A SITUATION WHERE HIGUCHI IS FORCED TO SHOW US HOW HE KILLS?
YOU HAVE AN IDEA?
I THINK SO. BUT BEFORE THAT, THERE'S SOMETHING THAT'S BEEN BUGGING ME...
...
YAGAMI-KUN, SORRY TO BRING THIS UP AGAIN, BUT...
I'M JUST GOING TO STRAIGHT OUT ASK.
WHAT?
?!
DO YOU REMEMBER HOW TO KILL?

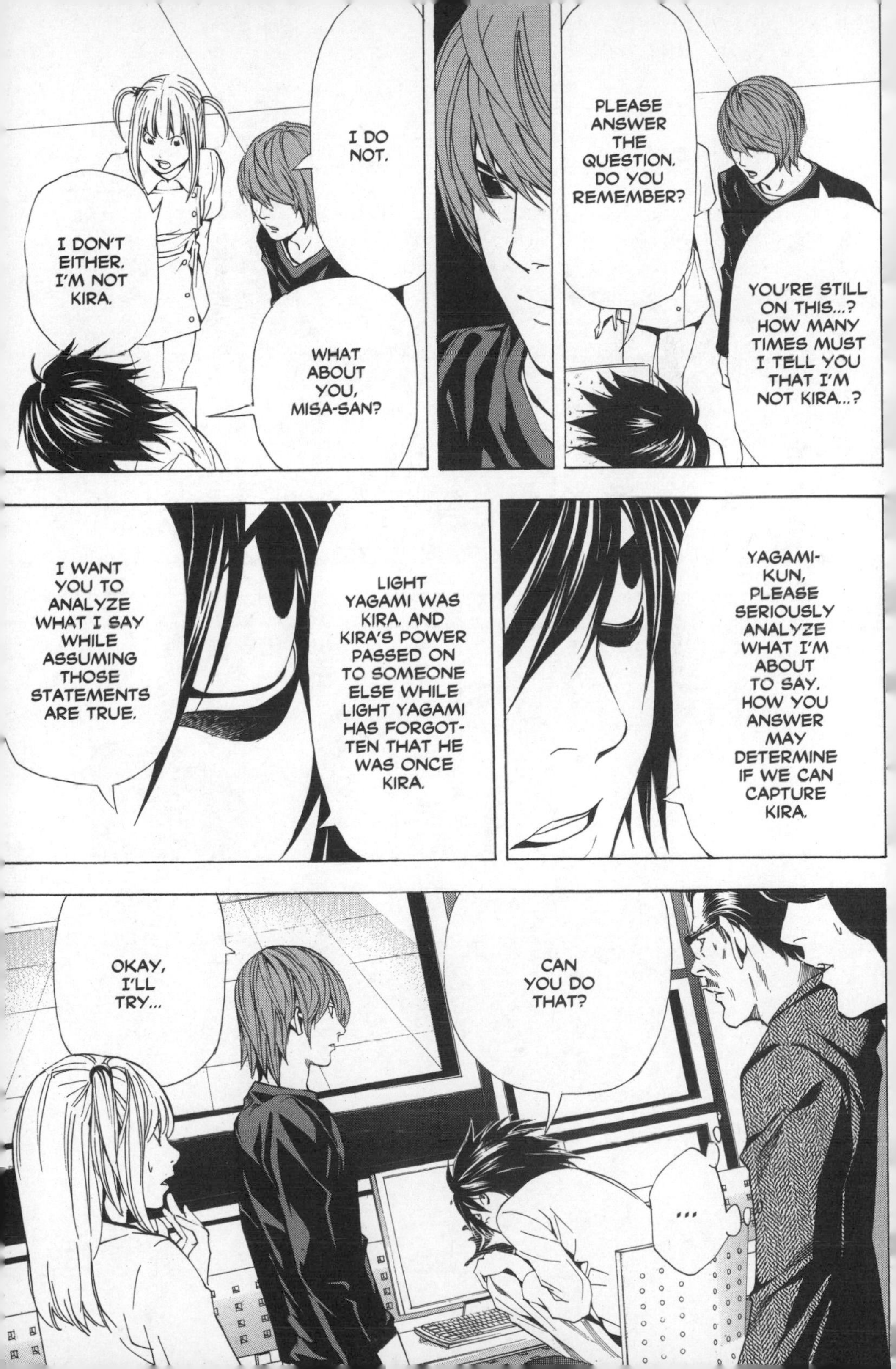
YOU'RE STILL ON THIS...? HOW MANY TIMES MUST I TELL YOU THAT I'M NOT KIRA...?
PLEASE ANSWER THE QUESTION. DO YOU REMEMBER?
I DO NOT.
WHAT ABOUT YOU, MISA-SAN?
I DON'T EITHER. I'M NOT KIRA.
YAGAMI-KUN, PLEASE SERIOUSLY ANALYZE WHAT I'M ABOUT TO SAY. HOW YOU ANSWER MAY DETERMINE IF WE CAN CAPTURE KIRA.
LIGHT YAGAMI WAS KIRA. AND KIRA'S POWER PASSED ON TO SOMEONE ELSE WHILE LIGHT YAGAMI HAS FORGOTTEN THAT HE WAS ONCE KIRA.
I WANT YOU TO ANALYZE WHAT I SAY WHILE ASSUMING THOSE STATEMENTS ARE TRUE.
CAN YOU DO THAT?
OKAY, I'LL TRY...
...

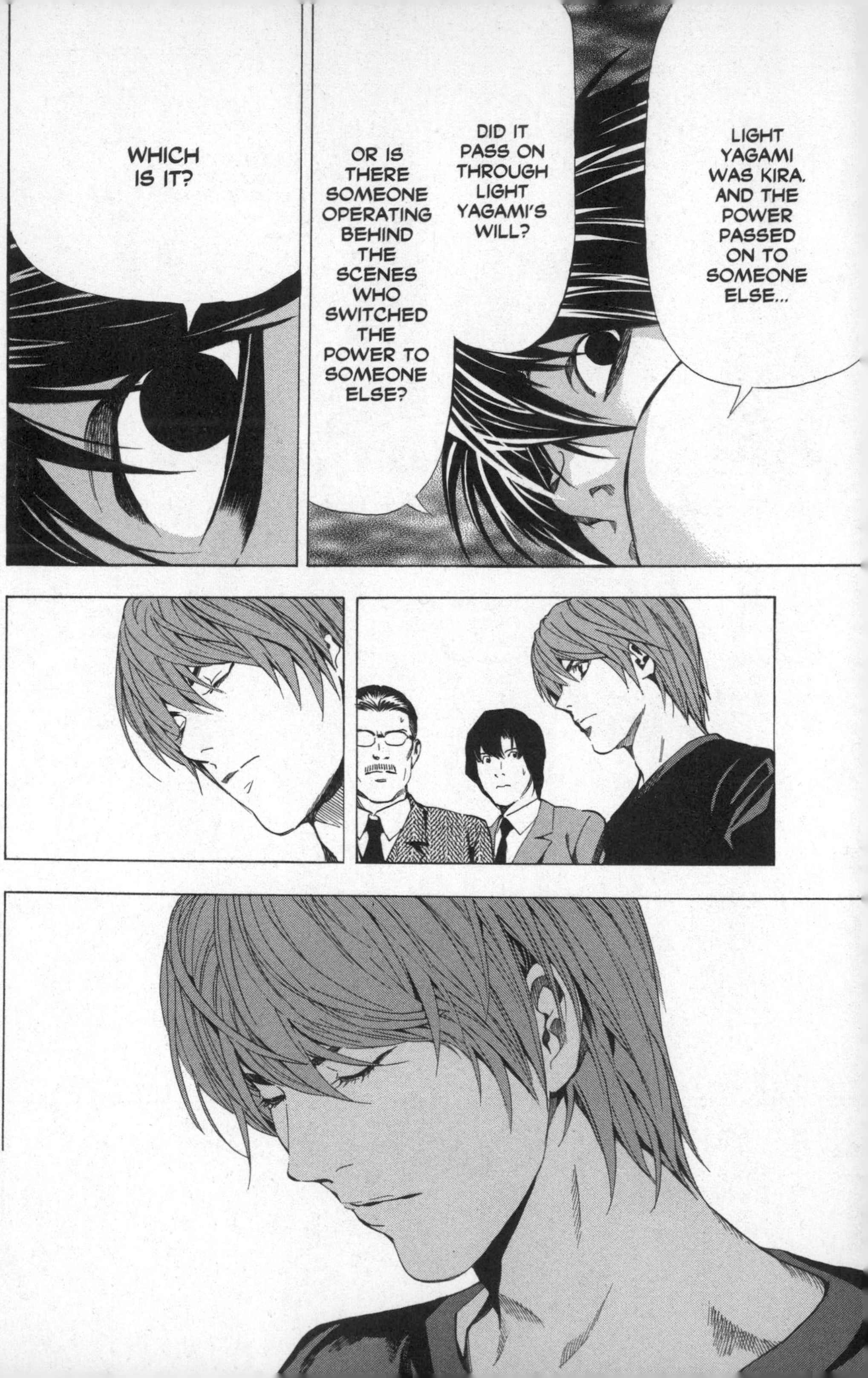
LIGHT YAGAMI WAS KIRA. AND THE POWER PASSED ON TO SOMEONE ELSE...
DID IT PASS ON THROUGH LIGHT YAGAMI'S WILL?
OR IS THERE SOMEONE OPERATING BEHIND THE SCENES WHO SWITCHED THE POWER TO SOMEONE ELSE?
WHICH IS IT?

READ THIS WAY

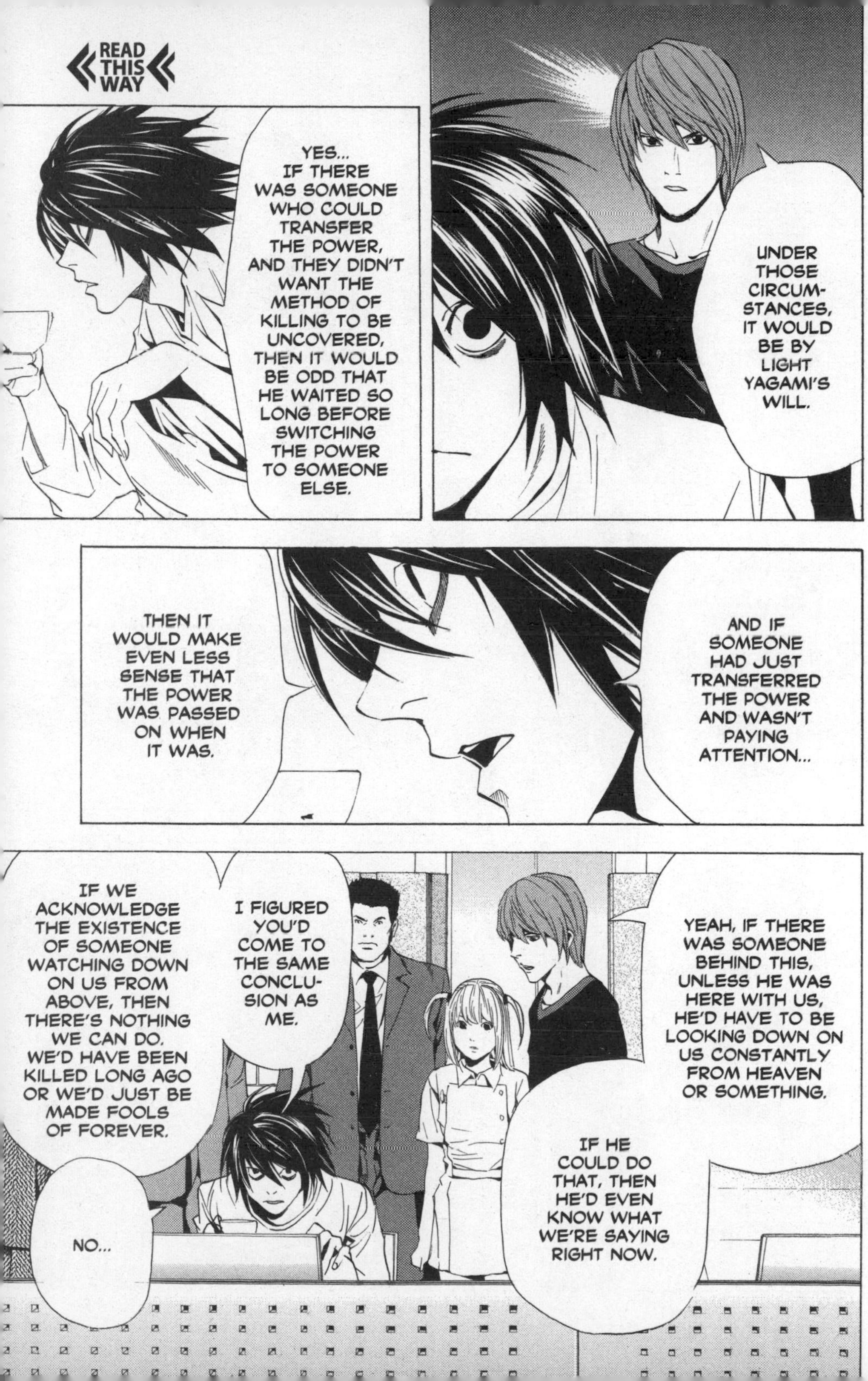
UNDER THOSE CIRCUMSTANCES, IT WOULD BE BY LIGHT YAGAMI'S WILL.
YES... IF THERE WAS SOMEONE WHO COULD TRANSFER THE POWER, AND THEY DIDN'T WANT THE METHOD OF KILLING TO BE UNCOVERED, THEN IT WOULD BE ODD THAT HE WAITED SO LONG BEFORE SWITCHING THE POWER TO SOMEONE ELSE.
AND IF SOMEONE HAD JUST TRANSFERRED THE POWER AND WASN'T PAYING ATTENTION...
THEN IT WOULD MAKE EVEN LESS SENSE THAT THE POWER WAS PASSED ON WHEN IT WAS.
YEAH, IF THERE WAS SOMEONE BEHIND THIS, UNLESS HE WAS HERE WITH US, HE'D HAVE TO BE LOOKING DOWN ON US CONSTANTLY FROM HEAVEN OR SOMETHING.
IF HE COULD DO THAT, THEN HE'D EVEN KNOW WHAT WE'RE SAYING RIGHT NOW.
I FIGURED YOU'D COME TO THE SAME CONCLUSION AS ME.
IF WE ACKNOWLEDGE THE EXISTENCE OF SOMEONE WATCHING DOWN ON US FROM ABOVE, THEN THERE'S NOTHING WE CAN DO. WE'D HAVE BEEN KILLED LONG AGO OR WE'D JUST BE MADE FOOLS OF FOREVER.
NO...

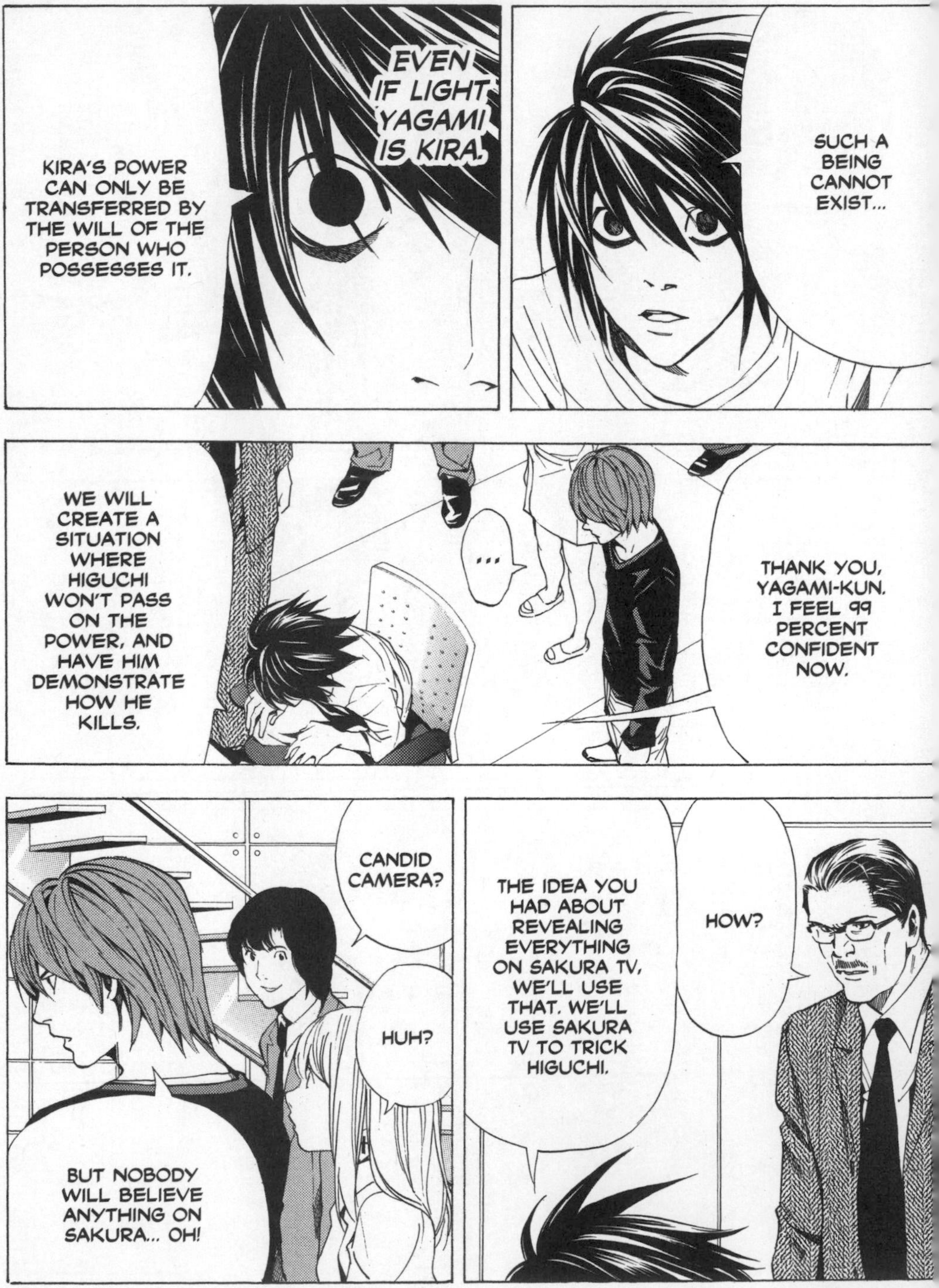
SUCH A BEING CANNOT EXIST...
EVEN IF LIGHT YAGAMI IS KIRA.
KIRA'S POWER CAN ONLY BE TRANSFERRED BY THE WILL OF THE PERSON WHO POSSESSES IT.
THANK YOU, YAGAMI-KUN. I FEEL 99 PERCENT CONFIDENT NOW.
...
WE WILL CREATE A SITUATION WHERE HIGUCHI WON'T PASS ON THE POWER, AND HAVE HIM DEMONSTRATE HOW HE KILLS.
HOW?
THE IDEA YOU HAD ABOUT REVEALING EVERYTHING ON SAKURA TV, WE'LL USE THAT. WE'LL USE SAKURA TV TO TRICK HIGUCHI.
CANDID CAMERA?
HUH?
BUT NOBODY WILL BELIEVE ANYTHING ON SAKURA... OH!

READ THIS WAY

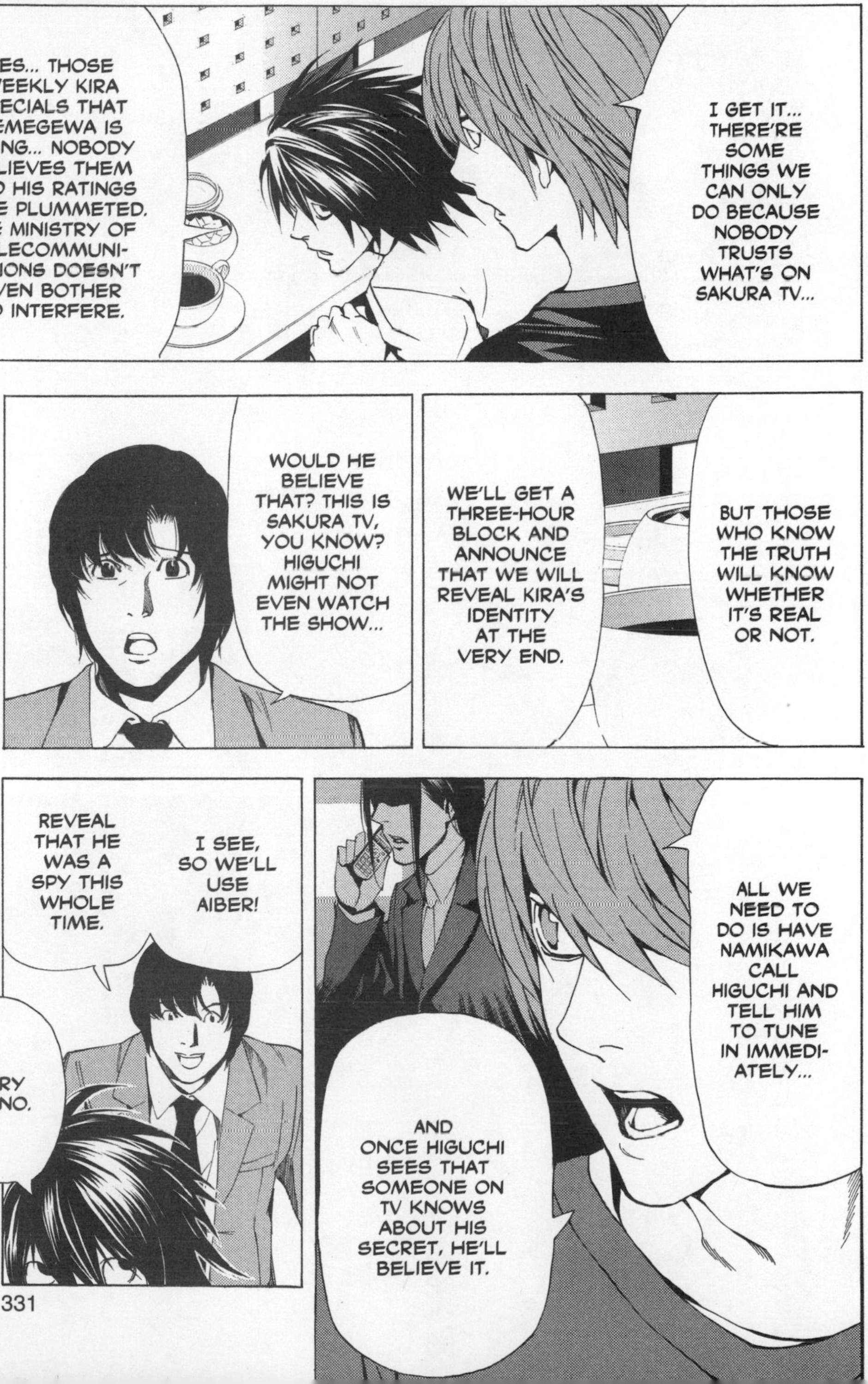
I GET IT... THERE'RE SOME THINGS WE CAN ONLY DO BECAUSE NOBODY TRUSTS WHAT'S ON SAKURA TV...
YES... THOSE WEEKLY KIRA SPECIALS THAT DEMEGEWA IS DOING... NOBODY BELIEVES THEM AND HIS RATINGS HAVE PLUMMETED. THE MINISTRY OF TELECOMMUNICATIONS DOESN'T EVEN BOTHER TO INTERFERE.
BUT THOSE WHO KNOW THE TRUTH WILL KNOW WHETHER IT'S REAL OR NOT.
WE'LL GET A THREE-HOUR BLOCK AND ANNOUNCE THAT WE WILL REVEAL KIRA'S IDENTITY AT THE VERY END.
WOULD HE BELIEVE THAT? THIS IS SAKURA TV, YOU KNOW? HIGUCHI MIGHT NOT EVEN WATCH THE SHOW...
ALL WE NEED TO DO IS HAVE NAMIKAWA CALL HIGUCHI AND TELL HIM TO TUNE IN IMMEDIATELY...
AND ONCE HIGUCHI SEES THAT SOMEONE ON TV KNOWS ABOUT HIS SECRET, HE'LL BELIEVE IT.
I SEE, SO WE'LL USE AIBER!
REVEAL THAT HE WAS A SPY THIS WHOLE TIME.
SORRY BUT NO.

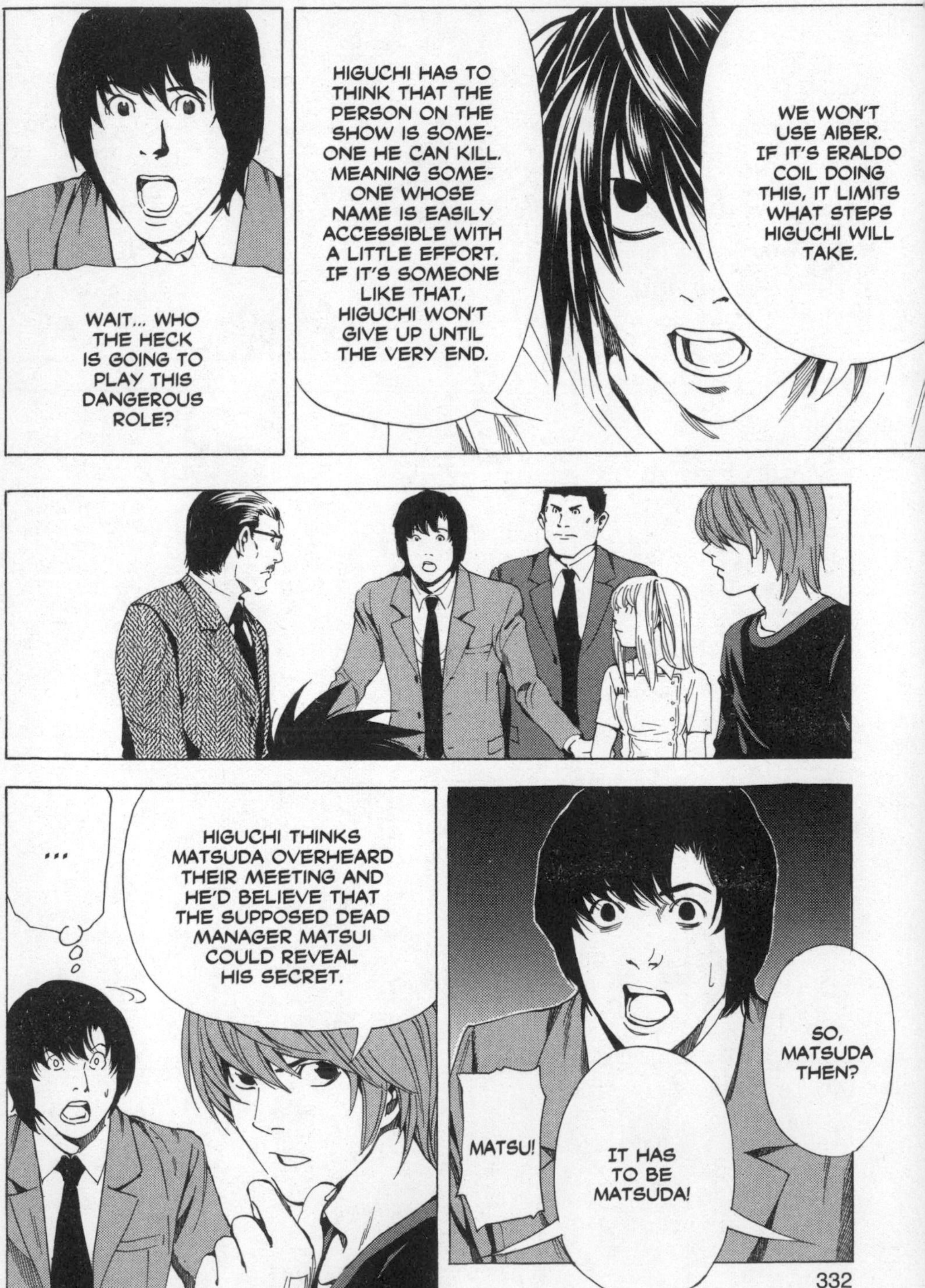
WE WON'T USE AIBER. IF IT'S ERALDO COIL DOING THIS, IT LIMITS WHAT STEPS HIGUCHI WILL TAKE.
HIGUCHI HAS TO THINK THAT THE PERSON ON THE SHOW IS SOME-ONE HE CAN KILL. MEANING SOME-ONE WHOSE NAME IS EASILY ACCESSIBLE WITH A LITTLE EFFORT. IF IT'S SOMEONE LIKE THAT, HIGUCHI WON'T GIVE UP UNTIL THE VERY END.
WAIT... WHO THE HECK IS GOING TO PLAY THIS DANGEROUS ROLE?
SO, MATSUDA THEN?
IT HAS TO BE MATSUDA!
MATSU!
HIGUCHI THINKS MATSUDA OVERHEARD THEIR MEETING AND HE'D BELIEVE THAT THE SUPPOSED DEAD MANAGER MATSUI COULD REVEAL HIS SECRET.
...

READ THIS WAY

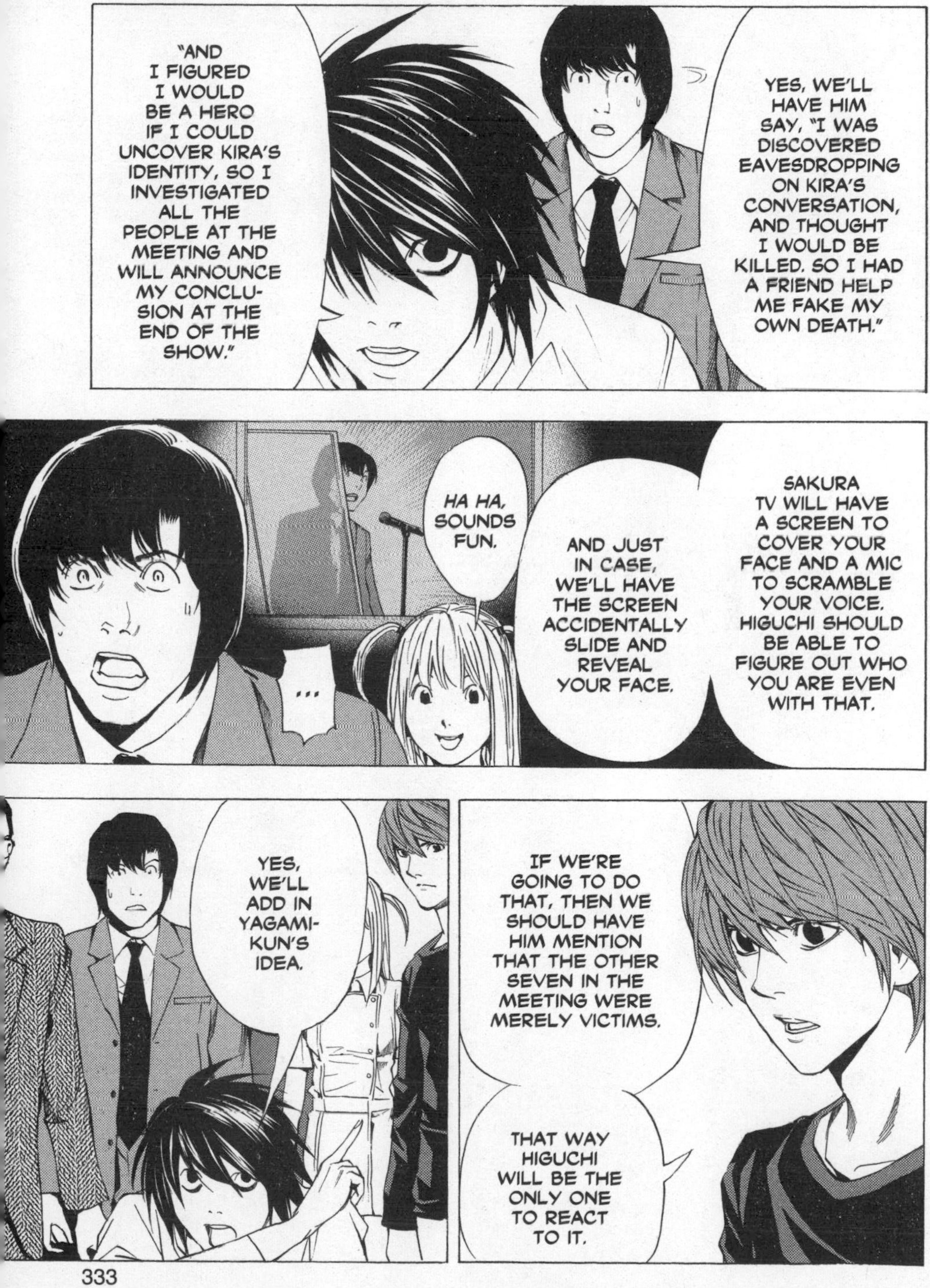
YES, WE'LL HAVE HIM SAY, "I WAS DISCOVERED EAVESDROPPING ON KIRA'S CONVERSATION, AND THOUGHT I WOULD BE KILLED. SO I HAD A FRIEND HELP ME FAKE MY OWN DEATH."
"AND I FIGURED I WOULD BE A HERO IF I COULD UNCOVER KIRA'S IDENTITY, SO I INVESTIGATED ALL THE PEOPLE AT THE MEETING AND WILL ANNOUNCE MY CONCLUSION AT THE END OF THE SHOW."
SAKURA TV WILL HAVE A SCREEN TO COVER YOUR FACE AND A MIC TO SCRAMBLE YOUR VOICE. HIGUCHI SHOULD BE ABLE TO FIGURE OUT WHO YOU ARE EVEN WITH THAT.
AND JUST IN CASE, WE'LL HAVE THE SCREEN ACCIDENTALLY SLIDE AND REVEAL YOUR FACE.
HA HA, SOUNDS FUN.
...
IF WE'RE GOING TO DO THAT, THEN WE SHOULD HAVE HIM MENTION THAT THE OTHER SEVEN IN THE MEETING WERE MERELY VICTIMS.
THAT WAY HIGUCHI WILL BE THE ONLY ONE TO REACT TO IT.
YES, WE'LL ADD IN YAGAMI-KUN'S IDEA.

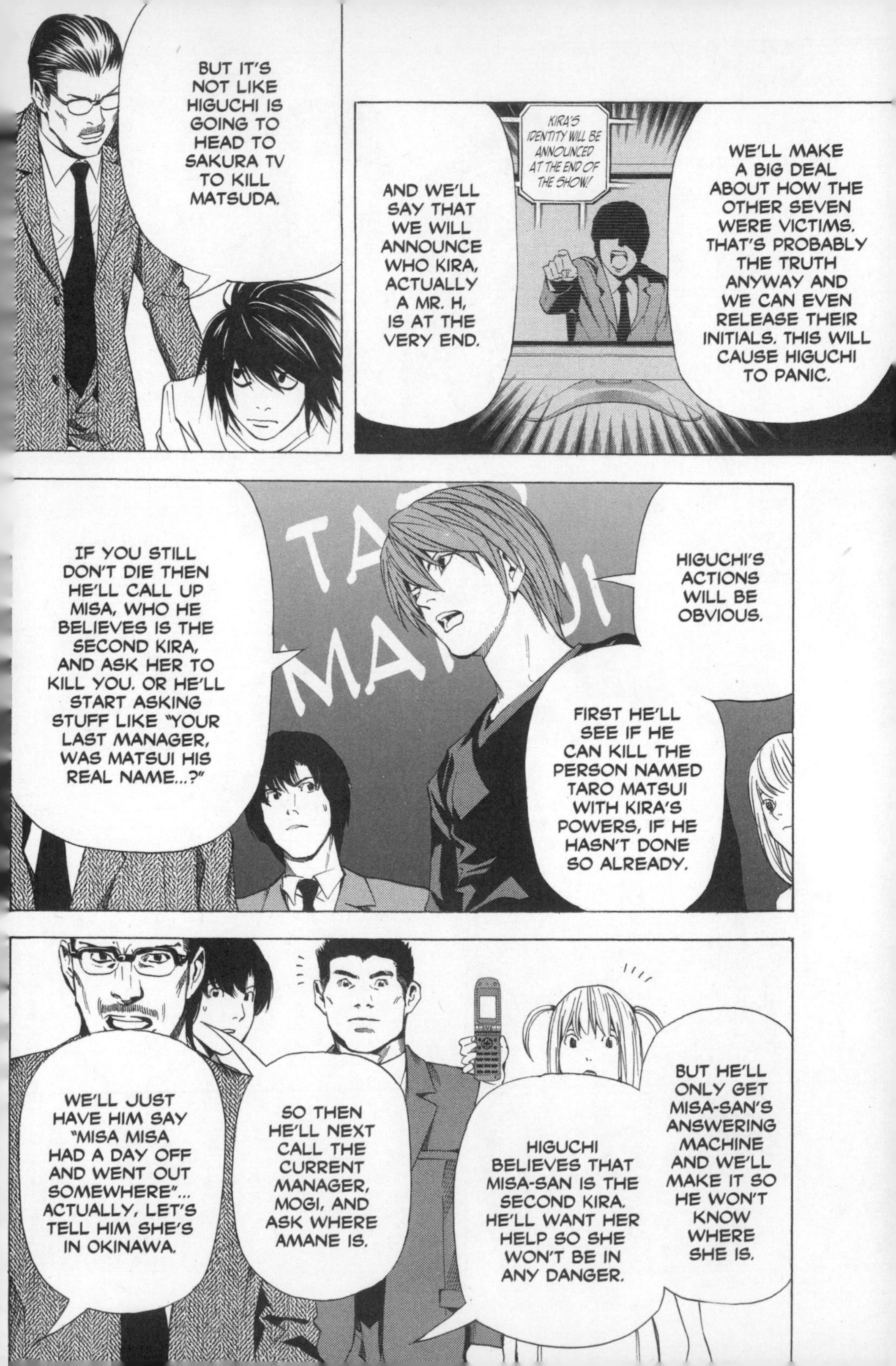
WE'LL MAKE A BIG DEAL ABOUT HOW THE OTHER SEVEN WERE VICTIMS. THAT'S PROBABLY THE TRUTH ANYWAY AND WE CAN EVEN RELEASE THEIR INITIALS. THIS WILL CAUSE HIGUCHI TO PANIC.
KIRA'S IDENTITY WILL BE ANNOUNCED AT THE END OF THE SHOW!
AND WE'LL SAY THAT WE WILL ANNOUNCE WHO KIRA, ACTUALLY A MR. H, IS AT THE VERY END.
BUT IT'S NOT LIKE HIGUCHI IS GOING TO HEAD TO SAKURA TV TO KILL MATSUDA.
HIGUCHI'S ACTIONS WILL BE OBVIOUS.
FIRST HE'LL SEE IF HE CAN KILL THE PERSON NAMED TARO MATSUI WITH KIRA'S POWERS, IF HE HASN'T DONE SO ALREADY.
IF YOU STILL DON'T DIE THEN HE'LL CALL UP MISA, WHO HE BELIEVES IS THE SECOND KIRA, AND ASK HER TO KILL YOU. OR HE'LL START ASKING STUFF LIKE "YOUR LAST MANAGER, WAS MATSUI HIS REAL NAME...?"
BUT HE'LL ONLY GET MISA-SAN'S ANSWERING MACHINE AND WE'LL MAKE IT SO HE WON'T KNOW WHERE SHE IS.
HIGUCHI BELIEVES THAT MISA-SAN IS THE SECOND KIRA. HE'LL WANT HER HELP SO SHE WON'T BE IN ANY DANGER.
SO THEN HE'LL NEXT CALL THE CURRENT MANAGER, MOGI, AND ASK WHERE AMANE IS.
WE'LL JUST HAVE HIM SAY "MISA MISA HAD A DAY OFF AND WENT OUT SOMEWHERE"... ACTUALLY, LET'S TELL HIM SHE'S IN OKINAWA.

READ THIS WAY

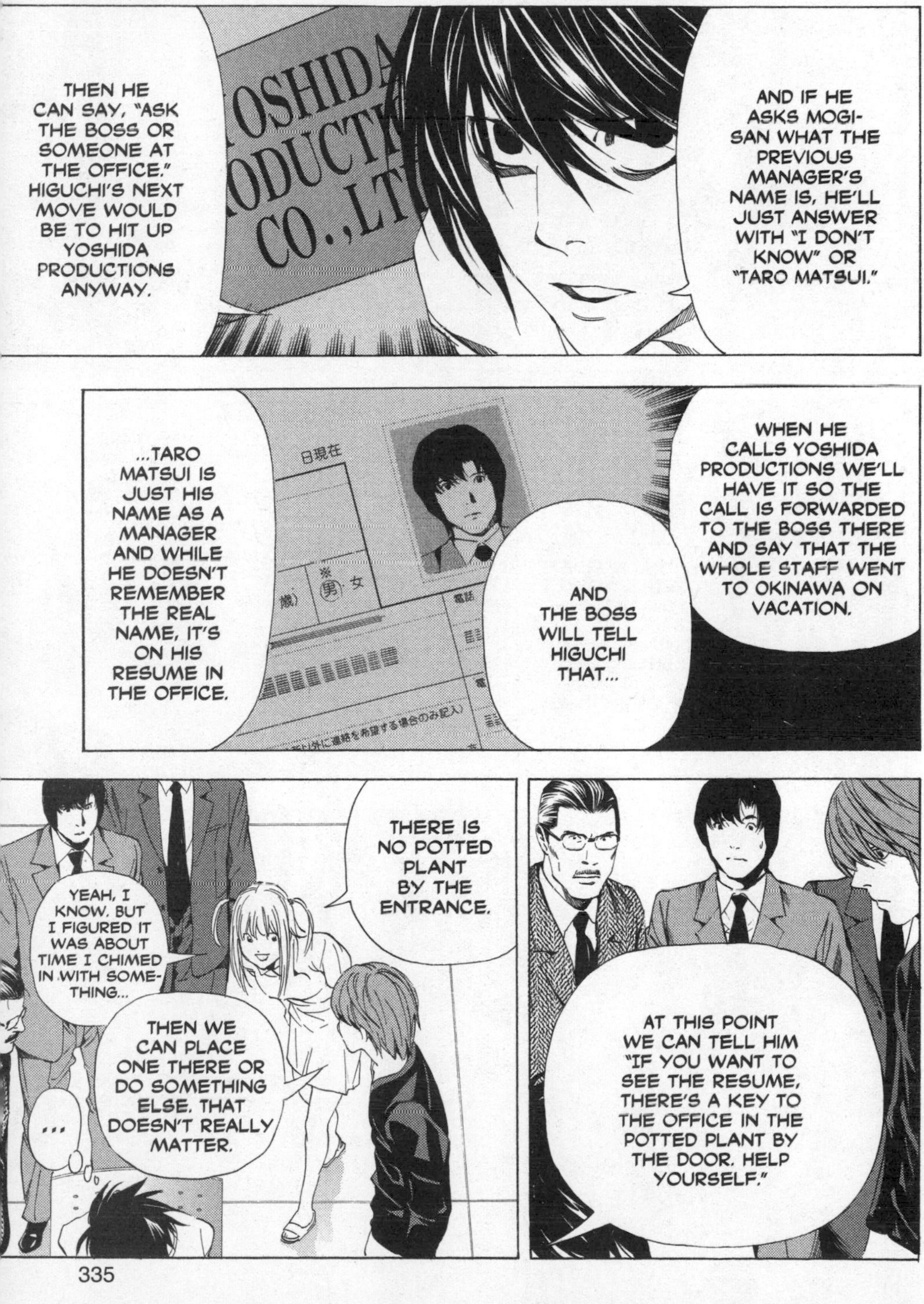
AND IF HE ASKS MOGI-SAN WHAT THE PREVIOUS MANAGER'S NAME IS, HE'LL JUST ANSWER WITH "I DON'T KNOW" OR "TARO MATSUI."
THEN HE CAN SAY, "ASK THE BOSS OR SOMEONE AT THE OFFICE." HIGUCHI'S NEXT MOVE WOULD BE TO HIT UP YOSHIDA PRODUCTIONS ANYWAY.
WHEN HE CALLS YOSHIDA PRODUCTIONS WE'LL HAVE IT SO THE CALL IS FORWARDED TO THE BOSS THERE AND SAY THAT THE WHOLE STAFF WENT TO OKINAWA ON VACATION.
AND THE BOSS WILL TELL HIGUCHI THAT...
...TARO MATSUI IS JUST HIS NAME AS A MANAGER AND WHILE HE DOESN'T REMEMBER THE REAL NAME, IT'S ON HIS RESUME IN THE OFFICE.
AT THIS POINT WE CAN TELL HIM "IF YOU WANT TO SEE THE RESUME, THERE'S A KEY TO THE OFFICE IN THE POTTED PLANT BY THE DOOR. HELP YOURSELF."
THERE IS NO POTTED PLANT BY THE ENTRANCE.
YEAH, I KNOW. BUT I FIGURED IT WAS ABOUT TIME I CHIMED IN WITH SOMETHING...
THEN WE CAN PLACE ONE THERE OR DO SOMETHING ELSE. THAT DOESN'T REALLY MATTER.
...

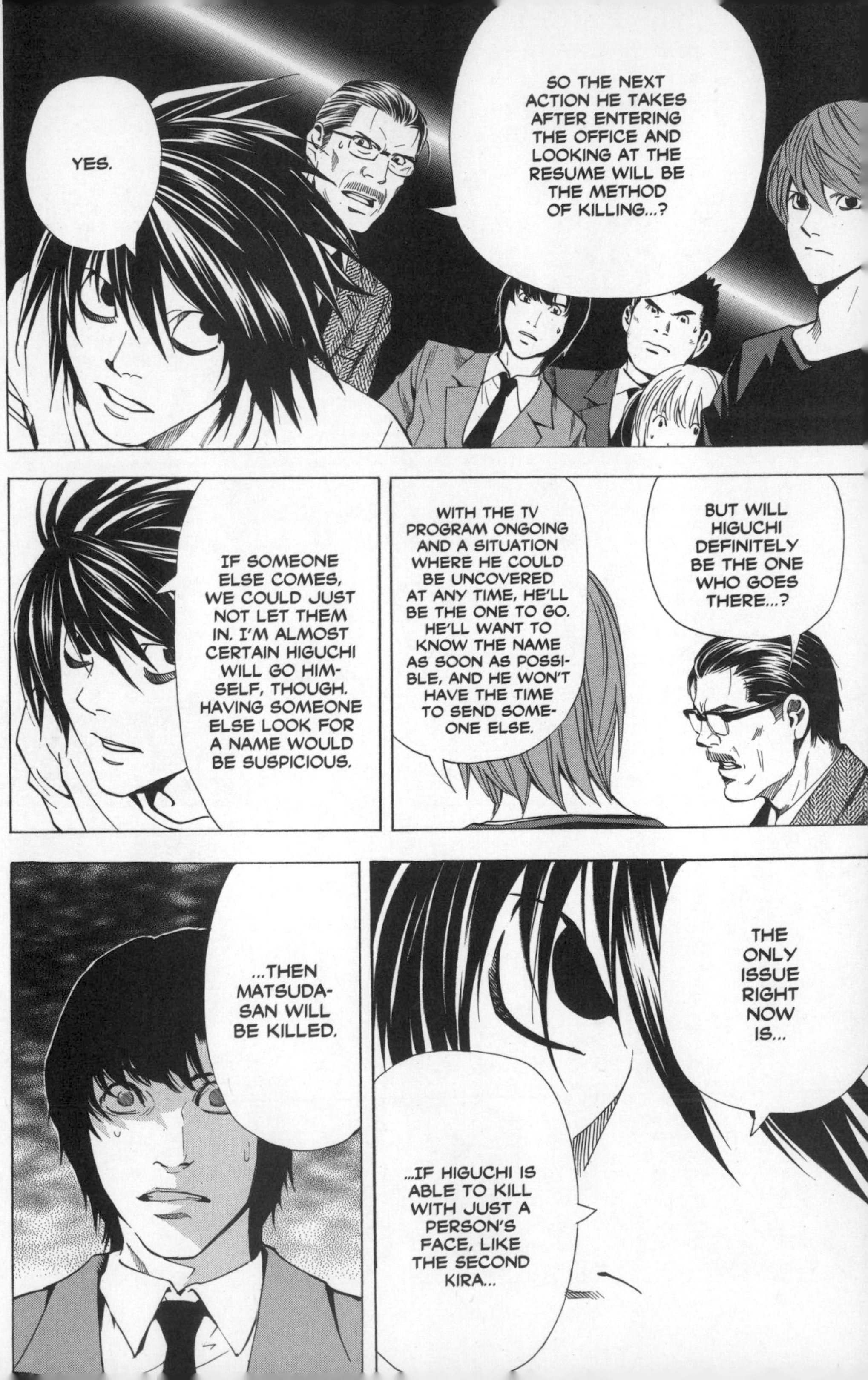
SO THE NEXT ACTION HE TAKES AFTER ENTERING THE OFFICE AND LOOKING AT THE RESUME WILL BE THE METHOD OF KILLING...?
YES.
BUT WILL HIGUCHI DEFINITELY BE THE ONE WHO GOES THERE...?
WITH THE TV PROGRAM ONGOING AND A SITUATION WHERE HE COULD BE UNCOVERED AT ANY TIME, HE'LL BE THE ONE TO GO. HE'LL WANT TO KNOW THE NAME AS SOON AS POSSIBLE, AND HE WON'T HAVE THE TIME TO SEND SOMEONE ELSE.
IF SOMEONE ELSE COMES, WE COULD JUST NOT LET THEM IN. I'M ALMOST CERTAIN HIGUCHI WILL GO HIMSELF, THOUGH. HAVING SOMEONE ELSE LOOK FOR A NAME WOULD BE SUSPICIOUS.
THE ONLY ISSUE RIGHT NOW IS...
...IF HIGUCHI IS ABLE TO KILL WITH JUST A PERSON'S FACE, LIKE THE SECOND KIRA...
...THEN MATSUDA-SAN WILL BE KILLED.

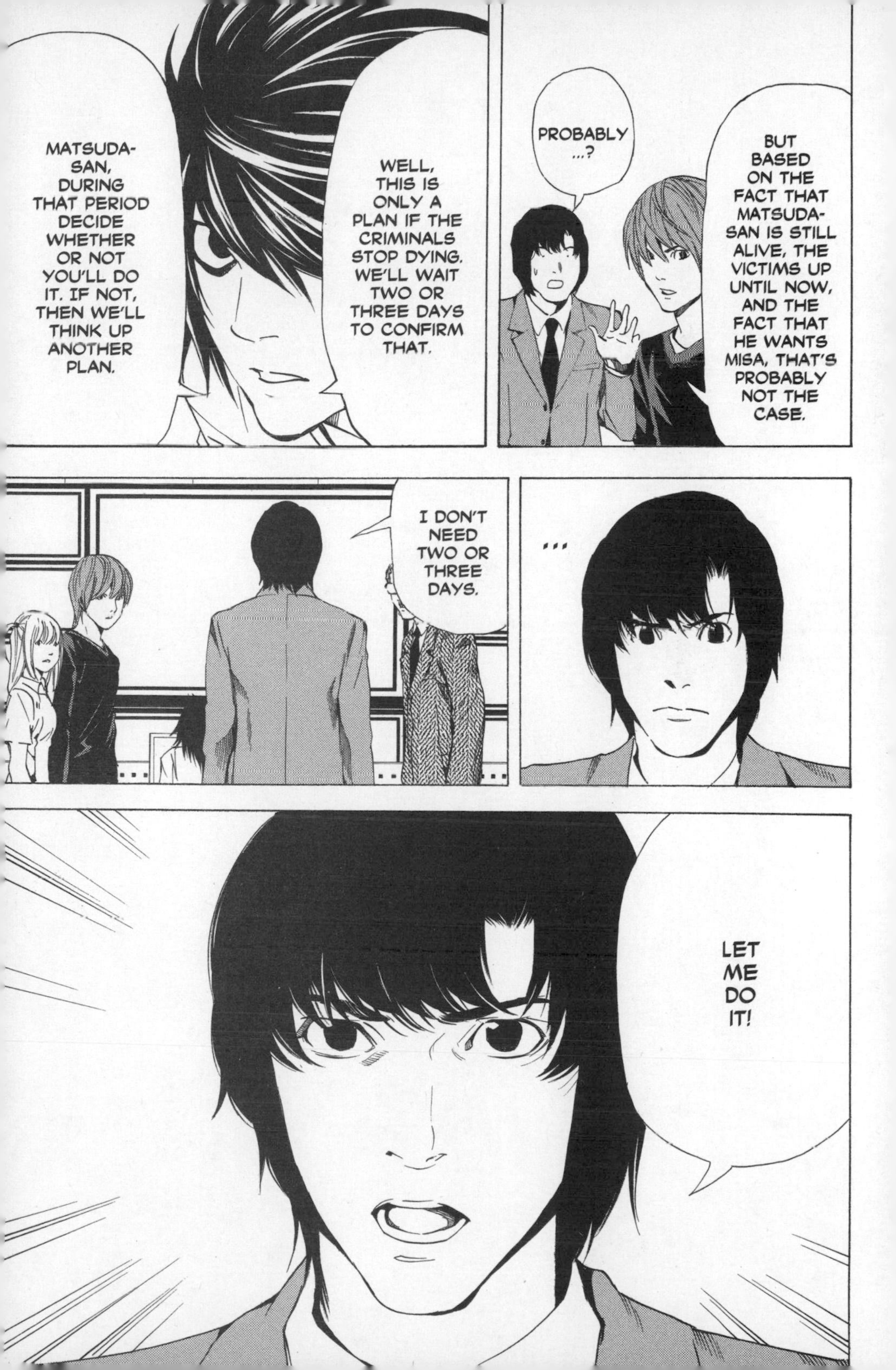
PROBABLY ...?
BUT BASED ON THE FACT THAT MATSUDA-SAN IS STILL ALIVE, THE VICTIMS UP UNTIL NOW, AND THE FACT THAT HE WANTS MISA, THAT'S PROBABLY NOT THE CASE.
WELL, THIS IS ONLY A PLAN IF THE CRIMINALS STOP DYING. WE'LL WAIT TWO OR THREE DAYS TO CONFIRM THAT.
MATSUDA-SAN, DURING THAT PERIOD DECIDE WHETHER OR NOT YOU'LL DO IT. IF NOT, THEN WE'LL THINK UP ANOTHER PLAN.
...
I DON'T NEED TWO OR THREE DAYS.
LET ME DO IT!

DEATH NOTE
HOW to USE it
XXXV

- If a DEATH NOTE owner accidentally misspells a name four times, that person will be free from being killed by the DEATH NOTE. However, if they intentionally misspell the name four times, the DEATH NOTE owner will die.

  デスノートに名前が書き込まれ死ぬ事を避ける為に
  故意に4度名前を間違えて書くと、書き込んだ人間は死ぬ。

- The person whose name was misspelled four times on purpose will not be free of death by a DEATH NOTE.

  故意に4度名前を間違えて書かれた人間は、
  4度間違えて書かれた事になりデスノートに名前を書き込まれても
  死ななくなる事にはならない。

chapter 50 Yotsuba

MIDO

LOOKS LIKE NAMIKAWA'S HERE.

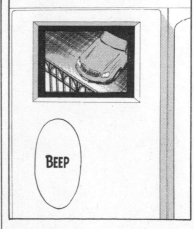

BEEP

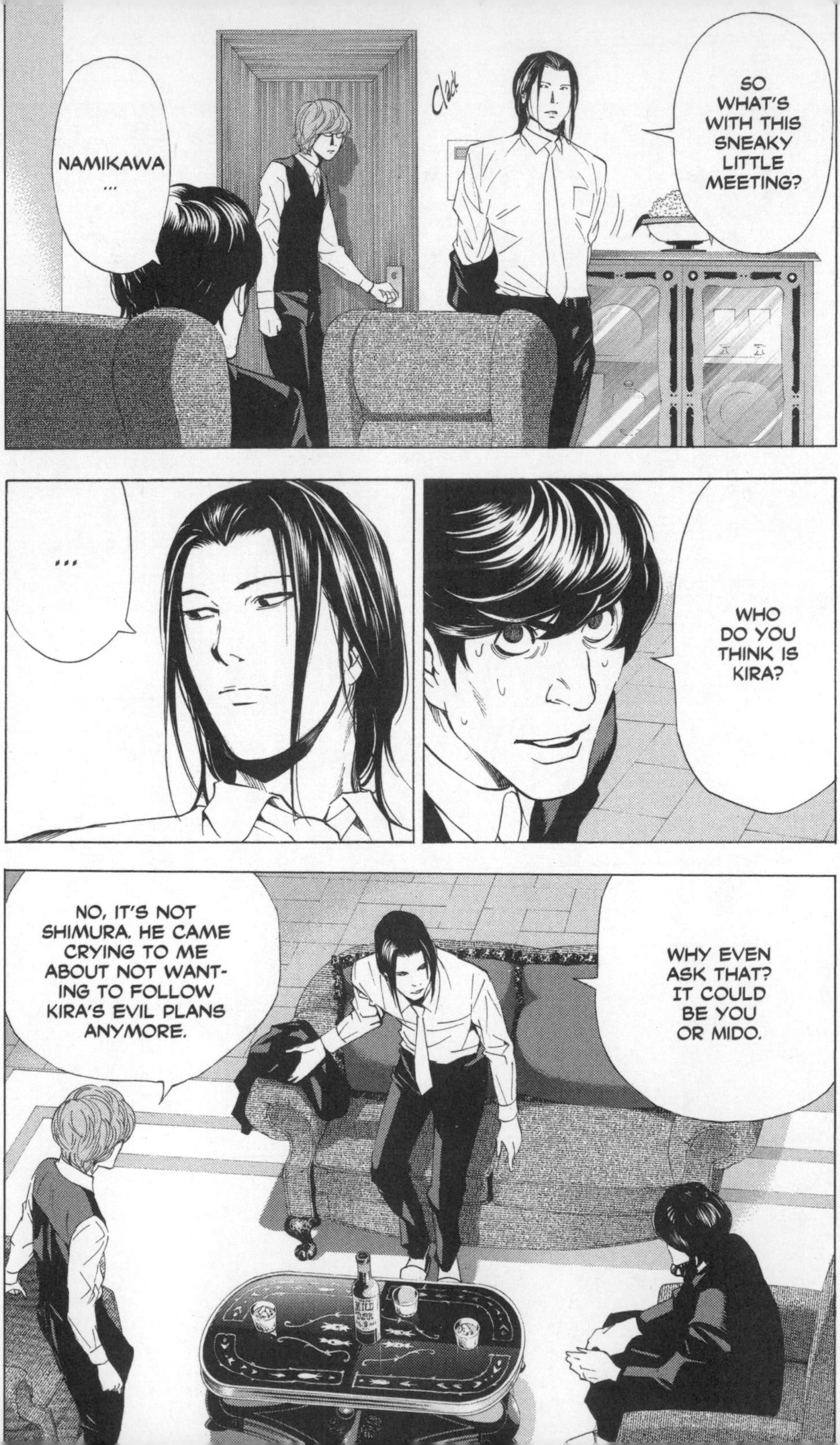
SO WHAT'S WITH THIS SNEAKY LITTLE MEETING?
Clack
NAMIKAWA ...
WHO DO YOU THINK IS KIRA?
...
WHY EVEN ASK THAT? IT COULD BE YOU OR MIDO.
NO, IT'S NOT SHIMURA. HE CAME CRYING TO ME ABOUT NOT WANTING TO FOLLOW KIRA'S EVIL PLANS ANYMORE.

READ THIS WAY

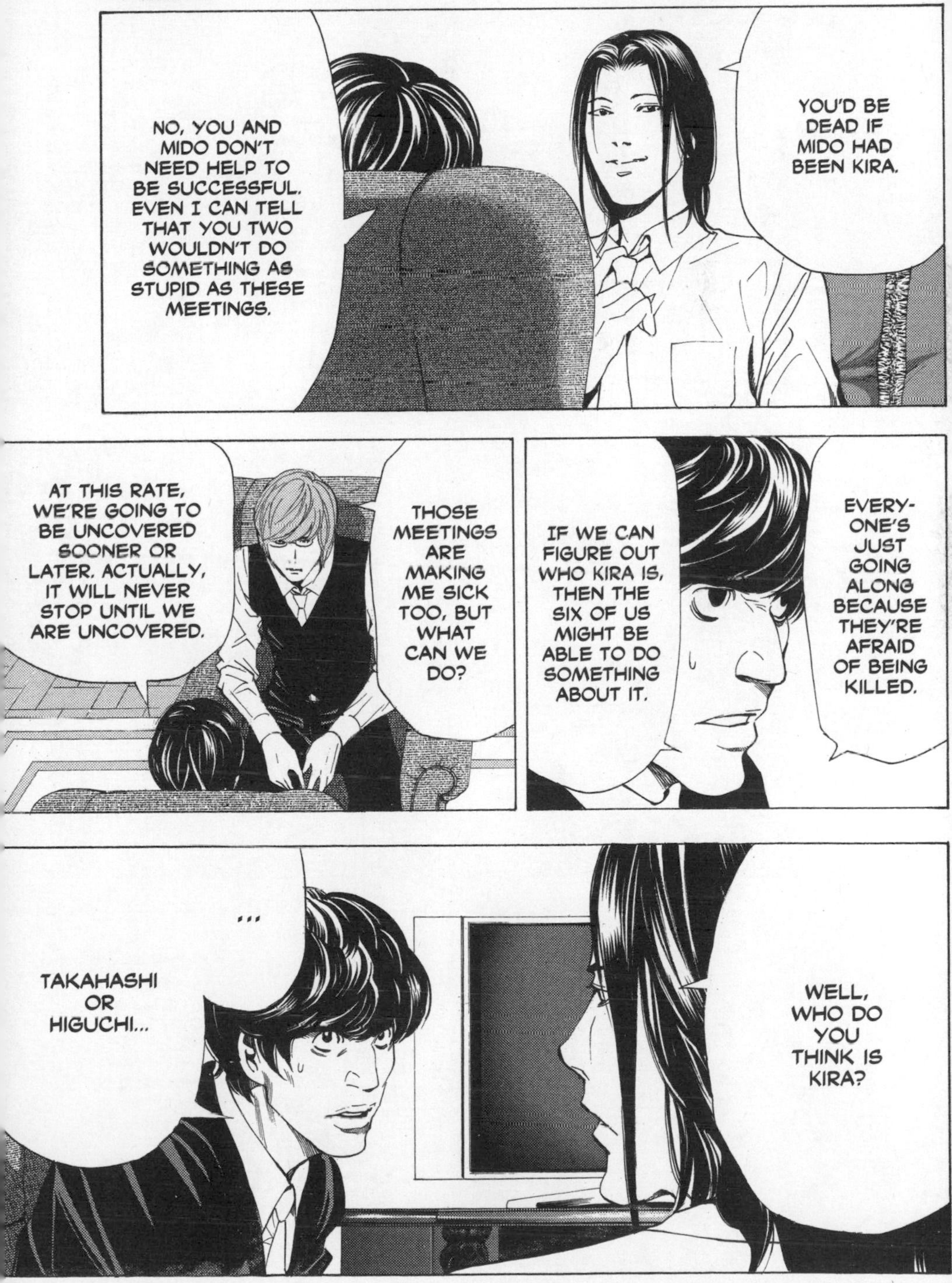
YOU'D BE DEAD IF MIDO HAD BEEN KIRA.
NO, YOU AND MIDO DON'T NEED HELP TO BE SUCCESSFUL. EVEN I CAN TELL THAT YOU TWO WOULDN'T DO SOMETHING AS STUPID AS THESE MEETINGS.
EVERY-ONE'S JUST GOING ALONG BECAUSE THEY'RE AFRAID OF BEING KILLED.
IF WE CAN FIGURE OUT WHO KIRA IS, THEN THE SIX OF US MIGHT BE ABLE TO DO SOMETHING ABOUT IT.
THOSE MEETINGS ARE MAKING ME SICK TOO, BUT WHAT CAN WE DO?
AT THIS RATE, WE'RE GOING TO BE UNCOVERED SOONER OR LATER. ACTUALLY, IT WILL NEVER STOP UNTIL WE ARE UNCOVERED.
WELL, WHO DO YOU THINK IS KIRA?
...
TAKAHASHI OR HIGUCHI...

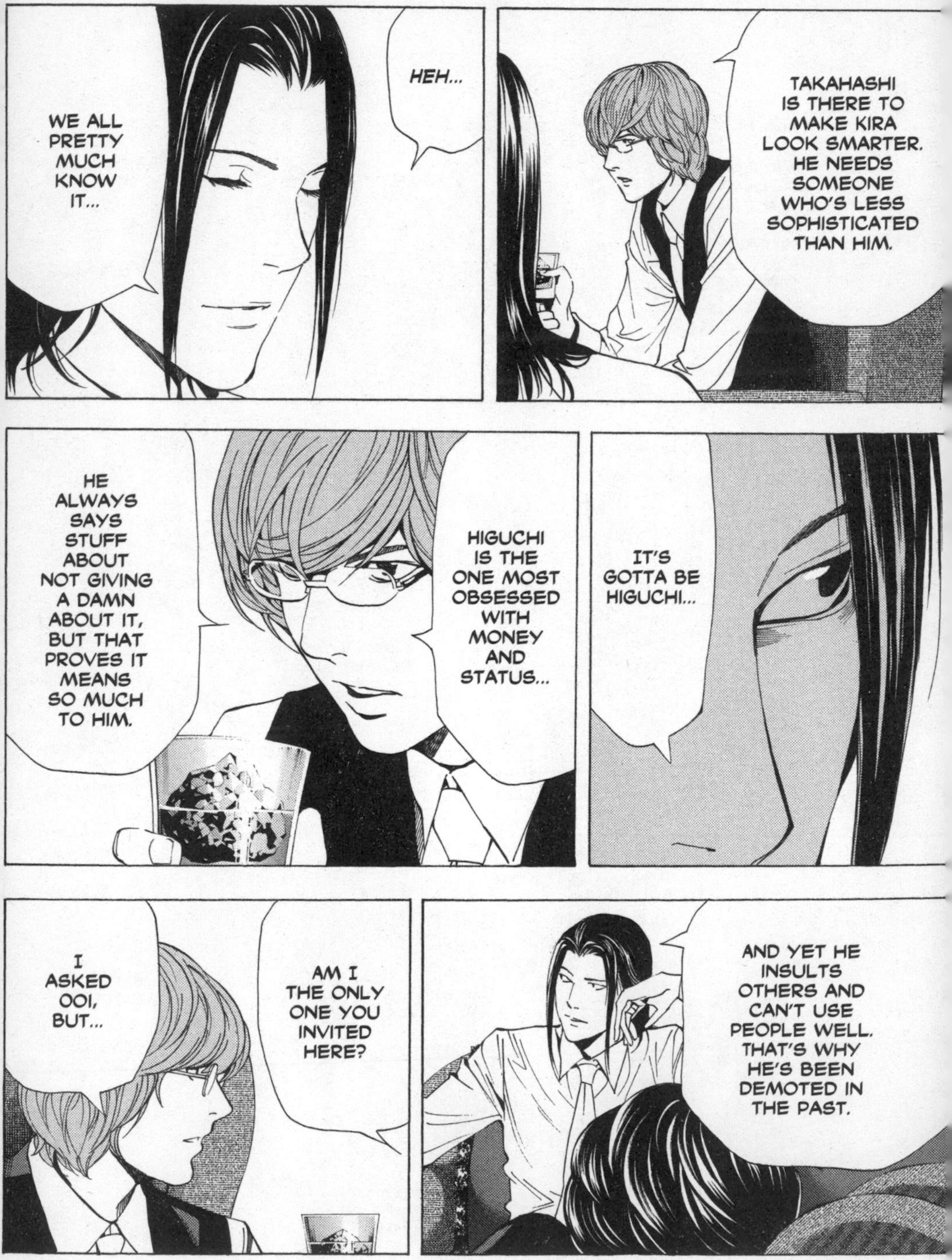
TAKAHASHI IS THERE TO MAKE KIRA LOOK SMARTER. HE NEEDS SOMEONE WHO'S LESS SOPHISTICATED THAN HIM.
HEH...
WE ALL PRETTY MUCH KNOW IT...
IT'S GOTTA BE HIGUCHI...
HIGUCHI IS THE ONE MOST OBSESSED WITH MONEY AND STATUS...
HE ALWAYS SAYS STUFF ABOUT NOT GIVING A DAMN ABOUT IT, BUT THAT PROVES IT MEANS SO MUCH TO HIM.
AND YET HE INSULTS OTHERS AND CAN'T USE PEOPLE WELL. THAT'S WHY HE'S BEEN DEMOTED IN THE PAST.
AM I THE ONLY ONE YOU INVITED HERE?
I ASKED OOI, BUT...

READ THIS WAY

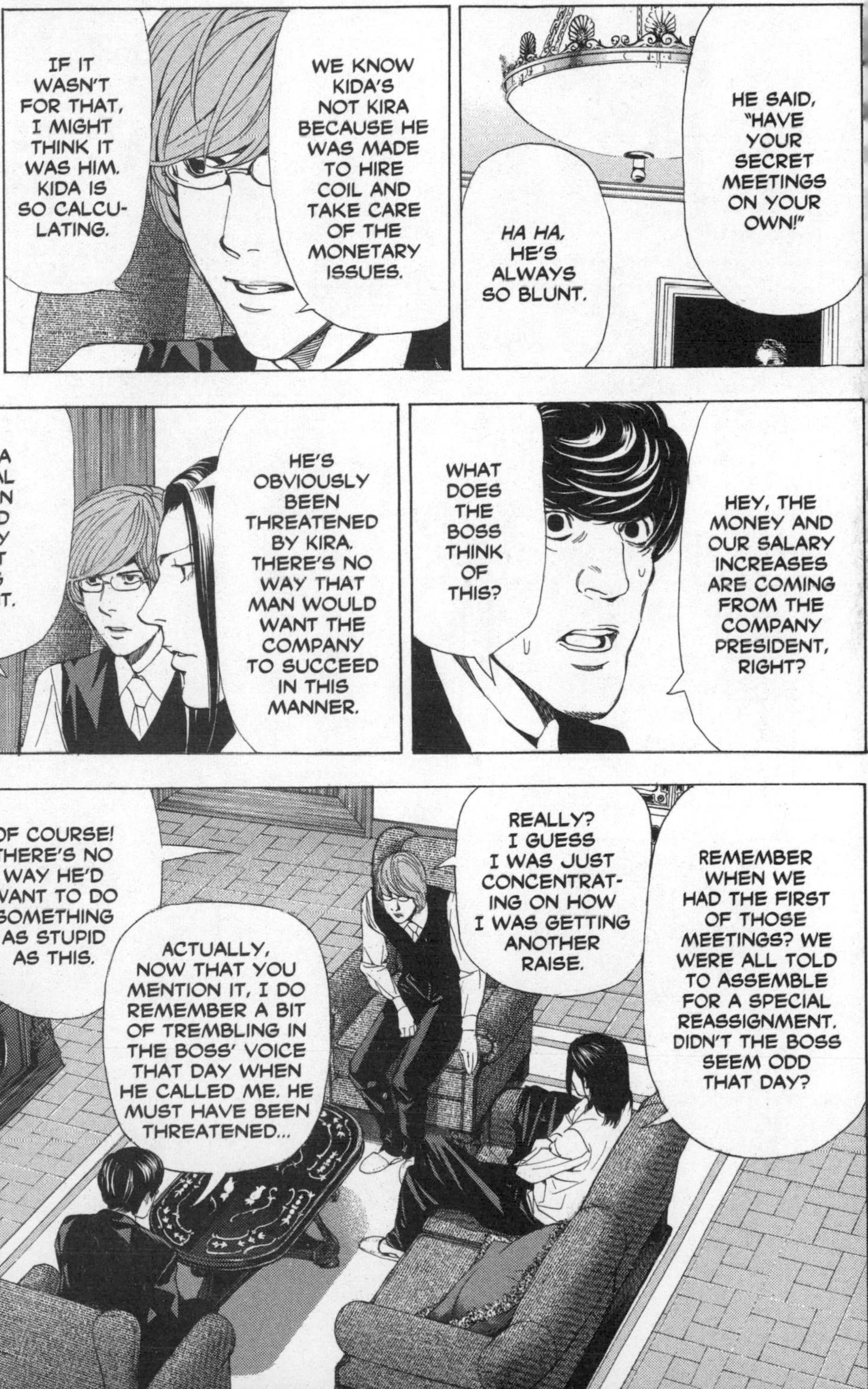
HE SAID, "HAVE YOUR SECRET MEETINGS ON YOUR OWN!"
HA HA, HE'S ALWAYS SO BLUNT.
WE KNOW KIDA'S NOT KIRA BECAUSE HE WAS MADE TO HIRE COIL AND TAKE CARE OF THE MONETARY ISSUES.
IF IT WASN'T FOR THAT, I MIGHT THINK IT WAS HIM. KIDA IS SO CALCU-LATING.
HEY, THE MONEY AND OUR SALARY INCREASES ARE COMING FROM THE COMPANY PRESIDENT, RIGHT?
WHAT DOES THE BOSS THINK OF THIS?
HE'S OBVIOUSLY BEEN THREATENED BY KIRA. THERE'S NO WAY THAT MAN WOULD WANT THE COMPANY TO SUCCEED IN THIS MANNER.
YEAH, A NORMAL PERSON WOULD WORRY ABOUT BEING CAUGHT.
REMEMBER WHEN WE HAD THE FIRST OF THOSE MEETINGS? WE WERE ALL TOLD TO ASSEMBLE FOR A SPECIAL REASSIGNMENT. DIDN'T THE BOSS SEEM ODD THAT DAY?
REALLY? I GUESS I WAS JUST CONCENTRAT-ING ON HOW I WAS GETTING ANOTHER RAISE.
ACTUALLY, NOW THAT YOU MENTION IT, I DO REMEMBER A BIT OF TREMBLING IN THE BOSS' VOICE THAT DAY WHEN HE CALLED ME. HE MUST HAVE BEEN THREATENED...
OF COURSE! THERE'S NO WAY HE'D WANT TO DO SOMETHING AS STUPID AS THIS.

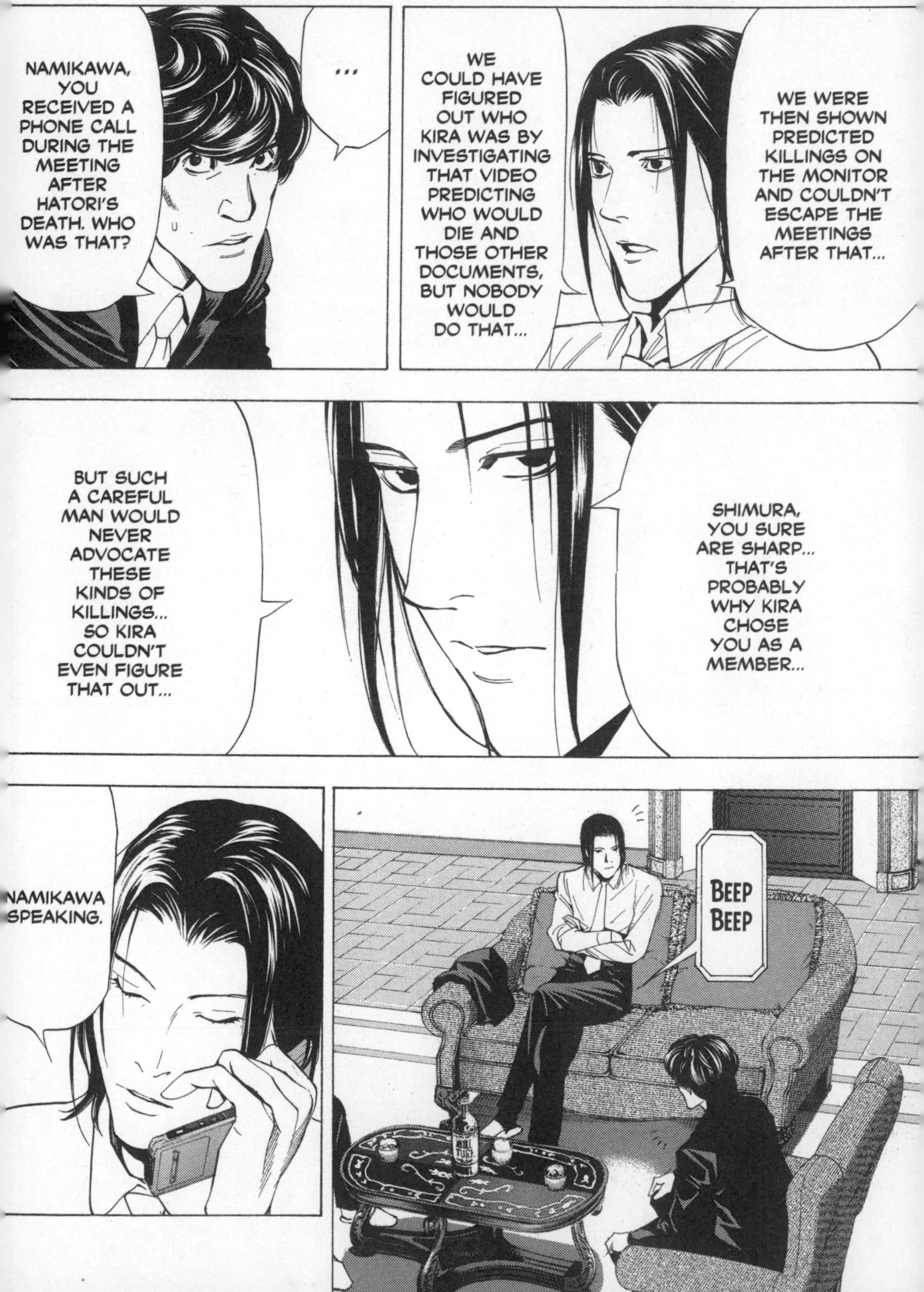
WE WERE THEN SHOWN PREDICTED KILLINGS ON THE MONITOR AND COULDN'T ESCAPE THE MEETINGS AFTER THAT...
WE COULD HAVE FIGURED OUT WHO KIRA WAS BY INVESTIGATING THAT VIDEO PREDICTING WHO WOULD DIE AND THOSE OTHER DOCUMENTS, BUT NOBODY WOULD DO THAT...
...
NAMIKAWA, YOU RECEIVED A PHONE CALL DURING THE MEETING AFTER HATORI'S DEATH. WHO WAS THAT?
SHIMURA, YOU SURE ARE SHARP... THAT'S PROBABLY WHY KIRA CHOSE YOU AS A MEMBER...
BUT SUCH A CAREFUL MAN WOULD NEVER ADVOCATE THESE KINDS OF KILLINGS... SO KIRA COULDN'T EVEN FIGURE THAT OUT...
BEEP BEEP
NAMIKAWA SPEAKING.

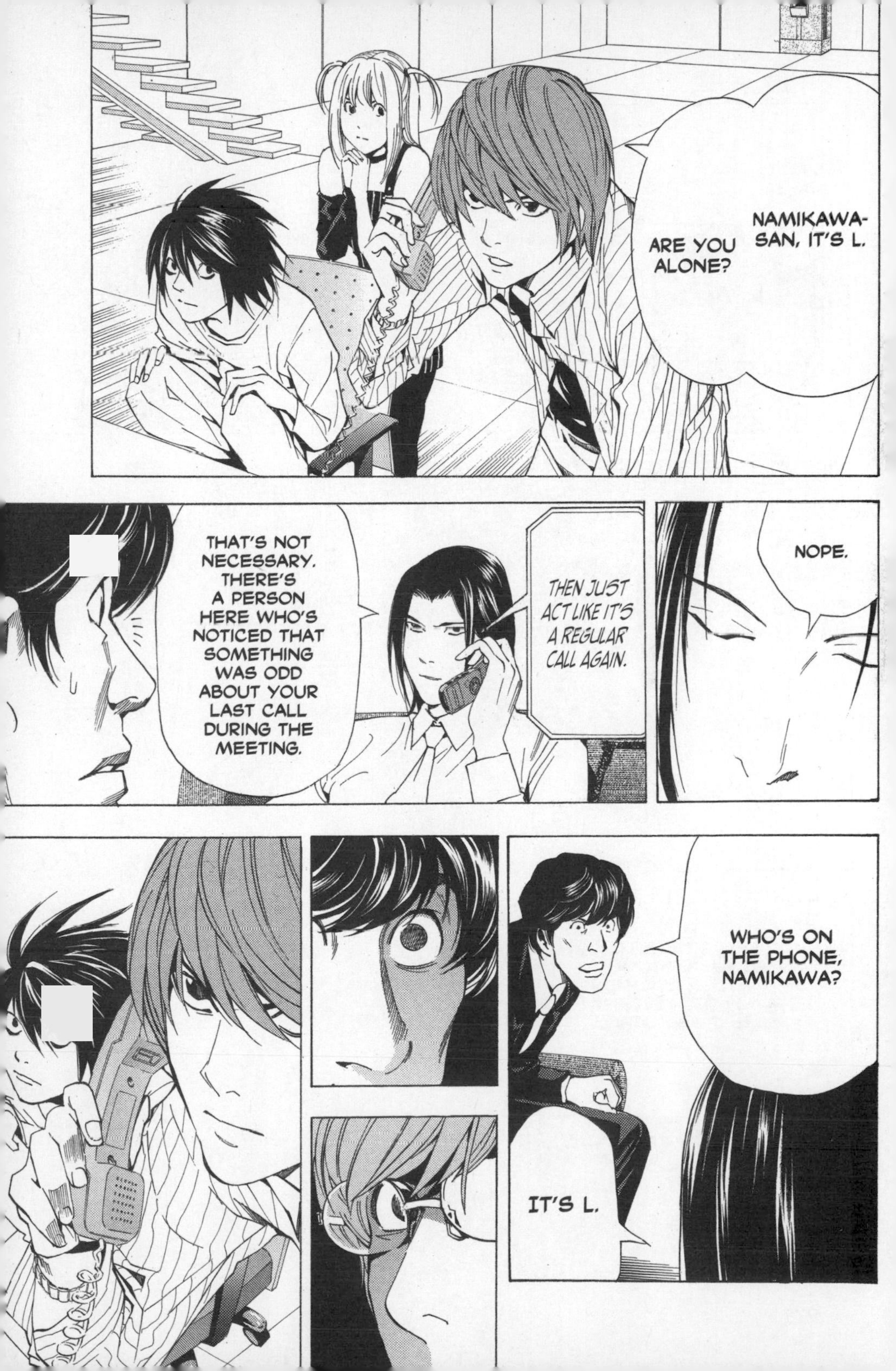
NAMIKAWA-SAN, IT'S L.
ARE YOU ALONE?
NOPE.
THEN JUST ACT LIKE IT'S A REGULAR CALL AGAIN.
THAT'S NOT NECESSARY. THERE'S A PERSON HERE WHO'S NOTICED THAT SOMETHING WAS ODD ABOUT YOUR LAST CALL DURING THE MEETING.
WHO'S ON THE PHONE, NAMIKAWA?
IT'S L.

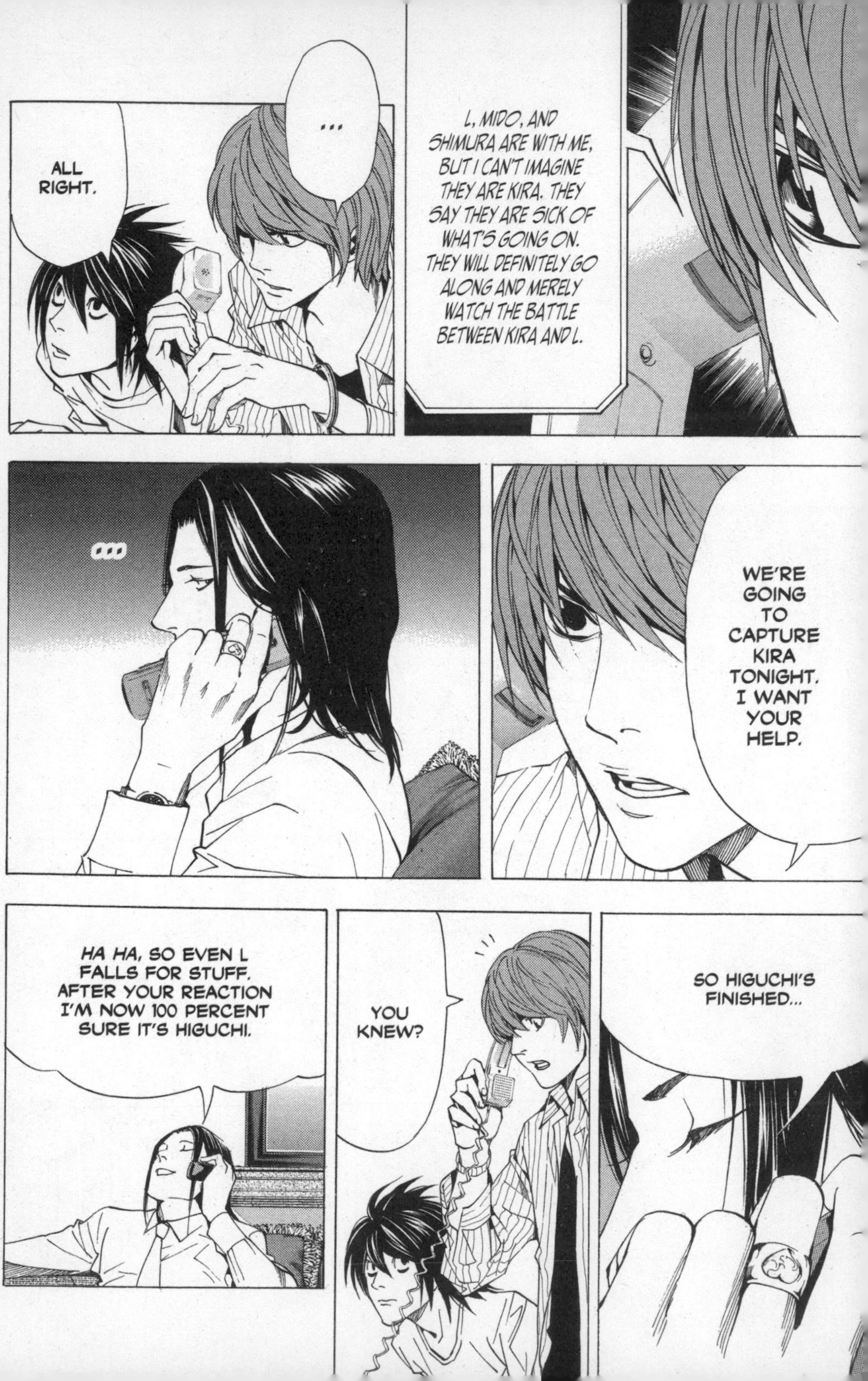
L, MIDO, AND SHIMURA ARE WITH ME, BUT I CAN'T IMAGINE THEY ARE KIRA. THEY SAY THEY ARE SICK OF WHAT'S GOING ON. THEY WILL DEFINITELY GO ALONG AND MERELY WATCH THE BATTLE BETWEEN KIRA AND L.
...
ALL RIGHT.
WE'RE GOING TO CAPTURE KIRA TONIGHT. I WANT YOUR HELP.
...
SO HIGUCHI'S FINISHED...
YOU KNEW?
HA HA, SO EVEN L FALLS FOR STUFF. AFTER YOUR REACTION I'M NOW 100 PERCENT SURE IT'S HIGUCHI.

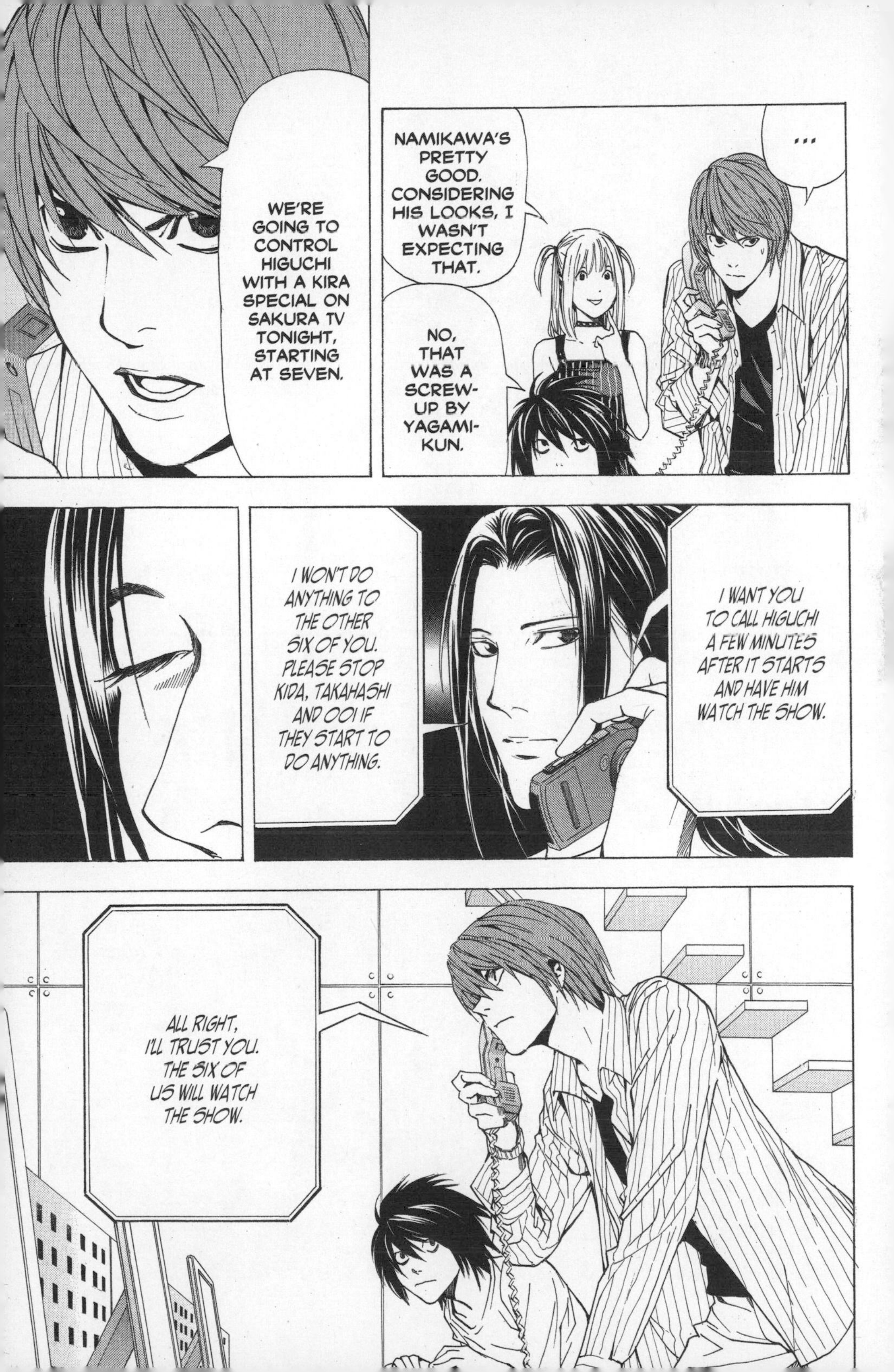
...
NAMIKAWA'S PRETTY GOOD. CONSIDERING HIS LOOKS, I WASN'T EXPECTING THAT.
NO, THAT WAS A SCREW-UP BY YAGAMI-KUN.
WE'RE GOING TO CONTROL HIGUCHI WITH A KIRA SPECIAL ON SAKURA TV TONIGHT, STARTING AT SEVEN.
I WANT YOU TO CALL HIGUCHI A FEW MINUTES AFTER IT STARTS AND HAVE HIM WATCH THE SHOW.
I WON'T DO ANYTHING TO THE OTHER SIX OF YOU. PLEASE STOP KIDA, TAKAHASHI AND OOI IF THEY START TO DO ANYTHING.
ALL RIGHT, I'LL TRUST YOU. THE SIX OF US WILL WATCH THE SHOW.

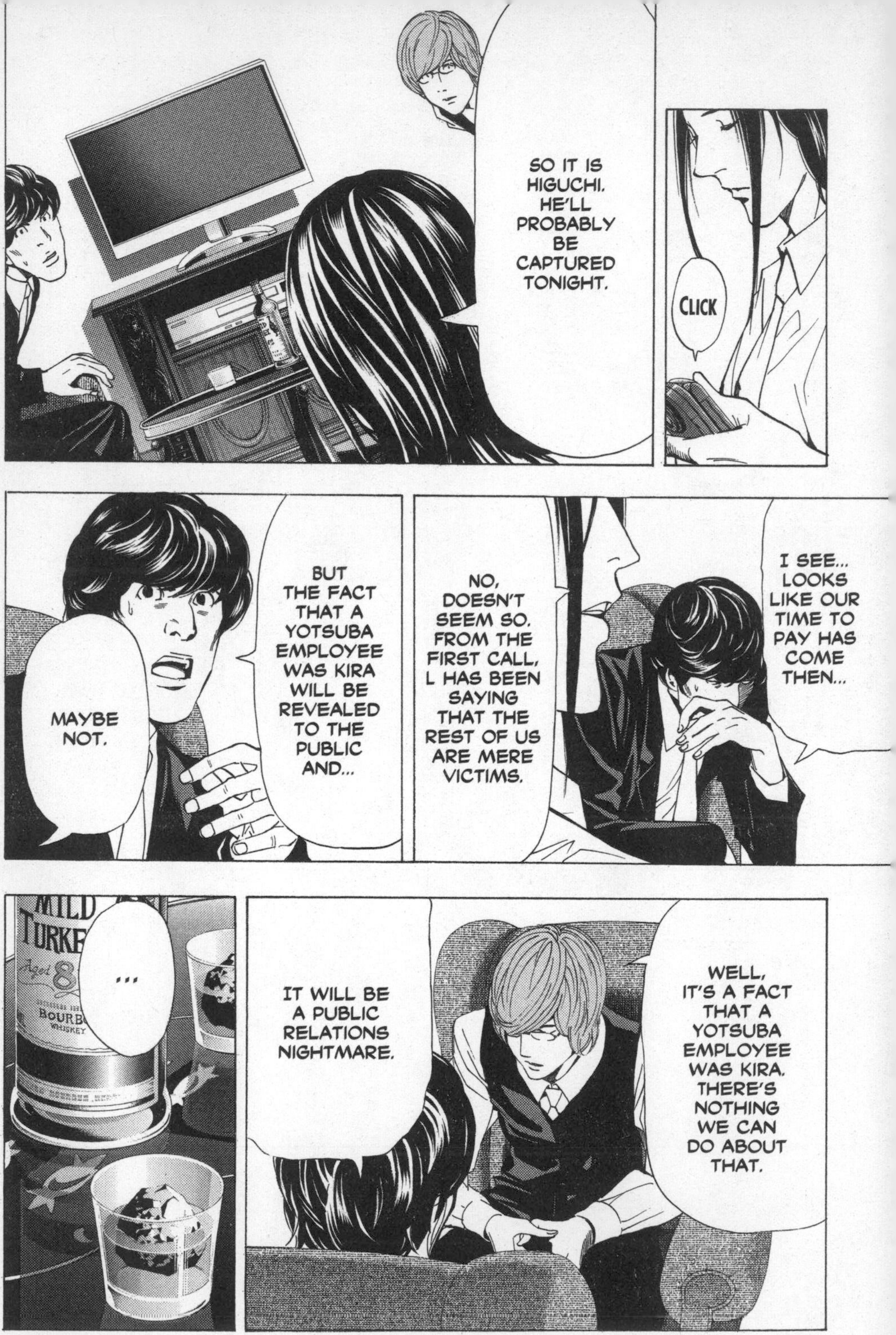
CLICK
SO IT IS HIGUCHI. HE'LL PROBABLY BE CAPTURED TONIGHT.
I SEE... LOOKS LIKE OUR TIME TO PAY HAS COME THEN...
NO, DOESN'T SEEM SO. FROM THE FIRST CALL, L HAS BEEN SAYING THAT THE REST OF US ARE MERE VICTIMS.
BUT THE FACT THAT A YOTSUBA EMPLOYEE WAS KIRA WILL BE REVEALED TO THE PUBLIC AND...
MAYBE NOT.
WELL, IT'S A FACT THAT A YOTSUBA EMPLOYEE WAS KIRA. THERE'S NOTHING WE CAN DO ABOUT THAT.
IT WILL BE A PUBLIC RELATIONS NIGHTMARE.
...

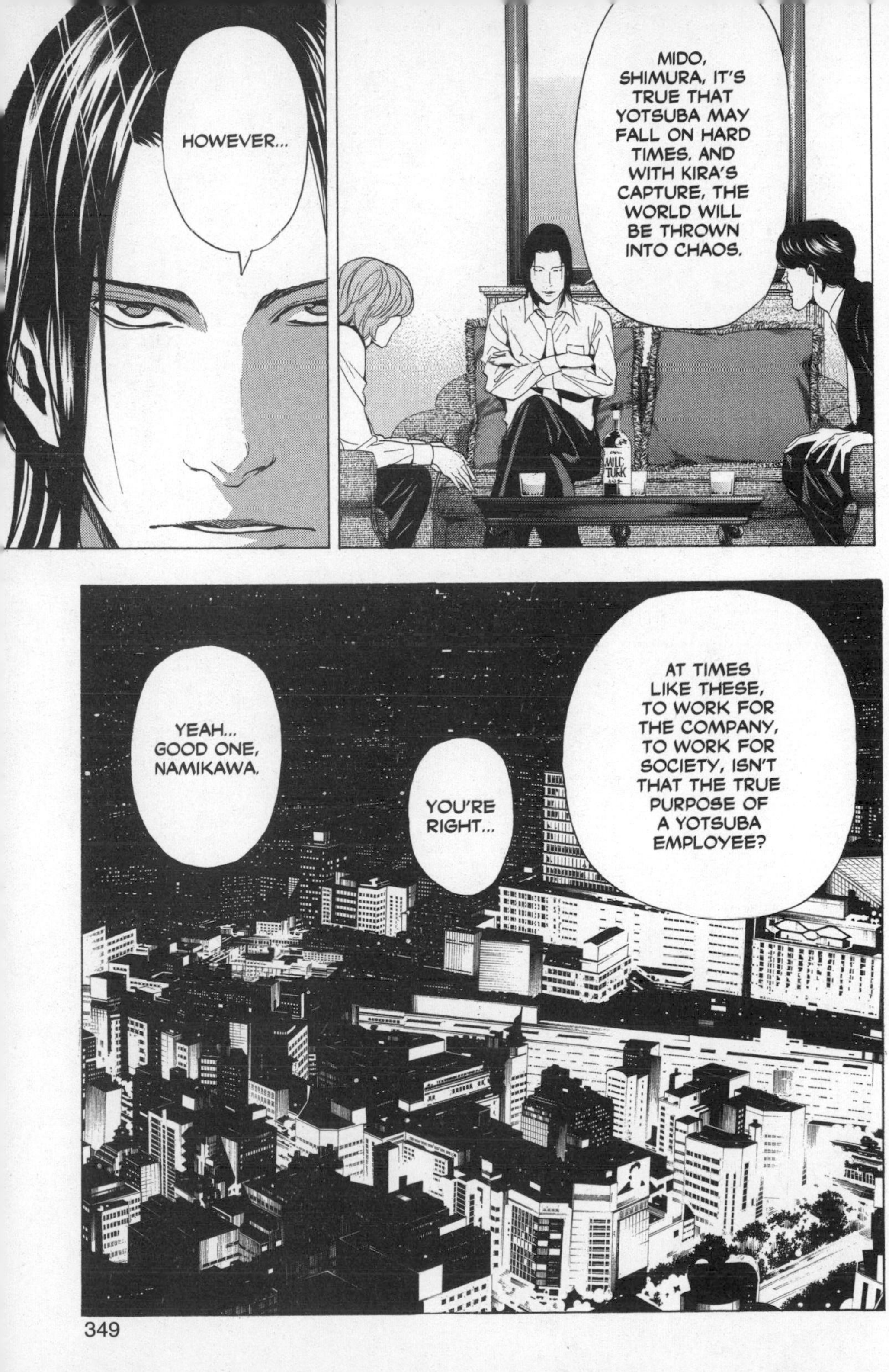
MIDO, SHIMURA, IT'S TRUE THAT YOTSUBA MAY FALL ON HARD TIMES. AND WITH KIRA'S CAPTURE, THE WORLD WILL BE THROWN INTO CHAOS.
HOWEVER...
AT TIMES LIKE THESE, TO WORK FOR THE COMPANY, TO WORK FOR SOCIETY, ISN'T THAT THE TRUE PURPOSE OF A YOTSUBA EMPLOYEE?
YOU'RE RIGHT...
YEAH... GOOD ONE, NAMIKAWA.

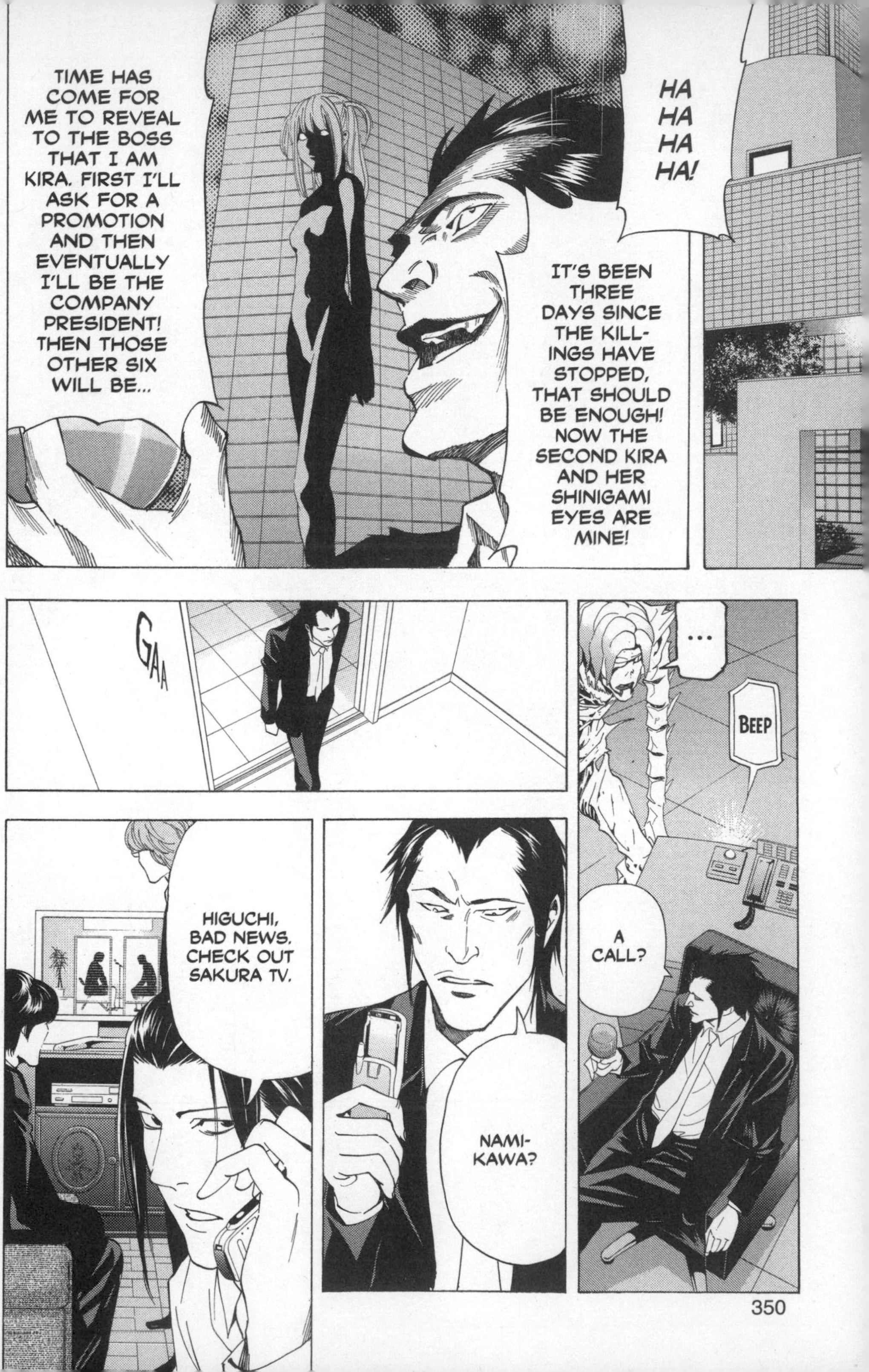
HA HA HA HA!
IT'S BEEN THREE DAYS SINCE THE KILL-INGS HAVE STOPPED, THAT SHOULD BE ENOUGH! NOW THE SECOND KIRA AND HER SHINIGAMI EYES ARE MINE!
TIME HAS COME FOR ME TO REVEAL TO THE BOSS THAT I AM KIRA. FIRST I'LL ASK FOR A PROMOTION AND THEN EVENTUALLY I'LL BE THE COMPANY PRESIDENT! THEN THOSE OTHER SIX WILL BE...
...
BEEP
A CALL?
GAA
NAMI-KAWA?
HIGUCHI, BAD NEWS. CHECK OUT SAKURA TV.

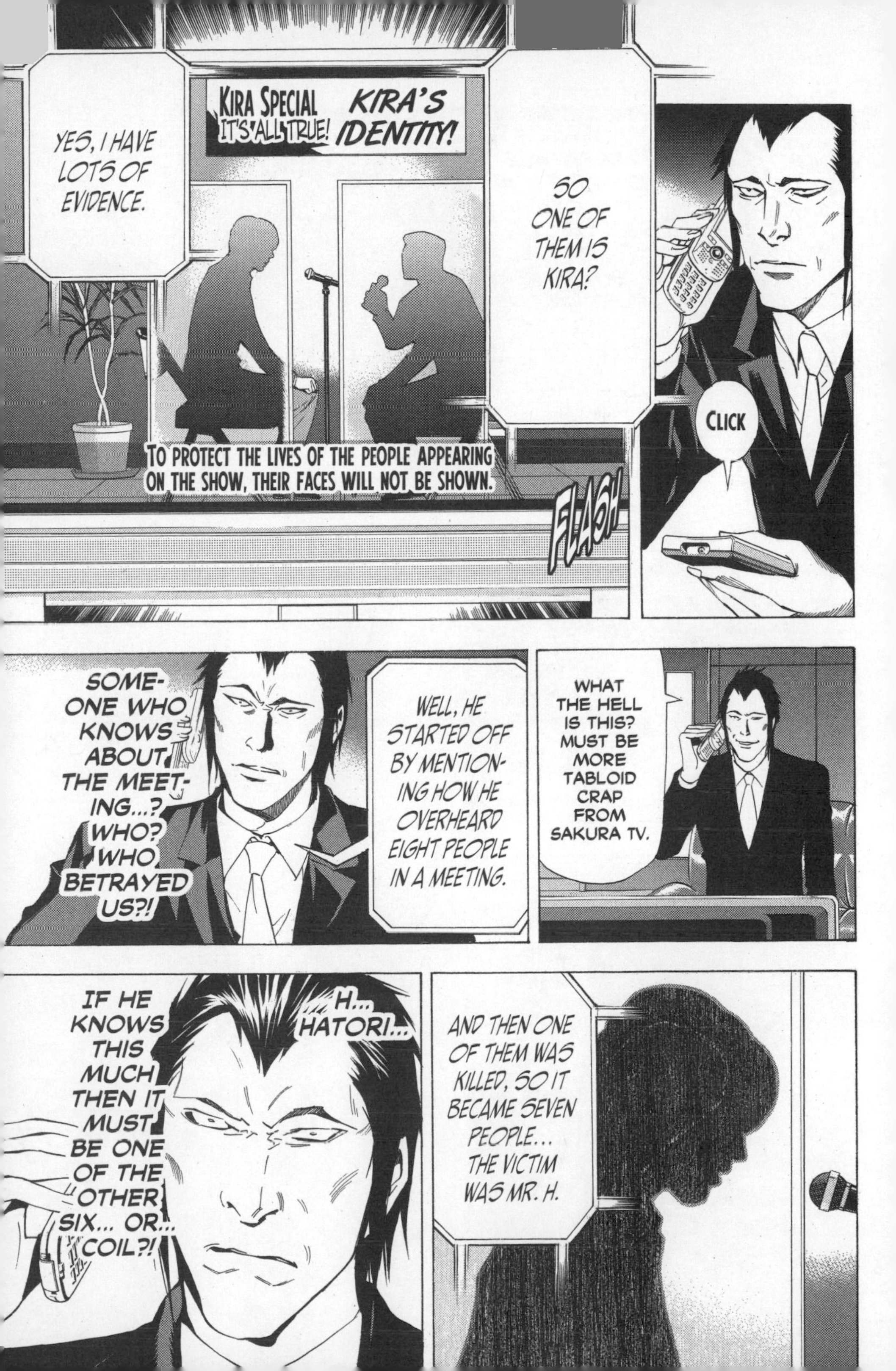
CLICK
FLASH
SO ONE OF THEM IS KIRA?
KIRA'S IDENTITY!
KIRA SPECIAL
IT'S ALL TRUE!
YES, I HAVE LOTS OF EVIDENCE.
TO PROTECT THE LIVES OF THE PEOPLE APPEARING ON THE SHOW, THEIR FACES WILL NOT BE SHOWN.
WHAT THE HELL IS THIS? MUST BE MORE TABLOID CRAP FROM SAKURA TV.
WELL, HE STARTED OFF BY MENTIONING HOW HE OVERHEARD EIGHT PEOPLE IN A MEETING.
SOMEONE WHO KNOWS ABOUT THE MEETING...? WHO? WHO BETRAYED US?!
AND THEN ONE OF THEM WAS KILLED, SO IT BECAME SEVEN PEOPLE... THE VICTIM WAS MR. H.
H... HATORI...
IF HE KNOWS THIS MUCH THEN IT MUST BE ONE OF THE OTHER SIX... OR... COIL?!

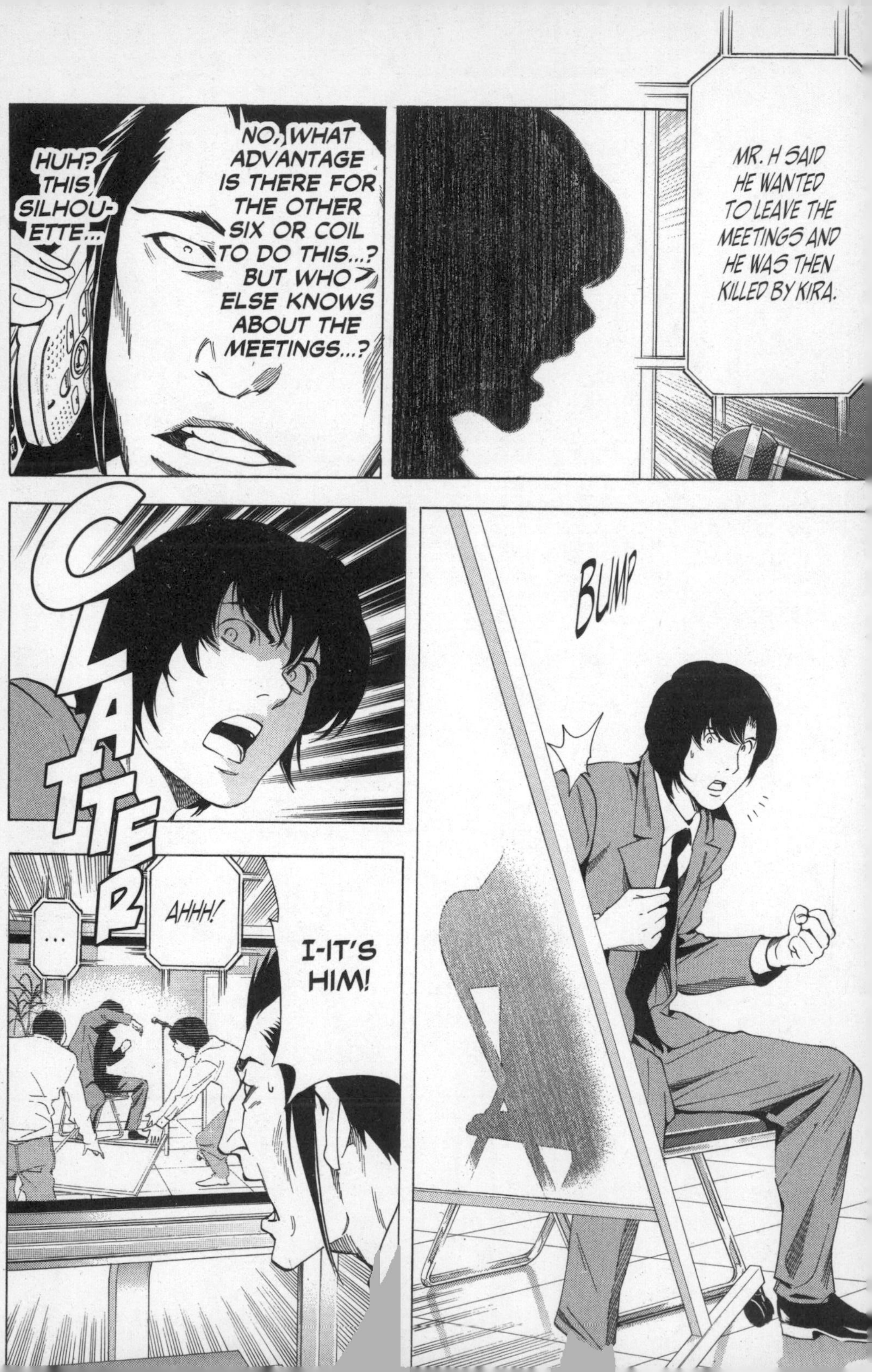
MR. H SAID HE WANTED TO LEAVE THE MEETINGS AND HE WAS THEN KILLED BY KIRA.
HUH? THIS SILHOU-ETTE...
NO, WHAT ADVANTAGE IS THERE FOR THE OTHER SIX OR COIL TO DO THIS...? BUT WHO ELSE KNOWS ABOUT THE MEETINGS...?
BUMP
CLATTER
I-IT'S HIM!
AHHH!
...

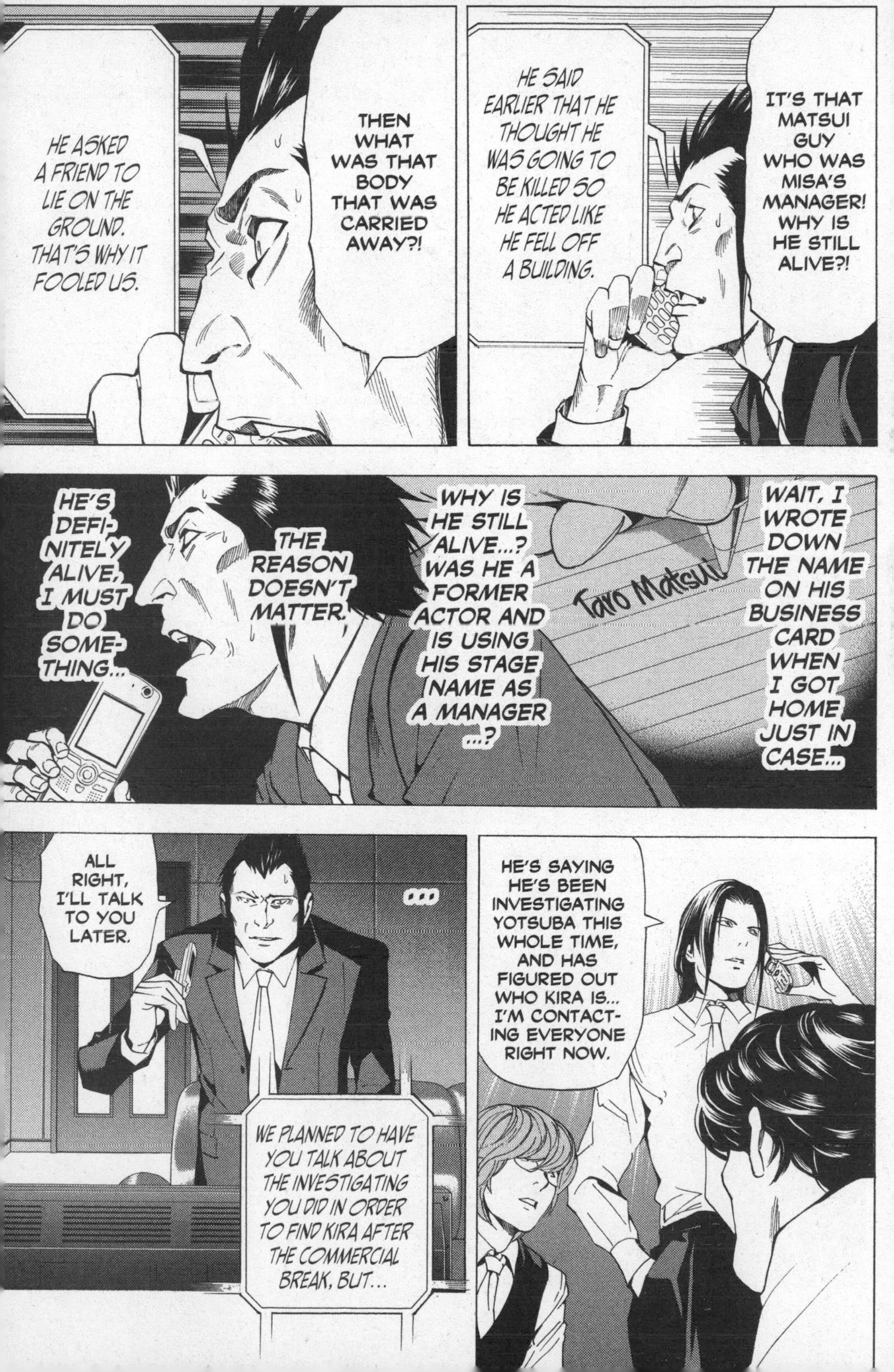

IT'S THAT MATSUI GUY WHO WAS MISA'S MANAGER! WHY IS HE STILL ALIVE?!
HE SAID EARLIER THAT HE THOUGHT HE WAS GOING TO BE KILLED SO HE ACTED LIKE HE FELL OFF A BUILDING.
THEN WHAT WAS THAT BODY THAT WAS CARRIED AWAY?!
HE ASKED A FRIEND TO LIE ON THE GROUND. THAT'S WHY IT FOOLED US.
WAIT, I WROTE DOWN THE NAME ON HIS BUSINESS CARD WHEN I GOT HOME JUST IN CASE...
Taro Matsui
WHY IS HE STILL ALIVE...? WAS HE A FORMER ACTOR AND IS USING HIS STAGE NAME AS A MANAGER ...?
THE REASON DOESN'T MATTER.
HE'S DEFINITELY ALIVE, I MUST DO SOMETHING...
HE'S SAYING HE'S BEEN INVESTIGATING YOTSUBA THIS WHOLE TIME, AND HAS FIGURED OUT WHO KIRA IS... I'M CONTACTING EVERYONE RIGHT NOW.
...
ALL RIGHT, I'LL TALK TO YOU LATER.
WE PLANNED TO HAVE YOU TALK ABOUT THE INVESTIGATING YOU DID IN ORDER TO FIND KIRA AFTER THE COMMERCIAL BREAK, BUT...

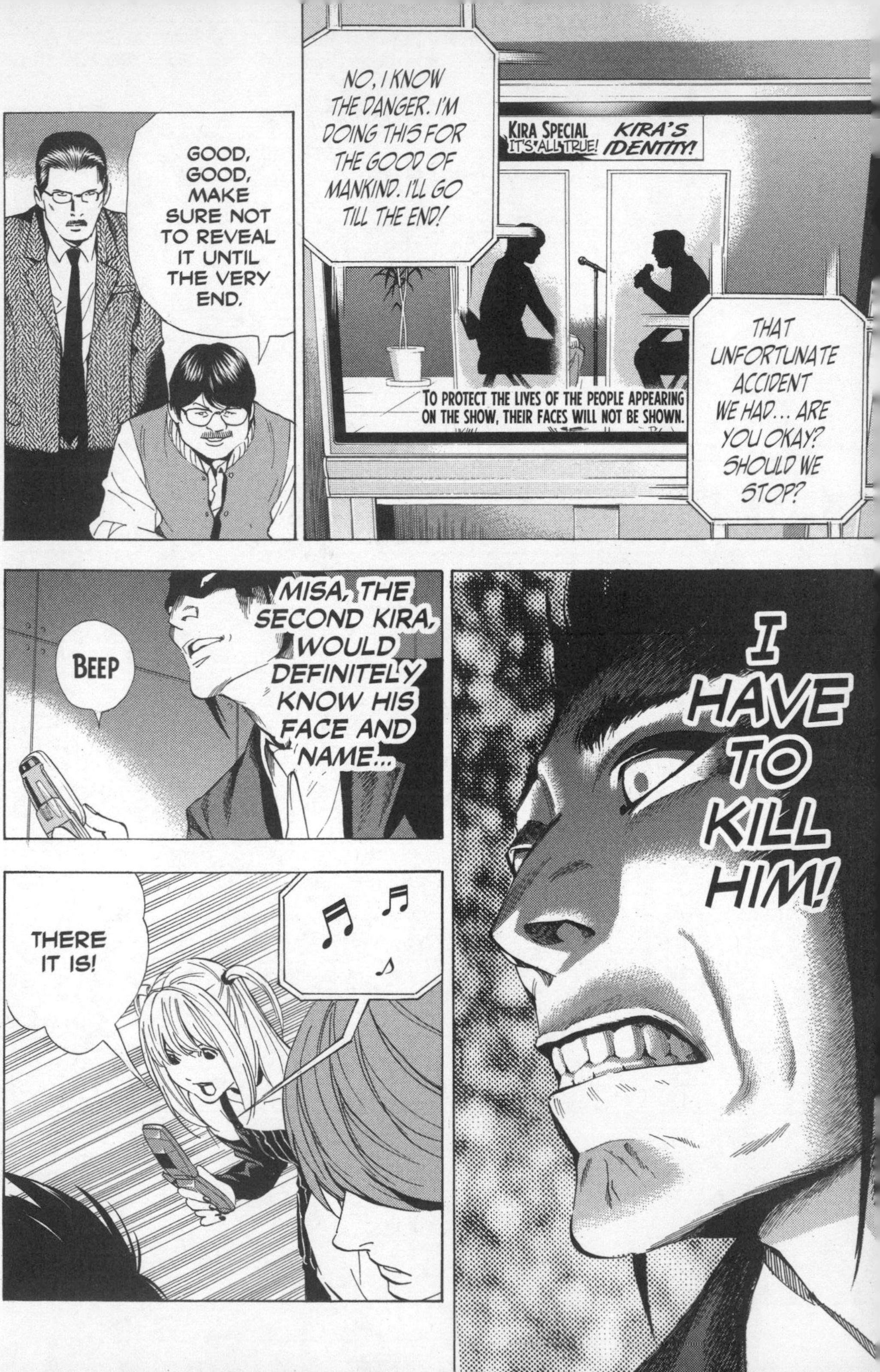
KIRA SPECIAL IT'S ALL TRUE! KIRA'S IDENTITY!
THAT UNFORTUNATE ACCIDENT WE HAD... ARE YOU OKAY? SHOULD WE STOP?
NO, I KNOW THE DANGER. I'M DOING THIS FOR THE GOOD OF MANKIND. I'LL GO TILL THE END!
TO PROTECT THE LIVES OF THE PEOPLE APPEARING ON THE SHOW, THEIR FACES WILL NOT BE SHOWN.
GOOD, GOOD, MAKE SURE NOT TO REVEAL IT UNTIL THE VERY END.
I HAVE TO KILL HIM!
MISA, THE SECOND KIRA, WOULD DEFINITELY KNOW HIS FACE AND NAME...
BEEP
THERE IT IS!

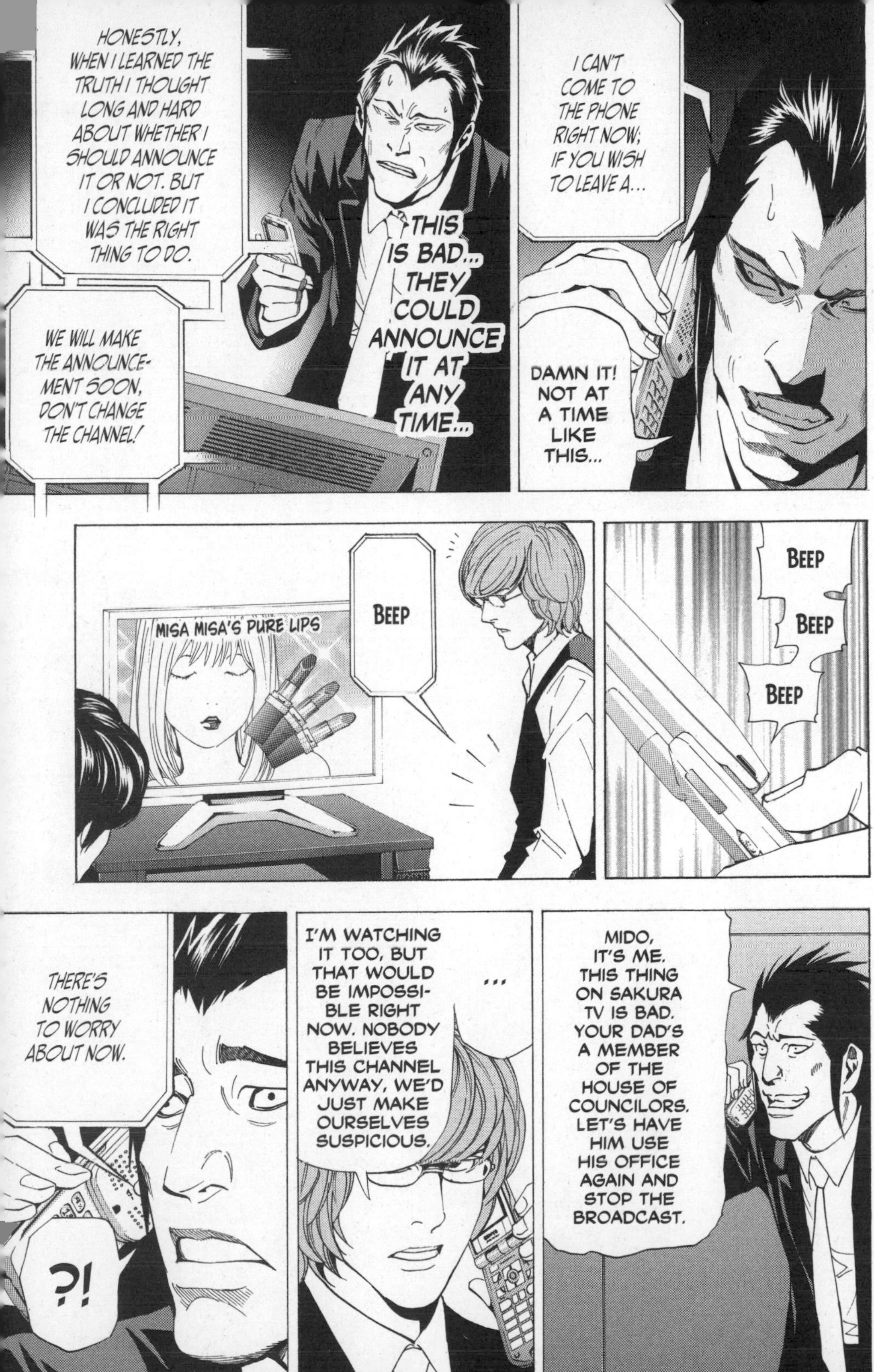
I CAN'T COME TO THE PHONE RIGHT NOW; IF YOU WISH TO LEAVE A...
DAMN IT! NOT AT A TIME LIKE THIS...
HONESTLY, WHEN I LEARNED THE TRUTH I THOUGHT LONG AND HARD ABOUT WHETHER I SHOULD ANNOUNCE IT OR NOT. BUT I CONCLUDED IT WAS THE RIGHT THING TO DO.
THIS IS BAD... THEY COULD ANNOUNCE IT AT ANY TIME...
WE WILL MAKE THE ANNOUNCE-MENT SOON, DON'T CHANGE THE CHANNEL!
BEEP
BEEP
BEEP
BEEP
MISA MISA'S PURE LIPS
MIDO, IT'S ME. THIS THING ON SAKURA TV IS BAD. YOUR DAD'S A MEMBER OF THE HOUSE OF COUNCILORS. LET'S HAVE HIM USE HIS OFFICE AGAIN AND STOP THE BROADCAST.
...
I'M WATCHING IT TOO, BUT THAT WOULD BE IMPOSSI-BLE RIGHT NOW. NOBODY BELIEVES THIS CHANNEL ANYWAY, WE'D JUST MAKE OURSELVES SUSPICIOUS.
THERE'S NOTHING TO WORRY ABOUT NOW.
?!

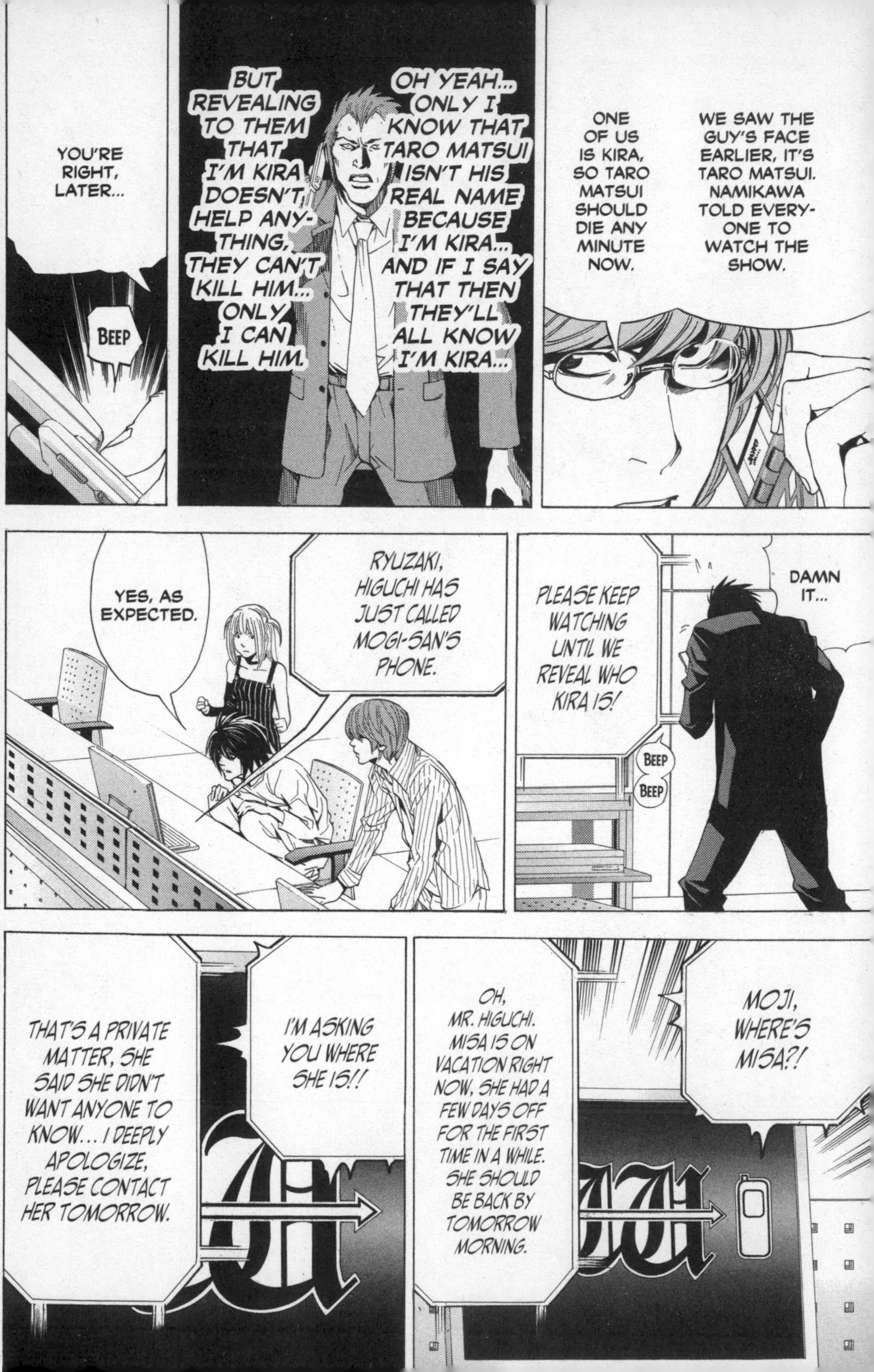
WE SAW THE GUY'S FACE EARLIER, IT'S TARO MATSUI. NAMIKAWA TOLD EVERYONE TO WATCH THE SHOW.
ONE OF US IS KIRA, SO TARO MATSUI SHOULD DIE ANY MINUTE NOW.
OH YEAH... ONLY I KNOW THAT TARO MATSUI ISN'T HIS REAL NAME BECAUSE I'M KIRA... AND IF I SAY THAT THEN THEY'LL ALL KNOW I'M KIRA...
BUT REVEALING TO THEM THAT I'M KIRA DOESN'T HELP ANYTHING, THEY CAN'T KILL HIM... ONLY I CAN KILL HIM.
YOU'RE RIGHT, LATER...
BEEP
DAMN IT...
PLEASE KEEP WATCHING UNTIL WE REVEAL WHO KIRA IS!
BEEP
BEEP
RYUZAKI, HIGUCHI HAS JUST CALLED MOGI-SAN'S PHONE.
YES, AS EXPECTED.
MOJI, WHERE'S MISA?!
OH, MR. HIGUCHI. MISA IS ON VACATION RIGHT NOW, SHE HAD A FEW DAYS OFF FOR THE FIRST TIME IN A WHILE. SHE SHOULD BE BACK BY TOMORROW MORNING.
I'M ASKING YOU WHERE SHE IS!!
THAT'S A PRIVATE MATTER, SHE SAID SHE DIDN'T WANT ANYONE TO KNOW... I DEEPLY APOLOGIZE, PLEASE CONTACT HER TOMORROW.

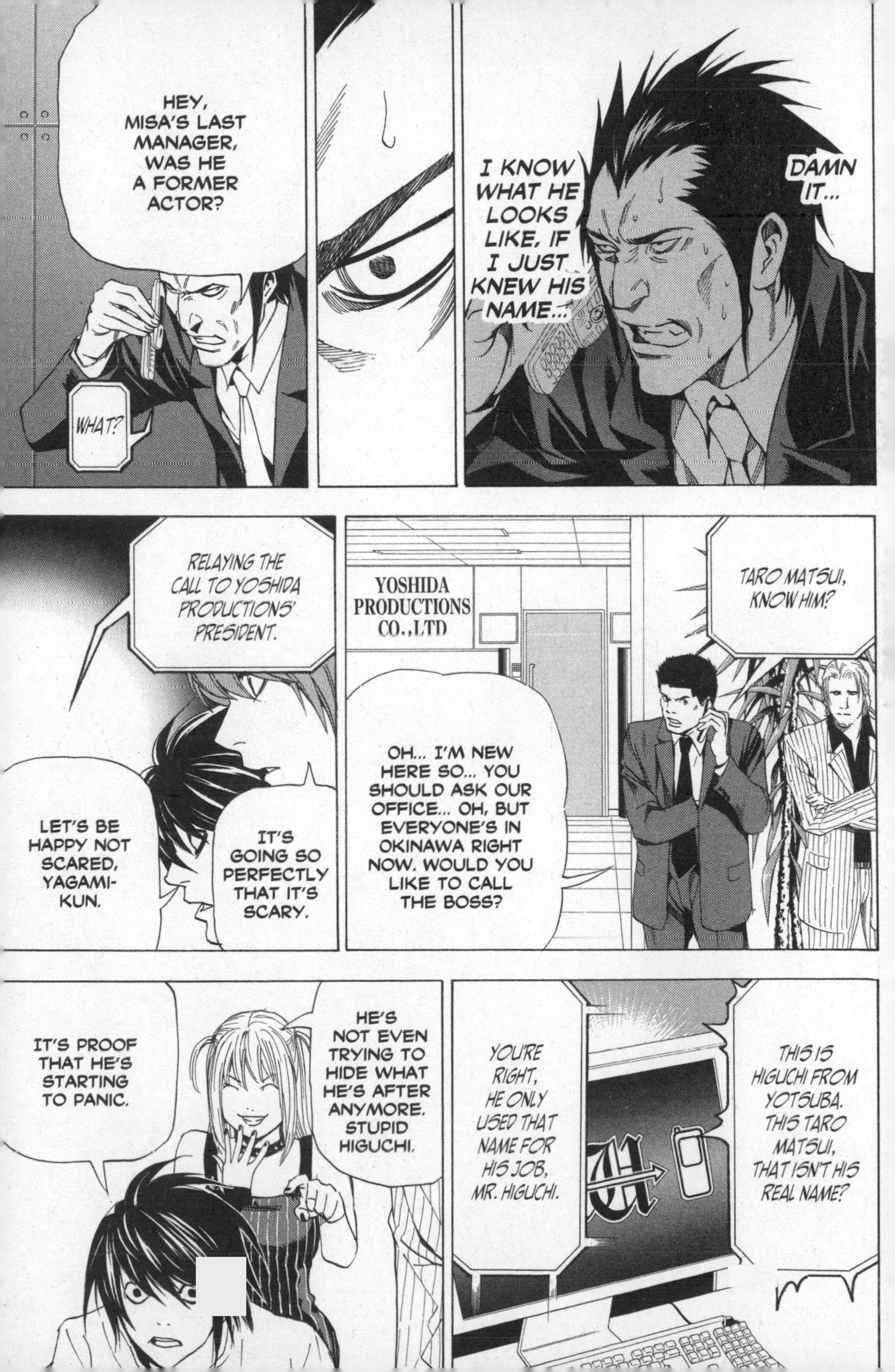
DAMN IT...
I KNOW WHAT HE LOOKS LIKE, IF I JUST KNEW HIS NAME...
HEY, MISA'S LAST MANAGER, WAS HE A FORMER ACTOR?
WHAT?
TARO MATSUI, KNOW HIM?
YOSHIDA PRODUCTIONS CO.,LTD
OH... I'M NEW HERE SO... YOU SHOULD ASK OUR OFFICE... OH, BUT EVERYONE'S IN OKINAWA RIGHT NOW. WOULD YOU LIKE TO CALL THE BOSS?
RELAYING THE CALL TO YOSHIDA PRODUCTIONS' PRESIDENT.
IT'S GOING SO PERFECTLY THAT IT'S SCARY.
LET'S BE HAPPY NOT SCARED, YAGAMI-KUN.
THIS IS HIGUCHI FROM YOTSUBA. THIS TARO MATSUI, THAT ISN'T HIS REAL NAME?
YOU'RE RIGHT, HE ONLY USED THAT NAME FOR HIS JOB, MR. HIGUCHI.
HE'S NOT EVEN TRYING TO HIDE WHAT HE'S AFTER ANYMORE. STUPID HIGUCHI.
IT'S PROOF THAT HE'S STARTING TO PANIC.

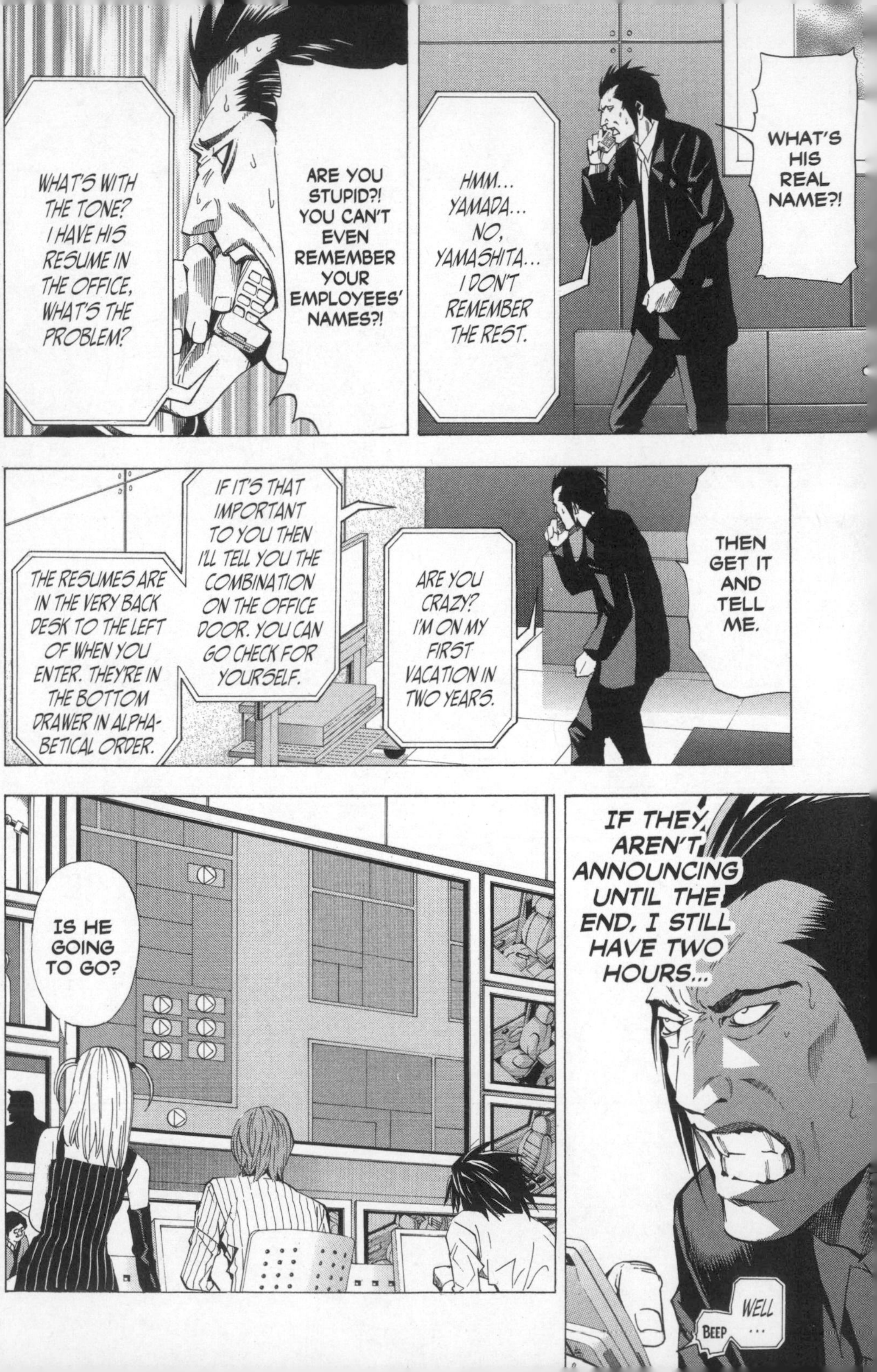
WHAT'S HIS REAL NAME?!
HMM... YAMADA... NO, YAMASHITA... I DON'T REMEMBER THE REST.
ARE YOU STUPID?! YOU CAN'T EVEN REMEMBER YOUR EMPLOYEES' NAMES?!
WHAT'S WITH THE TONE? I HAVE HIS RESUME IN THE OFFICE, WHAT'S THE PROBLEM?
THEN GET IT AND TELL ME.
ARE YOU CRAZY? I'M ON MY FIRST VACATION IN TWO YEARS.
IF IT'S THAT IMPORTANT TO YOU THEN I'LL TELL YOU THE COMBINATION ON THE OFFICE DOOR. YOU CAN GO CHECK FOR YOURSELF.
THE RESUMES ARE IN THE VERY BACK DESK TO THE LEFT OF WHEN YOU ENTER. THEY'RE IN THE BOTTOM DRAWER IN ALPHABETICAL ORDER.
IF THEY AREN'T ANNOUNCING UNTIL THE END, I STILL HAVE TWO HOURS...
WELL...
BEEP
IS HE GOING TO GO?

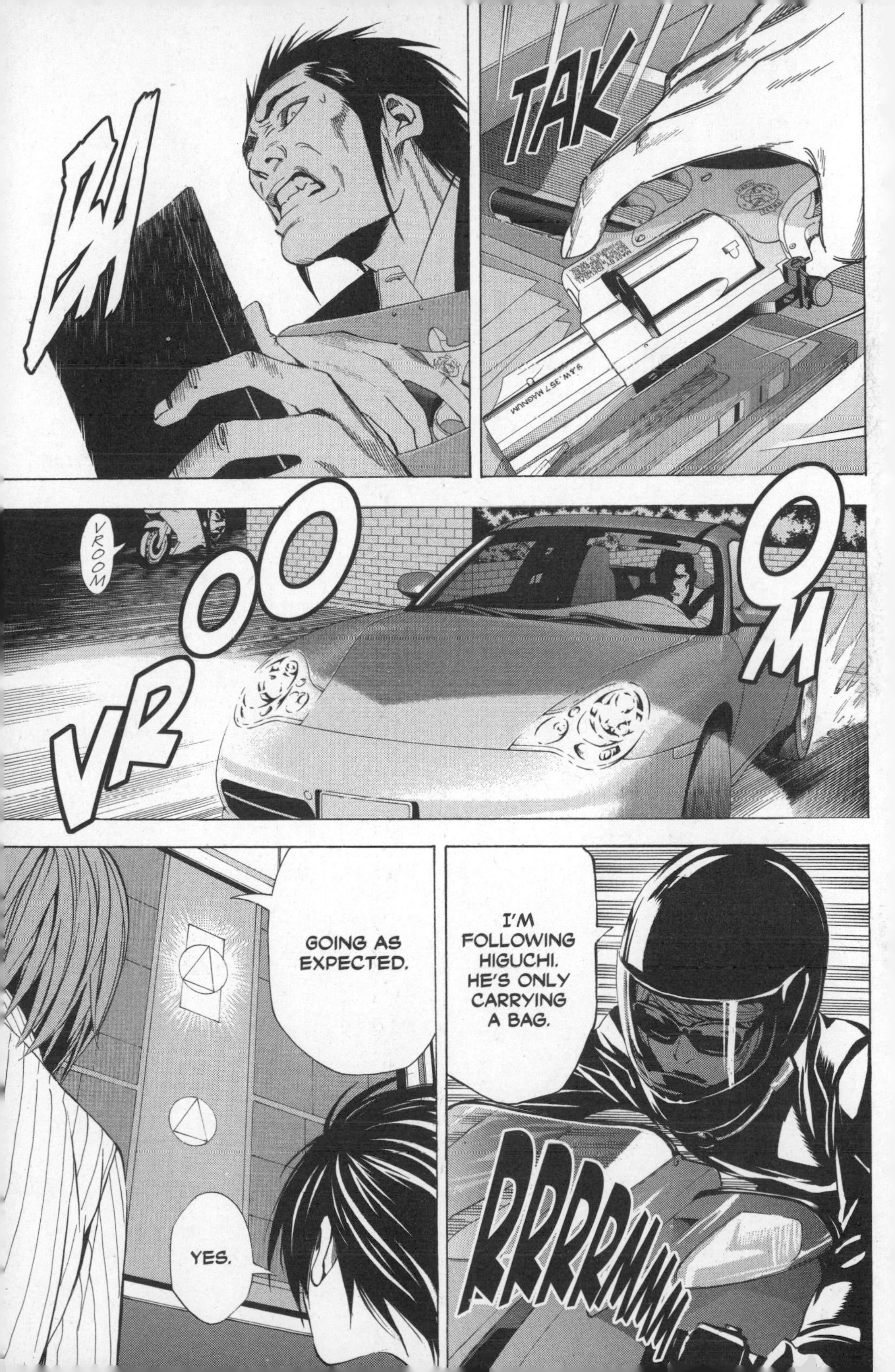
TAK
S.&W. .357 MAGNUM
BA
VROOOOM
VROOM
I'M FOLLOWING HIGUCHI. HE'S ONLY CARRYING A BAG.
RRRRMMM
GOING AS EXPECTED.
YES.

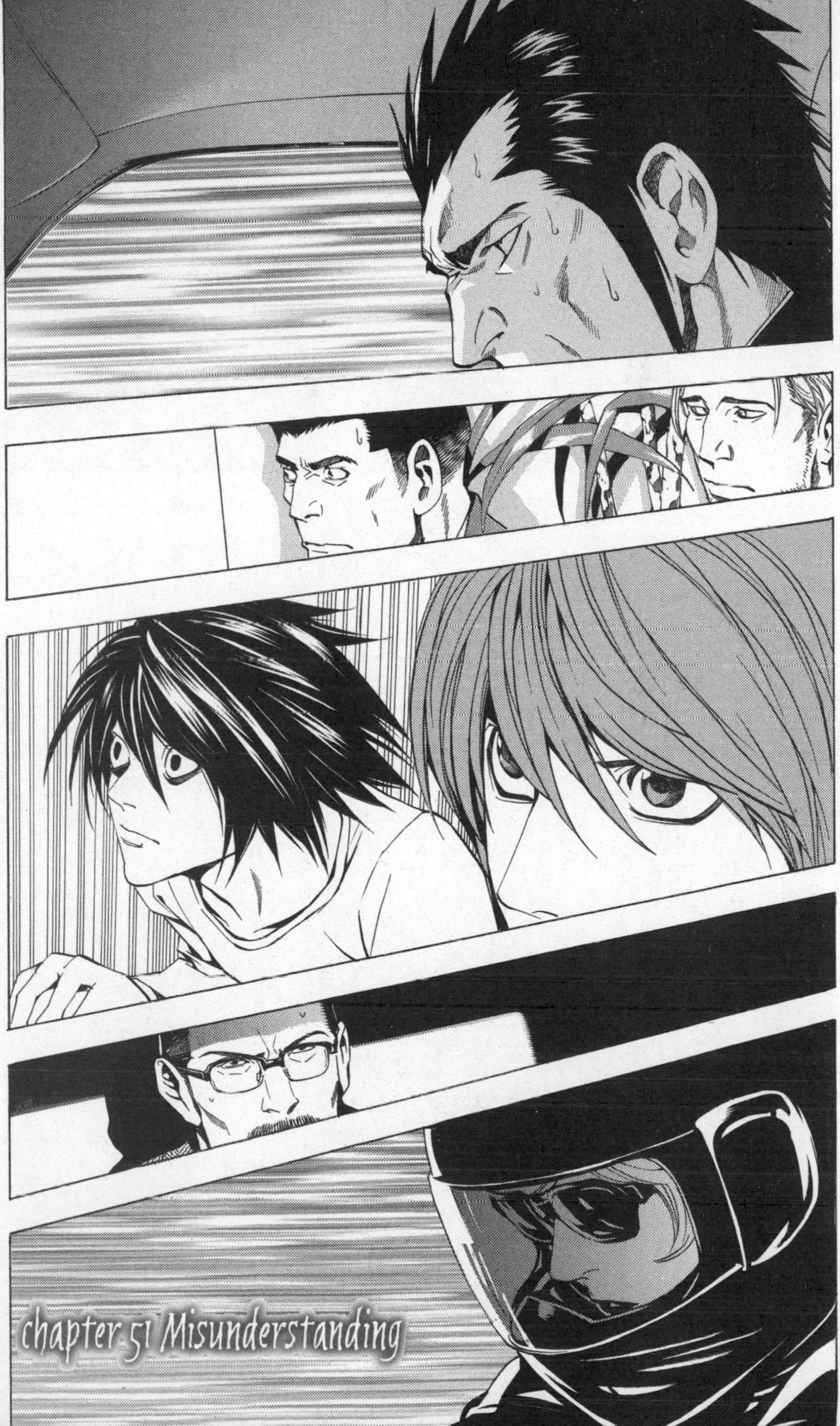
chapter 51 Misunderstanding

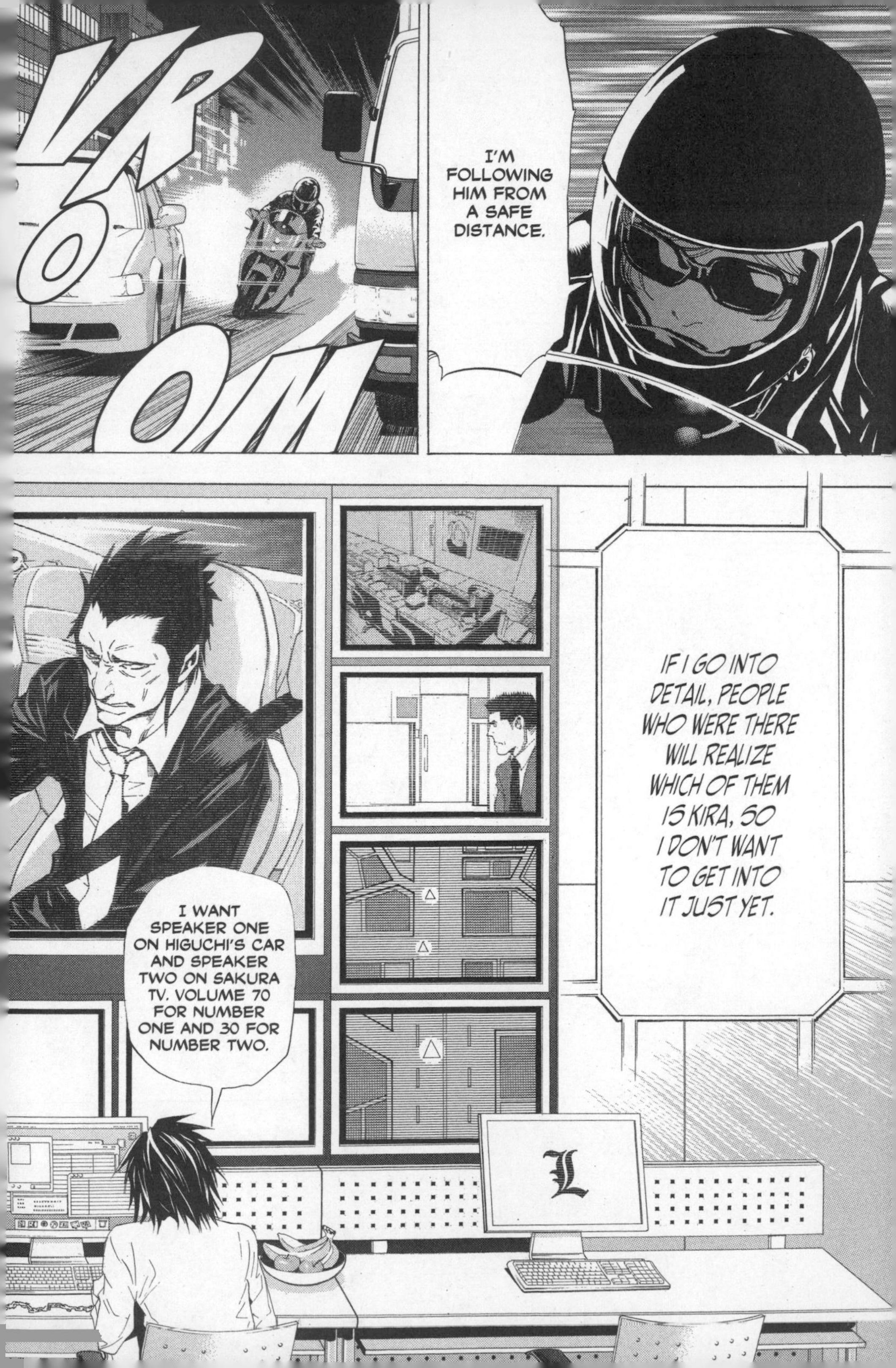
I'M FOLLOWING HIM FROM A SAFE DISTANCE.
VROOM
IF I GO INTO DETAIL, PEOPLE WHO WERE THERE WILL REALIZE WHICH OF THEM IS KIRA, SO I DON'T WANT TO GET INTO IT JUST YET.
I WANT SPEAKER ONE ON HIGUCHI'S CAR AND SPEAKER TWO ON SAKURA TV. VOLUME 70 FOR NUMBER ONE AND 30 FOR NUMBER TWO.
L

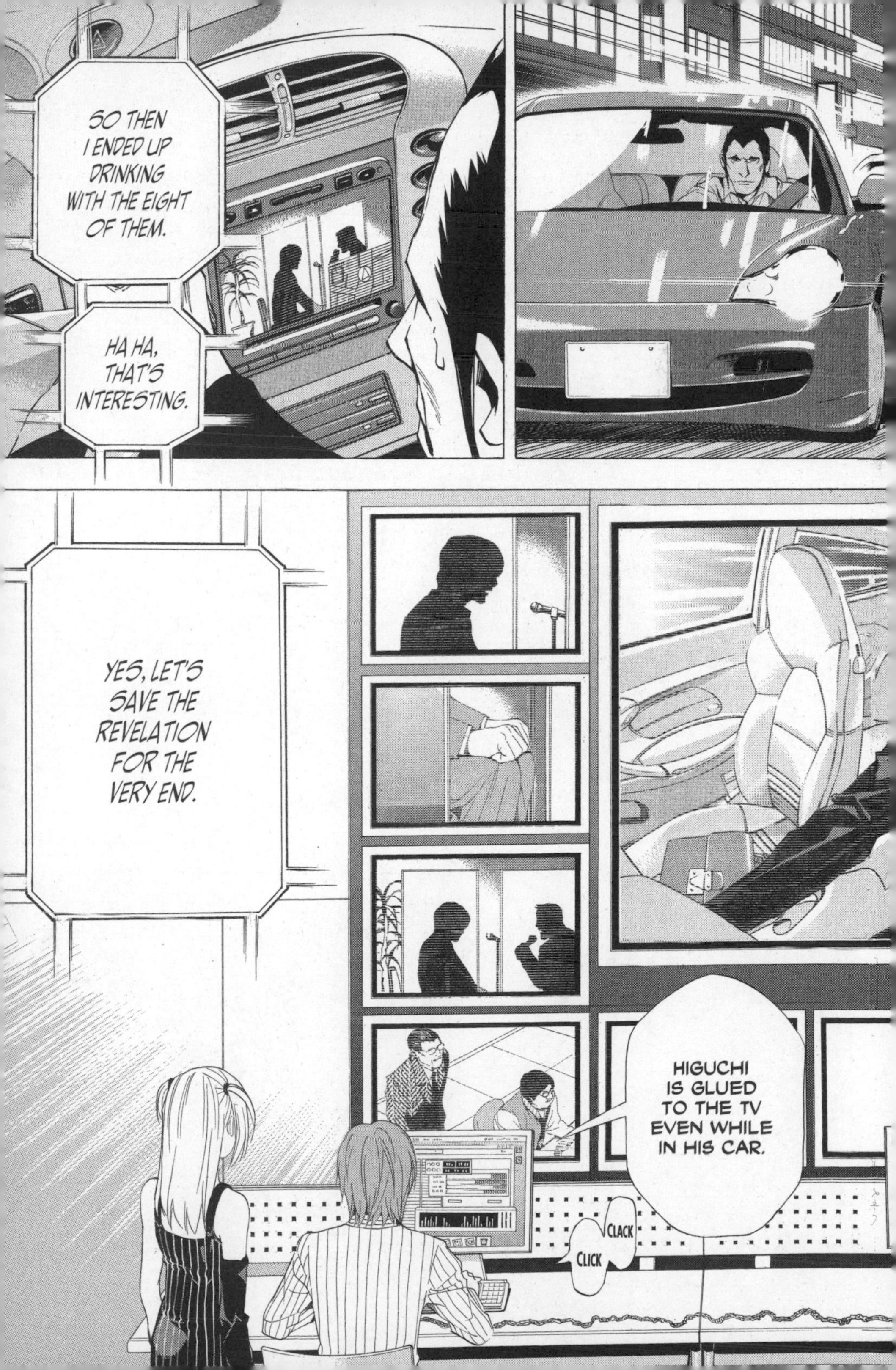
SO THEN I ENDED UP DRINKING WITH THE EIGHT OF THEM.
HA HA, THAT'S INTERESTING.
YES, LET'S SAVE THE REVELATION FOR THE VERY END.
HIGUCHI IS GLUED TO THE TV EVEN WHILE IN HIS CAR.
CLACK
CLICK

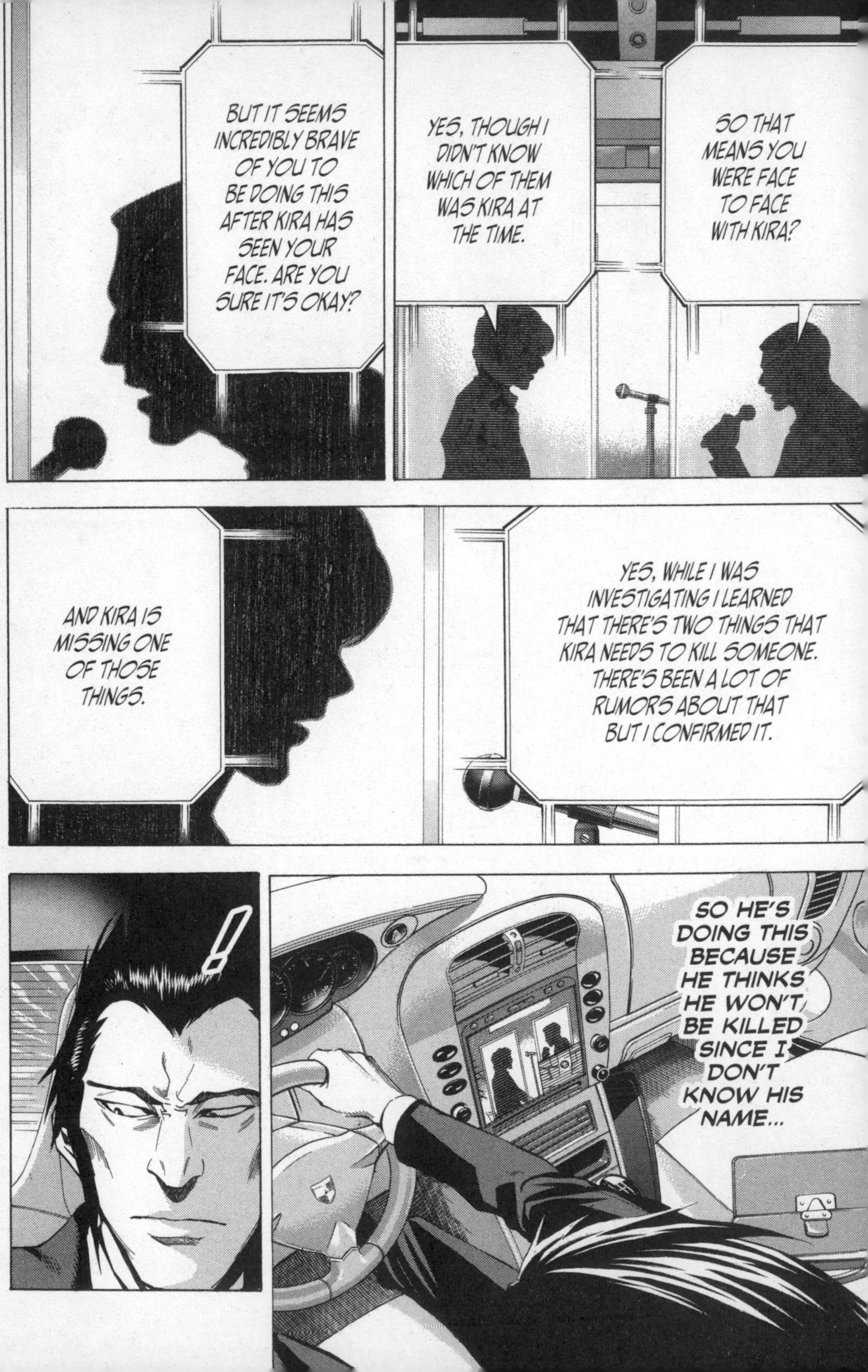
SO THAT MEANS YOU WERE FACE TO FACE WITH KIRA?
YES, THOUGH I DIDN'T KNOW WHICH OF THEM WAS KIRA AT THE TIME.
BUT IT SEEMS INCREDIBLY BRAVE OF YOU TO BE DOING THIS AFTER KIRA HAS SEEN YOUR FACE. ARE YOU SURE IT'S OKAY?
YES, WHILE I WAS INVESTIGATING I LEARNED THAT THERE'S TWO THINGS THAT KIRA NEEDS TO KILL SOMEONE. THERE'S BEEN A LOT OF RUMORS ABOUT THAT BUT I CONFIRMED IT.
AND KIRA IS MISSING ONE OF THOSE THINGS.
SO HE'S DOING THIS BECAUSE HE THINKS HE WON'T BE KILLED SINCE I DON'T KNOW HIS NAME...
!

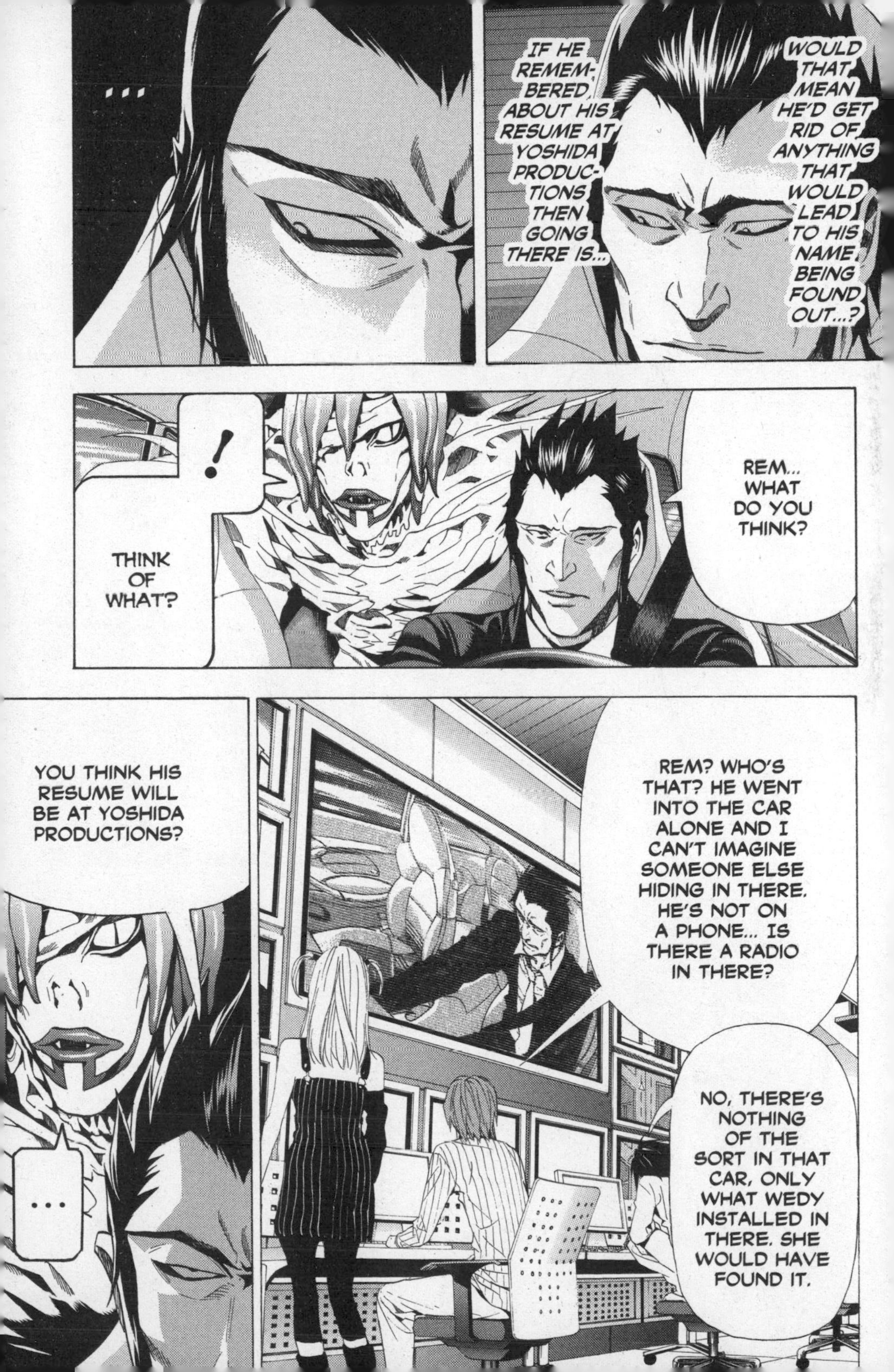
WOULD THAT MEAN HE'D GET RID OF ANYTHING THAT WOULD LEAD TO HIS NAME BEING FOUND OUT...?
IF HE REMEMBERED ABOUT HIS RESUME AT YOSHIDA PRODUCTIONS THEN GOING THERE IS...
...
REM... WHAT DO YOU THINK?
!
THINK OF WHAT?
REM? WHO'S THAT? HE WENT INTO THE CAR ALONE AND I CAN'T IMAGINE SOMEONE ELSE HIDING IN THERE. HE'S NOT ON A PHONE... IS THERE A RADIO IN THERE?
NO, THERE'S NOTHING OF THE SORT IN THAT CAR, ONLY WHAT WEDY INSTALLED IN THERE. SHE WOULD HAVE FOUND IT.
YOU THINK HIS RESUME WILL BE AT YOSHIDA PRODUCTIONS?
...

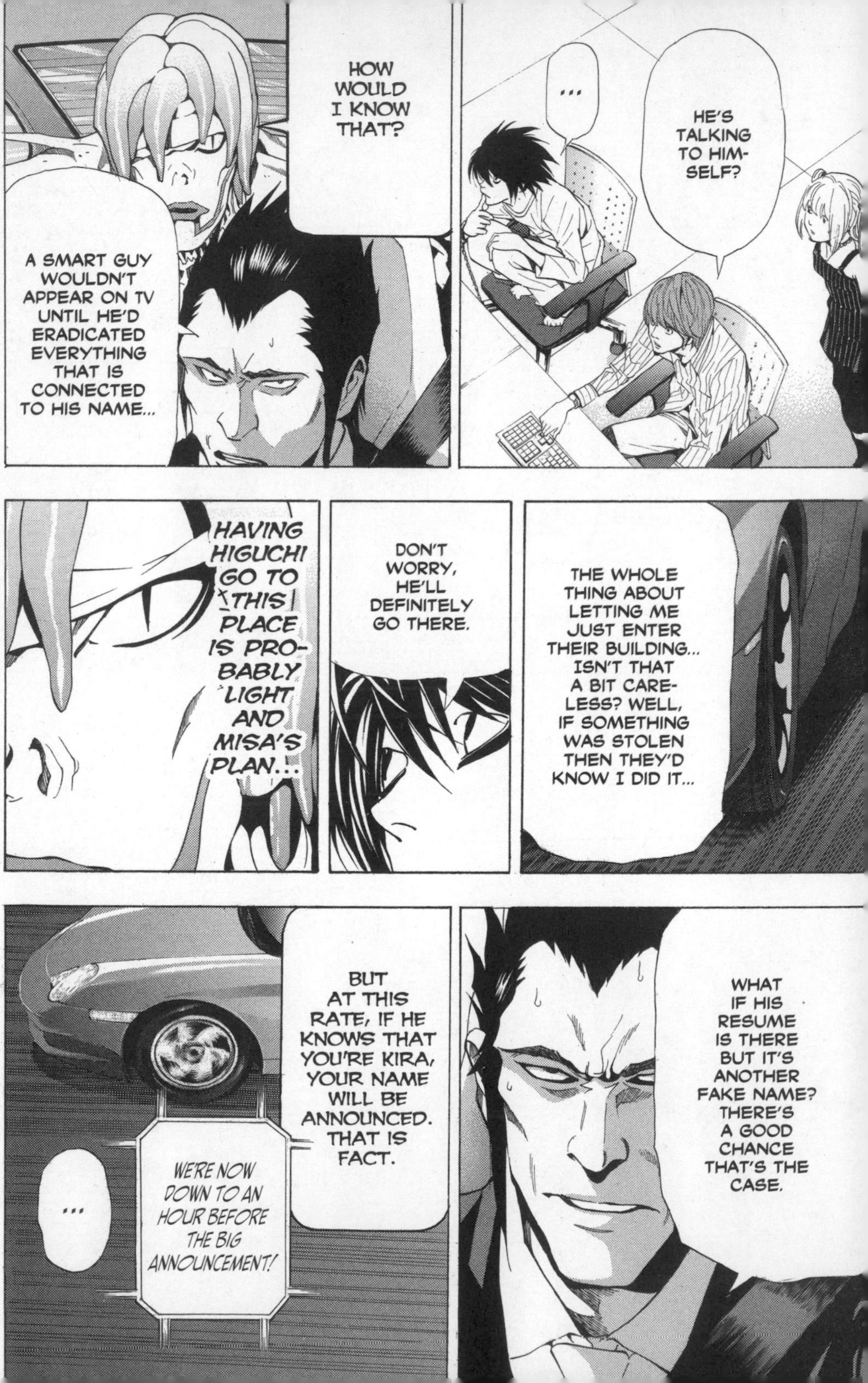
HE'S TALKING TO HIM-SELF?
...
HOW WOULD I KNOW THAT?
A SMART GUY WOULDN'T APPEAR ON TV UNTIL HE'D ERADICATED EVERYTHING THAT IS CONNECTED TO HIS NAME...
THE WHOLE THING ABOUT LETTING ME JUST ENTER THEIR BUILDING... ISN'T THAT A BIT CARE-LESS? WELL, IF SOMETHING WAS STOLEN THEN THEY'D KNOW I DID IT...
DON'T WORRY, HE'LL DEFINITELY GO THERE.
HAVING HIGUCHI GO TO THIS PLACE IS PRO-BABLY LIGHT AND MISA'S PLAN...
WHAT IF HIS RESUME IS THERE BUT IT'S ANOTHER FAKE NAME? THERE'S A GOOD CHANCE THAT'S THE CASE.
BUT AT THIS RATE, IF HE KNOWS THAT YOU'RE KIRA, YOUR NAME WILL BE ANNOUNCED. THAT IS FACT.
WE'RE NOW DOWN TO AN HOUR BEFORE THE BIG ANNOUNCEMENT!
...

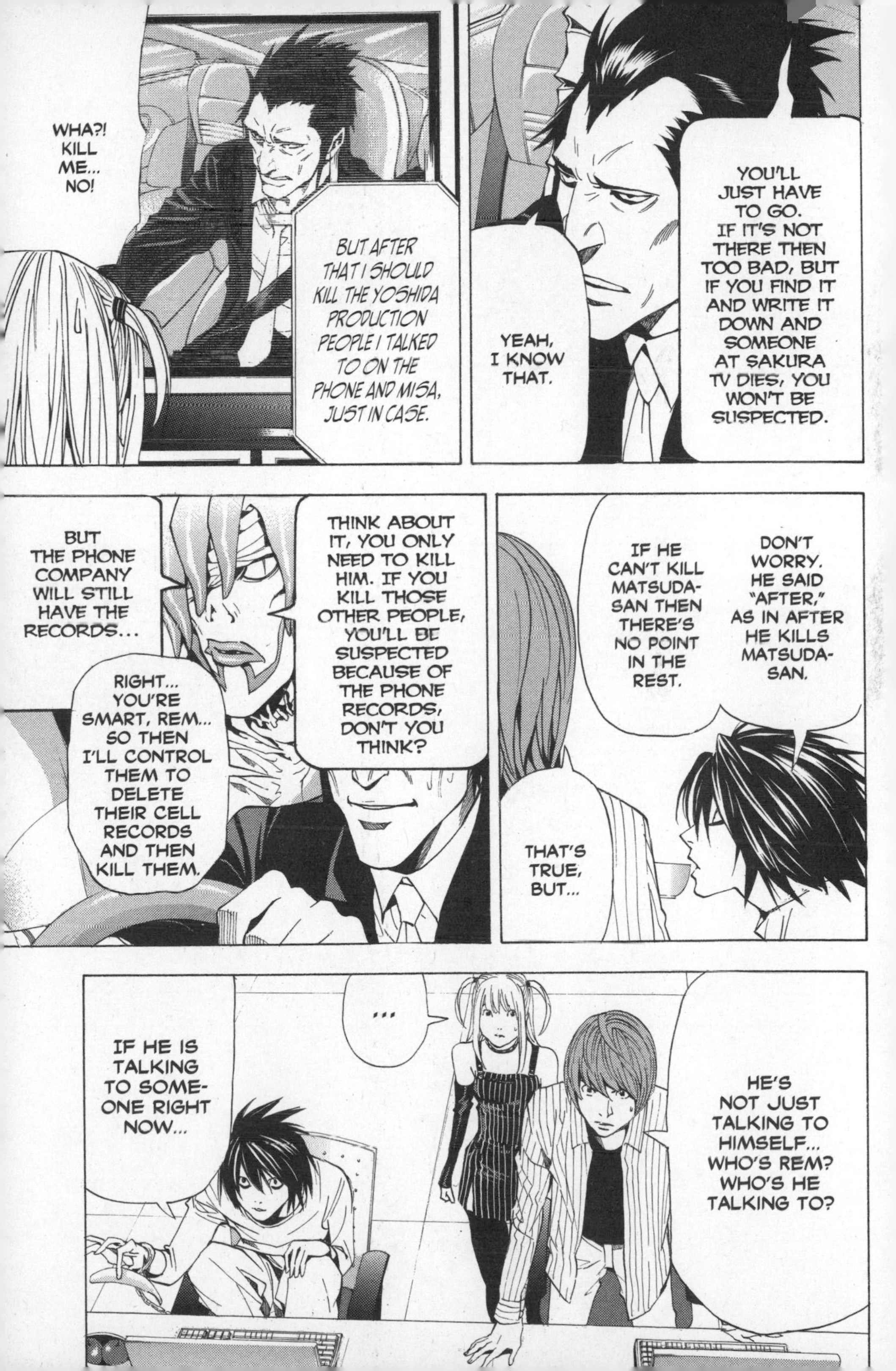
YOU'LL JUST HAVE TO GO. IF IT'S NOT THERE THEN TOO BAD, BUT IF YOU FIND IT AND WRITE IT DOWN AND SOMEONE AT SAKURA TV DIES, YOU WON'T BE SUSPECTED.
YEAH, I KNOW THAT.
WHA?! KILL ME... NO!
BUT AFTER THAT I SHOULD KILL THE YOSHIDA PRODUCTION PEOPLE I TALKED TO ON THE PHONE AND MISA, JUST IN CASE.
DON'T WORRY. HE SAID "AFTER," AS IN AFTER HE KILLS MATSUDA-SAN.
IF HE CAN'T KILL MATSUDA-SAN THEN THERE'S NO POINT IN THE REST.
THAT'S TRUE, BUT...
THINK ABOUT IT, YOU ONLY NEED TO KILL HIM. IF YOU KILL THOSE OTHER PEOPLE, YOU'LL BE SUSPECTED BECAUSE OF THE PHONE RECORDS, DON'T YOU THINK?
BUT THE PHONE COMPANY WILL STILL HAVE THE RECORDS...
RIGHT... YOU'RE SMART, REM... SO THEN I'LL CONTROL THEM TO DELETE THEIR CELL RECORDS AND THEN KILL THEM.
HE'S NOT JUST TALKING TO HIMSELF... WHO'S REM? WHO'S HE TALKING TO?
...
IF HE IS TALKING TO SOME-ONE RIGHT NOW...

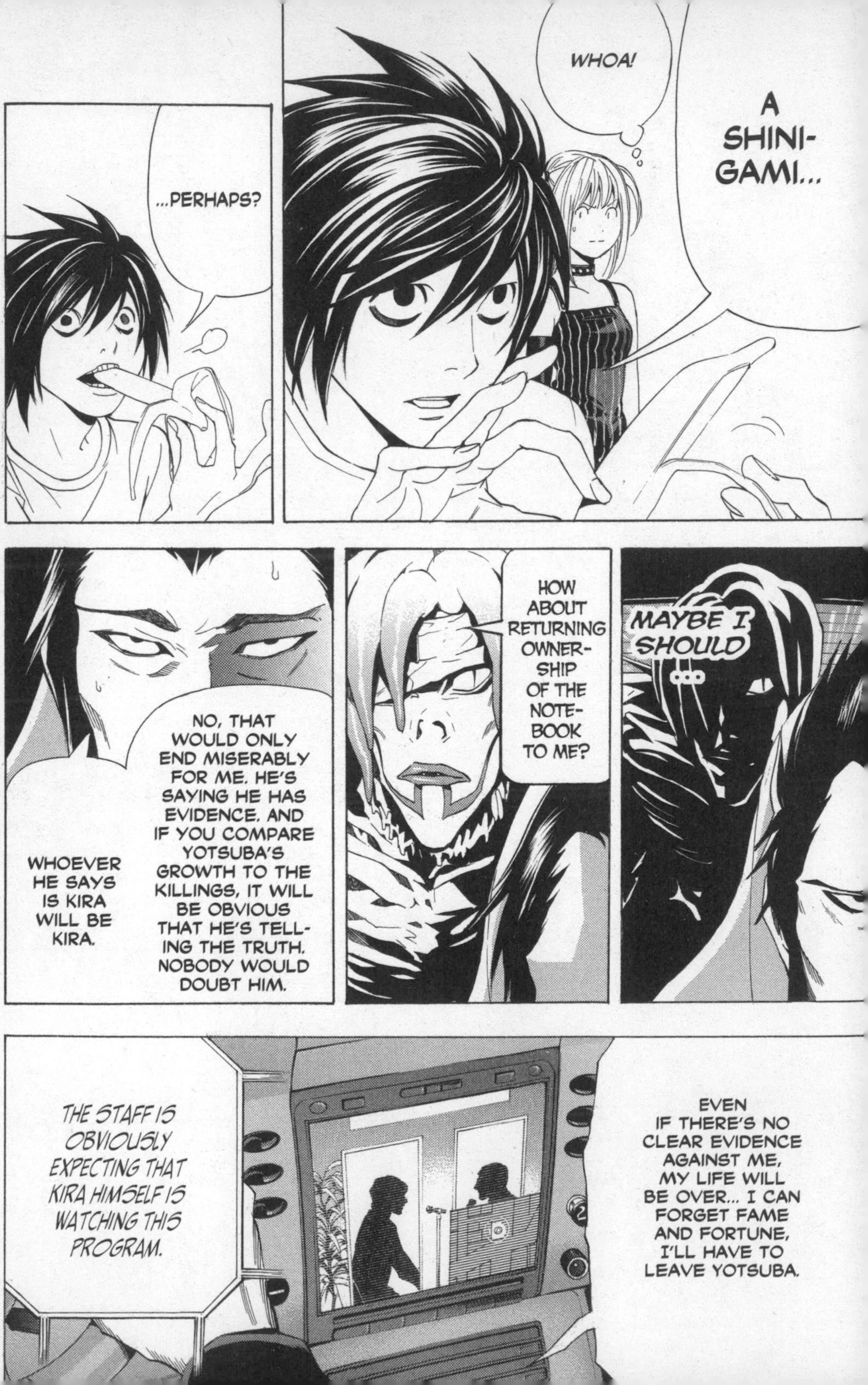
WHOA!
A SHINI-GAMI...
...PERHAPS?
MAYBE I SHOULD ...
HOW ABOUT RETURNING OWNERSHIP OF THE NOTEBOOK TO ME?
NO, THAT WOULD ONLY END MISERABLY FOR ME. HE'S SAYING HE HAS EVIDENCE. AND IF YOU COMPARE YOTSUBA'S GROWTH TO THE KILLINGS, IT WILL BE OBVIOUS THAT HE'S TELLING THE TRUTH. NOBODY WOULD DOUBT HIM.
WHOEVER HE SAYS IS KIRA WILL BE KIRA.
EVEN IF THERE'S NO CLEAR EVIDENCE AGAINST ME, MY LIFE WILL BE OVER... I CAN FORGET FAME AND FORTUNE, I'LL HAVE TO LEAVE YOTSUBA.
THE STAFF IS OBVIOUSLY EXPECTING THAT KIRA HIMSELF IS WATCHING THIS PROGRAM.

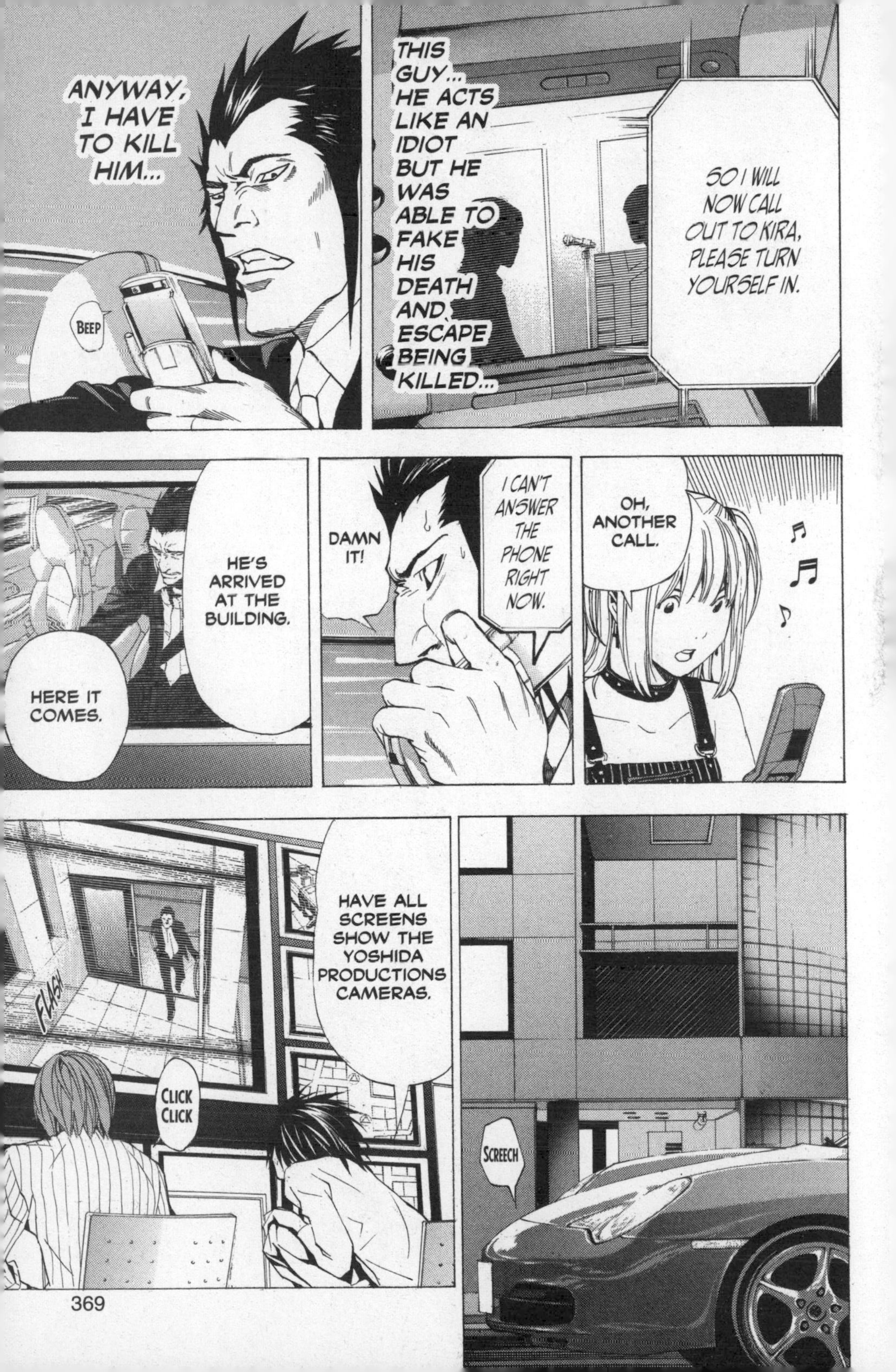
SO I WILL NOW CALL OUT TO KIRA, PLEASE TURN YOURSELF IN.
THIS GUY... HE ACTS LIKE AN IDIOT BUT HE WAS ABLE TO FAKE HIS DEATH AND ESCAPE BEING KILLED...
ANYWAY, I HAVE TO KILL HIM...
BEEP
OH, ANOTHER CALL.
I CAN'T ANSWER THE PHONE RIGHT NOW.
DAMN IT!
HE'S ARRIVED AT THE BUILDING.
HERE IT COMES.
SCREECH
HAVE ALL SCREENS SHOW THE YOSHIDA PRODUCTIONS CAMERAS.
CLICK CLICK
FLASH

CLACK

BEEP

BEEP

THE BOTTOM DRAWER ON THE FURTHEST DESK ON THE LEFT...

CLICK

RUSTLE

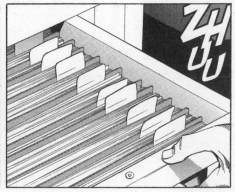

ZHUU

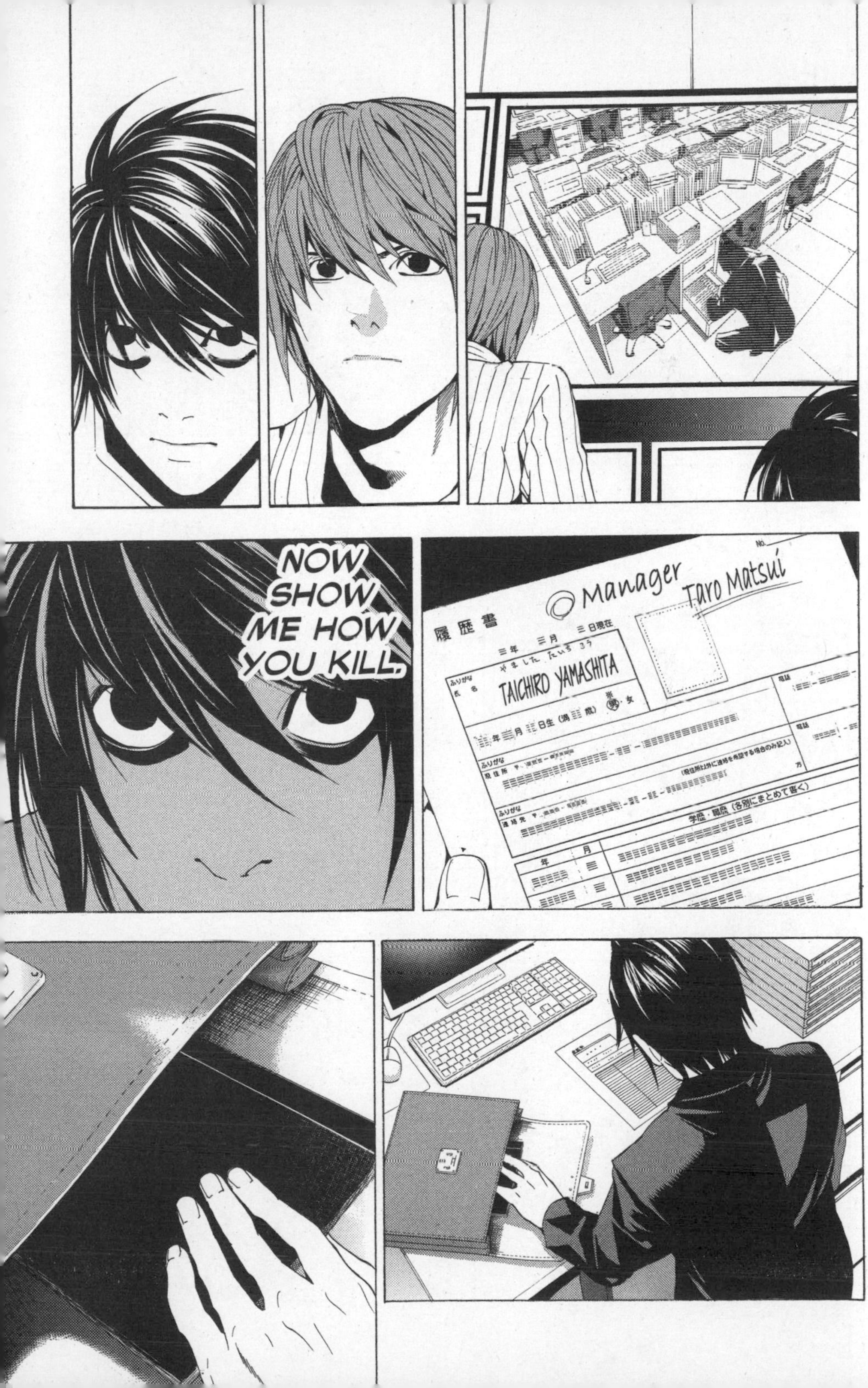
No.
Manager
Taro Matsui
履歴書
TAICHIRO YAMASHITA
NOW SHOW ME HOW YOU KILL.

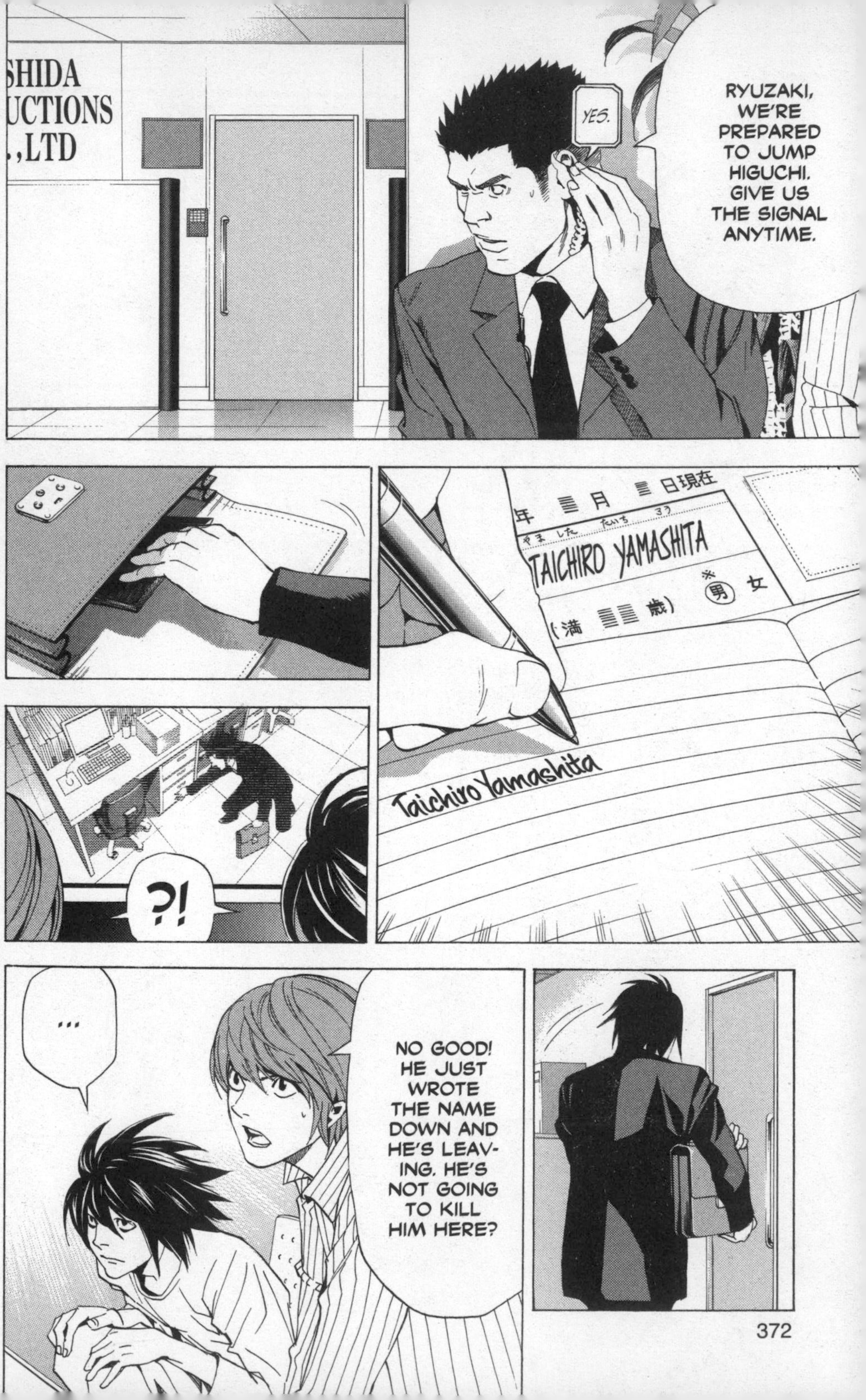
RYUZAKI, WE'RE PREPARED TO JUMP HIGUCHI. GIVE US THE SIGNAL ANYTIME.
YES.
SHIDA
UCTIONS
.,LTD
年 月 日現在
やました たいち ろう
TAICHIRO YAMASHITA
※ 男 女
(満 歳)
Taichiro Yamashita
?!
NO GOOD! HE JUST WROTE THE NAME DOWN AND HE'S LEAV-ING. HE'S NOT GOING TO KILL HIM HERE?
...

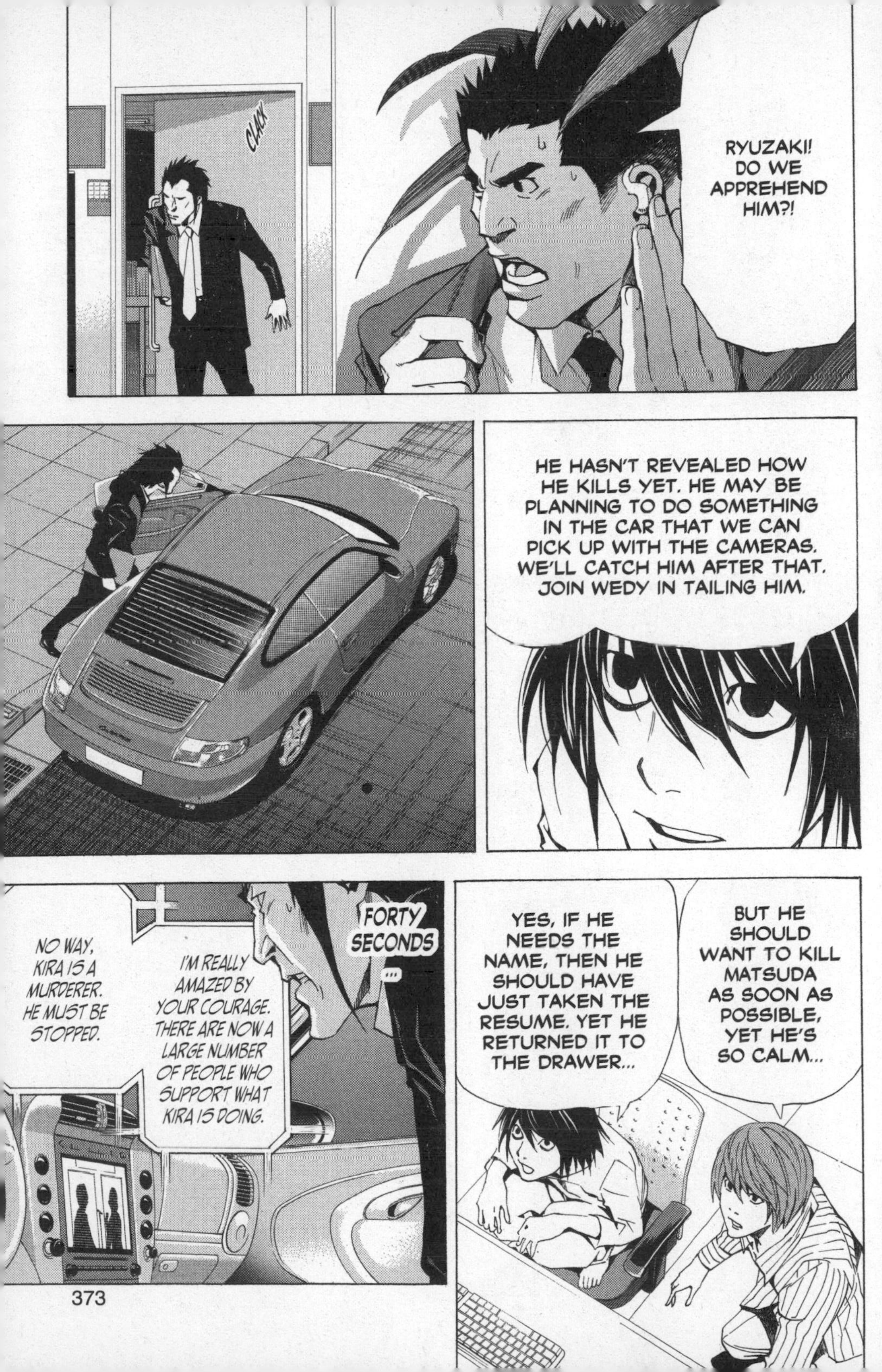
RYUZAKI! DO WE APPREHEND HIM?!
CLACK
HE HASN'T REVEALED HOW HE KILLS YET. HE MAY BE PLANNING TO DO SOMETHING IN THE CAR THAT WE CAN PICK UP WITH THE CAMERAS. WE'LL CATCH HIM AFTER THAT. JOIN WEDY IN TAILING HIM.
BUT HE SHOULD WANT TO KILL MATSUDA AS SOON AS POSSIBLE, YET HE'S SO CALM...
YES, IF HE NEEDS THE NAME, THEN HE SHOULD HAVE JUST TAKEN THE RESUME. YET HE RETURNED IT TO THE DRAWER...
FORTY SECONDS...
I'M REALLY AMAZED BY YOUR COURAGE. THERE ARE NOW A LARGE NUMBER OF PEOPLE WHO SUPPORT WHAT KIRA IS DOING.
NO WAY, KIRA IS A MURDERER. HE MUST BE STOPPED.

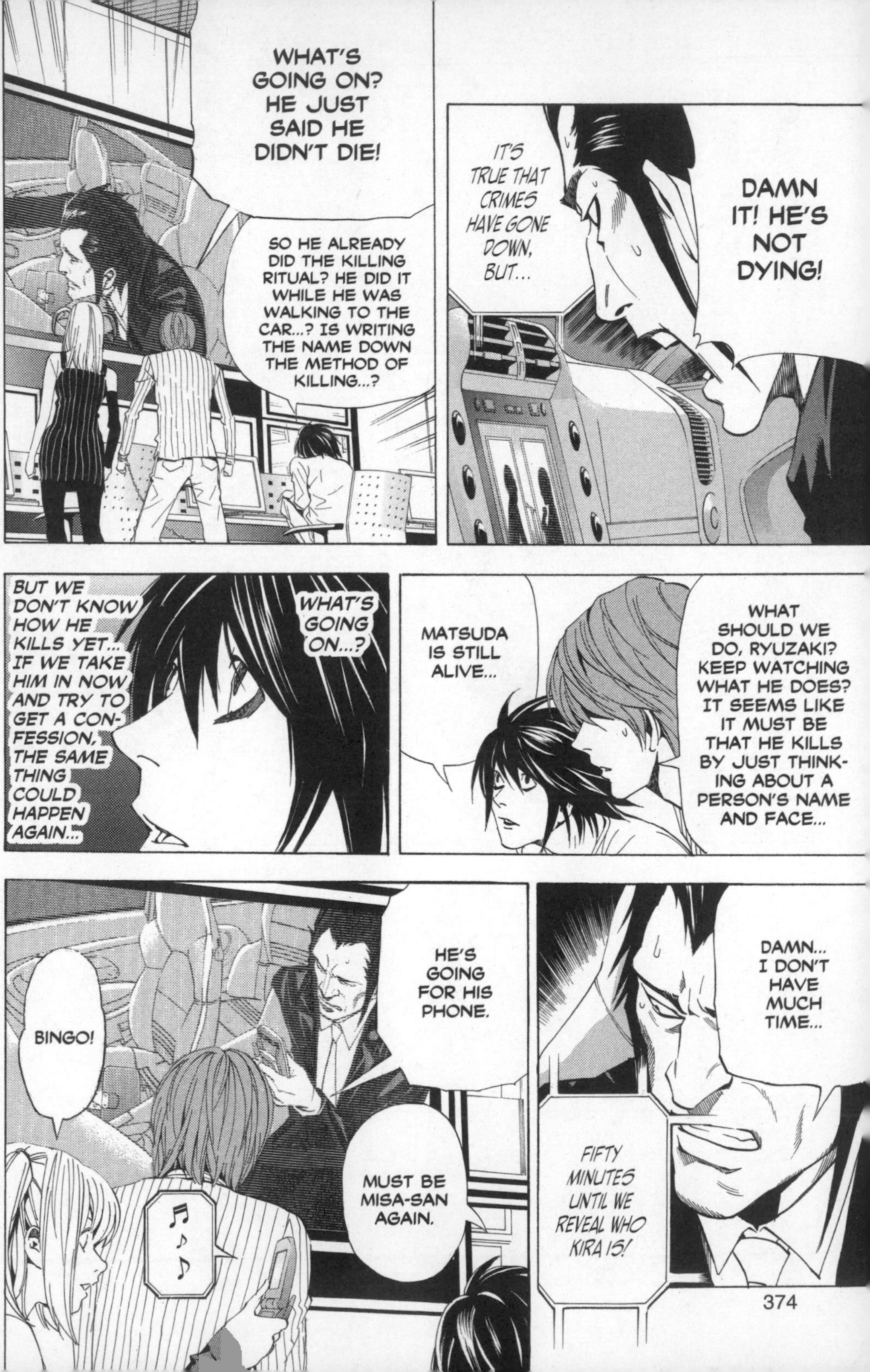
DAMN IT! HE'S NOT DYING!
IT'S TRUE THAT CRIMES HAVE GONE DOWN, BUT...
WHAT'S GOING ON? HE JUST SAID HE DIDN'T DIE!
SO HE ALREADY DID THE KILLING RITUAL? HE DID IT WHILE HE WAS WALKING TO THE CAR...? IS WRITING THE NAME DOWN THE METHOD OF KILLING...?
WHAT SHOULD WE DO, RYUZAKI? KEEP WATCHING WHAT HE DOES? IT SEEMS LIKE IT MUST BE THAT HE KILLS BY JUST THINKING ABOUT A PERSON'S NAME AND FACE...
MATSUDA IS STILL ALIVE...
WHAT'S GOING ON...?
BUT WE DON'T KNOW HOW HE KILLS YET... IF WE TAKE HIM IN NOW AND TRY TO GET A CONFESSION, THE SAME THING COULD HAPPEN AGAIN...
DAMN... I DON'T HAVE MUCH TIME...
FIFTY MINUTES UNTIL WE REVEAL WHO KIRA IS!
HE'S GOING FOR HIS PHONE.
BINGO!
MUST BE MISA-SAN AGAIN.
♬ ♪ ♪

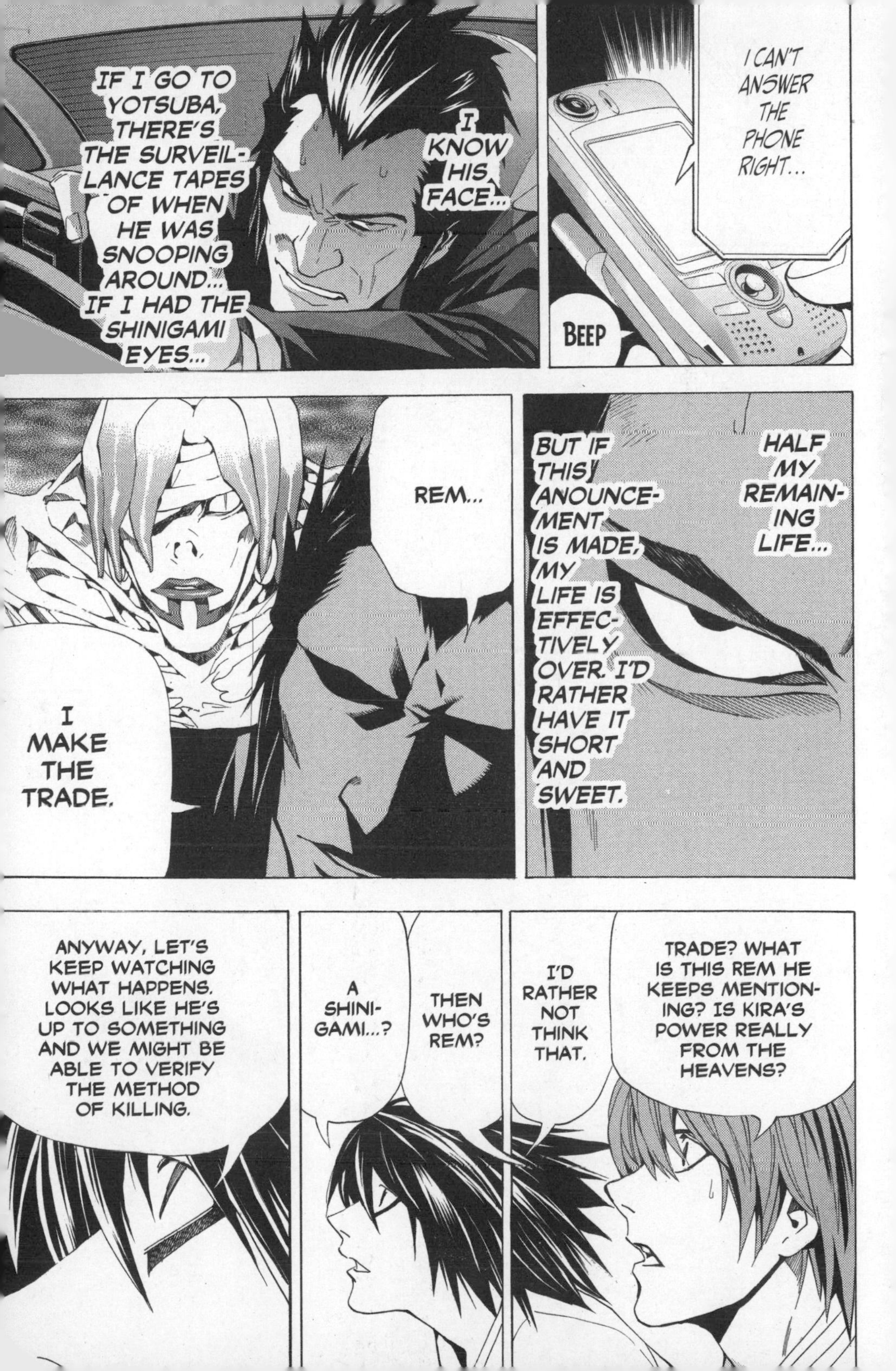

I CAN'T ANSWER THE PHONE RIGHT...
BEEP
I KNOW HIS FACE...
IF I GO TO YOTSUBA, THERE'S THE SURVEILLANCE TAPES OF WHEN HE WAS SNOOPING AROUND... IF I HAD THE SHINIGAMI EYES...
HALF MY REMAINING LIFE...
BUT IF THIS ANOUNCEMENT IS MADE, MY LIFE IS EFFECTIVELY OVER. I'D RATHER HAVE IT SHORT AND SWEET.
REM...
I MAKE THE TRADE.
TRADE? WHAT IS THIS REM HE KEEPS MENTIONING? IS KIRA'S POWER REALLY FROM THE HEAVENS?
I'D RATHER NOT THINK THAT.
THEN WHO'S REM?
A SHINIGAMI...?
ANYWAY, LET'S KEEP WATCHING WHAT HAPPENS. LOOKS LIKE HE'S UP TO SOMETHING AND WE MIGHT BE ABLE TO VERIFY THE METHOD OF KILLING.

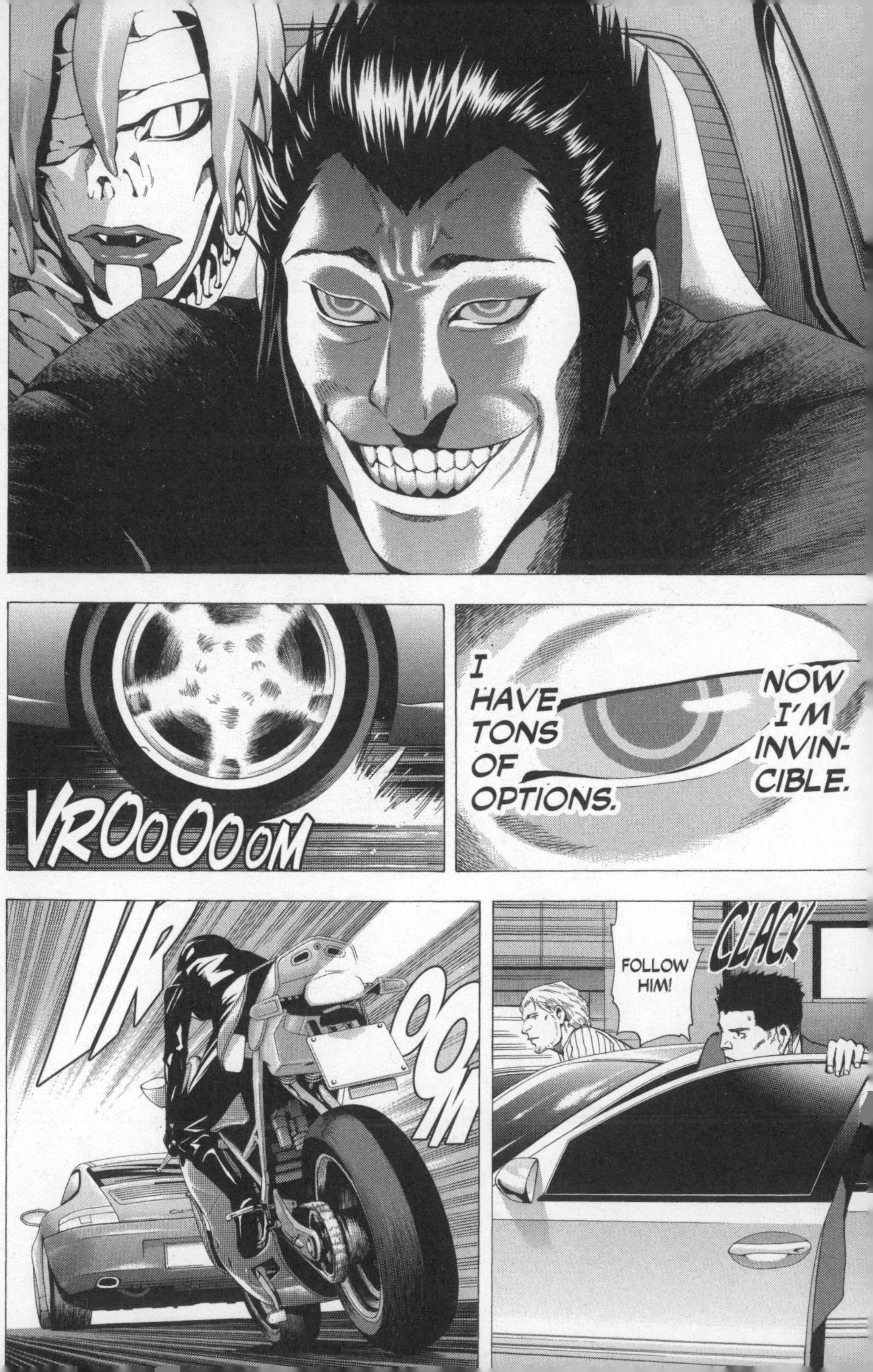
NOW I'M INVINCIBLE.
I HAVE TONS OF OPTIONS.
VROOOOOOM
CLACK
FOLLOW HIM!

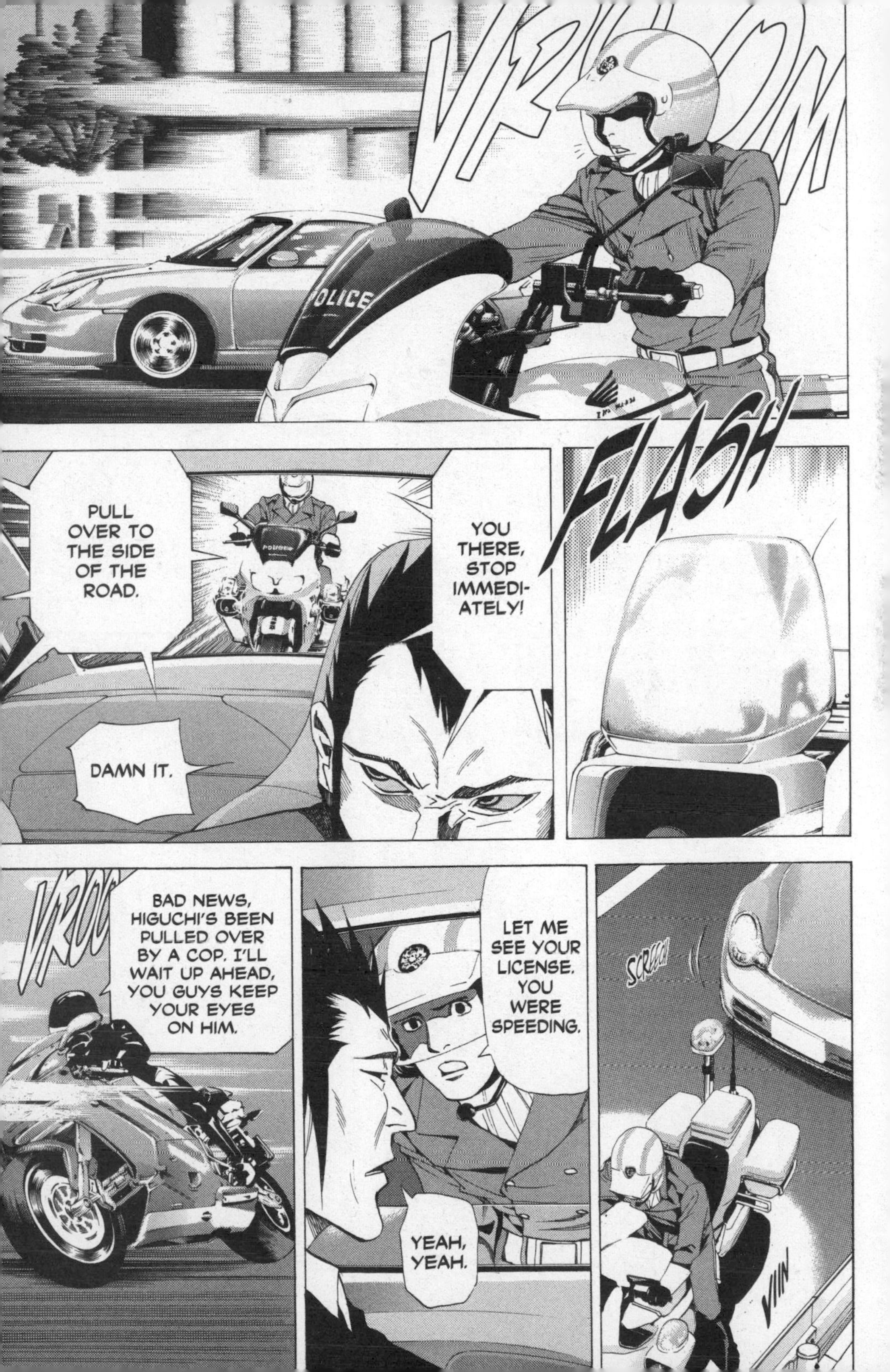
FLASH
YOU THERE, STOP IMMEDI-ATELY!
PULL OVER TO THE SIDE OF THE ROAD.
DAMN IT.
SCREEE
VIIN
LET ME SEE YOUR LICENSE. YOU WERE SPEEDING.
YEAH, YEAH.
BAD NEWS, HIGUCHI'S BEEN PULLED OVER BY A COP. I'LL WAIT UP AHEAD, YOU GUYS KEEP YOUR EYES ON HIM.

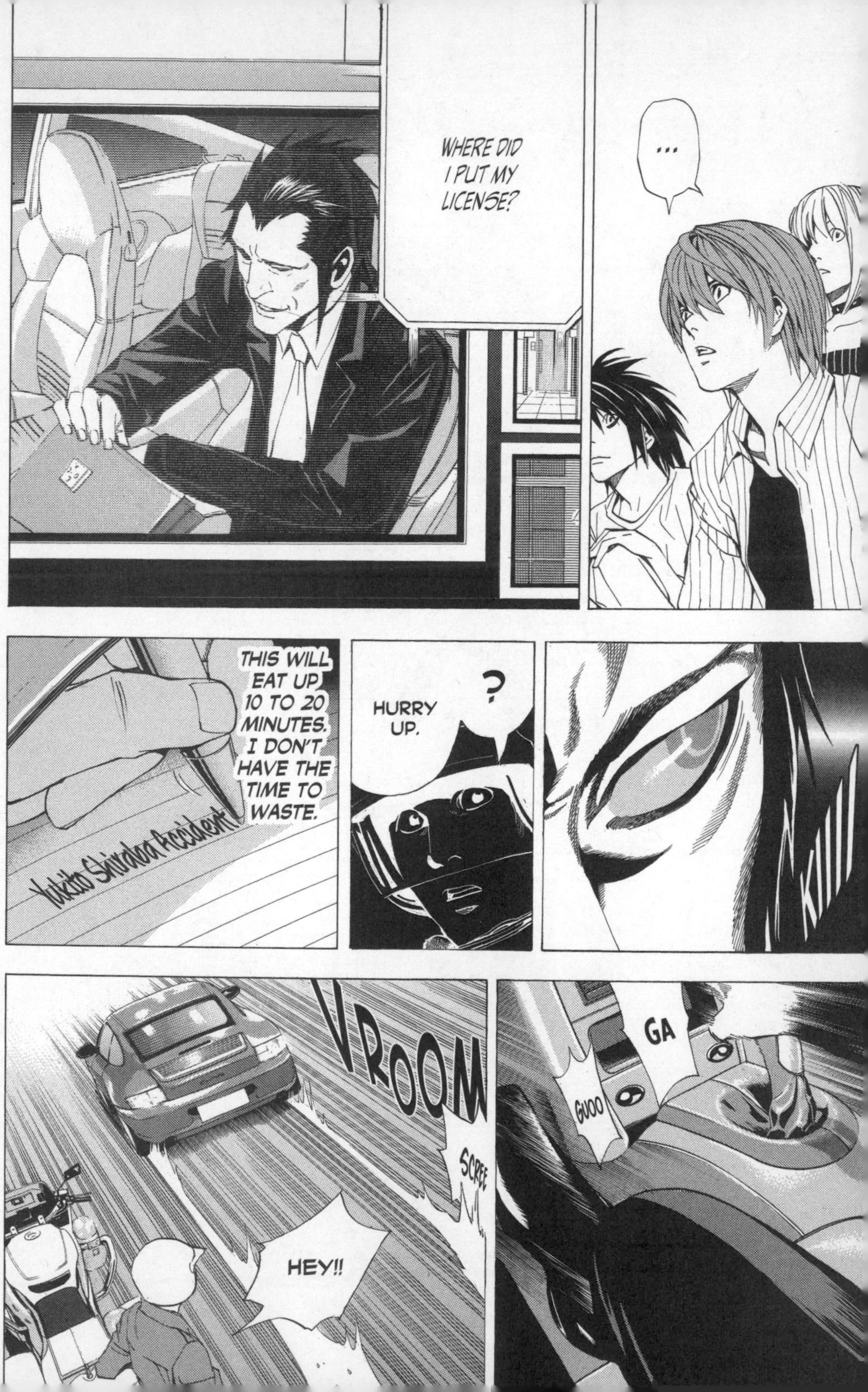
...
WHERE DID I PUT MY LICENSE?
KIIII
?
HURRY UP.
THIS WILL EAT UP 10 TO 20 MINUTES. I DON'T HAVE THE TIME TO WASTE.
GA
GUOO
VROOM
SCREE
HEY!!

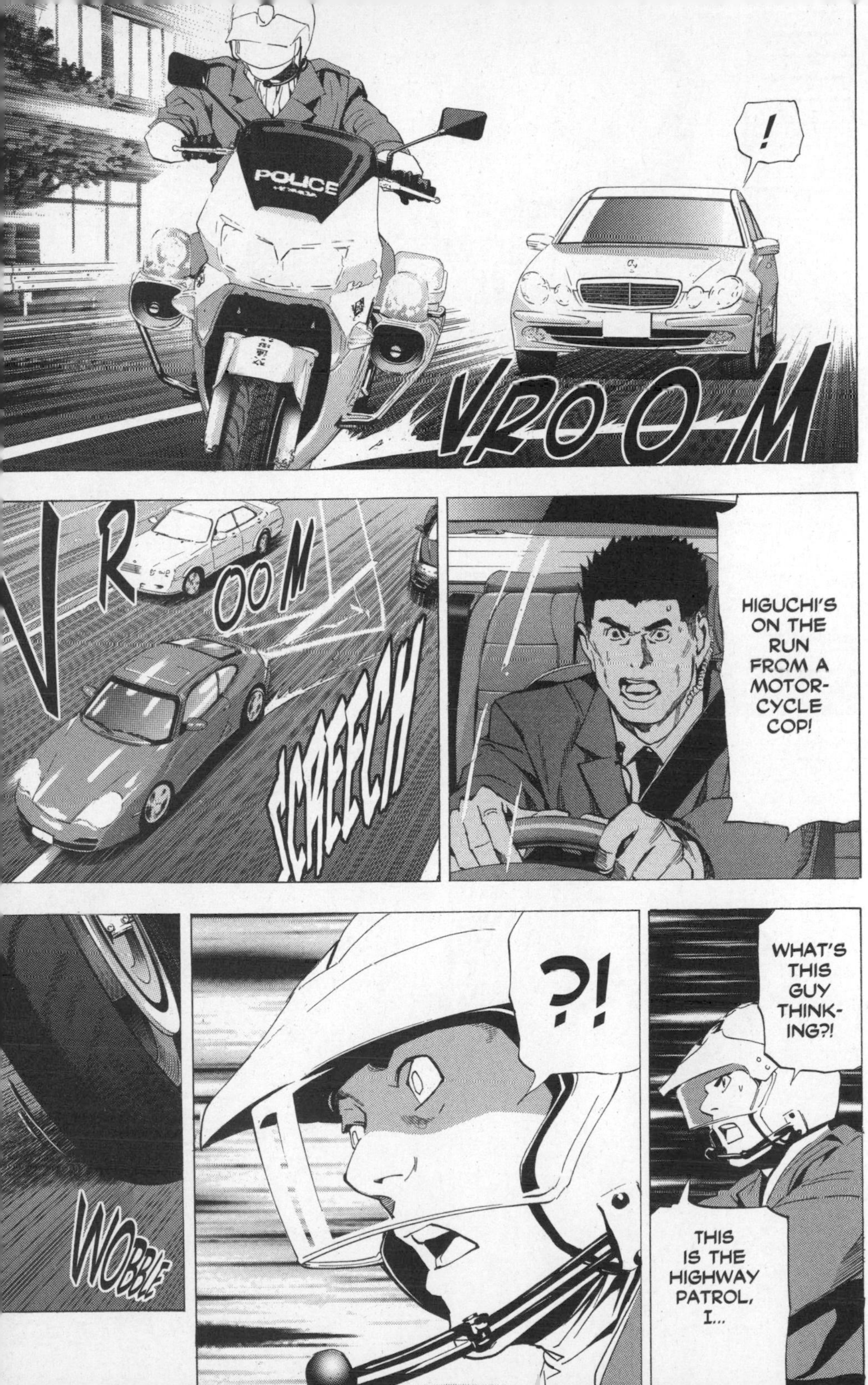
!
VROOM
HIGUCHI'S ON THE RUN FROM A MOTOR-CYCLE COP!
VROOM
SCREECH
WHAT'S THIS GUY THINK-ING?!
THIS IS THE HIGHWAY PATROL, I...
?!
WOBBLE

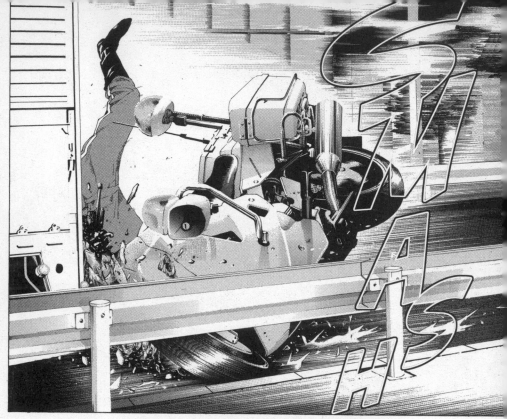

THIS IS BAD...

R-RYUZAKI... THE BIKE CRASHED INTO A TRUCK... IT'S A HORRIBLE ACCIDENT!

WHAT? KILLED IN AN ACCIDENT?!

READ THIS WAY

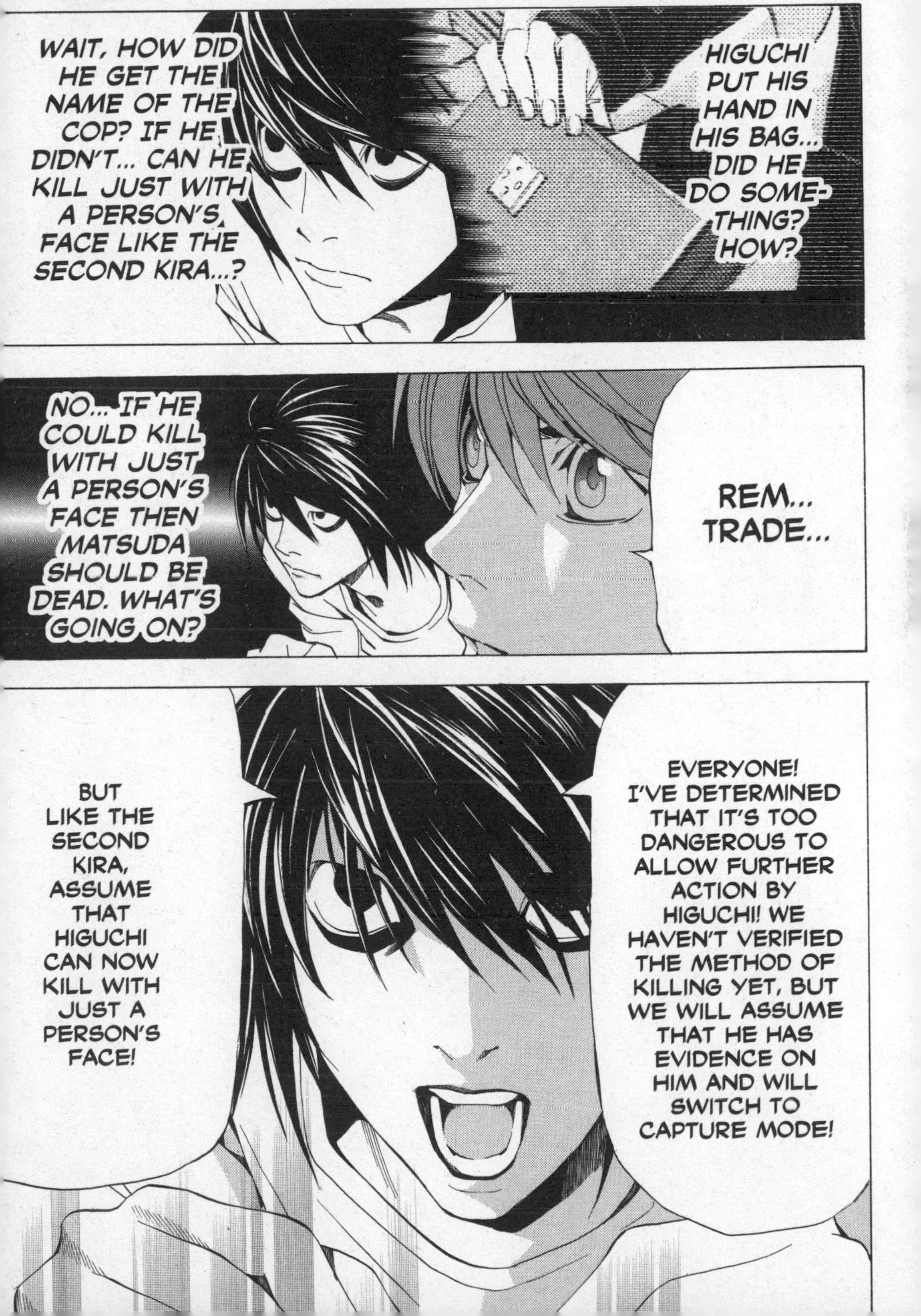
HIGUCHI PUT HIS HAND IN HIS BAG... DID HE DO SOMETHING? HOW?
WAIT, HOW DID HE GET THE NAME OF THE COP? IF HE DIDN'T... CAN HE KILL JUST WITH A PERSON'S FACE LIKE THE SECOND KIRA...?
REM... TRADE...
NO... IF HE COULD KILL WITH JUST A PERSON'S FACE THEN MATSUDA SHOULD BE DEAD. WHAT'S GOING ON?
EVERYONE! I'VE DETERMINED THAT IT'S TOO DANGEROUS TO ALLOW FURTHER ACTION BY HIGUCHI! WE HAVEN'T VERIFIED THE METHOD OF KILLING YET, BUT WE WILL ASSUME THAT HE HAS EVIDENCE ON HIM AND WILL SWITCH TO CAPTURE MODE!
BUT LIKE THE SECOND KIRA, ASSUME THAT HIGUCHI CAN NOW KILL WITH JUST A PERSON'S FACE!

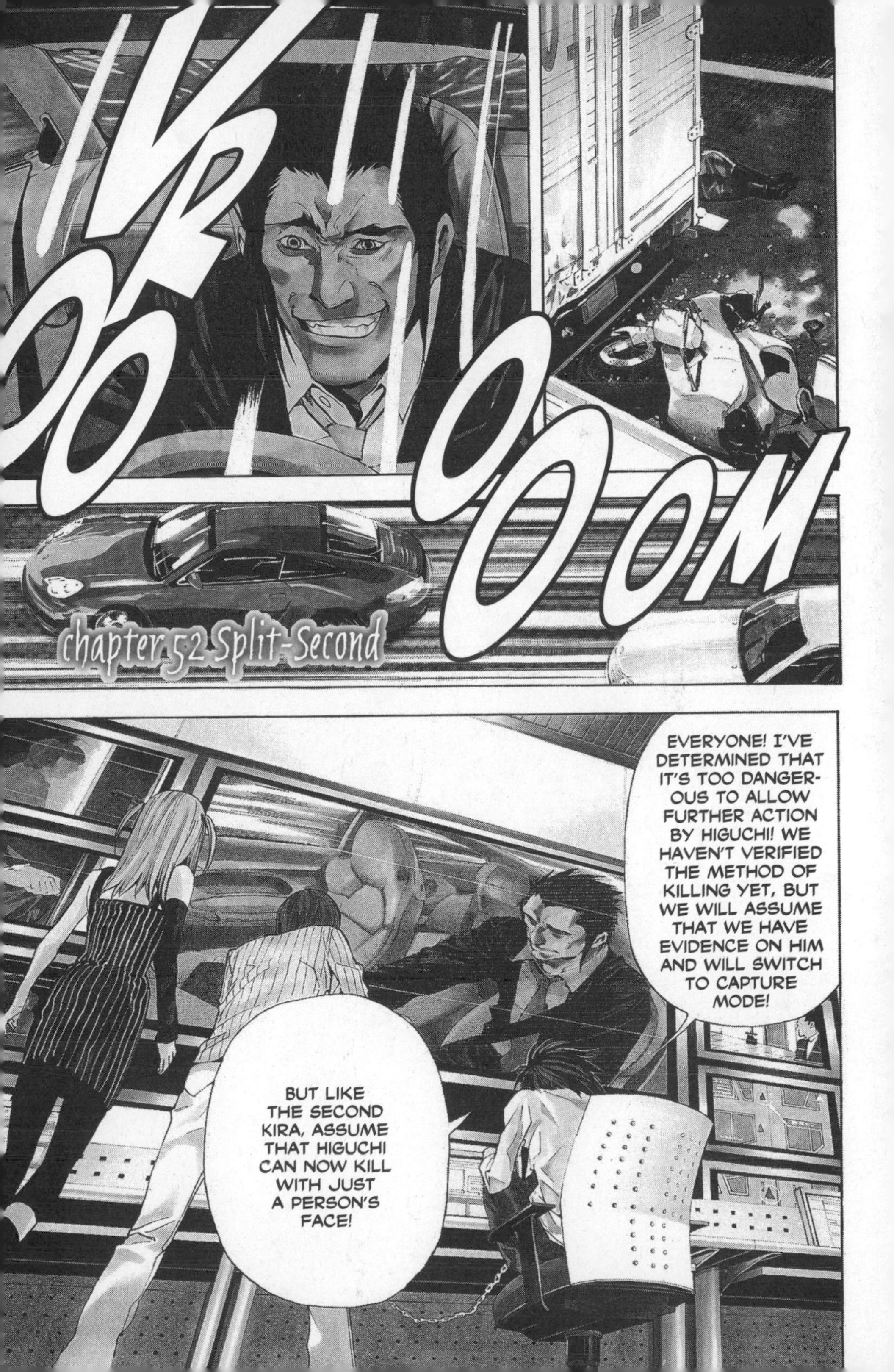
VROOOOOM
chapter 52 Split-Second
EVERYONE! I'VE DETERMINED THAT IT'S TOO DANGER-OUS TO ALLOW FURTHER ACTION BY HIGUCHI! WE HAVEN'T VERIFIED THE METHOD OF KILLING YET, BUT WE WILL ASSUME THAT WE HAVE EVIDENCE ON HIM AND WILL SWITCH TO CAPTURE MODE!
BUT LIKE THE SECOND KIRA, ASSUME THAT HIGUCHI CAN NOW KILL WITH JUST A PERSON'S FACE!

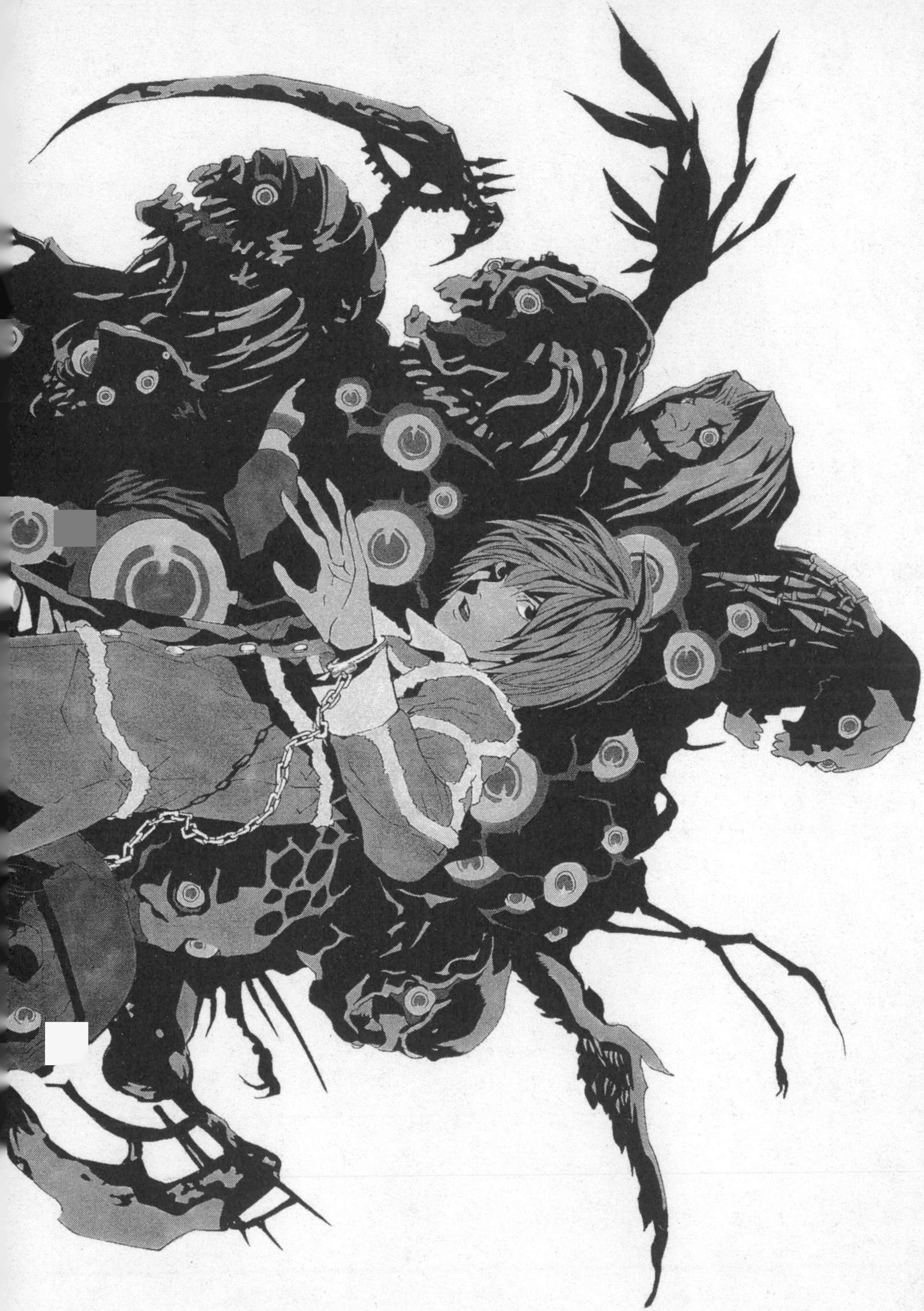

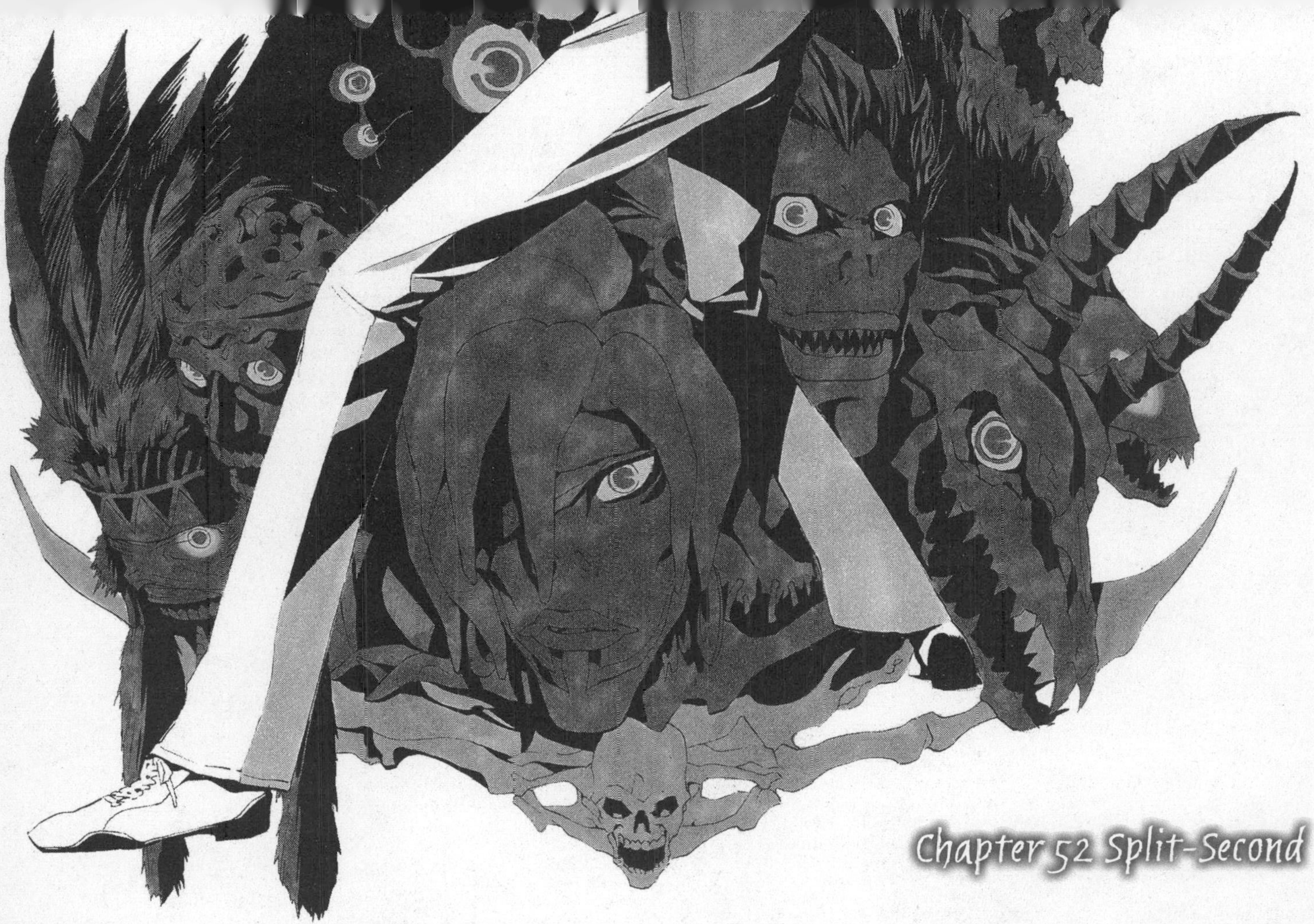

Chapter 52 Split-Second

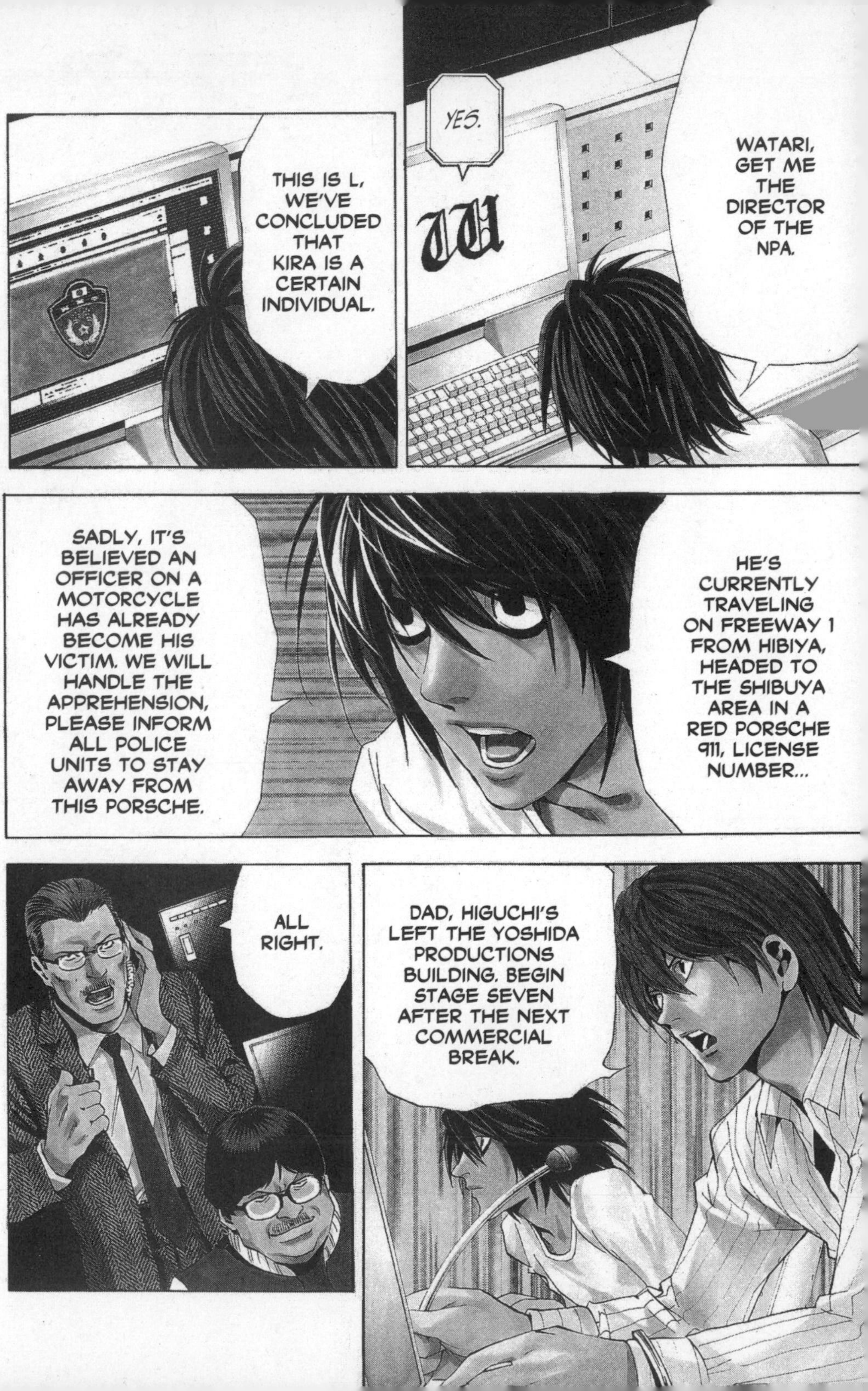
WATARI, GET ME THE DIRECTOR OF THE NPA.
YES.
THIS IS L, WE'VE CONCLUDED THAT KIRA IS A CERTAIN INDIVIDUAL.
HE'S CURRENTLY TRAVELING ON FREEWAY 1 FROM HIBIYA, HEADED TO THE SHIBUYA AREA IN A RED PORSCHE 911, LICENSE NUMBER...
SADLY, IT'S BELIEVED AN OFFICER ON A MOTORCYCLE HAS ALREADY BECOME HIS VICTIM. WE WILL HANDLE THE APPREHENSION, PLEASE INFORM ALL POLICE UNITS TO STAY AWAY FROM THIS PORSCHE.
DAD, HIGUCHI'S LEFT THE YOSHIDA PRODUCTIONS BUILDING. BEGIN STAGE SEVEN AFTER THE NEXT COMMERCIAL BREAK.
ALL RIGHT.

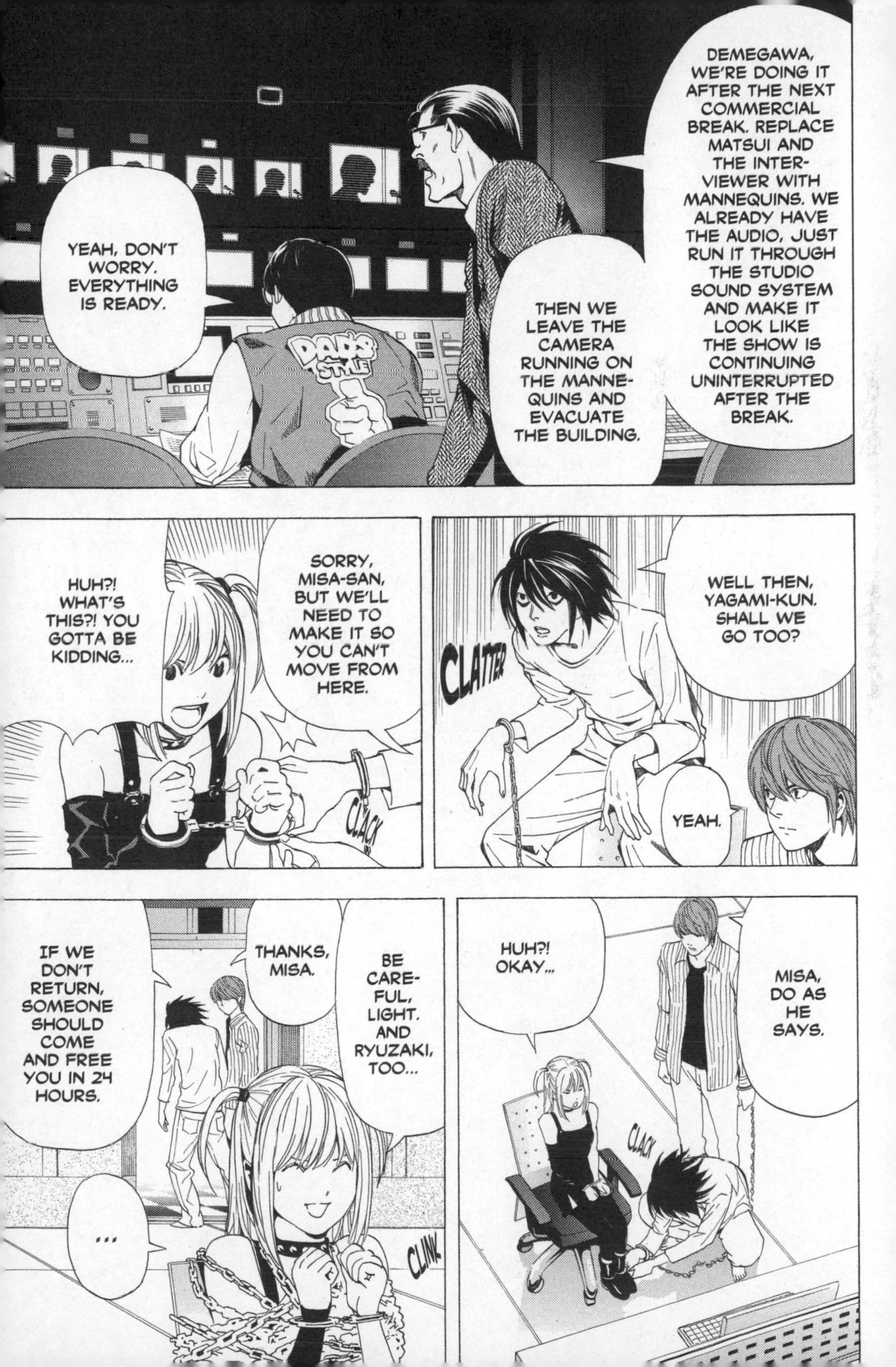
DEMEGAWA, WE'RE DOING IT AFTER THE NEXT COMMERCIAL BREAK. REPLACE MATSUI AND THE INTER-VIEWER WITH MANNEQUINS. WE ALREADY HAVE THE AUDIO, JUST RUN IT THROUGH THE STUDIO SOUND SYSTEM AND MAKE IT LOOK LIKE THE SHOW IS CONTINUING UNINTERRUPTED AFTER THE BREAK.
THEN WE LEAVE THE CAMERA RUNNING ON THE MANNE-QUINS AND EVACUATE THE BUILDING.
YEAH, DON'T WORRY. EVERYTHING IS READY.
WELL THEN, YAGAMI-KUN. SHALL WE GO TOO?
CLATTER
YEAH.
SORRY, MISA-SAN, BUT WE'LL NEED TO MAKE IT SO YOU CAN'T MOVE FROM HERE.
HUH?! WHAT'S THIS?! YOU GOTTA BE KIDDING...
CLACK
MISA, DO AS HE SAYS.
HUH?! OKAY...
CLACK
BE CARE-FUL, LIGHT. AND RYUZAKI, TOO...
THANKS, MISA.
IF WE DON'T RETURN, SOMEONE SHOULD COME AND FREE YOU IN 24 HOURS.
...
CLINK

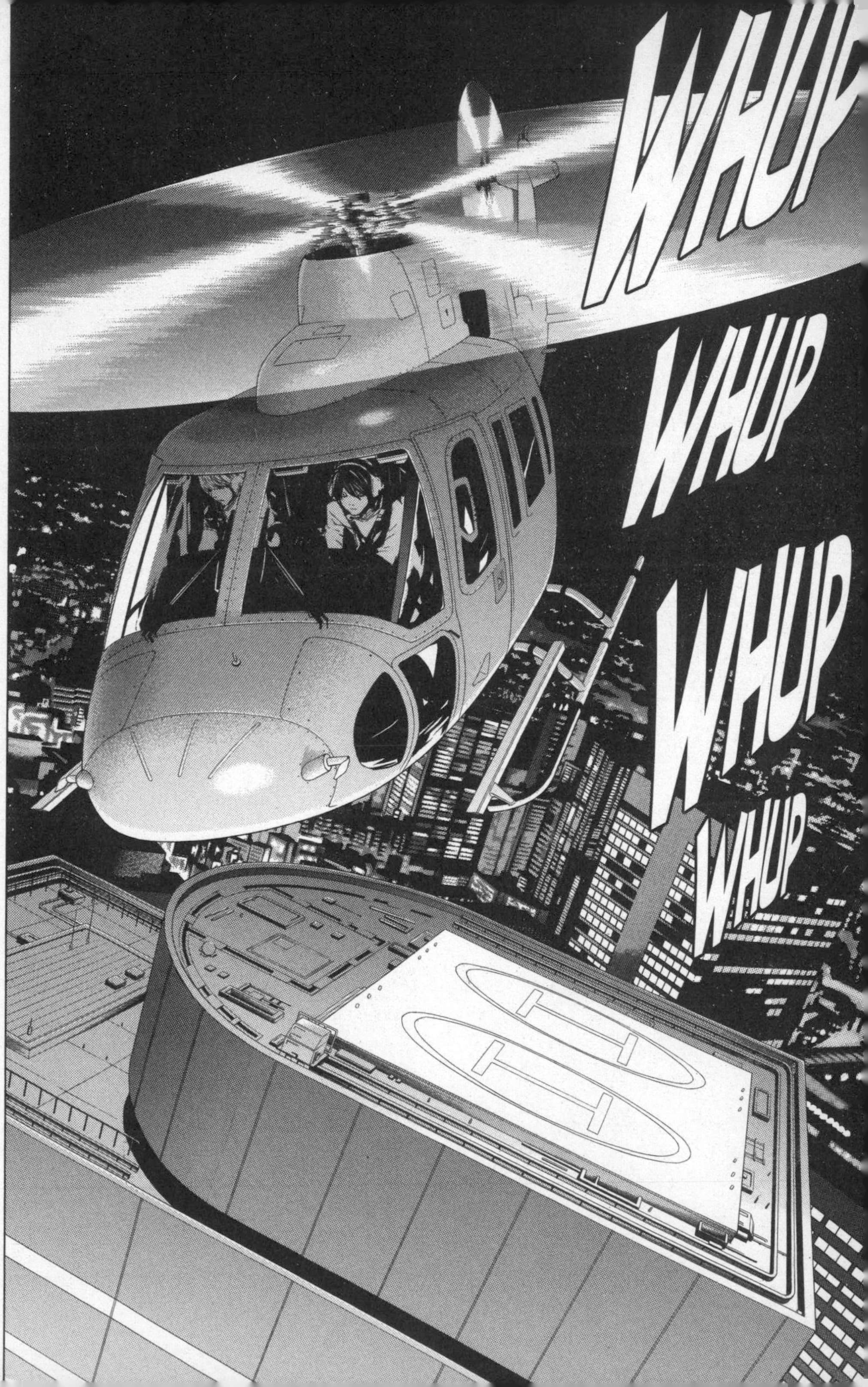
WHUP
WHUP
WHUP
WHUP

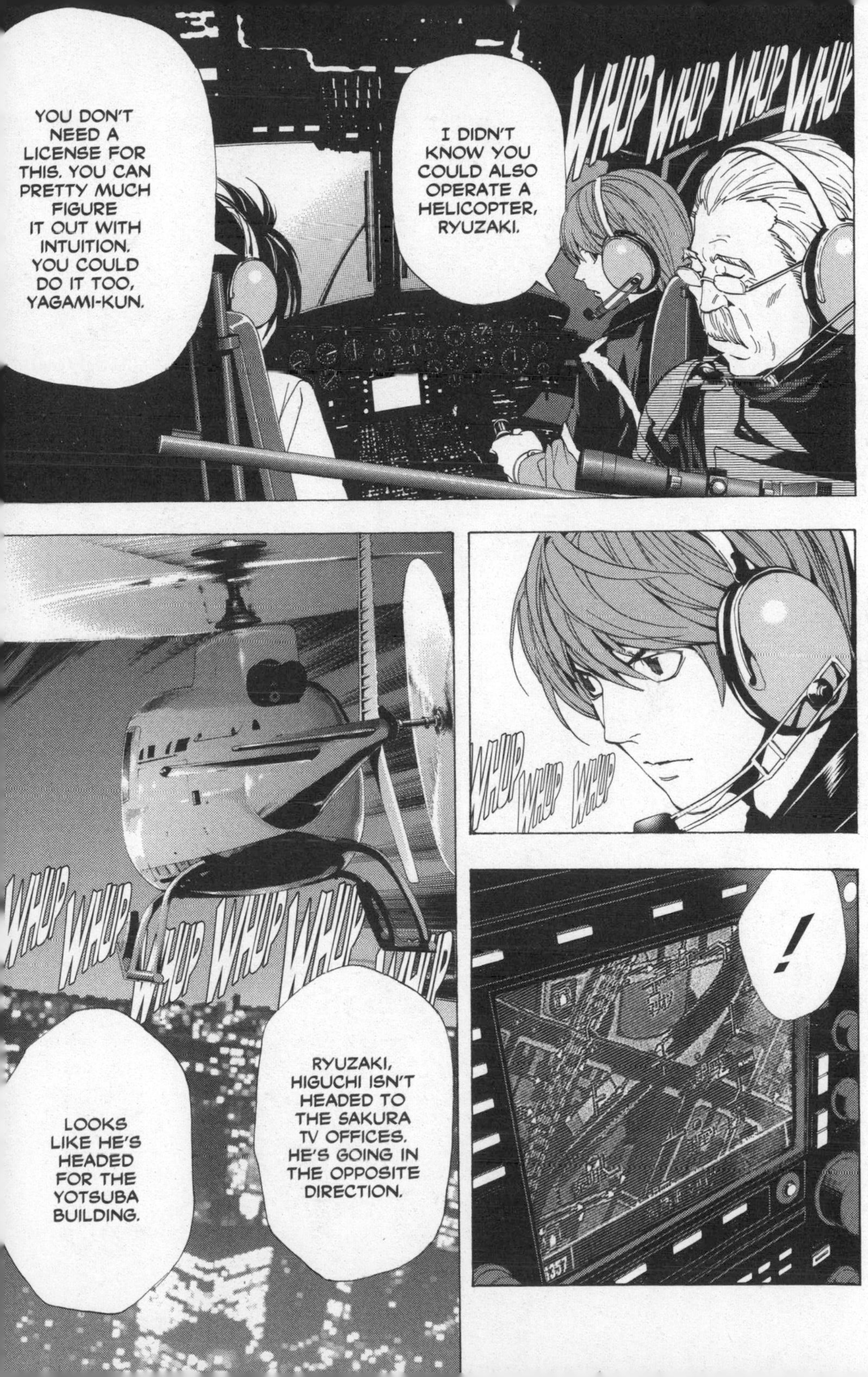
WHUP WHUP WHUP WHUP
I DIDN'T KNOW YOU COULD ALSO OPERATE A HELICOPTER, RYUZAKI.
YOU DON'T NEED A LICENSE FOR THIS. YOU CAN PRETTY MUCH FIGURE IT OUT WITH INTUITION. YOU COULD DO IT TOO, YAGAMI-KUN.
WHUP WHUP WHUP
!
WHUP WHUP WHUP WHUP WHUP
RYUZAKI, HIGUCHI ISN'T HEADED TO THE SAKURA TV OFFICES. HE'S GOING IN THE OPPOSITE DIRECTION.
LOOKS LIKE HE'S HEADED FOR THE YOTSUBA BUILDING.

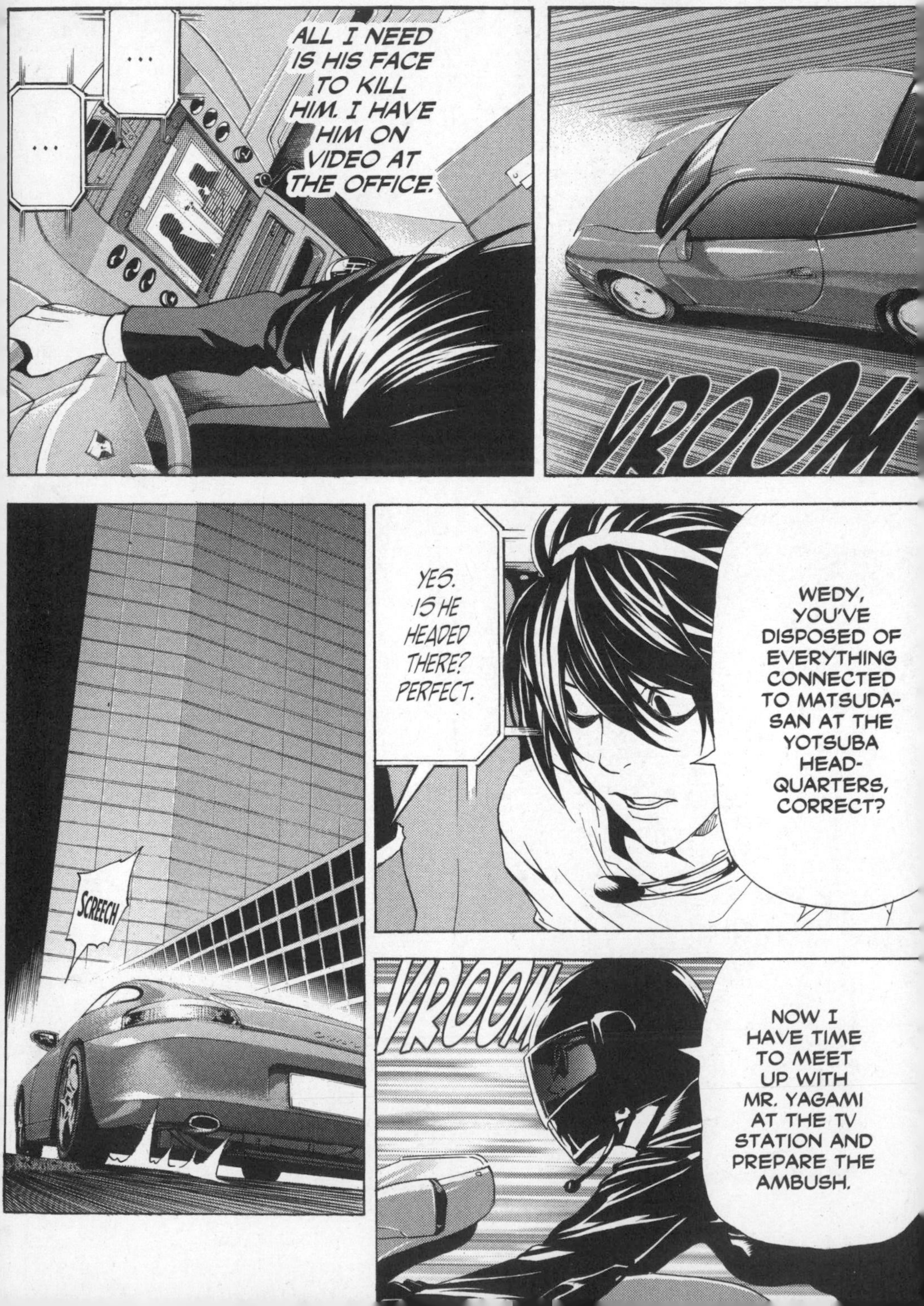
VROOM
ALL I NEED IS HIS FACE TO KILL HIM. I HAVE HIM ON VIDEO AT THE OFFICE.
...
...
WEDY, YOU'VE DISPOSED OF EVERYTHING CONNECTED TO MATSUDA-SAN AT THE YOTSUBA HEAD-QUARTERS, CORRECT?
YES. IS HE HEADED THERE? PERFECT.
NOW I HAVE TIME TO MEET UP WITH MR. YAGAMI AT THE TV STATION AND PREPARE THE AMBUSH.
VROOM
SCREECH

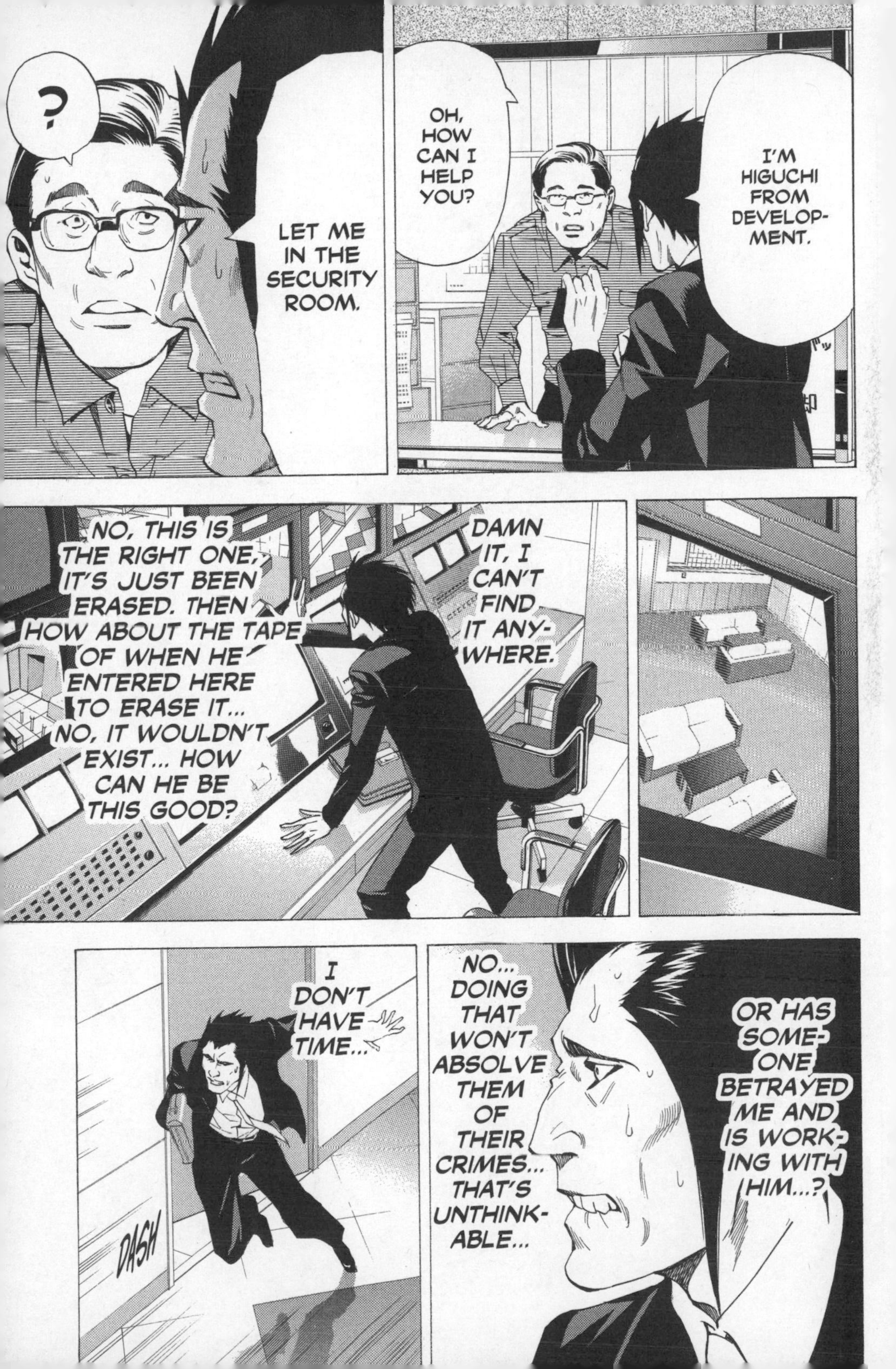
I'M HIGUCHI FROM DEVELOPMENT.
OH, HOW CAN I HELP YOU?
LET ME IN THE SECURITY ROOM.
?
DAMN IT, I CAN'T FIND IT ANYWHERE.
NO, THIS IS THE RIGHT ONE, IT'S JUST BEEN ERASED. THEN HOW ABOUT THE TAPE OF WHEN HE ENTERED HERE TO ERASE IT... NO, IT WOULDN'T EXIST... HOW CAN HE BE THIS GOOD?
OR HAS SOMEONE BETRAYED ME AND IS WORKING WITH HIM...?
NO... DOING THAT WON'T ABSOLVE THEM OF THEIR CRIMES... THAT'S UNTHINKABLE...
I DON'T HAVE TIME...
DASH

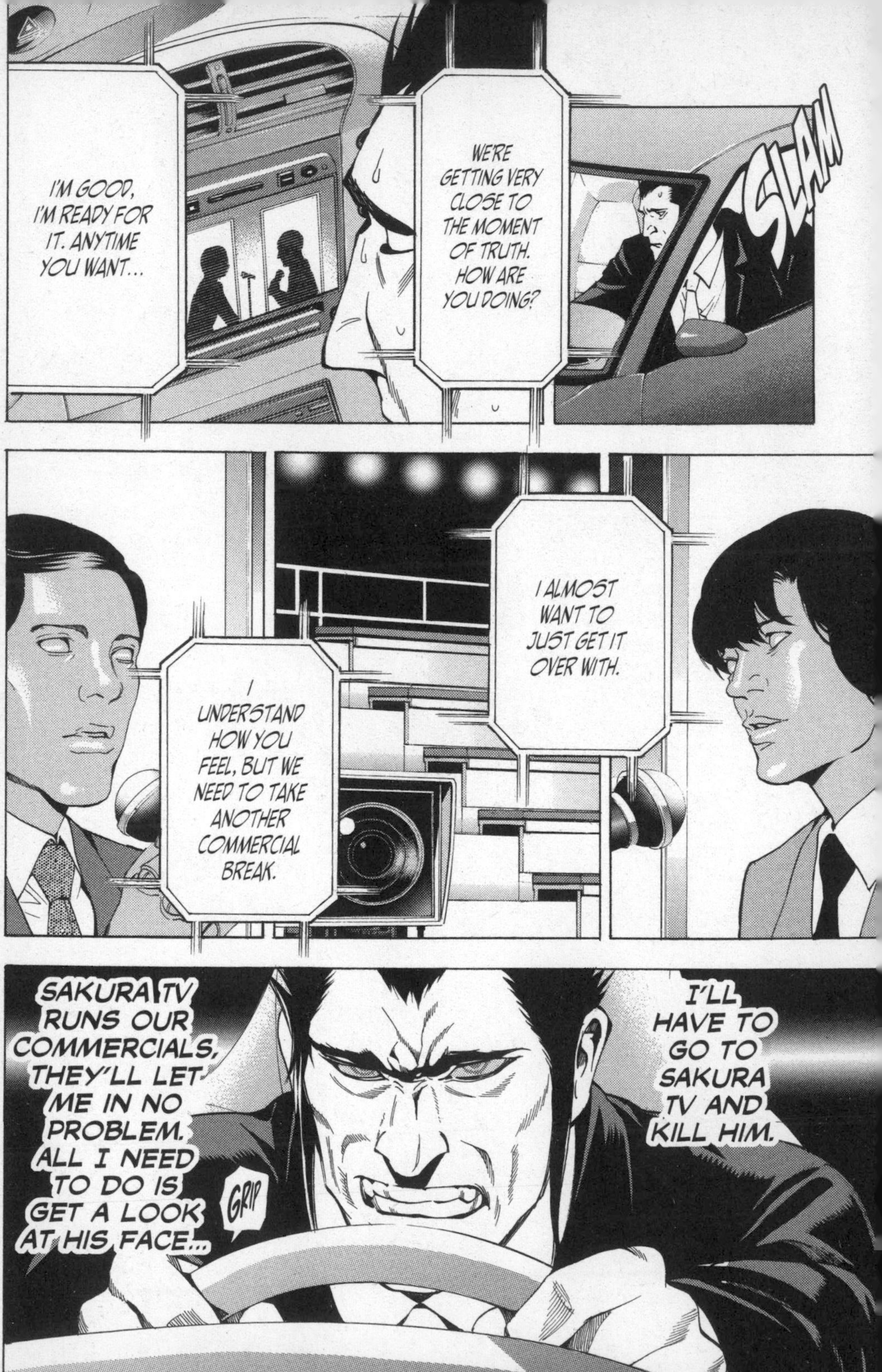
SLAM
WE'RE GETTING VERY CLOSE TO THE MOMENT OF TRUTH. HOW ARE YOU DOING?
I'M GOOD, I'M READY FOR IT. ANYTIME YOU WANT...
I ALMOST WANT TO JUST GET IT OVER WITH.
I UNDERSTAND HOW YOU FEEL, BUT WE NEED TO TAKE ANOTHER COMMERCIAL BREAK.
I'LL HAVE TO GO TO SAKURA TV AND KILL HIM.
SAKURA TV RUNS OUR COMMERCIALS, THEY'LL LET ME IN NO PROBLEM. ALL I NEED TO DO IS GET A LOOK AT HIS FACE...
GRIP

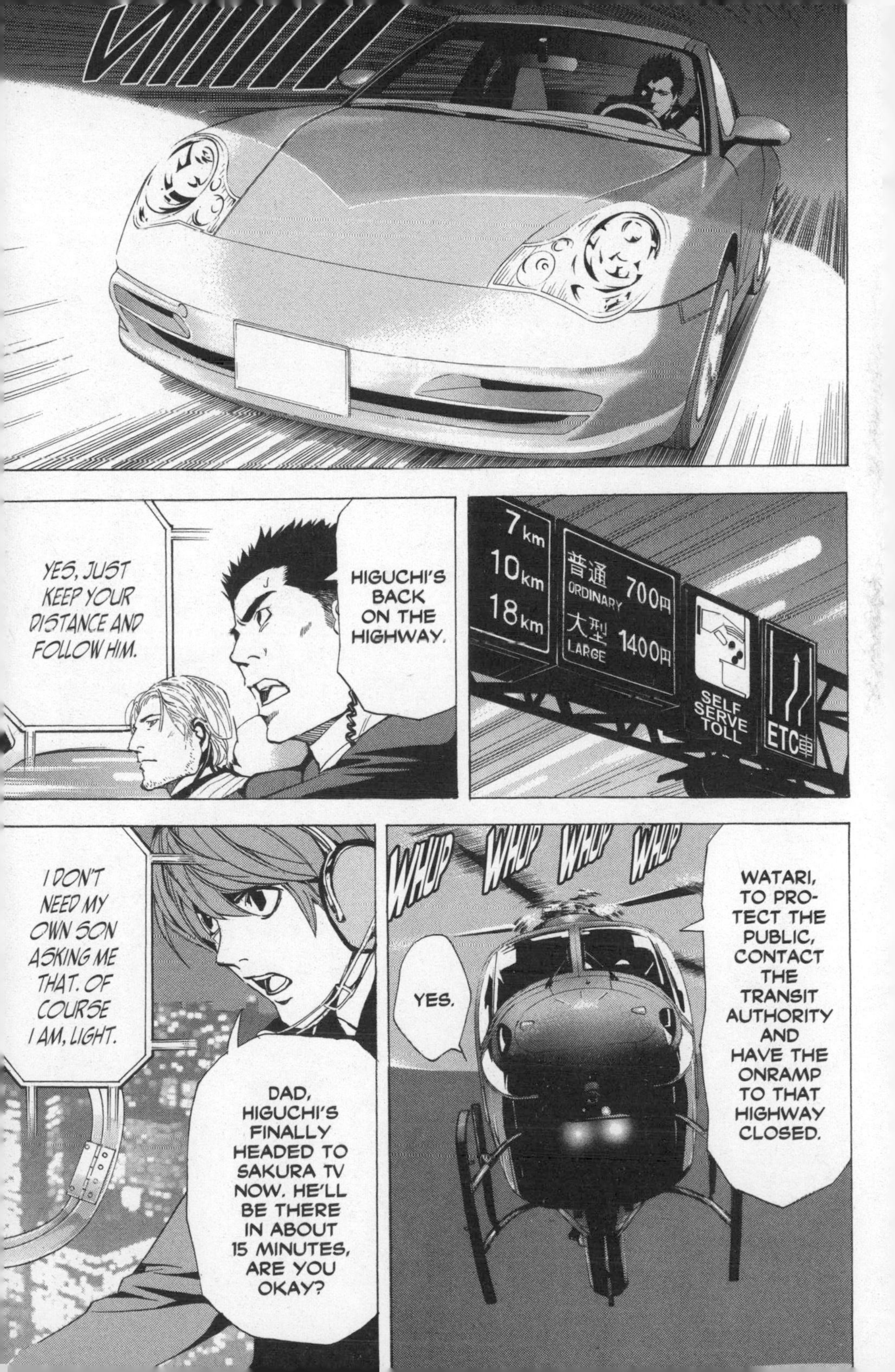
7km
10km
18km
普通 ORDINARY 700円
大型 LARGE 1400円
SELF SERVE TOLL
ETC車
HIGUCHI'S BACK ON THE HIGHWAY.
YES, JUST KEEP YOUR DISTANCE AND FOLLOW HIM.
WHUP WHUP WHUP WHUP
WATARI, TO PROTECT THE PUBLIC, CONTACT THE TRANSIT AUTHORITY AND HAVE THE ONRAMP TO THAT HIGHWAY CLOSED.
YES.
DAD, HIGUCHI'S FINALLY HEADED TO SAKURA TV NOW. HE'LL BE THERE IN ABOUT 15 MINUTES, ARE YOU OKAY?
I DON'T NEED MY OWN SON ASKING ME THAT. OF COURSE I AM, LIGHT.

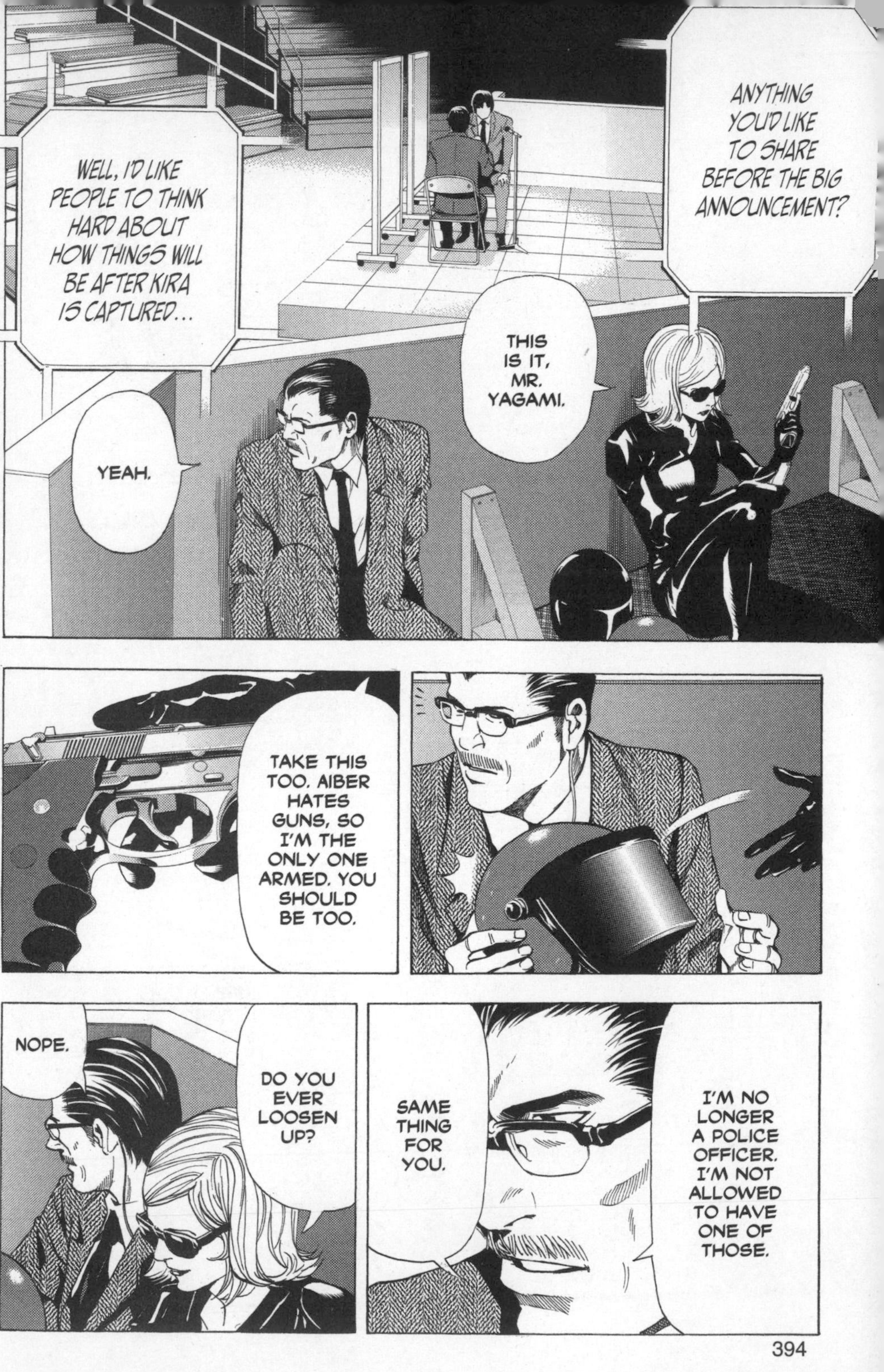
ANYTHING YOU'D LIKE TO SHARE BEFORE THE BIG ANNOUNCEMENT?
WELL, I'D LIKE PEOPLE TO THINK HARD ABOUT HOW THINGS WILL BE AFTER KIRA IS CAPTURED...
THIS IS IT, MR. YAGAMI.
YEAH.
TAKE THIS TOO. AIBER HATES GUNS, SO I'M THE ONLY ONE ARMED. YOU SHOULD BE TOO.
I'M NO LONGER A POLICE OFFICER. I'M NOT ALLOWED TO HAVE ONE OF THOSE.
SAME THING FOR YOU.
DO YOU EVER LOOSEN UP?
NOPE.

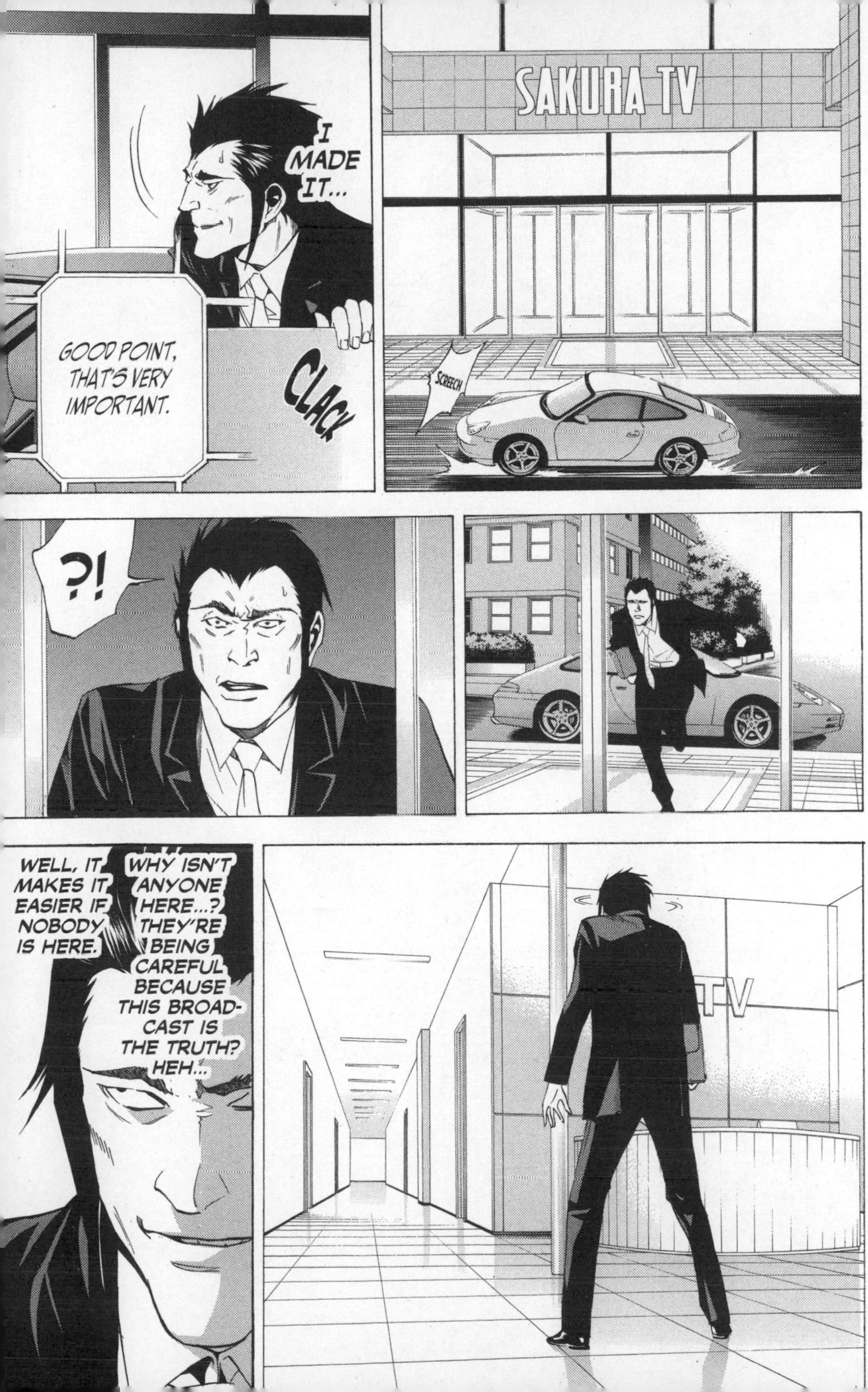
SAKURA TV
SCREECH
I MADE IT...
GOOD POINT, THAT'S VERY IMPORTANT.
CLACK
?!
TV
WHY ISN'T ANYONE HERE...? THEY'RE BEING CAREFUL BECAUSE THIS BROADCAST IS THE TRUTH? HEH...
WELL, IT MAKES IT EASIER IF NOBODY IS HERE.

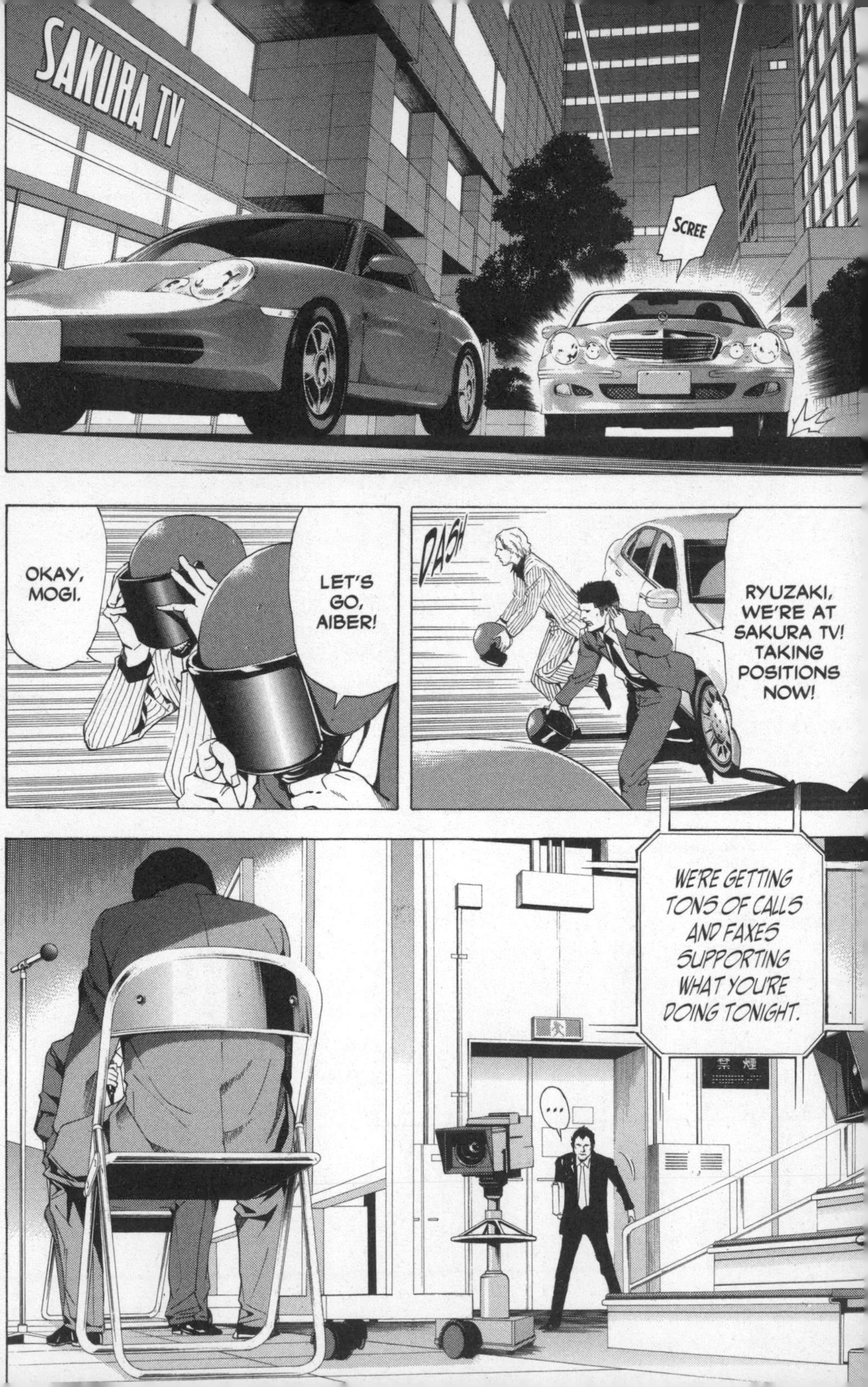
SAKURA TV
SCREE
RYUZAKI, WE'RE AT SAKURA TV! TAKING POSITIONS NOW!
DASH
LET'S GO, AIBER!
OKAY, MOGI.
WE'RE GETTING TONS OF CALLS AND FAXES SUPPORTING WHAT YOU'RE DOING TONIGHT.
...

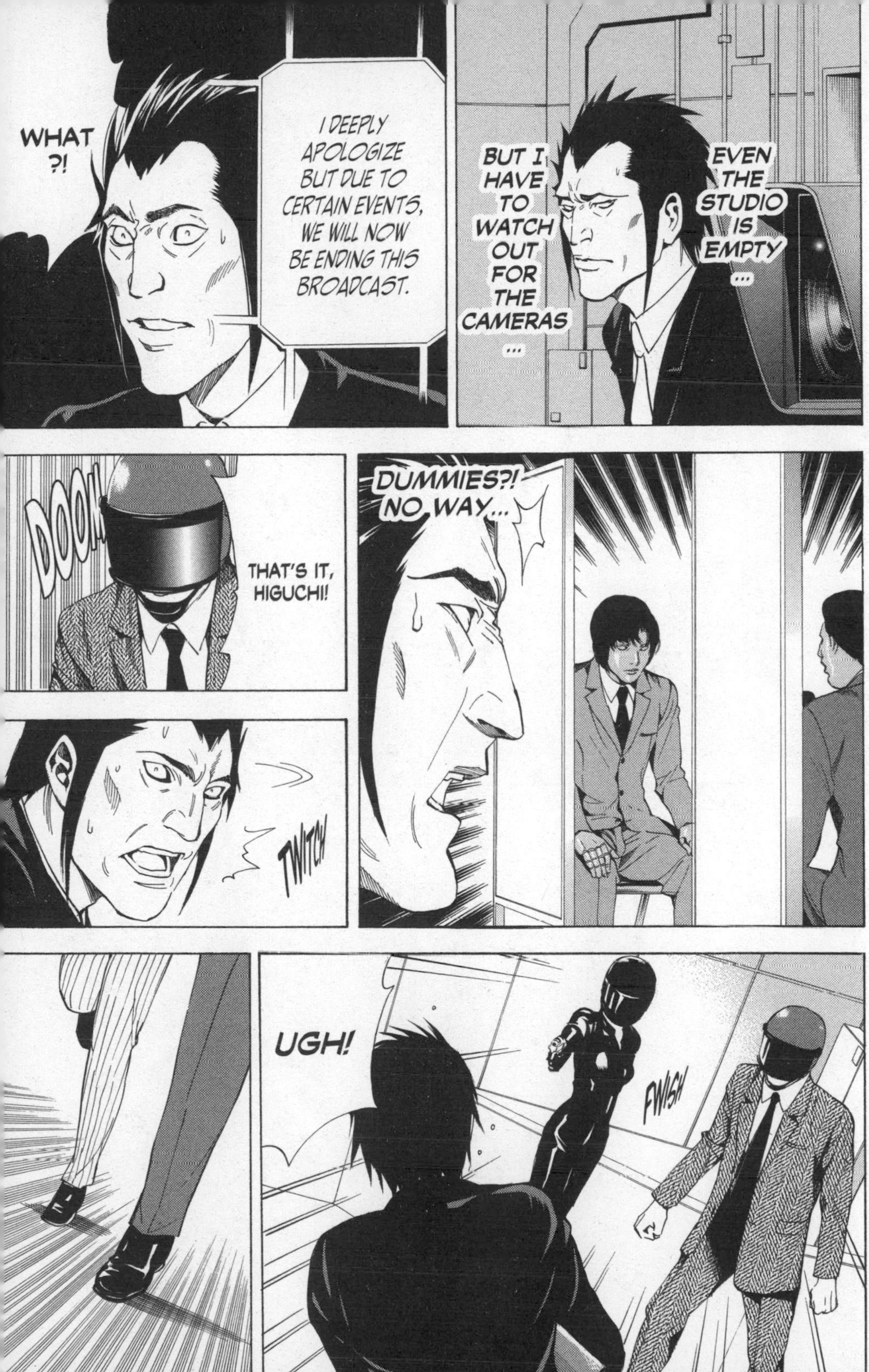
EVEN THE STUDIO IS EMPTY ...
BUT I HAVE TO WATCH OUT FOR THE CAMERAS ...
I DEEPLY APOLOGIZE BUT DUE TO CERTAIN EVENTS, WE WILL NOW BE ENDING THIS BROADCAST.
WHAT ?!
DUMMIES?! NO WAY...
DOOM
THAT'S IT, HIGUCHI!
TWITCH
FWISH
UGH!

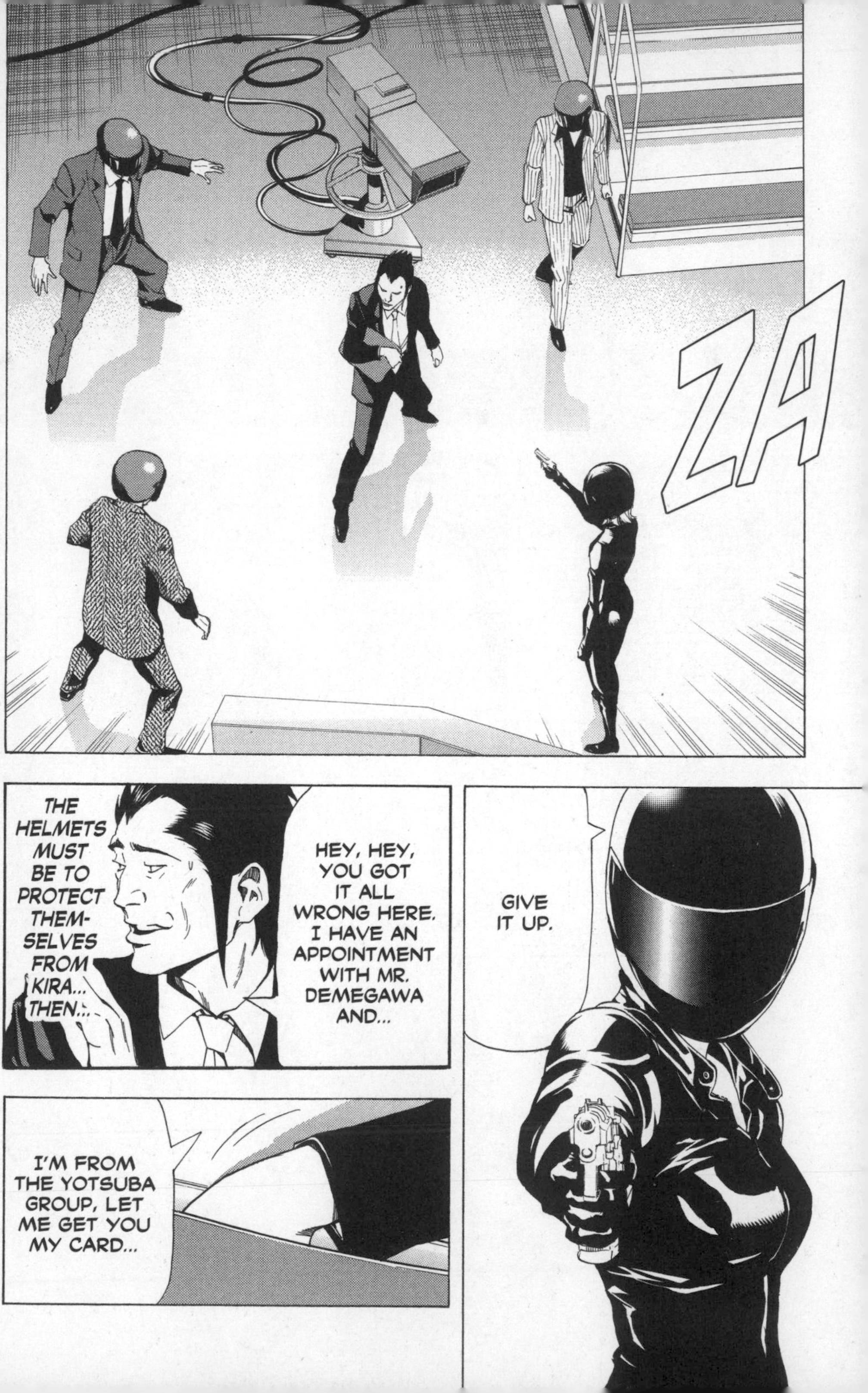
ZA
GIVE IT UP.
HEY, HEY, YOU GOT IT ALL WRONG HERE. I HAVE AN APPOINTMENT WITH MR. DEMEGAWA AND...
THE HELMETS MUST BE TO PROTECT THEM-SELVES FROM KIRA... THEN...
I'M FROM THE YOTSUBA GROUP, LET ME GET YOU MY CARD...

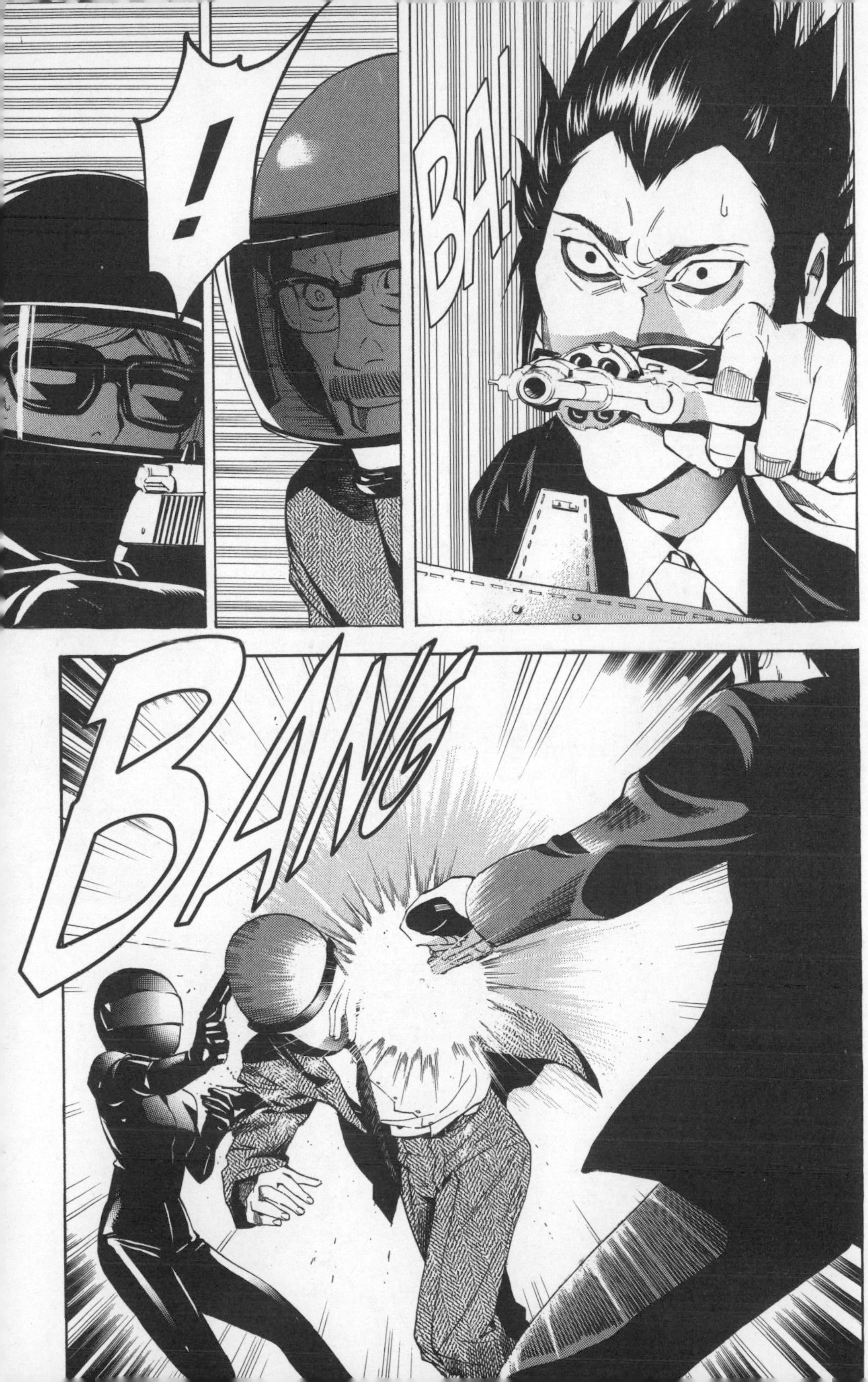
BA!
!
BANG

CHIEF!!

AIBER!

DASH

OH NO!

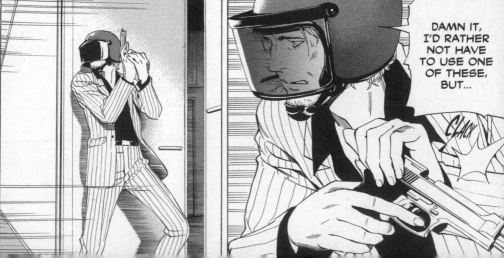

DAMN IT, I'D RATHER NOT HAVE TO USE ONE OF THESE, BUT...

CLACK

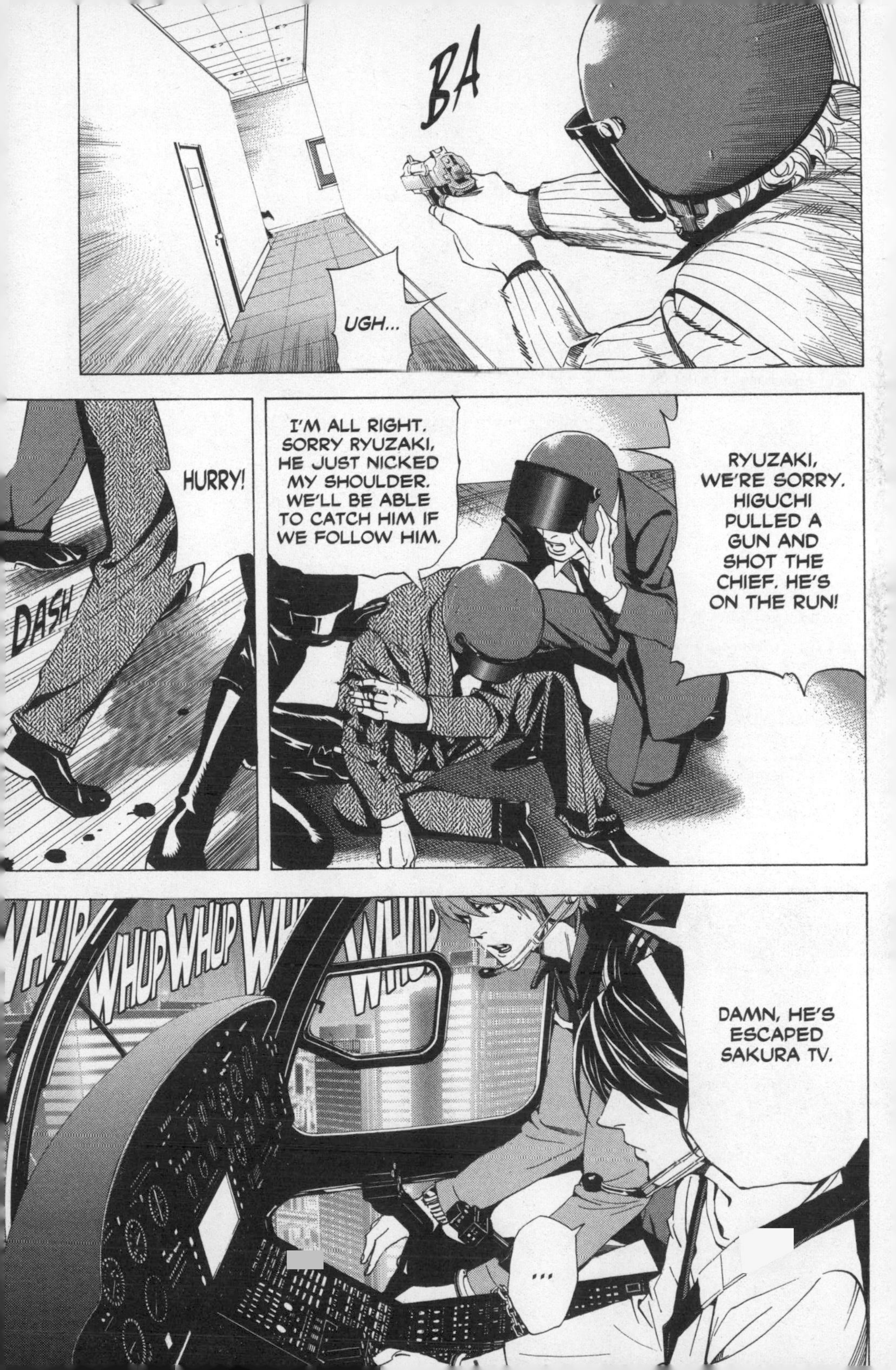
BA
UGH...
RYUZAKI, WE'RE SORRY. HIGUCHI PULLED A GUN AND SHOT THE CHIEF. HE'S ON THE RUN!
I'M ALL RIGHT. SORRY RYUZAKI, HE JUST NICKED MY SHOULDER. WE'LL BE ABLE TO CATCH HIM IF WE FOLLOW HIM.
HURRY!
DASH
DAMN, HE'S ESCAPED SAKURA TV.
WHUP WHUP
...

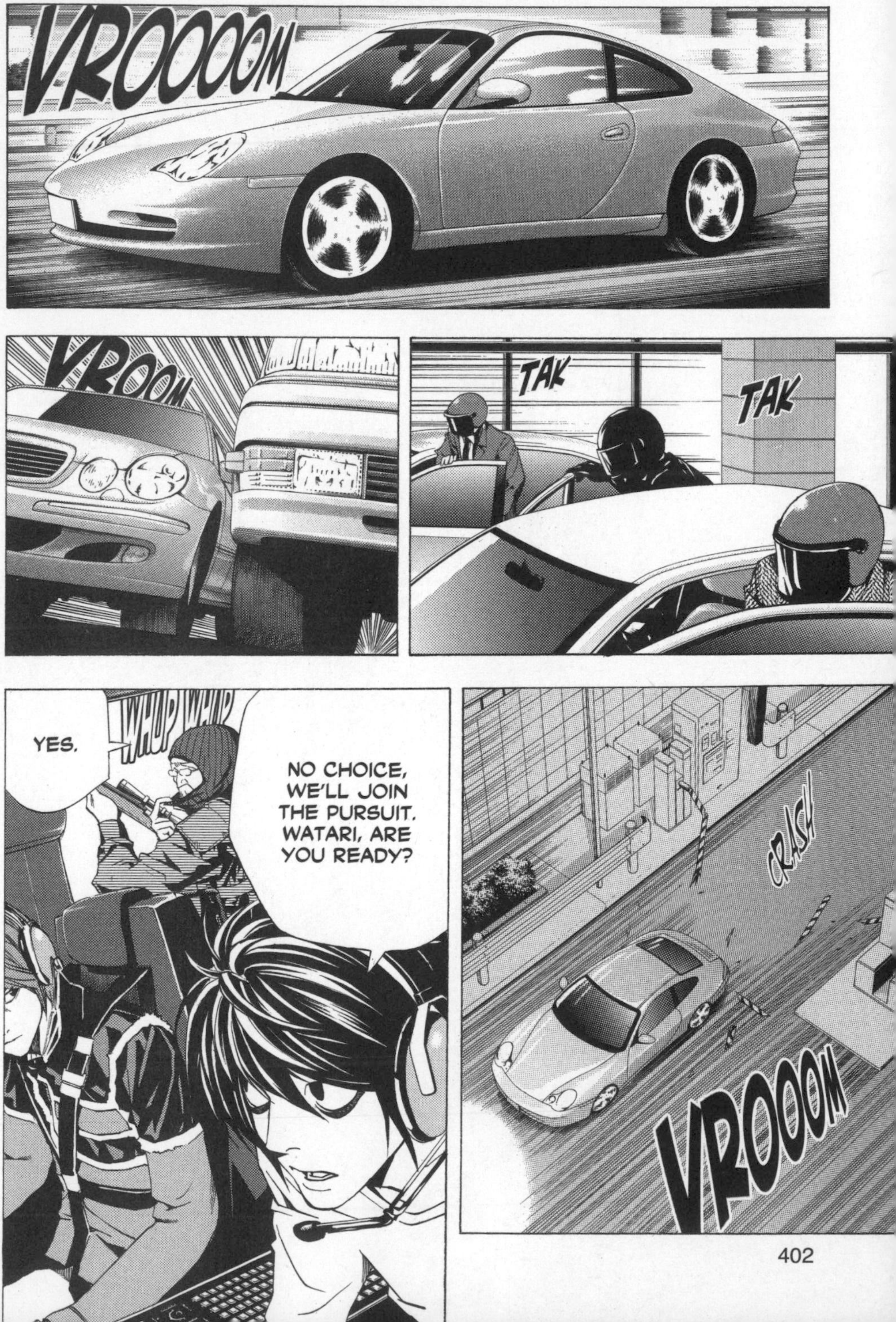
VROOOOM
TAK
TAK
VROOM
CRASH
VROOOM
NO CHOICE, WE'LL JOIN THE PURSUIT. WATARI, ARE YOU READY?
WHUP WHUP
YES.

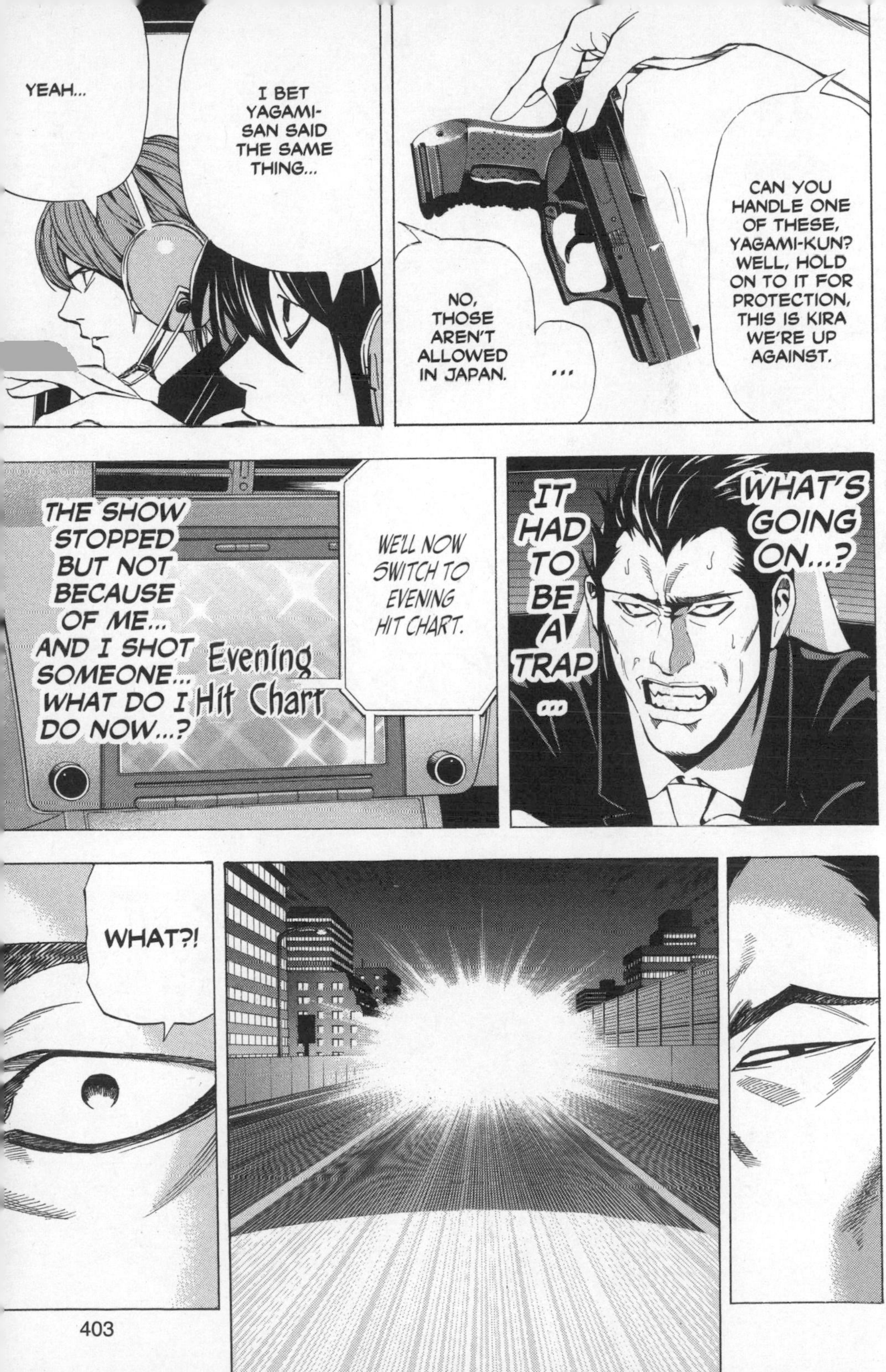
CAN YOU HANDLE ONE OF THESE, YAGAMI-KUN? WELL, HOLD ON TO IT FOR PROTECTION, THIS IS KIRA WE'RE UP AGAINST.
NO, THOSE AREN'T ALLOWED IN JAPAN.
...
I BET YAGAMI-SAN SAID THE SAME THING...
YEAH...
WHAT'S GOING ON...?
IT HAD TO BE A TRAP...
WE'LL NOW SWITCH TO EVENING HIT CHART.
Evening Hit Chart
THE SHOW STOPPED BUT NOT BECAUSE OF ME... AND I SHOT SOMEONE... WHAT DO I DO NOW...?
WHAT?!

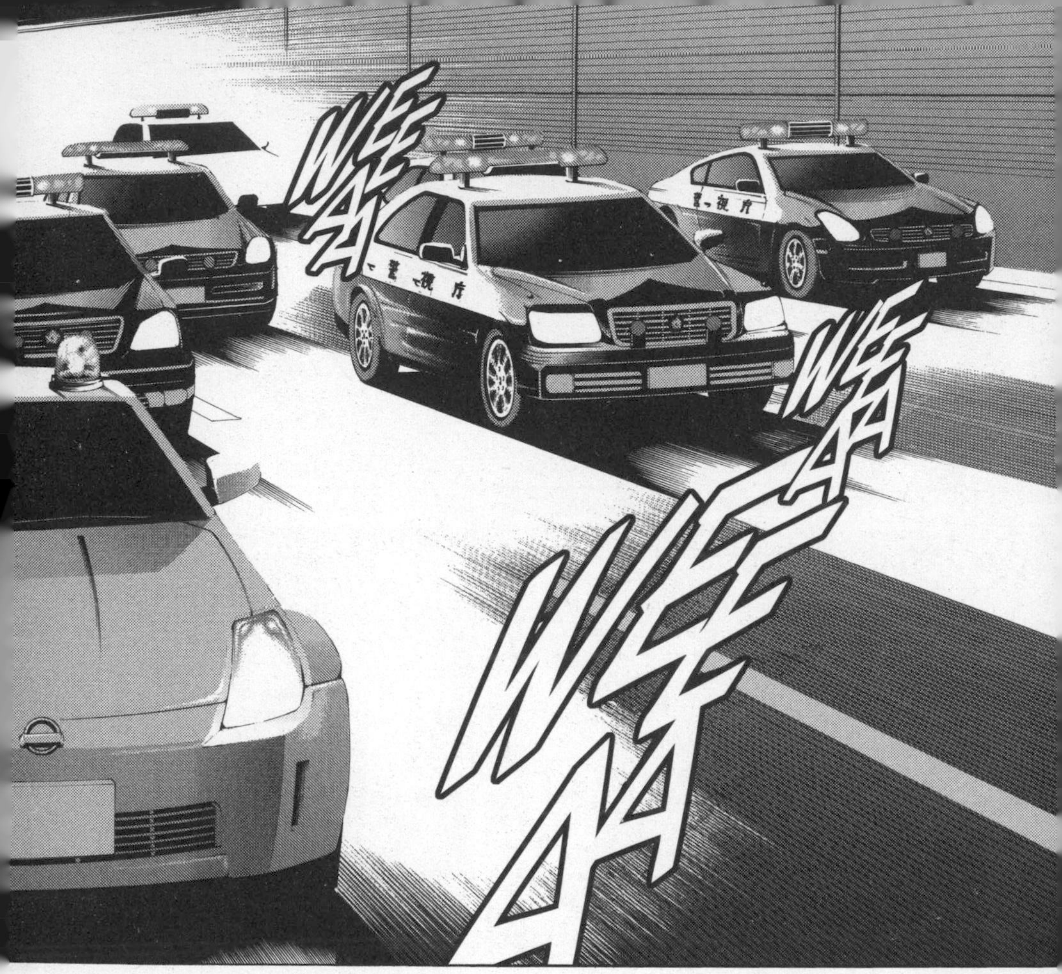
WEE AA
WEE AA
WEE AAA
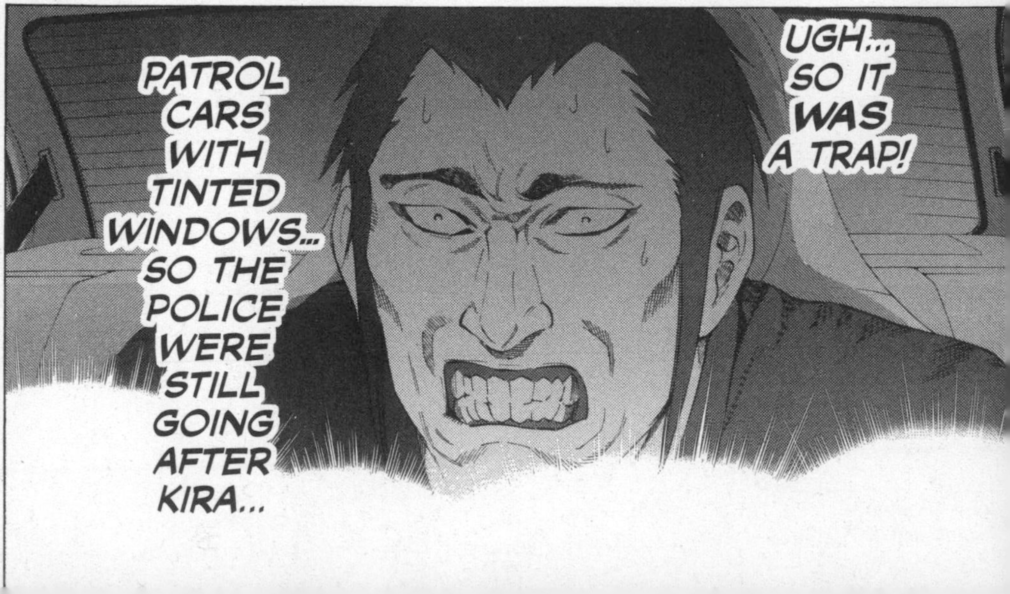
UGH... SO IT WAS A TRAP!
PATROL CARS WITH TINTED WINDOWS... SO THE POLICE WERE STILL GOING AFTER KIRA...

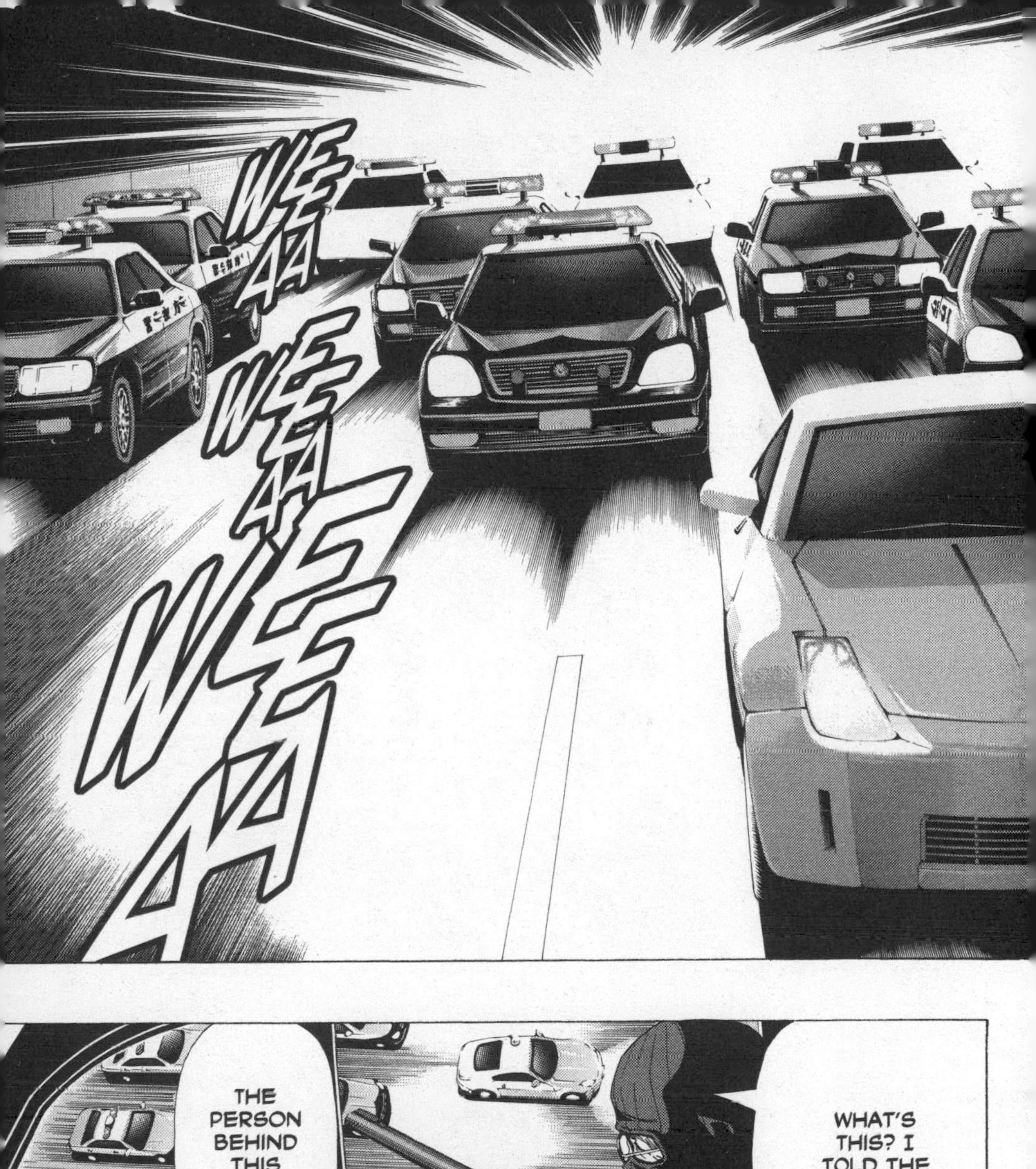

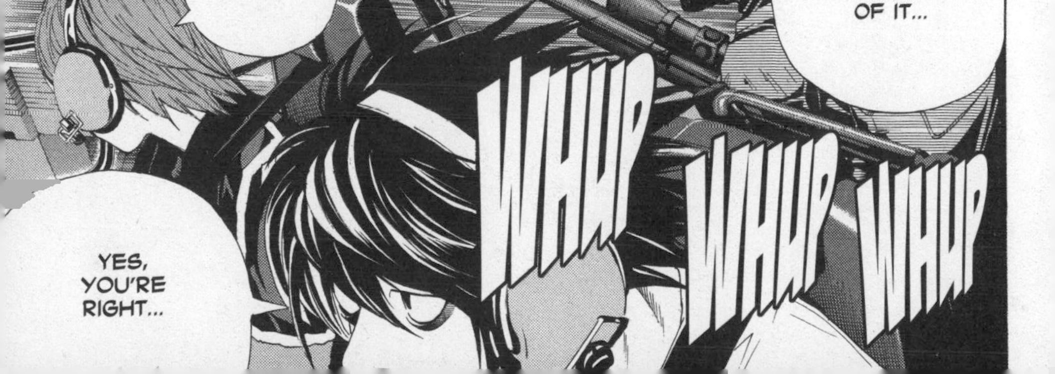

WHAT'S THIS? I TOLD THE POLICE TO STAY OUT OF IT...
THE PERSON BEHIND THIS MUST BE...
WHUP WHUP WHUP
YES, YOU'RE RIGHT...

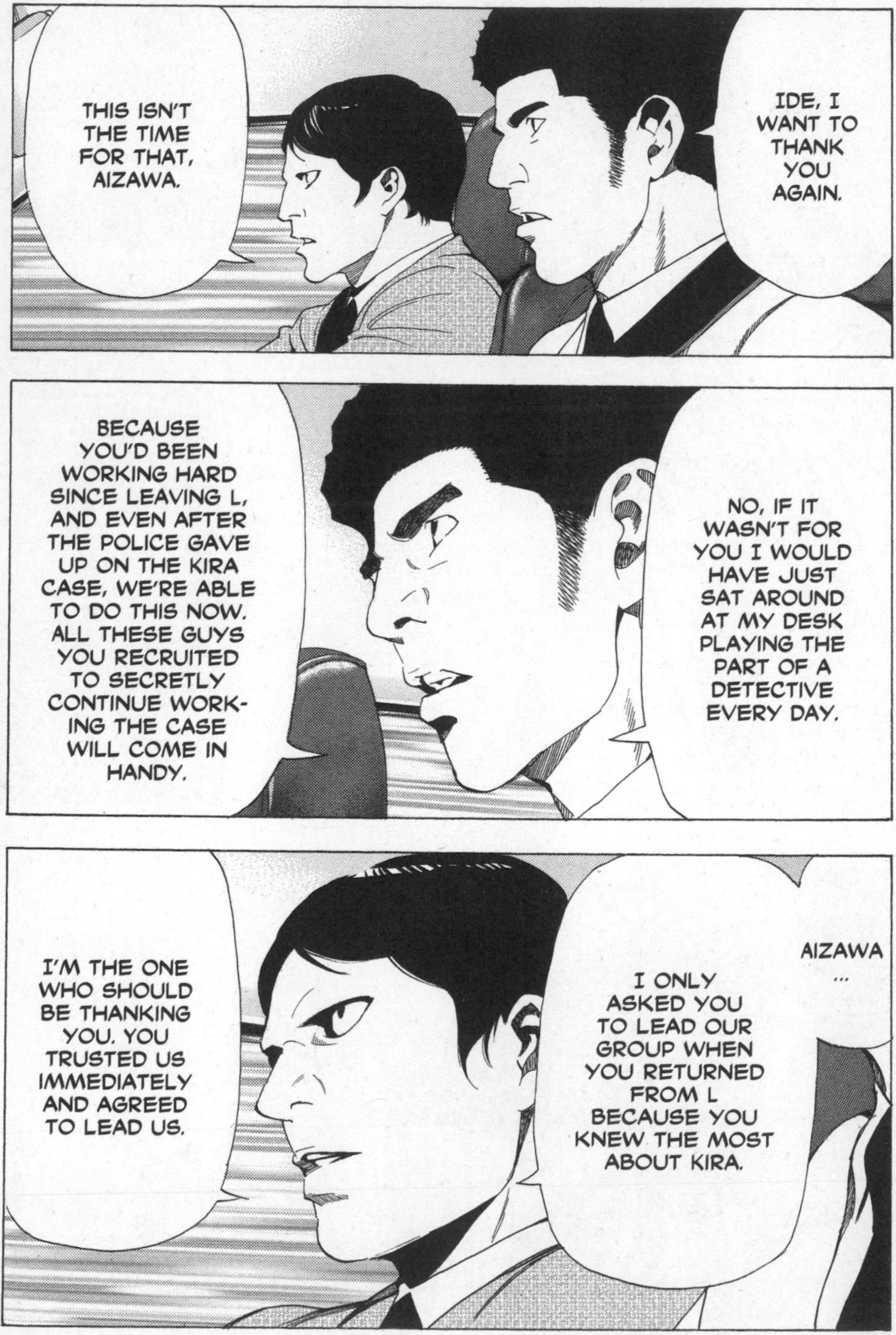
IDE, I WANT TO THANK YOU AGAIN.
THIS ISN'T THE TIME FOR THAT, AIZAWA.
NO, IF IT WASN'T FOR YOU I WOULD HAVE JUST SAT AROUND AT MY DESK PLAYING THE PART OF A DETECTIVE EVERY DAY.
BECAUSE YOU'D BEEN WORKING HARD SINCE LEAVING L, AND EVEN AFTER THE POLICE GAVE UP ON THE KIRA CASE, WE'RE ABLE TO DO THIS NOW. ALL THESE GUYS YOU RECRUITED TO SECRETLY CONTINUE WORKING THE CASE WILL COME IN HANDY.
AIZAWA ...
I ONLY ASKED YOU TO LEAD OUR GROUP WHEN YOU RETURNED FROM L BECAUSE YOU KNEW THE MOST ABOUT KIRA.
I'M THE ONE WHO SHOULD BE THANKING YOU. YOU TRUSTED US IMMEDIATELY AND AGREED TO LEAD US.

READ THIS WAY

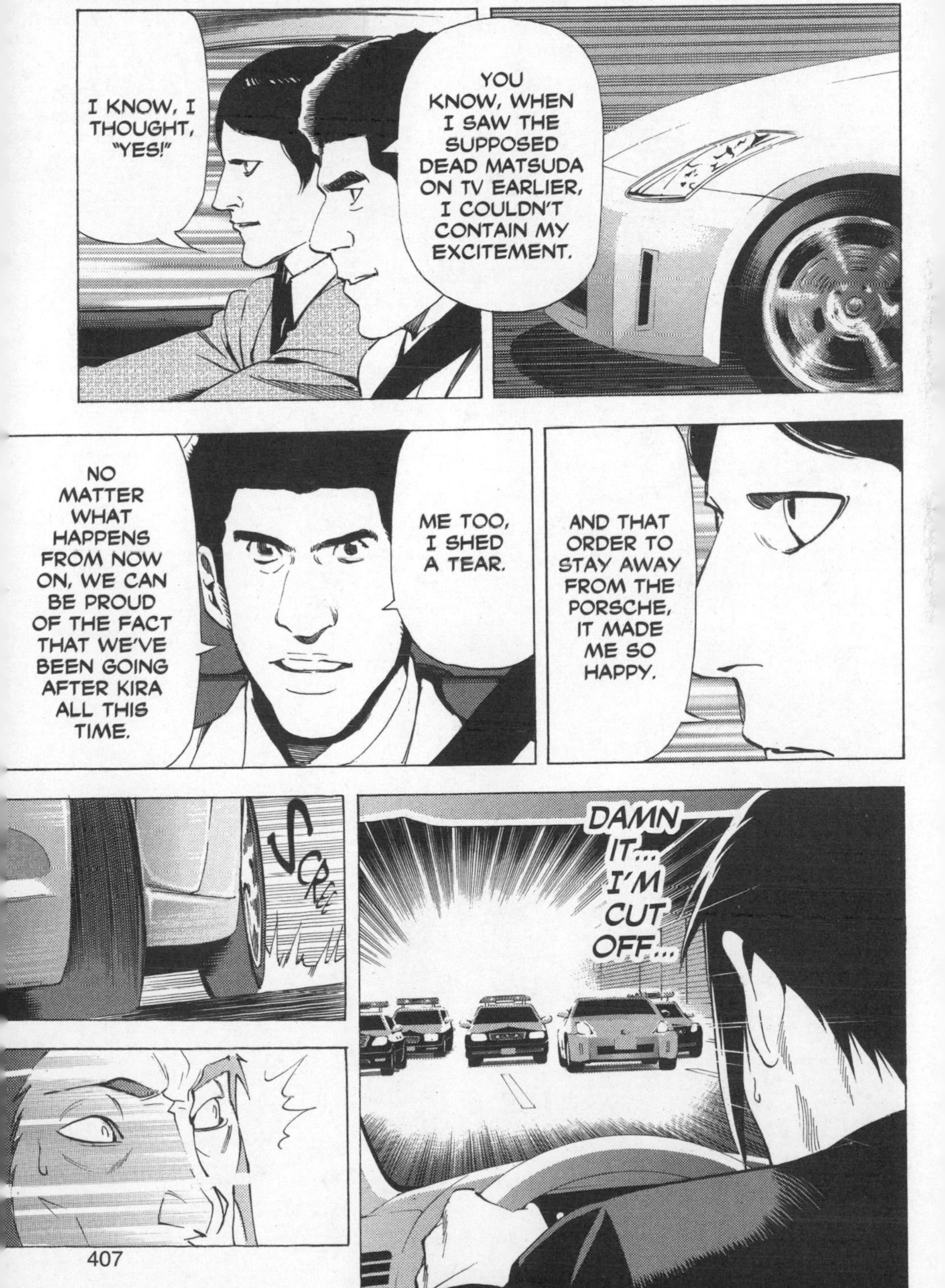

YOU KNOW, WHEN I SAW THE SUPPOSED DEAD MATSUDA ON TV EARLIER, I COULDN'T CONTAIN MY EXCITEMENT.
I KNOW, I THOUGHT, "YES!"
AND THAT ORDER TO STAY AWAY FROM THE PORSCHE, IT MADE ME SO HAPPY.
ME TOO, I SHED A TEAR.
NO MATTER WHAT HAPPENS FROM NOW ON, WE CAN BE PROUD OF THE FACT THAT WE'VE BEEN GOING AFTER KIRA ALL THIS TIME.
DAMN IT... I'M CUT OFF...
SCREE

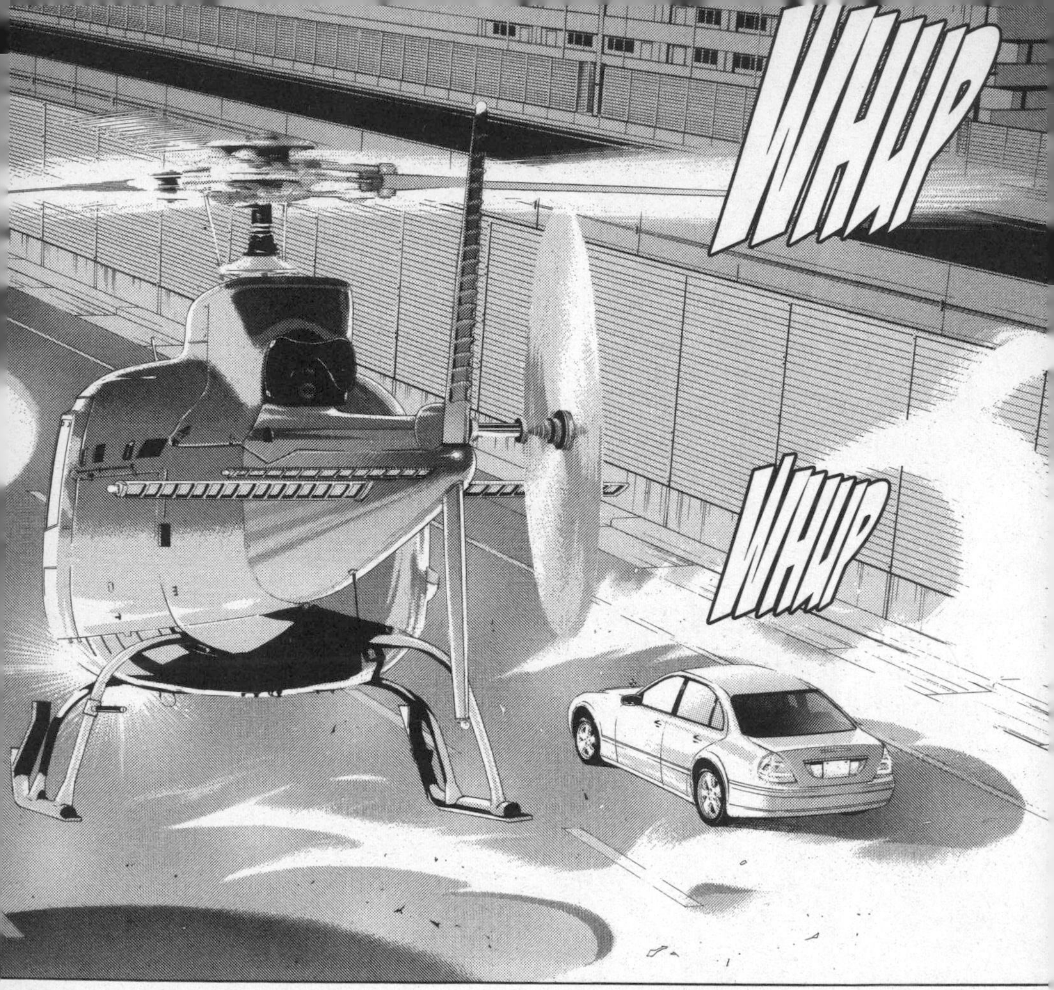
WHUP
WHUP
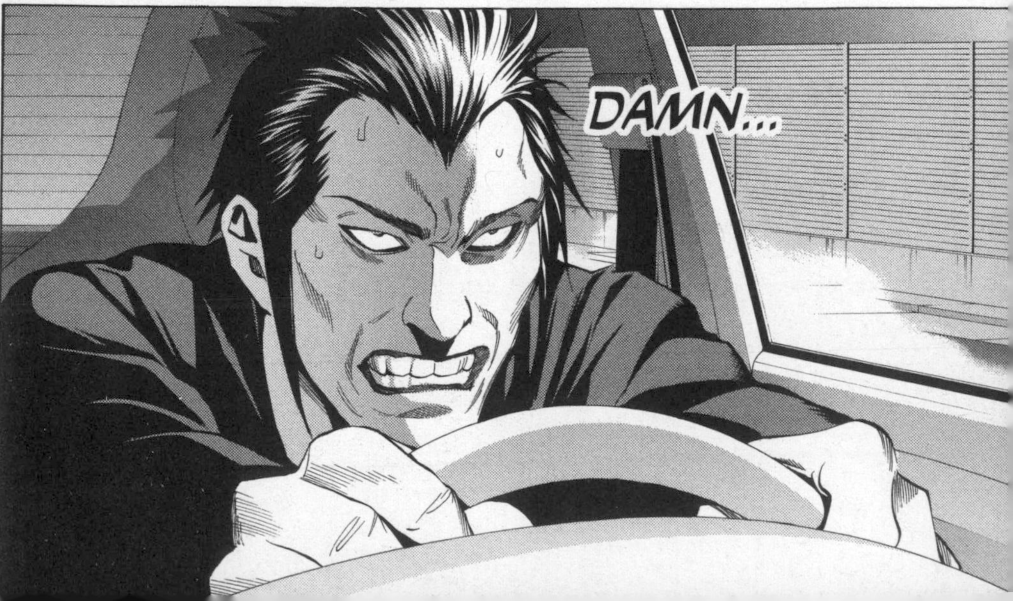
DAMN...

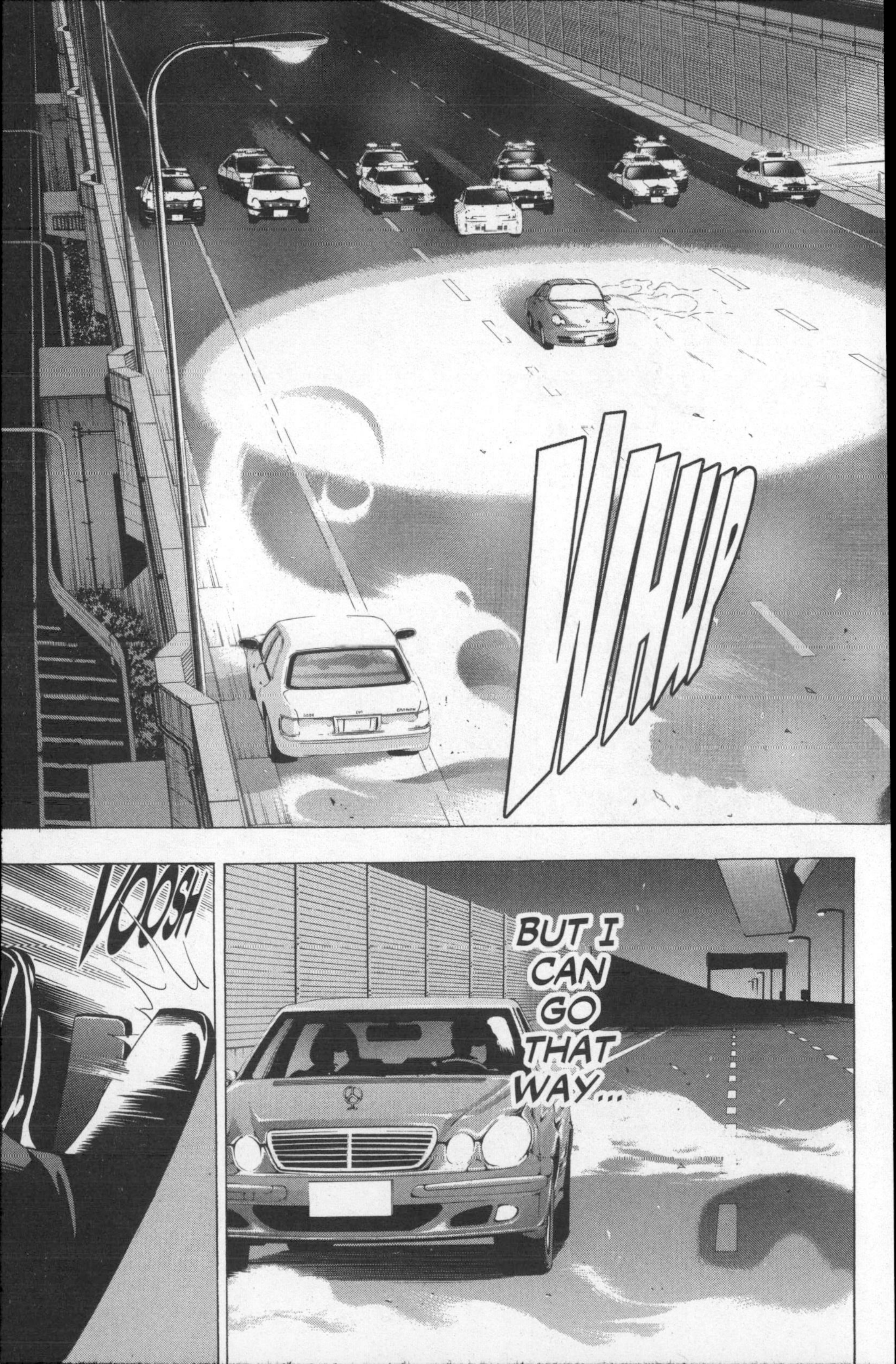
WHUD
BUT I CAN GO THAT WAY...
VOOSH

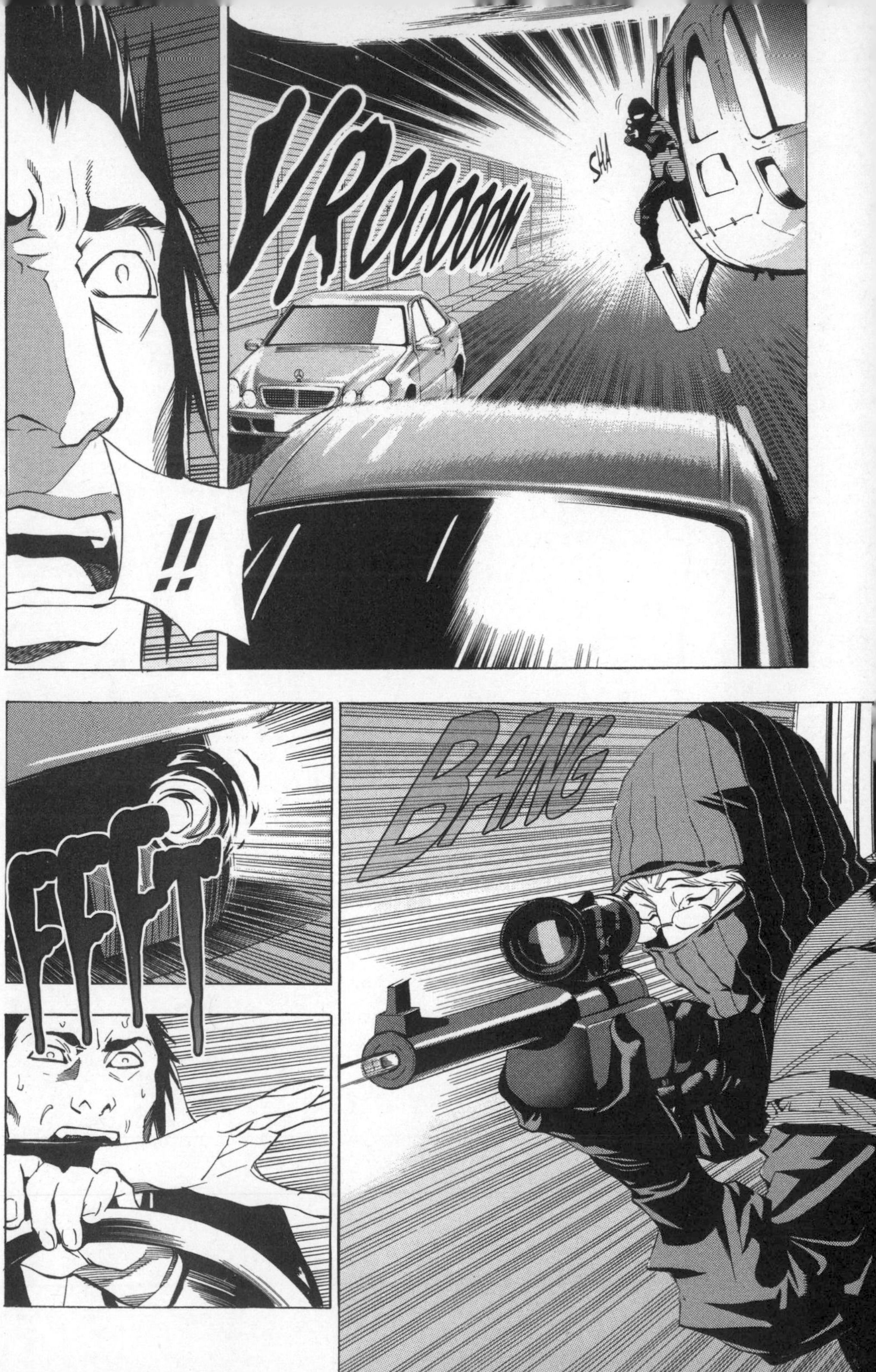
VROOOOOM
SHA
!!
BANG
FFFT

CRASH

WHIRL

SURROUND HIM SO HE CAN'T ESCAPE, KEEP YOUR WINDOWS UP.

SHYYY

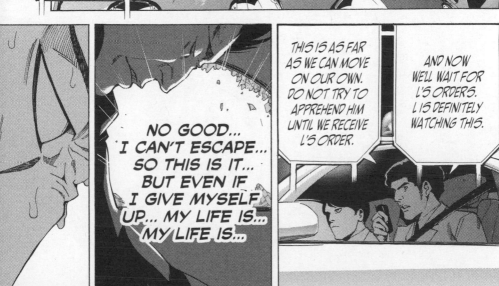

THIS IS AS FAR AS WE CAN MOVE ON OUR OWN. DO NOT TRY TO APPREHEND HIM UNTIL WE RECEIVE L'S ORDER.

AND NOW WE'LL WAIT FOR L'S ORDERS. L IS DEFINITELY WATCHING THIS.

NO GOOD... I CAN'T ESCAPE... SO THIS IS IT... BUT EVEN IF I GIVE MYSELF UP... MY LIFE IS... MY LIFE IS...

STAY BACK! EVERY-ONE STAY BACK!

SHA

WHAT THE HELL AM I DOING...? LIKE I CAN ESCAPE BY TAKING MYSELF HOSTAGE...

THIS IS BAD.

SO STUPID.

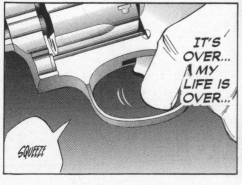

IT'S OVER... MY LIFE IS OVER...

SQUEEZE

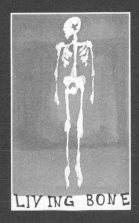

LIVING BONE

The other day I got an X-ray and saw my own
bones. It was a pretty shocking image to me. Am
I always talking about bones here because of all
those shinigami I'm drawing?

-Takeshi Obata

DEATH NOTE

Black Edition
III

SHONEN JUMP ADVANCED Manga Omnibus Edition
A compilation of the graphic novel volumes 5 and 6

Story by Tsugumi Ohba
Art by Takeshi Obata

Translation & Adaptation/Alexis Kirsch
Touch-up Art & Lettering/Gia Cam Luc
Design/Sam Elzway
Editor – Manga Edition/Pancha Diaz
Editor – Omnibus Edition/Elizabeth Kawasaki

Printed in the U.S.A.

Published by VIZ Media, LLC
P.O. Box 77010
San Francisco, CA 94107

12
First printing, May 2011
Twelfth printing, April 2021